IFIP Advances in Information and Communication Technology 363

IFIP – The International Federation for Information Processing

IFIP was founded in 1960 under the auspices of UNESCO, following the First World Computer Congress held in Paris the previous year. An umbrella organization for societies working in information processing, IFIP's aim is two-fold: to support information processing within ist member countries and to encourage technology transfer to developing nations. As ist mission statement clearly states,

> *IFIP's mission is to be the leading, truly international, apolitical organization which encourages and assists in the development, exploitation and application of information technology for the bene t of all people.*

IFIP is a non-profitmaking organization, run almost solely by 2500 volunteers. It operates through a number of technical committees, which organize events and publications. IFIP's events range from an international congress to local seminars, but the most important are:

- The IFIP World Computer Congress, held every second year;
- Open conferences;
- Working conferences.

The flagship event is the IFIP World Computer Congress, at which both invited and contributed papers are presented. Contributed papers are rigorously refereed and the rejection rate is high.

As with the Congress, participation in the open conferences is open to all and papers may be invited or submitted. Again, submitted papers are stringently refereed.

The working conferences are structured differently. They are usually run by a working group and attendance is small and by invitation only. Their purpose is to create an atmosphere conducive to innovation and development. Refereeing is less rigorous and papers are subjected to extensive group discussion.

Publications arising from IFIP events vary. The papers presented at the IFIP World Computer Congress and at open conferences are published as conference proceedings, while the results of the working conferences are often published as collections of selected and edited papers.

Any national society whose primary activity is in information may apply to become a full member of IFIP, although full membership is restricted to one society per country. Full members are entitled to vote at the annual General Assembly, National societies preferring a less committed involvement may apply for associate or corresponding membership. Associate members enjoy the same benefits as full members, but without voting rights. Corresponding members are not represented in IFIP bodies. Affiliated membership is open to non-national societies, and individual and honorary membership schemes are also offered.

Lazaros Iliadis   Chrisina Jayne (Eds.)

Engineering Applications of Neural Networks

12th INNS EANN-SIG International Conference, EANN 2011
and 7th IFIP WG 12.5 International Conference, AIAI 2011
Corfu, Greece, September 15-18, 2011
Proceedings Part I

 Springer

Volume Editors

Lazaros Iliadis
Democritus University of Thrace
68200 N. Orestiada, Greece
E-mail: liliadis@fmenr.duth.gr

Chrisina Jayne
London Metropolitan University
London N7 8DB, UK
E-mail: c.jayne@londonmet.ac.uk

ISSN 1868-4238   e-ISSN 1868-422X
ISBN 978-3-642-26954-7   ISBN 978-3-642-23957-1 (eBook)
DOI 10.1007/978-3-642-23957-1
Springer Heidelberg Dordrecht London New York

CR Subject Classification (1998): F.1, I.2, H.5, I.7, I.2.7, I.4.8

Typesetting: Camera-ready by author, data conversion by Scientific Publishing Services, Chennai, India

Printed on acid-free paper

Springer is part of Springer Science+Business Media (www.springer.com)

Preface

Artificial intelligence (AI) is a rapidly evolving area that offers sophisticated and advanced approaches capable of tackling complicated and challenging problems. Transferring human knowledge into analytical models and learning from data is a task that can be accomplished by soft computing methodologies. Artificial neural networks (ANN) and support vector machines are two cases of such modeling techniques that stand behind the idea of learning. The 2011 co-organization of the 12th Engineering Applications of Neural Networks (EANN) and of the 7th Artificial Intelligence Applications and Innovations (AIAI) conferences was a major technical event in the fields of soft computing and AI, respectively.

The first EANN was organized in Otaniemi, Finland, in 1995. It has had a continuous presence as a major European scientific event. Since 2009 it has been guided by a Steering Committee that belongs to the "EANN Special Interest Group" of the International Neural Network Society (INNS).

The 12th EANN 2011 was supported by the INNS and by the IEEE branch of Greece. Moreover, the 7th AIAI 2011 was supported and sponsored by the International Federation for Information Processing (IFIP).

The first AIAI was held in Toulouse, France, in 2004 and since then it has been held annually offering scientists the chance to present the achievements of AI applications in various fields. It is the official conference of the Working Group 12.5 "Artificial Intelligence Applications" of the IFIP Technical Committee 12, which is active in the field of AI. IFIP was founded in 1960 under the auspices of UNESCO, following the first World Computer Congress held in Paris the previous year.

It was the first time ever that these two well-established events were hosted under the same umbrella, on the beautiful Greek island of Corfu in the Ionian Sea and more specifically in the Department of Informatics of the Ionian University.

This volume contains the papers that were accepted to be presented orally at the 7th EANN conference and the papers accepted for the Applications of Soft Computing to Telecommunications (ASCOTE) Workshop, the Computational Intelligence Applications in Bioinformatics (CIAB) Workshop and the Second Workshop in Informatics and Intelligent Systems Applications for Quality of Life information Services (ISQLIS). The conference was held during September 15–18, 2011. The diverse nature of papers presented demonstrates the vitality of neural computing and related soft computing approaches and it also proves the very wide range of AI applications. On the other hand, this volume contains basic research papers, presenting variations and extensions of several approaches.

The response to the call for papers was more than satisfactory with 150 papers initially submitted. All papers passed through a peer-review process by at least two independent academic referees. Where needed a third referee was consulted to resolve any conflicts. In the EANN/AIAI 2011 event, 34% of the submitted manuscripts (totally 52) were accepted as full papers, whereas 21% were accepted as short ones and 45% (totally 67) of the submissions were rejected. The authors of accepted papers came from 27 different countries from all over Europe (e.g., Austria, Bulgaria, Cyprus, Czech Republic, Finland, France, Germany, Greece, Italy, Poland, Portugal, Slovakia, Slovenia, Spain, UK), America (e.g., Brazil, Canada, Chile, USA), Asia (e.g., China, India, Iran, Japan, Taiwan), Africa (e.g., Egypt, Tunisia) and Oceania (New Zealand). Three keynote speakers were invited and they gave lectures on timely aspects of AI and ANN.

1. Nikola Kasabov. Founding Director and Chief Scientist of the Knowledge Engineering and Discovery Research Institute (KEDRI), Auckland (www.kedri.info/). He holds a Chair of Knowledge Engineering at the School of Computing and Mathematical Sciences at Auckland University of Technology. He is a Fellow of the Royal Society of New Zealand, Fellow of the New Zealand Computer Society and a Senior Member of IEEE. He was Past President of the International Neural Network Society (INNS) and a Past President of the Asia Pacific Neural Network Assembly (APNNA). Title of the keynote presentation: "Evolving, Probabilistic Spiking Neural Network Reservoirs for Spatio- and Spectro-Temporal Data."
2. Tom Heskes. Professor of Artificial Intelligence and head of the Machine Learning Group at the Institute for Computing and Information Sciences, Radboud University Nijmegen, The Netherlands. He is Principal Investigator at the Donders Centre for Neuroscience and Director of the Institute for Computing and Information Sciences. Title of the keynote presentation: "Reading the Brain with Bayesian Machine Learning."
3. A.G. Cohn. Professor of Automated Reasoning Director of Institute for Artificial Intelligence and Biological Systems, School of Computing, University of Leeds, UK. Tony Cohn holds a Personal Chair at the University of Leeds, where he is Professor of Automated Reasoning. He is presently Director of the Institute for Artificial Intelligence and Biological Systems. He leads a research group working on knowledge representation and reasoning with a particular focus on qualitative "spatial/spatio-temporal reasoning, the best known being the well-cited region connection calculus (RCC). Title of the keynote presentation: "Learning about Activities and Objects from Video."

The EANN/AIAI conference consisted of the following main thematic sessions:

- AI in Finance, Management and Quality Assurance
- Computer Vision and Robotics
- Classification-Pattern Recognition
- Environmental and Earth Applications of AI
- Ethics of AI
- Evolutionary Algorithms—Optimization
- Feature Extraction-Minimization
- Fuzzy Systems
- Learning—Recurrent and RBF ANN
- Machine Learning and Fuzzy Control

- Medical Applications
- Multi-Layer ANN
- Novel Algorithms and Optimization
- Pattern Recognition-Constraints
- Support Vector Machines
- Web-Text Mining and Semantics

We would very much like to thank Hassan Kazemian (London Metropolitan University) and Pekka Kumpulainen (Tampere University of Technology, Finland) for their kind effort to organize successfully the Applications of Soft Computing to Telecommunications Workshop (ASCOTE).

Moreover, we would like to thank Efstratios F. Georgopoulos (TEI of Kalamata, Greece), Spiridon Likothanassis, Athanasios Tsakalidis and Seferina Mavroudi (University of Patras, Greece) as well as Grigorios Beligiannis (University of Western Greece) and Adam Adamopoulos (Democritus University of Thrace, Greece) for their contribution to the organization of the Computational Intelligence Applications in Bioinformatics (CIAB) Workshop.

We are grateful to Andreas Andreou (Cyprus University of Technology) and Harris Papadopoulos (Frederick University of Cyprus) for the organization of the Computational Intelligence in Software Engineering Workshop (CISE).

The Artificial Intelligence Applications in Biomedicine (AIAB) Workshop was organized successfully in the framework of the 12th EANN 2011 conference and we wish to thank Harris Papadopoulos, Efthyvoulos Kyriacou (Frederick University of Cyprus) Ilias Maglogiannis (University of Central Greece) and George Anastassopoulos (Democritus University of Thrace, Greece).

Finally, the Second Workshop on Informatics and Intelligent Systems Applications for Quality of Life information Services (2nd ISQLIS) was held successfully and we would like to thank Kostas Karatzas (Aristotle University of Thessaloniki, Greece) Lazaros Iliadis (Democritus University of Thrace, Greece) and Mihaela Oprea (University Petroleum-Gas of Ploiesti, Romania).

The accepted papers of all five workshops (after passing through a peer-review process by independent academic referees) were published in the Springer proceedings. They include timely applications and theoretical research on specific subjects. We hope that all of them will be well established in the future and that they will be repeated every year in the framework of these conferences.

We hope that these proceedings will be of major interest for scientists and researchers world wide and that they will stimulate further research in the domain of artificial neural networks and AI in general.

September 2011   Dominic Palmer Brown

Organization

Executive Committee

Conference Chair

Dominic Palmer Brown — London Metropolitan University, UK

Program Chair

Lazaros Iliadis — Democritus University of Thrace, Greece
Christina Jayne — London Metropolitan University, UK

Organizing Chair

Vassilis Chrissikopoulos — Ionian University, Greece
Yannis Manolopoulos — Aristotle University, Greece

Tutorials

Michel Verleysen — Universite catholique de Louvain, Belgium
Dominic Palmer-Brown — London Metropolitan University, UK
Chrisina Jayne — London Metropolitan University, UK
Vera Kurkova — Academy of Sciences of the Czech Republic, Czech Republic

Workshops

Hassan Kazemian — London Metropolitan University, UK
Pekka Kumpulainen — Tampere University of Technology, Finland
Kostas Karatzas — Aristotle University of Thessaloniki, Greece
Lazaros Iliadis — Democritus University of Thrace, Greece
Mihaela Oprea — University Petroleum-Gas of Ploiesti, Romania
Andreas Andreou — Cyprus University of Technology, Cyprus
Harris Papadopoulos — Frederick University, Cyprus
Spiridon Likothanassis — University of Patras, Greece
Efstratios Georgopoulos — Technological Educational Institute (T.E.I.) of Kalamata, Greece
Seferina Mavroudi — University of Patras, Greece
Grigorios Beligiannis — University of Western Greece, Greece

Adam Adamopoulos	University of Thrace, Greece
Athanasios Tsakalidis	University of Patras, Greece
Efthyvoulos Kyriacou	Frederick University, Cyprus
Elias Maglogiannis	University of Central Greece, Greece
George Anastassopoulos	Democritus University of Thrace, Greece

Referees

Abdullah Azween B.	Kermanidis Katia	Revett Kenneth
Abe Shigeo	Kitikidou Kiriaki	Ryman-Tubb Nick
Anagnostou K.	Koutroumbas K.	Sanguineti Marcello
Avlonitis M.	Kumpulainen Pekka	Schizas Christos
Berberidis K.	Kurkova V.	Serpanos D.
Bianchini M.	Lee Sin Wee	Shagaev Igor
Bukovsky I.	Levano Marcos	Sioutas S.
Canete J.Fernandez	Likas Aristidis	Sotiropoulos D.G.
Cottrell M.	Lorentzos Nikos	Steinhofel Kathleen
Cutsuridis V.	Magoulas George	Stephanakis I.
Fiasche M.	Malcangi Mario	Tsadiras Athanasios
Gegov Alexander	Mammone Nadia	Tsakalidis Athanasios
Georgiadis C.	Marcelloni F.	Tscherepanow Marko
Gnecco G.	Mitianoudis I.	Tsekouras G.
Hady Mohamed Abdel	Morabito Carlo	Vassilas N.
Hajek Petr	Francesco	Verykios Vassilios
Heskes T.	Mouratidis Haris	Vlamos Panayiotis
Jahankhani Pari	Olej Vladimir	Weller Peter
Kamimura Ryotaro	Papadopoulos H.	Xrysikopoulos V.
Karatzas K.	Pimenidis Elias	Zapranis A.
Karydis I.	Refanidis Ioannis	Zunino R.
Kazemian Hassan	Renteria Luciano Alonso	

Sponsoring Institutions

The 12th EANN / 7th AIAI Joint Conferences were organized by IFIP (International Federation for Information Processing), INNS (International Neural Network Society), the Aristotle University of Thessaloniki, the Democritus University of Thrace and the Ionian University of Corfu.

Table of Contents – Part I

Computer Vision and Robotics

Self Organizing Maps

Classification - Pattern Recognition

Medical Applications of AI

Environmental and Earth Applications of AI

Multi Layer ANN

Bioinformatics

The Applications of Soft Computing to Telecommunications (ASCOTE) Workshop

Computational Intelligence Applications in Bioinformatics (CIAB) Workshop

Informatics and Intelligent Systems Applications for Quality of Life information Services (ISQLIS) Workshop

Table of Contents – Part II

Fuzzy Systems

Learning and Novel Algorithms

Recurrent and Radial Basis Function ANN

Machine Learning

Generic Algorithms

Data Mining

Reinforcement Learning

Web Applications of ANN

Medical Applications of ANN and Ethics of AI

Environmental and Earth Applications of AI

Computational Intelligence in Software Engineering (CISE) Workshop

Artificial Intelligence Applications in Biomedicine (AIAB) Workshop

ART-Based Fusion of Multi-modal Information for Mobile Robots

Elmar Berghöfer[1], Denis Schulze[1,2],
Marko Tscherepanow[1], and Sven Wachsmuth[1,2]

[1] Applied Informatics, Faculty of Technology
[2] CITEC, Cognitive Interaction Technology, Center of Excellence,
Bielefeld University, Universitätsstraße 25, 33615 Bielefeld, Germany
{eberghoe,dschulze,marko,swachsmu}@techfak.uni-bielefeld.de

Abstract. Robots operating in complex environments shared with humans are confronted with numerous problems. One important problem is the identification of obstacles and interaction partners. In order to reach this goal, it can be beneficial to use data from multiple available sources, which need to be processed appropriately. Furthermore, such environments are not static. Therefore, the robot needs to learn novel objects. In this paper, we propose a method for learning and identifying obstacles based on multi-modal information. As this approach is based on Adaptive Resonance Theory networks, it is inherently capable of incremental online learning.

Keywords: sensor data fusion, incremental learning, Adaptive Resonance Theory.

1 Introduction

Mobile robots moving side by side with humans in a common environment are confronted with different types of problems. One example of such a problem is a situation where obstacles are blocking the planed route. The decision how to handle such a situation depends on the type of the obstacle. In general such an obstacle can be any type of physical object. Some of these may be fixed, such as pillars, tables or cupboards. Others are movable such as wheelchairs. Humans can block the robots path as well, but as a special case of obstacle the robot could ask a human to move out of its way. Furthermore, identifying humans as possible interaction partners would be of interest in most human robot interaction scenarios. An example of an environment for a mobile robot could be an office building or a hospital in which the robot has to deliver different things. The robot then has the possibility to interact with, manipulate (move), or circumnavigate objects and persons. In order to solve these tasks, the robot has to identify the type of occurring obstacles.

Robot systems, which can be applied in such scenarios, usually possess multiple sensor modalities, e.g. [16]. These sensor data need to be fused to take advantage of all of them so that the robot can act appropriately. Furthermore,

L. Iliadis and C. Jayne (Eds.): EANN/AIAI 2011, Part I, IFIP AICT 363, pp. 1–10, 2011.
© IFIP International Federation for Information Processing 2011

we assume that the environment may change; for instance, new obstacles or persons might appear. In this case, the robot should learn these objects. Therefore, this paper focuses on methods for the incremental learning of objects based on data from different sensors.

In Section 2, we discuss related work on this topic. Afterwards, our approach is presented in Section 3. In Section 4, we evaluate this approach based on data originating from a real robotic system. Finally, we summarise our most important results in Section 5 and give an outlook on possible future work.

2   Related Work

Established information fusion architectures applied in robotics [7,9] resort to predefined rules to find corresponding object representations in multiple sensor modalities. On the one hand, these approaches have the advantage that the results of different sensors (e.g., a laser scanner or a face detector, [7]) or different sub-architectures (e.g., speech recognition system and visual tracking system, [9]) can be used to integrate information for higher level processing systems like planners. On the other hand, it is often necessary to define new rules by hand, e.g. if a new sensor or new subsystem is integrated into the system.

In the scenario outlined in the introduction, a system is required that is able to automatically learn the correspondence between different sensor representations of a specific object. From the literature, several machine learning approaches are known that can be employed to perform this kind of sensor data fusion. For example, in [6] a time-delayed neural network (TDNN) is applied in an automatic lipreading system to fuse audio and visual data. In [11], another TDNN is applied to visual and audio data to detect when and where a person is speaking in a scene. A major drawback of these networks is the problem of catastrophic forgetting; i.e., learned associations from input data to output classes could be adversely influenced if the network trained online.

The majority of existing neural network architectures suffers from the problem that increasing stability causes a decrease of plasticity and vice versa, which is summarised in the so-called *stability-plasticity dilemma* [3]. In order to prevent these problems, neural networks based on the *Adaptive Resonance Theory* (ART) were developed. A first network realising this idea was published in 1987 [3]. It is usually referred to as ART1 and limited to unsupervised learning of binary data. Afterwards, a multitude of ART-based networks possessing different properties and application fields have been developed. In addition to unsupervised ART networks [1,5,12], supervised ARTMAP networks were introduced [4,14]. ART-based approaches have already been used for information fusion; for example, a sensor fusion approach using different sensors for distance measurement on a mobile B14 robot was proposed in [10].

The approach proposed in this paper was intended to connect several advantages of the above-mentioned concepts. Therefore, we developed a new ARTMAP network optimised for classification tasks based on multi-modal information. This novel ARTMAP network can learn the dependencies between different sensory representations of objects and retains the advantages of the already published ART approaches.

3 Our Approach

The following section deals with the theoretical background and a detailed description of our approach. Therefore, we firstly introduce some basic notations and concepts that are necessary for the understanding of the proposed simplified fusion ARTMAP (SiFuAM).

3.1 Basic Principles of ART Networks

The activation of ART networks is computed by means of the comparison of a bottom-up input vector and a top-down prototype. This prototype is represented by the weight vectors of the neurons in the output layer $F2$ of the network and for the most ART systems it can be interpreted as a region in the input space. An ART system learns a clustering of the input data. To achieve this, changes caused by new input vectors are restricted to similar prototypes and new input vectors that are too different will cause the net to create a new neuron representing a new cluster. As a result, vectors of low populated areas of the input space can be represented immediately, which makes the net flexible. While the learning rule guarantees that the regions only changes so that a data point in the input space that was covered once will not be excluded again. These properties of the ART architecture, render it capable of stable and plastic incremental learning.

For a basic understanding of the later described architectures, a description of Fuzzy ART [5] is required. The Fuzzy ART architecture is visualised in Fig. 1. The first layer of the network generates a so-called *complement coded* vector $\boldsymbol{I}$ from the input $\boldsymbol{a}$. This step is a normalisation process to prevent proliferation of generated clusters. $\boldsymbol{I}$ is defined as $\boldsymbol{I} = (\boldsymbol{a}, \boldsymbol{a}^c)$ and the elements of $\boldsymbol{u}^c$ are

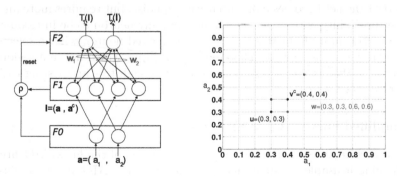

Fig. 1. Fuzzy ART architecture and functioning. The left subfigure shows the exemplary structure of a Fuzzy ART network for two-dimensional input vectors $\boldsymbol{a}$ that has learned two categories. The $F1$ layer performs the complement coding of the input vector. With complement coding, the weight vectors $\boldsymbol{w}_j$ can be interpreted as rectangular regions in the input space (right).

calculated by $a_i^c = 1 - a_i$. Each $F2$ neuron j represents one cluster and its activation $T_j(\boldsymbol{I})$ (note: j is used for indexing the output layer neurons, and J will be the index of the neuron with the highest activation) is given by:

$$T_j(\boldsymbol{I}) = \frac{|\boldsymbol{I} \wedge \boldsymbol{w}_j|}{\alpha + |\boldsymbol{w}_j|}, \ 0 < \alpha \ll 1, \ j = 0 \ldots N \ . \tag{1}$$

Where N is the number of $F2$ neurons, α is used to privilege small regions and $\wedge$ denotes the fuzzy AND operator: $x \wedge y = min(x, y)$ (used element by element on a vector). The applied vector norm $|\cdot|$ is the L1 Norm. After the best matching node J has been determined, its weight vector $\boldsymbol{w}_J$ will be used to calculate a matching value (2) for the represented category. The matching value will be compared to a value p called vigilance, which is a parameter controlling the generalisation of the net. As Fuzzy ART is using the complement coding, the vigilance defines also the maximum size of the hyper-rectangular regions.

$$\underbrace{\frac{|\boldsymbol{I} \wedge \boldsymbol{w}_J|}{|\boldsymbol{I}|}}_{\text{matching value}} \geq p, \ p \in [0, 1] \ . \tag{2}$$

If the vigilance criterion (2) is not fulfilled, the winner neuron will be reset (blocked for the current input), and the next best matching neuron will be determined. Otherwise, the net reaches resonance and the index of the winner neuron can be interpreted as the label of the cluster in which the input was categorised. The net learns new input by modifying the weight vector $\boldsymbol{w}_J$ of the winner neuron to represent the new information as given by:

$$\boldsymbol{w}_J^{new} = \beta(\boldsymbol{I} \wedge \boldsymbol{w}_J^{old}) + (1 - \beta)\boldsymbol{w}_J^{old}, \ \beta \in [0, 1] \ . \tag{3}$$

The parameter β defines the learning rate. The special case $\beta = 1$ is called fast-learning and causes the region to include the new point after a single learning step. For $\beta < 1$ the net becomes more insensitive to noise, but requires more input.

Another possibility is that the net can not find any neuron to be in resonance with the current input $\boldsymbol{I}$. In this case an uncommitted neuron will be selected, and its weight vector is set to $\boldsymbol{I}$. Therefore, a new input which lies in a region of the input space that is not covered by - or close enough to - an existing region will generate a new category.

3.2   Simplified Fuzzy ARTMAP (SFAM)

The SFAM architecture described in [14] is an extension of the FuzzyART architecture making it usable for supervised learning. A Fuzzy ART network is used as a part of the SFAM architecture (see Fig. 2), but the neurons in the $F2$ layer are extended with an associated class label. The training is supervised by the match-tracking algorithm. In contrast to Fuzzy ART, SFAM receives a sequence of pairs of an input vector $\boldsymbol{a}$ and an associated correct class label b. The input $\boldsymbol{a}$ is presented to the internal Fuzzy ART, then the class label of the winner neuron

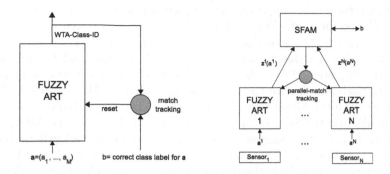

Fig. 2. SiFuAM in comparison to SFAM. An SFAM network (left) is trained with M-dimensional input vectors $\boldsymbol{a}$ and corresponding class labels b. In contrast, SiFuAM networks (right) receive N input vectors $\boldsymbol{a}^i$ from different sensor channels. These vectors are passed to individual ART modules. Then, a vector $\boldsymbol{z}$ comprising the concatenated output vectors of the ART modules is propagated to a common SFAM network which learns the corresponding class label b.

will be compared to the given class label b. Depending on matching or not, the vigilance of the Fuzzy ART may be raised temporarily to force the selection of another neuron. If necessary a new neuron will be committed.

A trained SFAM system can be used for class prediction of a given input $\boldsymbol{a}$. In this case, b is interpreted as the output.

3.3 Simplified Fusion ARTMAP (SiFuAM)

Our approach is based on the Fusion ARTMAP architecture [2,8]. Fusion ART-MAP has the benefit of reflecting the influence of single sensor channels on the classification. Because of our object identification scenario, we developed a simplified version, which we call the "Simplified Fusion ARTMAP" (SiFuAM). The design of the SiFuAM architecture is shown in Fig. 2. It consists of one Fuzzy ART module per input channel and a superior SFAM module. Due to the use of Fuzzy ART, the input vectors $\boldsymbol{a}^i$ of each channel were grouped into categories. A modified weight vector of the category will be used to create the input vector for the SFAM, while the input itself can be generated by different sensors or just different features calculated on the data from one physical sensor.

During learning, the SFAM network receives the correct class label b in addition to the actual input. A teaching input consists of $i = 1 \ldots N$ feature input vectors $\boldsymbol{a}^i$, and the target class label b. At the first step each ART^i module tries to assign its input to a known category. If that fails the ART module has to create a new category with $\boldsymbol{a}^i$ as its initial weight vector. When all ART networks have categorised their input, a vector $\boldsymbol{z}$ will be created from the weight vectors of the winner neurons. It is important to notice that the ART modules are not allowed to do a training step with their inputs yet. The input vector for the SFAM module is given by: $\boldsymbol{z}_c = (\boldsymbol{z}^1, \ldots \boldsymbol{z}^N)$, where the $\boldsymbol{z}^i$ are generated by:

$$\boldsymbol{z}^i = \beta(\boldsymbol{I}^i \wedge \boldsymbol{w}^i_J) + (1 - \beta)\boldsymbol{w}^i_J, \ \beta \in [0, 1] \ . \tag{4}$$

Here, $\boldsymbol{w}_j^i$ represents the weight vector of the winner neuron of the i'th Fuzzy ART module. The vector $\boldsymbol{z}^i$ of a Fuzzy ART represents $\boldsymbol{w}_j^i$ as if it was already trained with $\boldsymbol{I}^i$. If the SFAM categorises the concatenated vector $\boldsymbol{z}_c$ into a category whose class label matches b then all Fuzzy ART modules and the SFAM are doing a training step. If not, the so-called *parallel match-tracking* algorithm is activated, which searches for the least confidential Fuzzy ART module (ART$_{lc}$), i.e., the one with the lowest matching value (2). Then the vigilance of all Fuzzy ART modules and the SFAM will be raised just enough so that the ART$_{lc}$ resets the winner neuron. In doing so the least confidential channel will be blamed for the misclassification. Hence, not the whole network has to change but only the part which is most likely the reason for the mistake. The ART$_{lc}$ will choose another category and, therefore, another weight vector which leads also to a changed vector $\boldsymbol{z}_c$. This will be repeated until the SFAM classifies the input correctly. If all Fuzzy ART modules need to create a new category the SFAM has to create a new category as well which is labelled with b.

If the trained SiFuAM network is used for class prediction, b is the output.

4   Evaluation

Our approach was evaluated based on data originating from the Bielefeld Robot Companion (BIRON) [16]. For testing the learning system, a dataset from the data streams of two sensors was recorded: a colour camera ($1,600 \times 1,200$ pixels, approx. 120cm above the floor) and a laser range finder (LRF) (approx. 20cm above the floor) providing a $180°$ laser scan with 360 data points. The system should learn to identify and to distinguish persons from immobile, non-interactive obstacles, in particular pillars.

4.1   Data Collection

In order to render the output of both sensors compatible, only LRF data lying in the view angle ($86°$) of the camera were considered. From the camera image, two independent feature vectors were generated: a "face feature vector" (FFV) and a "structure feature vector" (SFV) reflecting the occurrence of vertical objects.

The FFV describes the fraction by which each pixel column of the camera image is covered by a face. A 1-dimensional Gaussian mask with 161 elements is used to calculate 21 weighted average values to reduce the dimension. The face hypotheses, their position, and size, were calculated by a face detector from the OpenCV[1] library based on [15].

The SFV is computed by means of a morphological opening operator with a structuring element of 1/3 of the image height and a width of one pixel. The resulting image is subtracted from the original image to remove all structures which do not have a high vertical dimension. Then, the structuring element is used in horizontal alignment for a morphological closing operation to remove all wide structures. Finally, a threshold is applied resulting in a new black and

---

[1] Version 2.1, http://opencv.willowgarage.com

white image. This threshold is chosen such that all values smaller than 20% of the maximal value are suppressed. The final 21-dimensional SFV is calculated similar to the FFV.

For the LRF data, only an averaging is made by a discrete 1-dimensional Gaussian mask of 3 elements, so that 1 value per degree was calculated (originally an element per 0.5 degree). Hence, the LRF vector is reduced to 86 elements, each of this corresponding to one degree of the region covered by the camera ($1°$ LRF represents 80 pixels of image width).

Following the assumption that not all of the information in the picture is required to identify an object, a sliding window is used to perform a search over a picture. Therefore, the picture is split into 17 overlapping slices of a width of 320 pixels with an offset of 80 pixels. Each slice is then represented by 5 values from the LRV and SFV as well as 18 values from the LRF vector corresponding to this image window.

The recorded dataset consist of 167 samples from 4 different persons and 200 samples from 2 different pillars. The centre of the person or the pillar was marked manually for each sample. All windows containing at least 50% of an object are labelled with the corresponding class label, 1 for humans and 2 for pillars. The slices which contain no object are marked with class label 0 for background, and are used as negative examples.

4.2 Results

The evaluation is done by a cross validation on the dataset, therefore the data elements from one person and one pillar are excluded for test and the rest were used for training set. So 8 different combinations of test and training sets were generated and the average test error was calculated. This was repeated for all combinations of the net parameters β in the range $[0.5, 1]$ and p in the range $[0, 0.99]$ ($p = 1$ results in a network just memorizing the input). Since the system is meant to be used in an online (sequential) learning scenario, each element from the training set was presented one at a time and only once.

For the interpretation, the classification performance of the two networks mainly two error rates are of interest, the false negative rate (FNR) and the false positive rate (FPR). The FNR accumulates the errors, where an object (person or pillar) was not detected, while the FPR accumulates the false positive detection in the background. Our net should not learn the background class as an object. Therefore, a rejection of background slices was not counted as an error. Minimizing the FPR could be done easily by rejecting every input, which certainly would be disadvantageous. Trying to reduce the FNR by finding objects everywhere is also an unwanted scenario. To optimize the classification result, the FNR and the FPR should be minimal at the same time. We use the harmonic mean accuracy (HMACC) because it has higher values where both errors have small values and it penalises big differences between them. Due to this the maximum of the HMACC is a good parameter choice. Its use for error analysis is also shown by Tscherepanow et al. in [13], and it is given by:

$$HMACC(p) = \frac{2}{\frac{1}{1-FNR(p)} + \frac{1}{1-FPR(p)}} . \tag{5}$$

As can be seen in Fig. 3(a), which shows the FNR for the SiFuAM respecting the different β and vigilance values, the change of β has a minor effect to the classification for our dataset. Therefore, the two plots on the right show the error rates only for the optimal values[2] of β of the SiFuAM and the SFAM. The third graph represents the HMACC.

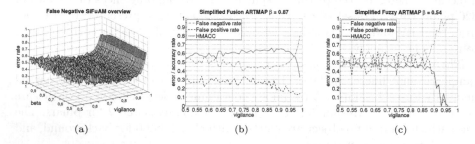

(a)   (b)   (c)

Fig. 3. Error Plots. The plot (a) exemplary shows the false negative rate of SiFuAM networks for all values of β. The other two plots show the error rates and the accuracy for SiFuAM (b) and SFAM (c) according to their best false negative value of β.

In Fig. 3, the HMACC value is plotted for the SiFuAM and SFAM where the SFAM has its best accuracy at vigilance $p = 0.52$ reaching a value of 0.52 and the SiFuAM has the best result at $p = 0.87$ reaching accuracy of 0.66. Also the fact that the SiFuAMs FPR curve has better values at high HMACCs has to be emphasised, because due to the use of the sliding window approach with the chosen values for window width and offset results in a higher number of windows representing background. Hence the absolute amount of possibilities to do a false positive prediction are twice as hight as those of performing a false negative. To illustrate which errors occur and in which quantity the following Table 1 shows the confusion matrices for the SiFuAM and SFAM with the best parameter values of each net.

The results show that the pillar class is more difficult to separate from the background than the person class. In general, SiFuAM predicts the correct class labels more often than SFAM. In particular, SiFuAM predicts less pillars and persons in background areas (false positive). Nevertheless, pillars are frequently considered as background by both types of networks. A reason for this can be that several sample images contain a bright background light caused by a large window close to the considered pillars, which compromised the SFV. In contrast, the pillar and person classes are better separated and only rarely mixed up.

---

[2] Averaged over all values of p.

Table 1. Confusion Matrices of SiFuAM ($\beta = 0.6$, $p = 0.87$) and SFAM ($\beta = 0.54$, $p = 0.52$). The percentage values are rounded. All rejections are counted as background predictions (background was not an object type to be learned).

correct \ prediction		background	person	pillar
SiFuAM	background	**11618 (79%)**	778 (5%)	2386 (16%)
	person	309 (23%)	**967 (73%)**	44 (3%)
	pillar	1443 (45%)	148 (5%)	**1585 (50%)**
SFAM	background	**7584 (51%)**	834 (6%)	6364 (43%)
	person	556 (42%)	**652 (49%)**	112 (8%)
	pillar	1628 (51%)	174 (5%)	**1374 (43%)**

5   Conclusion and Future Work

As shown in the previous section, the SiFuAM is able to learn a classification on a small set of data coming from real sensors of a mobile robot, even if they are partly very noisy. The SFAM which just uses a concatenated vector of all sensor data was outperformed by the SiFuAM especially in the FPR, which makes it more likely that considering effects of single sensor channels for learning is a good idea. Also analysing the weights after several training steps will give information of useless data channels that may be removed.

The classification was only done on sensor data snapshots. A future goal is, to use the SiFuAM directly embedded on a mobile robot system, where the sensor data are read out continuously. The use of time sequential information can increase the overall classification rate dramatically. For example a pillar is detected correctly in nearly every second image and has a low rate of false positives, hence analysing a short sequence of data can be used to generate hypothesis for pillar objects with a high reliability. Also better feature values for the LRF which are independent of the absolute distance of an object will be an advantage. Furthermore the ability of the net to incrementally learn online, can be used to learn new examples at any time labelled by a human tutor via human robot interaction.

Acknowledgements. This work was partially funded by the German Research Foundation (DFG) and Excellence Cluster 277 "Cognitive Interaction Technology".

References

1. Anagnostopoulos, G.C., Georgiopoulos, M.: Hypersphere ART and ARTMAP for unsupervised and supervised incremental learning. In: Proceedings of the International Joint Conference on Neural Networks, vol. 6, pp. 59–64 (2000)
2. Asfour, Y., Carpenter, G., Grossberg, S., Lesher, G.: Fusion ARTMAP: An adaptive fuzzy network for multi-channel classification. In: Proceedings of the International Conference on Industrial Fuzzy Control and Intelligent Systems, pp. 155–160 (1993)

3. Carpenter, G.A., Grossberg, S.: A massively parallel architecture for a self-organizing neural pattern recognition machine. Computer Vision, Graphics, and Image Processing 37(1), 54–115 (1987)
4. Carpenter, G.A., Grossberg, S., Markuzon, N., Reynolds, J.H., Rosen, D.B.: Fuzzy ARTMAP: A neural network architecture for incremental supervised learning of analog multidimensional maps. IEEE Transactions on Neural Networks 3(5), 698–713 (1992)
5. Carpenter, G.A., Grossberg, S., Rosen, D.B.: Fuzzy ART: Fast stable learning and categorization of analog patterns by an adaptive resonance system. Neural Networks 4, 759–771 (1991)
6. Cutler, R., Davis, L.: Look who's talking: speaker detection using video and audio correlation. In: Proceedings of the International Conference on Multimedia and Expo, pp. 1589–1592. IEEE, Los Alamitos (2000)
7. Fritsch, J., Kleinehagenbrock, M., Lang, S., Plötz, T., Fink, G.A., Sagerer, G.: Multi-modal anchoring for human-robot interaction. Robotics and Autonomous Systems 43(2-3), 133–147 (2003)
8. Harrison, R., Borges, J.: Fusion ARTMAP: Clarification, implementation and developments. Tech. Rep. 589, The University of Sheffield, Department of Automatic Control and Systems Engineering, Mappin Street, Sheffield S1 3JD (1995)
9. Jacobsson, H., Hawes, N., Kruijff, G.J., Wyatt, J.: Crossmodal content binding in information-processing architectures. In: Proceedings of the International Conference on Human Robot Interaction, pp. 81–88. ACM, New York (2008)
10. Martens, S., Gaudiano, P., Carpenter, G.: Mobile robot sensor integration with fuzzy ARTMAP. In: Proceedings of the International Symposium on Intelligent Control, pp. 307–312 (1998)
11. Stork, D., Wolff, G., Levine, E.: Neural network lipreading system for improved speech recognition. In: Proceedings of the International Joint Conference on Neural Networks, pp. 289–295. IEEE, Los Alamitos (1992)
12. Tscherepanow, M.: TopoART: A topology learning hierarchical ART network. In: Diamantaras, K., Duch, W., Iliadis, L.S. (eds.) ICANN 2010. LNCS, vol. 6354, pp. 157–167. Springer, Heidelberg (2010)
13. Tscherepanow, M., Jensen, N., Kummert, F.: An incremental approach to automated protein localisation. BMC Bioinformatics 9(445) (2008)
14. Vakil-Baghmisheh, M.T., Pavešić, N.: A fast simplified fuzzy ARTMAP network. Neural Processing Letters 17, 273–316 (2003)
15. Viola, P., Jones, M.: Robust real-time object detection. In: Second International Workshop on Statistical an Computational Theories of Vision (2001)
16. Wachsmuth, S., Siepmann, F., Schulze, D., Swadzba, A.: ToBI – Team of Bielefeld: The human-robot interaction system for RoboCup@Home 2010. Tech. rep., Bielefeld University, Applied Informatics (2010),
http://aiweb.techfak.uni-bielefeld.de/files/Team_ToBI_TDP_2010_0.pdf

Vision-Based Autonomous Navigation Using Supervised Learning Techniques

Jefferson R. Souza, Gustavo Pessin, Fernando S. Osório, and Denis F. Wolf

Mobile Robotics Laboratory, University of São Paulo (USP),
Av. Trabalhador São-Carlense, 400 - 13.560-970 - São Carlos, SP, Brazil
{jrsouza,pessin,fosorio,denis}@icmc.usp.br

Abstract. This paper presents a mobile control system capable of learn behaviors based on human examples. Our approach is based on image processing, template matching, finite state machine, and template memory. The system proposed allows image segmentation using neural networks in order to identify navigable and non-navigable regions. It also uses supervised learning techniques which work with different levels of memory of the templates. As output our system is capable controlling speed and steering for autonomous mobile robot navigation. Experimental tests have been carried out to evaluate the learning techniques.

Keywords: Robotic Vehicles Navigation, Trapezoidal Algorithm, Finite State Machine, Supervised Learning Techniques.

1 Introduction

Human driver errors are a major cause of accidents on roads. Frequently people get injuried or even die due to road traffic accidents (RTA). Also, bad road and weather conditions increase the risk of RTA. Autonomous vehicles could provide safer conditions in roads for individual or collective use. They also could increase efficiency in freight and provide some degree of independence to people unable to drive.

Several works in the literature have been focusing on navigation in outdoor environments. Competitions like DARPA Challenges [4] and ELROB [5] have been pushing the state of the art in autonomous vehicle control. Relevant results obtained in such competitions combine information obtained from a large number of complex sensors. Some approaches use five (or more) laser range finders, video cameras, radar, differential GPS, and inertial measurement units [4], [11]. Although there are several interesting applications for such technology, the cost of such systems is very high, which is prohibitive to commercial applications.

In this paper we propose a vision-based navigation approach based on a low cost platform. Our system uses a single camera to acquire data from the environment. It detects the navigable regions (roads), estimates the best trapezium on an image, acquires and trains different levels of memory of the templates that should be done in order to keep the robot in a safe path, and finally, control steering and accelerating of the robot.

L. Iliadis and C. Jayne (Eds.): EANN/AIAI 2011, Part I, IFIP AICT 363, pp. 11–20, 2011.
© IFIP International Federation for Information Processing 2011

Fig. 1 shows our test platform. The images are acquired and processed using an Artificial Neural Network (ANN) that identifies the road ahead of the robot.

Fig. 1. Pioneer 3-AT (P3-AT) test platform used in the experiments

We use two ANNs. The first one identifies navigable regions in which a template-based algorithm classifies the image and identifies the action that should be taken by P3-AT. After that, a Finite State Machine (FSM) is used to filter some input noise and reduce classification and/or control errors. In this paper noise is considered as variations in the road color, such as dirt road (mud or dust), shadows, and depressions. So, after obtaining the current state (template), which is the input of a new ANN that works with levels of memory of the templates. This ANN aims to learn the driver's behavior, providing smoother steering and levels of speed in the same way as the driver. We analyze six levels of template memory on the ANN searching to obtain the topology which provides the more reliable ANN. Also, we analyze many supervised ML algorithms to compare with this ANN in order to find the best among them.

This paper is organized as follows. Section 2 presents the related works. Section 3 describes the proposed method. Section 4 shows the experimental results and discussion. Finally, Section 5 presents the conclusion and future works.

2   Related Works

Autonomous Land Vehicle in a Neural Network (ALVINN) [12] is an ANN based navigation system that calculates a steer angle to keep an autonomous vehicle in the road limits. In this work, the gray-scale levels of a 30 x 32 image were used as the input of an ANN. In order to improve training, the original road image and steering were generated, allowing ALVINN to learn how to navigate in new roads. The disadvantages of this work are the low resolution of a 30 x 32 image (gray-scale levels) and the high computational time. The architecture has 960 input units fully connected to the hidden layer to 4 units, also fully connected to 30 units in output layer. Regarding that issue, this problem requires real time decisions therefore this topology is not efficient.

Later, the EUREKA project Prometheus [7] for road-following was successfully performed, which provided trucks with an automatic driving system to reproduce drivers in repetitive long driving situations. The system also included a function to warn the driver in dangerous situations. A limitation of this project was an excessive number of heuristics created by the authors to limit the false alarms caused by shadows or discontinuities in the color of the road surface.

Chan et al. [3] presents an Intelligent Speed Adaptation and Steering Control (ISASC) that allows the vehicle to anticipate and negotiate curves safely. This system uses Generic Self-Organizing Fuzzy Neural Network (GenSoFNN-Yager) which include the Yager inference scheme [10]. GenSoFNN-Yager has as main feature their ability to induce from low-level perceptual information in form of fuzzy IF-THEN rules. Results show the robustness of the system in learning from example human driving negotiating new unseen roads. The autonomous driver demonstrate that anticipation is not always sufficient yet, also large variations in the distribution of the rule were observed which imply a high complexity of the system, beyond the system be tested on a driving simulator.

The work [8] focus on the task of lane following, where a robot-car learns anticipatory driving from a human and visual sensory data. During the learning step the robot associates visual information with human actions. This information is derived from the street lane boundary that is detected in each image in real-time (based in [2]). In this work two modules were used, a reactive controller (RC) and a planner, which the former maps short-term information to a single steering control value, and the latter generates action plans, i.e. sequences for steering and speed control. The final steering command is a combination of planner and RC output. The advantages of this approach are react to upcoming events, cope with short lacks of sensory information, and use these plans for making predictions about its own state, which is useful for higher-level planning. Despite many advantages, due to the inertia of the robot it is less visible than what could be expected from the plotted signal. Also the system is not able to predict future states.

A more recent work, Markelic et al. [9], proposes a system that learns driving skills based on a human teacher. Driving School (DRIVSCO) is implemented as a multi-threaded, parallel CPU/GPU architecture in a real car and trained with real driving data to generate steering and acceleration control for road following. Besides, it uses an algorithm for detecting independently moving objects (IMOs) for spotting obstacles with stereo camera. A predicted action sequence is compared to the driver actions and a warning is issued if they are differing too much (assistance system). The IMO detection algorithm is more general in the sense that it will respond not only to cars, but to any sufficiently large (11 x 11 pixels) moving object. The steering prediction is very close to the human signal, but the acceleration is less reliable.

3   Proposed Method

Our approach (Fig. 2) is composed by 4 steps. In the first step an image is obtained and the road is identified using ANNs classification. In the second step, a template matching algorithm is used to identify the geometry of the road ahead of the robot. In the third, a FSM is used to filter noisy inputs and any

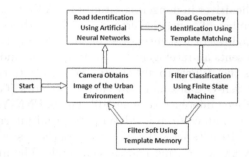

Fig. 2. The proposed method

classification error. Finally, a template memory is used in order to define the action that the robot should take to keep on road. These steps will be described in the next sub-sections.

3.1   Image Processing Step

We adopted the proposed method of Shinzato [13], which proposes to use ANNs to be applied into a road identification task. Based on the results, a system composed by six Multilayer Perceptron (MLP) ANNs was proposed to identify the navigable regions in outdoor environments (Fig. 3 (a)). The real image of the environment can be seen on Fig. 3 (b). The result of this ANNs output combination is a navigability map (as shown on Fig. 3 (c)). The image processing step divides the image into blocks of pixels and evaluates them as single units.

The ANNs are used to classify the blocks considering their attributes (output 0 to non-navigable and 1 to navigable). Each ANN contains an input layer with the neurons according to the image input features (see Table 1), one hidden layer with five neurons, and the output layer which has only one neuron (binary classification). However, after the training step, the ANN returns real values between 0 and 1, as outputs. These real values can be interpreted as the classification certainty degree of one specific block. The difference between the six ANNs is the set of image attributes used as input for each one. All these sets of attributes (see Table 1) are calculated during the block-segmentation of the image. The choice of these attributes was based on the results presented in the work [13].

After obtaining the six outputs of the ANNs referring to each block, the classifier calculates the average of these values to compose a single final output value. These values representing each block obtained from the original image form together the navigability map matrix. This matrix is used to locate the most likely navigable region. It is important to mention that the ANN is previously trained using supervised examples of navigable and non-navigable regions selected by the user one time on an initial image frame. After that, the trained ANN is integrated into the vehicle control system and used as the main source of information to the autonomous navigation control system.

Table 1. Input attributes of the ANNs (average = av, normalized = norm, entropy = ent, energy = en and variance = var)

ANNs	Input attributes
ANN1	U av, V av, B norm av, H ent, G norm en and H av
ANN2	V av, H ent, G norm en, G av, U av, R av,
	H av, B norm av, G norm av and Y ent
ANN3	U av, B norm av, V av, B var, S av, H av,
	G norm av and G norm ent
ANN4	U av, V av, B norm av, H ent, G norm en and H av
ANN5	V av, H ent, G norm en, G av, U av, R av,
	H av, B norm av, G norm av and Y ent
ANN6	U av, B norm av, V av, B var, S av, H av,
	G norm av and G norm ent

3.2   Template Matching Step

After obtaining the ANN classification, 7 different road templates are placed over the image in order to identify the road geometry. One of them identifies a straight road ahead, two identify a straight road in the sideways, two identify soft turns, and two identify hard turns (e.g. a straight road ahead Fig. 3 (d)). Each template is composed by a mask of 1s and 0s [15]. The value of each mask is multiplied by the correspondent value into the navigability matrix (values obtained from the ANN classification of the correspondent blocks of the image). The total score for each template is the sum of products. The template that obtains the higher score is selected as the best match. Only one template can obtain a high score, because we use probabilities as the decision criteria.

3.3   Finite State Machine Step

The FSM uses the result of the template matching step as input, which carries out a classification for the road detected in each captured frame. This classification is defined by the template which best fits the matrix and its position. The developed FSM is composed by 5 states (straight road, soft turns left and right, and hard turns left and right). Fig. 4 represents a state change of 'a' to 'b'. For example, 'a' represents a straight road state and 'b' soft turn left. To change the state in the FSM there must happen three consecutive equal states. In this work, we use the FSM with only 2 intermediate transitions between the states and have produced reasonable results. Detailed information can be seen in [15].

3.4   Template Memory Step

After obtaining the current state (e.g. template) by FSM, this current template is used as input in the template memory step. In this step, the levels of memory of the templates are stored in a queue, as $\{Template_t, Template_{t-1}, Template_{t-2}, ..., Template_{t-NTM}\}$. In this work, the $Template_t$ represents the current template, $Template_{t-1}$ the previous template, $Template_{t-2}$ one template before the previous. This is done successively, until the number of template memory (NTM) is reached, where t represents the time.

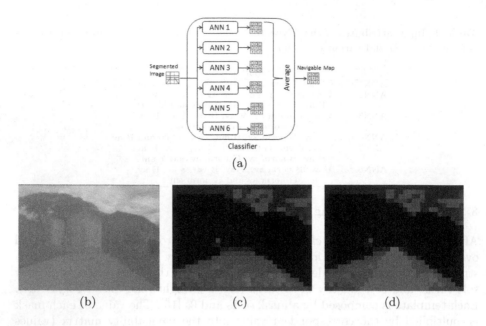

(a)

(b)   (c)   (d)

Fig. 3. Classifier structure (a), image real step (b), image processing step (c) and template matching (d)

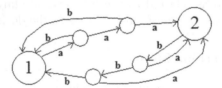

Fig. 4. Transition between 2 states with 2 intermediate states

In this step, an ANN second is used differently of the ANNs used in the image processing step. The basic network structure (Fig. 5) used is a feed-forward MLP, the activation function of the hidden neurons is the sigmoid function and the ANN learning is the resilient backpropagation (RPROP). The inputs are represented by templates memory and the outputs are the steer angle and speed. We compare the result of best ANN topology with others ML in order to find the best among them. Then, apply the best algorithm on the P3-AT robot to autonomous navigation in real-time.

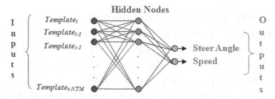

Fig. 5. The structure of the ANN

4   Experimental Results

The experiments were performed using the P3-AT shown on Fig. 1. It was equipped with a VIDERE DSG video camera. The GPS was used only to visualize the robot trajectory (Fig. 6). The image acquisition resolution was set to (320 x 240) pixels. The ANNs of the image processing step were executed using Fast Artificial Neural Network (FANN) [6], the ANN in the template memory step used Stuttgart Neural Network Simulator (SNNS) [14], and the supervised learning techniques used Waikato Environment for Knowledge Analysis (WEKA) [16]. For the development of the image acquisition, image processing and template matching algorithms, we used the OpenCV [1] library.

Fig. 6. GPS presents the performed path by P3-AT robot

In Table 2, we analyze six Levels of Memory of the Templates (LMT), which represent the architecture of the second ANN used in our proposed system. The ANN topology represents the numbers that we tested randomly in order to develop a well-defined architecture which is one of the goals of the paper. Half, Double and Equal shows the different architectures tested in this work, for example, LMT = 3 changes occur in the number of neurons in the intermediate layer of a Rprop MLP, where tested the architectures: 3-1-2 (Half), 3-3-2 (Equal) and 3-6-2 (Double), obtaining the cycle of the optimal point of generalization (OPG) and the values of mean squared error (MSE) for the validation set.

Fig. 7 shows the dispersion of the validation set on the 3D plan. We can observe that this data set is simple, but contains data very close. s1, s2, s3, s4 and s5 are the Rprop ANN outputs on the best ANN topology (3-3-2) from Table 2 (Test 1). These outputs represent the steering and speed control system of the P3-AT robot, for example, s1 (steering = 0.0000 and speed = 0.4000), s2 (steering = -0.0435 and speed = 0.2000), s3 (steering = 0.0435 and speed = 0.2000), s4 (steering = -0.0870 and speed = 0.1000) and s5 (steering = 0.0870 and speed = 0.1000). These values were obtained by the training set when the robot made an autonomously collect using only the assistance of the templates. We did not use the data collection from the human, but we obtained a response

Table 2. Results of ANN validation using different hidden layers

| ANN Topology | Mean Squared Error (MSE) (10^{-3}) | | | | |
	Test 1	Test 2	Test 3	Test 4	Test 5
1x0x2	7.79376	7.79377	7.79376	7.79376	7.79376
1x1x2	6.58673	6.58674	6.58673	6.58672	6.58664
1x2x2	0.00249	0.00271	0.00259	0.00235	0.00254
3x1x2	6.54093	6.54091	6.54093	6.54094	6.54093
3x3x2	**0.00006**	0.00195	0.00011	0.00573	0.00573
3x6x2	0.00047	0.00015	0.00637	0.05327	0.00189
5x2x2	0.00648	0.00619	0.00794	0.00679	0.00614
5x5x2	0.00076	0.00043	0.00008	0.00036	0.00769
5x10x2	0.00053	0.00243	0.01529	0.00132	0.00122
8x4x2	0.07995	0.09705	0.05762	0.00039	0.02225
8x8x2	0.02109	0.05366	0.04026	0.01900	0.15480
8x16x2	0.25874	0.06981	0.01869	0.12832	0.00054
10x5x2	0.03305	0.02345	0.03621	0.01560	0.01411
10x10x2	0.01385	0.01721	0.10243	0.06503	0.00952
10x20x2	0.07953	0.02662	0.00606	0.01197	0.00243
15x7x2	0.02513	0.00116	0.00884	0.00151	0.02031
15x15x2	0.00519	0.01556	0.01363	0.01643	0.06065
15x30x2	0.22430	0.01377	0.13015	0.00816	0.05283

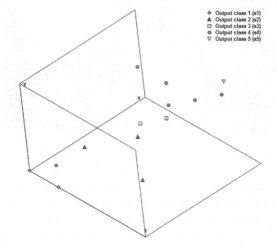

Fig. 7. Data dispersion of the validation set on 3D plan (most points are overlaped)

of the templates as shown Fig. 3 (c), to really make a safe collect, not allowing that the human supervisor to do interference in the behavior of the robot.

Table 3 shows the classification error of the supervised learning techniques using WEKA [16]. We can observe that the Bayes Network, AdaBoost and Sequential Minimal Optimization (SMO) algorithms presents the classification error similar (around 3%). Naives Bayes shows lower error compared with previous techniques. RBF network present the lower classification error compared Naive Bayes. Also shows the comparision with Support Vector Machine (SVM) for different kernel functions. Linear and Polynomial SVM present same values, but different incorrectly instances classified (see Table 4). The Sigmoid kernel function showed a larger error compared with previous techniques. Rprop shows a best classification compared Linear and Polynomial SVM (0% of error).

Table 3. Results of supervised learning techniques using the validation set

Supervised Learning Techniques	Instances Classification Error
Rprop MLP	**0,0000%**
Bayes Network	3,7152%
AdaBoost	2,7864%
Naive Bayes	1,5480%
SMO	2,7864%
RBF Network	0,6192%
Linear SVM	0,3096%
Polynomial SVM	0,3096%
RBF SVM	0,9288%
Sigmoid SVM	67,182%

Table 4 presents the confusion matrix of the three best techniques using the validation set from Table 3, this set contains 323 instances. We can observe that the Rprop, Linear SVM and Polynomial SVM classifiers are very similar, because the main difference between these techniques are only one classification. Linear and Polynomial SVM showed only an error of classification compared Rprop (Linear - error s2 classified and Polynomial - error s4 classified). Therefore, such algorithms are very close, but Rprop MLP correctly classified all the instances.

Table 4. Confusion matrix of the best techniques using the validation set

Rprop MLP					Linear SVM					Polynomial SVM					Classified
a	b	c	d	e	a	b	c	d	e	a	b	c	d	e	
88	0	0	0	0	88	0	0	0	0	88	0	0	0	0	s1
0	**106**	0	0	0	0	105	0	1	0	0	106	0	0	0	s2
0	0	**120**	0	0	0	0	120	0	0	0	0	120	0	0	s3
0	0	0	1	0	0	0	0	1	0	0	1	0	0	0	s4
0	0	0	0	**8**	0	0	0	0	8	0	0	0	0	8	s5

Experimental tests showed that the Rprop MLP output presents a better peformance in the robot behavior (see Video [1]).

5   Conclusion and Future Works

Autonomous vehicle navigation is a very important task in mobile robotics. This paper presented a vision-based navigation system which can be trained to identify the road and navigable regions using ANNs, template matching classification and a template memory algorithm. Our approach was evaluated using a mobile robot tested in outdoor road following experiments. The robot was able to navigate autonomously in this environment in straight line, soft turn, or hard turn left and right since one of our goals is to find the best architecture of the ANN to be applied in different environments. Our quantitative analysis also obtained reasonable results for the learning of ANNs with the respective architectures.

As future work, we plan to evaluate other classification methods and decision making algorithms. We also planning to held in other urban environments the

---

[1] Experiment video available in the Internet:
http://www.youtube.com/watch?v=H5UJu2JMljk

proposed method with GPS, in addition to integrate camera and LIDAR laser information in order to better deal with obstacles, bumps and depressions.

References

1. Bradski, G., Kaehler, A.: Learning OpenCV: Computer Vision with the OpenCV Library. O'Reilly, Sebastopol (2008)
2. Canny, J.F.: A Computational Approach to Edge Detection. IEEE Transactions on Pattern Analysis and Machine Intelligence 8(6), 679–698 (1986)
3. Chan, M., Partouche, D., Pasquier, M.: An Intelligent Driving System for Automatically Anticipating and Negotiating Road Curves. In: IROS, pp. 117–122 (2007)
4. Dahlkamp, H., Kaehler, A., Stavens, D., Thrun, S., Bradski, G.: Self-Supervised Monocular Road Detection in Desert Terrain. In: Robotics: Science and Systems (2006)
5. European Land-Robot, http://www.elrob.org/ (access on January 05, 2011)
6. Fast Artificial Neural Network, http://leenissen.dk/fann/ (access on June 02, 2010)
7. Graefe, V.: Vision for Intelligent Road Vehicles. In: Proc. IEEE IVS, pp. 135–140 (1993)
8. Markelic, I., Kulvicius, T., Tamosiunaite, M., Worgotter, F.: Anticipatory Driving for a Robot-Car Based on Supervised Learning. In: Pezzulo, G., Butz, M.V., Sigaud, O., Baldassarre, G. (eds.) Anticipatory Behavior in Adaptive Learning Systems. LNCS, vol. 5499, pp. 267–282. Springer, Heidelberg (2009)
9. Markelic, I., Kjaer-Nielsen, A., Pauwels, K., Jensen, L.B.W., Chumerin, N., Vidugiriene, A., Tamosiunaite, M., Rotter, A., Hulle, M.V., Kruger, N., Worgotter, F.: The Driving School System: Learning Automated Basic Driving Skills from a Teacher in a Real Car. IEEE Trans. on Intelligent Transp. Systems (2011)
10. Oentaryo, R.J., Pasquier, M.: GenSoFNN-Yager: A Novel Hippocampus-Like Learning Memory System Realizing Yager Inference. In: IJCNN, pp. 1684–1691 (2006)
11. Petrovskaya, A., Thrun, S.: Model Based Vehicle Tracking in Urban Environments. In: IEEE International Conference on Robotics and Automation, pp. 1–8 (2009)
12. Pomerlau, D.A.: ALVINN: An Autonomous Land Vehicle In a Neural Network. In: Advances In Neural Information Processing Systems (1989)
13. Shinzato, P.Y., Wolf, D.F.: A Road Following Approach Using Artificial Neural Networks Combinations. Journal of Intelligent and Robotic Systems (2010)
14. SNNS, http://www.ra.cs.uni-tuebingen.de/SNNS/ (access on November 20, 2010)
15. Souza, J.R., Sales, D.O., Shinzato, P.Y., Osório, F.S., Wolf, D.F.: Template-Based Autonomous Navigation in Urban Environments. In: 26th ACM Symposium on Applied Computing (SAC 2011), TaiChung, Taiwan, pp. 1381–1386 (2011)
16. WEKA, http://www.cs.waikato.ac.nz/ (access on April 17, 2011)

SOM-Based Clustering and Optimization of Production

Primož Potočnik, Tomaž Berlec, Marko Starbek, and Edvard Govekar

Faculty of Mechanical Engineering,
University of Ljubljana, Slovenia,
{primoz.potocnik,tomaz.berlec,marko.starbek,
edvard.govekar}@fs.uni-lj.si

Abstract. An application of clustering methods for production planning is proposed. Hierarchical clustering, k-means and SOM clustering are applied to production data from the company KGL in Slovenia. A database of 252 products manufactured in the company is clustered according to the required operations and product features. Clustering results are evaluated with an average silhouette width for a total data set and the best result is obtained by SOM clustering. In order to make clustering results applicable to industrial production planning, a percentile measure for the interpretation of SOM clusters into the production cells is proposed. The results obtained can be considered as a recommendation for production floor planning that will optimize the production resources and minimize the work and material flow transfer between the production cells.

Keywords: production optimization, clustering, SOM neural network, k-means clustering, hierarchical clustering.

1 Introduction

Modern production strives toward the optimization of production costs by methods such as lean production, [1] which involves defining the internal value system and consequently analyzing and optimizing the internal production flow. Related methods known as "group technology" (GT) [2] have been proposed to implement cellular manufacturing systems (CMS) that group machines into production cells. A number of methods have been proposed for cell formation. [3-6] A unified approach that combines assigning parts to individual machines and forming machines into cells is proposed in [7]. A clustering model is introduced in [8], exploiting similarities between products. The ART1 neural network-based cell formation in GT has been proposed by [9] and group technology based clustering is applied by [10].

In this paper, we develop a framework for production optimization for small and medium enterprises (SMEs) that are characterized by individual and small batch production with many different products in their production range. This paper's findings are based on data obtained from a Slovenian manufacturing company. We propose a clustering approach for the segmentation of various groups of products that can be organized into small production cells. Based on the representatives of each production cell, an efficient floor plan can be designed that will support lean production objectives.

L. Iliadis and C. Jayne (Eds.): EANN/AIAI 2011, Part I, IFIP AICT 363, pp. 21–30, 2011.

2 Data

The data considered in this paper are derived from the company KGL d.o.o., located in Slovenia. The company has been operating since 1985 in close relation to the automobile industry. The production line comprises mechanical services on CNC lathes and machining centres, pressing sheet metal, fabrication of cylinders for gasoline engines and assembling parts manufactured in blanks.

2.1 Collecting Data

Data were collected in the company in 2009 and comprise 252 products with descriptions of properties and operations required to manufacture each product. Table 1 presents 39 operations applied during production. Beside the operations, various features are attached to each product, such as: material, form, weight, volume, shape, number of assembly parts, dimensional accuracy, appearance of the product, number of possible variants, request for examination, the need of parts protection and the value of the product.

Table 1. List of operations applied during the production

No	Operation	No	Operation	No	Operation
1	Band cutting	14	Thermal cutting	27	Cutting on shears
2	Service-casting	15	Service-forging	28	Deploy profile
3	Broaching	16	Drilling	29	Single-spindle thread.
4	Multi-spindle thread.	17	CNC turning	30	3-axis CNC machin.
5	Brushing	18	Service-blasting	31	Service-deburring
6	Honing	19	Powder Coating	32	Dip galvanizing
7	Galvanic coating	20	Artificial aging	33	Carbonitrirating
8	Service-hardening	21	Washing	34	Precision polishing
9	Before assembly	22	Assembly 1	35	Hand deburring
10	Viewing area	23	Testing	36	Packaging
11	Chamfering machine	24	Tumble deburring	37	Compression-cutting
12	Remodeling	25	Compression	38	Progressive compress.
13	Progr. deep drawing	26	Deep Draw-transfer	39	Welding

2.2 Data Preprocessing

The data about required operations and features of the products need some preprocessing before being applied to various clustering algorithms. The following rules were applied to prepare the data:

1. Operations are encoded with a single value ('operation is not required' = -1, 'operation is required' = 1).
2. Materials are encoded with a single descriptor ('material not used' = -1, 'material used' = 1) for each possible material (Al/CuZn, SL, Fe).
3. Form is encoded with a single descriptor (-1,1) for each form applied (cast/forged, rod, platinum, band, profile/tube).
4. Shape is expressed as 'simple' = -1, 'combined' = 1.

5. Dimensional accuracy is originally expressed as ['0.1', '0.01', '0.001'] and we encode this property as '0.1' = -1, '0.01' = 0, '0.001' = 1 to keep proper ordering.
6. Appearance of the product is encoded as ordered variable: 'unimportant' = -1, 'important' = 0, and 'very important' = 1.
7. Request for examination is expressed as a single value: 'No request' = -1, 'Functional examination' = 1.
8. The need of parts protection is encoded with (-1,1) for each category (no protection, mechanical, anticorrosion).
9. Weight, Volume, Nr. assembly parts, Nr. of operations, Nr. of possible variants, and Value are expressed as real values and are therefore not encoded but only scaled into [-1,1] intervals.

Finally, constant operations (packaging and progressive deep drawing) were eliminated. Without prior knowledge about the relative importance of various operations, we assumed equal importance for all operations. This assumption was encoded into data by using the same scaling in interval [-1,1] for all the attributes. The preprocessed data comprises 58 attributes: 37 operations, 3 materials, 5 forms, 1 shape, 1 dimensional accuracy, 1 appearance, 1 request for examination, 3 protections, and 6 for real valued categories.

3 Clustering Algorithms

Several clustering algorithms were applied to the task of products clustering, as follows: hierarchical clustering, k-means clustering, and SOM neural network. An important ability of these algorithms is to also accept real-valued attributes, which is not possible with structures such as the ART1 neural network.

3.1 Hierarchical Clustering

Hierarchical clustering algorithms produce a nested series of partitions based on a criterion for merging or splitting clusters based on similarity [11]. In this paper, we apply agglomerative hierarchical clustering, with a Euclidean distance metric and several linkage methods: *single linkage*, *complete linkage*, *average linkage*, and *Ward linkage*.

3.2 *K*-means

The k-means is the simplest and most commonly used algorithm employing a squared error criterion [11]. It starts with a random initial partition and keeps reassigning the patterns to clusters based on the similarity between the pattern and the cluster centres until a convergence criterion is met.

3.3 SOM

A self-organizing map (SOM) was proposed by Kohonen [12]. In this paper, we examine a SOM algorithm with distances defined by the Euclidean distance metric, and two variants of two-dimensional grid (rectangular and hexagonal). We apply a two-dimensional grid with six clusters, arranged by two rows each with three elements. Such a topology seems to be well suited to production floor planning.

3.4 Evaluation of Clustering Results

Clustering validity measures fall broadly into three classes [13]:

   a)   *internal validation* (based on properties of the resulting clusters),
   b)   *relative validation* (running the algorithm with different parameters),
   c)   *external validation* (comparison with a given partition of the data).

In our case study, there is no possibility of evaluating the correct clustering based on external validation measures; therefore, we have to rely in internal and relative validation that makes clustering essentially a subjective visualization tool. Following the recommendation proposed in [13], we evaluate the clustering results based on silhouette values that seem to be a good internal validation measure and also provide good graphical representation of clustering quality. The silhouettes validation technique [14] calculates the *silhouette width* for each sample, the *average silhouette width* for each cluster and the overall *average silhouette width* for a total data set. In our study, we evaluate the clustering quality based on the average silhouette width for a total data set.

4   Clustering Results

In this section, we present and compare various clustering results, obtained by the proposed clustering algorithms. Results are presented for hierarchical clustering, k-means, and SOM clustering. Within each clustering method, various parameters are optimized in order to obtain the best results.

From the perspective of production planning, the company would prefer a small number of clusters, i.e. condensed production cells sharing the necessary tools and operation within confined space. The number of clusters should be around $K \approx 5$ but this is only a recommendation and not a strictly defined condition. Consequently, in our study we fix the number of clusters to be $K = 6$, which supports the application of a two-dimensional clustering architecture (3×2).

4.1   Hierarchical Clustering

Hierarchical clustering results based on Euclidean distance and several linkage methods are shown in Figure 1. Single linkage obviously yields the worst result, with an average silhouette $S = 0.1937$. Average and complete linkage give better clustering results, while the best result, $S = 0.4698$, is obtained by applying the Ward distance.

4.2   *K*-means

Due to the sensitivity of the k-means algorithm to become trapped in a local minimum, the algorithm was restarted 100 times from various random initial positions. This effectively converged into a unique solution, as presented in Figure 2. The obtained average silhouette value amounts to $S = 0.4742$, which slightly exceeds the result obtained by hierarchical clustering.

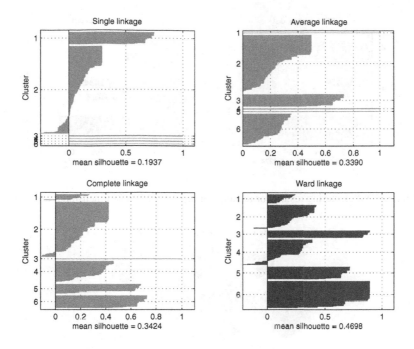

Fig. 1. Hierarchical clustering results compared by various linkage measures. Ward linkage results in best average silhouette value $S = 0.4698$.

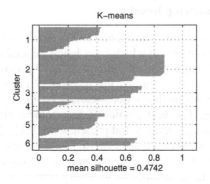

Fig. 2. K-means clustering, average silhouette value $S = 0.4742$

4.3 SOM

Two variants of SOM grid organization are explored: rectangular and hexagonal grid. For the distance metrics and for the neighbourhood distance functions, the Euclidean distance metric is applied. Figure 3 displays the clustering results for both topologies (rectangular and hexagonal). The best result is obtained by the hexagonal topology and yields an average silhouette of $S = 0.4743$. Figure 4 shows a hexagonal SOM topology with class labels and number of samples in each class.

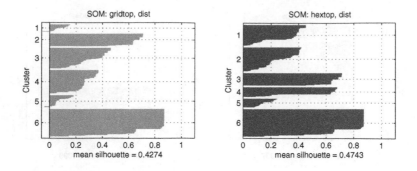

Fig. 3. SOM clustering results for rectangular and hexagonal 2-dimensional topology

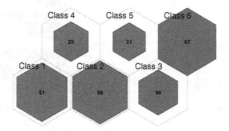

Fig. 4. Hexagonal SOM topology with class labels and number of samples in each class

4.4 Comparison of Clustering Results

The random initialization of the k-means and SOM clustering algorithm causes various final clustering arrangements in which class labels depend on initial conditions. In order to compare the silhouette plots of various clustering algorithms, the class labels should be aligned properly. We applied the method of class matching so that outcomes of various clustering methods were rearranged in a way that guarantees the highest cluster matching. The best results of hierarchical clustering, k-means, and SOM clustering are shown in Figure 5 and presented in Table 2. Table 2 also presents the similarity measure between various clustering approaches. The methods are compared to the SOM result with respect to the number of equally classified samples. After rearrangement, all three methods exhibit very similar results, with k-means and SOM being almost identical and hierarchical clustering diverging below 5%.

Table 2. Comparison of clustering results by average silhouette values

Method	Average silhouette S	Similarity to SOM
Hierarchical clustering	0.4698	95.2%
K-means	0.4742	99.6%
SOM	0.4743	100%

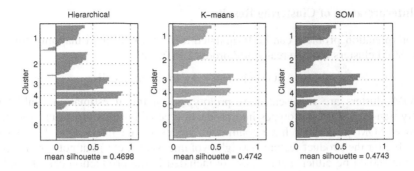

Fig. 5. Comparison of clustering results (hierarchical clustering, k-means, SOM)

The overall best result is considered to be obtained by SOM. Its average silhouette, $S = 0.4743$, is the highest score obtained in this study. The result is almost the same as k-means and only slightly exceeds hierarchical clustering, but there are two more advantages to support the selection of SOM clustering:

a)   SOM result has no negative silhouettes, which means there are no products that are classified in a wrong cluster,

b)   SOM topology shown in Figure 4 can be directly interpreted as a production floor plan.

SOM clusters maintain neighbourhood properties, which can be very helpful when designing a production floor plan. Operation clusters that are close to each other will probably share more equal operations and thus more material exchange than the clusters that are far apart. Therefore, we conclude that the SOM clustering method seems to be the most suitable approach for the task considered in this paper. The homogeneity of results obtained by various clustering methods only further supports the assumption that the obtained clustering result is meaningful and therefore applicable to production planning.

5   Application of Clustering Results

After obtaining a meaningful clustering result, the next step is to apply this result to the production environment. In this section, we propose an interpretation of clustering results that may yield an applicable industrial solution.

According to the SOM clustering result, six operation cells are arranged in a two-dimensional hexagonal grid. This architecture (shown in Figure 4) can already be interpreted as an initial production floor layout. The next question is about which operations should be contained in the arranged production cells. This leads to the interpretation problem of clustering results as described below.

5.1 Interpretation of Clustering Results

The interpretation problem can be formulated as how to define a mapping from obtained SOM clusters into the real world production cells:

SOM clusters → Production cells

As SOM clusters are represented by prototypes, an initial estimation could be to directly translate SOM prototypes into production cells, but this turns out to be inappropriate. SOM prototypes have continuous values in the interval [-1,1], which is acceptable for the product features (weight, volume, shape, etc.) but not for the operations that should be either included or not included in the production cell. Therefore, some kind of discretization of SOM prototypes should be performed for logical descriptors (such as operations, materials, form, shape, etc.).

We propose a percentile measure for the interpretation of SOM clusters into the production cells. For each operation in a particular cluster, we can provide a percentage of samples in this cluster, which should contain this operation (or property) in order for this operation (or property) to be included into the production cluster. Various percentile margins can be defined, such as: $p = \{50\text{th}, 75\text{th}, 100\text{th}\}$. For each percentile margin, the particular operation should be included into the production floor planning cell if at least $(100-p)\%$ of samples in a particular SOM cluster require this operation. The 100th percentile should be interpreted as a limit value: if at least one sample requires an operation, it should be included in the production cell.

Figure 6 presents SOM interpretation results based on various percentile margins $p = \{50\text{th}, 75\text{th}, 100\text{th}\}$. The result for $p = 50\text{th}$ seems to be under-populated as there

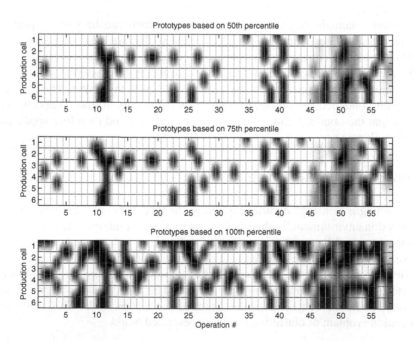

Fig. 6. Interpretation of SOM clusters into production cells based on percentile margins

are a significant number of operations missing in a complete production scheme because they are simply not frequently required by the production process. On the other side, the result for $p = 100$th is probably over-populated. An optimal arrangement can be expected somewhere between the 50th and 100th percentile margins; therefore, a 75th percentile margin can be taken as a guideline to successfully interpret SOM clusters into the production cells.

5.2 Finalization of Production Clusters

If SOM interpretation based on the 75th percentile is applied to cell arrangement, some operations are still not assigned to any production cell. This is a consequence of their rare application, but in practice the production process can not be completed unless all the required operations are available. Therefore, as a final stage, we propose assigning each missing operation into the cell that has the highest requirement for this operation among all cells. The final result is shown in Figure 7, where filled missing discrete operations are displayed in blue.

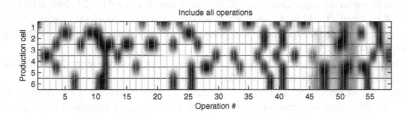

Fig. 7. Final interpretation of SOM clusters into production cells based on the 75th percentile margin and filling the empty operations

6 Conclusions

This paper presents an application of clustering methods to production planning. Various clustering methods, including hierarchical clustering, k-means and SOM clustering are applied to production data from the company KGL in Slovenia. The best results are obtained with SOM clustering, although the results are shown to be very consistent in comparison with other clustering methods. An interpretation method is proposed to translate the SOM clustering result into the production cells. The following two properties support the assumption that the resulting production cell arrangement is suitable for production planning:

a) Organization of production cells supports production of similar products in closed production units, which optimizes material and work flow, and reduces production costs. Clustering evaluation based on silhouette widths confirms good clustering quality, which means that the proposed clustering is meaningful.

b) Production cells are arranged according to SOM topology. This guarantees that neighbourhood properties of clusters are maintained and consequently, it can be expected that this will lead to the minimization of material and work piece exchange between production cells that are not close to each other.

The results reported can be considered as a recommendation to the production planning managers. We hope the proposed results will be a useful guidance to production planning in the company.

References

1. Hines, P., Tayor, D.: Going Lean, Lean Enterprise Research Centre, Cardiff Business School, Cardiff, UK (2000)
2. Kusiak, A.: The generalized group technology concept. International Journal of Production Research 25, 561–569 (1987)
3. Crama, Y., Oosten, M.: Models for machine-part grouping in cellular manufacturing. International Journal of Production Research 34, 1693–1713 (1996)
4. Shanker, K., Agrawal, A.K.: Models and solution methodologies for the generalized grouping problem in cellular manufacturing. International Journal of Production Research 35, 513–538 (1997)
5. Adenso-Díaza, B., Lozano, S., Racerob, J., Guerrerob, F.: Machine cell formation in generalized group technology. Computers & Industrial Engineering 41, 227–240 (2001)
6. Fan, Z.P., Chen, Y., Mab, J., Zhu, Y.: Decision support for proposal grouping: a hybrid approach using knowledge rules and genetic algorithms. Expert Systems with Applications 36, 1004–1013 (2009)
7. Foulds, L.R., Neumann, K.: A network flow model of group technology. Mathematical and Computer Modelling 38, 623–635 (2003)
8. Andrés, C., Albarracín, J.M., Tormo, G., Vicens, E., García-Sabater, J.P.: Group technology in a hybrid flowshop environment: A case study. European Journal of Operational Research 167, 272–281 (2005)
9. Yang, M.-S., Yanga, J.-H.: Machine-part cell formation in group technology using a modified ART1 method. European Journal of Operational Research 188, 140–152 (2008)
10. Morača, S., Hadžistević, M., Drstvenšek, I., Radaković, N.: Application of Group Technology in Complex Cluster Type Organizational Systems. Journal of Mechanical Engineering 56, 663–675 (2010)
11. Jain, A.K., Murty, M.N., Flynn, P.J.: Data clustering: a review. ACM Computing Survey 31, 264–323 (1999)
12. Kohonen, T.: Self-Organizing Maps, 2nd edn. Springer, Berlin (1997)
13. Brun, M., et al.: Model-based evaluation of clustering validation measures. Pattern Recognition 40, 807–824 (2007)
14. Rousseeuw, P.J.: Silhouettes: a Graphical Aid to the Interpretation and Validation of Cluster Analysis. Computational and Applied Mathematics 20, 53–65 (1987)
15. Rousseeuw, P.J.: Finding groups in data: An introduction to cluster analysis. Wiley, New York (1990)

Behavioral Profiles for Building Energy Performance Using eXclusive SOM

Félix Iglesias Vázquez[1], Sergio Cantos Gaceo[2],
Wolfgang Kastner[1], and José A. Montero Morales[2]

[1] Vienna University of Technology, Automation Systems Group,
Treitlstr. 1-3/ 4. Floor, A-1040 Vienna, Austria
{vazquez,k}@auto.tuwien.ac.at
https://www.auto.tuwien.ac.at
[2] La Salle (Universitat Ramon Llull), Electronics & Communication,
Passeig Bonanova 8, 08022 Barcelona, Spain
{scantos,montero}@salle.url.edu
http://www.salle.url.edu/portal/departaments/home-depts-DEC

Abstract. The identification of user and usage profiles in the built environment is of vital importance both for energy performance analysis and smart control purposes. Clustering tools are a suitable means as they are able to discover representative patterns from a myriad of collected data. In this work, the methodology of an eXclusive Self-Organizing Map (XSOM) is proposed as an evolution of a Kohonen map with outlier rejection capabilities. As will be shown, XSOM characteristics fit perfectly with the targeted application areas.

Keywords: pattern discovery, neural network, Self-Organizing Map, user behavior and profiling, energy performance simulation, building automation.

1 Introduction

Clustering techniques are usually deployed to discover representative patterns or profiles in diverse fields and applications. In this work, we focus on energy performance of buildings, and smart home and building control. Here reliable data are necessary to calculate and predict (energy) consumption. Besides information of the building structure, layout and physics, and environmental data (e.g. weather data), the identification of energy user models in the built environment is outstanding for energy efficiency purposes [14], but also for the evaluation of energy simulations [13]. Moreover, behavioral profiles (wrt. occupancy, setpoint temperatures, device usage, lighting habits, water usage, domestic hot water, heating, cooling, ventilation or electricity consumption, etc.) will improve and refine the way for a smarter control of sustainable buildings in the daily-life [8].

Self-Organizing Maps (SOM) have been previously used in similar scenarios, like usage patterns (e.g. [12]) or the identification of energy user profiles (e.g. [20]). A well-known problem in clustering is the existence of outlying elements

L. Iliadis and C. Jayne (Eds.): EANN/AIAI 2011, Part I, IFIP AICT 363, pp. 31–40, 2011.
© IFIP International Federation for Information Processing 2011

that disturb the reliability of the results. In this paper, we present eXclusive SOM (XSOM) as a SOM evolution. The main advantage of XSOM is the capability of rejecting and filtering non-representative and erratic data (outliers) that SOM classifies likewise, a problem already detected in previous works [15].

Therefore, the present work introduces the XSOM method and tests it in a behavioral profiling case with outliers, comparing it with SOM and K-means clustering performances. On the other hand, the importance of behavior and usage profiles in the building analysis and control is emphasized, as well as the convenience of using XSOM in this application field.

2   Behaviour Profiles and Uncertainties in Their Discovery

In the built environment, energy profiling is related to the analysis of the current or predicted energy performance of buildings. Nowadays, architects, construction engineers, and facility designers value the importance of energy profiling. Still, they are forced to rest their decisions on experienced knowledge or trust in values that often do not represent the reality. Obviously, the result is not as accurate as it should be, specifically in energy behavior issues [14].

Energy behavior describes the way (habits) in which inhabitants use or affect – in a direct or indirect fashion – the diverse energy resources of a dwelling. Modeling the behavior is important as these data are probably the dominant parameters adding uncertainties in the calculations of building energy performance [5]. In parallel, profiles allow a control system to guess the next steps in advance (e.g. [7], [17], [8]). Indeed, there is a high sensitivity in the user behavior or energy usage parameters, minor variations result in considerable differences. Unfortunately, often these inputs are not available and must be approximated, most of the times being not accurate [18].

As far as modeling the human behavior for the building optimization is concerned, absolute statements can hardly be established. It is often neither possible to determine exactly what the best model is nor to find the best method to obtain it. On the other hand, it is also difficult to abstract information from the discovered profiles or models. Moreover, it is even harder to assure that the profiles of a population will be suitable for another population (or give a measure of it). Also, only a few of today's buildings are monitored providing detailed information for a valid benchmarking. The scenario depicted above forces us to assume a certain level of uncertainty. We are convinced that the minimization of this uncertainty can only be achieved by intensive aggregation of real building data ending in comprehensive building usage information databases [6].

Clustering is the technique used to discover representative patterns within collected data. Seen from another point of view, it is the process of arranging samples into "sensible" clusters based on a pre-defined similarity (the similarity criterion is also part of the discussion regarding uncertainty). Due to the unsupervised nature of the clustering task, trying to find out the best clustering method for a certain scenario is not trivial. For instance, [22] have compared different clustering methods and show the difficulty to get absolute assessments because of the lack of benchmarks, [16] discuss the dependence on the data set characteristics, or [21] claim for significant improvements in the algorithms.

The outlier presence is also an additional question that adds complexity to the discovery of behavioral profiles. In statistics, the presence of outliers indicates some kind of problem. Often it is related to a sample which does not fit into the model, or an error in a measurement. In our case, there is neither an absolute mathematical definition nor a ubiquitous method to state whether or not a measured sample is an outlier (there is no reason to assume always normal distributions). Thus, an outlier has a flexible performance that strongly depends on the scenario, the nature of the samples, the distribution, and what we expect from the classification.

[4] emphasizes the necessity of analyzing and determining the outlier origins, in order to know if the outliers are helping us to discover new knowledge ("good outliers") or they are just noise ("bad outliers"). We fully agree with his conclusion that it requires not only an understanding of the mathematical properties of data but also relevant knowledge in the domain context in which the outliers occur. But it is also possible that the classification results are needed to obtain some of this relevant knowledge in the domain context. It is not unusual that many variables take part in the performance of the profiles and part of them are usually not collected or cannot be easily collected or abstracted, or even are hidden or unknown.

Though, there is a broad experience using SOM for user and usage patterns. Therefore, we are convinced that SOM algorithms are also a good choice to perform usage profile discovery in the built environment. However, results from previous energy usage scenarios suggested the mathematical analysis of available building data and pointed out the outlier presence. This caused the necessity of refining SOM in order to be able to reject outliers. The final result is the development of XSOM.

3 eXclusive SOM (XSOM)

Self-organizing Maps, also called Kohonen networks [11], are a kind of unsupervised and competitive artificial neural network widely deployed for clustering. They allow a mapping from one (usually high-dimensional) space to another (usually low-dimensional) space. In previous applications, we have tested their flexibility, accuracy, local minima and variable density management capabilities in comparison with other methods [9]. XSOM [8][1] tends to overperform SOM solutions mainly when the deployment of clustering tools is intended for pattern discovery. Remote samples which are considered outliers for XSOM are classified by SOM without any distinction. Therefore, output patterns in the SOM case can be significantly different to the ones in the XSOM case due to the corruption introduced by outliers. In some cases (like in our case study), the outlier

---

[1] The XSOM algorithm has been previously depicted in [8] (as ESOM).

presence can seriously affect the shape of the representatives and even the SOM ability to identify good clusters.

In order to achieve this filtering capability, the XSOM algorithm introduces a new parameter, called *tolerance*, that fixes the admitted level of appropriateness. In addition, XSOM also informs about the nearest cluster of each outlier. The main drawback of XSOM is the adjustment of the tolerance, it adds a new layer of complexity and discussion. Indeed, XSOM with a tolerance equal to infinite is just the normal SOM. Hence, SOM may be regarded as a specific case of XSOM.

4   Case Study: Water Consumption Profiling

4.1   Water Consumption Database

Our current research about energy usage profiles deploys the Leako System database. Leako is an enterprise from the Basque Country (Spain) specialized in central heating, Domestic Hot Water (DHW) and air conditioning installation, distribution, and metering. The Leako Database consists of hourly energy data obtained for seven years from more than 700 dwellings. The collected data comprise of heating (KWh), DHW (KWh), average indoor temperatures, and consumed amount of water. The latter was taken as database for this research.

The validity of profiles is based on the existence of trends and repetition patterns inside the data. The experience managing the database corroborates this statement but it is necessary to have a mathematical approach that supports it. For this reason, we started with an extensive analysis in order to validate the next assessments:

a) People keep habits.
b) Habits of some people are similar.

If every dwelling is analyzed independently and considered as a temporal series, stationary process criteria are not usually achieved and it does not allow to apply time series analysis and model estimation methods. Nevertheless, selecting a dwelling and analyzing the correlation between its days, after filtering absent days (no water consumption), the results very often conclude in a high number of correlated days (Pearson's correlation). Table 1 shows some collected data from random dwellings that corroborate the previous assessment.

If data concerning each dwelling are condensed or summarized through statistic procedures (or clustering tools), it is also possible to study the correlation between different dwellings in order to know if there exist similar habits between people. Some results are shown in Table 2.

For the model obtaining and the clustering tool preparation, the monitored raw data of the database are subjected to some transformations:

1. 0-days and incomplete data are removed.
2. Following the Spanish Technical Code for Buildings (CTE) characteristics [3], each dwelling is represented by a frame of 63 (7x3x3) cells. This transformation allows to map data to seven days a week, grouped in three periods of a day, classified by three seasons. Each cell shows the consumed liters per hour in a period of 8 hours.

Table 1. Correlation (ρ) between days for three dwellings selected at random

	Dwelling 1	Dwelling 2	Dwelling 3
Total days	2641	2634	1494
$af0$ (after filtering 0-days)	2384	1527	1274
$\rho_{0.6}(500)_{af0}{}^{*}$	1001	199	526
$\rho_{0.9}(100)_{af0}{}^{**}$	567	142	179

*: days that have a $\rho \geq 0.6$ with more than 500 other days.
**: days that have a $\rho \geq 0.9$ with more than 100 other days.

Table 2. Correlation (ρ) between dwellings

Total dwellings	685
$af0$ (after filtering 0-days)	668
$\rho_{0.6}(50)_{af0}{}^{*}$	426
$\rho_{0.9}(5)_{af0}{}^{**}$	74

*: dwellings that have a $\rho \geq 0.6$ with more than 50 other ones.
**: dwellings that have a $\rho \geq 0.9$ with more than 5 other ones.

3. Each dwelling consumption is related to a hypothetical user. This estimation is obtained from the Spanish Ministry of Health and Consumer Affairs.
4. Regardless of the fact that the data distribution is much narrower than in a normal distribution case, a second normalization – using mean and standard deviation – is executed [11].

4.2 Experiments and Parametrization of Clustering Methods

In order to evaluate XSOM for the usage pattern discovery in a building profiling case with outliers, different tests and comparisons have been undertaken.

XSOM is tested executing a sweep of tolerances and assessing the different performances. Later on, the performances are compared with SOM and K-means clustering methods. Except for the tolerance variation, the rest of the parameters have been equivalently chosen for SOM and XSOM. The application demands big spherical and globular clusters with high representativeness (marginal dense clusters are not important). The initial number of clusters has been fixed to 5 according to the maximum desired for the application and taking into account that SOM method does not present noticeable variations with a number of initial clusters between 5 and 10. The similarity function is based on Euclidean distance.

With regard to K-means method (using CLUTO tools [10]), the best performance is reached applying direct K-means methodology, with an initial number of 5 clusters, using Euclidean distances and the I_2 criterion for the optimization function. Different parametrizations and other approaches, like Repeated Bisection or Graph arrangements, have also been tested with worse results.

For the evaluation (i.e. the validity of the clustering method), the following outputs in each performance have been studied: *a)* Number of significant patterns (Ps). *b)* Number of outliers (nO). *c)* Form of patterns. *d)* Number of samples embraced in each cluster $(nP_j$, where j is the pattern identifier in the corresponding experiment). *e)* Distances between representatives. *f)* Distances and statistical data between representatives and their embraced samples.

4.3 Results

Table 3 shows a number of results obtained by different tolerance factors. As long as tolerance decreases, the number of outliers grows (Fig. 1). In parallel, the number of significant patterns rises. This is due to the disappearance of the outlier distortion, that appears when they are classified and accepted inside clusters. Outliers move the gravity center of the group and, thus, decisive differences between close elements are ignored. While SOM only detects one pattern, XSOM configurations detect more significant groups. In addition, the appearance of new clusters is also due to the fact that tolerance adjustment redefines the meaning of "outlier". Tolerance fixes how far samples can remain from the cluster center, so outliers are not only errors or samples that distort normal distributions. Summarizing, XSOM allows an outlier to be part of a new group of non-clustered members.

Table 3. Results in the tolerance sweep test

tol_m	Ps	nO	$\%O$	nP_1	nP_2	nP_3	nP_4	nP_5
∞	1	0	0.0%	659	13	4	6	2
158.70	1	23	3.4%	648	4	4	3	2
79.37	2	31	4.5%	538	110	4	1	0
39.68	2	43	6.3%	519	122	0	0	0
15.87	2	60	8.8%	404	220	0	0	0
7.94	3	72	10.5%	352	222	38	0	0
3.97	3	93	13.6%	376	191	24	0	0
1.59	3	201	29.4%	223	192	68	0	0
0.79	3	307	44.9%	184	97	95	0	0
0.32	4	541	79.1%	64	30	26	23	1

Paying attention to the distance values between the representative pattern and the samples in SOM, the existence of outliers can be confirmed (according to the common definition). Distances do not follow a normal distribution but their relationship is close to a logistic distribution that resembles normal distribution in shape but has a higher kurtosis. Most of the variance is due to odd extreme deviations [1]. A logistic distribution can be expressed as follows:

$$f(x, \sigma, \mu) = \frac{1}{2} + \frac{1}{2}tanh\left(\frac{x - \mu}{2\sigma}\right)$$

(1)

where μ stands for the mean and σ is the standard deviation. The usual definition of the (excess) kurtosis (γ_2) is shown in the next equation:

$$\gamma_2 = \frac{\mu_4}{\sigma^4} - 3 \tag{2}$$

where μ_4 is the fourth moment about the mean. Whereas in a normal distribution the excess kurtosis equals 0, in a logistical distribution it equals 1.2.

It is desirable to reach a good tolerance value that rejects a suitable number of outliers. Outliers-tolerance relationship fits an inversely proportional function (Fig. 1). According to this relationship, the compromise is reached when the increment of outliers and the increment of tolerance are balanced ($\Delta out = \Delta tol$). The tolerance that matches the previous conditions is close to 0.0158 (fifth experiment, Table 3) resulting in 8.8% of outliers in the whole population. In that case, XSOM identifies two patterns. The criterion applied to establish the selected tolerance can be widely discussed because it has been stated without a previous outlier definition and based on a commitment between the tolerance-outlier evolution. In any case, the tolerance sweep, in its medium values, always shows two main patterns that do not differ too much in shape and members.

The most remarkable question concerns the differences between SOM and XSOM comparison. In Fig. 2, SOM is compared against the most suitable XSOM performance (with a tolerance equal to 0.0158). While SOM considers a great group (96.3% of input samples) the XSOM classification delivers two groups (with 59.1% and 32.2% elements, respectively). Thus SOM ignores a well-defined group that represents 32% of the population in XSOM classification. Instead of that, it absorbs these elements into the group represented by the big pattern. As it can be noticed in Fig. 2, the outlines of most significant patterns in SOM and XSOM experiments are similar, but SOM has higher values in the whole range.

In the K-means case, the two main patterns embrace 42.3% and 24.1% of the inputs, respectively. The different performances are assessed based on the average similarities and standard deviations between the obtained patterns and the

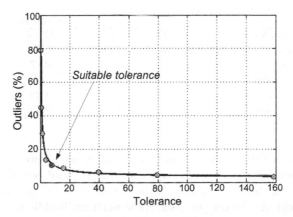

Fig. 1. Outliers vs tolerance

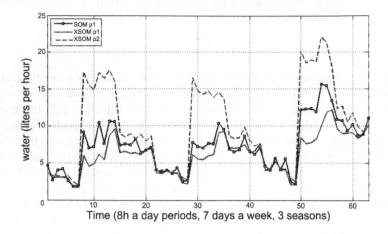

Fig. 2. SOM water pattern

patterns with their respective clustered samples. In any case, resulting representatives show distorted and even incoherent shapes. We conclude that approaches based on K-means methodology are poor to deal with the current scenario.

Without benchmarks or a a validation technique, it is difficult to establish a best method, but it is possible to submit the results to statistical analysis in order to know how close the input samples are to their representative patterns (internal cluster validity). Table 4 shows the evaluation. It discloses that elements classified in XSOM are very much closer to their own patterns than elements in SOM or K-means classifications. Therefore, the two patterns obtained in XSOM case are more representative than the others.

Table 4. Internal cluster validity in the three cases

		SOM	XSOM	K-means
P1	samples	96.3%	59.1%	42.3%
	distance (mean)	0.61	0.06	0.63
	distance (σ)	5.59	0.07	0.87
P2	samples	–	32.2%	24.1%
	distance (mean)	–	0.12	2.39
	distance (σ)	–	0.17	0.44

So far, Leako's technical experts confirm the existence of two trends in users. Besides water consumption, this also concerns heating and cooling energy consumption (backed up by the billing). These trends have not yet been carefully studied – this could also be due to geographic matters, building or family sizes, orientation, different systems, or other reasons.

5   Conclusions and Discussion

This paper studies the convenience of XSOM clustering for pattern discovery in a behavioural profiling case where outliers are existent. While in such a case SOM may fuse significant clusters and distort the representatives, XSOM is able to filter erratic data, obtain best representatives and identify members that must not be classified into any group. In other respects, XSOM also allows to apply other SOM enhancements and evolutions (e.g. [2]).

The main drawback of XSOM is the necessity to adjust a tolerance parameter. In the discussed use case, it has been deduced assuming that when the sensitivity regarding tolerance starts increasing quickly the clustering methodology is beginning to reject non-erratic samples.

The tolerance parameter introduces the concept of *focusing* in clustering. Perhaps it is difficult, or even impossible, to establish the right tolerance value in certain cases . In other words, an ambiguous scenario can admit different clustering solutions. Therefore, XSOM would improve SOM because it allows focusing or diverse granularity interpretations. In addition, tolerance sweeps imply a new hierarchical clustering approach that does not impose clustering shapes to the data as much as other agglomerative methods do [19]. Nevertheless, setting the right degree of tolerance for a given scenario is not a trivial issue which needs to be thoroughly analyzed in future work.

Despite the uncertainties and difficulties, it is worth applying clustering methods to discover behavior profiles for building energy performance and smarter control [17]. For instance, the water profiles obtained with XSOM have already been used to reach more realistic energy simulations in Spanish buildings (using Calener) and, combined with electricity usage profiles, for modeling occupancy in control application studies. Next planned activities include to deploy them to model DHW management systems and to optimize a predictive production.

Acknowledgements. The work presented in this paper was funded by the HdZ+ programme of the Austrian Research Promotion Agency FFG under the project 822170.

References

1. Balakrishnan, N.: Handbook of the Logistic Distribution. Marcel Dekker, New York (1992)
2. Berglund, E., Sitte, J.: The parameterless self-organizing map algorithm. IEEE Transactions on Neural Networks 17(2), 305–316 (2006)
3. Cantos, S., Iglesias, F., Vidal, J.: Comparison of standard and case-based user profiles in building's energy performance simulation. In: Eleventh International IBPSA Conference on Building Simulation 2009, pp. 584–590 (2009)
4. Cheng, J.G.: Outlier management in intelligent data analysis. Ph.D. thesis, University of London (2000)
5. Corrado, V., Mechri, H.E.: Effect of data uncertainty on energy performance assessment of buildings. In: Climamed 2007 Proceedings, pp. 737–758 (2007)

6. Crosbie, T., Dawood, N., Dean, J.: Energy profiling in the life-cycle assessment of buildings. Management of Environmental Quality: An International Journal 21, 20–31 (2010)
7. Heierman III, E.O., Cook, D.: Improving home automation by discovering regularly occurring device usage patterns. In: Third IEEE International Conference on Data Mining, pp. 537–540 (2003)
8. Iglesias Vázquez, F., Kastner, W.: Usage profiles for sustainable buildings. In: IEEE Conference on Emerging Technologies and Factory Automation, 2010, pp. 1–8 (2010)
9. Iglesias Vázquez, F., Kastner, W.: Clustering methods for occupancy prediction in smart home control. In: IEEE International Symposium on Industrial Electronics (2011) (unpublished)
10. Karypis, G.: CLUTO: A Clustering Toolkit. University of Minnesota, Dept. of Computer Science, Minneapolis, MN (2003), release 2.1.1
11. Kohonen, T.: The self-organizing map. Proceedings of the IEEE 78(9), 1464–1480 (1990)
12. Lingras, P., Hogo, M., Snorek, M.: Interval set clustering of web users using modified kohonen self-organizing maps based on the properties of rough sets. Web Intelligence and Agent Systems 2, 217–225 (2004)
13. Mahdavi, A., Pröglhöf, C.: User behaviour and energy performance in buildings. In: Int. Energy Economics Workshop TUV, IEWT 2009, pp. 1–13 (2009)
14. Mills, E.: Inter-comparison of north american residential energy analysis tools. Energy and Buildings 36(9), 865–880 (2004)
15. Mingoti, S.A., Lima, J.O.: Comparing som neural network with fuzzy c-means, k-means and traditional hierarchical clustering algorithms. European Journal of Operational Research 174(3), 1742–1759 (2006)
16. Qian, W., Zhou, A.: Analyzing popular clustering algorithms from different viewpoints. Journal of Software 13(8), 1382–1394 (2002)
17. Reinisch, C., Kofler, M.J., Iglesias, F., Kastner, W.: ThinkHome: Energy efficiency in future smart homes. EURASIP Journal on Embedded Systems 2011, 1–18 (2011)
18. Sabaté, J., Peters, C.: 50% CO2-reduction in Mediterranean social housing through detailed life-cycle analysis. In: Climamed 2007 Proceedings, pp. 927–959 (2007)
19. Theodoridis, S., Koutroumbas, K.: Pattern Recognition: Fourth Edition, 4th edn. Academic Press (Elsevier) (2003)
20. Verdu, S., Garcia, M., Franco, F., Encinas, N., Marin, A., Molina, A., Lazaro, E.: Characterization and identification of electrical customers through the use of self-organizing maps and daily load parameters. In: IEEE Conference on Power Systems Conference and Exposition, 2004, vol. 2, pp. 899–906 (2004)
21. Wu, J., Hassan, A.E., Holt, R.C.: Comparison of clustering algorithms in the context of software evolution, pp. 525–535. IEEE Computer Society, Los Alamitos (2005)
22. Zheng, X., Cai, Z., Li, Q.: An experimental comparison of three kinds of clustering algorithms. In: International Conference on Neural Networks and Brain, ICNN B 2005, vol. 2, pp. 767–771 (2005)

Hypercube Neural Network Algorithm for Classification

Dominic Palmer-Brown and Chrisina Jayne

London Metropolitan University, 166-220 Holloway Road,
London N7 8DB, UK
d.palmer-brown@londonmet.ac.uk
c.jayne@londonmet.ac.uk
http://www.londonmet.ac.uk/computing

Abstract. The Hypercube Neural Network Algorithm is a novel supervised method for classification. One hypercube is defined per class in the attribute space based on the training data. Each dimension of a hypercube is set to cover the full range of values in the class. The hypercube learning is therefore a rapid, one-shot form of learning. This paper presents three versions of the algorithm: hypercube without neurons; with simple neurons; and with adaptive activation function neurons. The methods are tested and evaluated on several diverse publically available data sets and compared with published results obtained on these data when using alternative methods.

Keywords: Hypercube Neural Network, Modal Learning, Adaptive Functions Neural Network, Classifictaion.

1 Introduction

This paper introduces a novel supervised learning method for classification based on the idea of a hypercube and the combination of hypercubes with neural modes of supervised learning. The attraction of the hypercube is that it directly encodes and represents the range of values of across patterns in each class and on each dimension, and thereby provides immediate separation of classes wherever there is at least one non-overlapping dimensional range between the two classes. The process is extremely efficient, requiring only a single pass through the training data, very few computational steps, and only one hypercube per class. The hypercube is a radical simplification of Nested Generalised Exemplar theory [1].

The modal learning approach to neural computing [2] is combined with the hypercube mode of learning. A principle of modal learning is that each mode tackles a different aspect of the learning task, and thus the learning problem is decomposed. Rather than attempting to enhance a mode so that it becomes more complex and computationally demanding without necessarily achieving a gain in classification/learning performance sufficient to justify the increase in complexity, the approach is to combine a selection of relatively simple and efficient modes in order to jointly solve the learning problem. The modes are

L. Iliadis and C. Jayne (Eds.): EANN/AIAI 2011, Part I, IFIP AICT 363, pp. 41–51, 2011.

combined within a single neural architecture. In this case we initially explore the hypercube mode and then its combination with the standard delta weight update learning rule for gradient descent in a single layer neural network, and then with the adaptive function neural network [3], which itself performs a modified delta rule in parallel with function adaptation.

The simplification of Nested Generalised Exemplar theory (NGE) [1] and associated hyperrectangle approaches [4] in hypercube learning avoids the NP-hard problem of determining an optimal number, location and size of the hypercubes. This simplification is achieved by stipulating one hypercube per class and allowing hypercubes to overlap. The patterns in overlapping regions are passed to the hypercube neuron to classify. The neuron is exclusively trained on patterns in the overlapping regions of the hypercube.

The nested generalised exemplar (NGE) theory is based on storing generalised examples in the form of hyperrectangles in a Euclidean n-space [1]. These hyperrectangles may overlap or nest. Each hyperrectangle has weights attached to it, which are modified during training. Once the training finishes, a test example is classified by computing the Euclidean distance between the example and each of the hyperrectangles representing the generalised exemplars. During the NGE training the number of hyperrectangles increases as training samples are presented. The existing hyperrectangle nearest to a training example expands. The performance of the NGE is compared with the k-nearest neighbour (kNN) algorithm in [4] in 11 domains and found to be significantly inferior to kNN in 9 of them. Several modifications of the NGE are suggested in [4] to improve the performance of the NGE such as avoiding overlapping hyperrectangles and batch training. Carpenter [5] et al. introduced the fuzzy ARTMAP based on fuzzy logic and adaptive resonance theory (ART). The category boxes used by the fuzzy ARTMAP with complement coding are similar to the hyperrectangles.

In this work we only require a fixed number of hypercubes which corresponds to the number of classes and a single pass through the data i.e. one shot learning; and there is no need to measure the distance from hypercube surface or hypercube volume. The problem of creating an optimal number of hyperrectangles for classification is NP-hard and several techniques have been suggested in the literature [6,7] to reduce the number of irrelevant hyperrectangles. For example, Garcia [8] suggests the use of evolutionary algorithms to select the most influential hyperrectangles in the NGE for classification tasks. In the hypercube algorithms presented here the problem is avoided by allowing hypercubes to overlap. A neural mode of learning is used to classify the patterns in the overlapping regions of the hypercube.

Other related work includes the Fuzzy Min-Max Neural Network [9] based on a fuzzy set of hyperboxes. A fuzzy set hyperbox is an n-dimensional box defined by a min point and a max point with a corresponding membership function. The min-max points are determined using an expansion-contraction process that can learn nonlinear class boundaries in a single pass through the data and provides the ability to incorporate new and refine existing classes without retraining. In the present work the hypercubes, like the hyperboxes, are allowed to expand and are bounded. However there is no contraction process necessary and overlapping between the hypercubes is permitted. Elesewhere, the hypercube topology has been applied in the form of distributed memory concurrent computers [10]. The idea of the hypercube in [10] is used to find efficient implementations of network algorithms with different connectivity patterns. It is not used for classification.

The rest of this paper is organized as follows: Section II introduces the Hypercube Neural Network (HNN) Algorithm. Section III presents the experiments, results and evaluation of the performance of the HNN. Finally, Section IV concludes the paper.

2   Hypercube Neural Network Algorithm

2.1   Hypercube without Neurons

One hypercube is assigned for each class in the data set. Assume that a given training set T consists of n patterns $(x_1, \ldots, x_n)$, where x_i belongs to R^d, where d is the dimensionality of the patterns. The training patterns x_i belong m classes. Let us denote a class c made of the patterns $(x_1^c, \ldots, x_k^c)$. A hypercube h^c is defined as

$$h^c = \{y^c \in R^d, hmin_j^c <= y_j^c <= hmax_j^c, j = 1, \ldots, d\},$$

where $hmin_j^c$ and $hmax_j^c$ are the minimum and maximum values on dimension j of all patterns in class c, i.e.

$$hmin_j^c = \min(x_{1j}^c, \ldots, x_{kj}^c),$$

$$hmax_j^c = \max(x_{1j}^c, \ldots, x_{kj}^c).$$

A pattern is said to belong to a hypercube if it is inside the hypercube. If the pattern belongs to only one hypercube then it is classified according to the class label of that hypercube. If a pattern belongs to more than one hypercube the pattern is classified as belonging to the hypercube that contains the maximum number of training patterns. If the hypercube corresponds to the correct class for the pattern then the classification error is 0, otherwise 1. The performance of the classification is measured as the percentage of the correctly classified patterns. In the case of the testing set the maximum number of dimensions containing the pattern determines which hypercube the pattern belongs to.

2.2   Hypercube with Simple Neurons

Using the training patterns we define m hypercubes corresponding to the m classes as described in A. We associate one neuron with each hypercube h^c and denote the weight vector for that neuron with

$$w^c = (w_1^c, .., w_d^c).$$

Sample architecture of the Hypercube Neural network is shown in (Fig. 1) for a 3 class problem.

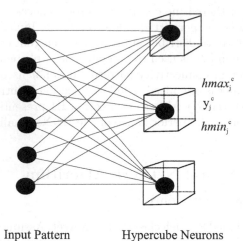

Input Pattern   Hypercube Neurons

Fig. 1. Hypercube Neural Network Architecture for 3 class problem

The weight components are initialized to $\frac{1}{d}$ at the beginning of the training process. Neurons are only trained with patterns that are in overlapping regions of hypercubes. In that case, we train the hypercube neurons of all the hypercubes to which the pattern belongs. The activation for each neuron is calculated as the sum of the weighted absolute differences between the pattern attributes values and the corresponding minimum hypercube values:

$$F(S) = F(\sum_{j=1}^{d} w_j^c \left| x_j^c - hmin_j^c \right|), \tag{1}$$

where F is the activation function. The activation function could be a simple linear function, a piecewise linear function, a sigmoid or an adaptive function. The $\left| x_j^c - hmin_j^c \right|$ terms in effect provide the coordinates of the pattern within the hypercube, taking the lower left vertex of the hypercube as the origin: in other words, the vector of the pattern within the hypercube space.

The weights associated with the neurons for those hypercubes that contain the pattern are updated using the formula:

$$w_{j,new}^c = w_{j,old}^c + \lambda e \left| x_j^c - hmin_j^c \right|, j = 1, .., d, \tag{2}$$

where λ is the learning rate for the weights set to a small number (e.g. 0.01) and e is the classification error. The classification error is determined as follows. If a pattern belongs to more than one hypercube then we check whether the pattern's class corresponds to the hypercube class and assign the classification error $e = 1 - F(S)$, otherwise $e = -F(S)$. If a pattern belongs to only one hypercube and the patterns' class corresponds to the class of the hypercube, then the error $e = 0$.

To calculate the performance of the method we use an approach that is similar to the way classification error is determined during the training process. If a pattern belongs to only one hypercube and the pattern's class coincides with the hypercube class then the classification error is 0, otherwise 1. In the case of the training set, when a pattern belongs to only one hypercube the classification error is 0. If the pattern belongs to more than one hypercube then the hypercube with the highest activation determines the membership of the pattern and subsequently the classification error, i.e. 0 if the class of the pattern and the hypercube's class are the same, 1 otherwise. If the pattern does not belong to any of the hypercubes then the highest number of dimensions within range determines the membership. When there is more than one hypercube with that maximum number of dimensions then the highest neuron activation is taken into account to define the membership and the classification error. Finally, if all of the pattern's dimensions are outside the range of the dimensions of all hypercubes then the classification error is set to 1. The performance is calculated as the percentage of the correctly classified patterns.

2.3 Hypercube with Adaptive Activation Functions

In this section we describe the algorithm when the associated activation functions with each neuron/hypercube are adaptive piecewise linear functions. The algorithm combines the simultaneous adaptation of both the weights and the shape of the individual neuron activation functions as in the case of the Adaptive Function Neural Network introduced in [3], [2]. This is a type of modal learning [11] which involves the strategic combination of modes of adaptation and learning within a single artificial neural network structure. Two or more modes may proceed in parallel in different parts of the neural computing structure (layers and neurons), or they occupy the same part of the structure, and there is a mechanism for allowing the neural network to switch between modes.

The algorithm is the same the one described in subsection B but the activation functions and the formula for updating the weights are different. Moreover, the activation functions are adapted during training. The weight components are initialised the same way as in B, but in addition they are normalised, in order to provide a stable range over which the functions can be adapted. We calculate the range of the intervals for the piecewise linear activation functions using the minimum and maximum value for the sums from formula (1) for all hypercrubes and training patterns. Then the activation functions values for each neuron are initialised to random numbers between 0 and 1 with function points evenly spaced across the calculated range. The number of points (intervals) in the activation piecewise functions is set according to the required precision. This is based on the smallest interval that is significant in the data set. During the training we calculate $F(S)$ using (1), and find the two neighbouring points that bound $F(S)$, which we denote with P_{i-1} and P_i.

We denote the values of the activation function at the points P_{i-1} and P_i as $Fval_i$ and $Fval_{i-1}$ respectively, and the slope of the activation function between these two points as $Fslope_i$. These values will be adapted in proportion to their proximity to $F(S)$. Following the algorithm from subsection B we update the weights and the activation functions in parallel for the hypercubes that contain a training pattern using:

$$w^c_{j,new} = w^c_{j,old} + \lambda e Fslope_i \left| x^c_j - hmin^c_j \right|, j = 1, \ldots, d$$

$$Fval^{new}_i = Fval_i + \mu e q_i$$

$$Fval^{new}_{i-1} = Fval_{i-1} + \mu e q_{i-1},$$

where the notations for the weights update are the same as in subsection B, $Fslope_i$ is the slope of the activation function at the particular interval, μ is the learning rate for the activation functions set to a small number (e.g. 0.1). The quantities q_i and q_{i-1} are the proximal-proportional values used to apportion the function adaptation across the two function points that bound the weighted sum input to the function, according to their proximity to the weighted sum input:

$$q_i = \frac{P_i - S}{P_i - P_{i-1}}$$

$$q_{i-1} = \frac{S - P_{i-1}}{P_i - P_{i-1}}$$

The classification error e is calculated the same way as in subsection B. Fig. 2 illustrates an adaptive linear piecewise function.

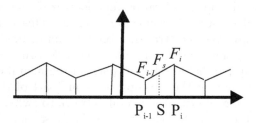

Fig. 2. Adaptive linear piecewise activation function

3   Experiments and Results

A range of data sets are chosen to represent a variety of learning challenges. They vary in terms of the number of input variables, the number of classes, and the level of separability of the classes. Since they are all known and freely available they provide useful benchmark comparisons with a number of neural computing and other machine learning techniques.

3.1   Data Sets

Animal data. The Animal data presents a simple classification problem. It is artificial data and consists of 16 animals described by 13 attributes such as size, number of legs etc. [12]. The 16 animals are grouped into three classes (the first one represents bird, the second represents carnivore and the third represents herbivore).

Breast Cancer Wisconsin. This data set was obtained from the University of Wisconsin Hospitals, Madison from Dr. William H. Wolberg [13], [14]. The data set used in the experiments consists of 683 patterns, 9 attributes and 2 classes with distribution 65.5% and 34.5%.

Ecoli. The Ecoli data set contains 336 patterns with 7 attributes and 8 classes, which are the 'localization sites' [15]. 91% of the patterns belong to 4 classes and the rest to the remaining 4 classes.

Iris data. The Iris data set has three classes setosa, virsicolor and virginica [16], [17]. The iris data has 150 patterns, each with 4 attributes. The class distribution is 33.3% for each of 3 classes. One of the classes is linearly separable from the other two, and the two are linearly inseparable from each other.

Optical and pen-based recognition of handwritten digits (OCR) data. The OCR data set [18], [19] consists of 3823 training and 1797 testing patterns. Each pattern has 64 attributes which are integer numbers between 0 and 16. There are 10 classes corresponding to the digits 0 to 9. The 64 attributes are extracted from normalised bitmaps of handwritten digits by 43 people.

The experiments with the OCR data set use the already existing division of training and testing Patterns, 3828 and 1797 respectively, as originally proposed by Kaynak [19]. This facilitates direct performance comparisons with alternative algorithms that have been applied to the same data.

Pima Indians Diabetes. The data set originates from the National Institute of Diabetes and Digestive and Kidney Diseases donated in 1990 by V. Sigillito, The Johns Hopkins University. It has 768 patterns, 8 numeric attributes and 2 classes with distribution 65% and 35%.

Tic-Tac-Toe Endgame. This data set encodes the complete set of possible board configurations at the end of tic-tac-toe games, where "x" is assumed to have played first [20]. The target concept is "win for x" (i.e., true when "x" has one of 8 possible ways to create a "three-in-a-row"). There are 958 patterns, 9 attributes and 2 classes with distribution 65.3% and 34.7%.

Yeast. This data set [15] consists of 1484 patterns, 7 attributes and 10 classes with most of patterns belonging to 4 classes.

Wine data. The Wine data set is the result of a chemical analysis of wines grown in the same region in Italy but derived from three different cultivars [21]. The analysis determines the quantities of 13 constituents (input variables) found in each of the three types of wines. There are 178 patterns with the following distribution: class 1 (59 patterns), class 2 (71 patterns), class 3 (48 patterns).

Zoo data. This is a simple data set with 101 patterns, 16 attributes and 7 classes.

3.2 Experiments

In the experiments, 20% selections of the patterns of each data set are allocated for testing and the remaining 80% form the training set. For each run the training and testing patterns are selected at random from the entire data set. The results are based on 10 runs. The Hypercube algorithm with a simple neuron requires the learning rate for the weight learning to be set as well as the number of epochs. The experiments for the data sets under investigation show that the algorithm is not sensitive to the learning rate which is set to a small number between 0.01 and 0.1. The number of epochs required for convergence is between 100 and 200. For the Hypercube algorithm with adaptive function the number of points for the piecewise functions has to be set, as well as the learning rates for the weights and the adaptive functions. The experiments reveal that 500 epochs are sufficient for training in all cases and the learning rates have to be small numbers between 0.01 and 0.1. The algorithm is most sensitive on the number of function points which varies between 10 and 50 for the data sets under consideration.

3.3   Results

Table 1 presents the results from the experiments. The notations in the Table 1 are as follows: HC is the hypercube algorithm without neurons, HCN is the hypercube algorithm with a simple neuron and HCAF is the hypercube algorithm with adaptive function. Table 2 presents comparative results for 7 of the data sets based on the results with three other algorithms: the classic Nearest Neighbour Classifier (1NN), the Batch Nested Generalised Exemplar(BNGE) and the

Table 1. Mean % correct classification for train and test sets based on 10 runs. Standard deviation is given in italic below the mean %.

Method	HC train	HC test	HCN train	HCN test	HCAF train	HCAF test
Animal	100	92	100	100	100	100
st. dev.	*0*	*11.2*	*0*	*0*	*0*	*0*
Breast	90.3	90.1	93.9	92.3	98.2	96.5
st. dev	*1.1*	*2.2*	*2.0*	*2.7*	*0.6*	*1.7*
Ecoli	78.5	72.9	92	82.4	99.6	84.4
st. dev.	*1.3*	*5.1*	*0.9*	*2.6*	*0*	*2.7*
Iris	95.1	94.4	98.9	94.6	98.8	95.8
st. dev.	*1.9*	*2.9*	*0.8*	*1.2*	*1.3*	*1.4*
OCR	36	36	97	91	99	92
st. dev.	*0*	*0*	*0*	*0*	*0*	*0*
Pima	67.6	66.4	67.5	65.5	77.1	76.6
st. dev.	*1.3*	*1.8*	*1.6*	*2.5*	*0.7*	*3.1*
Tic-tac	65.5	36.9	98.7	98.2	98.7	98.2
st. dev.	*1.1*	*3.7*	*0.4*	*0.9*	*0.4*	*0.6*
Wine	94.7	93.1	100	96.7	100	98.3
st. dev.	*0.9*	*3.2*	*0*	*2.2*	*0*	*2.2*
Yeast	35.2	34.8	54.3	51.3	57.4	55.9
st. dev.	*0.9*	*2.8*	*1.5*	*2.5*	*1.1*	*1.5*
Zoo	96.3	75	98.3	94	100	96.5
st. dev.	*5.7*	*5.4*	*0.4*	*5.1*	*0*	*2.4*

Evolutionary Selection by CHC (EHS-CHC)[8]. The BNGE is a batch version of the first NGE model and it addresses some of the limitations of NGE [4]. We compare with these methods because BNGE appears to yield the best results for the 7 data sets in Table 2, while the EHS-CHC gives the best results average results over all data sets as reported in [8]. The HCAF average results are better than the average results of the BNGE and EHS-CHC over the selected 7 data sets. HCAF gives better results in 4 of the data sets compared to BNGE and is very close in 2 others. HCAF performs better in 6 data sets in comparison to EHS-CHC.

The results for the Breast cancer and OCR data sets are comparable to the results obtained with other classifiers. For example, 95.9% (96.5% for HCAF) accuracy is reported for the Breast cancer data set in [22] using a multisurface method of pattern separation and linear programming. Using combination of four learning modes, Snap-Drift and Adaptive Functions in [2], 94.99% (92% for HCAF) accuracy is obtained for the OCR data set.

Table 2. Mean % correct classification test sets - comparison with classic and best hyperrectangle methods

Method	1NN	HCAF	BNGE	EHS-CHC
Ecoli	80.7	84.4	82.16	81.54
Iris	93.3	95.8	96	94.0
Pima	70.33	76.6	72.78	75.01
Tic-tac	73.07	98.2	92.07	92.06
Wine	95.52	98.3	96.6	94.31
Yeast	50.47	55.9	57.35	56.34
Zoo	92.81	96.5	96.83	95.00
Average	*79.45*	*86.53*	*84.83*	*84.04*

4   Conclusions

Hypercube is computationally very efficient, especially in comparison to NGE methods. Both in terms of computation and classification, the results achieved demonstrate the advantages of a simplified hypercube method that is treated as a mode of learning. Rather than perform the computationally intensive process of optimising hyperrectangles, we achieve high levels of classification by combining hypercubes with other modes. Whilst these modes carry a computational overhead, they are only invoked for the minority of patterns that reside in the overlapping regions of hypercubes. Each class is characterised by only one hypercube and a single neuron, and so the computation required scales linearly with the number of classes. The combination of the hypercube and neural modes of learning proves effective on the range of data sets considered in this work. Further investigation will focus on combining hypercubes with alternative unsupervised and supervised forms of modal learning, and applying the techniques to wider range of problems including large scale data sets. A receiver operating characteristic (ROC) analysis will be also carried out to evaluate the prosed algorithms in terms of true positive, false positive, false negative and tru engative values.

References

1. Salzberg, S.: A nearest hyperrectangle learning method. Machine Learning 6, 251–276 (1991)
2. Kang, M., Palmer-Brown, D.: A Modal Learning Adaptive Function Neural Network Applied to Handwritten Digit Recognition. Information Sciences 178(20), 3802–3812 (2008)
3. Kang, M., Palmer-Brown, D.: A Multilayer Adaptive Function Neural Network (MADFUNN) for Analytical Function Recognition. In: IJCNN (2006) part of the IEEE World Congress on Computational Intelligence, WCCI 2006, Vancouver, BC, Canada, pp. 1784–1789 (2006)
4. Wettschereck, D., Dietterich, T.G.: An experimental comparison of the nearest-neighbor and nearest-hyperrectangle algorithms. Machine Learning 19(1), 5–27 (1995)
5. Carpenter, G.A., Grossberg, S., Markuzon, N., Reynolds, J.H., Rosen, D.B.: Fuzzv ARTMAP: A Neural Network Architecture for Incremental Supervised Learning of Analog Multidimensional Maps. IEEE Transactions on Neural Networks 3(5), 698–712 (1992)
6. Wilson, D.R., Martinez, T.R.: Reduction Techniques for Instance-Based Learning Algorithms. Machine Learning 38(3), 257–286 (2000)
7. Garcia, S., Cano, J.R., Herreraa, F.: A memetic algorithm for evolutionary prototype selection: A scaling up approach. Pattern Recognition 41(8), 2693–2709 (2008)
8. Garcia, S., Derracb, J., Luengob, J., Carmonab, C., Herreraa, F.: Evolutionary Selection of Hyperrectangles in Nested Generalized Exemplar Learning. Applied Soft Computing (2010), doi:10.1016/j.asoc.2010.11.030
9. Simpson, P.K.: Fuzzy min-max neural networks. I. Classification. IEEE Transactions on Neural Networks 3(5), 776–786 (1992), doi:10.1109/72.159066
10. Furmanski, G.C.F.: Hypercube Algorithms for Neural Network Simulation The Crystal_Accumulator and the Crystal_Router. In: Proceedings of the Third Conference on Hypercube Concurrent Computers and Applications: Architecture, Software, Computer Systems, and General Issues, vol. 1, pp. 714–724 (1988)
11. Palmer-Brown, D., Lee, S.W., Draganova, C., Kang, M.: Modal Learning Neural Networks. WSEAS Transactions on Computers 8(2), 222–236 (2009)
12. Ritter, H., Kohonen, T.: Self-Organizing Semantic Maps. Biological Cybernetics 61, 241–254 (1989)
13. Mangasarian, O.L., Wolberg, W.H.: Cancer diagnosis via linear programming. SIAM News 23(5), 1–18 (1990)
14. William, H., Wolberg, Mangasarian, O.L.: Multisurface method of pattern separation for medical diagnosis applied to breast cytology. Proceedings of the National Academy of Sciences, U.S.A. 87, 9193–9196 (1990)
15. Horton, P., Nakai, K.: A Probablistic Classification System for Predicting the Cellular Localization Sites of Proteins. Intelligent Systems in Molecular Biology, 109–115 (1996)

16. Fisher, R.A.: The use of multiple measurements in taxonomic problems. Annual Eugenics 7, part II, 179–188 (1936); also in Contributions to Mathematical Statistics. John Wiley, NY (1950)
17. Duda, R.O., Hart, P.E.: Pattern Classification and Scene Analysis, p. 218. John Wiley & Sons, New York (1973)
18. Alpaydin, E., Kaynak, C.: Cascading Classifiers. Kybernetika 34, 369–374 (1998)
19. Kaynak, C.: Methods of Combining Multiple Classifiers and Their Applications to Handwritten Digit Recognition. MSc Thesis, Institute of Graduate Studies in Science and Engineering, Bogazici University (1995)
20. Aha, D.W.: Incremental constructive induction: An instance-based approach. In: Proceedings of the Eighth International Workshop on Machine Learning, pp. 117–121 (1991)
21. Forina, M., Lanteri, S., Armanino, C., et al.: PARVUS–an extendible package for data exploration, classification and correlation. Institute of Pharmaceutical and Food Analysis and Technologies, Via Brigata Salerno, 16147 Genoa, Italy (1991)
22. Wolberg, W.H., Mangasarian, O.L.: Multisurface method of pattern separation for medical diagnosis applied to breast cytology. Proceedings of the National Academy of Sciences 87, 9193–9196 (1990)

Improving the Classification Performance of Liquid State Machines Based on the Separation Property

Emmanouil Hourdakis and Panos Trahanias

Institute of Computer Science,
Foundation for Research and Technology – Hellas (FORTH),
Heraklion, Greece

Abstract. Liquid State Machines constitute a powerful computational tool for carrying out complex real time computations on continuous input streams. Their performance is based on two properties, approximation and separation. While the former depends on the selection of class functions for the readout maps, the latter needs to be evaluated for a particular liquid architecture. In the current paper we show how the Fisher's Discriminant Ratio can be used to effectively measure the separation of a Liquid State Machine. This measure is then used as a fitness function in an evolutionary framework that searches for suitable liquid properties and architectures in order to optimize the performance of the trained readouts. Evaluation results demonstrate the effectiveness of the proposed approach.

Keywords: Liquid State Machines, Separation, Fisher Discriminant Ratio.

1 Introduction

Liquid State Machines (LSMs) are based on the concept of using biologically realistic neural networks for processing continuous input channels of information [9,10]. Their powerful computational abilities can be attributed to the capacity of these networks to transform the temporal dynamics of an input signal into a high dimensional spatio-temporal pattern, which preserves recent and past information about the input. This information can be retrieved with a high degree of accuracy using certain types of classifiers.

Following their introduction [9], LSMs have been used in various pattern classification tasks, including speech recognition [14] and movement prediction [2]. The notion behind LSMs has also been extended to problem domains outside computational modeling, where researchers use physical mediums for the implementation of the liquid, such as a bucket of water [5] or real cell assemblies [3].

An LSM consists of three components: *(i)* the liquid, i.e. a pool M of spiking neurons that accepts input from different sources and outputs a series of spike trains, *(ii)* a filter L that is applied on the output of the liquid in order to create a state matrix S, and *(iii)* one or more memoryless readout maps that are trained to extract information from S. The main conception behind this setup is that the complex dynamics of the input are transformed by the liquid to a high dimensional space, in a way that

L. Iliadis and C. Jayne (Eds.): EANN/AIAI 2011, Part I, IFIP AICT 363, pp. 52–62, 2011.

preserves their recent and past properties. This can be compared to a pool of water with a stone thrown in it. The disturbances that are caused in the liquid could be used by a trained observer to deduce the properties of the motion of the stone before entering the water.

To improve the classification performance of an LSM, one must ensure that for two different input histories, the liquid states produced are significantly different [8]. This property, known as separation, has recently received increased attention in the literature, due to its close correlation with the performance of the LSM. In [9] the separation between two different liquid states is calculated by measuring the Euclidean distance of their state vector, i.e. the filtered neuron output sampled at one time instance. A similar geometric interpretation has been given by [7], who measure the separation of the liquid as the Euclidean distance between the centroids of the states that belong to different classes. In [3], the authors use spike train distance metrics instead of Euclidean distance. From the perspective of a classification system, it has been suggested that the rank of the state matrix S can be used to measure the quality of the liquid [8]. According to this measure, the larger the number of linear independent variables produced by a liquid state, the better the classification that can be performed by the LSM.

Attempts to improve the performance of an LSM in the literature have shown that it is very difficult to devise a proper measure or structural criterion to optimize the quality of the liquid. For example in [18] the authors have concluded that randomly generated liquids outperform any attempt to structurally modify the LSM. In [17] the authors use both reinforcement learning and genetic algorithms in order to optimize the classification performance of the LSM. Finally in [16] the authors use the centroid separation measure in order to drive the synaptic modification of the LSM.

In the current paper we propose a criterion that measures the separation of the liquid states that correspond to different classes based on the class means and variances. The classification performance of an LSM is subsequently improved by employing an evolutionary framework to minimize the introduced criterion. Experimental results attest on the performance and accuracy of the proposed approach.

2 Separation Measure

Similarly to Support Vector Machines, the liquid of the LSM acts as a kernel that transforms the low-dimensional space of an input signal to the spatio-temporal space of the liquid. When used for classification, it is important that this transformation yields liquid states that are well separated across different classes. Thus an appropriate measure of the quality of the LSM is a criterion that incorporates the liquid means and variances in order to compute the separation of the data. For a classification task of ω_i different classes we define three quantities.

(a) The between-class scatter matrix:

$$S_b = \sum_{i=1}^{M} P_i \, (\mu_i - \mu_0)(\mu_i - \mu_0)^T \tag{1}$$

where $\mu_0 = \sum_{i=1}^{M} P_i \mu_i$ is the global mean vector for all M classes, P_i is the a priori probability of class ω_i, and μ_i is the mean of the liquid states that correspond to class ω_i.

(b) The within-class scatter matrix:

$$S_w = \sum_{i=1}^{M} P_i \Sigma_i \tag{2}$$

where Σ_i is the covariance matrix of the liquid states that correspond to class ω_i, and P_i is as eq. 1.

(c) The covariance matrix S_m with respect to the μ_0 global mean:

$$S_m = S_w + S_b \tag{3}$$

The trace of the S_m matrix adequately describes the sum of the variances of the features around the global mean, while the trace of the S_w matrix is the sum of the feature variances computed for all classes. Consequently, the separation between different classes can be determined using the following quantity:

$$FDR = trace\{S_w^{-1} S_m\} \tag{4}$$

which is the generalization of the Fisher Discriminant Ratio [FDR, 19] to more than two classes.

To apply the FDR measure on an LSM we sample the spatio-temporal patterns of the liquid's action potentials with respect to each input. These are used to construct the state matrix S:

$$S = \begin{bmatrix} s_{11} & \cdots & s_{1j} \\ \vdots & \ddots & \vdots \\ s_{i1} & \cdots & s_{ij} \end{bmatrix} \tag{5}$$

where s_{ij} is the filtered output of the jth spiking neuron in the liquid and i is the index of the time window in which the outputs of the neurons are sampled. For each task, we create n matrices S, each corresponding to a different class. The FDR measure is then calculated based on eqs. 1-4.

3   Genetic Algorithm Based Liquid Evolution

The separation of the liquid is positively correlated with the performance of the LSM [8]. Consequently, one can improve the classification performance of the trained readouts by designing a liquid that has a high separation measure. To accomplish this we minimize the FDR (eq. 4) of a liquid using genetic algorithms (GAs). GAs are a stochastic optimization method that can optimize complex functions by exploiting their parameter space [6]. Due to their ability to find good solutions in multi-modal and non-differentiable functions they have been extensively used to optimize the performance of neural networks. In these cases researchers encode properties such as the architecture, weights or neuronal models of the network and exploit them in order to minimize some objective optimization function (see [15] for a review). To evolve the LSM we utilize three types of properties: *(i)* the parameters of the neurons in the liquid, *(ii)* the architecture of the liquid, and *(iii)* the local properties of each architecture. The effect these parameters have on the liquid performance is discussed in the following.

The first part of the chromosome encodes the firing threshold of all neurons in the liquid and the mean of the Gaussian noise added to the neurons' output on every step. These two parameters control the responsiveness and generalization properties of each neuron. In the first case, if the firing threshold of a neuron is low, then it will require to integrate more spikes before firing a post-synaptic potential, making the liquid less responsive to the perturbations of the low input signals. The second parameter controls the mean of the white noise added to each neuron, which affects the generalization properties of the training.

The second part of the chromosome encodes three different architectures for the LSM. Each architecture specifies a different way for connecting the inputs to the liquid, and the inter-liquid connectivity (Fig. 1). In architecture 1, all input neurons are connected to all neurons within the liquid. Thus all task information is integrated in overlapping liquid locations. This is the original setup suggested by [9]. In the second architecture the neurons that encode the input from different sources project to different locations in the liquid. In this case, the resulting LSM will produce a state vector whose entries correspond to particular input properties. The third architecture also incorporates the properties of the input, but discriminates it depending on whether they are temporally varying or static throughout the classification task. Temporally varying inputs project to different locations within the liquid, while the constant input signals are propagated to all neurons.

Architecture 1   Architecture 2   Architecture 3

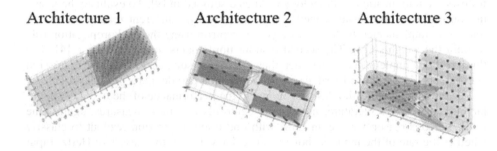

Fig. 1. The three architectures used in the genetic algorithm, shown from a different perspective in order to highlight how the components are connected together. In each architecture the liquid component of the LSM is shaded with red, while the inputs with green.

The last part of the chromosome encodes the properties common to all architectures. These include the size of the liquid map and the locality of the connections in the liquid (i.e. the size of the neighborhood that each neuron is allowed to connect to). Because of the exponential descending output of the dynamic synapses of the LSM [10], the last parameter affects the chaotic dynamics of the liquid, i.e. the period in which a certain input has an effect on the liquid state.

To evolve the chromosomes we use 3 different operators, mutation, crossover and selection. Mutation was implemented by adding a random number drawn from a

Gaussian distribution, with zero mean and standard deviation that starts from 1 and decreases linearly until it reaches 0 in the final generation. To perform crossover, the GA selects (with probability 0.5) a bit from each parent chromosome in order to form a child. Selection was implemented using a roulette wheel function.

4 Experimental Results

In the current section we evaluate the performance of the FDR measure and the GA optimization framework on a number of different classification tasks. For this reason, we focus on two issues: *(i)* the ability of the proposed measure to predict the quality of the liquid in an LSM, and *(ii)* whether the optimization framework can reduce the error of the readouts by minimizing the FDR.

4.1 Measure Evaluation

To evaluate the FDR measure we use three classification tasks, which incorporate different methods for encoding the input. This is important since diverse input encodings can have a different effect on the liquid dynamics. Population codes [11] provide a consistent representation of the input by using distributed and partially overlapping neuron groups in order to encode the values of a variable. In contrast, rate codes [11] produce a higher homogeneity when used as input because they employ the same neuron to represent different input values. Consequently in the three tasks discussed below, rate codes are used to encode the input in two cases, whereas population codes are used in the third case. The liquid in all the aforementioned classification tasks follows the initialization and topology settings discussed in [9]. To evaluate the measure on different classification methods we employ four different readouts: the first readout is implemented with a multi-layer perceptron using the backpropagation rule to train the weights [12]. The second readout implements linear regression [4]. The third readout implements a classifier that uses least squares to find the regression coefficients [4], while the fourth the p-Delta rule on a parallel perceptron layer [1].

For the first classification task, we compare the performance of the two most popular measures in the literature, namely the centroids and rank measures, against the FDR. For this reason we use an LSM with one linear regression readout to classify whether the rate of the input is above a particular value, in this case five Hertz. Input is encoded as a random Poisson rate and applied for 1000ms to a pool of Leaky Integrate and Fire [13] spiking neurons. The liquid used for this purpose consists of a pool of 125 spiking neurons, arranged in a 3 dimensional grid. States are sampled every 10ms for 1 second and input to the 4 readout units.

The FDR, Rank and Centroids measures were *(a)* calculated for the two state vectors S_1 and S_2 from eq. 5 that correspond to classes ω_1 and ω_2, and *(b)* compared against the performance of a linear regression readout for 16 different simulations (Fig. 2).

A good measure should be positively correlated with the error of any trained readout that is used to extract information from the liquid. As Fig. 2 shows there is a clear correlation between the value of the error of a readout map and the value of the FDR measure (for both cases high values close to 1 are colored with red shades, while low values close to 0 are colored with blue). Furthermore, the results presented in Fig. 2 show

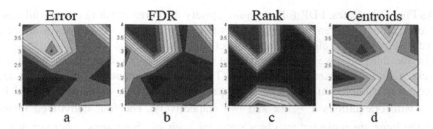

Fig. 2. Evaluation of the FDR, Rank and Centroids measures against their ability to predict the performance of the linear readout map of an LSM. In each subplot the x,y axes correspond to different configurations for an LSM. The color in each x,y entry corresponds to the value of the error (for subplot a) or the negative value of the measure (for subplots b,c,d).

that the proposed measure outperforms the Centroids measure and, at the same time, performs better than the Rank measure. By comparing Fig. 2a and Fig. 2b, it is evident that the FDR measure can predict with satisfying accuracy the performance of the linear regression readout and, therefore, the separation of the liquid in the LSM (readout error/FDR correlation was 0.86). Due to space limitations we do not provide the corresponding contour plots for the other three readouts, although we note that the results were similar to the ones presented in Fig. 2.

The second task requires the LSM to classify two different motions of an object, based on the projection of its image on a 9x9 grid of receptive field neurons. The output of the retina field is encoded as a group of 81 neurons, each one corresponding to a different cell. These neurons fire random Poisson spikes of 30Hz when their corresponding cell in the retina field is occupied, and at a rate of 5Hz otherwise. This output is then projected to a liquid with 63 neurons, where we record the post-synaptic potentials of the neurons for 3 sec (3000ms). Information from the liquid response is used to classify whether the movement on the retina belongs to either one of the two behaviors for 9 different simulations. The error is calculated by subtracting the readout value from the actual behavior being performaned for each step of the simulaton, and normalized to 1. Due to space limitations, results are not presented for this task in the form of contour plots but rather as graphs of the errors of the readouts against the FDR (Fig. 3).

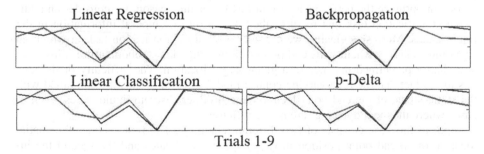

Fig. 3. Graphs of the FDR measure (blue line) against the readout error (red line) of linear regression, backpropagation, linear classification and pDelta methods. The x-axis corresponds to the 9 different trials of the simulation, while the y-axis shows the output of the corresponding error and measure.

As Fig. 3 illustrates, FDR follows quite closely the corresponding error in all cases. The correlation between the FDR measure and the readout error was in all cases above 0.8, indicating a close relationship between the two.

For the third task we use an LSM that must classify the type of three different objects, a circle, a square and a hexagon. To encode the input we first sharpen each image using a Laplacian filter and consequently convolve it with 4 different Gabor filters with orientations π, $\frac{\pi}{2}$, 2π and $-\frac{\pi}{2}$ respectively. The four convolved images from the input are projected into four neuronal grids of 25 neurons, where each neuron corresponds to a different location in the Gabor output. Information from the liquid response is classified by the above mentioned four readouts for 9 different simulations (Fig. 4).

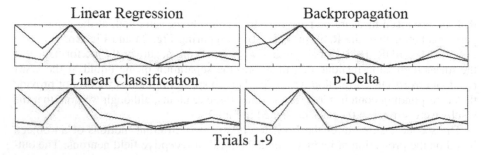

Trials 1-9

Fig. 4. Graphs of the FDR measure (blue line) against the readout error (red line) of linear regression, backpropagation, linear classification and pDelta methods. The x-axis corresponds to the 9 different trials of the simulation, while the y-axis shows the output of the corresponding error and measure.

The results presented above for all three tasks, indicate that the FDR measure can describe the quality of the liquid over a broad range of tasks and input encodings.

4.2 Liquid Optimization

In the current section we evaluate the extent to which the aforementioned GA framework can optimize the performance of an LSM. For this reason, we consider an additional classification task that requires the integration of temporal information in the liquid states. More specifically, we consider a binary classification task in which an LSM must classify whether the end point of a moving planar robotic arm is closer (or not) than a predefined distance to a given target location. The difficulty of the task lies in the fact that the time-varying control model of the arm must be combined with the static signal of the end point location and produce discrete liquid states, even in cases where the input dynamics are not so different.

Input in this case consists of two different channels. The first encodes the spatial location of an end point position in (x, y) space coordinates and the second the inverse kinematics of different arm trajectories. Input joint positions are generated by creating different trajectories using a two-link planar arm based on one start position (Fig. 5a), three speed profiles (Fig. 5b) and five random ending positions for the train and test sets (Fig. 5c,d). The training set consists of the trajectories between the initial position (Fig. 5a) and a random end position (Fig. 5c). The test set is generated using a different set of ending positions (Fig. 5d).

To determine the trajectory between a starting and ending position, a random speed profile is chosen from the templates in Fig. 5b. The joint configurations of the robot across the pathway of a trajectory are obtained using an iterative solution to the inverse kinematics problem based on the pseudo-inverse of the robot's Jacobian.

To encode the target position we use a population code with 10 neurons for each dimension (i.e. the x, y coordinates). Thus for the two dimensional space 20 input neurons are used. The simulated robotic arm that is employed in the experiments consists of 2 joints, namely elbow and shoulder, which are also encoded using population codes.

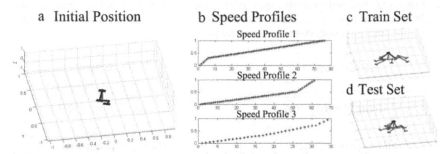

Fig. 5. a. The initial position of the robot's arm. **b.** The three speed profiles used to generate random movements. **c.** The five different configurations of the arm of the robot for the five ending positions of the train set. **d.** The five different configurations of the arm for the test set.

The classification task we consider requires the LSM to predict whether in the next location, the end point of the robot's arm will be closer than a predefined distance to the object in x, y coordinates. To classify a given location correctly, the LSM must make a prediction on the speed of the arm at any given time. Hence, the liquid state must integrate information about the location of the robot's end-point effector position in previous time steps. To generate the different liquid states we have run 100 simulations for the train set kinematics and 30 simulations for the test set kinematics. To learn the classification task, these liquid states were input to 4 readout units, namely a feedforward neural network, a parallel perceptron layer, a linear regression and a linear classification readout.

Even though the results reported here regard the optimal individual produced by the genetic algorithm, it should be noted that similar results were obtained for all chromosomes in the last generation. The GA was run for 18 generations in order to minimize the FDR criterion (Fig. 6). As the four rightmost plots in Fig. 6 show, while the genetic algorithm was used to minimize the FDR measure, it also reduced the error on all four readout maps.

The subplots in Fig. 6 demonstrate how the GA was able to optimize the performance of the LSM by reducing the classification error of the readouts. The error was reduced from 0.3 to 0.1 in all four readouts maps (Fig. 6, right four subplots), simply by optimizing the FDR measure on the liquid (Fig. 6, left subplot) during the evolutionary process. The improvement in the liquid performance is also evident when we examine the output of the four classifiers in the optimal individual produced by the GA. As Fig. 7 shows, all the readouts are able to classify different movements with a high degree of accuracy.

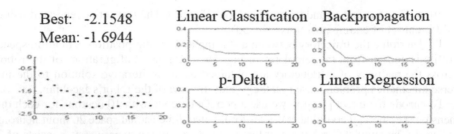

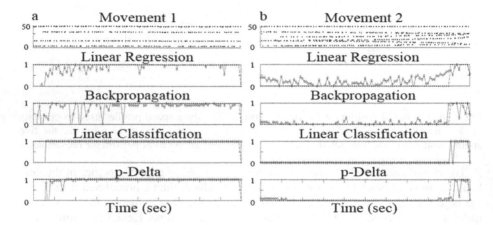

Fig. 6. The results from the evolution of the LSM for 18 generations of the 100 individuals. The left plot shows the best and mean fitness (y-axis) of the population on each generation (x-axis). The right set of four plots shows the average error of the four readouts across the generations (y-axis) of the 100 individuals (x-axis) in the final population.

Fig. 7. The output of the four trained readouts for two sample movements (four bottom sub-plots) and the input projected to the liquid (top subplot)

In the first example (plot a), the robot's arm never reaches the target location in a distance closer than required. In the second (plot b), it approximates the end location in the final 10 simulation steps. In both plots, we show the stimulus input to the liquid (top graph of plots a,b), the output of the four readouts (blue lines in bottom four graphs of plots a,b) and the target for each readout (red lines in bottom four graphs of plots a,b). Each graph is labeled with the corresponding readout map. The x-axis represents the simulation time in 100ms intervals for all graphs.

5 Discussion

In the current paper we presented a method for improving the computational capabilities of LSMs by focusing on the separation property of the liquid. This was measured using the Fisher's Discriminant Ratio, a measure that is maximized when the class means are far from each other, and the class variances are as small as possible. To evaluate the FDR measure against a broad range of classification tasks, we incorporated different types of neuron encodings for the input. As the results show, the FDR criterion accurately predicts the performance of the readouts without having any knowledge of the algorithm used to train them. Due to this fact, the GA, by minimizing the value of the FDR criterion, also improved the performance of all four classifiers.

In contrast to other criterions, the FDR is a supervised measure, i.e. requires the class labels in order to compute the quantities in eqs. 1-3. Consequently, the evolutionary framework that was presented is also supervised. We consider this a benefit of the method, since it allows the design of liquid architectures that will be suited for the specific dynamics of the classification task.

The proposed methodology will be used to develop a large-scale model of movement imitation and observational learning. In this context, the FDR measure can be employed to optimize the performance of the LSMs that underpin the agent's perception and motor control system. We also plan to investigate whether projecting the liquid states along the eigenvectors of the argument of the FDR measure, can further improve class separation.

References

1. Auer, P., Burgsteiner, H., Maass, W.: A learning rule for very simple universal approximators consisting of a single layer. Neural Nets 21, 786–795 (2008)
2. Burgsteiner, H., Kroll, M., Leopold, A., Steinbauer, G.: Movement prediction from real-world images using a liquid state machine. Applied Intelligence 27(2), 99–109 (2007)
3. Dockendorf, K.P., Park, I., He, P., Principe, J.C., DeMarse, T.B.: Liquid state machines and cultured cortical networks: The separation property. BioSystems 95(2), 90–97 (2009)
4. Duda, R.O., Hart, P.E., Stork, D.G.: Pattern Classification. Wiley, Chichester (2000)
5. Fernando, C., Sojakka, S.: Pattern recognition in a bucket. Advances in ALife, 588–597 (2003)
6. Fogel, D.B.: An introduction to simulated evolutionary optimization. IEEE Trans. Neural Networks 5, 3–14 (1994)
7. Goodman, E., Ventura, D.: Spatiotemporal pattern recognition via liquid state machines. In: Intl. Joint Conf. Neural Networks, IJCNN, pp. 3848–3853 (2006)
8. Legenstein, R., Maass, W.: Edge of chaos and prediction of computational performance for neural circuit models. Neural Nets 20(3), 323–334 (2007)
9. Maass, W., Natschlaeger, T., Markram, H.: Real-time computing without stable states: A new framework for neural computation based on perturbations. Neural Computation 14(11), 2531–2560 (2002)
10. Natschlager, T., Markram, H., Maass, W.: Computer models and analysis tools for neural microcircuits. A practical guide, pp. 123–138 (2003)
11. Rieke, F.: Spikes: Exploring the neural code. MIT Press, Cambridge (1999)
12. Rumelhart, D., Hinton, G., Williams, R.: Learning Internal Representations by Error Propagation. In: Parallel Distributed Processing: Explorations in the Microstructure of Cognition, vol. 1. MIT Press, Cambridge (1986)
13. Stein: Some models of neuronal variability. Biophysical Journal 7, 37–68 (1967)
14. Verstraeten, D., Schrauwen, B., Stroobandt, D.: Isolated word recognition with the liquid state machine: a case study. In: 13th European Symp. Artificial Neural Nets (ESANN), vol. 95(6), pp. 435–440 (2005)

15. Yao, X.: Evolving artificial neural networks. Proc. of the IEEE 87(9), 1423–1447 (1999)
16. Norton, D., Ventura, D.: Improving the performance of liquid state machines through iterative refinement of the reservoir. Neurocomputing 73, 2893–2904 (2010)
17. Kok, S.: Liquid State Machine Optimization, Master Thesis, Utrecht University (2007)
18. Matser, J.: Structured liquids in liquid state machines, Master Thesis, Utrecht University (2010)
19. Fisher, R.A.: "The Use of Multiple Measurements in Taxonomic Problems" (PDF). Annals of Eugenics 7(2), 179–188 (1936)

A Scale-Changeable Image Analysis Method

Hui Wei, Bo Lang, and Qing-song Zuo

Laboratory of Cognitive Model and Algorithm, School of Computer Science and Technology,
Fudan University, Shanghai, China
weihui@fudan.edu.cn, blang2004@gmail.com, qingsong.zuo@gmail.com

Abstract. The biological vision system is far more efficient than machine vision system. This is due to the former has rich neural layers for representation and process. In order to obtain a non-task-dependent image representation schema, the early phase of neural vision mechanism is worth simulating. We design a neural model to simulate non-classical receptive field of ganglion cell and its local feedback control circuit, and find it can represent image, beyond pixel level, self-adaptively and regularly. The experimental results prove this method can represent image faithfully with low cost, and can produce a compact and abstract approximation to facilitate successive image segmentation as well as integration operation. This representation schema is good at extracting spatial relationship from different components of image, thus it can be applied to formalize image semantics. Further it can be applied to object recognition or image classification tasks in future.

Keywords: Neurons, non-classical receptive field, image representation, feedback control circuit.

1 Introduction

The function of any representation scheme is to capture the essential features of an image and make those features accessible at higher processing layers. The target of image representation is to discover what objects are in an image, and how about their spatial relations. Human vision system generates an internal representation for the external stimulus and requires an internal data structure recording the spatial distribution of stimulus. Such a fundamental data structure is also required by computer vision for recording the image. A better representation should characterize an image by the spatial relationships between them such that a later processing can be adapted to preserver or enhance these relationships.

In order to achieve this goal, a bio-inspired image representation model based on non-classical receptive field (nCRF) is constructed, in which every nCRF denotes a unit of visual information processing, basic, structural and functional. Ganglion cell (GC) merges all stimuli occurring in its RF and reports a composite message upwards for further processing. By means of these dense and regular RFs, many GCs can realize a general representation for any outside stimuli.

Image representation is of primary importance for developing effective image processing and analysis techniques. However, due to lack of a complete

L. Iliadis and C. Jayne (Eds.): EANN/AIAI 2011, Part I, IFIP AICT 363, pp. 63–68, 2011.
© IFIP International Federation for Information Processing 2011

understanding of the human vision system and the existence of an infinite number of probable image patterns, it is extremely difficult to construct a universal model for various natural scene images. Facing this dilemma, researchers in this field have resorted to designing separate models for different applications. Some mechanisms proposed for image representation range from color histogram to feature statistics, from spatial frequency based to region based, and from color detection to topology detection. For a more extensive review of image representation techniques, see [1], [2], [3], [4]. Another image representation scheme using a set of block pattern models was constructed in which each model a small image block is satisfying certain intensity variation constraints. Although many representation schemes have been proposed, local image patterns was characterized by their statistical properties (i.e. pixels) in most of them. Those operations only differentiating and labeling pixels, this is far away from grasping semantic of an image. As we known, an image is an array of pixels, and this kind of discrete and separate structure cannot manifest semantic organization of image in-depth. Assembled or clustered pixels are more meaningful and effective than single pixel. So a novel representation fashion that can make pixels clustered into some sets or regions is required. Our formulation is unique in that each RF represents explicitly a basic image unit and is described by block-grained. Each block is a compact unit including semantic and every of them should be perfectly divisible units. There is a vivid metaphor describing it, holding a dozen of small tones must be much easier than holding 10-thousands grains of sands with same weight. Integrating pixels of image and use a set to pocket them is an indispensible step in image understanding. It provided a heuristic approach that integrating properly and reducing the load of memory will greatly facilitate semantic emerging.

The arrangement of this paper is as follows. In section II, we formalize the design of the image representation model based on nCRF. Some experiment results are presented in Section III. Finally, in Section IV, we conclude the paper by summarizing the main result and suggesting possible future investigations.

2 Formulations of the Multi-layer Computational Model Based on nCRF

2.1 A Computational Model for RF Self-adaptive Adjusting Dynamically

Neurophysiological shows that the horizontal cell (HC) with a wide range of electrical synaptic connections, it can receive inputs from large areas of receptor cells (RCs). When a disinhibitory nCRF are solely and fully stimulated by grating patches with low spatial frequency, large area horizontal cells can be simultaneously activated. It affects the activities of RCs by means of spatial summation and feedback and then elicits the (GC) responses to the stimuli within the disinhibitory nCRF through bipolar cells (BCs). Moreover, the amacrine cell (AC) connects many of the nearby GCs in the horizontal direction through its extensive dendritic branches. ACs also interconnect with each other. The breadth of AC's connection exceeds far beyond GC's CRF surround, So AC is properly related to the formation of nCRF with a wide range. Thus, HC and AC play the role of information integration in the outer and inner plexiform layer respectively. GC receive inputs from many neurons in the outer and inner plexiform layer, hence HC and AC are properly connected with the formation of nCRF of retinal GC. Figure 1 shows the details of computational model. According to the computational model show in Fig. 1. The RF's size can self-adaptive adjusting according to the color changing of region is uniform or sharp.

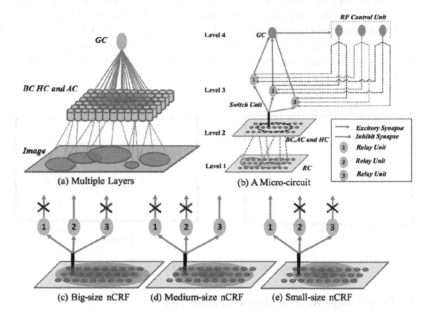

(a) Multiple Layers   (b) A Micro-circuit

(c) Big-size nCRF   (d) Medium-size nCRF   (e) Small-size nCRF

Fig. 1. A multi-layer neural architecture and how a GC adjusts its nCRF dynamically (a)is a multiple layers architecture. For the sake of clarity, only one GC and its nCRF is drawn. A nCRF has three rings with positive, negative and positive weight values. (b) This is a neural circuit of nCRF adjusting dynamically, which is a small function unit of (a) in detail. Because a neuron can change its output projection direction according to changing stimulus, nCRF can dynamically change its size. This can be realized by three relay neurons and three switch neurons. A switch neuron imposes its backward control on three relay neurons, and selectively permits only one relay outputting its signal upwards to GC. The relay neuron may have a chance to join one of three different rings of nCRF(c)-(d). With the different switch is turning on ,the same neuron may exclusively participate in forming one of rings of a nCRF. Then a size-changing nCRF come into being. (c) is big one, (d) is middle one and (e) is small one.

3   Experiments Results

A series of experiments is performed, from several single attributes to the whole function one-by-one, to test the efficiency of nCRF based representation model.

3.1   The Relationship between Entropy and Number of RF

Information entropy is a key concept in information theory. If this concept is applied in image description, it can measure the extent of color change in an image. If we define the quantity of information contained in an image as the number of blocks it contains, then according to the equation of entropy, we get:

$$I[M] = \left(\sum_{i=1}^{n} -p(m_i) \log_2(p(m_i)) \right) = E\left[-\log_2 p(m_i) \right]$$. where M is a set of

classes of blocks with different sizes, M = {m1, m2, ..., mn}, and each class has multiple occurrences, meaning there can be a number of blocks of the same size. A set {p(mi)} defines the numerical likelihood that all classes occur. I[M] represents the information entropy of an image. In terms of the same strategies used in two previous experiments, we calculated information entropies of 300 images, and sorted them into a sequence based on these values.

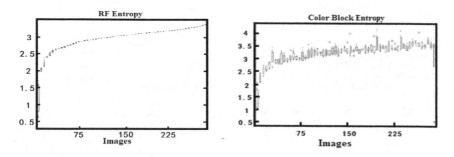

Fig. 2. RF-based entropy and block-based entropy

3.2 Multiscale Image Representation Using nCRF

There exists hierarchical structure among biological tissue of vision, characteristics of external object and the image process. Therefore, the image feature must be described clearly by vision image with multi-scale. Utilizing wavelet transform, a unified mathematic description of the scale of vision image can be achieved with multiscale or multiresolution analysis. The wavelet $\psi(x)$ is stretched as $\psi(x/a)$ (a denote scale) to construct a set of primary functions. When the value of a arises, the primary function can represent the global feature of image, on the contrary, while it descends, it can be used to search for the detailed information of image.

From the pattern of nCRF, the equivalent functional form of single GC or LGN cell for performing calculation in local scope, and the exhaustive distribution of GC and LGN array on the whole vision, it can be concluded that the process of GC and LGN array for image is very similar to the wavelet transform. In fact, DOG function, which is widely used by researcher, is a wavelet function itself, too. A distinctive feature of wavelet transform is the multiscale analysis, which can use different observing scale to detect and represent different size characteristics. The RF of GC and LGN are capable of dynamically changed, it realized the effective extraction and representation for local characteristics of stimulation. For example, the large continuous areas are suitable for being represented by large-sized RF, while the details of image are suitable for being represented by small-sized RF. In this regard, the nervous system shows the adaptability and suitability of the structure and functionality. To explore the mathematical essence of the physiological mechanism, wavelet transform is a very appropriate tool for description. Fig. 3 illustrates the close association between image processing result from the nCRF mechanism and wavelet transformation.

The experiment result shows that:

(1) With the increasing of level of wavelet transformation, the details of image are gradually faded and the regional characteristic of image emerges simultaneously. The characteristic in these space positions can be exactly rep-resented by the lag-er-size RF.
(2) The details of image can be exactly represented by the small-size RF.
(3) Multi-scale analysis come from wavelet transform can be represented by Multi-size RF.

It can be found that nCRF is an image analysis using neural computation actually, of which function is similar to wavelet transform. This method is credible because its foundation of mathematic is derived from wavelet transform. Although computation ability may not exceed wavelet transform, the representation based on neuron can achieve the synchronous enhance effect in a certain scope by means of synchronous oscillations, and make them prominent from the whole group of neurons. All of these may be the mechanism of neurons, of which can realize the image integration and segmentation.

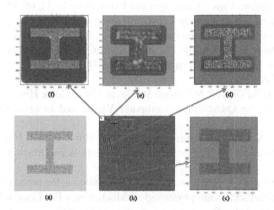

Fig. 3. Multiscale image representation using nCRF. The red circle denotes the RF with different size. (a) is original image. (b) is an image after wavelet transform.(c) is the distribution of minimum-size RF, which able to represent the details of face in the image. (d) is the distribution of medium-size RF. (e) is the distribution of large-size RF. (f) is the distribution of full-size RF, which able to represent the region with homogeneous color in the image.

4 Discussion

The feasibility for image representation based on nCRF is studied in this work. The real effect of nCRF is newly thought as increasing the encoding efficiency and lowering the redundancy of cells. Visual system can be regarded as a system of information processing and encoding according to information theory [12]. If visual system takes adaptation to natural stimulus as its evolutional goal, it can certainly employ the most effective encoding method for natural images. Since natural images have high relativity, the visual information inputting to RCs is largely redundant [13]. They found that the modulation of nCRF increases the selectivity of the responses of V1 neurons in and the sparsity of the response distribution of groups of neurons. The narrow effective bandwidth of the response curve of single neuron does not decrease the amount of information. Therefore, they thought that the modulation of nCRF help improve the encoding efficiency of visual information. For this purpose, two measures should be taken: first, increase the encoding efficiency of single cell and fully utilized the dynamic characteristics of the cell itself; second, reduce as much as possibly the redundancy in cells possibly and use as few cells as possible to transfer information, which remains the principal problem for our future work.

Acknowledgments. This work is supported by 973 Program (Project No. 2010CB327900), the NSFC major project (Project No. 30990263) and Shanghai Key Laboratory of Intelligent Information Processing, China (Grant No. IIPL-09-009).

References

1. Eauqueue, J., Boujemaa, N.: Region-based Image Retrieval: Fast Coarse Segmentation and Fine Color Description. Vision Languages and Computing 15(1), 69–95 (2004)
2. Deng, Y., Manjunath, B.S., Kenney, C.: An Efficient Color Representation For Image Retrieval. IEEE Transaction on Image Processing 10(1), 140–147 (2001)
3. Saykol, E., Gudukbay, U., Ulusoy, O.: A Histogram Based Approach For Object Based Query By Shape And Color In Image And Video Database. Image and Vision Computing 23, 1170–1180, 2005 (1999)
4. Jeong, S., Won, C.S., Gray, R.M.: Image Retrieval Using Color Histograms Generated By Gauss Mixture Vector Quantization. Computer Vision and Image Understanding 9(1-3), 44–46 (2004)
5. Wang, Y., Mitra, S.K.: Image Representation Using Block Pattern Models And Its Image Processing Applications. IEEE Trans. on Pattern Analysis and Machine Intelligence 15(4) (1993)
6. Allman, J., Miezin, F., McGuiness, E.: Stimulus Specific Responses From Beyond The Classical Receptive Field: Neurophysiological Mechanisms For Local Global Comparisons On Visual Neurons. Annu. Rev. Neurosci. 8, 407–430 (1985)
7. Fitzoatrick, D.: Seeing Beyond The Receptive Field In Primary Visual Cortex. Current Opinion in Neurobiology 10, 438–443 (2000)
8. Sillito, A.M., Grieve, K.L., Jones, H.E., Cudeiro, J., Davis, J.: Visual Cortical Mechanisms Detecting Local Fical Orientation Discontinuities. Nature 378, 492–496 (1995)
9. Wilson, H.R., Richards, W.A.: Curvature and Separation Discrimination at Texture Boundaries. Opt. Soc. Am. A 9, 1653–1662 (1992)
10. Krieger, G., Zetzsche, C.: Nonlinear Image Operators For The Evaluation Of Local Intrinsic Dimensionality. IEEE Trans Image Process 5, 1026–1041 (1996)
11. http://www.eecs.berkeley.edu/Research/Projects/CS/vision/bsds/
12. Zetzsche, C., Röhrbein, F.: Nonlinear And Extra-Classical Receptive Field Properties And The Statistics Of Natural Scenes. Network 12, 331–350 (2001)
13. Ruderman, D.L., et al.: Statistics Of Natural Images: Scaling In The Woods. Phys. Rev. Lett. 73, 814–817 (1994)

Induction of Linear Separability through the Ranked Layers of Binary Classifiers

Leon Bobrowski

Faculty of Computer Science, Bialystok Technical University,
ul. Wiejska 45A, Bialystok
and
Institute of Biocybernetics and Biomedical Engineering, PAS, Warsaw, Poland
leon@ibib.waw.pl

Abstract. The concept of *linear separability* is used in the theory of neural networks and pattern recognition methods. This term can be related to examination of learning sets (classes) separation by hyperplanes in a given feature space. The family of K disjoined learning sets can be transformed into K linearly separable sets by the ranked layer of binary classifiers. Problems of the ranked layers deigning are analyzed in the paper.

Keywords: Learning sets, linear separability, formal neurons, binary classifiers, ranked.

1 Introduction

The *Perceptron* model and the error-correction learning algorithm of formal neurons played a fundamental role in the early neural networks [1], [2]. The key concept here was the linear separability of learning sets. The convergence in a finite number of steps of the classical error correction algorithm depends on the linear separability of learning sets. Introducing a positive margin into error correction procedure allowed to ensure the convergence in a finite number of steps of the modified learning algorithms, also when the learning sets are not linearly separable [3], [4]. The perceptron criterion function linked to the error error-correction learning algorithm belongs to the family of *convex and piecewise linear* (*CPL*) criterion functions. Minimizing the *CPL* functions allows for, inter alia, effective designing of linear classifiers, linear forecasting models designing or carrying out selection of features subsets by using the *relaxed linear separability* (*RLS*) method [5].

The most popular algorithms currently used in data mining are the *support vector machines* (*SVM*) [6]. The *SVM* algorithms are also linked to linear separability of learning sets. An essential part of these algorithms is the linear separability induction through the application of kernel functions. The selection of the appropriate kernel functions is still an open and difficult problem in many practical problems.

A family of K disjoined learning sets can be transformed into K linearly separable sets as a result of the transformation by ranked layer of formal neurons [4], [7]. This result can be extended on the ranked layer of arbitrary binary classifiers. The proof of the theorem concerning induction of linear separability through ranked layer of binary classifiers is given in this paper.

L. Iliadis and C. Jayne (Eds.): EANN/AIAI 2011, Part I, IFIP AICT 363, pp. 69–77, 2011.

2 Separable Learning Sets

Let us assume that m objects O_j $(j = 1,....,m)$ are represented as the so called feature vectors $\mathbf{x}_j = [x_{j1},...,x_{jn}]^T$, or as points in the n-dimensional feature space $F[n]$ ($\mathbf{x}_j \in F[n]$). Components (*features*) x_i of the feature vector $\mathbf{x}$ represent numerical results of different measurements on a given object O ($x_i \in \{0,1\}$ or $x_i \in R$).

We assume that the feature vector $\mathbf{x}_j(k)$ $(j = 1,......, m)$ has been labelled in accordance with the object $O_j(k)$ *category* (*class*) ω_k $(k = 1,....,K)$. The learning set C_k contains m_k feature vectors $\mathbf{x}_j(k)$ assigned to the k-th category ω_k

$$C_k = \{\mathbf{x}_j(k)\} \quad (j \in I_k) \tag{1}$$

where I_k is the set of indices j of the feature vectors $\mathbf{x}_j(k)$ assigned to the class ω_k.

Definition 1. The learning sets C_k (1) are *separable* in the feature space $F[n]$, if they are disjoined in this space ($C_k \cap C_{k'} = \emptyset$, if $k \neq k'$). This means that the feature vectors $\mathbf{x}_j(k)$ and $\mathbf{x}_{j'}(k')$ belonging to different learning sets C_k and $C_{k'}$ cannot be equal:

$$(k \neq k') \Rightarrow (\forall j \in I_k) \; and \; (\forall j' \in I_{k'}) \; \mathbf{x}_j(k) \neq \mathbf{x}_{j'}(k') \tag{2}$$

We are also considering separation of the sets C_k (1) by the hyperplanes $H(\mathbf{w}_k,\theta_k)$ in the feature space $F[n]$:

$$H(\mathbf{w}_k,\theta_k) = \{\mathbf{x}: \mathbf{w}_k^T\mathbf{x} = \theta_k\}. \tag{3}$$

where $\mathbf{w}_k = [w_{k1},....,w_{kn}]^T \in R^n$ is the weight vector, $\theta_k \in R^1$ is the threshold, and $(\mathbf{w}_k)^T\mathbf{x}$ is the inner product.

Definition 2. The feature vector $\mathbf{x}_j$ is situated on the *positive side* of the hyperplane $H(\mathbf{w}_k,\theta_k)$ (3) if and only if $(\mathbf{w}_k)^T\mathbf{x}_j > \theta_k$. Similarly, vector $\mathbf{x}_j$ is situated on the *negative side* of $H(\mathbf{w}_k,\theta_k)$ if and only if $(\mathbf{w}_k)^T\mathbf{x}_j < \theta_k$.

Definition 3. The learning sets (1) are *linearly separable* in the n-dimensional feature space $F[n]$ if each of the sets C_k can be fully separated from the sum of the remaining sets C_i by some hyperplane $H(\mathbf{w}_k,\theta_k)$ (3):

$$(\exists k \in \{1,...,K\}) \; (\exists \mathbf{w}_k,\theta_k) \; (\forall \mathbf{x}_j(k) \in C_k) \; \mathbf{w}_k^T\mathbf{x}_j(k) > \theta_k.$$
$$\textbf{and} \quad (\forall \mathbf{x}_j(i) \in C_i, i \neq k) \; \mathbf{w}_k^T\mathbf{x}_j(i) < \theta_k \tag{4}$$

In accordance with the inequalities (4), all the vectors $\mathbf{x}_j(k)$ from the set C_k are situated on the positive side of the hyperplane $H(\mathbf{w}_k,\theta_k)$ (3) and all the vectors $\mathbf{x}_j(i)$ from the remaining sets C_i are situated on the negative side of this hyperplane.

3 Layers of Binary Classifiers

The binary classifiers $BC_i(\mathbf{v})$ operate on feature vectors $\mathbf{x}$ ($\mathbf{x} \in F[n]$) and are characterized by such a decision rule $r_i(\mathbf{v}; \mathbf{x})$ which depends on the vector of parameters $\mathbf{v}$ ($\mathbf{v} \in R^N$) and has the binary output of $r_i = r_i(\mathbf{v}; \mathbf{x})$ ($r_i \in \{0, 1\}, i = 1,...,m$).

Definition 4. The *activation field* $A_i(\mathbf{v})$ of the i-th binary classifier $BC_i(\mathbf{v})$ with the decision rule $r_i(\mathbf{v};\mathbf{x})$ is the set of such a feature vectors $\mathbf{x}$ which activate this classifier

$$A_i(\mathbf{v}) = \{\mathbf{x}: r_i(\mathbf{v}; \mathbf{x}) = 1\} \tag{5}$$

A layer composed of L binary classifiers $BC_i(\mathbf{v}_i)$ with the decision rules $r_i(\mathbf{v}_i;\mathbf{x})$ produces output vectors $\mathbf{r}(\mathbf{V};\mathbf{x}) = [r_1(\mathbf{v}_1;\mathbf{x}),...,r_L(\mathbf{v}_L;\mathbf{x})]^T$, where $\mathbf{V} = [\mathbf{v}_1^T,...,\mathbf{v}_L^T]^T$. The layer of L binary classifiers $BC_i(\mathbf{v}_i)$ transforms feature vectors $\mathbf{x}_j(k)$ from the learning sets C_k (1) into the sets R_k of the binary output vectors $\mathbf{r}_j(k) = \mathbf{r}(\mathbf{V};\mathbf{x}_j(k))$.

$$R_k = \{\mathbf{r}_j(k)\} \quad (j \in I_k) \tag{6}$$

Under certain conditions, it is possible to achieved the linear separability (4) of the sets R_k (6). These conditions are analyzed in the paper.

Consider a few examples of binary classifiers $BC_i(\mathbf{v}_i)$.

i. Formal neurons $FN(\mathbf{w}_i, \theta)$

The formal neuron $FN(\mathbf{w}, \theta)$ with the weight vector $\mathbf{w} = [w_1,...,w_n]^T \in R^n$ and the threshold θ ($\theta \in R$) can be characterized by the below decision rule $r_{FN}(\mathbf{w}, \theta; \mathbf{x})$:

$$\textit{if } \mathbf{w}^T\mathbf{x} > \theta \textit{ then } r_{FN}(\mathbf{w}, \theta; \mathbf{x}) = 1, \textit{ else } r_{FN}(\mathbf{w}, \theta; \mathbf{x}) = 0 \tag{7}$$

The formal neuron $FN(\mathbf{w},\theta)$ is activated ($r_{FN}(\mathbf{w}, \theta; \mathbf{x}) = 1$) if and only if the weighed sum $w_1x_1+...+ w_n x_n$ of n inputs x_i ($x_i \in R$) is greater than the threshold θ. This decision rule $r_{FN}(\mathbf{w}, \theta; \mathbf{x})$ depends on $n + 1$ parameters w_i ($i = 1,...,n$) and θ. The activation field $A_i(\mathbf{v})$ (5) is in this case the half space $A_{FN}(\mathbf{w},\theta) = \{\mathbf{x}: \mathbf{w}^T\mathbf{x} > \theta\}$.

ii. Logical elements $LE_i(\mathbf{w}, \theta)$

The i-th *logical element* $LE_i(\mathbf{w},\theta)$ ($i = 1,..., L$) can be defined as the formal neuron (7) with only one entry $x_{k(i)}$ ($x_{k(i)} \in R$), where $k(i)$ is the number of the distinguished entry $k(i) \subseteq \{1,...,n\}$). The decision rule $r_{LEi}(w_{k(i)},\theta_i; \mathbf{x})$ of the i-th logical element $LE_i(\mathbf{w},\theta)$ can be given similarly to (7) as:

$$\textit{if } w_{k(i)}x_{k(i)} > \theta \textit{ then } r_{LEi}(w_{k(i)},\theta_i; \mathbf{x}) = 1, \textit{ else } r_{LEi}(w_{k(i)},\theta_i; \mathbf{x}) = 0 \tag{8}$$

The above decision rule $r_{LEi}(w_{k(i)},\theta_i; \mathbf{x})$ depends on two parameters: $w_{k(i)}$ and θ_i. The hyperplane $H(w_{k(i)},\theta_i) = \{\mathbf{x}: w_{k(i)}x_{k(i)} = \theta_i\}$ (3) in the feature space $F[n]$ is parallel to all axes x_1 except the axis $x_{k(i)}$ ($l = 1,...,n$ *and* $l \neq k(i)$) and perpendicular to the axis $x_{k(i)}$.

iii. Radial binary classifiers $RC(\mathbf{w}_{0i},\rho_i)$

The decision rule $r_{RC}(\mathbf{w}_0,\rho; \mathbf{x})$ of the radial classifier $RC(\mathbf{w}_0,\rho)$ can be defined in the below manner by using the distance $\delta(\mathbf{w}_0,\mathbf{x})$ between the point $\mathbf{x}$ and the center of the ball $\mathbf{w}_0 = [w_{01},...,w_{0n}]$.

$$\textit{if } \delta(\mathbf{w}_0,\mathbf{x}) \leq \rho \textit{ then } r_{RC}(\mathbf{w}_0,\rho; \mathbf{x}) = 1, \textit{ else } r_{RC}(\mathbf{w}_0,\rho; \mathbf{x}) = 0 \tag{9}$$

The radial classifier $RC(\mathbf{w}_0,\rho)$ is excited ($r_{RC}(\mathbf{w}_0,\rho; \mathbf{x}) = 1$) if and only if the distance $\delta(\mathbf{w}_0,\mathbf{x})$ is no greater than the radius ρ. The decision rule $r_{RC}(\mathbf{w}_0,\rho; \mathbf{x})$ (9) of the radial classifier $RC(\mathbf{w}_0,\rho)$ depends on the $n + 1$ parameters $\mathbf{w}_0 = [w_{01},...,w_{0n}]^T$ and ρ. The activation field $A_{RC}(\mathbf{w}_0, \rho)$ (5) of the radial classifier $RC(\mathbf{w}_0,\rho)$ is the ball with the center $\mathbf{w}_0$ and the radius ρ. The shape of this activation field $A_{RC}(\mathbf{w}_0, \rho)$ depends of the choice of the distance function $\delta(\mathbf{w}_0,\mathbf{x})$. A few examples of distance functions $\delta(\mathbf{w}_0,\mathbf{x})$ are given below [3]:

$$\delta_E(\mathbf{w}_0,\mathbf{x}) = ((\mathbf{x} - \mathbf{w}_0)^T(\mathbf{x} - \mathbf{w}_0))^{1/2} \quad \text{- the } \textit{Euclidean distance}$$
$$\delta_M(\mathbf{w}_0,\mathbf{x}) = ((\mathbf{x} - \mathbf{w}_0)^T\Sigma^{-1}(\mathbf{x} - \mathbf{w}_0))^{1/2} \quad \text{- the } \textit{Mahalanobis distance}$$
$$\delta_{L1}(\mathbf{w}_0,\mathbf{x}) = \sum_{i=1,\dots,N} |w_{0i} - x_i| \qquad \text{- the } L_1 \text{ distance} \tag{10}$$

4 Properties of the Ranked Layers of Binary Classifiers

The strategy of the ranked layers designing allows to find a layer with such a property that the sets R_k (6) of transformed vectors $\mathbf{r}_j(k) = \mathbf{r}(V;\mathbf{x}_j(k))$ become linearly separable (4). The proposed multistage designing procedure involves finding a sequence of *admissible cuts* by binary classifiers $BC_i(\mathbf{v}_i)$ with the decision rules $r_i(\mathbf{v}_i; \mathbf{x})$ (5).

Definition 5. The binary classifier $BC_i(\mathbf{v}_i)$ with the decision rule $r_i(\mathbf{v}_i; \mathbf{x})$ (5) is *admissible* in respect to a given learning set $C_{k'}$ from the family (1) if and only if $n_{k'}$ ($n_{k'} > 0$) elements $\mathbf{x}_j(k')$ of this set activate the classifier and none of elements $\mathbf{x}_j(k)$ from other sets C_k ($k \neq k'$) activate the classifier $BC_i(\mathbf{v}_i)$

$$(\forall k' \in \{1,\dots,K\}) \ (\exists \mathbf{x}_j(k') \in C_{k'}) \ r_i(\mathbf{v}_i; \mathbf{x}_j(k')) = 1, \textit{ and}$$
$$(\forall \mathbf{x}_j(k) \in C_k, \textit{ where } k \neq k') \ r_i(\mathbf{v}_i; \mathbf{x}_j(k)) = 0 \tag{11}$$

The activation field $A_i(\mathbf{v}_i)$ (4.1) of the admissible binary classifier $BC_i(\mathbf{v}_i)$ contains some elements $\mathbf{x}_j(k')$ of only one learning set $C_{k'}$ (1).

Let us describe the multistage procedure of the ranked layer designing from binary classifiers $BC_i(\mathbf{v})$ on the basis of the learning sets C_k (1).

Ranked layer designing procedure (12)

Stage i. (Start)

- put $n = 1$ and define the sets $C_k[n]$: $(\exists k \in \{1,\dots,K\})$ $C_k[n] = C_k$

Stage ii. (Admissible classifier)

- find parameters $\mathbf{v}_{i(n)}$ of classifier $BC_{i(n)}(\mathbf{v}_{i(n)})$ admissible (11) to some set $C_{k(n)}[n]$.

Stage iii. (Admissible reduction (*cut*) of the set $C_{k(n)}[n]$)

- delay such feature vectors $\mathbf{x}_j$ which activate the classifier $BC_{i(n)}(\mathbf{v}_{i(n)})$

$$C_{k(n)}[n+1] = C_{k(n)}[n] - \{\mathbf{x}_j(k(n)) \in C_{k(n)}[n]: r_{i(n)}(\mathbf{v}_{i(n)}; \mathbf{x}_j(k(n))) = 1\} \tag{13}$$

Stage iv. (Stop criterion)

if all the sets $C_k[n+1]$ are empty *then stop*
else increase the index n by one ($n \rightarrow n+1$) *and go to* the *Stage ii.*   □

It can be seen that each binary classifiers $BC_i(\mathbf{v}_i)$ added to the layer reduces (13) the set $C_{k(n)}[n]$ by at least one feature vector $\mathbf{x}_j(k(n))$. Based on this property, it can be proved that if the learning sets C_k (1) are separable (2), then after finite number L of steps the procedure will be stopped. The following Lemma results.

Lemma 2. The number L of binary classifiers $BC_i(\mathbf{v}_i)$ in the ranked layer is no less than the number K of the learning sets C_k (1) and no greater than the number m of the feature vectors $\mathbf{x}_j(k)$ in these sets.

$$K \leq L \leq m \tag{14}$$

The minimal number $L = K$ of binary classifiers $BC_i(\mathbf{v}_i)$ appears in the ranked layer when whole learning sets C_k (1) are reduced (13) during successive steps n. The maximal number $L = m$ of elements appears in the ranked layer when only single elements $\mathbf{x}_j(k)$ are reduced during successive steps n.

In accordance with the postulate of *a large admissible reduction,* the number $n_{k(n)}[n]$ of the reduced elements $\mathbf{x}_j(k(n))$ $(\mathbf{x}_j(k(n) \in C_{k(n)}[n])$ during each step n (13) should be as large as possible [4]. In order to fulfill this postulate the below rule can be introduced:

The set $C_{k(n)}[n]$ reduced during the n-th designing step should be characterized by the largest number $n_{k(n)}[n]$ of reduced elements $\mathbf{x}_j(k(n))$:

$$(\forall k \in \{1,...,K\}) \; n_{k(n)}[n] \geq n_k[n] \tag{15}$$

The sequence of the parameters $\mathbf{v}_{i(1)}$ appears as the result of the procedure (12):

$$\mathbf{v}_{i(1)}, \mathbf{v}_{i(2)},..., \mathbf{v}_{i(L)} \tag{16}$$

Additionally, the class indices $k(n)$ of the sets $C_{k(n)}[n]$ reduced (13) during successive steps n can be obtained

$$k(1), k(2),..., k(L) \tag{17}$$

The parameters $\mathbf{v}_{i(n)}$ (16) define the decision rule $r_{i(n)} = r_{i(n)}(\mathbf{v}_{i(n)};\mathbf{x})$ $(r_{i(n)} \in \{0, 1\})$ of the binary classifiers $BC_{i(n)}(\mathbf{v}_{i(n)})$ in the ranked layer

$$BC_{i(1)}(\mathbf{v}_{k(1)}), BC_{i(2)}(\mathbf{v}_{i(2)}),..., BC_{i(L)}(\mathbf{v}_{i(L)}) \tag{18}$$

Feature vectors $\mathbf{x}_j(k)$ from the learning sets C_k (1) are transformed by the ranked layer of L classifiers (18) into vectors $\mathbf{r}_j(k) = [r_{j1},...,r_{jL}]^T$ with L binary components r_{ji} $(r_{ji} \in \{0, 1\})$ which are related to the category ω_k.

$$(\forall k \in \{1,...,K\}) \; (\exists \mathbf{x}_j(k) \in C_k)$$
$$\mathbf{r}_j(k) = [r_{i(1)}(\mathbf{v}_{i(1)};\mathbf{x}_j(k)),..., r_{i(L)}(\mathbf{v}_{i(L)};\mathbf{x}_j(k))]^T \tag{19}$$

The transformed vectors $\mathbf{r}_j(k)$ (19) can be represented in the below manner by L – dimensional vectors $\mathbf{q}_n = [q_{n1},..., q_{nL}]^T$ $(l = 1,..., L)$ with the binary components q_{lj}

$$\mathbf{q}_1 = [1, q_{12},...,r_{1L}]^T$$
$$\mathbf{q}_2 = [0,1, q_{23},...,r_{2L}]^T$$
....
$$(20)$$
....
$$\mathbf{q}_L = [0,0,...,0,1]^T$$

It is assumed in the above representation that each component q_{nj} with $j > n$ can be set to any binary value $q_{nj} = 1$ or $q_{nj} = 0$. In result, each vector $\mathbf{q}_n$ (20) can represent more than one transformed vector $\mathbf{r}_j(k)$ (19).

The vectors $\mathbf{q}_n = [q_{n,1},...,q_{n,L}]^T$ (20) can be used in the below decision rule, which results from the procedure (12) of the ranked layers designing

$$\textit{if } (\forall i: 0 < i < n) \ q_{n,i} = 0 \ \textit{and } q_{n,n} = 1, \textit{ then } \ \mathbf{q}_n \in \omega_{k(n)} \qquad (21)$$

where $k(n)$ is the index (17) of the set $C_{k(n)}$ reduced during the n–th stage.

The rule (21) links the vectors $\mathbf{q}_n$ (20) to particular classes ω_k. This rule is based only on the content of the n-th admissible cut (13) of the set $C_{k(n)}$. In this manner, each class ω_k can be represented by the set Q_k of the related vectors $\mathbf{q}_n(k)$ (20).

$$Q_k = \{\mathbf{q}_n(k): k(n) = k\}, \qquad (22)$$

where $k \in \{1,..., K\}$ and the distinguished index $k(n)$ is determined by (17).

Theorem 1. The sets Q_k (22) are linearly separable (4).

Proof: The proof is based on the example of such parameters $\mathbf{w}_k$, θ_k, which fulfil the inequalities (4) [7]. Let us introduce the L-dimensional vector $\mathbf{a} = [a_1,...,a_L]^T$ with the components a_i specified below

$$(\forall i \in \{1,..., L\}) \quad a_i = 1/2^i \qquad (23)$$

The weight vector $\mathbf{w}_k = [w_{k1},...,w_{kL}]^T$ is defined on the basis of the sequence (17) in accordance with the below rule

$$(\forall i \in \{1,..., L\}) \ \textit{if } k(i) = k, \textit{then } w_{ki} = a_i \ \textit{else } w_{ki} = - a_i \qquad (24)$$

It can be directly verified that all the inequalities (4) are fulfilled by the vectors $\mathbf{w}_k$ with the components w_{ki} (24) and the threshold $\theta_k = 0$. This means that the sets Q_k (22) are linearly separable (4). □

Corollary. The sets $R_k = \{\mathbf{r}_j(k)\}$ (6) of the transformed vectors $\mathbf{r}_j(k)$) related to particular categories ω_k are linearly separable (4).

$$(\forall k \in \{1,..., K\}) \ (\exists \mathbf{w}_k) \ (\forall \mathbf{r}_j(k) \in R_k) \ (\mathbf{w}_k)^T \mathbf{r}_j(k) > 0$$
$$\textit{and} \quad (\forall \mathbf{r}_j(k') \in R_{k'}, k \neq k') \ (\mathbf{w}_k)^T \mathbf{r}_j(k') < 0 \qquad (25)$$

The transformation (25) of the feature vectors $x_j(k)$ by the ranked layer allows to replace the separable (2) learning sets C_k (1) by the sets $R_k = \{r_j(k)\}$ (6) which are linearly separable (25). Let us remark that the *Theorem* 1 is also valid if the ranked layer is composed of different types of binary classifiers $BC_i(v_i)$.

5 Examples of Implementations of the Ranked Layer Designing Procedure

Let us consider at the beginning, the procedure ranked layer designing from logical elements $LE_i(w,\theta)$ (8). The decision rule $r_{LEi}(w_{k(i)},\theta_i;x)$ (8) of the *i*-th logical element $LE_i(w,\theta)$ depends on only one feature $x_{k(i)}$. The decision rule $r_{LEi}(w_{k(i)},\theta_i;x)$ (8) can be decomposed into two rules $r_i^+(x)$ and $r_i^-(x)$ and represented in the below manner for each feature x_i $(i = 1,...,n)$:

$$(\forall i \in \{1,...,n\})\; \textit{if } x_i > \theta_i^+,\; \textit{then } r_i^+(x) = 1\; \textit{else } r_i^+(x) = 0 \qquad (26)$$

and

$$(\forall i \in \{1,...,n\})\; \textit{if } x_i < \theta_i^-,\; \textit{then } r_i^-(x) = 1\; \textit{else } r_i^-(x) = 0 \qquad (27)$$

where θ_i^+ and θ_i^- are two numerical parameters $(\theta_i^+ \in R^1$ and $\theta_i^- \in R^1)$.

In accordance with the *admissible reduction* principle (11), the parameters θ_i^+ and θ_i^- should ensure the homogenous reduction of the maximal numbers $n^+(i)$ and $n^-(i)$ of elements $x_j(k)$ belonging to only one learning set C_k (1). The term *homogenous reduction* (11) means that the condition $r_i^+(x) = 1$ (26) is fulfilled by $n^+(i)$ elements $x_j(k)$ of only one learning set C_k (1). Similarly, the condition $r_i^-(x) = 1$ (27) should be fulfilled by $n^-(i)$ elements $x_j(k')$ of only one learning set $C_{k'}$ (1).

In order to satisfy the postulate of *a large admissible reduction* the below rules can be used

$$(\forall i \in \{1,...,n\})\; n(i) = max\{\, n^+(i),\, n^-(i)\},\, and$$
$$n(i') = max\{\, n(1),..., n(L)\}, \qquad (28)$$

where $n(i)$ is the maximal number of elements $x_j(k)$ from one learning set C_k (1), which can be reduced by using the *i*-th feature x_i (coordinates x_i)and the rule (26) or (27), i' is the index of such a coordinate $x_{i'}$ which allows to reduce the maximal number $n(i')$ of elements $x_j(k')$ belonging to only one learning set $C_{k'}$ (1).

The rule (28) allows to determine the class indices $k(n)$ (17) of the sets $C_{k(n)}[n]$ reduced (13) during successive steps n of the *Ranked layer designing procedure* (12). The optimal threshold value $\theta(n)$ can be determined on the basis of the rules (26) and (27). The optimal threshold value $\theta(n)$ should result in the maximal number $n(i')$ (28) of elements $x_j(k)$ of one learning set C_k (1) reduced during each step n. The rules (28) and include the selection of the optimal threshold values θ_i^+ and θ_i^- for each coordinate x_i. The optimal threshold values θ_i^+ (26) and θ_i^- (27) should result in the maximal numbers $n^+(i)$ and $n^-(i)$ of the reduced elements $x_j(k)$ of one learning set C_k

(1). The implementation of the ranked layers design rules is relatively simple in the case of logical elements $LE_i(\mathbf{w},\theta)$ (8). For small data sets (1), such rules can even be implemented without a computer, based on handwritten calculations.

Let us consider now the layer of formal neurons $FN(\mathbf{w}_i, \theta_i)$ (7) which can be linked to the hyperplanes $H(\mathbf{w}_i,\theta_i)$ (3).

Definition 6. The hyperplane $H(\mathbf{w}_{k'},\theta_{k'})$ (3) is *admissible* (*Definition* 5) to a given set $C_{k'}[n]$ from the family $\{C_k[n]\}$ (13) if and only if $n_{k'}$ ($n_{k'} > 0$) elements $\mathbf{x}_j(k')$ of this set is situated on the positive side of the hyperplane $H(\mathbf{w}_{k'},\theta_{k'})$ and all elements $\mathbf{x}_j(k)$ from other sets C_k ($k \neq k'$) are situated on the negative side of this hyperplane:

$$(\forall k' \in \{1,\ldots,K\})\ (\exists \mathbf{x}_j(k') \in C_{k'}[n])\ \ \mathbf{w}_{k'}^{T}\mathbf{x}_j(k') > \theta_{k'},\ and$$

$$(\forall \mathbf{x}_j(k) \in C_k[n],\ where\ k \neq k')\ \ \mathbf{w}_{k'}^{T}\mathbf{x}_j(k) < \theta_{k'} \tag{29}$$

The sequence of admissible hyperplanes $H(\mathbf{w}_i,\theta_i)$ (3) should be consisted with the *Ranked layer designing procedure* (12). The parameters $\mathbf{w}_i$ and θ_i of admissible hyperplanes $H(\mathbf{w}_i,\theta_i)$ (3) define the formal neurons $FN(\mathbf{w}_i,\theta_i)$ (7) of the ranked layer.

The hyperplane $H(\mathbf{w}_{k'},\theta_{k'})$ (3) admissible (*Definition 5*) to a given set $C_{k'}[n]$ from the family $\{C_k[n]\}$ (13) can be obtained through minimization of the convex and piecewise linear (*CPL*) criterion functions $\Psi_{k'}(\mathbf{w},\theta)$ [7]. The preceptron criterion function belongs to the *CPL* family [4]. The criterion function $\Psi_{k'}(\mathbf{w},\theta)$ can be defined on the basis of the positive G_k^{+} and the negative G_k^{-} sets of feature vectors $\mathbf{x}_j$ from the sets $\{C_k[n]\}$ (13)

$$G_{k'}^{+} = \{\mathbf{x}_j\colon \mathbf{x}_j \in C_{k'}[n]\}\ \ and\ \ G_{k'}^{-} = \{\mathbf{x}_j\colon \mathbf{x}_j \in \underset{k \neq k'}{\cup} C_k[n]\} \tag{30}$$

Each element $\mathbf{x}_j$ of the set $G_{k'}^{+}$ defines the positive penalty function $\varphi_j^{+}(\mathbf{w},\theta)$

$$(\forall \mathbf{x}_j \in G_{k'}^{+})$$

$$if\ \ \mathbf{w}^{T}\mathbf{x}_j - \theta \leq 1,\ then\ \varphi_j^{+}(\mathbf{w},\theta) = 1 - \mathbf{w}^{T}\mathbf{x}_j + \theta,\ else\ \varphi_j^{+}(\mathbf{w},\theta) = 0 \tag{31}$$

Similarly, each element $\mathbf{x}_j$ of the set $G_{k'}^{-}$ defines the negative penalty function $\varphi_j^{-}(\mathbf{w},\theta)$

$$(\forall \mathbf{x}_j \in G_{k'}^{-})$$

$$if\ \ \mathbf{w}^{T}\mathbf{x}_j - \theta \geq -1,\ then\ \varphi_j^{-}(\mathbf{w},\theta) = \mathbf{w}^{T}\mathbf{x}_j - \theta \geq -1,\ else\ \varphi_j^{-}(\mathbf{w},\theta) = 0 \tag{32}$$

The criterion functions $\Psi_{k'}(\mathbf{w},\theta)$ is the sum of the functions $\varphi_j^{+}(\mathbf{w},\theta)$ and $\varphi_j^{-}(\mathbf{w},\theta)$

$$\Psi_{k'}(\mathbf{w},\theta) = \Sigma\ \varphi_j^{+}(\mathbf{w},\theta) + \lambda\ \Sigma\ \varphi_j^{-}(\mathbf{w},\theta) \tag{33}$$

where λ ($\lambda > 0$) is a positive parameter (*price*).

Minimization of the function $\Psi_{k'}(\mathbf{w},\theta)$ allows to find optimal parameters $(\mathbf{w}_{k'}^{*},\theta_{k'}^{*})$:

$$min\ \Psi_{k'}(\mathbf{w},\theta) = \Psi_{k'}(\mathbf{w}_{k'}^{*},\theta_{k'}^{*}) \geq 0 \tag{34}$$

The basis exchange algorithms which are similar to the linear programming allow to find efficiently minimum $\Psi_{k'}(w_{k'}{}^*,\theta_{k'}{}^*)$ of the criterion function $\Psi_{k'}(w,\theta)$ (33) [7]. It can be shown that the optimal parameters $(w_{k'}{}^*,\theta_{k'}{}^*)$ (34) obtained from the function $\Psi_{k'}(w,\theta)$ (39) with a sufficiently large parameter λ define the admissible hyperplane $H(w_{k'}{}^*,\theta_{k'}{}^*)$ (29) [4]. The optimal parameters $(w_{k'}{}^*,\theta_{k'}{}^*)$ allows to define the formal neurons $FN(w_{k'}{}^*,\theta_{k'}{}^*)$ (7) of the ranked layer in accordance with the *Ranked layer designing procedure* (12).

6 Concluding Remarks

Separable learning sets C_k (2) can always be transformed into such sets R_k (6) which are linearly separable (4). The linear separability is induced through the transformation of elements $x_j(k)$ of the learning sets C_k (1) by the ranked layer of binary classifiers $BC_i(v_i)$. The paper contains a proof of this property.

The paper also contains examples of designing ranked layers of formal neurons $FN(w_i, \theta_i)$ (7) and logical elements $LE_i(w_i,\theta_i)$ (8). Efficient designing ranked layers of radial classifiers $RC(w_0,\rho)$ (9) is still an open problem from computational point of view.

Acknowledgment. This work was supported by the by the NCBiR project N R13 0014 04, and partially financed by the project S/WI/2/2011 from the Białystok University of Technology, and by the project 16/St/2011 from the Institute of Biocybernetics and Biomedical Engineering PAS.

References

1. Rosenblatt, F.: Principles of neurodynamics. Spartan Books, Washington (1962)
2. Minsky, M.L., Papert, S.A.: Perceptrons. MIT Press, Cambridge (1969)
3. Duda, O.R., Hart, P.E., Stork, D.G.: Pattern classification. J. Wiley, New York (2001)
4. Bobrowski, L.: Eksploracja danych oparta na wypukłych i odcinkowo-liniowych funkcjach kryterialnych (Data mining based on convex and piecewise linear (CPL) criterion functions), Technical University Białystok (2005) (in Polish)
5. Bobrowski, L., Łukaszuk, T.: Feature selection based on relaxed linear separability. Biocybernetics and Biomedcal Engineering 29(2), 43–59 (2009)
6. Vapnik, V.N.: Statistical Learning Theory. J. Wiley, New York (1998)
7. Bobrowski, L.: Design of piecewise linear classifiers from formal neurons by some basis exchange technique. Pattern Recognition 24(9), 863–870 (1991)

Classifying the Differences in Gaze Patterns of Alphabetic and Logographic L1 Readers – A Neural Network Approach

André Frank Krause[1,3], Kai Essig[1,3], Li-Ying Essig-Shih[2], and Thomas Schack[1,3]

[1] Faculty of Sport Science, Dept. Neurocognition & Action
{andre_frank.krause,kai.essig,thomas.schack}@uni-bielefeld.de
[2] cultureblend IIT GmbH Universitätsstraße 25
essigshih@cultureblend.de
[3] Cognitive Interaction Technology, Center of Excellence
Bielefeld University, D-33615 Bielefeld, Germany

Abstract. Using plain, but large multi-layer perceptrons, temporal eye-tracking gaze patterns of alphabetic and logographic L1 readers were successfully classified. The Eye-tracking data was fed directly into the networks, with no need for pre-processing. Classification rates up to 92% were achieved using MLPs with 4 hidden units. By classifying the gaze patterns of interaction partners, artificial systems are able to act adaptively in a broad variety of application fields.

1 Introduction

With the technical progress and the minituarization of electronic devices, eye tracking became more and more popular in the recent years. The term eye tracking denotes the process of monitoring and recording the participants' gaze positions when they look at 2D or 3D stimuli. Researchers are interested in exact *gaze positions* and their temporal course, i.e., *spatial-temporal scan paths*. The analysis of eye movements yields valuable insights into the cognitive processes underlying information processing ("eyes are a window to the mind") [1] [2] - providing answers to questions like: " Which information are perceived as valuable?", "What is the temporal order of perceived objects?", "Where had the participants problems to understand important scene information (signified by a high number of fixations or long fixation durations)?". Eye tracking is of high interest in different research areas: Linguists are interested in the relations between the perception of spoken or written text and visual attention. Computer scientists are interested in the development of suitable human-computer interfaces for inutitive terminals or robotic systems.

Neural Networks have been developed with their main feature beeing their learning ability: They have the ability to learn a particular task autonomously from training data, whithout the need of explicit programming [3]. Neural nets have been applied to the field of eye tracking to reliably estimate the 3D gaze point from a participant's binocular eye-position data [4]. Neural nets have been used to analyze the diagnostic significance of dyslexis eye movements [5]. The authors measured eye movements of 52 school children (normal readers, mentally disabled readers and dyslexics) during a reading task. Using

L. Iliadis and C. Jayne (Eds.): EANN/AIAI 2011, Part I, IFIP AICT 363, pp. 78–83, 2011.

a self-organizing map, the three groups formed individual clusters and could be clearly classified. [6] validate if the way a person reads influence the way they understand information and propose a novel method of detecting the level of engagement in reading based on a person's gaze-pattern. They organized some experiments in reading tasks of over thirty participants and the experimental outputs are classified with Artificial Neural Networks with approximately 80% accuracy. All these approaches have in common that the gaze data needs a high amount of pre-processing before it can serve as an input for the neural networks. Recent experiments revealed, that deep, big feedforward networks trained with standard online backpropagation can achive excellent classification results without any preprocessing of the input data [7] - making them a suitable tool for the flexible analysis of raw gaze-movement data. Here, we feed eye-tracking data, recoded in a reading experiment with German and Chinese natives, without any pre-processing into a feedforward network to classify the scan path as belonging to a Chinese or German reader. Eye-tracking combined with neural networks enable artificial systems to react adaptively in a broad variety of application fields.

2 Eye Movements in Reading

While reading, the visual information is projected on different areas of the retina, i.e., the foveal, parafoveal, and peripheral area. The fovea is the area of highest visual resolution in the retina. Because of the limited size of the fovea ($2°$ of the visual field), only a small text area (around 8 letters) can be sharply analyzed during each fixation [8]. Figure 1 shows the perceptual span for the foveal and parafoveal areas during reading. Although humans are able to dissociate their attention from the foveal direction of gaze (Duchowsky, 2003), complex information processing tasks, like reading, require a strong coupling of gaze movements and attention [9]. During a fixation the eye remains directed at the same spot for a longer period (while reading: 200-400 ms), enabling visual information processing of the fixated region. Approximately 90% of the viewing time is spent on fixations [10].

Because only the fovea allows clear vision, the eye has to be moved so that different parts of the text can be processed in sequence. These movements are called *saccades*. Saccades are jerky eye movements from one fixation to another. During saccades the pupil is accelerated up to $1000°/s$, and an angular velocity of more than $300°$ per second is reached [11]. Saccade velocity and durations vary with the writing system, the individual fluency of the reader and the diffculty of the text.

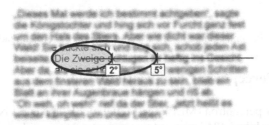

Fig. 1. The perceptual span for the foveal and parafoveal area during text reading

Eye movement research with participants of different native languages revealed, that L1-Readers with an alphabetic writing system (e.g., English and German) have a slightly bigger perceptual span than those of a syllabographical and logographical writing system, such as Japanese or Chinese readers [12][13]. Furthermore, experienced readers have a larger perceptual span than beginners, i.e., the perceptual span can be widened by exercise [14]. Additionally, the perceptual span is larger when reading a simple compared to a complex text [15][13].

3   Data Collection

The eye movements of thirteen german native speakers (5 females and 8 males) and thirteen Chinese native speakers (9 females, 4 males), with an age between 26 and 37 years, were recorded while they read silently German text passages. The Chinese native speakers were required to have passed the DSH (German abbreviation for Deutsche Sprachprüfung für den Hochschulzugang), a language exam required to study at German higher education institutions and be at least enrolled for one year at a German high school. For the experiment, two literature text passages were used. Text A, is an excerpt from "'Der Richter und sein Henker"', Friedrich Dürrenmatt with 195 words (1027 letters). Text B is an excerpt from the novel "'Fabian. Die Geschichte eines Moralisten"', Erich Kästner with 201 words (1084 letters). The text was splitted in 4 sections and then presented in Times New Roman 16pt, double spaced, black colour on a gray background on a computer screen with 1024x768 pixel resolution (see Figure 2). For the experiment, an SMI Eyelink I eye tracker was used to record participants' eye movements. The collected eye-tracking data consists of (x,y) coordinates of all recorded fixations as well as the fixation durations in ms. The maximum length of scanpaths was 424 frames.

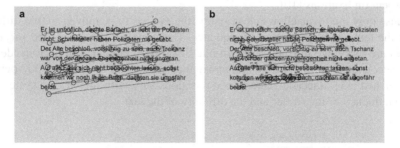

Fig. 2. Example scanpaths of a (a) chinese and (b) german reader

4   Multilayer Perceptron Classification

To train a multilayer perceptron (MLP), the Matlab©2010b Neural Network Toolbox was used. The network had 424 input and two output neurons with a sigmoidal activation function (tanh). Each output neuron represents one class, with class 1 (logographic)

coded as $\begin{pmatrix} 1 & 0 \end{pmatrix}$ and class 2 (logographic) as $\begin{pmatrix} 0 & 1 \end{pmatrix}$. The training data fed into the net had three data channels: the x- and the y-component of the scan path and the fixation duration (f). Before training, the temporal input data was scaled into the range $[-1, 1]$ and spatially unfolded into the input vector $\mathbf{u} = (x_0, y_0, f_0, \ x_1, y_1, f_1 \ .... \ x_n, y_n, f_n)$. The default training algorithm for pattern classification used by the toolbox is Levenberg-Marquardt backpropagation. All toolbox options were kept at their default values, except the stopping criterion "'failed evaluation runs'". The maximum allowed number of failed evaluation runs was increased to 50 (default = 7). This increased the classification performance slightly without impairing generalization. N-fold cross validation (N=10) was applied to estimate the classification performance.

Fig. 3a shows the performance of a single layer perceptron (N=100 training repetitions with different random network initialisations) compared to MLPs with hidden layers sizes from 1 to 10. The figure shows, that already a single layer perceptron can classify the data (median value 83%). The best network found had a classification performance of 88%. Adding a hidden layer improves performance (Fig. 3b). MLPs with 4 hidden units show a best performance of 92% and a median performance of 84%.

Adding more hidden layers did not improve the performance. 100 MLPs with two hidden layers and hidden layer sizes ranging from 1 to 15 were trained (N=100 repetitions of the training process with random initial network weights). Best mean value found was 84.3% and the best overall network had 92% classification performance. Fig. 4 shows mean and maximal performance for MLPs with two hidden layers.

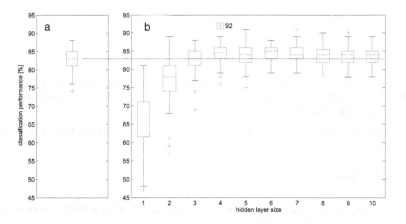

Fig. 3. Classification performance depending on the number of neurons in the hidden layer. Boxplots show n=100 repetitions of 10-fold crossvalidation runs over the training data. a) Performance of a single layer perceptron for comparison. b) Performance of perceptrons with one hidden layer.

4.1 Contribution of Data Components

To analyse the contribution of the several components of the eye tracking data, an MLP with four hidden units was trained (N=100 repetitions) seperately for each data channel. Fig. 5 shows that training the networks given each channel alone did not reach the performance of the networks that were fed with all three data channels. The figure also

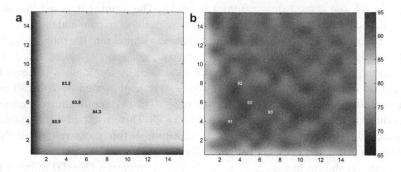

Fig. 4. a) Mean and b) maximum classification performance (colour coded) of MLPs with two hidden layers. N=100 training repetitions were performed. No combination of hidden layer sizes (1 to 15 units) resulted in an improvement over the single hidden layer MLPs.

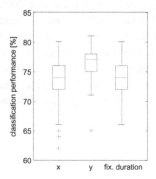

Fig. 5. Contribution of the eye-tracking data components. A MLP with 4 units in the hidden layer was used, N=100 training repetitions. The input to the network was either the x-, the y-component of the scan path or the fixation duration, only.

indicates that the vertical component of the scanpath contributes the most to classification success.

5   Conclusions

Given raw, non-preprocessed eye-tracking data, a simple feedforward network could be trained to achieve a high classification rate on an experimental data set regarding the reading performance of German versus Chinese L1-readers. The temporal eye-tracking data was spatially unfolded into a high number of network inputs.

A possible application scenario can be information terminals that are able to detect persons having difficulties reading the presented on-screen language and automatically offer a language selection menu. Also, a pre-evaluation of reading performance of aspirants for specialised professions (translators) are imaginable.

The process of recording data in empirical studies and test it in an adequate simulation will be important for further understanding of interaction scenarios. The question is, if the data which was measured in the real world, is also reflected in simulated behavior. One example would be humanoid robots. Will a robot perform like a grown up or more like a child, when fed with recorded data of adults or childrens? The automatic classification of the gaze behavior and human movement data will be of high importance to this field of research.

References

1. Essig, K.: Vision-Based Image Retrieval (VBIR) - A New Approach for Natural and Intuitive Image Retrieval. VDM Verlag, Saarbrücken (2008)
2. Duchowski, A.: Eye Tracking Methodology: Theory and Practice. Springer, London (2003)
3. Haykin, S.: Neural Networks: A Comprehensive Foundation. Prentice Hall PTR, Upper Saddle River (1994)
4. Essig, K., Pomplun, M., Ritter, H.: A neural network for 3d gaze recording with binocular eye trackers. International Journal of Parallel, Emergent and Distributed Systems 21(2), 79–95 (2006)
5. Macaš, M., Lhotská, L., Novák, D.: Bio-inspired methods for analysis and classification of reading eye movements of dyslexic children. Technical report, University in Prague, Algarve, Portugal (October 3-5, 2005)
6. Vo, T., Mendis, B.S.U., Gedeon, T.: Gaze pattern and reading comprehension. In: Wong, K.W., Mendis, B.S.U., Bouzerdoum, A. (eds.) ICONIP 2010, Part II. LNCS, vol. 6444, pp. 124–131. Springer, Heidelberg (2010)
7. Ciresan, D.C., Meier, U., Gambardella, L.M., Schmidhuber, J.: Deep big simple neural nets excel on handwritten digit recognition. CoRR (2010)
8. Just, M.A., Carpenter, P.A.: The psychology of reading and language comprehension. Allyn and Bacon, Boston (1987)
9. Essig-Shih, L.Y.: Effekte simultanen Hörens und Lesens auf das L2-Lesen: Eine Eyetracking-Studie im BereichDeutsch als Fremdsprache. PhD thesis, University of Bielefeld (2008)
10. Irwin, J.W.: Teaching reading comprehension process. Allyn & Bacon, Boston (1991)
11. Rötting, M.: Parametersystematik der Augen- und Blickbewegungen für arbeitswissenschaftliche Untersuchungen. Shaker, Aachen (2001)
12. Inhoff, A.W., Liu, W.: The perceptual span and oculomotor activity during the reading of chinese sentences. Journal of Experimental Psychology: Human Perception and Performance 24, 20–34 (1998)
13. Rayner, K., Sereno, S.C.: Eye movements in reading. Psycholinguistic studies. In: Handbook of Psycholinguistics, pp. 57–81. Academic Press, San Diego (1994)
14. Nerius, D. (ed.): Deutsche Orthographie. 3. Aufl. Dudenverlag, Mannheim (2000)
15. Rayner, K., Carroll, P.J.: Issues and problems in the use of eye movement data in study reading comprehension. In: New Methods in Reading Comprehension Research, pp. 129–150. Erlbaum, Hillsdale (1984)

Subspace-Based Face Recognition on an FPGA

Pablo Pizarro and Miguel Figueroa

Department of Electrical Engineering, Universidad de Concepción
{ppizarroj,miguel.figueroa}@udec.cl

Abstract. We present a custom hardware system for image recognition, featuring a dimensionality reduction network and a classification stage. We use Bi-Directional PCA and Linear Discriminant Analysis for feature extraction, and classify based on Manhattan distances. Our FPGA-based implementation runs at 75MHz, consumes 157.24mW of power, and can classify a 61×49-pixel image in $143.7\mu s$, with a sustained throughput of more than 7,000 classifications per second. Compared to a software implementation on a workstation, our solution achieves the same classification performance (93.3% hit rate), with more than twice the throughput and more than an order of magnitud less power.

1 Introduction

During the last few decades, automatic face recognition has evolved greatly. This development involved increased algorithmic complexity, which translates into long computation time and high energy consumption. Software implementations of most highly effective methods require the performance of a state-of-the-art workstation to operate in real time. Their cost, size and power requirements preclude their use in embedded and portable electronic systems. This has motivated the development of custom hardware implementations of face recognition algorithms, which can exploit the parallelism available in silicon integrated circuits, achieving high performance with much smaller die area and power than general-purpose microprocessors.

To accomplish high performance, neural network based on linear subspaces are normally used, mainly because VLSI technology favors architectures that feature regular computation and local or structured communication. Often the net- work is trained (and retrained) offline in software and the coeficients are then transfered onto the chip, greatly simplifying the implementation.

This paper presents a custom hardware implementation of an image classification algorithm for face recognition. The algorithm uses Bi-Dimensional Principal Components Analysis (BDPCA) and Linear Discriminant Analysis (LDA) for dimensionality reduction and feature extraction, and a Manhattan distance metric to perform the classifcation. We implemented our design on a Xilinx Spartan 3 XC3S1000 FPGA and tested it with the Yale database of face images. Our chip, compared to a floating-point software implementation of the algorithm, achieves the same classifcation hit rate of 93.3% and classifies an image in half the time ($143.7\mu s$), while consuming only 157.24mW of power.

L. Iliadis and C. Jayne (Eds.): EANN/AIAI 2011, Part I, IFIP AICT 363, pp. 84–89, 2011.

2   Design

2.1   Algorithm and Testing

To select a suitable algorithm to implement, we analyzed different designs and assessed their classification performance and hardware cost. We considered four algorithms for feature extraction: Eigenfaces (PCA), Fisherfaces (PCA+LDA), BDPCA and BDPCA+LDA [3,1,5]. Both PCA and BDPCA project the images, for these tests onto a 24-dimensional space, while LDA projects to 14 dimensions. For classification Euclidean and Manhattan distances are tested.

We used the Yale database as input data, which consists of 15 subjects, with 11 images of each, showing variations in lighting and facial expressions and details. The images are 8-bit grayscale, and were centered and resized to a resolution of 61×49 pixels using the Matlab Image Processing toolbox. We use 5 images of each subject for training, and 6 of each subject for testing. The procedure is performed 3 times, changing the selection for training and test images. We computed the mean classification hit rate and standard deviation for each experiment.

Fisherfaces achives the best recognition rate (97.8%) with lowest standard deviation. However, BDPCA+LDA achieves the second best performance (93%) with a memory usage 40 times lower than Fisherfaces and 3-4 times fewer arithmetic operations. The classification has a better performance using Manhattan distance. Based on the results, we chose to implement our hardware solution with BDPCA+LDA for feature extraction, and Manhattan distance for classification.

2.2   Architecture

Fig. 1(a) depicts the architecture of our image classifier. The classification is performed in three steps. First, the chip reads the image from external RAM and performs BDPCA dimensionality reduction. The second stage arranges the resulting matrix as a row vector and projects it onto the LDA feature space. Finally, the classifier computes the Manhattan distance between the vector and a database of reference face images in feature space, selecting the class based on the smallest distance. The BDPCA and LDA projection matrices and the classifier reference vectors are small, heavily reused, and require fast access, therefore they are stored in on-chip RAM. These matrices and reference vectors are calculated offline in a computer and are then transfered to the chip

Fig. 1(b) illustrates the three steps scheduled in a pipelined fashion. BDPCA projection is the slowest stage because it is the most computationally intensive, and is further limited by the external RAM access time. When the projected matrix is available, LDA projection starts concurrently with BDPCA projection for the next image. Distance computation and classification starts as soon as the first results from LDA are available, thus the two stages largely overlap.

2.3   Hardware Platform

We implemented the architecture on a Xilinx Spartan 3 XC3S1000 FPGA chip with 24 18-bit embedded multipliers and 24 18-Kbit block RAM modules [4].

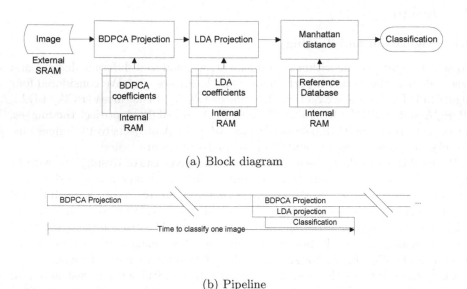

(a) Block diagram

(b) Pipeline

Fig. 1. Architecture of the image classifier

Because the FPGA does not feature floating-point hardware, we wrote our Verilog HDL descriptions using fixed-point arithmetic. We tested the system on a Digilent Nexys FPGA development board [2], which contains a Spartan 3 chip and an external 16 MByte RAM. The RAM interfaces to the FPGA through a 16-bit data bus, allowing us to read two pixels from the test image per each 80ns memory cycle. Currently, this memory bandwidth limits the performance of our classifier, as discussed in Section 3.

2.4   Implementation of BDPCA

Fig. 2 shows our pipelined implementation of the BDPCA algorithm. Module (M) reads the test image from external RAM, 2 pixels per memory cycle. Module (1) stores the 61×4 eight-bit coefficient matrix W_c in internal RAM and streams its elements at a rate of two 4-word rows per cycle. Modules (2) and (3) perform the multiplies and adds to implement the first projection (multiplication by W_c), streaming 4 words per cycle to the next stage. Module (4) stores the 49×6 eight-bit coefficient matrix W_r in internal RAM and streams it at 2 words per cycle to module (5), which performs the multiplies of the second projection (multiplication by W_r), streaming eight 16-bit words of the result per cycle. Finally, module (6) accumulates the results using a register file stored in internal RAM, thus finishing the BDPCA projection. The resulting 4×6 matrix of 16-bit coefficients is stored in the register file, which is available to the LDA projector.

All 6 modules overlap their operation in a pipelined fashion. Because of limited external RAM bandwidth, the module processes 2 pixels of the input image every

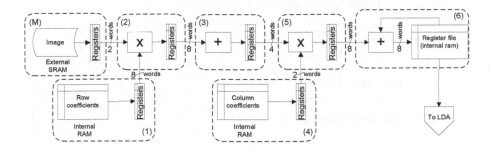

Fig. 2. Implementation of BDPCA

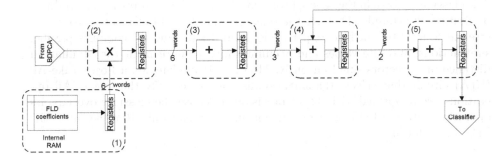

Fig. 3. Implementation of LDA

7 clock cycles, with an initial latency of 13 cycles. With a faster memory, the module could process 2 pixels every 3 clock cycles with a latency of 6 cycles.

2.5 Implementation of LDA

Fig. 3 shows the LDA projector. As Fig. 1(b) shows, the module starts when BDPCA results are available in the register file. The block reads the 4×6 resulting matrix from BDPCA as a 24-element row vector. Module (1) stores the 14×24 LDA matrix using 16-bit coefficients, and streams it at a rate of 6 coefficients per cycle. Module (2) multiplies the 6 coefficients by 6 elements of the BDPCA vector, generating 6 results that are accumulated in a 3-stage pipeline by modules (3) to (4). Without this pipeline, the accumulation becomes the critical path of the circuit and limits the clock frequency. The module outputs 32-bit results, which are then used by the classifier.

As with the BDPCA block, all operations in the LDA projector are pipelined. The block produces a 32-bit element of the output vector in the feature space every 8 clock cycles, with an initial latency of 6 cycles.

Table 1. Implementation results at 75[MHz]

Classification hit rate			93.3%
Estimated speed	Limited by RAM bandwidth	1 image	143.7 μs
		throughput	7,045 images/second
	Not limited by RAM bandwidth	1 image	62.5 μs
		throughput	16,447 images/second
Estimated power consumption		Quiescent	99.41 mW
		Dynamic	57.83 mW
		Total	157.24 mW

2.6   Implementation of the Classifier

The classifier, shown in Fig. 4, starts operating when the LDA projector produces its first result. Module (1) stores the reference database 14-element vectors, and streams four 32-bit coefficients per cycle. Modules (2) and (3) compute parallel subtractions, absolute values and accumulations to implement the Manhattan distance on 4 vectors simultaneously. Module (4) implements a Loser-Take-All (LTA) circuit that selects the smallest distance to classify the image. All operations are performed with 32-bit precision. Because the classifier overlaps its operation with the LDA projector, it outputs its result only 10 cycles after the LDA block finishes.

3   Experimental Results

We synthesized a gate-level implementation of the classifier from our Verilog HDL code using the Synopsys Synplicity hardware compiler and mapped it onto a Xilinx Spartan 3 FPGA using the Xilinx place-and-route tool. The circuit achieves maximum throughput with a clock frequency of 75Mhz, limited by the access time of the external RAM. Table 1 shows the performance results for our implementation. We repeated the experiment of Section 2.1 with the Yale database on the FPGA, comparing its classification performance to the software implementation. Our fixed-point circuit achieves a hit rate of 93.3%, slightly better than the software for this particular dataset, but the difference is negligible

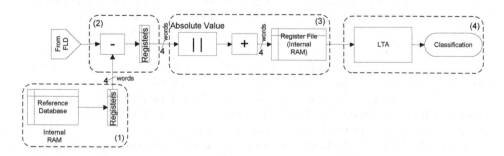

Fig. 4. Implementation of the classifier

(0.3%). The circuit classifies one image in 143.7μs, with a sustained through-put of 7,045 classifications per second. This is more than twice the throughput achieved by the software version running on a state-of-the-art workstation. Removing the limitation imposed by the external RAM, the performance more than doubles. We also estimated the power consumption using the Xilinx Xpower tool, showing that the circuit dissipates 157.24mW.

The utilization of combinational logic, flip-flops and RAM is less than 40%, the circuit is currently limited by the hardware multipliers (we use 22 out of 24 available on the chip). If we used a more complex classifier (e.g. an RBF network), we would need to reuse the multipliers with an increase in logic complexity.

4   Conclusions

We have described the architecture and implementation of a custom hardware digital implementation of a face recognition algorithm. Our solution uses BD-PCA and LDA for feature extraction, and Manhattan distance for classification. We selected these algorithms based on their measured performance and their implementation cost in hardware. Our architecture makes use of parallelism and pipelined execution to maximize throughput limited by hardware resources. The resulting implementation on a Xilinx Spartan 3 FPGA achieves 93.3% classification hit rate on several experiments using the Yale database, which is equivalent to a floating-point software version. Compared to software running on a state-of-the-art microprocessor, our circuit performs more than twice as fast, with a reduction of more than one order of magnitude in power.

Acknowledgments. This work was funded by CONICYT Grant PFB-0824. Simulation and synthesis were done with EDA software donated by Synopsys.

References

1. Delac, K., Grgic, M., Liatsis, P.: Appearance-based statistical methods for face recognition. In: 47th International Symp. on ELMAR, 2005, pp. 151–158 (2005)
2. Digilent. Digilent Nexys Board Reference Manual (2007)
3. Turk, M., Pentland, A.: Face recognition using eigenfaces. In: Procs. of IEEE Computer Society Conference on Computer Vision and Pattern Recognition, CVPR 1991, pp. 586–591 (June 1991)
4. Xilinx. Spartan-3 Generation FPGA User Guide (2008)
5. Zuo, W., Zhang, D., Yang, J., Wang, K.: BDPCA plus LDA: a novel fast feature extraction technique for face recognition. IEEE Transactions on Systems, Man, and Cybernetics, Part B: Cybernetics 36(4), 946–953 (2006)

A Window-Based
Self-Organizing Feature Map (SOFM) for Vector
Filtering Segmentation of Color Medical Imagery

Ioannis M. Stephanakis[1,2], George C. Anastassopoulos[3,4], and Lazaros Iliadis[4,5]

[1] Hellenic Telecommunication Organization S.A. (OTE),
99 Kifissias Avenue, GR-151 24, Athens, Greece
stephan@ote.gr
[2] Technological Educational Instutute of Pireaus,
GR-122 44, Pireaus, Greece
[3] Democritus University of Thrace, Medical Informatics Laboratory, GR-681 00,
Alexandroupolis, Greece
anasta@med.duth.gr
[4] Hellenic Open University, Parodos Aristotelous 18, GR-262 22, Patras, Greece
[5] Department of Forestry & Management of the Environment and Natural Resources,
Democritus University of Thrace, GR-68200, Orestiada, Hellas
liliadis@fmenr.duth.gr

Abstract. Color image processing systems are used for a variety of purposes including medical imaging. Basic image processing algorithms for enhancement, restoration, segmentation and classification are modified since color is represented as a vector instead of a scalar gray level variable. Color images are regarded as two-dimensional (2-D) vector fields defined on some color space (like for example the RGB space). In bibliography, operators utilizing several distance and similarity measures are adopted in order to quantify the common content of multidimensional color vectors. Self-Organizing Feature Maps (SOFMs) are extensively used for dimensionality reduction and rendering of inherent data structures. The proposed window-based SOFM uses as multidimensional inputs color vectors defined upon spatial windows in order to capture the correlation between color vectors in adjacent pixels. A 3x3 window is used for capturing color components in uniform color space ($L^*u^*v^*$). The neuron featuring the smallest distance is activated during training. Neighboring nodes of the SOFM are clustered according to their statistical similarity (using the Mahalanobis distance). Segmentation results suggest that clustered nodes represent populations of pixels in rather compact segments of the images featuring similar texture.

Keywords: Vector Filtering, Color Segmentation, Self-Organizing Feature Maps (SOFM), Medical Imaging.

1 Introduction

Color image processing systems [1] are used for a variety of purposes, ranging from capturing and rendering scenes in entertainment, industry, scientific exploration and

L. Iliadis and C. Jayne (Eds.): EANN/AIAI 2011, Part I, IFIP AICT 363, pp. 90–100, 2011.

medical praxis [2]. Processing of color imagery for feature and edge extraction [3] underlies several image processing algorithms for pattern recognition in industrial and scientific applications, computer vision systems and image coding methods. Color medical images may be enhanced or segmented using such techniques as vector filtering and tensor analysis [4], [5]. Colors are perceived as combinations of the three primary colors, red (R), green (G) and blue (B). The attributes generally used to distinguish one color from another are brightness, hue and saturation. There are several standard color spaces that are widely used in image processing like RGB, CMY, HIS, YIQ and others. All systems can be calculated from the tristimuli R, G, B by appropriate transformations. However, these models are not uniform color spaces [6]. In a uniform color space - such as $L^*u^*v^*$ or $L^*a^*b^*$ [7] - the difference between two colors can be simply measured by their Euclidean distance. In $L^*u^*v^*$ color space, u^* and v^* represent color chromaticities and L^* stands for the intensity.

1.1 Vector Filtering for Color Images

Color images are two-dimensional (2-D) vector fields defined on color spaces. Filtering schemes operate on the premise that an image can be subdivided into small regions, each of which can be treated as stationary [8]. Several window shapes and sizes may be used. The most commonly used window is of rectangular shape. Vector filtering is based on the ordering of aggregated distances $D_i = \sum_{j=1}^{N} d(\mathbf{x}_i, \mathbf{x}_j)$ or aggregated similarities $D_i = \sum_{j=1}^{N} s(\mathbf{x}_i, \mathbf{x}_j)$ within the sliding window and is non-linear in nature [9]. The most popular vector filter is the Vector Median Filter (VMF). Non-linear and linear approaches may be combined together in successive processing steps [10]. The proposed approach implements a Self-Organizing Feature Map (SOFM) whose trained neurons may be viewed as the possible outputs of a non-linear vector operator defined upon a 3x3 rectangular sliding window. The trained neurons capture structural as well as color local information of the underlying segment of the image. Linear statistical analysis in $L^*u^*v^*$ color space is carried out as a second processing step. The number of non-zero eigenvalues of the distributions of the training vectors indicates the dimensionality of the probability distributions of the local patterns that are represented by a neuron of the SOFM.

Traditional image filtering techniques usually applied scalar filters on each channel separately since each individual channel of a color image can be considered as a monochrome image. However, this does not take into account the correlation that exists between the color components of natural images when represented in a correlated color space.

1.2 Dimensionality Reduction Algorithms and Self-Organizing Feature Maps

The SOFM [11] is an efficient method for cluster analysis of a high-dimensional feature space onto 2-D arrays of reference vectors. SOFMs are considered as unsupervised learning algorithms and they are frequently used when there exists no-apriori knowledge about the distributions of the features (see for example [12]).

Recent advancements in the subject include Visualization-induced SOM (ViSOM) [13] and other multidimensional scaling (MDS) techniques for structural dimensionality reduction like the ISOMAP (isometric feature mapping) algorithm. Dimensionality reduction is associated as well with principal component analysis (PCA), multilinear principal component analysis (MPCA), linear discriminant analysis (LDA), marginal Fisher analysis and other approaches [14]. Dimensionality reduction should be targeted at removing the dimensions that are unreliable for the classification in order to boost classification accuracy. Retaining small eigenvalues results in overfitting models and complicates calculations. A processing step that involves linear subspace analysis for the local distributions that are represented by a neuron of a SOFM yields a better understanding of the local statistics and improves clustering results.

2   A Window-Based 2-D SOFM Model for Rendering Color Correlation

2.1 Model Formulation

There are three basic steps involved in the application of the SOFM algorithm after initialization, namely, sampling, similarity matching and updating. These three steps are repeated until map formation is completed. The algorithm is summarized as follows:

1. *Initialization.* Choose the initial values for the weight vectors $\mathbf{w}_j(0)$, which in the proposed approach are comprised by the color vectors within a sliding window of $N\mathrm{x}M$ pixels, i.e. $\mathbf{w}_j = \begin{pmatrix} L_{j,1}^* & L_{j,2}^* & \cdots & L_{j,MxN}^* \\ u_{j,1}^* & u_{j,2}^* & \cdots & u_{j,MxN}^* \\ v_{j,1}^* & v_{j,2}^* & \cdots & v_{j,MxN}^* \end{pmatrix}$

    where index j equals 1, 2,..., L.

2. *Sampling.* Choose randomly a window and the corresponding color array

$$\mathbf{v}(m,n) = \begin{pmatrix} L^*(m-\frac{M}{2},n-\frac{N}{2}) & \cdots & L^*(m,n) & \cdots & L^*(m+\frac{M}{2},n+\frac{N}{2}) \\ u^*(m-\frac{M}{2},n-\frac{N}{2}) & \cdots & u^*(m,n) & \cdots & u^*(m+\frac{M}{2},n+\frac{N}{2}) \\ v^*(m-\frac{M}{2},n-\frac{N}{2}) & \cdots & v^*(m,n) & \cdots & v^*(m+\frac{M}{2},n+\frac{N}{2}) \end{pmatrix}.$$

3. *Similarity Matching.* Find the best-matching (winning) neuron $i(\mathbf{v})$ at time t, using the minimum complex Euclidean distance:

$$i(\mathbf{v}) = \arg \min_j \sum_{k=1}^{MxN} d(\mathbf{w}_{j,k}, \mathbf{v}_k), \tag{1}$$

where $j = 1,2,..., L$. Scaling should be used in non-uniform color spaces.

4. *Updating.* Adjust the synaptic weight vectors of all neurons, using the update formula

$$\mathbf{w}_j(t+1) = \begin{cases} \mathbf{w}_j(t) + \eta\ (t)\big(\mathbf{v}(t) - \mathbf{w}_j(t)\big), & j \in \Lambda_{i(v)}(t) \\ \mathbf{w}_j(t), & \text{otherwise} \end{cases} \qquad (2)$$

where $\eta(t)$ is the learning-rate parameter and $\Lambda_{i(v)}(t)$ is the neighborhood function centered around the winning neuron $i(\mathbf{v})$. $\Lambda_{i(x,v)}(t)$ are varied dynamically during learning for best results.

5. *Continuation.* Continue with step 2 until no noticeable changes in the feature map are observed.

Alternative, such distances as the weighted Minkowski metric, the Canberra distance and various similarity measures that are obtained by using different commonality and totality concepts [15] may be used instead of the Euclidean distance.

2.2 Clustering

The correlations of local color differences within the sliding window for color vectors represented by neuron i are grouped into matrix $\mathbf{R}'_i$, which is defined as,

$$\mathbf{R}'_i = E[\Delta\mathbf{v}(m,n)\Delta\mathbf{v}^T(m,n)]. \qquad (3)$$

Assuming stationarity within the sliding window one may write,

$$\mathbf{R}'_i = \begin{pmatrix}
\mathbf{R}_i(0,0) & \mathbf{R}_i(0,1) & \mathbf{R}_i(0,2) & \mathbf{R}_i(1,0) & \mathbf{R}_i(1,1) & \mathbf{R}_i(1,2) & \mathbf{R}_i(2,0) & \mathbf{R}_i(2,1) & \mathbf{R}_i(2,2) \\
\mathbf{R}_i(0,1) & \mathbf{R}_i(0,0) & \mathbf{R}_i(0,1) & \mathbf{R}_i(1,-1) & \mathbf{R}_i(1,0) & \mathbf{R}_i(1,1) & \mathbf{R}_i(2,-1) & \mathbf{R}_i(2,0) & \mathbf{R}_i(2,1) \\
\mathbf{R}_i(0,2) & \mathbf{R}_i(0,1) & \mathbf{R}_i(0,0) & \mathbf{R}_i(1,-2) & \mathbf{R}_i(1,-1) & \mathbf{R}_i(1,0) & \mathbf{R}_i(2,-2) & \mathbf{R}_i(2,-1) & \mathbf{R}_i(2,0) \\
\mathbf{R}_i(1,0) & \mathbf{R}_i(1,-1) & \mathbf{R}_i(1,-2) & \mathbf{R}_i(0,0) & \mathbf{R}_i(0,1) & \mathbf{R}_i(0,2) & \mathbf{R}_i(1,0) & \mathbf{R}_i(1,1) & \mathbf{R}_i(1,2) \\
\mathbf{R}_i(1,1) & \mathbf{R}_i(1,0) & \mathbf{R}_i(1,-1) & \mathbf{R}_i(0,1) & \mathbf{R}_i(0,0) & \mathbf{R}_i(0,1) & \mathbf{R}_i(1,-1) & \mathbf{R}_i(1,0) & \mathbf{R}_i(1,1) \\
\mathbf{R}_i(1,2) & \mathbf{R}_i(1,1) & \mathbf{R}_i(1,0) & \mathbf{R}_i(0,2) & \mathbf{R}_i(0,1) & \mathbf{R}_i(0,0) & \mathbf{R}_i(1,-2) & \mathbf{R}_i(1,-1) & \mathbf{R}_i(1,0) \\
\mathbf{R}_i(2,0) & \mathbf{R}_i(2,-1) & \mathbf{R}_i(2,-2) & \mathbf{R}_i(1,0) & \mathbf{R}_i(1,-1) & \mathbf{R}_i(1,-2) & \mathbf{R}_i(0,0) & \mathbf{R}_i(0,1) & \mathbf{R}_i(0,2) \\
\mathbf{R}_i(2,1) & \mathbf{R}_i(2,0) & \mathbf{R}_i(2,-1) & \mathbf{R}_i(1,1) & \mathbf{R}_i(1,0) & \mathbf{R}_i(1,-1) & \mathbf{R}_i(0,1) & \mathbf{R}_i(0,0) & \mathbf{R}_i(0,1) \\
\mathbf{R}_i(2,2) & \mathbf{R}_i(2,1) & \mathbf{R}_i(2,0) & \mathbf{R}_i(1,2) & \mathbf{R}_i(1,1) & \mathbf{R}_i(1,0) & \mathbf{R}_i(0,2) & \mathbf{R}_i(0,1) & \mathbf{R}_i(0,0)
\end{pmatrix} \qquad (4)$$

which is a block symmetrical matrix and $\mathbf{R}_i(\Delta m, \Delta n)$ are 3x3 correlation submatrices for difference color vectors in $L^* u^* v^*$ color space $(\Delta m, \Delta n)$ pixels apart. A single linear neuron implementing a Hebbian-type adaptation rule for the training of its synaptic weights can evolve into a filter for the first principal component of the input distribution, $\mathbf{R}_i \mathbf{u}_i^0 = \lambda_i^0 \mathbf{u}_i^0$ ([16]). Several generalizations for multiple principal component analysis exist. Nevertheless one may apply the Householder transformation (see for example [17]) in order to obtain the eigenvectors and the eigenvalues for such a matrix by multiplying $\mathbf{R}'_i$ from the left and from the right by a sequence of matrices of the form $\mathbf{P}_k = diag\ \{1 \cdots \mathbf{A}_k \cdots 1\} - \mathbf{U}_k \big(\mathbf{H}_k^{-1}\big)_{3\times3} \mathbf{U}_k^{'T}\big)$, where,

$$\mathbf{P}_1 = diag \; \{ \begin{bmatrix} \mathbf{u}_1^T(0,0) \\ \mathbf{u}_2^T(0,0) \\ \mathbf{u}_3^T(0,0) \end{bmatrix}, 1, 1 \cdots \} - \begin{bmatrix} \mathbf{0} \\ \mathbf{R}_i(0,1) \\ \mathbf{R}_i(0,2) \\ \vdots \end{bmatrix} \left(\sum_{(m,n)\neq(0,0)} \begin{bmatrix} \lambda_1(m,n)\mathbf{u'}_1^T(m,n) \\ \lambda_2(m,n)\mathbf{u'}_2^T(m,n) \\ \lambda_3(m,n)\mathbf{u'}_3^T(m,n) \end{bmatrix} \right)^{-1} \begin{bmatrix} \mathbf{0} & \mathbf{u}_1^T(0,1) & \mathbf{u}_1^T(0,2) \\ \mathbf{0} & \mathbf{u}_2^T(0,1) & \mathbf{u}_2^T(0,2) \\ \mathbf{0} & \mathbf{u}_3^T(0,1) & \mathbf{u}_3^T(0,2) \end{bmatrix} \cdots$$

for $k=1$ with $\mathbf{u}_l^T(m,n)\mathbf{R}_i(m,n)\mathbf{u'}_l(m,n) = diag\{\lambda_l(m,n),0,0\}$ and likewise for other k.

2.3 Segmentation

Image segmentation consists of determining K disjoint segments of an image, denoted as I, that are compact in image space, feature smooth boundaries and are homogeneous regarding color distribution within each region, i.e. a partition

$$P(I) = \{R_1, R_2, R_3, \ldots, R_K\}, \tag{5}$$

where $R_i \cap R_j = \varnothing$ with $i, j \subset [1, K]$ and $i \neq j$. Segmentation algorithms seek to outline salient regions of an image. Often, their goal is to detect boundaries or interfaces between different regions. Such operators as the "Canny operator" for color edge detection and the Cumani operator are used [18]. Bayesian methods, level-set methods [19], active contour models [20], Gibbs models [21], watershed methods [22] and texture analysis methods [23] are widely used approaches. Segmentation algorithms are implemented as a first processing step in pattern classification, robot vision, medical image analysis, image coding and many other disciplines.

3 Numerical Simulations

3.1 Original Images

The medical images used to apply the proposed approach to image segmentation are selected from a histological database that has been developed in the University Hospital of the Democritus University of Thrace (DUTH), Greece, as well as standard medical images in free internet databases. The image in Fig. 1.a depicts a Bone – Haversian System (UCLA Histology Collection). This is an example of compact bone. A Haversian system consists of concentric layers (lamellae) of bone surrounding a central Haversian canal in which blood vessels and nerves are located. The osteocytes are found within small lacunae. Fig. 1.c depicts a right and a left kidney (University Hospital, DUTH). There is intensive heterogeneity in the fixation of the radioisotope in the cortex of the right and left kidneys. Also, there are defective areas of radioisotope uptake in the upper and lower poles of both kidneys (particularly in the lower poles) as a scar. Figs. 1.b and 1.d illustrate the distributions of $L^*u^*v^*$ color vectors respectively.

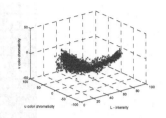

Fig. 1. a Bone - Haversian System (UCLA Histology Collection)

Fig. 1. b Distribution of vectors in $L^* u^* v^*$ color space

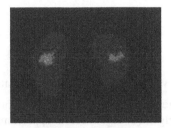

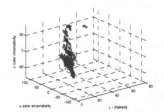

Fig. 1. c Right and left kidney (University Hospital, DUTH)

Fig. 1. d Distribution of vectors in $L^* u^* v^*$ color space

3.2 Initialization and Training

A 15 by 15 node SOFM initialized uniformly in a 3x3x3 dimensional space is used to obtain representative points of the initial distribution. The training cycle consists of 100 epochs for both images and the learning rate parameter varies dynamically. The SOFMs for the average color vectors within the 3x3 sliding window after training are depicted in Figs. 2.a and 2.d. The corresponding color windows are illustrated in Figs. 2.b and 2.e. One may utilize the obtained values in order to construct a color reduced image, i.e. $Color \in \{Color(\mathbf{w}_1) \cdots Color(\mathbf{w}_j) \cdots Color(\mathbf{w}_L)\}$.

The color reduced images for the two cases under consideration are given in Fig. 2.c and 2.f.

Fig. 2. a Distribution of average color vectors in a sliding 3x3 window (Fig. 1.a)

Fig. 2. b 15x15 SOFM after training

Fig. 2. c Color reduced image

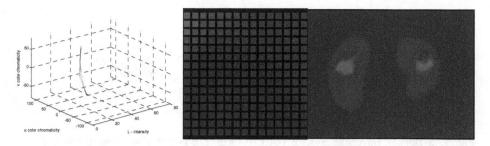

Fig. 2. d Distribution of average **Fig. 2. e** 15×15 SOFM   **Fig. 2. f** Color reduced image
color vectors in a sliding 3×3   after training
window (Fig. 1.c)

3.3 Clustering and Segmentation

The local difference distribution of $\Delta \mathbf{v} = (\mathbf{w}_j - \mathbf{v})$ for $i(\mathbf{v}) = j$ is approximated by
the eigenvectors corresponding to its largest eigenvalues. Standard SVD algorithms
indicate that pdfs featuring a dimensionality of eight (8) eigenvectors approximate at
least 90% of the power spectrum of the local distributions (see Figs. 3.a and 3.b for
both images). Nevertheless for the sake of simplicity only the three (3) largest
eigenvectors - denoted as $\mathbf{w}_{j,1}^e$, $\mathbf{w}_{j,2}^e$ and $\mathbf{w}_{j,3}^e$ - are used in order to measure the
similarity between local distributions. The similarity between local pdfs according to
the Mahalanobis distance [24] is estimated as,

$$\frac{1}{2}(\mathbf{w}_j - \mathbf{w}_k)^{\mathrm{T}}[\mathbf{w}_{j,1}^e \frac{1}{\lambda_1}\left(\mathbf{w}_{j,1}^e\right)^{\mathrm{T}} + \mathbf{w}_{j,2}^e \frac{1}{\lambda_2}\left(\mathbf{w}_{j,2}^e\right)^{\mathrm{T}} + \mathbf{w}_{j,3}^e \frac{1}{\lambda_3}\left(\mathbf{w}_{j,3}^e\right)^{\mathrm{T}} +$$
$$\mathbf{w}_{k,1}^e \frac{1}{\lambda_1}\left(\mathbf{w}_{k,1}^e\right)^{\mathrm{T}} + \mathbf{w}_{k,2}^e \frac{1}{\lambda_2}\left(\mathbf{w}_{k,2}^e\right)^{\mathrm{T}} + \mathbf{w}_{k,3}^e \frac{1}{\lambda_3}\left(\mathbf{w}_{k,3}^e\right)^{\mathrm{T}}](\mathbf{w}_j - \mathbf{w}_k) < th \tag{6}$$

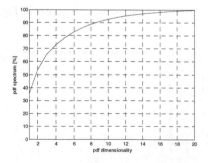

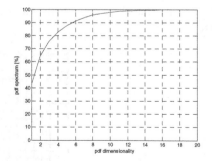

Fig. 3. a Spectrum of eigenvalues vs. number of eigenvectors (Bone - Haversian System)

Fig. 3. b Spectrum of eigenvalues vs. number of eigenvectors (Right and left kidney)

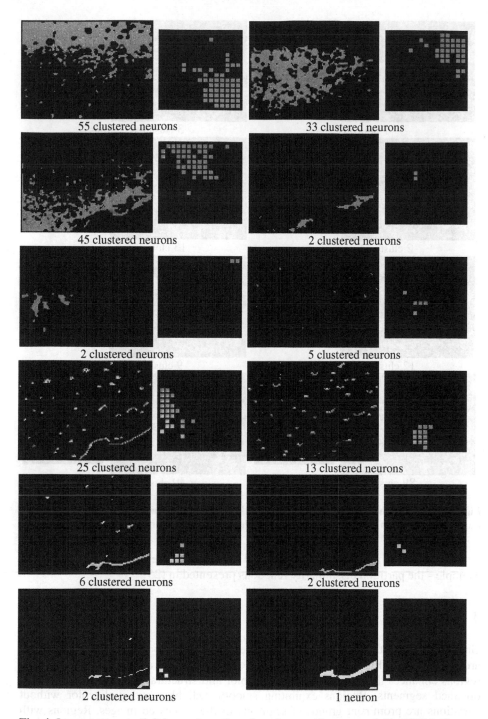

Fig. 4. Image segments (left images) attributed to clusters of neurons of the SOFM after training (depicted on the right images) for the Bone - Haversian System (Fig. 1a)

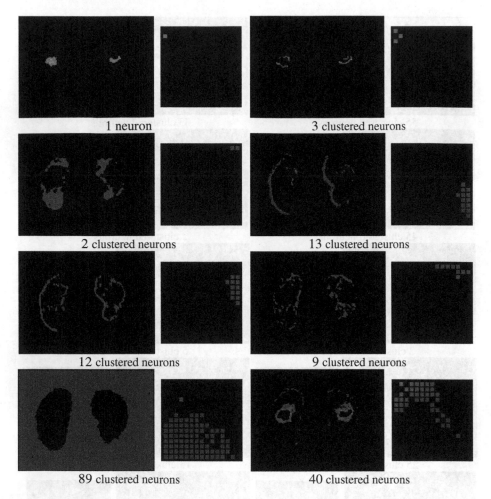

1 neuron   3 clustered neurons

2 clustered neurons   13 clustered neurons

12 clustered neurons   9 clustered neurons

89 clustered neurons   40 clustered neurons

Fig. 5. Image segments (left images) attributed to clusters of neurons of the SOFM after training (depicted on the right images) for the right and left kidney in Fig. 1b

One may use alternative measures and clustering schemes as well like - for example - the partition dissimilarity functions presented in [25].

4 Discussion

Groups of segments for the two images as well as the corresponding clustered neurons are presented in Figs. 4 and 5. Spatial nearest-neighbor assignment of pixels to regions enhances their compactness. Both color and structural details characterize the obtained segments. Regions exhibiting smooth red, blue and pink color without variations are prominent groups of segments in the processed images. Regions with textural variations of red and blue color as well as directional variations of pink and blue are grouped separately. Background clusters most of the neurons in Fig. 1.c and forms a segment of the image by itself. Different segments correspond to different tissues and underlying biological structures. The number of eigenvectors chosen to represent local distributions of color vectors affects both the accuracy of the segmentation algorithm and its execution time. The size of the sliding window is also a crucial factor that affects the execution time of the proposed algorithm.

References

1. Ramanath, R., Snyder, W.E., Yoo, Y., Drew, M.S.: Color Image Processing Pipeline. IEEE Signal Processing Mag. 22(1), 34–43 (2005)
2. Cucchiara, R., Grana, C.: Color Analysis, Segmentation and Retrieval in Medical Imaging
3. Koschan, A., Abidi, M.: Detection and Classification of Edges in Color Images. IEEE Signal Processing Mag. 22(1), 64–73 (2005)
4. Karvelis, P.S., Fotiadis, D.I.: Enhancement of Multispectral Chromosome Image Classification Using Vector Median Filtering. In: Proc. 15th Int. Conference on Conceptual Structures (ICCS 2007), Sheffield, England (2007)
5. Mosaliganti, K., Janoos, F., Irfanoglu, O., Ridgway, R., Machiraju, R., Huang, K., Saltz, J., Leone, G., Ostrowski, M.: Tensor Classification of N-Point Correlation Function Features For Histology Tissue Segmentation. Medical Image Analysis 13, 156–166 (2009)
6. Robertson, A.R.: The CIE 1976 Color-difference Formulae. Color Research and Applications 2, 7–11 (1977)
7. Tominaga, S.: Color Classification of Natural Color Images. Color Research and Applications 17, 230–239 (1992)
8. Pitas, I., Venetsanopoulos, A.N.: Nonlinear Digital Filters, Principles and Applications. Kluwer, Norwell (1990)
9. Lukac, R., Smolka, B., Martin, K., Plataniotis, K.N., Venetsanopoulos, A.N.: Vector Filtering for Color Imaging. IEEE Signal Processing Mag. 22(1), 74–86 (2005)
10. Astola, J., Haavisto, P., Neuvo, Y.: Vector Median Filters. Proc. IEEE 78(4), 678–689 (1990)
11. Kohonen, T.: Self-Organizing Maps. Series in Information Sciences. Springer, Berlin (1995)
12. Stephanakis, I., Anastassopoulos, G., Iliadis, L.: Color Segmentation Using Self-Organizing Feature Maps (SOFMs) Defined Upon Color and Spatial Image Space. In: Proc. 20th International Conference on Artificial Neural Networks, Thessaloniki, Greece (2010)
13. Yin, H.: ViSOM – A Novel Method for Multivariate Data Projection and Structure Visualization. IEEE Trans. Neural Networks 13(1), 237–243 (2002)
14. Jiang, X.: Linear Subspace Learning-Based Dimensionality Reduction. IEEE Signal Processing Mag. 28(2), 16–26 (2011)
15. Plataniotis, K.N., Androutsos, D., Venetsanopoulos, A.N.: Adaptive Fuzzy Systems for Multichannel Signal Processing. Proc. IEEE 87(9), 1601–1622 (1999)
16. Oja, E.: A Simplified Neuron Model as a Principal Component Analyzer. Journal of Mathematical Biology 15, 267–273 (1982)
17. Golub, G.H., Van Loan, C.F.: Matrix Computations, 2nd edn. Johns Hopkins University Press, Baltimore (1989)
18. Koschan, A., Abidi, M.: Detection and Classification of Edges in Color Images. IEEE Signal Processing Mag. 22(1), 64–73 (2005)

19. Malladi, R., Sethian, J.A., Vermuri, B.C.: Shape Modeling With Front Propagation: A Level set Approach. IEEE Trans. on Pattern Analysis and Machine Intelligence 17(2), 158–174 (1995)
20. Caselles, V., Kimmel, R., Sapiro, G.: Geodesic Active Contours. International Journal on Computer Vision 22(1), 61–97 (1997)
21. Chen, T., Metaxas, D.: A Hybrid Framework for 3D Medical Image Segmentation. Medical Image Analysis 9, 547–565 (2005)
22. Vincent, L., Soille, P.: Watersheds in Digital Spaces: An Efficient Algorithm Based on Immersion Simulations. IEEE Trans. Pattern Analysis and Machine Intelligence 13(6), 583–598 (1991)
23. Haralik, R., Shanmugam, K., Dinstein, I.: Textural Features for Image Classification. IEEE Trans. on Systems, Man and Cybernetics, 610–621 (1973)
24. McLachlan, G.J.: Discriminant Analysis and Statistical Pattern Recognition, p. 12. Wiley Interscience, Hoboken (1992)
25. Logeswari, T., Karnan, M.: An Improved Implementation of Brain Tumor Detection Using Segmentation Based on Hierarchical Self Organizing Maps. International Journal of Computer Theory and Engineering 2(4), 591–595 (2010)

Neural Network Rule Extraction
to Detect Credit Card Fraud

Nick F. Ryman-Tubb and Paul Krause

University of Surrey, Department of Computing, Guildford, Surrey, GU2 7XH, UK
n.ryman-tubb@surrey.ac.uk, p.krause@surrey.ac.uk

Abstract. Neural networks have represented a serious barrier-to-entry in their application in automated fraud detection due to their black box and often proprietary nature which is overcome here by combining them with symbolic rule extraction. A Sparse Oracle-based Adaptive Rule extraction algorithm is used to produce comprehensible rules from a neural network to aid the detection of credit card fraud. In this paper, a method to improve this extraction algorithm is presented along with results from a large real-world European credit card data set. Through this application it is shown that neural networks can assist in mission-critical areas of business and are an important tool in the transparent detection of fraud.

Keywords: fraud detection, credit card, neural applications, rule extraction, neuro-symbolic, data mining.

1 Introduction

The Oxford dictionary defines fraud as, *"wrongful or criminal deception intended to result in financial or personal gain"*. Fraud can involve the use of stolen credit, debit, fuel or gift cards, opening a bank account through identity theft, concealing the source of illegally or criminally received money, making a wrongful or exaggerated claim for medical expenses through insurance or social security claims, etc. Fraud can be found in on-line shopping, computer gaming, telecommunications, banking, social security, tax evasion, customs fraud, insurance claims, payments and financial services, to the illegal sale of endangered species. The list of crimes and their targets is disappointingly long.

Public perceptions of fraud are often tempered by a belief that it is a "white-collar" crime which targets the wealthy, government and big business and is of less concern as the effects are cushioned for the victim [1]. However, violent criminals are increasingly moving into fraud [2] so that fraud can involve the threat of violence including murder. In the USA, the fear of fraud supersedes that of terrorism, computer and health viruses and personal safety [3]. In the UK the Attorney General described fraud as, *"second only to drug trafficking in causing harm to the economy and society."* [4]. Today, the proceeds from fraud are paying for organised crime, drug smuggling and terrorism [5]. It was estimated that in the UK fraud cost £30bn in 2010, that is 1.3% of the entire UK economic output [6]. In the US, the fraud cost was

L. Iliadis and C. Jayne (Eds.): EANN/AIAI 2011, Part I, IFIP AICT 363, pp. 101–110, 2011.

estimated at $994bn in 2008 [7]. Whatever country, it seems that fraud is large and there is a human cost for each individual act of fraud [8].

The detection of fraud is a complex scientific and business challenge. The datasets are large and therefore need to be properly sampled as it becomes computationally impractical to use the natural population. Real world transactional data is noisy, unbalanced, computationally expensive to maintain and highly dimensional. Such data is skewed, has uneven distributions and contains a mixture of symbolic and continuous variables. The dataset is sparse - there is a large quantity of transactional data which contain only a small number of example frauds. Often researchers are unable to report on real fraud datasets due to their sensitivity with many published papers using either synthetic or small datasets; where there is no reason to believe that the conclusions drawn will hold true when they are scaled-up to large, real-world applications [9], [10].

1.1 Payment Card Fraud

One common type of fraud is payment card fraud – this is the criminal act of deception through the use of a physical plastic card or card information without the knowledge of the cardholder. When a transaction takes place, the details of that transaction are processed by the acquiring bank for authorisation. It is reported that in 2009, the USA total card fraud losses cost banks and merchants $8.6 billion [11] and in the UK £609.9 million [12]. To detect this fraud, organisations use a range of methods; manual methods and some form of automated Fraud Management System (FMS) [13]. The FMS is often a rule-based system that stores and uses knowledge in a transparent way and is easy for a Fraud-Analyst to modify and interpret. Rules provide a convenient mechanism for explaining decisions. However, the generation of comprehensible rules is an expensive and time-consuming task, requiring a high degree of skill both in terms of the developers and the Fraud-Analysts concerned. The performance of the FMS is dependent upon the skill of the Fraud-Analyst and how past data and events are interpreted by them.

An alternative to rules is the use of a learning approach that does not require expert knowledge but learns from examples given in transaction data. A model is formed that can then be used on new transactions to make a decision. The ability of such a model to generalise is fundamental. One such method is to use supervised neural networks that have been widely used to learn from fraud data [9], [14], [15].

Supervised neural networks are essentially a collection of large numbers of real-valued parameters (weights, etc.) with no obvious method to determine their meaning. The knowledge is represented by the distributed weights between the connections, the threshold values and activation functions. The uptake and use of neural networks has been hampered by their "black box" nature and the requirement for often proprietary software to implement the neural network model to be deployed on a server within a mission-critical part of the business – a serious barrier-to-entry in the automated use of FMS.

1.2 Mission Critical Application

Once a transaction is made a decision has to be taken to accept or refer/decline the payment. This authorisation process is part of a real-time payments system, which means that the FMS is mission critical – it's failure will cause damage to the business in terms of both money and reputation. It is for this reason that many businesses are reluctant to deploy a FMS that is based on a neural network, where the exact method of fraud detection is kept hidden and they are reliant on their supplier. Many businesses require a transparent approach to fraud detection so that both Fraud-Analysts and management teams can understand exactly why a decision to refer/decline is being made.

A practical solution to promote the widespread use of neural networks within FMS is to use them off-line. One approach is to use the neural network to create evolving models that automatically learn from patterns in transaction data of payment cards that can then be used to extract knowledge in the form of symbolic rules. The rules can be formatted into human-readable ANSI SQL statements that can then be deployed within an existing live Fraud Server environment. This will allow existing FMS systems (that support SQL) to be used and reduce the need for expensive and time consuming creation of manual rules and reliance on Fraud-Analysts.

1.3 Rule Generation

There are a number of rule induction algorithms that can be used to generate rules from a dataset. One common method is the decision tree - based on information gain [16]. In applications where the dataset is large and contains noise, such as fraud detection, this approach and others have been found to generate a large number of rules where each rule has many conditions and are unfortunately difficult to understand. A key objective for a FMS is to use as few rules as possible – as a "global" view of the fundamental fraud factors is generally preferred over actual accuracy. Neural networks have shown considerable promise in terms of accuracy with generalisation for fraud detection. There are two key approaches to rule extraction from a neural network: (1) Decompositional, (2) Pedagogical. A decompositional approach is where rules are created using heuristic searches that guide the process of rule extraction [17], [18] by decomposing the neural network architecture and therefore produce rules that represent the internal architecture. Since there is no reason for individual neurons to represent a recognisable "concept", the extracted rules are often not sufficiently comprehensible. A pedagogical approach is where a set of global rules are extracted from the neural network in terms of the relationships between only the inputs and the outputs [19], [20]. These individual rules are then combined into a set of rules that describes the neural network as a whole. The main difficulty with this approach is that the size of the search space is large so that a straightforward search is not practical in real-world problems, where even a small number of input neurons (fields) mean an unrealistic level of computing power is required.

2 SOAR Extraction

The Sparse Oracle-based Adaptive Rule (SOAR) extraction algorithm is detailed in [21] and uses sensitivity analysis to avoid the exhaustive decision boundary searches of other neural rule extraction algorithms e.g. [22], [23], [24]. The SOAR algorithm shown in Figure 1, is independent of the neural structure and here uses a standard Multi-Layer Perceptron (MLP) as a Neural "Oracle" which was chosen as a classifier to produce good generalisation and noise-tolerance. Sparse fraud examples are used as the initial search space "seeds" – since (randomly) locating fraud points on the decision boundary in a large search space would be otherwise inefficient. SOAR has the following steps:

1. Continuous valued fields are converted into discreet literals using a well known clustering algorithm called ART2 [25] that is applied to group together similar fraud examples. The algorithm creates a new cluster when the input does not belong to the cluster that was determined as most probable, based on a user defined parameter. The Euclidean distance measure is used for measuring similarities between the input pattern and the exemplars in each cluster.

2. The trained MLP neural system is used as an oracle, to interrogate.

3. Prototypes are formed by grouping similar examples from the fraud dataset class to reduce complexity.

4. The prototype generated is "expanded" to cover the largest area on the decision boundary that continues to represent a single class e.g. *{genuine, fraud}*. This is accomplished using the neural network as an oracle where the binary digits in each literal in the prototype are sequentially activated e.g., $\{1,0,...0\}$, $\{0,1,...0\}$ until $\{0,0,...1\}$ and the class membership determined by the oracle. In the case of a discretised numeric type each b_i represents a contiguous real range and so the search is simplified by only having to activate each in turn, $(\{b_1,b_2,b_m\}, \oplus)=1$. Only fields that represent continuous values are expanded since it would make no sense to expand an unordered nominal field. The aim is to capture the generalisation of the neural model while covering as much of the space contiguously as is possible. This is then used to create a propositional rule as a list of antecedents as a combination of the expanded input fields.

5. The rules are optimised to avoid overlap, duplication and redundancy. This step includes rule pruning to remove rules that have a large estimated error and those which never "fire" (have zero coverage) for the training set.

6. A false-positive ratio is calculated for each rule using the Training Dataset. Those rules that have a large ratio (i.e. produce a large number of false-positives compared to the correct number of frauds detected) are removed.

Since the fraud data examples are sparse, the above procedure is computationally efficient. This approach will approximate the classification capability of the neural network by creating a set of rules. The optimisation steps 5 and 6 above aim to improve comprehensibility by reducing the number of rules and approximation errors.

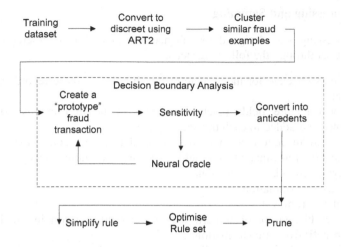

Fig. 1. SOAR Extraction Framework

2.1 Extended SOAR Extraction

In [21] the algorithm only extracted rules for the fraud class. The algorithm has been extended here, called SOAR II, so that steps 3 and 4 are repeated to extract rules for a sample of the genuine class. For those points that overlap/intersect within the two sets of rules, false positives will be generated and the fraud rule is "trimmed" so as to remove the overlap. To compare the performance of the two versions of SOAR extraction experiments were completed using the same dataset with both approaches.

3 Experimental Results

A dataset was provided by a large European company that processes a high volume of transactions per day. The fraud class priors are highly skewed. It has been shown that such a class imbalance may not allow learning algorithms to create good models [26] so sampling has been used. This sampled dataset was created from a natural population of transactions over a fixed time period so as to be representative of the natural population containing all of the known fraud, shown in Table 1.

Table 1. European Credit Card Fraud Dataset for Natural Population

Feature	Total
Transactions	60m
Cards	8m
Number of Fraud Transactions	4,000
Value of Fraud Transactions	€1m
A *priory* transaction fraud	1:15,000

3.1 Pre-processing and Sampling

The pre-processing was designed to enhance the modelling characteristics of the provided dataset through the following steps:

- All records checked for incomplete or missing data. These records are ignored if found.
- Additional feature fields (such as average spend in previous 30-days) are calculated and added to each transaction record.
- Attempts are made to identify outliers in the data and to remove them.
- Assessing the relevance of each field (to ensure maximum entropy).
- Identifying redundancy in the data.
- Relevance determination.
- Redundancy removal.
- Frequency histograms of numeric data are created to ascertain which variables could benefit from transformation.
- Frequency analysis of symbolic data is undertaken to ascertain which low frequency variables could benefit from being grouped (into SQL tables).
- Re-weighting and splitting.

The pre-processing splits the transaction data into two datasets, shown in Table 2.

Table 2. Sampled Datasets

Training Dataset	Consists of a randomly selected proportion of the transaction data where the class is known. This information is used by the training algorithm to train the neural network to learn the relationships within the data.
Validation Dataset	Consists of a sample of data where the outcome is known and is used only once the model has been completed to validate the accuracy of the model.

3.2 Neural Network Training

A three layer MLP architecture was selected as is was the common choice in the previously mentioned research and so is representative of the range of classifiers that could be used. All neuron values were in the range [0,1] using a standard sigmoidal activation function. The training of the neural network is an iterative process that requires considerable processing power to complete where the more transactions presented the longer the algorithm will take. For this reason a Training Dataset was created as a sub-sample shown in Table 3. The Training Dataset used a small sub-sample of 40,000 transaction records with 2,800 example fraud transactions. The remaining 1,200 fraud transactions were reserved as "unseen" in a Validation Dataset to produce performance metrics given in Table 4. The MLP was then trained using this Training Dataset by interleaving and repeating the fraud examples with the genuine examples so that they were re-balanced. The Conjugate Gradient Descent (CGD) [27] training algorithm was then used. Using a Constructive Algorithm [28] the number of hidden neurons in the hidden layer was automatically determined by starting at a single neuron and then dynamically growing the layer by adding

Table 3. Dataset Distribution

	Total Sample	Training Dataset		Validation Dataset	
Total Transaction Records	1,100,000	40,000	4%	1,060,000	96%
Containing Fraud Records	4,000	2,800	70%	1,200	30%
Value of Fraud Records	€1,000,000	€703,000		€297,000	

additional neurons until the stopping criteria is reached; in this case, the final MLP had 60 discreet inputs, 10 hidden and 1 output neuron.

3.3 Rule Extraction

Once the neural network was trained, the SOAR and SOAR II extraction algorithms were applied to the Training Dataset and two rule sets created. A confusion matrix was used to evaluate the performance of both the trained neural network and the extracted rule set using the Validation Dataset. The metrics used for calculating accuracy and precision are given in equations (1), (2) and (3).

$$accuracy = \frac{TP + TN}{TP + FN + FP + TN}. \tag{1}$$

$$precision_{genuine} = \frac{TP}{TP + FP}. \tag{2} \qquad precision_{fraud} = \frac{FP}{TP + FP}. \tag{3}$$

While the standard evaluation metrics are important, in the practical application of the approach these need to be projected into the real world. Businesses that deploy a FMS generally have a case management system to review the fraud alerts generated by the rules and have a maximum number of alerts that they can reasonably review in a day. Therefore, performance needs to be projected to the natural population with reference to the number of alerts per day:

$$Sampling\ Rate\ S_g = \frac{\#Transactions\ Natural}{\#Transactions\ Sample}. \tag{4}$$

$$Segmentation\ Rate\ R_t = \frac{\#Transactions\ Training}{\#Transactions\ Validation}. \tag{5}$$

$$Transaction\ FP\ Ratio = \frac{\left(FP.S_g.R_t\right)}{TP}. \tag{6}$$

$$Transaction\ alerts\ per\ day\ T_d = \frac{(FP.S_g.R_t)+(TP.R_t)}{Days\ in\ period}. \tag{7}$$

$$Transaction\ correctly\ alerted\ per\ day\ T_{dc} = \frac{T_d}{FP}. \tag{8}$$

Here, S_g is calculated as 53 (4), R_t is 0.04 (5) and the resulting performance metrics are given in Table 4, where a "card" is a sequence of transactions linked by a single card number. The number of antecedents in each rule is a good measure on human comprehensibility; shorter and simpler rules are more straightforward to understand than complex rules.

Table 4. Evaluation using the Validation Dataset only

	Neural	SOAR I	SOAR II
#Rules	-	47	**44**
Average Antecedents	-	9.4	**9.4**
Accuracy (1)	63%	91%	**93%**
Precision$_{genuine}$ (2)	63%	91%	**93%**
Precision$_{fraud}$ (3)	88%	87%	**73%**
Transaction False Positive Rate (6)	1:468	1:219	**1:215**
Transactions alerted per day (7)	7,385	1,734	**1,778**
Transactions correctly alerted per day (8)	8	8	**8**
Cards alerted per day	975	238	**201**
Cards correctly alerted per day	1.7	1.7	**1.6**

For reasons of space, just the top rule from the SOAR II extraction algorithm is presented - this single rule captures over 30% of all frauds in the Validation Dataset. Separate SQL tables of values are created during the pre-processing clustering/grouping stage, e.g. L1 could contain {France, Germany, Spain, Italy, Netherlands}, meaning true if any one of the countries listed is in the transaction field.

```
IF RECORDTYPE=(SA) AND COUNTRY=(L1) AND CODE=(CODE1) AND PRDCODE=(10) AND
NETW=(ID1) AND TRANSTYPE=(5) AND IND=(1) THEN FRAUD
```

In SQL:

```
SELECT * FROM [TRANSACTIONS] WHERE RECORDTYPE IN
(SELECT A FROM SA) AND COUNTRY IN (SELECT A FROM L1)
AND CODE IN (SELECT A FROM CODE1) AND PRDCODE=10 AND
NETW IN (SELECT A FROM ID1) AND TRANSTYPE=5 AND IND=1;
```

3.4 Analysis

From Table 4, SOAR II has extracted three fewer rules than the original algorithm with a similar accuracy but at the expense of the fraud precision; those rules that have been omitted in SOAR II were generated from genuine transactions that completely overlap the fraud transactions in the Training Dataset – they are therefore impossible to classify into a single class as they are indistinguishable from each other. The rules in both cases outperform the neural network in terms of accuracy. It is suggested that the rules are able to outperform as the boundaries located are crisp boundaries so that the (inaccurate) generalisation of the neural model is not captured in the extraction. This tends to create rules that do not cover the decision boundary correctly as evidenced by the reduced precision which tends to reduce the false-positive rate suffered by the neural network. The false-positive rate is further reduced by pruning those rules that exhibit a high rate, reducing precision but contributing to improved accuracy. There is no such equivalent process for the neural network. The Fraud-Analysts found that the SOAR II rules were easier to understand and identified both already known patterns as well as previously unknown patterns of fraud.

4 Conclusions

Accurate rules can be extracted from a trained neural network that can then be inspected and applied in a live FMS environment. This removes the fear of applying neural networks within a mission critical part of a business. The rules are easy to understand and can be produced rapidly, reducing the workload on Fraud-Analysts. SOAR II extraction used on a regular basis has the promise of enabling a more dynamic FMS that can respond to the changing patterns of fraud. It is anticipated that the SOAR II extraction approach can be applied to many other areas of fraud detection where transparency of the decision is important.

Acknowledgments. This work was supported in part by Retail Decisions Europe Ltd.

References

1. Transnational Financial Crime Program, The International Centre for Criminal Law Reform & Criminal Justice Policy, Vancouver, Canada: Drawing conclusions about financial fraud: crime, development, and international co-operative strategies in China and the West (2008)
2. IdentityTheft.com Inc.,
   http://www.identitytheft.com/index.php/article/
   stolen_credit_terroist_attacks
3. Unisys-Corporation: Research shows economic crisis increases Americans' fears about fraud and ID theft (2009)
4. Button, M., Johnston, L., Frimpong, K.: The fraud review and the policing of fraud: Laying the foundations for a centralized fraud police or counter fraud executive? Policing, 241–250 (2008)
5. Everett, C.: Credit card fraud funds terrorism. Computer Fraud & Security (5) (2003)
6. BBC News, http://news.bbc.co.uk/1/hi/business/8473167.stm
7. Association of Certified Fraud Examiners: Report to the Nation on Occupational Fraud and Abuse (2008)
8. European Healthcare Fraud & Corruption Network: The Human Cost of Fraud (2010)
9. Aleskerov, E., Freisleben, B., Rao, B.: CARDWATCH: a neural network based database mining system for credit card fraud detection. In: Computational Intelligence for Financial Engineering (CIFEr), pp. 220–226. IEEE Press, Los Alamitos (1997)
10. Rong-Chang, C., Shu-Ting, L., Xun, L.: Personalized Approach Based on SVM and ANN for detecting credit card fraud. In: International Conference on Neural Networks and Brain, pp. 810–815. IEEE Press, Los Alamitos (2005)
11. Crosman, P.: Card fraud costs U.S. payment providers $8.6 billion per year. Bank Systems & Technology (2010)
12. UK Payments Administration: Card fraud facts and figures (2009)
13. Cybersource: Seventh annual UK online fraud report: trends, key metrics, informed decisions (2011)

14. Brause, R., Langsdorf, T., Hepp, M.: Neural data mining for credit card fraud detection. In: 11th International Conference on Tools with Artificial Intelligence, p. 103. IEEE Press, Los Alamitos (1999)
15. Ghosh, S., Reilly, D.L.: Credit card fraud detection with a neural network. In: International Conference on System Sciences, Hawaii, pp. 621–630. IEEE Press, Los Alamitos (1994)
16. Quinlan, J.R.: Induction of decision trees. Machine Learning 1, 81–106 (1986)
17. Towell, G.G., Shavlik, J.W.: Extracting refined rules from knowledge-based neural networks. Machine Learning 13(1), 71–101 (1993)
18. Setiono, R.: Extracting rules from neural networks by pruning and hidden-unit splitting. Neural Computation 9(1), 205–225 (1997)
19. Craven, M., Shavlik, J.W.: Using sampling and queries to extract rules from trained neural networks. In: International Conference on Machine Learning, pp. 37–45. Morgan Kaufmann, San Francisco (1994)
20. Thrun, S.: Advances in Neural Information Processing Systems-Extracting rules from artificial neural networks with distributed representations. MIT Press, Cambridge (1995)
21. Ryman-Tubb, N., d'Avila Garcez, A.S.: SOAR - Sparse Oracle-based Adaptive Rule extraction: knowledge extraction from large-scale datasets to detect credit card fraud. In: World Congress on Computational Intelligence, Barcelona, Spain, pp. 1–9. IEEE Press, Los Alamitos (2010)
22. Barakat, N., Diederich, J.: Learning-based rule-extraction from support vector machines. In: 12th International Conference on Computer Theory and Applications, IEEE Press, Los Alamitos (2004)
23. Barakat, N., Diederich, J.: Eclectic rule-extraction from support vector machines. International Journal Computational Intelligence 2(1), 59–62 (2005)
24. Engelbrecht, A.P., Viktor, H.L.: Engineering applications of bio-inspired artificial neural networks-Rule improvement through decision boundary detection using sensitivity analysis. Springer, Heidelberg (1999)
25. Carpenter, G.A., Grossberg, S.: ART2: Self-organization of stable category recognition codes for analog input patterns. Applied Optics 26, 4919–4930 (1987)
26. Chawla, N.V., Bowyer, K.W., Hall, L.O., Kegelmeyer, W.P.: SMOTE: Synthetic Minority Over-sampling TEchnique. Journal of Artificial Intelligence Research 16, 341–378 (2002)
27. Fletcher, R., Powell, M.J.D.: A rapidly convergent descent method for minimization. Computing Journal 6, 163–168 (1963)
28. Hirose, Y., Yamashita, K., Hijiya, S.: Backpropagation algorithm which varies the number of hidden units. In: International Joint Conference on Neural Networks, p. 625. Elsevier, Amsterdam (1989)

A Neuro-Fuzzy Hybridization Approach to Model Weather Operations in a Virtual Warfare Analysis System

D. Vijay Rao[1], Lazaros Iliadis[2], and Stefanos Spartalis[3]

[1] Institute for Systems Studies and Analyses
Defence Research and Development Organisation,
Metcalfe House, Delhi 110054, India
{doctor.rao.cs@gmail.com}
[2] Department of Forestry & Management of the Environment and Natural Resources
Democritus University of Thrace, GR-68200, Orestiada, Hellas
liliadis@fmenr.duth.gr
[3] Department of Production Engineering and Management
Democritus University of Thrace, GR-68200, Orestiada, Hellas
sspart@pme.duth.gr

Abstract. Weather operations play an important and integral part of planning, execution and sustainment of mission operations. In this paper, a neuro-fuzzy hybridization technique is applied to model the weather operations and predict its impact on the effectiveness of air tasking operations and missions. Spatio-temporal weather data from various meteorological sources are collected and used as the input to a neural network and the predicted weather conditions at a given place is classified based on fuzzy logic. The corresponding fuzzy rules are generated forming the basis for introducing the weather conditions in the evaluation of the effectiveness of the military mission plans. An agent-based architecture is proposed where agents representing the various weather sensors feed the weather data to the simulator, and a weather agent developed using neuro-fuzzy hybridization computes the weather conditions over the flight plan of the mission. These rules are then used by the Mission Planning and Execution system that evaluates the effectiveness of military missions in various weather conditions.

Keywords: Military simulation, Weather Modeling, Neuro-Fuzzy hybridization, Mission effectiveness, agent-based architecture.

1 Introduction

Virtual Warfare Analysis systems constitute an important class of applications that have proved to be an important tool for military system analyses and an inexpensive alternate to live training exercises. Air Wargame Simulation System (AWGSS) is a virtual warfare analysis software that has been developed for planning, analysis and evaluating air tasking operations [1],[2]. In the design and development of such applications, modeling the complexity and battle dynamics, assessing, and predicting

L. Iliadis and C. Jayne (Eds.): EANN/AIAI 2011, Part I, IFIP AICT 363, pp. 111–121, 2011.

the outcomes of mission plans quantitatively under various real-world conditions is a very difficult endeavor [3],[4]. One such phenomenon that bears an important and critical success factor in achieving the military objectives is weather operations [1]. Weather operations [5] are an integral part of planning, execution, and sustainment of military operations and critical to commanders' battle space awareness and decision making across the range of military operations. Operational environment and weather conditions play an important role in deciding the suitability of the weapon for a target. For instance, poor weather and conflict induced environmental conditions such as smoke from bombing may degrade or block the infrared, electro-optical or laser targeting sensors required for delivery of guidance ordnance. Laser Guided Bombs cannot be used in poor weather where target illumination cannot be seen, or where it is not possible to get target designator in close distance. However, poor visibility does not affect satellite guided bombs. Only comparatively inaccurately unguided bombs could be delivered in poor weather. These factors change the decisions taken by the pilots on Execute/Call-off mission, Change mission route and/or profile of weapon delivery, change in the class of weapons to deliver in the light of sensors performance, re-prioritize the target, and/or change the Time-on-target of the mission or even abort the mission [1],[2]. In this paper, ANFIS a neuro-fuzzy hybridization technique is used to model the weather conditions and predict the Mission_Effectiveness_Factor.

2   An Agent-Based Architecture to Model Military Operations

Agent-oriented system development aims to simplify the construction of complex systems by introducing a natural abstraction layer on top of the object-oriented paradigm composed of autonomous interacting actors. It has emerged as a powerful modeling technique that is more realistic for today's dynamic warfare scenarios than the traditional models which were deterministic, stochastic or based on differential equations. These approaches provide a very simple and intuitive framework for modeling warfare and are very limited when it comes to representing the complex interactions of real-world combat because of their high degree of aggregation, multi-resolution modeling and varying attrition rate factors. The effects of random individual agent behavior and of the resulting interactions of agents are phenomenon that traditional equation-based models simply cannot capture. The traditional approaches of computers to warfare simulation used algorithms that aggregated the forces on each side, such as differential equations or game theory, effectively modeling the entire battle space with a single process. These mathematical theories treat the opposing sides as aggregates, and do not consider the detailed interactions of individual entities.

Agent-based models give each entity its own thread of execution, mimicking the real-world entities that affect military operations [3]. The Environment Agent is a lightweight agent that determines the current environmental conditions over the area of operation selected for the mission.

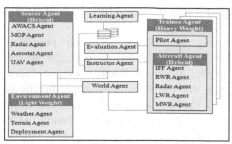

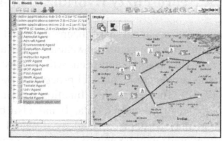

Fig. 1. Agent architecture for AWGSS

Fig. 2. Mission Planning with weather constraints

It receives information from weather, terrain and deployment agent and provides an information service to the world agent after its own process of reasoning. This information is then used by other agents such as Manual Observation Post (MOP), *Pilot*, Unmanned Air Vehicle (UAV), Identification Friend/Foe (IFF), Radar Warning Receiver (RWR), Missile Warning Receiver (MWR), Laser Warning Receiver (LWR), *Mission Planning, Sensor Performance, Target Acquisition* and *Damage Assessment and Computation*. The weather agent is an important agent that that has functions such as *Get_Visibility(), Get_Temperature()* and *Get CloudCover()*. The weather agents's reasoning has been designed using ANFIS, a neuro-fuzzy hybridization technique that is used to predict the Mission_Success_Factor(), considering the weather conditions along the mission route.

Surface aviation weather observations include weather elements and forecasts pertaining to flying. A network of airport stations provides routine up-to-date surface weather information. Upper-air weather data is received from sounding balloons (radiosonde observations) and pilot weather reports that furnish temperature, humidity, pressure, and wind data. Aircraft in flight also report turbulence, icing and height of cloud tops. The weather radar provides detailed information about precipitation, winds, and weather systems. Doppler technology allows the radar to provide measurements of winds through a large vertical depth of the atmosphere. Terminal Doppler weather radars are used to alert and warn airport controllers of approaching wind shear, gust fronts, and heavy precipitation which could cause hazardous conditions for take-off, landing and diversion. Low-level wind shear alert systems provide pilots and controllers with information on hazardous surface wind conditions (on and near airbases) that create unsafe operational conditions. Visible, infrared and other types of images of clouds are taken from weather satellites in orbit. Weather is a continuous, multi-dimensional, spatio-temporally data intensive, dynamic and partly chaotic process. Traditionally, two main approaches for weather forecasting are followed: Numerical Weather Prediction and Analogue forecasting. For the AWGSS application, it is needed to consider the past weather conditions at given places of operation and predict the weather for simulation of mission tasks in real-time. In this paper, the ANFIS neuro-fuzzy hybridization technique is used to predict the weather conditions along the mission route and study the effects of weather in the virtual warfare scenario analysis in terms of pilot decisions in mission planning, performance of sensors, and target identification and damage assessment.

3 A Neuro-Fuzzy Hybridization Approach to Weather Prediction

The weather agent has been designed using ANFIS to give the predicted Mission_Success_factor in weather constraints. In the following section, the neuro-fuzzy hybridization approach will be discussed. Both neural networks and fuzzy systems are dynamic, parallel processing systems that estimate input–output functions [6],[7],[8]. They estimate a function without any mathematical model and learn from experience with sample data. It has also been proven that 1) any rule-based fuzzy system may be approximated by a neural net and 2) any neural net (feed-forward, multilayered) may be approximated by a rule-based fuzzy system. Fuzzy systems can be broadly categorized into two families. The first includes linguistic models based on collections of IF–THEN rules, whose antecedents and consequents utilize fuzzy values. The Mamdani model falls in this group where the knowledge is represented as it is shown in the following expression.

$$R^i : If \ X_1 \ is \ A_1^i \ and \ X_2 \ is \ A_2^i ....and \ X_n \ is \ A_m^i, then \ y^i \ is \ B^i$$

The second category, which is used to model the Weather prediction problem is the Sugeno-type and it uses a rule structure that has fuzzy antecedent and functional consequent parts. This can be viewed as the expansion of piece-wise linear partition represented as shown in the rule below.

$$R^i : If \ X_1 \ is \ A_1^i \ and \ X_2 \ is \ A_2^i ....and \ X_n \ is \ A_m^i, then \ y^i = a_0^1 + a_1^i X_1 + ...+ a_n^i X_n$$

$$\bar{A} \cap \bar{B} = \left\{ \left(x, \mu_{\bar{A} \cap \bar{B}}(x) \right) | \mu_{\bar{A} \cap \bar{B}}(x) = \mu_{\bar{A}}(x)^\wedge \mu_{\bar{B}}(x) = \min\left(\mu_{\bar{A}}(x), \mu_{\bar{B}}(x) \right) \right\} \tag{1}$$

The conjunction "and" Operation between fuzzy sets known as *Linguistics*, for the implementation of the Mamdani rules is done by employing special Fuzzy Operators called T-Norms [6]. The ANFIS uses by default the Minimum T-Norm which is the case here and it can be seen in the above equation 1. The approach approximates a nonlinear system with a combination of several linear systems, by decomposing the whole input space into several partial fuzzy spaces and representing each output space with a linear equation. Such models are capable of representing both qualitative and quantitative information and allow relatively easier application of powerful learning techniques for their identification from data. They are capable of approximating any continuous real-valued function on a compact set to any degree of accuracy [9],[10]. This type of knowledge representation does not allow the output variables to be described in linguistic terms and the parameter optimization is carried out iteratively using a nonlinear optimization method.

Fuzzy systems exhibit both symbolic and numeric features. Neuro-fuzzy computing [8],[11] is a judicious integration of the merits of neural and fuzzy approaches, enables one to build more intelligent decision-making systems. Neuro-fuzzy hybridization is done broadly in two ways: a neural network equipped with the capability of handling fuzzy information [termed fuzzy-neural network] and a fuzzy system augmented by neural networks to enhance some of its characteristics like flexibility, speed, and adaptability [termed neural-fuzzy system]. ANFIS is an adaptive network that is functionally equivalent to a fuzzy inference system and referred to in literature as "adaptive network based fuzzy inference system" or "adaptive neuro-fuzzy inference system" (Fig.3) [9],[10],[13],[14]. In the ANFIS model, crisp input series are converted to fuzzy inputs by developing triangular, trapezoidal and sigmoid membership functions for each input series. These fuzzy inputs are processed through a network of transfer functions at the nodes of different layers of the network to obtain fuzzy outputs with linear membership functions that are combined to obtain a single crisp output the predicted Mission_Success_Factor, as the ANFIS method permits only one output in the model. The following equations 2,3,4 correspond to triangular, trapezoidal and sigmoid membership functions.

$$\mu_s(X) = \begin{cases} 0 \text{ if } X < a \\ (X-a)/(c-a) \text{ if } X \in [a,c) \\ (b-X)/(b-c) \text{ if } X \in [c,b] \\ 0 \text{ if } X > b \end{cases} \quad (2)$$

$$\mu_s(X) = \begin{cases} 0, & \text{if } X \leq a \\ (X-a)/(m-a), & \text{if } X \in (a,m) \\ 1, & \text{if } X \in [m,n] \\ (b-X)/(b-n), & \text{if } X \in (n,b) \\ 0, & \text{if } X \geq b \end{cases} \quad (3)$$

$$f(x;a,c) = \frac{1}{1+e^{-a(x-c)}} \quad (4)$$

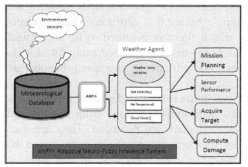   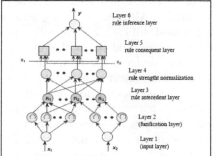

Fig. 3. Weather agent's architecture and behaviors   **Fig. 4.** ANFIS architecture to design the Weather agent

Weather conditions of interest to AWGSS [15],[16],[17],[18] are classified as Precipitation (Drizzle, Rain, Snow, Snow-grains, Ice crystals, Ice pellets and Hail), Obscuration (Mist, Fog, Dust, Sand, Haze, Spray, Volcanic ash, Smoke) and Others (Dust/Sand whirls, Squalls, Funnel cloud, Tornado or Water spout, Sandstorm, Dust-storm). Temperature, Clouds, Height of cloud base, Wind speed and direction, Icing, Precipitation, Visibility, Fog, Mist, Rain, Thunderstorm, Haze, dust/sand whirls and squall speeds are quantified using linguistic fuzzy variables. Target Identification factor: Rapid and certain target detection and identification are the dominant factors in the success of all air-to-ground attacks. The ability of tactical fighters to penetrate enemy defenses and to acquire and identify ground targets successfully within weather constraints is a keystone of success in a mission. It has been observed that aerial observers respond to targets in a manner indicating that detection / identification represents a continuum rather than discrete phenomena. At one extreme the response is based on the ability to merely discriminate the existence of a military object among non-military objects (detection) [19],[20],[21]. At the other extreme the observer can describe the object in precise detail (identification). Factors considered for computing the Target Identification factor are target size, percent contrast, illumination, terrain, weather conditions, altitude and speed of the aircraft at time of target acquisition. **Target Size:** As target size increases, probability of correct target identification increases. It may vary from small to large tactical targets, including personnel, trucks, and tanks to big targets as bridges, runways and taxi-tracks. **Contrast:** Target/Ground Brightness Contrast is expressed as a percentage. **Illumination:** Detection performance increases as illumination increases. Effects of decreases in illumination occurring after sunset and before sunrise are very important and need to be considered. **Terrain:** Types of terrain have been defined in terms such as number of slope changes per unit area and average slope change. Four different terrain types have been defined-fairly smooth, moderately rough, rough, and very rough. As the roughness of terrain increases, percent terrain view decreases, and decrease in detection performance is observed. **Weather:** Temperature, humidity, and wind effects the performance of sensors (such as Radars) deployed, where as conditions such as Precipitation, icing, wind, visibility, fog, rain, date and time of operation, clouds, and storm effect the pilots' decisions in planning and executing the missions. **Altitude:** The relationship between altitude and target detection/identification is normally one in which there is assumed to be an optimal altitude; above and below this optimum altitude, detection is reduced. As altitude increases, detection performance decreases. As altitude is increased beyond an optimal point, detection probability falls off rapidly.

Data on all these factors are collected from meteorological department databases, handbooks and experimental field trials and heuristic knowledge from experts and defense analysts (in questionnaire form) are collected and recorded. They are then represented as decision matrices and decision trees which form the basis to design the membership functions and rules. The rules are then executed in the mission processing module and defuzzified to obtain the damage to target [22]. These results are then compared to the expected output and fine-tuned before storing in the rule base. A decision to include the new rule or not is provided to the commander. Missions and results of the missions are stored as a case-base for retrieval and reuse of missions plans in new situations. The following fuzzy linguistic variables used in the design of the game rules are as follows:

Mission_Success_Factor (with weather constraints): **[1-10]** {Very Low: **[0.0 - 3.5]**; Low with Moderate Risk **[2.5 - 5.5]**; Medium with Controllable Risk **[4.5 - 7.5]**; High with Moderate Risk **[6.5 - 8.0]**; Very High with Low Risk **[7.5-10.0]**} **Temperature:** [Very Low, Low, Moderate, High, Very High] **Fog-Haze:** [Shallow, Patches, Low Drifting, Blowing, Showers, Thunderstorm, Freezing, Partial] **Wind-Speed:** [Light, Moderate, Heavy] **Clouds/Cloud Base**: [Shallow, Patches, Low Drifting, Blowing, Showers, Thunderstorm, Partial]; [Height (ft)] **Visibility:** [Low, Medium, Clear]

Turbulence: [Clear, Low, Medium, Heavy] **Storm/Squalls:** [Clear, Low, Medium, Heavy] **Sky Cover:** [Clear, Few, Scattered, Broken, Overcast, Vertical Visibility]

Terrain: **[1-100]** {Fairly Smooth **[0 -22]**; Moderately Rough **[14 - 49]**; Rough **[45-81]**; Very Rough **[75 - 100]**}. **Target Size (in feet):** {Very small: **[0 -100]**; Small:

[70 – 190]; Medium sized: [160 – 300]; Large: [270 – 400]; Fairly Large: [360 – 500]; Extremely Large: [450 – 900]} **Damage:** Offset (in meters): {Very Less:[0-23]; Less:[16-36]; Medium: [34-57]; Large: [56-80]; Very Large [78-100]} **Weapon Target Match:** [0 -10] {Poor: [0-3.6]; Average: [3.36 – 6.669]; Good: [6.73 – 14.2]}

Target Identification Factor: [0 -10] {Very poorly identified: [0-1.19]; Poorly identified [0.96 – 2.43]; Average identification [2.34 – 5.61]; Good identification [5.43 – 7.55]; Excellent identification [7.35 – 10]} **Relative Damage (Damage relative to intended damage):** [0 - 100] {Mild: [0-18]; Moderate: [16-36]; Average: [34-57]; Severe: [56-80]; Fully Damaged: [78-96]}.

Data from meteorological database is used to train the network to apply a hybrid method whose membership functions and parameters keep changing until the weather forecast error is minimized (Fig.5(a),(b)). Then the resulting model is applied to the test data of the mission time and places en-route from take-off base, target and landing base.

4 Results Discussion

The fuzzy variables are used to calculate the Mission success factor based on the prevailing weather conditions generated by the ANFIS model, target identification factor and firing of the rules to compute the relative damage to the target (Fig. 2). Offset is calculated using actual altitude, actual vertical flight path angle, actual wind speed and observed altitude, observed altitude, observed vertical flight path angle, observed wind speed by the weapon system trajectory calculation module and the aircraft speed as the input variables (Table 3). Offset is a measure of induced error, wind induced error, and vertical flight path angle induced error.

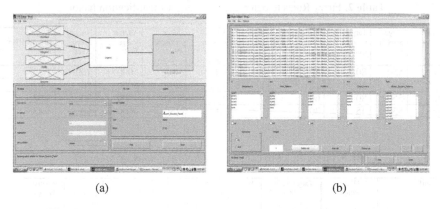

(a)   (b)

Fig. 4. (a),(b): ANFIS and Rules for computing Mission Success Factor

Case Mission ID # 001: Consider a large area-target of size of 550 ft to be attacked, where the fuzzy variables *target-ground contrast* 80%, the *terrain*, rated 8, is fairly smooth, aircraft altitude is 900 ft, aircraft range is 5000 ft is flying at 100 knots speed.

The *target identification factor* for this target is computed as "good" with value 7.32. (*In the tables below* * *denotes the Missions planned and executed when considering the Weather conditions.*)

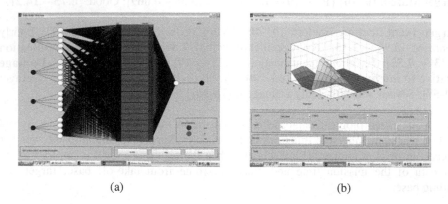

(a)   (b)

Fig. 5. (a),(b) ANFIS Rules and Surface Plot for the different Weather conditions in AWGSS

Table 1. Fuzzy Rules to determine the Mission Success factor in Weather conditions

MissionID	Temperature	Fog-Haze	Wind Speed (m/s)	Clouds/ Base	Visibility	Turbulence	Storm/ Squalls	**Mission Success Factor**
#001	Moderate	Clear	Low-Drifting	Clear	Clear	Low	Clear	8.4
#001*	Very Low	Moderate	High	Low	Poor	High	Clear	3.7
#002	Moderate	Clear	Moderate	Scattered	Clear	Low	Clear	9.8
#002*	Very High	Haze	High	Low	Poor	Low	Squall	7.1

Table 2. Fuzzy Rules to determine the Target Identification factor

MissionID	Target Size(ft)	Target-Ground Contrast%	Illumination (foot candles)	Terrain	Weather_ Mission Success Factor	Aircraft Altitude (feet)	Aircraft Range (feet)	Aircraft Speed (knots)	Target Identification Factor
#001	550	80	40	8	8.4	900	5000	100	7.32
#001*	550	45	20	8	3.7	900	5000	80	5.67
#002	550	80	60	7	9.8	750	4000	80	8.03
#002*	550	45	30	7	7.1	750	4000	60	6.43

Table 3. Fuzzy Rules to compute the *Relative damage to target*

MissionID	Offset (meters)	Target Radius (km)	Weapon-Target Match	Weapon Delivery Mode	Target Identification Factor	Relative damage
# 001	29.03	0.09	6	6	7.32	28.91
#001*	37.54	0.09	6	6	5.67	13.55
# 002	6.07	90.0	9	9	8.03	88.74
#002*	12.65	90.0	9	9	6.43	65.92

Table 4. Fuzzy attributes to determine the *offset* of the weapon from the intended target

Mission ID #	Apparent Altitude(km)	Apparent Angle (degrees)	Apparent Wind velocity (km/hr)	Actual Altitude(km)	Actual Angle(degrees)	Actual Wind velocity (km/hr)	Aircraft speed(km/hr)	Offset (meters)
001	1.65	-26.9	-25.24	1.67	-26.9	-25.24	829.8	29.03
002*	1.65	-26.9	-23.9	1.67	-26.9	-25.24	820.1	37.54
002	1.65	-25.2	-28	1.65	-25.2	-30.4	830.2	6.07
002*	1.65	-25.2	-22	1.65	-25.2	-30.4	824.7	12.65

In this mission, on firing the rules for inference, the offset from the desired point of impact is 29m, considered "less"(i.e. fairly accurate targeting); *weapon-target match* is 6 (average), "good" *target identification factor* 7.32, the relative damage caused is 28.92 which is a "moderate" damage to the target. We consider two scenarios of weather conditions at the given place and time or the mission plan (Fig.2). Weather conditions are identified based on the place and time of missions. The ANFIS model computes the Mission_Success_Factor as 8.4 when no weather conditions are considered, and reduces to 3.7 when weather conditions are considered in the AWGSS (Table1, 2). These conditions also reduce the Relative Damage from 28.91 to 13.55 (Table 3) and *offset* of the weapon hitting away from the intended target increased from 29.03 to 37.54 (Table 4).

Case Mission ID # 002: Another mission planned by the commander where a similar target is chosen with the fuzzy variables as shown in Tables 1 and 2. While the offset has reduced to 6m, considered "very less" (i.e. very accurate targeting), choosing a different weapon system and delivery improved the weapon-target match to 9 ("good"), and mode of weapon delivery 9, the *target identification factor* also improved to 8.033 (considered "excellent"), and the relative damage caused is 88.74, which is a "substantial" damage to the target (Tables 2, 3). Weather conditions are again identified based on the place and time of missions. The ANFIS gives the Mission_Success_factor as 9.8 when no weather conditions are considered, and reduces to 7.1 when weather conditions are considered in the AWGSS (Table1, 2). These conditions also reduce the Relative Damage from 28.91 to 13.55 (Table 3) and *offset* of the weapon hitting away from the intended target increased from 6.07 to 12.05 (Table 4). These attributes form the antecedents of the fuzzy rule and the consequent is shown in the last column of the tables. For all the missions that the pilots plan in the wargame exercises, these fuzzy game rules are used to infer the expected damage caused to the target. These missions form a part of a case-base which is used as part of the *'learning'* by the system for future instructional use.

5 Conclusions

A novel approach using ANFIS is presented in this research paper. More specifically, a neuro-fuzzy hybridization technique is employed to model the operations of the weather agent in a virtual warfare analysis system called AWGSS that is designed using an agent-based architecture. The system is applied to compare the results obtained in the presence of weather in combat simulation exercises. The results that are predicted by the weather agents after a pilot application and the rules that are generated to predict the Mission_Success_Factor are found to be very satisfactory in predicting the mission's performance in the presence of different weather conditions over different regions of the mission route. This concept induces a realistic methodology to introduce weather conditions in the AWGSS by using ANFIS as the reasoning and inference system in the weather agent. A future research effort will include working on ways for optimizing the rules for specific weather conditions like extreme weather phenomena and also on the improvement of the overall system's performance. Of course the whole idea and the framework of the developed system can be applied also in other wider problems like watching and taking real time measures for the cases of natural disasters.

Acknowledgments. We thank Air Marshal "Doc" Vaidya and Air Cmde S P Ojha, College of Air Warfare for the useful insights and discussions on air warfare tactics and game rules development; and the scientists of the air wargaming team for their enthusiasm.

References

1. Vijay Rao, D.: The Design of Air Warfare Simulation System. Technical report, Institute for Systems Studies and Analyses (2011)
2. Vijay Rao, D., Jasleen, K.: A Fuzzy Rule-based approach to design game rules in a mission planning and evaluation system. In: Papadopoulos, H., Andreou, A.S. (eds.) 6th IFIP Conference on Artificial Intelligence Applications and Innovations, Cyprus. Springer, Heidelberg (October 2010)
3. Vijay Rao, D., Saha, B.: An Agent oriented Approach to Developing Intelligent Training Simulators. In: SISO Euro-SIW Conference, Ontario, Canada (June 2010)
4. Banks, J. (ed.): Handbook of Simulation: Principles, Methodology, Advances, Applications, and Practice. John Wiley and Sons, New York (1998)
5. Maqsood, I., Khan, M.R., Abraham, A.: An ensemble of neural networks for weather forecasting. Nerual Computing & Applications 13, 112–122 (2004)
6. Cox, E.: The Fuzzy Systems Handbook, 2nd edn. Academic Press, New York (1999)
7. Castellanos, F., James N.: Average Hourly Wind speed forecasting with ANFIS. In: 11th American Conference on Wind Engineering, San Juan, Puerto Rico (June 2009)
8. Taher, J., Zomaya, A.Y.: Artificial Neural Networks in Handbook of Nature-Inspired and Innovative Computing. In: Zomaya, A.Y. (ed.) Integrating Classical Models with Emerging Technologies, pp. 147–186. Springer, USA (2006)
9. Jang, J.S.R.: ANFIS: Adaptive Network-based fuzzy inference systems. IEEE Trans. on Systems, Man and Cybernetics 23(3), 665–685 (1993)
10. Jang, J.S.R., Sun, C.T., Mizutani, E.: Neuro-Fuzzy and Soft Computing: A Computational approach to Learning and Machine Intelligence. Prentice Hall, New Jersey (1997)
11. Pedrycz, W.: Computational Intelligence-An Introduction. CRC Press, USA (1998)
12. Hiramatsu, A., Van-Nam, H., Yoshiteru, N.: A Behavioral decision model based on Fuzzy Targets in decision making using weather information. Journal of Advanced Computational Intelligence and Intelligent Informatics 12(5), 435–442 (2008)
13. Mitra, S., Hayashi, Y.: Neuro-Fuzzy Rule Generation: Survey in Soft Computing Framework. IEEE Trans. Neural Networks 11(3), 748–768 (2000)

14. Mendel, J.M.: Uncertain Rule-Based Fuzzy Logic Systems-Introduction and New Directions. Prentice Hall PTR, Upper Saddle River (2001)
15. Federal Aviation Administration, The Weather Forecast, R & D Review (1), USA (2006)
16. Pierce, C., Hirsch, T., Bennett, A.C.: Formulation and evaluation of a post-processing algorithm for generating seamless, high resolution ensemble precipitation forecasts, Forecasting R & D Tech. Report No. 550, Exeter, UK (November 2010)
17. Bovis, K., Dow, G., Dumelov, R., Keil, M.: An assessment of deployment strategies for targeting observations, Tech. Rep. No. 515, Meteorological research and Development, UK (2008)
18. Das, A.K., Saxena, R., Roy Bhowmik, S.K.: NWP Inputs of IMD for use in Operational Fog Forecasting, IMD Forecaster-Users interactive workshop Fog monitoring and Forecasting services, India Meteorological Services, New Delhi (December 2010)
19. Iliadis, L.: Intelligent Information Systems and Risk estimation. A Stamoulis publ. (2007)
20. Meitzler, T.J., Singh, H., Sohn, E.: Fuzzy Logic Technique to Determine Search Time and Probability of Detection for Targets of Interest in Background Scenes, TACOM Research Development and Engineering Center, Warren, MI (2002)
21. Celmiņs, A.: Vulnerability assessment of fuzzy targets. Fuzzy Sets and Systems 68(1), 29–38 (1994)
22. MATLAB Fuzzy Logic Toolbox

Employing Smart Logic to Spot Audio in Real Time on Deeply Embedded Systems

Mario Malcangi

DSP&RTS Laboratory
DICo - Università degli Studi di Milano, Via Comelico 39,
20135 Milano, Italy
malcangi@dico.unimi.it

Abstract. Audio mining is currently the subject of several research efforts, especially because of its potential to speed up search for spoken words in audio recordings. This study explores a method for approaching the problem from the bottom. It proposes a framework based on smart logic, mainly fuzzy logic, and on an audio model applicable to any kind of audio recording, including music.

Keywords: Audio mining, audio spotting, fuzzy logic, phone unit, spoken term detection, phonetic search, keyword-spotting.

1 Premises

Audio is the most powerful information medium available because of peculiarities that fit well with the requirements of the emerging technology found in embedded systems. Such technology will be very pervasive in the next generation of computing and communication devices. Because of those devices' deep level of embedding, audio will be the preferred interaction medium. There are several reasons for this.

Audio can embed much more information than any other analog medium. Not only does it represent semantic information; the same audio frame contains behavioral, environmental, psychological, and expressive information. Another important peculiarity of audio as information medium is that only audio one can be accessed in eyes-free or hands-free mode. This means that very simple human-to-machine interfaces (HMIs) could be employed in the next generation of embedded devices.

Audio is a one-dimensional signal, storage and processing are simpler and less resource-hungry than for other signal-information media, such as video. This feature is very important in developing embedded devices, because storage and processing power are always limited resources.

Researchers are very interested in using audio as interaction medium for text retrieval in spoken documents (conference speeches, broadcast news, etc.) to provide smart access to spoken audio and audio corpora, including music. Such research is targeted at several application areas, mainly spoken document retrieval, media monitoring, and personal entertainment.

L. Iliadis and C. Jayne (Eds.): EANN/AIAI 2011, Part I, IFIP AICT 363, pp. 122–129, 2011.

2 Introduction

Using audio to access audio information is a relatively new research issue, mainly focusing on the problem of retrieving spoken documents in large audio archives. Advances in automatic speech recognition (ASR) technology have allowed for developing search engines based on the uttered word, an audio version of the text-based, word-spotting engines targeted at text documents.

ASR-based word spotting is effective but consumes vast computing resources, primarily due to the huge recognition vocabulary required. This prevents such solutions from being applicable to limited-resource systems like embedded devices. Limiting the recognizer vocabulary leads to some words not being found, which curtails practical usefulness.

A new approach to the problem of word spotting in uttered documents is based on phonetic search [1] , [2]. The goal is to spot elementary sounds like phones rather than whole words. This approach obviously minimizes problems related to vocabulary size, at the expense of very intensive computing efforts needed to implement the phonetic segmentation of utterances efficiently and reliably. Less challenging is the task of pattern matching applied to phonetic units. The main problem that arises is related to the very short duration of phonetic units compared to the duration of a word. The word-matching approach used in ASR applications (based on dynamic time warping, DTW, and hidden Markov models, HMM) is not enough robust if not supported by a smart decision logic.

A phonetic matcher based on artificial neural networks (ANNs) proves to be more reliable than word matchers based only on DTW and HMM . The disadvantage of the ANN-based solution is its need to be trained for the set of words to be spotted. This is not a disadvantage for a phonetic recognizer because training is required only once and only for a very limited set of patterns.

This research investigates the capacity of a fuzzy-logic engine to work as a phone-pattern matcher and how such capabilities can be extended to the task audio-pattern matching for application to the more general problem of the audio-spotting [3] , [4]. Audio segmentation based on fuzzy-logic processing has been successfully used to separate uttered words (end-point detection) [5], as well as to separate phone units [6] within each uttered word. The peculiarity of fuzzy-logic processing is mainly related to nature of its computing model, which is essentially data-driven [7] ,[8] . The same inference engine can be applied to a different problem when the appropriate set of rules and membership functions is available.

The aim of the research was to model a fuzzy-logic-based, audio-segmentation engine and accompanying fuzzy decision logic that would support decisions at spotting time when a search and retrieval application is to be executed on an audio stream (speech, music [9], sounds, etc.). To do this, hard-computing (digital signal processing algorithms) and soft-computing (fuzzy logic) methods were combined to yield a solution that matches the limited resources (computing power and memory footprint) available on deeply embedded systems.

3 Framework of Audio-Spotting System

The whole audio-spotting system consists of an indexing engine that finds occurrences of the elementary audio units (phonemes, stationary sounds, musical tones, etc.) in a given audio pattern (uttered word, audio event, musical theme, etc.) to be spotted in an audio stream. The system consists of two main subsystems: the audio-unit-segmentation subsystem and the audio-spotting subsystem (Fig. 1).

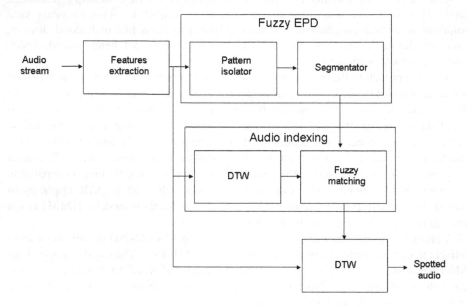

Fig. 1. Architecture of audio-spotting system

The audio-unit-segmentation subsystem consists of a feature-extraction preprocessor and a fuzzy-logic engine trained to identify the end points of audio units in the incoming audio stream. The segmentation subsystem implements a set of digital signal-processing algorithms to measure certain key, audio-signal features (energy, dominant frequency, pitch, etc.) that help identify the separation point of the audio-units. The fuzzy-logic engine processes the (fuzzified) audio features and infers about the end-points of each audio unit embedded in the audio stream.

The audio-spotting subsystem consists of a DTW-based, pattern-matching processor and a fuzzy-logic engine tuned to infer about the spotting. The pattern-matching processor executes continuous alignment between the target audio to be spotted and a portion of the audio stream. The alignment data and the extracted audio features are fed to the fuzzy-logic engine, which evaluates whether the audio stream can be indexed as spottable.

Each time a spottable portion of audio stream is identified, full audio-spotting is then executed on the target audio pattern. This process can be run at the same time as the index processing (real-time execution) or later, after the whole stream has been indexed (off-line execution).

4   Audio Feature Measurements

A set of audio features [10] is measured from the audio pattern to be spotted in the audio stream. The audio features to be measured are those required by the segmentation and pattern-matching smart logic that implements the audio-spotting system.

Short-time computation is applied to the audio signal based on an N-points time window as follows:

$$w(m) = 0.54 - 0.46\cos(2\pi m/(N-1)), \text{ for } 0 \leq m \leq N-1$$
$$w(m) = 0, \text{ otherwise} \tag{1}$$

For each window, the following feature measurements are executed: short-time energy $E(n)$, short-time zero-crossing rate $ZCR(n)$, and short-time dominant frequency $P_n(k)$.

$$E(n) = \sum_{m=0}^{N-1} [s(m)w(n-m)]^2 \tag{2}$$

$$ZCR(n) = \sum_{m=0}^{N-1} 0.5 \square sign(s(m)) - sign(s(m-1)\square w(n-m)$$
$$\tag{3}$$
$$sign(s(n)) = 1, \text{ for } x(n) \geq 0$$
$$sign(s(n)) = \text{ otherwise}.$$

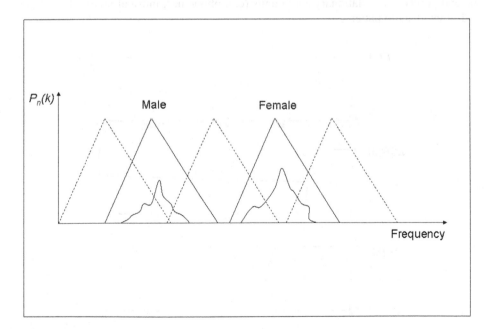

Fig. 2. Dominant frequency distribution in uttered speech maps speaker gender

$$P_n(k) = \sum_{m=0}^{N-1} s(m)w(n-m)s(m-k)w(n-m+k) \qquad (4)$$

Such audio features are very useful for classifying stationary audio units into classes. For example, $P_n(k)$, when the audio is an utterance, features the gender of the speaker (male (low), female (high)), as shown in the $P_n(k)$ diagram (Fig. 2).

5 Audio Segmentation and Indexing Based on Fuzzy Logic

Three separate tasks were implemented using fuzzy logic:

- Audio end-point detection
- Audio segmentation
- Audio indexing

The same engine was trained for each of the above tasks, generating the needed set of rules and membership functions. The engines for audio end-point detection and audio segmentation have the same set of membership functions to fuzzify their inputs (audio features) and use different sets of rules to make inferences about the audio pattern. Both evaluate the end point of the audio pattern. The former evaluates the audio boundaries of the whole pattern to be spotted, while the second evaluates the end points of the stationary audio units (e.g. phonemes, musical notes, etc.) of the end-pointed audio pattern.

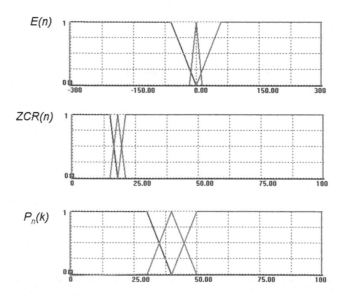

Fig. 3. Membership functions for fuzzifying audio energy, zero-crossing rate, and short-time dominant frequency

The audio-indexing engine matches each stationary audio unit so as to index it in the processed audio stream. To accomplish this, the measured audio features and the score of the DTW audio-spotter are fuzzified and processed using an appropriately tuned set rules.

The membership functions for fuzzifying the audio features used as inputs for the fuzzy engine are derived directly from the distribution of the crisp measurements of such features.

The rules evaluate the fuzzy inputs as follows :

....

IF ZCR(n) IS Low
     AND E(n) IS Average
     AND P(n) IS High
     THEN Segment IS Vowel

....

IF ZCR(n) IS High
     AND E(n) IS Average
     AND P(n) IS Low
     THEN Segment IS Consonant

....

The defuzzifying membership functions are all of the singleton type.

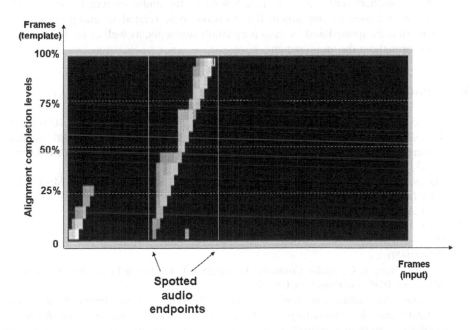

Fig. 4. Pattern matching executed by sliding along the whole audio stream to find best alignment of the template (audio pattern to be spotted) into the audio stream (input)

6 DTW-Based Audio Spotter

Audio spotting is executed by a DTW-based audio-pattern-matching engine, which continuously executes alignment between an audio-pattern template and the occurrence of such patterns in the audio stream. The alignment process consists of searching the audio stream for the starting point of a pattern that is the same as the template. Because the position of pattern to be spotted is unknown, pattern matching needs to be executed by sliding along the whole audio stream (Fig. 4). Using the indexing information, the pattern matcher focuses its action only on the indexed part of the audio stream, thus significantly reducing the time needed to complete the spotting process.

The DTW-based audio spotter uses dynamic-time warping to align the template pattern with the target pattern. It uses the method for similarity evaluation suggested in the work of Christiansen and Rushforth [11].

7 Conclusion

The proposed framework for smart audio spotting enables faster optimization of the method that exhaustively searches audio information for an audio pattern. It optimizes exhaustive search by indexing the audio stream in terms of the occurrence of a set of stationary audio patterns that belong to the audio pattern to be spotted. Fuzzy logic was used to implement the decision logic related to end-pointing the audio pattern to be spotted and its stationary audio segments, as well as to index audio segments throughout the audio stream.

References

1. Wallace, R.G., Vogt, R.J., Sridharan, S.: A Phonetic Search Approach to the 2006 NIST Spoken Term Detection Evaluation. In: Proceedings Interspeech 2007 - 8th Annual Conference of the International Speech Communication Association, Antwerp, Belgium, pp. 2385–2388 (2007)
2. Manos, A.S., Zue, V.W.: A segment-based Wordspotter Using Phonetic Filler Models. In: IEEE International Conference on Acoustics, Speech, and Signal Processing, ICASSP 1997, April 21-24, vol. 2, pp. 899–902 (1997)
3. Ying, Y., Woo, P.: Speech Recognition Using Fuzzy Logic. In: Proceedings of IJCNN 1999 – International Joint Conference on Neural Networks, July 10-16, vol. 5, pp. 2962–2964 (1999)
4. Hale, C., Nguyen, C.: Audio Command Recognition Using Fuzzy Logic. In: Proceedings of Wescon 1995, San Francisco, CA (November 7, 1995)
5. Malcangi, M.: Improving Speech Endpoint Detection Using Fuzzy Logic-based Methodologies. In: Proceedings of the Thirteenth Turkish Symposium on Artificial Intelligence and Neural Networks, Izmir, Turkey (June 10-11, 2004)
6. Malcangi, M.: Softcomputing Approach to Segmentation of Speech in Phonetic Units. International Journal of Computer and Communications 3(3), 41–48 (2009)

7. Malcangi, M.: Soft-computing Approach to Fit a Speech Recognition System on a Single-chip. In: Proceedings of 2002 International Workshop System-on-Chip for Real-Time Applications, Banff, Canada (July 6-7, 2002)
8. Ciota, Z.: Improvement of Speech Processing Using Fuzzy Logic Approach. In: Proceedings of IFSA World Congress and 20th NAFIPS International Conference (2001)
9. Cano, P., Kaltenbrunner, M., Mayor, O., Batlle, E.: Statistical Significance in Song-Spotting in Audio. In: Proceedings of the International Symposium on Music Information Retrieval (October 2001)
10. O'Shaughnessy, D.: Speech Communication – Human and Machine. Addison-Wesley, Reading (1987)
11. Christiansen, R.W., Rushforth, C.K.: Detecting and Locating Key Words in Continuous Speech Using Linear Predictive Coding. IEEE Transactions ASSP-25 (1977)

Quantization of Adulteration Ratio of Raw Cow Milk by Least Squares Support Vector Machines (LS-SVM) and Visible/Near Infrared Spectroscopy

Ching-Lu Hsieh[1,*], Chao-Yung Hung[2], and Ching-Yun Kuo[3]

[1] Department of Biomechatronics Engineering, National Pingtung University of Science and
Technology, Taiwan, R.O.C.
Tel.: 886-8-7703202#7583
chinglu@mail.npust.edu.tw
[2]Department of Biomechatronics Engineering,
National Pingtung University of Science and Technology, Taiwan, R.O.C.
[3] Animal Research Institute, Council of Agriculture, Executive Yuan, Taiwan, R.O.C.

Abstract. Raw cow milk has short supply market in summer and over supply in winter, which causes consumers and dairy industry concern about the quality of raw milk whether is adulated with reconstituted milk (powdered milk). This study prepared 307 raw cow milk samples with various adulteration ratios 0%, 2%, 5%, 10%, 20%, 30%, 50%, 75%, and 100% of powdered milk. Least square support vector machine (LS-SVM) was applied to calibrate the prediction model for adulteration ratio. Grid search approach was used to find the better value of network parameters of γ and σ^2. Results show that R^2 ranges from 0.9662 to 0.9777 for testing data set with plate surface and four concave regions. Scatter plot of testing data showed that adulteration ratio above 10% clearly differs from 0% samples.

Keywords: LS-SVM, Raw milk, Cow milk, Adulteration detection, NIR.

1 Introduction

For thousand years, milk has been an important nutrient source for people. There are more than 50,000 milking cows in Taiwan which produce over 300,000 tons of raw milk annually with a value of about US$ 230 million [1]. In terms of our planet, about 578 million tons of fresh and whole cow's milks are produced with a value of more than 148 billion US dollars per year [2]. Thus, dairy is an important and influential industry.

Weather in Taiwan is hot and humidity during summer, but winter is cooler. This causes dairy industry faces a problem of milk shortages in summer and oversupply in winter. Hu [3] reported that consumption index of cow's milk in summer (Jun. to Oct.) was 101.3-137.4, whereas in winter (Dec. to Mar.), it was 68.1-87.4. This situation makes consumers' worry that whether the raw milk or fresh milk is adulterated with reconstituted (powdered) milk [4]. Milk factories are also concerned

---

* Corresponding author.

L. Iliadis and C. Jayne (Eds.): EANN/AIAI 2011, Part I, IFIP AICT 363, pp. 130–139, 2011.

that farmers may dilute the raw milk with powdered milk. Therefore, milk factories and consumer agencies need to confirm the quality of raw milk.

Milk may be adulterated either intentionally or accidentally during production and processing. Harding [5] stated that there are many potential adulterants in liquid milk, such as water, neutralizers, salt, sugar, or solid contents. Borin et al. [6] reported adulteration of powdered milk in Brazil and mentioned that the most frequent contaminants were whey, starch, and sucrose that range from 20 to 25%, which does not cause detectable flavor changes. But occasionally contaminant ratio may be as high as 60%. In Taiwan, the media reported that an adulteration ratio of 30% reconstituted milk in fresh milk has been found. Therefore, many researches have been conducted to detect milk contaminants.

For example, Lin et al., [7] used a modified MAD (Metachromatic Agar-Diffusion) technique to detect DNase activity in synthetic raw milk so as to detect reconstituted milk in raw milk. Ding and Chang [4] reported that milk powder is one of the most common forms of adulteration in fresh milk sold in the summer in Taiwan. They used an amino acid analyzer to detect furosine so as to identify the adulteration of milk powder in raw and UHT (ultra-high temperature) treated milk. These studied methods are time consuming and require higher skills.

Water, proteins, lactose and other components (such as somatic or body cell, micro-organisms, antibiotics etc.) are the main composition of milk [8]. Usually, normal milk has an opalescent white to yellowish color because of light dispersion. Conventional testing of compositional quality for milk is a lengthy, labor-intensive, and expensive process, making such methods unsuitable for routine use in quality control [9]. Thus, an infrared (IR) absorption technique that provides faster and easier working conditions, has been adopted in milk analysis.

Association of Official Agricultural Chemists [10] stated that analysis of milk by IR is based on absorption of IR energy at specific wavelengths. For instance, CH groups in fatty acid chains of fat molecules absorb at 3.48 μm. The IR spectra usually show the fundamental vibration of molecules where the near infrared (NIR, 750-2500 nm) or visible wavelength (Vis, 400-750 nm) indicate the overtone or combination of molecule vibration and electron transition of constituents [11]. Thus, visible/NIR spectroscopy has been intensively used to evaluate the quality of milk or the adulteration of milk or dairy products. For example, Schmilovitch et al. [12] used NIR to analyze fat and total soluble solids (TSS) content of fresh milk. Chen et al. [13] applied MLR and multiplicative scatter correction method to determine the fat content in raw milk. Kawasaki et al. [14] developed a sensor system for milking robots. The system was equipped with NIR in order to measure fat, protein and lactose, somatic cell count, and milk urea nitrogen of unhomogenized milk.

Visible/NIR spectrum contain high dimensional data usually needs chemometrics to downsize its data dimensions. Spectral calibration tries to find the relationship between spectral absorption of specific wavelength and target composition, which can be applied in further prediction for unknown samples. Neural network has been proven its ability in function fitting that correlates the dependent variable y and independent variables x with y=f(x). Least squares-support vector machine (LS-SVM) that was originally proposed by Suykens and Vandewalle [15] are becoming a popular tool for data classification and function estimation. LS-SVM is modified from support vector machine (SVM) that is a supervised learning methods used for classification and regression analysis. The LS-SVM is based on the margin-maximization theory performing structural risk minimization. However, it is easier to train than the SVM, as it requires only the solution to a convex linear problem, and not a quadratic problem as in the SVM [15]. Yu et al. [16] compared partial least squares regression (PLSR) with LS-SVM in alcohol content, titratable acidity, and pH prediction and found LS-SVM was slightly better. Siuly and Wen [17] used LS-SVM to cluster EEG signal. Zuao et al. [18] employed on-line LS-SVM for gas prediction. Borin et al. [6] used LS-SVM and NIR spectroscopy for quantification of adulterants (starch, whey, or sucrose) in powdered milk.

In summary, the aims of this study are as follows:

1. take Vis/NIR spectroscopy for raw cow milk samples that were adulterated in various percentages of powdered milk
2. apply LS-SVM approach to quantify the ratio of adulteration
3. use grid search method to test the parameters of LS-SVM so as to find a better model for detecting the percentage of powdered milk in row milk.

Therefore, this study is the first that applies LS-SVM to quantify the adulteration ratio of powdered milk in raw cow milk.

2 Materials and Methods

2.1 Sample Preparation

Raw cow milk samples were collected from a dairy farm near our campus, and they were delivered to our laboratory within 2 hr. in ice box. Sampling process was conducted from Jul. 2010 to Nov. 2010. Powdered milk was made by diluting powdered cow milk with water on the basis of protein composition of raw milk. Protein ratio was chosen as criteria because it is easy changed after processed. After the powdered milk was prepared, it was mixed with raw milk in volume ratio of 0:100 (0%), 2:98 (2%), 5:95 (5%), 10:90(10%), 20:80 (20%), 30:70 (30%), 50:50 (50%), 75:25 (75%) and 100:0 (100%).Number of samples in each ratio and batch were listed in Table 1.

Table 1. Number of prepared samples at each test batch

Batch	0%	2%	5%	10%	20%	30%	50%	75%	100%	Total
1	3	3	3	3	3	3	3	3	3	27
2	9	9	9	9	9	9	9	9	9	81
3	9	9	9	9	9	9	9	9	9	81
4	13	11	11	12	15	11	15	15	15	118
Total	34	32	32	33	36	32	36	36	36	307

Each sample was scanned to record its visible/NIR spectrum and was analyzed to obtain its compositions. Monochrometer (FOSS NIRS 6500, NIRSYSTEM, US) was used to obtain sample spectrum in a range of 400 nm to 2498 nm at 2-nm intervals. A quartz cuvette of light path 0.5 mm was used to record transmittance spectrum of sample at 25 ℃. Milk composition analyzer (Expert, Scopo Electric, Europe) was employed to observe fat, protein, SNF (solid-not-fat), lactose, and density. From 307 samples, 207 samples were randomly selected as training data set while the remaining samples (100) were used as testing data set.

To correct the baseline shift and smoothing noise on spectral data, each spectrum was proceed with baseline treatment, Savitzky–Golay smoothing with 4th order 11 data points, and standard normal variate scaling. These data processes were supported by a PLS-Toolbox (Eigenvector co.) compatible to MATLAB.

2.2 LS-SVM

To deal with linear or nonlinear multivariate calibration, the LS-SVM uses a estimation function to map input vectors (training vectors) x_i into a higher dimensional space by the function ϕ. $K(x_i,x_j)= \phi(x_i)^T\phi(x_j)$ is called the kernel function that generally have four basic forms: 1) linear: $K(x_i,x_j)= x_i^Tx_j$; 2) polynomial: $K(x_i,x_j)= (px_i^Tx_j+r)d$, p>0; 3) radial basis function (RBF): $K(x_i,x_j)=\exp(-q\| x_i-x_j\|^2)$,q>0; 4) sigmoid $K(x_i,x_j)= \tanh(mx_i^Tx_j+r)$, where d, m, p, q, and r are kernel parameters. Therefore, a LS-SVM function estimation is to minimize a cost function (C) that has a regression error, as follows [15]:

$$C =\frac{1}{2}w^T w+\frac{1}{2}\gamma\sum_{i=1}^{N}e_i^2$$

(1)

such that

$$y_i = w^T \phi(x_i)+b+e_i$$

(2)

Analyzing Eq. (1) and Eq. (2), we may have a typical problem of convex optimization which can be solved by using the Lagrange multipliers method [16] as follows:

$$L =\frac{1}{2}\|w\|^2 +\gamma\sum_{i=1}^{N}e_i^2 -\sum_{i=1}^{N}\alpha_i\{w^T \phi(x_i)+b+e_i - y_i\}$$

(3)

where $y_i=[y_1, ..., y_N]^T$, $e_i=[e_1, ..., e_N]^T$, and $i=[\alpha_1,..., \alpha_N]^T$; By conducting $\partial L(w, b, e,\alpha)/\partial w$, $\partial L(w, b, e,\alpha)/\partial b$, $\partial L(w, b, e,\alpha)/\partial e$, and $\partial L(w, b, e,\alpha)/\partial \alpha$, and setting the first derivative to zero, we obtain the optimal solution for training data as equations:

$$\frac{\partial L}{\partial w}= w-\sum_{i=1}^{N}\alpha_i\phi(x_i)=0 \qquad w=\sum_{i=1}^{N}\alpha_i\phi(x_i)$$

thus,

(4)

$$\frac{\partial L}{\partial e}=\sum_{i=1}^{N}\gamma e-\alpha=0 \qquad \alpha=\gamma e$$

thus,

(5)

Combining eq.(4) and eq.(5), we have

$$w=\sum_{i=1}^{N}\alpha_i\phi(x_i)=\sum_{i=1}^{N}\gamma e_i\phi(x_i)$$

(6)

γ (Gamma) is the regularization constant that balances the model's complexity and the training errors. For nonlinear regression, the kernel function meets Mercer's mapping, then it has formulation [15]:

$$y_i = \sum_{i=1}^{N} \alpha_i K(x_i, x) + b + e_i$$

(7)

For a point y_j to be evaluated it is:

$$y_j = \sum_{i=1}^{N} \alpha_i K(x_i, x_j) + b$$

(8)

Testing of the kernel function is cumbersome and it depends on each case. For simple and low dimensional problems, kernel function of linear can be adopted, while in high dimensional and nonlinear problems, RBF of Gaussian, $\exp(-\|x_i\text{-}x_j\|^2/(2\sigma^2))$, is commonly used. The σ^2 (sigma2) is the width of the Gaussian function. By careful selection on these parameters, a good generalization model could be achieved.

2.3 Performance Evaluation

There are three problems need to be solved when LS-SVM is used, which are kernel function, input feature subset, and kernel parameters. However, no systematic methodology is available for selection the kernel function. In here, a RBF kernel of Gaussian function was used because it was a nonlinear function and could reduce the computational complexity of the training procedure [19]. In order to find proper parameter, a grid search technique and leave one out 10 folds cross-validation were used. Grid search is a two-dimensional minimization procedure based on exhaustive search in a limited range. Leaves one out cross-validation fits a model on the training data points except one and the performance of the model is estimated based on the one point left out. This procedure is repeated for each data point. After the model was set, the testing data were evaluated to the model again. Parameter γ controls the trade-off between structural risk minimization principle and empirical risk minimization. Parameter σ^2 affects the value of function regression error. Small values of σ^2 yield a large number of regressors and eventually it can lead to over fitting. On the contrary, a large value of σ^2 can lead to a less number of regressors, but finally not so accurate. These LS-SVM calculations were conducted using MATLAB 7.0 (The Math Works, USA) and a free LS-SVM toolbox (LS-SVM v 1.5, Suykens, Leuven, Belgium) [20].

3 Results and Discussion

3.1 Composition of Samples

Some important statistics of sample compositions are shown in Table 2. These results indicate that adulteration do modify the composition of samples. Duncan test for these samples also suggests possible groups with 5% significant level. For instance, groups for fat are 3 and 0% to 20% and 50% and 100% are the group a. All samples of adulteration ratio of 0%, 2%, 5%, 10%, and 20% have no significant difference in each composition. This result may suggest too less adulteration will not have statistical difference in composition.

Table 2. Statistics for sample compositions

Adulteration ratio	Fat (%)	SNF (%)	Density (kg/m³)	Protein (%)	Lactose (%)	Water (%)
0%	3.95 #^{ab}	8.45 ᵃ	1.0284 ᵃ	3.17 ᵃ	4.63 ᵃᵇ	87.60 ᶜ
2%	3.90 ᵃᵇᶜ	8.47 ᵃ	1.0285 ᵃ	3.18 ᵃ	4.65 ᵃ	87.63 ᶜ
5%	3.85 ᵃᵇᶜ	8.46 ᵃᵇ	1.0284 ᵃ	3.17 ᵃ	4.64 ᵃᵇ	87.69 ᵇᶜ
10%	3.82 ᵃᵇᶜ	8.42 ᵃᵇᶜ	1.0284 ᵃ	3.16 ᵃᵇ	4.62 ᵃᵇ	87.76 ᵇᶜ
20%	3.85 ᵃᵇᶜ	8.38 ᵃᵇᶜ	1.0282 ᵃ	3.14 ᵃᵇᶜ	4.59 ᵃᵇᶜ	87.77 ᵇᶜ
30%	3.81 ᵇᶜ	8.32 ᵃᵇᶜ	1.0280 ᵃᵇ	3.13 ᵃᵇᶜ	4.57 ᵃᵇᶜ	87.88 ᵃᵇ
50%	3.90 ᵃᵇᶜ	8.27 ᵇᶜ	1.0278 ᵃᵇ	3.11 ᵇᶜ	4.54 ᵇᶜ	87.84 ᵃᵇᶜ
75%	3.77 ᶜ	8.23 ᶜ	1.0277 ᵇ	3.10 ᶜ	4.51 ᶜ	88.00 ᵃ
100%	3.96 ᵃ	8.38 ᵃᵇᶜ	1.0277 ᵇ	3.13 ᵃᵇᶜ	4.56 ᵃᵇᶜ	87.66 ᵇᶜ
Mean±S.D.	3.89±0.25	8.37±0.37	1.0281±0.0014	3.14±0.11	4.59±0.20	87.75±0.42
Maximum	4.17	9.11	1.0301	3.36	5.54	88.81
Minimum	3.08	7.88	1.0226	2.99	4.33	87.04
Duncan Groups	3	3	2	3	3	3

\# Same letter means same group under Duncan's grouping test.

Boxplot of SNF composition is shown Fig.1. Other similar plots can be obtain to corresponding to other compositions: fat, density, protein, lactose, and water. They are omitted due to space limitation. Figure shows that mean value decreases as adulteration increases, but the 100% adulterated group has higher mean than that of 75% group. This indicates that powered milk contained similar composition of raw milk. But samples of various adulterations will change the composition.

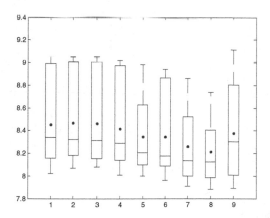

Fig. 1. Boxplot for SNF composition (%) of test samples (xabel 1 to 9 represent adulteration ratio 0% to 100%)

Mean spectra of partial region are shown in Fig. 2 to demonstrate the difference of each adulterated sample. Line on the figure is the average of samples for the adulteration ratio. They have trends of higher ratio samples have lower absorbance, except 2% samples that have the highest value. Reason for that needs more study.

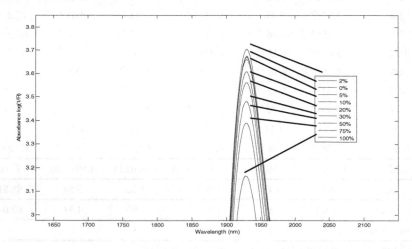

Fig. 2. Average spectra of adulterated samples (No. of samples = 307)

3.2 Grid Search for Training Data and Testing Data

Parameter of γ(gamma) and σ^2(sigma2) of LS-SVM were tested from 1E-15 to 1E+15 in 1E3 step. Coefficient of determination R^2 for training set at each test are shown in mesh plot (Fig.3), which shows a zigzag surface ranging from 0.9588 to 0.9873. From Fig. 3 we found that two regions of near γ(1E-5), σ^2 (1E0) and γ(1E0), σ^2 (1E0) have higher R^2.

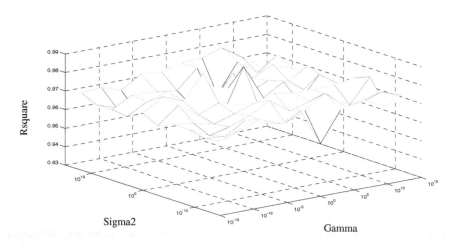

Fig. 3. Mesh plot of R^2 (Rsquare) for training data at combination of γ (Gamma) and σ^2 (Sigma2) for LS-SVM

Contour plot for testing set are shown in Fig.4. Basically it shows a plate surface that R^2 ranges from 0.9662 to 0.9777 with four regions of concave. These four concaves are easily identified in contour plot, which they are near γ(1E-10), σ^2(1E5); γ(1E-5), σ^2(1E0); γ(1E0), σ^2(1E-5); and γ (1E0), σ^2(1E0).

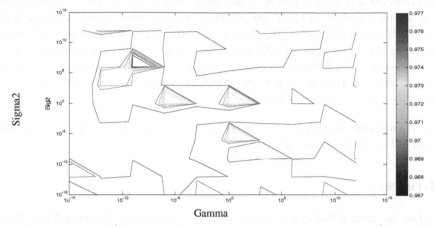

Fig. 4. Contour plot of R^2 for testing data at combination of γ (Gamma) and σ^2 (Sigma2) for LS-SVM

To evaluate the accuracy of prediction, parameters of LS_SVM were set to γ (1E-5), σ^2 (1E-5) that is not a concave region. The R^2 for testing set is 0.9775 and its scatter plot for 100 samples is in Fig. 5. From the plot, we learned that 100% have the most identical prediction, and 0%, 2%, 5%, and 10% are predicted widely. When the adulteration is higher than 10%, most samples have prediction value differs from 0%, which suggested that the sensibility for the model is about 10%. For benefit, 20% to 30% adulteration ratio is more attractive in market. Therefore, 10% sensibility has its application potential in market.

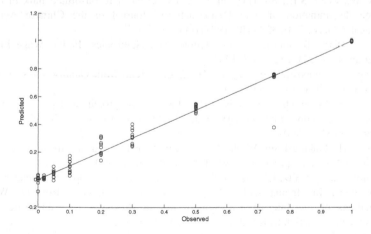

Fig. 5. Scatter plot of testing set for observed value and predicted valued. (Noted value has been normalized. No. of samples = 100).

4 Conclusion

This study applied LS-SVM and visible near infrared spectroscopy to quantize adulteration ratio of powdered milk in raw cow milk. Network parameter of γ and σ^2 were examined with grid search approach both from 1E-15 to 1E+15. Results show that R^2 for training data set has a zigzag surface with two obvious peaks of near γ(1E-5), σ^2(1E0) and γ(1E0), σ^2(1E0). Results also showed that based on 100 testing samples, most regions have high R^2 except four concaves regions. Parameters γ and σ^2 were chosen to 1E-5 that is not concave region and had R^2 0.9775. Its scatter plot indicated that most samples can be correctly separated from 0% when it is adulteration ratio is equal or higher than 10%.

Acknowledgments. Authors appreciate Council of Agriculture, the Executive Yuan, Taiwan, R.O.C. for financial support.

References

1. COA, Agricultural Statistics Yearbook. Council of Agriculture, Executive Yuan, Taipei, Taiwan, p. 126 (2009) (in Chinese)
2. FAOSTAT (2008), http://faostat.fao.org/default.aspx
3. Hu, Y.W.: Analysis of consumer's behavior for cow milk and goat milk in Taiwan. Grains and Livestock 241, 18–27 (1993) (in Chinese)
4. Ding, H.C., Chang, T.C.: Detection of reconstituted milk in fresh milk. Journal of the Chinese Agricultural Chemical Society 23(4), 406–411 (1986) (in Chinese)
5. Harding, F.: Adulteration of milk. In: Harding, F. (ed.) Milk Quality, ch. 5, pp. 60–74. Chapman & Hall, Wiltshire (1995a)
6. Borin, A., Ferrao, M., Mello, C., Maretto, D., Poppi, R.: Least-squares support vector machines and near infrared spectroscopy for quantification of common adulterants in powdered milk. Analytica Chimica Acta 579, 25–32 (2006)
7. Lin, C.W., Chen, S.H., Su, H.P., Ju, C.C.: Detection of reconstituted milk in raw milk through determination of milk Dnase activity. Journal of the Chinese Agricultural Chemical Society 25(3), 332–340 (1987) (in Chinese)
8. Berg, J.: Diary Technology in the Tropics and Subtropics, Pudoc Wageningen, the Netherlands, pp. 223–242, 1–45 (1988)
9. Harding, F.: Composition quality. In: Harding, F. (ed.) Milk Quality, ch. 6, pp. 75–96. Chapman & Hall, Wiltshire (1995b)
10. AOAC official methods of analysis. 972.16 Fat, lactose, protein, and solids in milk. Mid-infrared spectroscopic method. Association of Official Analytical Chemists, Arlington, VA, pp. 816–818 (1990)
11. Norris, K.H.: Making Light Work: Advances in Near Infrared Spectroscopy. In: Murray, I., Cowe, I.A. (eds.), pp. 596–602. VCH Press, New York (1991)
12. Schmilovitch, Z., Maltz, E., Austerweill, M.: Fresh raw milk composition analysis by NIR spectroscopy. In: Ipema, A.H., Lippus, A.C., Metz, J.H.M., Rossing, W. (eds.) Proceedings of the International Symposium on Prospects for Automatic Milking, Wageningen, Netherlands, EAAP Publication No.65 (1992)

13. Chen, J.Y., Iyo, C., Terada, F., Kawano, S.: Effect of multiplicative scatter correction on wavelength selection for near infrared calibration to determine fat content in raw milk. Journal of Near Infrared Spectroscopy 10(4), 301–307 (2002)
14. Kawasaki, M., Kawamura, S., Tsukahara, M., Morita, S., Komiya, M., Natsuga, M.: Near-infrared spectroscopic sensing system for on-line milk quality assessment in a milking robot. Computers and Electronics in Agriculture 63, 22–27 (2008)
15. Suykens, J.A.K., Vandewalle, J.: Least squares support vector machine classifiers. Neural Processing Letters 9, 293–300 (1999)
16. Yu, H.Y., Niu, X.Y., Lin, H.J., Ying, Y.B., Li, B.B., Pan, X.X.: A feasibility study on on-line determination of rice wine composition by Vis–NIR spectroscopy and least-squares support vector machines. Food Chemistry 113, 291–296 (2009)
17. Siuly, Y., Wen, P.: Clustering technique-based least square support vector machine for EEG signal classification. Computer Methods and Programs in Biomedicine (2010), doi:10.1016/j.cmpb.2010.11.014
18. Zuao, X., Wang, G., Zhao, K., Tan, D.: On-line least squares support vector machine algorithm in gas prediction. Mining Science and Technology 19, 194–198 (2009)
19. Wu, D., He, Y., Feng, S., Sun, D.W.: Study on infrared spectroscopy technique for fast measurement of protein content in milk powder based on LS-SVM. Journal of Food Engineering 84, 124–131 (2008)
20. LS-SVM v 1.5,
    http://www.esat.kuleuven.be/sista/lssvmlab/home.html

Support Vector Machines versus Artificial Neural Networks for Wood Dielectric Loss Factor Estimation

Lazaros Iliadis[1,*], Stavros Tachos[2], Stavros Avramidis[3], and Shawn Mansfield[3]

[1] Democritus University of Thrace , Department of Forestry & Management of the Environment & Natural Resources, 193 Pandazidou st., 68200 N Orestiada, Greece
[2] Aristotle University of Thessaloniki, Greece
[3] University of British Columbia, Department of Wood Science, Vancouver, Canada
liliadis@fmenr.duth.gr, staxos@gmail.com,
stavros.avramidis@ubc.ca

Abstract. This research effort aims in the estimation of Wood Loss Factor by employing Support Vector Machines. For this purpose experimental data for two different wood species were used. The estimation of the dielectric properties of wood was done by using various Kernel algorithms as a function of both ambient electro-thermal conditions applied during drying of wood and basic wood chemistry. Actually the best fit neural models that were developed in a previous effort of our research team were compared to the Kernels' approaches in order to determine the optimal ones.

Keywords: Wood Loss Factor, Gaussian Support Vector Machines, Polynomial Support Vector Machines, Artificial Neural Networks.

1 Introduction

It has been shown in the literature that the knowledge of dielectric properties of wood can be used to determine its density and moisture content nondestructively. On the other hand this knowledge can lead to the detection of hand knots, spiral grain, and other defects [14]. From a theoretical perspective a better understanding of the molecular structure of wood and wood-water interactions can be obtained [9]. Various approaches towards this direction have been reported in the literature, namely the radio frequency vacuum drying [11][12][13] and the high frequency electric field heating, such as the veneer and finger-joint gluing and parallam manufacturing [19]. Thus, estimation of the dielectric constant (ε'), the loss tangent ($tan\delta$) and the loss factor (ε'') plays a catalytic role in the process of design, control, optimization and simulation.

Recently Koumoutsakos [11] has shown that ε'' is proportional to the thermal energy transferred to the wood, during radio frequency vacuum drying (RFV) process. RFV heating is a volumetric method where thermal energy is produced simultaneously through a pile of lumber which is placed inside an electromagnetic field. In this process the moisture starts its transportation from the center to the

---

* Corresponding author.

L. Iliadis and C. Jayne (Eds.): EANN/AIAI 2011, Part I, IFIP AICT 363, pp. 140–149, 2011.
© IFIP International Federation for Information Processing 2011

surface as soon as the wood is exposed to the field [1]. In fact, the electric power converted to thermal is given by the following formula 1.

$$PD = 5.56 \times 10^{-11} E^2 f \varepsilon'' \tag{1}$$

It should be clarified that PD is the power density in W/m^3, E is the field strength in V/m and f is the frequency measured in Hz.

Research efforts in the past have shown that there exists a strong relationship between the dielectric properties and wood attributes studied plus field frequency applied [18][19].

It is a fact that despite all conducted research so far, there is very little respective knowledge regarding the effect of wood chemical composition on the determination of ε''. Actually, Norimoto [15][16] have investigated the dielectric properties of some wood chemical constituents as a function of frequency and temperature, but no attempt was made towards the correlation of their percent content in the cell-wall composition to the gross wood ε'' values.

Another point that motivated this study is the fact that the data that have been used so far to construct such models have originated from assorted species, under different thermo-physical conditions and variable frequencies and thus, they are not suitable to be employed in drying modeling [2].

This research effort aims in the development of Support Vector Machines models (Gaussian, Fuzzy weighted and Polynomial) capable of determining reliably the value of ε'' based on ambient electro-thermal conditions and also on basic wood chemistry. On the other hand a comparative study is performed with a previous study of our research team that used Artificial Neural Networks (ANNs) for the same purpose [2]. This comparison aims in the determination of the optimal approaches that can be used to offer reliable and most of all cost and time effective approximation.

2 Materials and Methods

2.1 Obtaining the Experimental Data

This study employees ε'' values and macro-physical data that were already published by Zhou and Avramidis [22]. According to Zhou and Avramidis all sapwood and all-heartwood western hemlock [*Tsuga heterophylla* (Raf.) Sarg.], and all-heartwood western red cedar [*Thuja plicata* Donn] specimens were evaluated in the radial direction (thickness) and at various moisture contents and temperature levels were exposed to two levels of electric field voltage. After the exposure was terminated the ε'' values were calculated indirectly by performing heating studies at a 13.56 MHz fixed frequency with a laboratory size RFV dryer [22] [2].

Also the above described wood species were analyzed by Zhou and Avramidis [22] regarding their chemical composition as follows: air dried wood samples were ground in a Wiley Mill to pass a 40-mesh screen and extracted in a Soxhlet apparatus with acetone for 12 hours, and extractives determined gravimetrically [2]. According to Zhou and Avramidis [22], the content of Lignin was determined using a modified Klason approach derived from the TAPPI standard method T222 om-98. For more details refer to [22].

2.2 5-Fold-Cross Validation

Cross-validation is a methods for estimating generalization error based on "resampling" [21] [7] [8] [17]. The resulting estimates of generalization error are often used for choosing among various models. In k-fold cross-validation, the data are divided into k subsets of (approximately) equal size. The model is trained k times, each time leaving out one of the subsets from training, but using only the omitted subset to compute whatever error criterion interests you. If k equals the sample size, this is called "leave-one-out" cross-validation. The division of the data set was done by the use of MATLAB's *crossvalind* function, which is included in the Bioinformatics Toolbox.

2.3 ε-SV Regression (ε-SVR)

Support Vector Machines (SVM) are keeping the training error foxed while at the same time they are minimizing the confidence interval [10]. Their primary target was pattern recognition [3]. Now they are used for both regression and classification. Vapnik [20] [10] introduced the following loss function that ignores errors less than a predefined value $\varepsilon > 0$

$$\left| y - f\left(\vec{x}\right) \right|_{\varepsilon} = \max\left\{ 0 \ , \ \left| y - f\left(\vec{x}\right) \right| - \varepsilon \right\} \tag{2}$$

It is a fact that the ε-SVR algorithm offers in many cases the optimal function of the form: $f\left(\vec{x}\right) = k\left(\vec{w}, \vec{x}\right) + b \qquad \vec{w}, \vec{x} \in R^{N}, \ b \in R$ (3). The whole idea is based on the determination of the function with the minimum testing error. The problem in this case is that the minimization of the above function is not possible due to the fact that the probability distribution P is unknown. Consequently, the actual solution can be reached by minimizing the following normalized risk function 4.

$$\frac{1}{2}\left\| \vec{w} \right\|^{2} + C_{SVR} \cdot R_{emp}^{\varepsilon}\left[f \right] \tag{4}$$

$R_{emp}^{\varepsilon}\left[f \right]$ is the function of empirical risk $R_{emp}\left[f \right] = \frac{1}{p}\sum_{i=1}^{p} L\left(f, \vec{x}_i, y_i \right)$ (5)

whereas the loss function is $L(f, \vec{x}_i, y_i) = \left| y_i - f\left(\vec{x}_i\right) \right|_{\varepsilon}$ (6) and it ignores errors less

than ε. Also it is clear that $\left\| \vec{w} \right\|^{2}$ is related to the complexity of the model, whereas C_{SVR} is a constant value determining the point that relates $R_{emp}^{\varepsilon}\left[f \right]$ to $\left\| \vec{w} \right\|^{2}$ [6].

Obviously, the objective which is the Minimization of the above risk function 4 can be phased as a specific optimization problem which phases the constraints described below: The aim is the minimization of the following function:

$$\tau\left(\overrightarrow{w},\overrightarrow{\xi},\overrightarrow{\xi^*}\right)=\frac{1}{2}\left\|\overrightarrow{w}\right\|^2+C_{SVR}\cdot\frac{1}{p}\sum_{i=1}^{p}\left(\xi_i+\xi_i^*\right) \qquad (7)$$

The constraints in this case are: $\left(k\left(\overrightarrow{w},\overrightarrow{x_i}\right)+b\right)-y_i\le\varepsilon+\xi_i$ (8) and

$y_i-\left(k\left(w\cdot x_i\right)+b\right)\le\varepsilon+\xi_i^*$ (9) and of course $\xi_i,\xi_i^*\ge0$ (10). Obviously (and this

can be seen in the following figure 1) ξ_i^*,ξ_i are the distances of the training data set points from the e-zone. All of the errors that are smaller than ε are ignored. As it is clearly shown, ξ_i stands for the distance of a point that can be found above the e-tube

zone and ξ_i^* stands for the distance of a point that is located below the e-tube zone. It is well known that in the case of the application of Lagrange multipliers the problem would correspond to a double optimization one as follows: Maximize

$$W\left(a,a^*\right)=-\varepsilon\sum_{i=1}^{p}\left(a_i^*+a_i\right)+\sum_{i=1}^{p}\left(a_i^*-a_i\right)y_i-\frac{1}{2}\sum_{i,j=1}^{p}\left(a_i^*-a_i\right)\left(a_j^*-a_j\right)k\left(x_i,x_j\right) \qquad (11)$$

subject to $\sum_{i=1}^{p}\left(a_i-a_i^*\right)=0$ (12) and $a_i^{(*)}\in\left[0,\dfrac{C_{SVR}}{p}\right]$ (13).

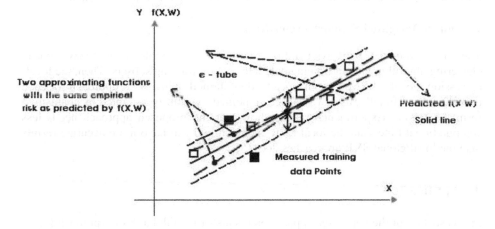

Fig. 1. ε-SVR for Regression

Based on Vapnik and Kecman [20][10], the optimization problem can be solved by the use of the following linear extension of the kernel functions (14) and (15)

$$w=\sum_{i=1}^{p}\left(a_i^*-a_i\right)\overrightarrow{x_i} \qquad (14)$$

$$f\left(\vec{x}, a, a^*\right) = \sum_{i=1}^{p}\left(a_i^* - a_i\right)k\left(\vec{x}, \vec{x_i}\right) + b \tag{15}$$

where b is estimated by the following function 16

$$b = average_i\left\{\varepsilon \cdot sign\left(a_i - a_i^*\right) + y_k - \sum_j\left(a_j - a_j^*\right)k\left(\vec{x_j}, \vec{x_i}\right)\right\} \tag{16}$$

The training set vectors $\vec{x_i}$ related to nonzero values of $\left(a_i - a_i^*\right)$ are called SVM. The following function 17 presents the Radial Basis function (RBF) kernel

$$f\left(\vec{x}, a, a^*\right) = \sum_{i=1}^{p}\left(a_i^* - a_i\right)\exp\left\{\frac{-\left\|\vec{x} - \vec{x_i}\right\|^2}{2 \cdot \sigma_{RBF}^2}\right\} + b \tag{17}$$

The involved parameters $\left\{\sigma_{RBF}, \gamma, \varepsilon\right\}$ are very significant and they determine to a great level of extend the good fit of the ε-SVR. It should be specified that σ_{RBF} is the RBF kernel's standard deviation, γ has a constant value that determines the point where the empiric error is related to complexity and finally the parameter ε is the width of the ε-zone. In statistics, when we consider the Gaussian probability density function σ_{RBF} is called the *standard deviation*, and the square of it, the variance.

2.4 Fuzzy Weighted Support Vector Regression

The fuzzy weighted SVR with a fuzzy partition first employs the fuzzy c-mean clustering algorithm to split training data into several training subsets. Then, the local-regression models (LRMs) are independently obtained by the SVR approach for each training subset. Finally, those LRMs are combined by a fuzzy weighted mechanism to form the output. Experimental results show that the proposed approach needs less computational time than the local SVR approach and can have more accurate results than the local/global SVR approaches does [5].

3 Application

In this section of the paper, the application results of the Global SVR approach for all existing data vectors will be presented thoroughly. The regression was done for different kernels, namely the Gaussian (RBF) the Fuzzy weight SVM and the Polynomial one. In order to perform Global SVR a global regression model was developed.

The regression was performed by the use of the LIBSVM v2.9 (http://www.csie.ntu.edu.tw/~cjlin/libsvm/) [4] which is encoded in C++ and offers a Matlab Interface. In this specific application the RBF-Kernel was applied.

3.1   Performing Trial and Error for the Gaussian Kernel

The initial data set comprised of one hundred forty-four (144) sets of experimental data, where the ε'' was measured under different temperature and moisture conditions and for various types of chemical composition.

During Training and Testing, several hundreds of experiments were performed in order to determine the optimal parameters' values.

More specifically in the case of the Gaussian (RBF) Kernel, 400 experimentation cases (applications of the 5-fold cross validation) were constructed with the integer value of σ_{RBF} ranging from 1 to 20 and with the value of the parameter γ ranging from 1 to 14. In the same case the e parameter took real values from the following set {0.003, 0.004, 0.005, 0.006, 0.007, 0.008, 0.009, 0.1, 0.12, 0.14, 0.16, 0.18,0.20, 0.22} This means that totally 400*14=5600 trials were performed during the 5-fold cross validation process.

The Root Mean Square Errors (RMSE) produced in each Training or Testing cycle were stored and then they were averaged each time 5-fold cross validation was employed. In each trial the initial data set was divided into five subsets (4 training and one testing) where five training and testing cycles were performed (each time changing the testing set in a round robin manner). Totally 5600 Average Root Mean Square Errors were obtained (ARMSE) one for each 5-fold cross validation cycle and for each unique combination of the parameters, together with the corresponding % Mean Average Percent Error (MAPE).

In the case of the Gaussian Kernel the optimal SVM model was produced for the $\sigma_{RBF}=$ 2 and for the value of the parameter $\gamma=12$ in the case with e=0.04 as it is shown in the following table 1.

Table 1. Performance of the Optimal Gaussian Kernel

Optimal Gaussian Kernel SVM (5-fold cross validation)

Value of σ_{RBF}	Value of γ	Value of e	Mean RMSE Training	Mean RMSE Testing	MAPE Training	MAPE Testing
2	12	0.04	0.00009664	0.0001501	2.4824596	3.7328347

The following figures 2 and 3 present the evolution of the Mean RMSE and of the MAPE respectively, according to the values of the e parameter for the Gaussian Kernel. It is clearly shown that the best model should have an e value equal to 0.04.

For the case of the Polynomial Kernel, the σ_{RBF} again took integer values from 1 to 20 and the parameter γ from 1 to 14. However the e parameter took real values from the following set {0.005, 0.1, 0.15, 0.20, 0.25}. The performance of the best fit Polynomial Kernel is shown in the following table 2 and it was achieved for $\sigma_{RBF}=3$ $\gamma=18$ and e=0.1

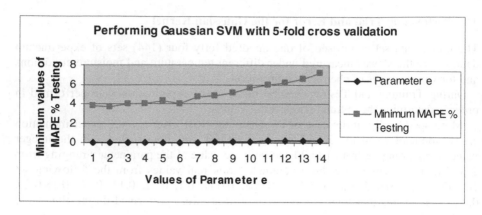

Fig. 2. Evolution of the Mean RMSE for different values of the parameter

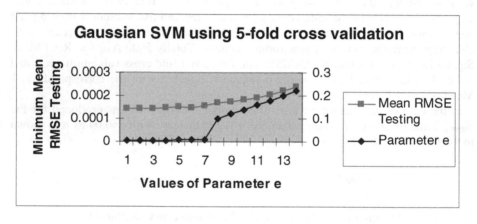

Fig. 3. Evolution of the MAPE for different values of the e parameter

Table 2. Performance of the Optimal Polynomial Kernel

Optimal Polynomial Kernel SVM (5-fold cross validation)

Value of σ_{RBF}	Value of γ	Value of e	Mean RMSE Training	Mean RMSE Testing	MAPE Training	MAPE Testing
3	18	0.1	0.000485	0.000549	11.74819	14.01062

For the Fuzzy weight Support Vector Machine the σ_{RBF} again took integer values from 1 to 20 and the parameter γ from 1 to 14. Also the e parameter took real values from the following set {0.005, 0.1, 0.15, 0.20, 0.25}. The performance of the best fit Fuzzy weight SVM is shown in the following table 3 and it was achieved for $\sigma_{RBF}=3$ $\gamma=16$ and e=0.05

Table 3. Performance of the Optimal Fuzzy weight SVM

Optimal Fuzzy weight SVM (5-fold cross validation)

Value of σ_{RBF}	Value of γ	Value of e	Mean RMSE Training	Mean RMSE Testing	MAPE Training	MAPE Testing
3	16	0.05	0.000488	0.000542	12.13017	14.12399

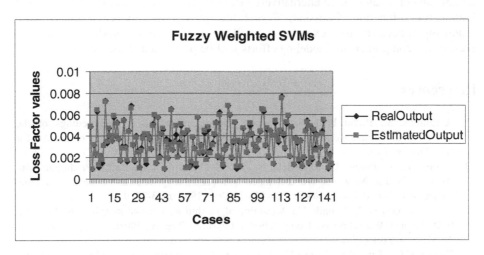

Fig. 4. Actual versus estimated values of Loss Factor for Fuzzy Weighted SVMs

3.2 Discussion – Comparative Analysis

The results of the e-SVM regression were compared to the results of the Artificial Neural Network that was developed by our research team in a previous study [2] and also the results of the three SVM kernels were compared to each other.

In [2] the optimal ANN that estimated wood loss factor for the same input variables was found to be a multi layer Back propagation one, with Sigmoid transfer function. It was found to have eleven (11) processing elements in the input layer, nine (9) neurons in the hidden layer and of course one neuron in the output layer [2].

Table 4. Performance of the optimal ANN for the estimation of loss factor in wood

Optimal ANN RMSE Training	Optimal ANN R^2 Training	Optimal ANN RMSE Testing	Optimal ANN R^2 Testing
0.017	R^2=0.9989	0.0382	R^2=0.9945

The above table 4 presents the performance of the best fit ANN. It is clearly shown that the Gaussian Kernel approach has by far much lower RMS error than the Polynomial and the Fuzzy weight SVM and also than the best fit ANN. Thus it can be considered the most reliable modeling approach.

This research effort is quite new and processes a high degree of innovation due to the fact that similar research has not been performed in wood science literature before. It is the final part of a wider effort to produce rational and useful Soft Computing regression models towards the estimation of wood dielectric properties.

It has been clearly shown that all three Kernel approaches and the ANN model are reliable and they can be used alternatively in wood industry applications. However the Radial Basis function (Gaussian) Kernel has proven to produce a much more promising model. Further experiments will be performed to produce more data vectors and complimentary modeling efforts will be performed in the future.

References

1. Avramidis, S.: Radio Frequency Vacuum Drying of wood. In: Proceedings of the International Conference of cost Action E1 5 Wood Drying. Theme State of the Art for Kiln Drying (1999)
2. Avramidis, S., Iliadis, L., Mansfield, S.: Wood Dielectric Loss Factor Prediction with Artificial Neural Networks Wood Science and Technology. Journal of the International Academy of Wood Science 40(7), 563–574 (2006) ISSN: 0043-7719
3. Boser, B., Guyon, I., Vapnik, V.: A training algorithm for optimal margin classifiers. In: Fifth Annual Workshop on Computational Learning Theory, Pittsburgh, pp. 144–152. ACM, New York (1992)
4. Chang C.C., Lin C.J.: LIBSVM A Library for Support Vector Machines (2009), http://www.csie.ntu.edu.tw/~cjlin/libsvm/
5. Chuang, C.C.: Fuzzy Weighted Support Vector Regression with a Fuzzy Partition. IEEE Transaction on Systems, Man, and Cybernetics, Part B: Cybernetics 37(3), 630–640 (2007)
6. Davy, M.: An Introduction to Support Vector Machines and other kernel algorithms. In: Proc. of the 9th Engineering Applications of Neural Networks Conference, Lille, France (2005)
7. Efron, B., Tibshirani, R.J.: An Introduction to the Bootstrap. Chapman & Hall, London (1993)
8. Hjorth, J.S.U.: Computer Intensive Statistical Methods Validation, Model Selection, and Bootstrap. Chapman & Hall, London (1994)
9. Kabir, M.F., Daud, W.M., Khalid, K.b., Sidek, H.A.: Temperature dependence of the dielectric properties of rubber wood. Wood and Fiber Science 33(2) (2001)
10. Kecman, V.: Learning and Soft Computing. MIT Press, USA (2001)
11. Koumoutsakos, A., Avramidis, S., Hatzikiriakos, S.: Radio frequency vacuum drying Part I. Theoretical model. Drying Technol. 19(1), 65–84 (2001a)
12. Koumoutsakos, A., Avramidis, S., Hatzikiriakos, S.: Radio frequency vacuum drying Part II. Experimental model evaluation. Drying Technol. 19(1), 85–98 (2001b)
13. Koumoutsakos, A., Avramidis, S., Hatzikiriakos, S.: Radio frequency vacuum drying Part III. Two dimensional Model, Optimization and Validation. Drying Technol. 21(8), 1399–1410 (2003)
14. Martin, P., Collet, R., Barthelemy, P., Roussy, G.: Evaluation of wood characteristics: Internal scanning of the material by microwaves. Wood Sci. Technol. 21, 361–371 (1987)

15. Norimoto, M.: Dielectric properties of wood. Wood Research 60(59), 106–152 (1976)
16. Norimoto, M., Hayashi, S., Yamada, T.: Anisotropy of dielectric constants in coniferous wood. Holzforschung 32, 167–172 (1978)
17. Shao, J., Tu, D.: The Jackknife and Bootstrap. Springer, New York (1995)
18. Siau, J.F.: Wood: influence of moisture on physical properties. Department of Wood Science and Forest Products, VPI&SU (1995)
19. Torgovnikov, G.I.: Dielectric properties of wood and wood-based material. Springer, Heidelberg (1993)
20. Vapnik, V.N., Golowich, S., Smola, A.: Support Vector method for function approximation regression estimation and signal processing. In: Advances in Neural Information Processing Systems, vol. 9, pp. 281–287. MIT Press, Cambridge (1997)
21. Weiss, S.M., Kulikowski, C.A.: Computer Systems That Learn. Morgan Kaufmann, San Francisco (1991)
22. Zhou, B., Avramidis, S.: On the loss factor of two B.C. softwoods. Wood Sci. and Technol. 33(4), 299–310 (1999)

Time-Frequency Analysis of Hot Rolling Using Manifold Learning*

Francisco J. García[1], Ignacio Díaz[1], Ignacio Álvarez[1],
Daniel Pérez[1], Daniel G. Ordonez[1], and Manuel Domínguez[2]

[1] Universidad de Oviedo, Área de Ingeniería de Sistemas y Automática
{fjgarcia,idiaz,ialvarez,dperez,dgonzalez}@isa.uniovi.es
[2] Universidad de León, Instituto de Automática y Fabricación
diemdg@unileon.es

Abstract. In this paper, we propose a method to compare and visualize spectrograms in a low dimensional space using manifold learning. This approach is divided in two steps: a data processing and dimensionality reduction stage and a feature extraction and a visualization stage. The procedure is applied on different types of data from a hot rolling process, with the aim to detect *chatter*. Results obtained suggest future developments and applications in hot rolling and other industrial processes.

Keywords: Hot rolling, dimensionality reduction, ISOMAP, spectrogram analysis.

1 Introduction

Ever since its inception in the end of sixteenth-century, metal rolling has become one of the most important industrial process in the world. Huge amounts of material and money are driven by the rolling industry, so it is so important to have a method not only for describing the observed behaviour of the process, but also for identifying the nature of a problem. Due to the high amount of variables involved, trying to find relationships among them appears to be a good aproach for dimensionality reduction (DR).

The selection of a set of variables that describes operating modes in industrial processes is closely related to DR. One of the most important DR technique is Principal Component Analysis (PCA)[1], described by Pearson in 1901. After PCA, other DR techniques have been proposed, such as Multidimensional Scaling (MDS) methods, Independent Component Analysis (ICA)[2] or Self-Organizing Maps (SOM)[3]. However, in the last 10 years, a new trend in DR, based on nonlinear models, appeared and a new collection of algorithms have been proposed. These algorithms –called local embeddings– involve a local optimization by defining local models of the k nearest neighbours and an alignment

---

* This work has been financed by a grant from Research Fund for Coal and Steel of the European Community and by the spanish Ministry of Science and Education and FEDER funds under grants DPI2009-13398-C02-01/02.

L. Iliadis and C. Jayne (Eds.): EANN/AIAI 2011, Part I, IFIP AICT 363, pp. 150–155, 2011.
© IFIP International Federation for Information Processing 2011

in order to obtain the global coordinates of each model, usually implying a singular value decomposition (SVD). Some of the most known of these techniques are isometric feature mapping or ISOMAP[4], local linear embedding (LLE)[5], laplacian eigenmaps (LE)[6] and local tangent subspace alignment (LTSA)[7].

Faults appeared in rolling process provoke important economic losses to the final product, so it is necessary to detect them in an early state, which is usually performed by analizing the frequency content of signals. A common source of problems in rolling is *chatter* [8], which is an unexpected powerful vibration that affects the quality of rolled material by causing an unacceptable variation of thickness. The frequency band related to chatter appears at 100-300 Hz, so monitoring this band is a possibility to detect it. A good way to visualize that information is the *spectrogram*, which provides a time-varying spectral representation that shows how the spectral density of the signal varies with time [9], making it possible to visually detect defects. Spectrograms can be understood as vectors of high dimensionality, making it possible to use them as inputs for DR techniques in order to divide them into different groups of data. In this paper we propose a method based on the use of embedding methods for the visulization of differences in spectrograms, applying it to vibration, speed and torque data of a hot rolling mill, showing not only the data structure, but also features of the different spectrograms. This paper is organized as follows: section 2 describes the method applied, section 3 shows a description of the experiment, section 4 submits the results and finally section 5 includes the conclusions obtained.

2   Spectrogram Analysis Using Manifold Learning

As proposed in [4][5][7], DR techniques are a good approach for image classification. From an industrial point of view, spectrograms can be understood as images of the process, because they provide time-frequency information about the state of the involved variables. The proposed method takes advantage of the analogy between spectrogram and image applying DR techniques. The procedure is divided into two parts: firstly spectrograms and ISOMAP projections of different coils are computed and secondly information about main features of process is visualized in a similar way to component planes [3] (See Fig. 1).

2.1   Computation of ISOMAP Projections

Due to the nature of the rolling process, it is common to do a spatial sampling of signals, where harmonics are independent from speed, therefore this procedure is performed at first. Considering a measured variable $y(t)$ at a regular time interval T_m, the sequence obtained is $y'_k = y(t'_k)$, where $t'_k = k \cdot T_m$. Spatial resampling needs a speed measurement $\mathbf{v} = [v_0, v_1, \ldots, v_k]$, either linear or rotatory, to know the spatial points where the original data was sampled $\mathbf{x} = [x_0, x_1, \ldots]$. Afterwards, selecting a spatial sampling rate (e_m) allows to obtain a signal regularly sampled at fixed space intervals –each e_m– $\mathbf{y} = [y_0, y_1, \ldots]^T$ where $y_k = y(t_k)$, with $t_k = 0$ for $k = 0$ and $t_k = t_{k-1} + \frac{e_m}{v_k}$ for $k = 1, 2, \ldots$. Since actual data

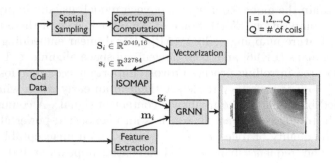

Fig. 1. Flowchart describing the method applied

is regular time sampled, the values of the spatial sampled data are obtained through linear interpolation.

The next step in our method is to compute the spectrogram of variables. Given a discrete signal $y_k = [y_0, y_1, \ldots, y_{n-1}]^T$, the Short-Time Fourier Transform (STFT) at a time n is defined as $Y(\omega, m) = \sum_{n=-\infty}^{\infty} y_{n-m}\omega_n e^{-j\omega n} = \sum_{n=0}^{R-1} y_{n-m}\omega_n e^{-j\omega n}$, where ω_n is a window function of length R. The *spectrogram* is a graphical display of the magnitude of $STFT$, $|Y(\omega, m)|$. This representation provides simplicity, robustness and ease of interpretation of the information contained in the frequency content. In Fig. 2, appearance of work roll (a), vibration (b), time (c) and spatial (d) spectrograms for a chattered coil are shown. Note that the strong 30 rev^{-1} harmonic in the spatial spectrogram matches the periodicity of the marks in the work rolls for a whole turn, regardless the rolling speed. This makes such kind of representation a proper invariant descriptor of spatial phenomena typically involved in chatter effect.

Because of this type of visualization, it is possible to stablish a logical analogy between spectrogram and image. After spectrogram computation, the obtained matrix is converted into a vector with the aim to apply a DR technique. Being **S**

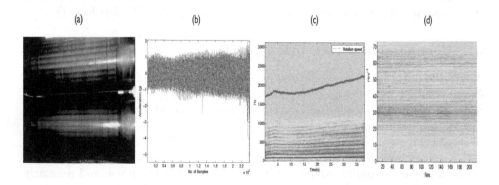

Fig. 2. Typical case of chattered coil

the spectrogram matrix of dimension $(\frac{R}{2}+1) \times M$, each spectrogram can be represented as a vector $\mathbf{s} = [s_0, \ldots, s_p]^T$, where $s_{r+(m-1)(\frac{R}{2}+1)} = S_{r,m}$. The ISOMAP algorithm [4] was applied to $\mathbf{s}$. The ISOMAP algorithm is a DR technique where geodesic distance on a weighted graph is incorporated with the classical scaling, obtaining low-dimensional embedding of a set of high-dimensional data points.

2.2   Feature Extraction and Visualization

The first step of this stage is the extraction of relevant features from the signals being analysed. Considering a variable y_k of length N, a windowed Fast Fourier Transform (FFT) –as an efficient algorithm for Discrete Fourier Transform (DFT), avoiding Gibbs effect– is applied in order to obtain its spectral information, as $Y_i = \sum_{k=0}^{N-1} w(k) y_k e^{-j2\pi k/N}$, for $i = 0, \ldots, N-1$, where Y_i is a complex sequence describing the amplitudes and phases of the signal harmonics and $w(k)$ is a Hanning window. In this case, a N-length window is used, so there is only one value of energy for each harmonic. The energy in bands around p specified center frequencies $f_1, f_2, \cdots, f_p$ with predefined bandwidths $B_1, B_2, \cdots, B_p$ can be computed by summing up the squares of the harmonics inside this bands, in order to obtain a p-dimensional feature vector $\mathbf{m} = [m_1, m_2, \ldots, m_p]^T$, where $m_i = \sqrt{\sum_{\frac{k}{NT} \in [f_i - \frac{B_i}{2}, f_i + \frac{B_i}{2}]} ||\mathbf{Y}_k||^2}$. Finally, features extracted for each analysed signal can be arrange in a *data matrix* $\mathbf{M} = (\mathbf{m}_n) = [\mathbf{m}_1, \mathbf{m}_2, \ldots]$, where $\mathbf{m}_n$ represents the column feature vector of coil n. In addition to the frequency features, specific feature extraction derived from process domain knowledge can be added (see Section 3). The visualization of component planes requires the application of a interpolation algorithm to estimate the value of each feature at every point in the 2D visualization space. In this paper, the Specht's [10] algorithm, *general regression neural network* (GRNN) is applied to match the extracted features and ISOMAP projections.

3   Experiment

The method described here was applied to data from a hot rolling finishing facility. The analysed signals were acceleration at driver-side (Acc DS, 6250 Hz), as a measure of vibration, the root mean square of velocity, both at operator side and at driver side (VRMS OS and VRMS DS, 10 Hz), upper roll torque (Torque OS, 500 Hz) and, finally, rotation speed of rolls (Rot Sp, 500 Hz). Only data during rolling stage was analysed. Two states of rolling –*non-chatter* and *chatter*, which leads to low quality coils– were taken into account in order to understand the results obtained with this method. The total size of the sample is 111 coils, comprising both states of rolling. Due to the original difference in the sampling frequency between Acc DS and Rot Sp signals, Acc DS signal was decimated in order to have a unique sample rate. A spatial sample rate of $212.16\ rev^{-1}$ was selected using the minimum spatial distance between two samples in the data. Spectrogram computation was applied to Acc DS signal of every coil, with a window size of 4096 and an overlapping of 90%. To have equal sized spatial spectrograms, only the first 30 revolutions of rolling were considered, resulting in a total size of 32784 elements for each spectrogram to be projected with the ISOMAP algorithm. The dimensionality reduction stage of spectrograms involved the application of the ISOMAP algorithm with $K = 30$ and output dimensionality of 2. Apart from frequency features, the mean of the difference between each element of VRMS OS and VRMS DS was added, as $\mu_v = \frac{1}{N} \sum_{i=0}^{N-1} (v_{d_i} - v_{o_i})$. Finally, component planes generation was computed with value of $\sigma = 0.003$ in GRNN with the aim to obtain a smooth degradation of the color of the planes for the difference of *chatter* and *non-chatter* group.

4   Results

The application of the method obtains the ISOMAP projections shown in Fig. 3 (top). ISOMAP is able to make a clusterization of the high-dimensional input data, obtaining two clusters (chatter and non-chatter), being remarkable that coils number 14 and 15 which appear isolated. It can be observed that these two coils happen to appear just before a long series of chattered coils. Component planes of ISOMAP are visualized in Fig. 3 (bottom). In this representation, two different color zones dependent from the value of the feature analysed are distinguished . The effect of the σ value stablished for the GRNN algorithm, smoothing the color in each plane, can also be observed. This representation provides information about the value of the feature analysed in each plane. In addition, component planes characterize two zones, related to chatter and non-chatter coils. Such representations combine the visualization of the cluster structure of the data with the visual display of the value of different features associated to

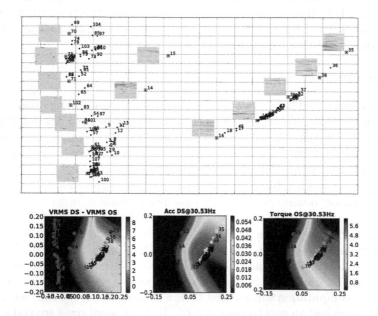

Fig. 3. ISOMAP projections and component planes of coils analysed

each coil. Also, it is noteworthy the explanatory power in the definition of chatter of VRMS DS-VRMS OS, which is an unusual feature for detecting chatter.

5 Conclusions

In this paper we have proposed a method to explore the visualization of spectrograms in a low dimensionality as an use of ISOMAP, similar to image classification in [4]. This method was applied to data from a hot rolling process in order to detect different states of rolling. The resulting projections show that different spectrograms produce low dimensional structures that can be efficiently unfolded with ISOMAP, distinguishing chatter, non-chatter and transition coils before chatter appears, which suggests that there is a difference in the frequency content of rolling that could be potentially used as to estimate when chatter could appear. Another contribution are component planes of ISOMAP, which provides information about analyzed features of the process, differentiating chatter and non chatter coils. These results suggest the potential use of the proposed method not only in hot rolling, but also in other kinds of batch process monitoring or in fault detection where time-frequency behavior of one or more variables bear information on process quality or fault conditions.

References

1. Jollife, I.: Principal component analysis (1986)
2. Hyvarinen, A.: Survey on independent component analysis. Neural Computing Surveys 2, 94–128 (1999)
3. Kohonen, T.: Self-Organizing Maps, 3rd extended edn. Springer Series in Information Sciences, vol. 30. Springer, Heidelberg (2001)
4. Tenenbaum, J.B., de Silva, V., Langford, J.C.: A global geometric framework for nonlinear dimensionality reduction. Science 290, 2319–2323 (2000)
5. Roweis, S.T., Saul, L.K.: Nonlinear dimensionality reduction by locally linear embedding. Science 290, 2323–2326 (2000)
6. Belkin, M., Niyogi, P.: Laplacian eigenmaps for dimensionality reduction and data representation. Neural computation 15(6), 1373–1396 (2003)
7. Zhang, Z., Zha, H.: Principal manifolds and nonlinear dimension reduction via local tangent space alignment. SIAM Journal of Scientific Computing 26(1), 313–338 (2004)
8. Drevermann, J., Fieweger, M., Jckel, I.: Prozess-und zustandsberwachung an einem fertiggerst. In: Akida 2010, Aachen, Germany (November 17-18, 2010)
9. Boashash, B. (ed.): Time-Frequency Signal Analysis and Processing A Comprehensive Reference. Elsevier Science, Amsterdam (2003)
10. Specht, D.F.: A general regression neural network. IEEE Transactions on Neural Networks 2(6), 568–576 (1991)

Application of Radial Bases Function Network and Response Surface Method to Quantify Compositions of Raw Goat Milk with Visible/Near Infrared Spectroscopy

Ching-Lu Hsieh[1,*], Chao-Yung Hung[2], and Mei-Jen Lin[3]

[1] Department of Biomechatronics Engineering, National Pingtung University of Science and Technology, Taiwan, R.O.C.
Tel.: 886-8-7703202#7583
`chinglu@mail.npust.edu.tw`
[2] Department of Biomechatronics Engineering,
National Pingtung University of Science and Technology, Taiwan, R.O.C.
[3] Department of Animal Science,
National Pingtung University of Science and Technology. Taiwan, R.O.C.

Abstract. Raw goat milk pricing is based on the milk quality especially on fat, solid not fat (SNF) and density. Therefore, there is a need of approach for composition quantization. This study applied radial basis function network (RBFN) to calibrate fat, SNF, and density with visible and near infrared spectra (400~2500 nm). To find the optimal parameters of goal error and spread used in RBFN, a response surface method (RSM) was employed. Results showed that with the optimal parameters suggested by RSM analysis, R^2 difference for training and testing data set was the smallest which indicated the model was less possible of overtraining or undertraining. The R^2 for testing set was 0.9569, 0.8420 and 0.8743 for fat, SNF and density, respectively, when optimal parameters were used in RBFN.

Keywords: Raw goat milk, Radial basis function network, Response surface method, NIR.

1 Introduction

Goat milk provides abundant nourishment that has been treated as an important daily supply especially for the people at the stage of recovery or youth. Price of goat milk usually higher than cow milk either in raw or fresh format. Dairy factory evaluates milk price based on its quality, such as the ratio of fat, SNF (Solid Not Fat), and density, which drives dairy farmer's attention on monitoring the constituents of milk. Therefore, a quick method for measuring goat milk composition is highly needed.

For decades, near infrared (NIR, 700~25000 nm, or 0.7~25 µm) or infrared (IR, 25~50 µm) has been proven high performance in qualitative and quantitative analysis for agriculture, food, and pharmacy industry. For milk quality evaluation and

---

* Corresponding author.

L. Iliadis and C. Jayne (Eds.): EANN/AIAI 2011, Part I, IFIP AICT 363, pp. 156–161, 2011.

quantization, AOAC [1] suggested that some milk components are good correlated to IR energy absorption, such as, CH groups in fatty acid chains of fat molecules absorb at 3.48 μm. Many studies have been conducted on cow milk [2,3,4], but studies on raw goat milk are comparatively less, meanwhile most approaches used in previous researches usually needs chemometrics that users usually hard to follow the theory.

Artificial neural networks (ANN) have been extensively used in many fields because it can perform a curve-fitting operation in a multidimensional space even it has been thought as a black box. After properly training, ANN model can be applied straightforwardly. Thus, it is a good option for dairy farmers for online application. One drawback of ANN is that they are highly nonlinear in the parameters and their parameter estimation may be trapped at a local minimum in learning process. One alternative to highly nonlinear-in-the-parameter neural networks is the radial bases function network (RBFN) [5]. The performance of an RBFN depends upon the choices of the number and the centers of hidden units. Most choice of centers is to let each data point in the training set correspond to a center. In this case the number of degree of freedoms in the network is equal to the number of training data. In some cases, such as data contaminated by noise, then the overfitting phenomenon will occur. One of possible way to access overfitting condition is to separate samples into training data set and testing data set, then compare the performance on each set. In this study, we used response surface method (RSM) to tune network parameters so as to avoid or lessen overtraining or undertraining problem. Therefore, this article has three purposes:

1. obtain visible/NIR spectroscopy of raw goat milk samples mixed with 0%, 2%, 5%, 10%, 20%, 30%, 50%, 70% and 100% reconstituted milk to vary sample compositions
2. apply RBFN to quantify the compositions of the goat milk, i.e., fat, SNF, and density
3. use RSM to study the effect of RBFN parameters, i.e., goal error and spread so as to find the optimum model parameters.

2 Materials and Methods

2.1 Sample Preparation

Raw goat milk samples were collected in the morning from a dairy farm near our campus, and they were sent to our laboratory within 2 hr. Sampling process was conducted from Oct. 2010 to Nov. 2010. In order to have different composition, reconstituted goat milk were made by diluting powdered goat milk with water on the basis of protein of raw milk. It means the reconstitutes goat milk samples have as close as protein ratios to raw goat milk samples. After the reconstituted milk was prepared, it was mixed with raw milk in volume ratio of 0:100 (0%), 2:98 (2%), 5:95 (5%), 10:90 (10%), 20:80 (20%), 30:70 (30%), 50:50 (50%), 75:25 (75%), and 100:0 (100%). Thus total 324 test samples were prepared.

Each sample was scanned to record its visible/NIR spectrum. Sample was also analyzed by milk composition analyzer (Expert, Scopo Electric, Europe) on fat, protein, SNF (solid-not-fat), lactose, and density. But, only fat, SNF, and density were studied in here. Monochrometer (FOSS NIRS 6500, NIRSYSTEM, US) was used to obtain spectrum (400~2498 nm at 2 nm intervals). From all tested samples, 216 samples were randomly selected as training set while the remaining samples (108) were used as testing set.

To correct the baseline shift and to smooth noise on spectral data, each spectrum was proceed with baseline treatment, Savitzky–Golay smoothing with 4th order 11 data points, and standard normal variate scaling. These data processes were supported by a PLS-Toolbox (Eigenvector co.) compatible to MATLAB.

2.2 Radial Basis Function Networks

A RBFN is one whose output is symmetric around an associated center, c_i. That is, $\phi(x) = \phi(\|x - c_i\|)$, where $\|.\|$ is a vector norm or distance, such as, Euclidean distance. A radial basis neuron with input p (R×1 dimension) and with a bias b, then its output can be formulated as $f(\|w-p\|b)=f(n)$. One transfer function f of radial basis neuron support by MATLAB is

$$radbas(n) = e^{-n^2}$$

(1)

A RBFN is a supervised network and it takes matrices of input vectors P and target vectors T, and a spread constant for the radial basis layer. The spread determines the width of an area in the input space to which each neuron responds. Thus spread should be large enough to overlap the regions of input space. Thus, designing an RBN involves selecting the goal error and width of RBFN. In here, RBFN function was supported by Neural Network Toolbox (MATLAB).

2.3 Response Surface Method

Response y are affected by variables ξ_1, ξ_2, ..., ξ_k that are usually called the natural variables. In many RSM works it is convenient to transform the natural variables to coded variables x_1, x_2, ..., x_k. In terms of the coded variables, the response function can be written as [6]

$$\eta = f(x_1, x_2, ..., x_k)$$

(2)

For the case of two independent variables, the second order model is

$$\eta = \beta_0 + \beta_1 x_1 + \beta_2 x_2 + \beta_{11} x_{11}^2 + \beta_{22} x_{22}^2 + \beta_{12} x_1 x_2$$

(3)

Many applications of RSM involve fitting and checking the adequacy of a second order model. An experimental design called central composite design (CCD) has been widely used for fitting a second-order response surface. Natural variables and coded variables of each CCD observation is listed in Table 1 suggested by previous run. Model performance of RBN was evaluated by coefficient of determination R^2 for training set (R_c^2) and test set (R_v^2). These analyses were conducted by MATLAB. Thus, RBFN was trained with each error goal and spread parameter listed on Table 1.

Table 1. Central composite design for RBN

Observation	Error Goal	Spread	Coded variable	
	ξ_1	ξ_2	x_1	x_2
1	0.001	0.5	-1	-1
2	0.1	0.5	1	-1
3	0.001	1.5	-1	1
4	0.1	1.5	1	1
5	0.000373	1	-1.414	0
6	0.3726	1	1.414	0
7	0.01	0.3344	0	-1.414
8	0.01	1.707	0	1.414
9	0.01	1	0	0
10	0.01	1	0	0
11	0.01	1	0	0
12	0.01	1	0	0

3 Results and Discussion

3.1 RSM and RBN Performance

Based on the CCD experiment, 12 observations in Table 1 were examined by RBFN (MATLAB) and each corresponding R^2 for training set (R_c^2) and test set (R_v^2) are shown in Table 2. The highest R_c^2 for fat, SNF, and density are 0.9943, 0.9917, and 0.9902, respectively, while the highest R_v^2 are 0.9549, 0.8208, and 0.8599. R_v^2 is smaller than the corresponding R_c^2, therefore overtraining problem might exist.

Table 2. The performance of RBFN at each central composite design observation

Obs.	Coded variable		Fat		SNF		Density	
	X_1	X_2	R_c^2	R_v^2	R_c^2	R_v^2	R_c^2	R_v^2
1	-1	-1	0.9847	0.9492	0.9778	0.8209	0.9754	0.8599
2	1	-1	0.3376	0.4460	0.0994	0.0546	0.2095	0.1603
3	-1	1	0.9850	0.9506	0.9779	0.7755	0.9739	0.7751
4	1	1	0.3698	0.4598	0.1146	0.1009	0.2332	0.1882
5	-1.414	0	0.9943	0.9549	0.9917	0.6872	0.9902	0.7392
6	1.414	0	0.2295	0.2267	0.0133	0.0010	0.0746	0.0122
7	0	-1.414	0.8538	0.8587	0.7817	0.6321	0.7639	0.6341
8	0	1.414	0.8521	0.8617	0.7841	0.7045	0.7379	0.6171
9	0	0	0.8585	0.8955	0.7855	0.7367	0.7526	0.7372
10	0	0	0.8585	0.8955	0.7855	0.7367	0.7526	0.7372
11	0	0	0.8585	0.8955	0.7855	0.7367	0.7526	0.7372
12	0	0	0.8585	0.8955	0.7855	0.7367	0.7526	0.7372

R_c^2 is for training data set, and R_v^2 is for test data set.

Three conditions of goal error and spread suggested in the optimal regions were set on the RBFN and run the model again. Results show the highest R_v^2 is 0.9569, 0.8420 and 0.8743 for fat, SNF and density, respectively. The corresponding R_c^2 is 0.9573, 0.9181, and 0.9255 respectively. These parameters show less problem on model overtraining or model undertraining because they have the lowest difference between R_c^2 and R_v^2. The epochs for these optimal tests were 25 for fat, 50 for SNF, and 25 for density. The numbers of centers of these optimal RBFN were 37 for fat, 63 for SNF, and 49 for density. Scatter distribution of 108 testing samples on fat for observation and prediction are shown in Fig. 1. Model used is the RSM optimal model. Results shown the prediction error randomly occurred that made the data points distribute randomly beneath or above the identical line.

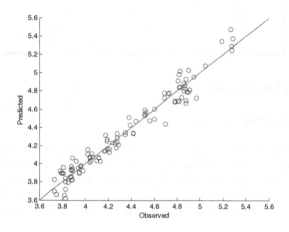

Fig. 1. Scatter plot of observation and prediction of testing set for fat (%) at the optimal parameters of goal error 0.0028 and spread 1.0

4   Conclusion

Parameters of goal error and spread of radial basis function networks (RBFN) were tested under the assistance of response surface method (RSM). The optimal parameters were found and validated for three raw goat milk compositions: fat, solid not fat (SNF), and density. Result shows that RSM suggested the optimal parameters for fat in RBF were goal error 0.0028 and spread 1.0, while for SNF were goal error 0.0037 and spread 0.9 and for density were goal error 0.0028 and spread 0.7. With these optimal parameters the R_v^2 was 0.9569, 0.8420 and 0.8743 for fat, SNF and density, respectively.

Acknowledgments. This study was finally supported by Council of Agriculture, the Executive Yuan, Taiwan, R. O. C.

References

1. AOAC official methods of analysis. 972.16 Fat, lactose, protein, and solids in milk. Mid-infrared spectroscopic method. Association of Official Analytical Chemists, Arlington, VA, pp. 816–818 (1990)
2. Schmilovitch, Z., Maltz, E., Austerweill, M.: Fresh raw milk composition analysis by NIR spectroscopy. In: Ipema, A.H., Lippus, A.C., Metz, J.H.M., Rossing, W. (eds.) Proceedings of the International Symposium on Prospects for Automatic Milking, Wageningen, Netherlands, EAAP Publication No.65 (1992)
3. Martin, I.G., Hierroa, J.M., Sanchoa, R.M., Estebana, J.S., Quintanab, A.V., Revilla, I.: Determination of the percentage of milk (cow's, ewe's and goat's) in cheeses with different ripening times using near infrared spectroscopy technology and a remote reflectance fibre-optic probe. Analytica Chimica Acta 604, 191–196 (2007)
4. Mouazen, A.M., Dridi, S., Rouissi, H., De Baerdemaeker, J., Ramond, H.: Feasibility study on using visible-near infrared spectroscopy coupled with factorial discriminant analysis technique to identify sheep milk from different genotypes and feeding systems. Journal of Near Infrared Spectroscopy 15(6), 359–369 (2007)
5. Chen, S., Cowan, C.F.N., Grant, P.M.: Orthogonal Least Squares Learning Algorithm for Radial Basis Function Networks. IEEE Transactions on Neural Networks 2(2), 302–309 (1991)
6. Myers, R.H., Montgomery, D.C.: Response Surface Methodology, pp. 1–78. John Wiley & Sons, Chichester (1995)

Transferring Models in Hybrid Reinforcement Learning Agents

Anestis Fachantidis, Ioannis Partalas, Grigorios Tsoumakas,
and Ioannis Vlahavas

Department of Informatics
Aristotle University of Thessaloniki
54124 Thessaloniki, Greece
{afa,partalas,greg,vlahavas}@csd.auth.gr

Abstract. The main objective of transfer learning is to reuse knowledge acquired in a previous learned task, in order to enhance the learning procedure in a new and more complex task. Transfer learning comprises a suitable solution for speeding up the learning procedure in Reinforcement Learning tasks. In this work, we propose a novel method for transferring models to a hybrid reinforcement learning agent. The models of the transition and reward functions of a source task, will be transferred to a relevant but different target task. The learning algorithm of the target task's agent takes a hybrid approach, implementing both model-free and model-based learning, in order to fully exploit the presence of a model. The empirical evaluation, of the proposed approach, demonstrated significant results and performance improvements in the 3D Mountain Car task, by successfully using the models generated from the standard 2D Mountain Car.

1 Introduction

Reinforcement Learning (RL) is popular for its ability to deal with complex problems using limited feedback. However, RL algorithms often require a considerable amount of training, especially when they are applied to problems with very large and/or continuous state spaces.

Besides this, data efficiency is another important factor. Data efficiency refers to the ability of an agent to compute a good policy with less data. In the case of RL less data means less interaction with the environment which is specially important in real world applications such as robotics, where much interaction with the environment needs time and can be costly. Two of the most important approaches to speed up the learning process and boost data efficiency are Transfer Learning and Model - Based RL algorithms.

Whereas direct RL algorithms compute for long periods before finding good policies *Model-based algorithms* learn an explicit model of the environment and at the same time, the value function which determines the agent's policy. The model generated from this learning process can either be used for generating simulated experiences or for planning.

L. Iliadis and C. Jayne (Eds.): EANN/AIAI 2011, Part I, IFIP AICT 363, pp. 162–171, 2011.

Transfer learning refers to the process of using knowledge that has been acquired in a previous learned task, the *source task*, in order to enhance the learning procedure in a new and more complex task, the *target task*. The more similar those two tasks are, the easier it is to transfer knowledge between them.

The key insight of our approach is to achieve maximum data efficiency and knowledge exploitation by combining transfer learning with model based learning. We do so by adopting a hybrid Dyna-like approach for our agent, in order to maximize the use of the model. The proposed approach is dubbed ***Transfer learning in Model-based Reinforcement Learning Agents*** (TiMRLA). The empirical evaluation, of the proposed approach, demonstrated significant results and performance improvements in the 3D Mountain Car task, by successfully using the models generated from the standard 2D Mountain Car.

2   Learning the Model of a Source Task

In order to capture the dynamics of the source task environment we have to learn models of its transition and reward functions. Our main concern here is to achieve a balanced presence of the state space in the training sample and maximize the accuracy of the learned models.

To gather experiences and generate the source's task model, we use the model-based RL algorithm *Model Based Policy Improvement* (MBPI) [4]. MBPI is a model-based learning algorithm that can learn, on-line, the model of a task from real, gathered, experiences. Thereafter, MBPI uses that model to generate simulated experiences and learns directly from them using Sarsa.

In continuous domains, a value approximation technique is necessary in order to approximate the value of a state using nearby state values. We use the Cerebral Model Articulation Controller (CMAC) [1], a well-known tile coding function approximation scheme.

Our specific choice of the MBPI model-based learning algorithm in the source task, should not be considered as a limitation of the method as every other model-based RL algorithm can be equally considered, as long as it can provide us with models of the reward and transition functions of the task. The simulated experiences, in the form of a tuple $< s, a, r, s' >$, form a training set that will be used to learn the transition and reward functions of the task.

In our specific implementation, we use two cascade neural networks to learn the models of these functions. Cascade neural networks were chosen as the characteristics of this type of networks were considered suitable for the RL scheme [7].

Next, the agent of the source task starts to learn and progressively creates the requested models. Every e episodes MPBI learns a new model of the transition and reward functions, based on all the gathered experiences so far. In our implementation these new models are kept only if their Validation mean square error (MSE) is less than that of the previously generated models. We choose Validation MSE and not Train MSE to avoid overfitting and test the ability of the model to predict from unseen data, such as those in the validation data set.

3   Transfer Learning with TiMRLA

The TiMRLA algorithm (see Algorithm 3.3) consists of two learning mechanisms which are set up to be compatible. This hybrid-learning approach is followed, as explained later, in order to make maximum use of the source's task model.

3.1   Model-Based Learning

TiMRLA implements model based learning by generating mental (non-real) experiences from a model and directly learning from them with Sarsa (policy improvement) (line 30). This model can either be a source task model thus implementing transfer learning, or the new target task model being trained while learning in the target task. In the beginning of each episode the two models compete for being the current episode's "Model" (line 7). The choice is based on their error on predicting the afterstates from the current agent's state, this error is calculated as the euclidean distance between a predicted state and the one experienced (line 23).

3.2   Direct Learning

Direct learning is implemented using Sarsa(λ) accompanied with eligibility traces for temporal-credit assignment. This is a model-free approach but in our implementation is accompanied by a model-based mechanism, *Action Determinant*, that assists the model-free learning process. This approach could be considered closer to that of Reward Shaping [3]. Reward Shaping is a methodology in which directly altering and adjusting the reward an agent receives, can improve its performance by biasing certain state-action values according to some prior knowledge. A simple, in form, quantity called Action Determinant is being calculated in every step (line 17). This quantity is calculated for each action α and consists of two parts. The first, $CMAC.V(s'_{model})$ is according to our model, the value of the state following our current state if action α was to be applied. The second part of the quantity, r_{model} is the reward predicted from our model for the specific state-action pair (s, α). For each action $\alpha \in A$ the sum of the two quantities is summed with the respective $Q(s, a)$ value thus creating $|A|$ new values. These values will be used for action selection with real experiences. So, when being greedy, the agent will make a more informed choice of actions based on the CMAC weights of the predicted afterstates and on the predicted reward.

3.3   Transfer Learning

Learning in the source task provided us with the best, in terms of Validation MSE, Neural Networks. These three networks are used by TiMRLA to predict next states, whether they are terminal, and their rewards.

We describe the flow of the proposed algorithm as it executes in the target task. In lines 1-3 some basic initializations are done. The weights in the CMAC, representing our value function $Q(s, a)$, are all set to zero and the initial model to be used is the Source Model. In the beginning of each episode we obtain the start state and we select an action (ϵ-greedy) with respect to the policy. Next, takes place the process of choosing the model that will be used (lines 7-9) in the specific episode. In lines 12-13 we obtain for each step, the current state and its reward. We then optionally calculate the quantities for the Action Determinant by predicting the next state and its value, according to our function approximator as also the reward. This is calculated for each action and passed as a parameter to the function that implements the ϵ-greedy action selection (line 19). Next model-free learning with Sarsa(λ) takes place, with its update rule using an added "CMAC" notation to emphasize the fact that these values come from the approximation of the CMAC.

Next, in lines 21-24 and for each even numbered step (not in every step, for robustness) the two models (target and source) are queried for the new state s' (already known) based on the preceding state-action pair (s, a). We then compute and compare two euclidean distances $d(s', s'_{target})$ and $d(s', s'_{source})$ where the second argument in the distances, represents the state predictions of the two models. The distances are stored in a tabular form with a window of 1000 distances and the two mean errors are calculated for that window. As mentioned before, at the start of each episode, based on this averaged error (distance), TiMRLA chooses to use the target or the source task model (the one with the less error).

In the next lines the flow continues with the MBPI algorithm for policy improvement using generated experiences from the model.

4   Experiments

4.1   Generalized Mountain Car

The mountain car domain was originally proposed by [6] and extended by [8]. In the standard 2D task an underpowered car must be driven up to a hill. The state of the environment is described by two continuous variables, the horizontal position $x \in [-1.2, 0.6]$, and velocity $v_x \in [-0.007, 0.007]$. The actions are {Neutral, Left and Right} which modify the velocity by $-0.001, 0$ and 0.001 respectively. At each time step, an amount of $-0.0025 * \cos 3x$ is added to the velocity, in order to take gravity into account.

Each episode starts with the car at the bottom of the hill and ends when x becomes greater than 0.5. At each time step, the agent selects among the three available actions and receives a reward of -1. The objective is to move the car to the goal state, as fast as possible. The main difficulty in this environment is that the force of gravity is greater than the force that the engine is capable to provide. Therefore, the agent controlling the underpowered car must move back and forth, in order to exploit the effect of gravity to its favour and manage to reach the goal state.

The 3D mountain car extends the 2D task by adding an extra spatial dimension. The 3D task was originally proposed in [12]. The state is composed by four continuous variables, the coordinates in space x, and $y \in [-1.2, 0.6]$, as well

Algorithm 1. Transferring Models in Reinforcement Learning Agents - TiMRLA

1: $Q \leftarrow Q_0 \ D \leftarrow 0$
2: $Model \leftarrow SourceModel$
3: **repeat** for each episode
4:      $s \leftarrow StartStateFromEnvironment()$
5:      $\alpha \leftarrow Select\_e\_GreedyAction(Q, ActionDeterminant[])$
6:      **if** $TargetModel.error < SourceModel.Error$ **then**
7:          $Model \leftarrow TargetModel$
8:      **end if**
9: **until** end
10: **repeat** for each step
11:      $s'_{mdl} \leftarrow nextStateFromEnvironment$
12:      $r \leftarrow reward$
13:      **for** each action α in A **do**
14:          $s'_{mdl} \leftarrow Model.PredictState(s', \alpha)$
15:          $r_{mdl} \leftarrow Model.PredictReward(s', \alpha)$
16:          $ActionDeterminant[\alpha] \leftarrow \text{CMAC}.V(s'_{mdl}) + r_{mdl}$
17:      **end for**
18:      $\alpha' \leftarrow Select\_e\_GreedyAction()$
19:      $CMAC.Q(s, \alpha) \leftarrow CMAC.Q(s, \alpha) + a(r + \gamma CMAC.Q(s', \alpha') - CMAC.Q(s, \alpha))$
20:      $s'_{trg} \leftarrow TargetModel.PredictState(s, a)$
21:      $s'_{src} \leftarrow SourceModel.PredictState(s, a)$
22:      $SourceModel.Error \leftarrow SourceModel.Error + d(s'_{src}, s')^2$
23:      $TargetModel.Error \leftarrow TargetModel.Error + d(s'_{trg}, s')^2$
24:      $s \leftarrow s'; \alpha \leftarrow a'$
25:      **if** $NonTrainingPeriodElpased = false$ **then**
26:          $D \leftarrow D \cup (s, \alpha, r, s')$
27:      **else**
28:          $LearnTargetModel(D)$
29:          $ImprovePolicy(Q)$ //Using MBPI in our case
30:      **end if**
31: **until** s' terminal

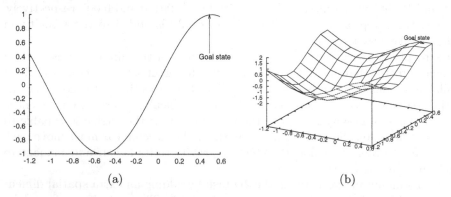

Fig. 1. (a) The Mountain Car 2D task. (b) The Mountain Car 3D task.

as the velocities v_x and $v_y \in [-0.07.0.07]$. The available actions are {Neutral, West, East, South, Nourth}. The Neutral action has no impact on the velocity of the car. The West and East actions add -0.001 and 0.001 to v_x respectively, while South and North add -0.001 and 0.001 to v_y respectively. Additionally, in order to simulate the effect of gravity, at each time step, $-0.0025 * \cos 3x$ and $-0.0025 * \cos 3y$ is added to v_x and v_y respectively. Each episode starts with the car at the bottom of the basin. The goal state is reached when $x \geq 0.5$ and $y \geq 0.5$. At each time step, the agent receives a reward of -1. In this work we use the mountain car software[1] that is based on version 3.0 of the RL-Glue library[2] [9].

4.2   Setup

After thorough experimentation we concluded to a set of parameters for the MBPI agent in the source task. We set ϵ to 0.5 decaying by a factor of 0.99, the step-size parameter α to 0.2 and γ, the discounting factor, to 1 as this task is an episodic one.Also, depth d of the MBPI algorithm was set to 1 as [4] show that a greater depth decreases the overall learning performance.

As the standard MBPI algorithms specifies, after every e episodes, training of the networks takes place based on the set of experiences D gathered so far. We set e to 40 episodes. The neural networks produced are compared with the previously used, based on their MSE, finally keeping the best of them.

As our methodology allows for different state and action variables between the source and the target task, we used manual inter-task mappings. For our experimental domain this is successfully done in [11]. Manual mapping of the different actions and states should not be seen as a limitation of the method, as there exist methods that are able to automatically learn these mappings [12]. Table 1 presents the inter-task mapping that we used in our experiments.

Table 1. Inter-task Mappings used by TiMRLA to construct target task instances from source task data

3D action	2D action	3D variable	2D variable
Neutral	Neutral	x	x
North	Right	v_x	v_x
East	Right	y	x
South	Left	v_y	v_x
West	Left		

For the model-based learning part of the algorithm, we got the best results by setting the model-based policy improvement period to 1, which means that policy improvement takes place in every episode. The iterations n were set to 2000, and e and the step-size parameter a, was set to 0 (greedy) and 0.07 respectively. The above values of the parameters are those who gave us the best results.

---

[1] Available at http://library.rl-community.org/
[2] Available at http://glue.rl-community.org/

Finally, for the optional part of our algorithm that specifies the Action Determinant, we run the experiments for both versions of TiMRLA, with and without Action Determinant (TiMRLA+AD).

Both versions of the TiMRLA agent were compared with the standard Sarsa(λ) with a CMAC function approximator. In order to isolate and evaluate the effect of transferring the source model, the two agents had exactly the same parameters for learning from real experiences, with ϵ set to 0.5 , a to 0.2 and γ to 1.

5   Results and Discussion

Figure 2 presents the average cumulative reward that is obtained by each algorithm against the learning episodes.

The graphs were produced from 20 independent trials per method and with a smoothing-averaging window of 20 episodes for clarity purposes. They show a clear performance gain of the proposed algorithm TiMRLA over the standard model-free agent, which is also statistically significant at $p < 0.05$ (one-tail t test). Its performance demonstrates the positive effect of transferring a model from a source task and also that this model can still assist learning even after many episodes.

Clearly, TiMRLA+AD, shows a more unstable performance having a slight performance gain at the start that decreases gradually after 300 episodes. Its average reward difference with the standard model-free agent is still statistically significant at p<0.05 but for the first 400 episodes. This feature for model based assisting in the action selection, although promising, needs major adjustments such as proper decaying of its influence that will allow the method to positively influence learning in the beginning and gradually decrease its effect.

Furthermore we calculated the mean predictive accuracy of the mountain car 2D model. The mean euclidean distance of a real afterstate s' to the predicted one was 0.018 for the state variables x and y.

For the simulated experiences, it is important to note that the best results were obtained with policy improvement taking place in every episode. This shows us that the models succeeded in producing real-like experiences that were positively influencing the learning algorithm just like complementary steps. Although that, the tuned value for the step-size parameter was 0.07 being less than that used for the real experiences which was set to 0.2. This can be seen as a reasonable consequence of using approximate models since they are error prone and can produce at times, errors that could negatively alter the learning procedure.

Finally, an interesting finding is that the best results were obtained with the simulated actions ϵ parameter set to zero. We hypothesize that the model-based learning part, favours greedy action selection because the agent explores anyway by just being placed at random start states. This sub-optimal placing is the exploration mechanism in the agent's mental experiences, and he balances by implementing greedy action selection.

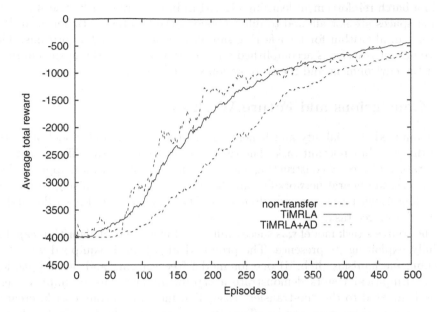

Fig. 2. Average reward in a period of 500 episodes. The curves are smoothed with a window of 20 episodes.

6   Related Work

This section presents related work in transfer learning and contrasts it with the proposed approach. For a broader review of transfer learning in reinforcement learning domains the reader can refer to a comprehensive survey of the field [10].

Fernadez and Veloso [2] propose an approach that reuses past policies from solved source tasks to speed up learning in the target task. A restriction of this approach is that the tasks (source and target) must have the same action and state space. Our method allows the state and action spaces to be different between the target and the source task.

Advice based methods have been proposed in [13,15]. Taylor and Stone [13] proposed a method that uses a list of learned rules from the source task as advice, to guide the learning procedure in the target task. The authors introduce three different utilization schemes of the advice. Furthermore, Torrey et al. [15] export rules in first-logic order and translate them into advices.

Taylor et al. [14] proposed a method, named *Transfer via inter-task mappings*, that initializes the weights of the target task, using the learned weights of the source task, by utilizing mapping functions. The method depends strongly on the function approximation scheme that is used in both tasks, as the function that transfers the weights is altered according to the approximation method.

The transfer of samples have also been proposed in [11,5]. Lazaric et al. [5] proposed a method that uses samples gathered in the source task, in order to train a batch reinforcement learning algorithm in the target task. The state and action spaces are not allowed to differ between the two tasks. Taylor et al. [11] present an algorithm for transferring samples in model-based algorithms. The procedure of transfer is accomplished on-line, that is, when the agent interacts with the environment and the state-action space can change.

7   Conclusions and Future Work

We examined the viability and benefits of transferring the full model of a task to a different but relevant task. The tasks are allowed to have different actions and state variables by constructing and using the right inter-task mappings. The use of cascade neural networks in an RL scheme showed promising results by providing us with accurate enough models of the transition and reward function of the the source task.

The source's task model was successfully used from a novel algorithm capable of fully exploiting its presence. The proposed algorithm is equipped with two learning mechanisms (hybrid) one for model-free learning and one for model-based. Empirical results demonstrate a significant performance improvement when compared to the "no-transfer" case. The model of a source task, created with supervised learning, can be efficiently used in a standard model-free learning algorithm either through a model-based add-on module, or directly, with approaches such as that of Reward Shaping. Moreover concurrent learning with the two mechanisms can be compatible as also feasible and efficient.

Proposals for future work include the evaluation of the method with the use of different model-based algorithms and the improving, upon our design, of the model-free learning mechanism with the use of more sophisticated forms of Reward Shaping. Also, the development of new hybrid learning algorithms may further demonstrate the advantages of this approach. Finally, a lot of work has to be done in the field of trustworthy and informative evaluation metrics, in the context of transfer learning for Reinforcement Learning.

References

1. Albus, J.S.: A new approach to manipulator control: The cerebellar model articulation controller (cmac). Journal of Dynamic Systems, Measurement, and Control 97, 220 (1975)
2. Fernández, F., Veloso, M.: Probabilistic policy reuse in a reinforcement learning agent. In: 5th International Joint Conference on Autonomous Agents and Multiagent Systems, pp. 720–727 (2006)
3. Gullapalli, V., Gullapalli, V., Barto, A.G.: Shaping as a method for accelerating reinforcement learning. In: Proceedings of the 1992 IEEE International Symposium on Intelligent Control, pp. 554–559. IEEE, Los Alamitos (1992)
4. Kalyanakrishnan, S., Stone, P., Liu, Y.: Model-based reinforcement learning in a complex domain (2008)
5. Lazaric, A., Restelli, M., Bonarini, A.: Transfer of samples in batch reinforcement learning. In: ICML 2008: Proceedings of the 25th International Conference on Machine Learning, pp. 544–551 (2008)

6. Moore, A.: Variable resolution dynamic programming: Efficiently learning action maps in multivariate real-valued state-spaces. In: Proceedings of the Eighth International Conference on Machine Learning (1991)
7. Rivest, F., Precup, D.: Combining td-learning with cascade-correlation networks (2003)
8. Singh, S.P., Sutton, R.S.: Reinforcement learning with replacing eligibility traces. Machine Learning 22(1-3), 123–158 (1996)
9. Tanner, B., White, A.: Rl-glue: Language-independent software for reinforcement-learning experiments. Journal of Machine Learning Research 10, 2133–2136 (2010)
10. Taylor, M., Stone, P.: Transfer learning for reinforcement learning domains: A survey. Journal of Machine Learning Research 10, 1633–1685 (2009)
11. Taylor, M.E., Jong, N.K., Stone, P.: Transferring instances for model-based reinforcement learning. In: Daelemans, W., Goethals, B., Morik, K. (eds.) ECML PKDD 2008, Part II. LNCS (LNAI), vol. 5212, pp. 488–505. Springer, Heidelberg (2008)
12. Taylor, M.E., Kuhlmann, G., Stone, P.: Autonomous transfer for reinforcement learning. In: AAMAS 2008: Proceedings of the 7th International Joint Conference on Autonomous Agents and Multiagent Systems, pp. 283–290 (2008)
13. Taylor, M.E., Stone, P.: Cross-domain transfer for reinforcement learning. In: ICML 2007: Proceedings of the 24th International Conference on Machine Learning, pp. 879–886 (2007)
14. Taylor, M.E., Stone, P., Liu, Y.: Transfer learning via inter-task mappings for temporal difference learning. Journal of Machine Learning Research 8, 2125–2167 (2007)
15. Torrey, L., Shavlik, J., Walker, T., Maclin, R.: Skill acquisition via transfer learning and advice taking. In: Fürnkranz, J., Scheffer, T., Spiliopoulou, M. (eds.) ECML 2006. LNCS (LNAI), vol. 4212, pp. 425–436. Springer, Heidelberg (2006)

Anomaly Detection from Network Logs Using Diffusion Maps

Tuomo Sipola, Antti Juvonen, and Joel Lehtonen*

Department of Mathematical Information Technology
University of Jyväskylä, Finland
{tuomo.sipola,antti.juvonen}@jyu.fi, joel.lehtonen@iki.fi

Abstract. The goal of this study is to detect anomalous queries from network logs using a dimensionality reduction framework. The fequencies of 2-grams in queries are extracted to a feature matrix. Dimensionality reduction is done by applying diffusion maps. The method is adaptive and thus does not need training before analysis. We tested the method with data that includes normal and intrusive traffic to a web server. This approach finds all intrusions in the dataset.

Keywords: intrusion detection, anomaly detection, n-grams, diffusion map, data mining, machine learning.

1 Introduction

The goal of this paper is to present an adaptive way to detect security attacks from network log data. All networks and systems can be vulnerable to different types of intrusions. Such attacks can exploit e.g. legitimate features, misconfigurations, programming mistakes or buffer overflows [15]. This is why *intrusion detection systems* are needed. An intrusion detection system gathers data from the network, stores this data to logfiles and analyzes it to find malicious or anomalous traffic [19]. Systems can be vulnerable to previously unknown attacks. Because usually these attacks differ from the normal network traffic, they can be found using anomaly detection [2].

In modern networks clients request and send information using queries. In HTTP traffic these queries are strings containing arguments and values. It is easy to manipulate such queries to include malicious attacks. These injection attacks try to create requests that corrupt the server or collect confidential information [18]. Therefore, it is important to analyze data collected from logfiles.

An *anomaly* is a pattern in data that is different from the well defined normal data [2]. In network data, this usually means an intrusion. There are two main approaches for detecting intrusions from network data: *misuse detection* and *anomaly detection* [19]. Misuse detection means using predefined attack signatures to detect the attacks, which is usually accurate but detecting new types of

---

* Now with C2 SmartLight Oy.

L. Iliadis and C. Jayne (Eds.): EANN/AIAI 2011, Part I, IFIP AICT 363, pp. 172–181, 2011.

attacks is not possible. In anomaly detection the goal is to find actions that some-how deviate from normal traffic. This way it is possible to detect previously un-known attacks. However, not all anomalous traffic is intrusive. This means there might be more false alarms. Different kinds of machine learning based methods, such as self-organizing maps and support vector machines, have been used in anomaly detection [20,23]. Information about other anomaly detection methods can be found in the literature [19]. *Unsupervised anomaly detection* techniques are most usable in this case, because no normal training data is required [2].

This study takes the approach of dimensionality reduction. Diffusion map is a manifold learning method that maps high-dimensional data to a low-dimensional diffusion space [5]. It provides tools for visualization and clustering [6]. The basic idea behind any manifold learning method is the eigen-decomposition of a similarity matrix. By unfolding the manifold it reveals the underlying structure of the data that is originally embedded in the high-dimensional space [1]. Diffusion maps have been applied to various data mining problems. These include vehicle classification by sound [21], music tonality [10], sensor fusion [12], radio network problem detection [25] and detection of injection attacks [8]. Advantages of this approach are that the dimensionality of the data is reduced and that it can be used unsupervised [2].

2   Method

2.1   Feature Extraction

First let us define an n-gram as a consecutive sequence of n characters [7]. For example, the string *ababc* contains unique 2-grams *ab*, *ba* and *bc*. The 2-gram *ab* appears twice, thus having frequency of 2. A list of tokens of text can be represented with a vector consisting of n-gram frequencies [7]. Feature vector describing this string would be $x_{ababc} = [2, 1, 1]$. The only features extracted are n-gram frequencies. Furthermore, syntactic features of the input strings might reveal the differences between normal and anomalous behavior. Computed n-grams can extract features that describe these differences.

The frequencies are collected to a feature matrix X whose rows correspond to lines in logfiles and columns to features. These n-gram frequencies are key-value fields, variable-length by definition. Key strings are ignored and 2-grams are produced from each parameter value. The count of occurrences of every occurring 2-gram is summed. In practice n-gram tables produced from real-life data are very sparse, containing columns in which there are only zero occurrences. To minimize the number of columns, the processing is done in two passes. If a column contains no variation between entries, that column is not present in the final numeric matrix X. That makes it reasonable to use diffusion maps to process n-gram tables directly with no further preprocessing.

2.2   Dimensionality Reduction

The number of extracted features is so large that dimensionality reduction is performed using diffusion maps. It is a manifold learning method that embeds the original high-dimensional space into a low-dimensional diffusion space. Anomaly detection and clustering are easier in this embedded space [6].

The recorded data describe the behavior of the system. Let this data be $X = \{x_1, x_2, \ldots, x_N\}, x_i \in \mathbb{R}^n$. Here N is the number of samples and n the dimension of the original data. In practice the data is a $N \times n$ matrix with features as columns and each sample as rows.

At first, an affinity matrix W is constructed. This calculation takes most of the computation time. The matrix describes the distances between the points. This study uses the common Gaussian kernel with Euclidean distance measure, as in equation 1 [6,16].

$$W_{ij} = \exp\left(-\frac{\|x_i - x_j\|^2}{\epsilon}\right) \tag{1}$$

The affinity neighborhood is defined by ϵ. Choosing the parameter ϵ is not trivial. It should be large enough to cover the local neighborhood but small so that it does not cover too much of it [21].

The rows of the affinity matrix are normalized using the diagonal matrix D, which contains the row sums of the matrix W on its diagonal.

$$D_{ii} = \sum_{j=1}^{N} W_{ij} \tag{2}$$

P expresses normalization that represents the probability of transforming from one state to another. Now the sum of each row is 1.

$$P = D^{-1}W \tag{3}$$

Next we need to obtain the eigenvalues of this transition probability matrix. The eigenvalues of P are the same with the conjugate matrix in equation 4. The eigenvectors of P can be derived from $\tilde{P}$ as shown later.

$$\tilde{P} = D^{\frac{1}{2}}PD^{-\frac{1}{2}} \tag{4}$$

If we substitute the P in equation 4 with the one in equation 3, we get the symmetric probability matrix $\tilde{P}$ in equation 5. It is called the normalized graph Laplacian [4] and it preserves the eigenvalues [16].

$$\tilde{P} = D^{-\frac{1}{2}}WD^{-\frac{1}{2}} \tag{5}$$

This symmetric matrix is then decomposed with singular value decomposition (SVD). Because $\tilde{P}$ is a normal matrix, spectral theorem states that such a matrix is decomposed with SVD: $\tilde{P} = U\Lambda U^*$. The eigenvalues on the diagonal of $\Lambda = \mathrm{diag}([\lambda_1, \lambda_2, \ldots, \lambda_N])$ correspond to the eigenvalues of the same matrix $\tilde{P}$ because it is symmetric. Matrix $U = [u_1, u_2, \ldots, u_N]$ contains in its columns the N eigenvectors u_k of $\tilde{P}$. Furthermore, because $\tilde{P}$ is conjugate with P, these two matrices share their eigenvalues. However, to calculate the right eigenvectors v_k of P, we use equation 6 and get them in the columns of $V = [v_1, v_2, \ldots, v_N]$ [16].

$$V = D^{-\frac{1}{2}}U \tag{6}$$

The coordinates of a data point in the embedded space using eigenvalues in Λ and eigenvectors in V are in the matrix Ψ in equation 7. The rows correspond to the samples and the columns to the new embedded coordinates [6].

$$\Psi = V\Lambda \tag{7}$$

Strictly speaking, the eigenvalues should be raised to the power of t. This scale parameter t tells how many time steps are being considered when moving from data point to another. Here we have set it $t = 1$ [6].

With suitable ϵ the decay of the spectrum is fast. Only d components are needed for the diffusion map for sufficient accuracy. It should be noted that the first eigenvector v_1 is constant and is left out. Using only the next d components the diffusion map for original data point x_i is presented in equation 8. Here $v_k(x_i)$ corresponds to the ith element of kth eigenvector [6].

$$\Psi_d : x_i \rightarrow [\lambda_2 v_2(x_i), \lambda_3 v_3(x_i), \ldots, \lambda_{d+1} v_{d+1}(x_i)] \tag{8}$$

This diffusion map embeds the known point x_i to a d-dimensional space. Dimension of the data is reduced from n to d. If desired, the diffusion map may be scaled by dividing the coordinates with λ_1.

2.3   Anomaly Detection

After obtaining the low-dimensional presentation of the data it is easier to cluster the samples. Because spectral methods reveal the manifold, this clustering is called spectral clustering. This method reveals the normal and anomalous samples [13]. Alternatively, k-means or any other clustering method in the low-dimensional space is also possible [17]. Another approach is the density-based method [25].

Only the first few low-dimensional coordinates are interesting. They contain most of the information about the manifold structure. We use only the dimension corresponding to second eigenvector to determine the anomaly of the samples. At 0, this dimension is divided into two clusters. The cluster with more samples is considered normal behavior. Conversely, the points in the other cluster are considered anomalous [22,11,13]. The second eigenvector acts as the separating feature for the two clusters in the low-dimensional space. The second eigenvalue is the solution to the normalized cut problem, which finds small weights between clusters but strong internal ties. This spectral clustering has probabilistic interpretation: grouping happens through similarity of transition probabilities between clusters [22,14].

3   Results

3.1   Data Acquisition

The data is acquired from a large real-life web service. The logfiles contain mostly normal traffic, but they also include anomalities and actual intrusions. The logfiles are from several Apache servers and are stored in *combined log format*. Listing below provides an example of a single logline. It includes information about the user's IP-address, time and timezone, the HTTP request including used resource and parameters, Apache server response code, amount of data sent to the user, the web page that was requested and used browser software.

```
127.0.0.1 - - [01/January/2011:00:00:01 +0300]
"GET /resource?parameter1=value1&parameter2=value2 HTTP/1.1"
200 2680 "http://www.address.com/webpage.html"
"Mozilla/5.0 (SymbianOS/9.2;...)"
```

The access log of a web site contains entries from multiple, distinct URLs. Most of them point to static requests like images, CSS files, etc. We are not focused to find anomalies at those requests because it is not possible to inject code via static requests unless there are major deficiencies in the HTTP server itself. Instead, we are focused in finding anomalies from dynamic requests because those requests are handled by the Web application, which is run behind the HTTP server.

To reach this goal, the access log entries are grouped by the resource URL. That is the part between host name and parameters in the HTTP URL scheme. Those resources containing only HTTP GET requests with no parameters are ignored. Each remaining resource is converted to a separate numerical matrix. In this matrix, a row represents a single access log entry, and a column represents an extracted feature.

Feature extraction is done in two passes. In the first pass the number of features is determined, and in the second pass the resulting matrix is produced. In our study we extracted the number of occurrences of 2-grams produced from HTTP GET parameters. These frequencies are normalized with logarithm in order to scale them. This ensures that the distances between the samples are comparable.

3.2   Data Analysis

To measure the effectiveness of the method the data is labeled so that classification accuracy can be measured. However, this labeling is not used for training the diffusion map. The class labels are not input for the method.

Diffusion map reveals the structure of the data, and all the anomalies are detected. The n-gram features of the data are mapped to a lower dimensions. Figure 1 shows the resulting low-dimensional diffusion space with $\epsilon = 100$. The normal behavior lies in the dense area to the lower right corner. Anomalous points are to the left of 0.

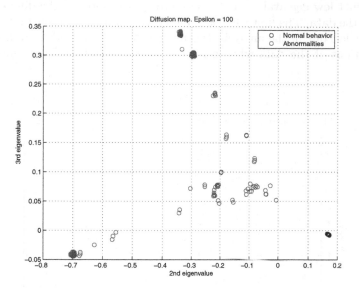

Fig. 1. Two-dimensional diffusion map of the dataset

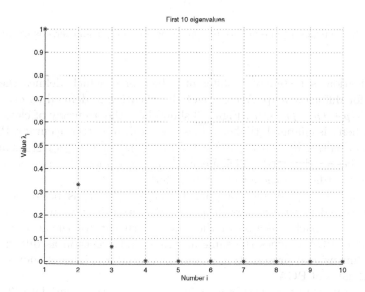

Fig. 2. Eigenvalues of transition matrix with $\epsilon = 100$

Figure 2 shows that the eigenvalues converge rapidly with $\epsilon = 100$. This means that the first few eigenvalues and eigenvectors cover most of the differences observed in the data. The first value is 1 and corresponds to the constant eigenvector that is left out in the analysis. Eigenvalues $\lambda_2 = 0.331$ and $\lambda_3 = 0.065$ cover large portions of the data when compared to the rest that have values below 0.005.

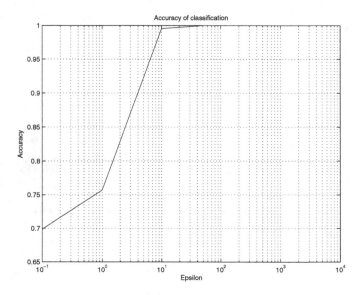

Fig. 3. Accuracy of classification changes when the parameter ϵ is changed

Classification is tested with different values of ϵ, which defines the neighborhood for diffusion map. Accuracy of classification is defined as $accuracy = (tp + tn)/(tp + fp + fn + tn)$. Figure 3 shows how the accuracy of classification changes when ϵ is changed. Higher values of ϵ result in better accuracy. Precision of classification is defined $precision = tp/(tp + fp)$. The precision stays at 1 once any anomalies are detected, which means that all the anomalies detected are real anomalies regardless of the accuracy [9, p. 361].

For comparison, principal component analysis (PCA) is performed on the same normalized feature matrix [9, p. 79]. Results are very similar to the diffusion map approach, because of the simple structure of the feature matrix. Furthermore, PCA reaches the same accuracy and precision as diffusion map. The low-dimensional presentation is also very similar. Figure 4 shows the first two coordinates of PCA.

We also apply support vector machines (SVM) to the same data [9, p. 337–344]. LIBSVM implementation is used [3]. We use one-class SVM with RBF kernel function. A subset of the data is used in the model selection for SVM (500 lines randomly selected). Then the rest of the data is used to test the method.

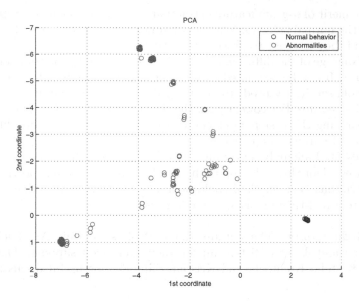

Fig. 4. PCA of the dataset, first two coordinates. The Y-axis of this figure has been reversed for better visual comparison with diffusion map.

The data labels are unknown, so the training data is not "clean" and contains some intrusions as well. It is possible to find the right parameters (ν and γ) for model selection if pre-specified true positive rate is known. The parameters which give a similar cross-validation accuracy can be selected [3]. However, this kind of information is not available. Fully automatic parameter selection for OC-SVM could be achieved by using more complicated methods, such as evolving training model method [24]. In this study the parameter selection is done manually. At best the accuracy is 0.999 and precision 0.998.

4   Conclusion

The goal of this study is to find security attacks from network data. This goal is met since all the known attacks are found. The proposed anomaly detection scheme could be used for query log analysis in real situations. In practice the boundary between normal and anomalous might not be as clear as in this example. However, the relative strangeness of the sample could indicate how severe an alert is.

The diffusion map framework adapts to the log data. It assumes that the data lies on a manifold, and finds a coordinate system that describes the global structure of the data. These coordinates could be used for further analysis of characteristics of anomalous activities.

Because all the methods perform extremely well, the data in question is rather sparse and the discriminating features are quite evident from the feature matrix.

This is the merit of n-gram feature extraction which creates a feature space that separates the normal behavior in a good manner. The features describe the data clearly, and they are easy to process afterwards.

One advantage of the diffusion map methodology is that it has only one meta-parameter, ϵ. It can be estimated with simple interval search. If for some reason the threshold sensitivity needs to be changed, ϵ gives the flexibility to adapt to the global structure. For comparison, the SVM we used has two parameters, ν and γ. Searching the best parameters for the application gets more difficult as the number of parameters increases.

The presented anomaly detection method performs well on real data. As an unsupervised algorithm this approach is well suited to finding previously unknown intrusions. This method could be applied to offline clustering as well as extended to a real-time intrusion detection system.

Acknowledgements. The authors thank Professors Amir Averbuch, Timo Hämäläinen and Tapani Ristaniemi for their continued support. Thanks are extended to Juho Knuuttila and Kristian Siljander for useful discussions and ideas.

References

1. Bengio, Y., Delalleau, O., Roux, N.L., Paiement, J.F., Vincent, P., Ouimet, M.: Spectral Dimensionality Reduction. In: Feature Extraction. Studies in Fuzziness and Soft Computing, pp. 519–550. Springer, Heidelberg (2006)
2. Chandola, V., Banerjee, A., Kumar, V.: Anomaly detection: A survey. ACM Comput. Surv. 41(3), 1–58 (2009)
3. Chang, C.C., Lin, C.J.: LIBSVM: a library for support vector machines (2001), http://www.csie.ntu.edu.tw/~cjlin/libsvm
4. Chung, F.R.K.: Spectral Graph Theory, p. 2. AMS Press, Providence (1997)
5. Coifman, R.R., Lafon, S., Lee, A.B., Maggioni, M., Nadler, B., Warner, F., Zucker, S.W.: Geometric diffusions as a tool for harmonic analysis and structure definition of data: Diffusion maps. Proceedings of the National Academy of Sciences of the United States of America 102, 7426 (2005)
6. Coifman, R.R., Lafon, S.: Diffusion maps. Applied and Computational Harmonic Analysis 21(1), 5–30 (2006)
7. Damashek, M.: Gauging similarity with n-grams: Language-independent categorization of text. Science 267(5199), 843 (1995)
8. David, G.: Anomaly Detection and Classification via Diffusion Processes in Hyper-Networks. Ph.D. thesis, Tel-Aviv University (2009)
9. Han, J., Kamber, M.: Data mining: concepts and techniques. Morgan Kaufmann, San Francisco (2006)
10. İzmirli, Ö.: Tonal-atonal classification of music audio using diffusion maps. In: 10th International Society for Music Information Retrieval Conference (ISMIR 2009) (2009)
11. Kannan, R., Vempala, S., Vetta, A.: On clusterings: Good, bad and spectral. J. ACM 51, 497–515 (2004)
12. Keller, Y., Coifman, R., Lafon, S., Zucker, S.: Audio-visual group recognition using diffusion maps. IEEE Transactions on Signal Processing 58(1), 403–413 (2010)

13. von Luxburg, U.: A tutorial on spectral clustering. Statistics and Computing 17, 395–416 (2007)
14. Meila, M., Shi, J.: Learning segmentation by random walks. In: NIPS, pp. 873–879 (2000)
15. Mukkamala, S., Sung, A.: A comparative study of techniques for intrusion detection (2003)
16. Nadler, B., Lafon, S., Coifman, R., Kevrekidis, I.G.: Diffusion maps – a probabilistic interpretation for spectral embedding and clustering algorithms. In: Barth, T.J., Griebel, M., Keyes, D.E., Nieminen, R.M., Roose, D., Schlick, T., Gorban, A.N., Kégl, B., Wunsch, D.C., Zinovyev, A.Y. (eds.) Principal Manifolds for Data Visualization and Dimension Reduction. Lecture Notes in Computational Science and Engineering, vol. 58, pp. 238–260. Springer, Heidelberg (2008)
17. Ng, A.Y., Jordan, M.I., Weiss, Y.: On spectral clustering: Analysis and an algorithm. In: Advances in Neural Information Processing Systems, vol. 14, pp. 849–856. MIT Press, Cambridge (2001)
18. Nguyen-Tuong, A., Guarnieri, S., Greene, D., Shirley, J., Evans, D.: Automatically hardening web applications using precise tainting. In: Sasaki, R., Qing, S., Okamoto, E., Yoshiura, H. (eds.) Security and Privacy in the Age of Ubiquitous Computing. IFIP AICT, vol. 181, pp. 295–307. Springer, Boston (2005)
19. Patcha, A., Park, J.: An overview of anomaly detection techniques: Existing solutions and latest technological trends. Computer Networks 51(12), 3448–3470 (2007)
20. Ramadas, M., Ostermann, S., Tjaden, B.: Detecting anomalous network traffic with self-organizing maps. In: Vigna, G., Krügel, C., Jonsson, E. (eds.) RAID 2003. LNCS, vol. 2820, pp. 36–54. Springer, Heidelberg (2003)
21. Schclar, A., Averbuch, A., Rabin, N., Zheludev, V., Hochman, K.: A diffusion framework for detection of moving vehicles. Digital Signal Processing 20(1), 111–122 (2010)
22. Shi, J., Malik, J.: Normalized cuts and image segmentation. IEEE Transactions on Pattern Analysis and Machine Intelligence 22(8), 888–905 (2000)
23. Tran, Q., Duan, H., Li, X.: One-class support vector machine for anomaly network traffic detection. China Education and Research Network (CERNET) (2004)
24. Tran, Q.A., Zhang, Q., Li, X.: Evolving training model method for one-class svm. In: IEEE International Conference on Systems, Man and Cybernetics, vol. 3, pp. 2388–2393 (2003)
25. Turkka, J., Ristaniemi, T., David, G., Averbuch, A.: Anomaly detection framework for tracing problems in radio networks. In: Proc. to ICN 2011 (2011)

Large Datasets: A Mixed Method to Adapt and Improve Their Learning by Neural Networks Used in Regression Contexts

Marc Sauget[1], Julien Henriet[1], Michel Salomon[2],
and Sylvain Contassot-Vivier[3]

[1] Femto-ST, ENISYS/IRMA, F-25210 Montbéliard Cedex, France
[2] LIFC, EA 4269, University of Franche-Comté,
BP 527, F-90016 Belfort Cedex, France
[3] LORIA, UMR CNRS 7503, University Henri Poincaré Nancy-1, France
marc.sauget@univ-fcomte.fr

Abstract. The purpose of this work is to further study the relevance of accelerating the Monte-Carlo calculations for the gamma rays external radiotherapy through feed-forward neural networks. We have previously presented a parallel incremental algorithm that builds neural networks of reduced size, while providing high quality approximations of the dose deposit [4]. Our parallel algorithm consists in an optimized decomposition of the initial learning dataset (also called learning domain) in as much subsets as available processors. However, although that decomposition provides subsets of similar signal complexities, their sizes may be quite different, still implying potential differences in their learning times. This paper presents an efficient data extraction allowing a good and balanced training without any loss of signal information. As will be shown, the resulting irregular decomposition permits an important improvement in the learning time of the global network.

Keywords: Pre-clinical studies, Doses Distributions, Neural Networks, Learning algorithms, External radiotherapy, Data extraction.

1 Introduction

The work presented in this paper takes place in a multi-disciplinary project called *Neurad* [1], involving medical physicists and computer scientists whose goal is to enhance the treatment planning of cancerous tumors by external radiotherapy [12]. The final objective of our work is to propose a new tool to evaluate the result of an external radiotherapy treatment. In our previous works [2,4], we have proposed an original approach to solve scientific problems whose accurate modeling and/or analytical description are/is difficult. A short review of this problem is described in [10]. One of the major originality of that work is to use a Monte-Carlo simulator to build a very accurate dataset instead of measured data [6] (less accurate and sparser).

L. Iliadis and C. Jayne (Eds.): EANN/AIAI 2011, Part I, IFIP AICT 363, pp. 182–191, 2011.

More precisely, the *Neurad* project proposes a new mechanism to simulate the dose deposit during a clinical irradiation. Our method consists in using a set of neural networks (one per processor), which act as universal approximators, in combination with a specific computational code. Each neural network predicts the dose delivered in a homogeneous environment on a subdomain of the domain to be treated, whereas a specific algorithm expresses the rules to manage any heterogeneous environment. The feasibility of this original project has been clearly established in [12]. It was shown that our approach results in an accuracy similar to the Monte-Carlo one and fulfills the time constraints of the external radiotherapy evaluation. The accuracy of a neural network is a crucial issue; therefore it is the subject of many research works on neural network learning algorithms.

The main idea of our work is to improve the performance of our incremental learning algorithm [3,4] by an efficient decomposition of the learning set. We have already proposed an optimized decomposition method based on an evaluation of the signal complexities of each data subset [17]. This approach provides subsets of similar signal complexities, however these subsets may have different sizes. So, although that decomposition offers a better homogeneity in the learning times of the subsets than classical decompositions, it can still be enhanced. A way to further improve the learning step is to work on the subsets sizes. More precisely, the work presented thereafter is motivated by the following question:

> "*If two data sets have the same complexity, why do they not have the same number of data samples?*".

2   Extraction of a Representative Set from Massive Data

Our study deals with the construction of a representative dataset from a larger database, in order to train a neural network. The data samples have the following characteristic: they are usually regularly spaced and often they contain statistical noise. These samples could not be used directly to obtain an efficient data learning. Indeed, the larger is the dataset, the longer is the learning time. When the dataset is too large, the neural network behaves more like a database with a low generalization (interpolation) capacity. In our first studies we have removed the statistical noise, but the limits of this approach were rapidly reached. Therefore, we are now looking for a method that limits the size of the dataset and captures the salient characteristics of the original dataset to be approximated.

There are many solutions in the literature to limit the size of a dataset. In particular, Jankowski and Grochowski present in [8,11] a state of the art of these methods in the context of neural networks used for classification. On the one hand they describe solutions that filter data to remove noise and on the other hand, they present ones doing data selection based on a good value repartition or using a mask. Another solution is to keep only the most homogeneous data to build the dataset [7,9]. However, those solutions are not fully adapted to neural networks used as universal approximators where the data must reflect the signal on the entire domain while preserving the sharp variations. In the classifier

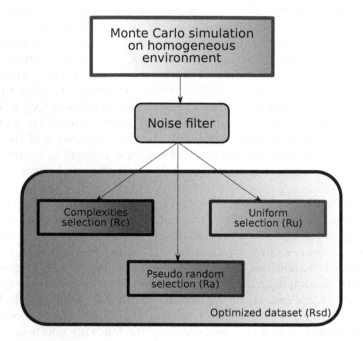

Fig. 1. A mixed selection method for optimized dataset decomposition

context, the most important data are at the frontiers between the different data classes and their accuracy must be preserved whereas other parts can be sparser and less accurate.

In this paper, we present an innovative method to select data samples based on the combination of two existing solutions together with a selection based on the complexities (see Fig. 1). As shown in the following, the proposed method is designed for neural networks used as approximators. The interest of this method is to improve the learning time thanks to a suitable selection of the data samples, leading to an optimized dataset decomposition. That approach prevents over-fitting due to the presence of useless noising data and reduces the computational cost of the learning step [19].

2.1   Conservation of the Global Aspect of the Signal

The general aspect of the signal could be easily guaranteed by the use of a uniform grid applied to the ranges of the dataset. The first tool used to build our dataset is very simple: the position of the new uniform grid is evaluated and we select the corresponding samples to build the subset R_u. The resolution of that grid could be quite low because its only interest is to constrain the learning on the global aspect of the signal. Its particularities will be taken into account by another group of data samples selected according to their complexities.

2.2   Conservation of the Particularities of the Signal

The most difficult point during the learning phase of a neural network used as a universal approximator is to keep its general aspect without forgetting the quality of interpolation in local areas having an important gradient value. The equilibrium between these two parts is always difficult to preserve. The solution presented here consists in only selecting the most important values taking into account their local complexity. Our notion of *data complexity* has already been presented in [17]. We recall here that, in order to evaluate the local complexity $lC_{i,j}$ at spatial point (i,j), we use the variations between that point and a given set of its neighbors (x,y), each of them being distance weighted. So, the local complexity at point (i,j) has the following form:

$$lC_{i,j} = \sum_{x=i-r}^{i+r} \sum_{y=j-r,(x,y)\neq(i,j)}^{j+r} \frac{|f(x,y) - f(i,j)|}{||\overrightarrow{(x,y)} - \overrightarrow{(i,j)}||} \tag{1}$$

where parameter r defines the size of the neighborhood taken into account.

The algorithm used to select n points is described in Algorithm 1. This algorithm evaluates the complexities of every point according to (1) and produces a decreasing order sorted list. Once the list is built, the algorithm returns a subset of the initial dataset composed of the n most characteristic points. The resulting subset corresponds to the R_c data subset.

Algorithm 1. Most particular points selection

Require: Dataset viewed as elements set $E = \{e_1, e_2, \dots\}$,
    $|E| = m$, and $n < m$ is the number of points to select.

1: $R_c = \{\}$, $R_p = \{\}$
2: **for** i = 1 to m **do**
3:    c = evaluateComplexity(e_i)
4:    decreasingOrderInsertion(e_i, c, R_p)
5: **end for**
6: append($R_c, R_p\{1, n\}$)
7: **return** R_c

2.3   Homogeneous Density of the Complexity Classes

The combination of the two previous methods does not ensure that the obtained dataset provides an optimal learning. In [15], the authors have shown for a neural network used as a classifier that a dataset is composed of a few sets of data samples with the same complexity. They called such a set a class and also showed that the different classes should have the same density (number of samples).

In our case, the neural network is used as an approximator, so the data samples values are just discretized to define the complexity classes induced by a dataset.

Hence, we firstly compute the complexity classes considering the data samples that compose subsets R_u and R_c. Secondly, once the classes are identified, new data samples are selected from the initial dataset to complete the classes that are not sufficiently represented. The objective is to obtain classes with similar densities, in order to respect the quality constraint. The new data samples selected to complete R_u and R_c are chosen with a classical random method, they define the data subset R_a.

2.4   Global Building of the Dataset

To obtain each dataset affected to a single processor, more precisely a subset of the global dataset, the process is as follows.

Firstly, the initial global dataset is decomposed in p subsets, where p is the number of available processors, using our URB based decomposition described in [17]. Since the resulting decomposition is irregular, the subsets have different sizes. In order to have similar sizes, we impose that all the subsets (R_{sd}) have N data samples: the size of the smaller subset in the decomposition. Obviously, this last subset keeps all its data samples, while in the remaining $p - 1$ subsets, some data samples must be discarded.

The second step, which reduces the size of the larger R_{sd} subsets, uses the three methods previously described to select for each of them the N data samples that will be retained. In fact, R_u, R_c, and R_a are computed for each subset R_{sd} such that these data subsets have each N data samples. Then, the reduced subset R_{sd} is built by picking elements from its corresponding sets R_u, R_c, and R_a, according to the respective proportions α, β and γ, such that:

$$\alpha = \frac{\|R_{sd} \cap R_u\|}{N}, \quad \beta = \frac{\|R_{sd} \cap R_c\|}{N}, \quad \gamma = \frac{\|R_{sd} \cap R_a\|}{N} \qquad (2)$$

where $\alpha + \gamma + \beta = 1$. In a first approach, similar ratios might be used ($\alpha = \gamma = \beta = 1/3$), but this choice could not be retained because R_a is not a real data subset. Indeed, its main interest is to guarantee the equilibrium between the complexity classes. 20% of the data subset R_a (γ) are sufficient and necessary to balance the complexities. The most important data are provided by R_u, thus 50% of the data samples from R_{sd} are selected in it. Finally, the remaining samples correspond to the 30% (β) most characteristic ones in R_c.

Once the p data subsets of N samples have been built, they are learned using our fault-tolerant parallel algorithm [4].

3   Experimental Results

In this section, both quality and performance of our approach are experimentally assessed. Our algorithm has been implemented in standard C++ with Open-MPI [14] for the parallel part. All the experiments have been performed using the computing resources from the *Mesocenter of Franche-Comté* [13]: a cluster consisting of 8-core nodes (two Intel Xeon Nehalem quad-core processors) with 12GB RAM.

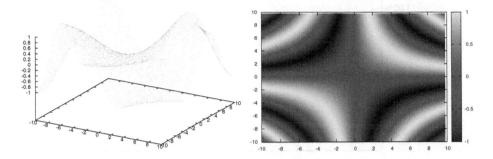

Fig. 2. Synthetic dataset generated from the function: $f(x,y) = sin(0.1 * x * y)$

3.1   Generic Function

The objective of our method is to provide an accurate learning using only a selection of samples from a large dataset. To perform a first evaluation, we have built a synthetic dataset using a generic 2D function given in Fig. 2. The dataset is composed of 10000 points uniformly distributed over the two dimensions.

We have evaluated the training times to obtain the desired accuracy of learning in two cases. In the former case, the domain decomposition method presented in [4] has been used with the entire dataset. In the latter case, a filtered version of the dataset has been used. The decomposition method allows us to obtain different subdomains with a relative similarity of complexities. We have also chosen to limit the size of each data subset using as reference the size of the smaller subset obtained with the decomposition mechanism. Several dataset decompositions have been tested and for each one we give the average size of the data subsets.

The results are presented in Table 1. They show the average learning time of the subdomains for each decomposition, as well as the standard deviation. This last information allows us to check the good balancing of the training times between the subdomains. Finally, the last column indicates the speedup between the average learning time obtained with the full dataset and the one obtained with the filtered one. We show with this first test the good performance of our data subset reduction method: an average speedup value of 3 can be observed. Furthermore, the speedup remains almost constant, whatever the decomposition degree used. This observation can be explained by the structure of the function, since it presents only a few parts with important gradient values which are also regularly distributed on the studied domain. Let us notice that the cumulative size of all the subdomains resulting from a decomposition is greater than the size of the initial global dataset (10000 samples in this case). Indeed, to ensure a homogeneous quality of the results of our parallel algorithm [4] throughout the global domain, each subdomain must have a small overlapping area with all its neighbors, thus some data samples belong to several subdomains.

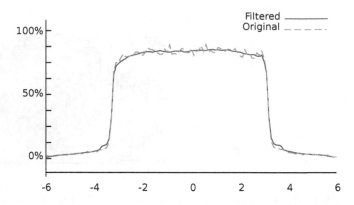

Fig. 3. The impact of the filtering step

3.2   Radiotherapy Context

In the radiotherapy context, we use data resulting from a Monte-Carlo simulation that represents an irradiation in a homogeneous environment. The first part is the evaluation of the initial dataset obtained with a Monte-Carlo simulator [5]. These data are very dense and quite noisy. To enhance the learning process, a first treatment is used to limit the negative impact of the noise, as shown in Fig. 3. We use a simple filter to reduce the noise. Figure 4 presents a comparative view of the original data and the final data obtained from our selection process. These curves correspond to the dose deposit for a single material. The next step is the learning process. The neural networks obtained after the learning phase are then used in conjunction with a specific algorithm to compute the result of an irradiation in any kind of environment, potentially heterogeneous [18].

To evaluate the behavior of our algorithm, we have chosen a restricted learning set. This configuration allows us to verify the interest of our algorithm without requiring a very long learning time. In fact, we have chosen to use only two materials (tissue and bones) and one configuration of irradiation. Since we use a grid of 120×100 points, the dataset is obviously composed of 120×100×2 samples. Each sample is characterized by seven components: the position in the three spatial dimensions; the material density; its distance from the irradiation source and the beam width (minimum and maximum values).

Table 1. Performances of the learning phase for the generic function

Subdomains	Original dataset			Selective dataset			Speedup
	Size	Average times (s)	SD	Size	Average times (s)	SD	
4	2962	393	92	1155	131	14	3.0
8	1591	173	61	519	59	5	2.9
16	846	92	37	221	29	3	3.1

Table 2. Performances of the learning phase for the dose deposit curves

Subdomains	Original dataset			Selective dataset			Speedup
	Size	Average times (s)	SD	Size	Average times (s)	SD	
4	14520	1054	887	7258	297	84	3.5
8	4249	541	611	3035	113	17	4.7
16	3546	276	371	846	055	11	5.0

The tests have be performed with different decomposition degrees to evaluate the accuracy of the learning and to determine the limits of our solution. The objective of this work is to reduce the time of the learning step without affecting the final quality. So, the learning time is the essential parameter to take into account to validate our dataset construction. In all cases, the given times are only the learning times, they do not include any other data manipulation. The training stops when the specified accuracy is reached.

Table 2 shows the average learning time for each training case, as well as the standard deviation. As for the generic function in the previous subsection, this last information allows us to check the good balancing of the subdomains training times. Note that the load balancing is a very important parameter because it indicates the degree of use of all the computing resources during the training step. These results, together with the speedup information, show that the use of a selected dataset efficiently improves the learning time without inducing any significant accuracy loss (controlled during the learning process). So, we obtain in all cases a good speedup (values ranging from 3 to 5) with a very good improvement (reduction) of the standard deviation. We can also notice that with real data, like the radiotherapy case, the speedup is not as regular as in the previous case, with the generic function. We explain this difference by the fact that the parts of the dose deposit curves that exhibit an important gradient are less regularly distributed (as it was the case for the generic function). Thus, as one could expect, the size of the data subsets is not the only parameter having an impact on the learning time.

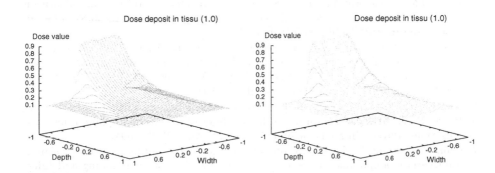

Fig. 4. General aspect of the dose deposit curves (left: original set, right: selected points)

4 Conclusion and Future Work

In this paper, we have presented a simple and efficient method to build an optimized learning dataset from data produced by a physical simulation. Thanks to this method, both data size and noise can be reduced without loosing any information. Hence, this approach significantly reduces the learning times without impacting the final quality.

Qualitative and quantitative evaluations of the algorithm have been performed experimentally on artificial and real datasets. The use of an artificial dataset points out that this method is not restricted to the specific radiotherapy context. The tests with real datasets confirm the good behavior of our algorithm, whether in terms of quality or performance, for complex datasets. The low standard deviation values show that the method gives well-balanced decompositions, and consequently smaller learning times.

In the following of the *Neurad* project, it will be necessary to test our different algorithms in real conditions, which means with complete datasets required in the medical operational context. A training using a full dataset, as well as a dose deposit calculation in real 3D images will allow us to fully validate our project.

Acknowledgements. The authors thank the LCC (Ligue Contre le Cancer) for the financial support, the Franche-Comté county and the APM (Agglomération du Pays de Montbéliard).

References

1. Bahi, J.M., Contassot-Vivier, S., Makovicka, L., Martin, E., Sauget, M.: Neurad. Agence pour la Protection des Programmes. No: IDDN.FR.001.130035.000.S.P.2006.000.10000 (2006)
2. Bahi, J.M., Contassot-Vivier, S., Makovicka, L., Martin, É., Sauget, M.: Neural network based algorithm for radiation dose evaluation in heterogeneous environments. In: Kollias, S.D., Stafylopatis, A., Duch, W., Oja, E. (eds.) ICANN 2006. LNCS, vol. 4132, pp. 777–787. Springer, Heidelberg (2006)
3. Bahi, J.M., Contassot-Vivier, S., Sauget, M.: An incremental learning algorithm for functional approximation. Advances in Engineering Software 40(8), 725–730 (2009), doi:10.1016/j.advengsoft.2008.12.018
4. Bahi, J.M., Contassot-Vivier, S., Sauget, M., Vasseur, A.: A parallel incremental learning algorithm for neural networks with fault tolerance. In: Palma, J.M.L.M., Amestoy, P., Daydé, M.J., Mattoso, M., Lopes, J.C. (eds.) VECPAR 2008. LNCS, vol. 5336, pp. 174–187. Springer, Heidelberg (2008)
5. BEAM-nrc: NRC of Canada, http://www.irs.inms.nrc.ca/BEAM/beamhome.html
6. Blake, S.W.: Artificial neural network modelling of megavoltage photon dose distributions. Physics in Medicine and Biology 49, 2515–2526 (2004)
7. Chu, C.K., Deng, W.S.: An interpolation method for adapting to sparse design in multivariate nonparametric regression. Journal of Statistical Planning and Inference 116(1), 91–111 (2003)
8. Grochowski, M., Jankowski, N.: Comparison of instance selection algorithms ii. results and comments. In: Rutkowski, et al. [16], pp. 580–585

9. Guo, G., Zhang, J.S., Zhang, G.Y.: A method to sparsify the solution of support vector regression. Neural Comput. Appl. 19(1), 115–122 (2010)

10. Haas, O., Goodband, J.: Artificial Neural Networks in Radiation Therapy. In: Intelligent and Adaptive Systems in Medicine. Series in Medical Physics and Biomedical Engineering, pp. 213–258. Taylor & Francis, Abington (2008)

11. Jankowski, N., Grochowski, M.: Comparison of instances seletion algorithms i. algorithms survey. In: Rutkowski, et al. [16], pp. 598–603

12. Makovicka, L., Vasseur, A., Sauget, M., Martin, E., Gschwind, R., Henriet, J., Salomon, M.: Avenir des nouveaux concepts des calculs dosimétriques basés sur les méthodes de Monte Carlo. Radioprotection 44(1), 77–88 (2009),
    http://dx.doi.org/10.1051/radiopro/2008055

13. Computing Mesocenter of Franche-Comté, http://meso.univ-fcomte.fr

14. Open Source High Performance Computing, http://www.open-mpi.org

15. Pan, F., Wang, W.: Finding representative set from massive data. Tech. rep., IEEE International Conference on Data Mining (2005)

16. Rutkowski, L., Siekmann, J.H., Tadeusiewicz, R., Zadeh, L.A. (eds.): ICAISC 2004. LNCS (LNAI), vol. 3070. Springer, Heidelberg (2004)

17. Sauget, M., Laurent, R., Henriet, J., Salomon, M., Gschwind, R., Contassot-Vivier, S., Makovicka, L., Soussen, C.: Efficient domain decomposition for a neural network learning algorithm, used for the dose evaluation in external radiotherapy. In: Diamantaras, K.I., Duch, W., Iliadis, L.S. (eds.) ICANN 2010, Part I. LNCS, vol. 6352, pp. 261–266. Springer, Heidelberg (2010)

18. Vasseur, A., Makovicka, L., Martin, E., Sauget, M., Contassot-Vivier, S., Bahi, J.M.: Dose calculations using artificial neural networks: a feasibility study for photon beams. Nucl. Instr. and Meth. in Phys. Res. B 266(7), 1085–1093 (2008)

19. Wu, A., Hsieh, W.W., Tang, B.: Neural network forecasts of the tropical pacific sea surface temperatures. Neural Networks 19(2), 145–154 (2006), earth Sciences and Environmental Applications of Computational Intelligence

Evolutionary Algorithm Optimization of Edge Delivery Sites in Next Generation Multi-service Content Distribution Networks

Ioannis Stephanakis[1] and Dimitrios Logothetis[2]

[1] Hellenic Telecommunication Organization S.A. (OTE),
99 Kifissias Avenue, GR-151 24, Athens, Greece
stephan@ote.gr
[2] Ericsson Hellas S.A., 40.2 km Attica Avenue
GR-190 02, Peania, Greece
dimitris.logothetis@ericsson.com

Abstract. In the past decade or so we have been experiencing an extraordinary explosion of data volumes first in wireline networks and recently even in mobile wireless networks. Optimizing bandwidth utilization is critical for planning and deploying efficient networks that are capable of delivering new services like IPTV over cost-oriented implementations. Models of distributed content caching in the access network have been employed - for example - as analytical optimization tools in order to tackle associated problems. A modified *capacitated quality-of-service network* (QoS) model is proposed herein in order to optimize the placement of the sites of surrogate media servers (central offices-COs) on the access part of a content distribution network (CDN). The novelty of the proposed approach lies in the fact that *capacitated quality-of-service network* optimization is cast as an optimization problem over two rather than one optimization variables-objectives. Implementation cost and link delay as determined by capacity/utilization requirements are the optimization functionals-objectives. Optimization of the network architecture is carried out via a multiobjective evolutionary algorithm that encodes all possible edges between the first level aggregation points of the access network. Proper priorities are assigned to different types of traffic according to class of service. Two main services are considered, namely live broadcast/IPTV and video on demand services (VoD). The media servers/COs are incorporated into the infrastructure of the access nodes in a step-by-step fashion modifying the traffic requirements between source and sink nodes of the optimal configurations of the access network. The evolution of the Pareto front is investigated in each case.

Keywords: content distribution networks, multiobjective optimization, evolutionary algorithms, capacitated minimum spanning tree, quality of service.

1 Introduction

In the past decade or so we have been experiencing an extraordinary explosion of data volumes first in wireline networks and recently even in mobile wireless networks.

L. Iliadis and C. Jayne (Eds.): EANN/AIAI 2011, Part I, IFIP AICT 363, pp. 192–202, 2011.

Technological advances in broadband access technologies, devices and new bandwidth hungry services like IPTV are occasionally cited as explanations to the above mentioned trend. In order to cope with this issue operators are asked to invest in capacity in all parts of the transport network. These investments are not always justified from the underlying revenues from the services. It is therefore of paramount importance for operators to optimize the bandwidth utilization of the underlying transport network by employing techniques like content caching. A next generation network (NGN) is a multi-service functional network, capable to differentiate between users and applications through policies of quality of service (QoS), the application of access and security guidelines and by providing virtual private networks (VPNs) to its users [1]. The NGN is characterized by [2]: (1) support of a wide range of services, applications and mechanisms based on service building blocks (including real time/streaming/non-real time services and multimedia); (2) broadband capabilities with end-to-end QoS and transparency; (3) unrestricted access to different service providers by all users; (4) a variety of identification schemes which can be resolved to IP addresses for the purposes of routing in IP networks, *etc.* A content distribution network (CDN) integrated in currently deployed next generation infrastructure – be it IMS (IP Multimedia Subsystem) core or an MPLS based gigabit router core network - consists of a head-end platform (including the EPG, the encryption-conditional access system, user redirection functionality and the account management-billing system) and a group of cache-media servers (primary servers/Video Hub Offices and surrogate servers/Central and Intermediate Offices that deliver content to users on behalf of content providers). These components are usually owned by the network provider/ISPs whereas local insertion points that multiplex user-created content and advertisements may complete the distribution network [3], [4]. The services offered to the customers are differentiated and include live broadcast/IPTV, video on demand (VoD) and personal video recorder, radio channels, interactive services, multimedia games, teletext and others. Access network may be pure optical or both optical and copper (ADSL/VDSL) based on some FTTx architecture.

Designing a content distribution network (CDN) includes the dimensioning of the head-end platform, decisions regarding the placement and the connections of the cache-media servers, dimensioning of the cache-media servers themselves [5], traffic engineering to accommodate for the offered services [6], [6] and grooming the access network.

1.1 Multiobjective Optimization with Evolutionary Algorithms

Multiobjective optimization is the process of simultaneously optimizing two or more conflicting objectives subject to certain constraints. Evolutionary multiobjective optimization (EMOO) uses evolutionary genetic algorithms - the so-called multiobjective evolutionary algorithms (MOEA) - to tackle such optimization problems [8]. Genetic algorithms (GA) take as inputs populations of genomes representing individual non-optimal solutions scattered across state space. A genome in the context of network design represents a specific topology of node sites and connections between them. New populations are created through mutation and crossover operations (i.e topology variations stemming from one and two parent topologies) in order to gain a different set of possibilities. The fitness of each individual of the population is evaluated and the best individuals are then retained to create new generations of improved solutions. The population will search state space and converge on the best solution over many generations. Multi-objective genetic algorithms optimize against a collection of fitness parameters. Sequential switching objective optimization, aggregation and weighting of all objectives to form a scalar fitness, cooperative fitness sharing of the various objectives, Pareto selection using non-dominated individuals, Pareto simulated annealing and min-max optimization are some of the distinct approaches to multiobjective optimization. Evolutionary algorithms such as the Non-dominated Sorting Genetic Algorithm-II (NSGA-II) [9] and Strength Pareto Evolutionary Approach 2 (SPEA-2) [10] are the state-of-the-art implementations of the aforementioned concepts based upon Pareto optimality [11].

Definition 1. A solution $\mathbf{x} \in \Omega$ is said to be Pareto Optimal with respect to Ω if and only if there is no $\mathbf{x}' \in \Omega$ for which $\mathbf{v} = F(\mathbf{x}') = \left(f_1(\mathbf{x}'), ..., f_k(\mathbf{x}')\right)$ dominates $\mathbf{u} = F(\mathbf{x}) = \left(f_1(\mathbf{x}), ..., f_k(\mathbf{x})\right)$ for the entire variable space.

2 Analytical Formulation

Communication network models include *centralized network models, backbone network models* and *reliable network models*. Core and access networks shall be optimized separately. Access network is usually modeled as a centralized network where all communication is to and from a central site (backbone node). Optimal topology for such a problem corresponds to a tree in a graph $G=(V,E)$ with all but one of the nodes in V corresponding to the terminals/edge nodes. The remaining node refers to the central site and edges in E correspond to the feasible communication wiring. A spanning tree on G is a maximal, acyclic subgraph of G; that is, it connects all of G's nodes and contains no cycles. A spanning tree's cost is the sum of the costs of its edges; a spanning tree with the smallest possible cost is a minimum spanning tree (MST) on G. Terminals/edge nodes may be thought of as the first level aggregation points of the DSLAM multiplexers whereas the root node may be thought of as the second level aggregation point which is part of the backbone core.

The *extended capacitated minimum spanning tree* (cMST) problem is formulated by Lin and Gen [12]. It is modeled using an edge-weighted undirected graph $G=(V,E,Q,U)$ with n nodes and m edges. Its objective is to minimize the communication cost (defined as a kind of performance measures for NGN's QoS) while considering the following constraints: (1) consider the capabilities of the network; (2) different priority for different types of service; (3) dynamic environment [13]. cMST is an NP-hard problem. The proposed approach modifies the aforementioned communication model as follows:

$$\min f = \sum_{(i,j) \in E} \left(\sum_{l=1}^{L} w_l \, \Gamma\left(\min\{0, y_{ij} - u_{ij}\}\right) \right) \tag{1}$$

$$\min z(\mathbf{x}) = \sum_{(i,j)\in E} c_{ij} x_{ij} \tag{2}$$

$$\text{s.t.} \sum_{(i,j)\in E} x_{ij} = n-1 \tag{3}$$

$$\sum_{(i,j)\in A_S} x_{ij} = |S| - 1 \text{ for any set } S \text{ of nodes} \tag{4}$$

$$\sum_{(i,j)\in E} y_{ij} - \sum_{(k,i)\in E} y_{kj} = \begin{cases} q_{st}^l & i = s \\ 0 & i \in V - s, t, \forall\, (s,t) \in q_{s,t}^l, \forall\, l \\ -q_{st}^l & i = t \end{cases} \tag{5}$$

$$y_{ij} \geq 0 \quad \forall\, i,j \tag{6}$$

$$x_{ij} \in \{0,1\}, \quad \forall\, (i,j) \in E \tag{7}$$

where $i,j,k = 1,2,\ldots,n$ are the indices of the nodes and

$n = |V|$: number of nodes

$m = |E|$: number of edges

$q_{st}^l \in \mathbf{Q}$: requirement regarding traffic of type l from souse node s to sink node t

$c_{ij} \in \mathbf{C}$: cost of each edge $(i,j) \in E$

$u_{ij} \in \mathbf{U}$: capacity of edge (i,j)

$w_l \in \mathbf{W}$: priority of type l communication service

$d_{ij} \in \mathbf{D}$: delay of edge (i,j) defined as a performance measure for NGN's QoS,

$$d_{ij} = \sum_l w_l \Gamma(q_{ij}^l - u_{ij})$$

$\Gamma(y_{ij}^l - u_{ij})$: a function for delay definition of service type l

The decision variable x_{ij} indicates whether we select edge (i,j) as part of the chosen spanning tree whereas the decision variable y_{ij} stands for the resulting traffic for the selected requirements at source and sink nodes according to Eq. 5 (note that if variable $y_{ij} > 0$ then $x_{ij} = 1$, else $x_{ij} = 0$).

The sites of the cash-media servers define the source nodes in the access network whereas the terminal/edge nodes stand for the sink nodes. The proposed approach starts by assuming that a cache-media server is incorporated at the central node and solving the optimization problem defined by Eqs. 1 and 2. Additional cache-media servers are placed gradually at intermediate nodes of the optimal topologies. Such nodes are to be thought of as both sink and terminal nodes. Optimization is carried out at successive steps since the traffic requirements q_{st}^l of the edges are modified after separate optimizations. The overall cost $z(\mathbf{x})$ depends upon the capacity of the selected edges u_{ij} and the total number of the cash-media servers incorporated into the access network.

2.1 Scenarios

Each node but the central code is assumed to serve a certain number of active IPTV users. The traffic requirements are determined by the behavior of the active users and the commercial offerings of the provider. The bandwidth allocated to each active user serves for the broadcast of live IPTV, radio and on-line multimedia content of the first priority whereas part of it is allocated to the delivery of best-effort data services including video-on-demand. The central node broadcasts all IPTV and radio channels of the provider platform to the intermediate cache-media servers. Such a traffic requirement is denoted as q^0. Paths from the central node to the intermediate cache-media servers deliver traffic of lower priority as well, which is assumed to be constant and is denoted as q^1. Active users that are not served by intermediate cache-media servers are assigned to the central node. Thus graph G is divided into $K+1$ subgraphs, $G=\{G_0, G_1 \ldots G_K\}$, where K is the number of intermediate cache-media servers and each subgraph represents a subtree structure featuring an intermediate cache-media server at its root. The egress traffic requirements at the root equal the sum of the traffic requirements at its leaves whereas the ingress traffic requirement equals q^0.

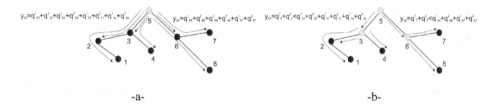

Fig. 1. Sample topologies of cMSTs depicting traffic requirements (a- media delivery site is incorporated to the central node and -b- media delivery sites incorporated to the central and two intermediate nodes).

2.2 Outline of the Algorithm

Several algorithms have been proposed to solve for the optimum cMST. Not all approaches utilize multiobjective optimization models (see for example [15] and [16]). The proposed algorithm utilizes PrimPred encoding of the edges from which the optimum tree may be constructed [14]. Let $P(t)$ and $C(t)$ be parents and offspring in current generation t. The evolutionary multiobjective optimization algorithm is written in Matlab code. It is outlined as follows:

```
Procedure: PrimPred-based GA for capacitated QoS models
Input: network data (V, E, Q, U)
       GA parameters (popSize, maxGen, p_M, p_c)
Output: Pareto optimal solutions E for K intermediate
        media servers
```

```
Begin
    t ← 0 ;
    initialize P(t);
    calculate objectives f(P) and z(P);
    create Pareto E(P);
    evaluate fitness of individuals of P(t);
    while (not terminating condition) do
            create C(t) from P(t) by crossover routine;
            create C(t) from P(t) by mutation routine;
            calculate objectives f(C) and z(C);
            update Pareto E(P,C);
            evaluate fitness of individuals of P(t)∪C(t);
            select P(t+1) from P(t) and C(t)
            t ← t+1 ;
    end
    output Pareto optimal solutions E(P,C)
End
```

2.3 Encoding Schemes for Crossover and Mutation

A recombination operator builds an offspring spanning tree that consists mostly or entirely of the edges found in the offspring's parents. This is accomplished by applying random-tree algorithms to the union of the parent spanning trees, i.e. $G_{cr} = (V, T_1 \cup T_2)$. Mutation reintroduces genetic information into the population. A mutation operator makes a small change in a parent solution usually by replacing an edge of a spanning tree topology with another feasible edge. This may be implemented either by choosing an edge at random from $E\text{-}T$ and introducing it in T or creating two sub-trees and replacing the edge that connects them. The first approach creates a cycle which is resolved by removing a random edge from it.

Several fitness schemes may be accommodated in the context of the proposed algorithm.

2.4 Fitness Considerations

Evaluating the Pareto front does not depend upon the specific fitness scheme that it is used. *Interactive Adaptive-weight Fitness Assignment* evaluates the maximum and the minimum extreme points of the two objectives, i.e. $[f_{max}\ z_{max}]$ and $[f_{min}\ z_{min}]$, and calculates the corresponding adaptive weights $w_1 = \dfrac{f_{max}\, f_{min}}{f_{max} - f_{min}}$ and

$w_2 = \dfrac{z_{max}\, z_{min}}{z_{max} - z_{min}}$. The interactive adaptive-weight fitness assignment for each member of the population is given as,

$$eval(v_k) = w_1(1/f_k - 1/f_{max}) + w_2(1/z_k - 1/z_{max}) + p(v_k), \quad \forall k \in popSize \qquad (8)$$

A penalty $p(v_k)$ is assigned to all dominated solutions.

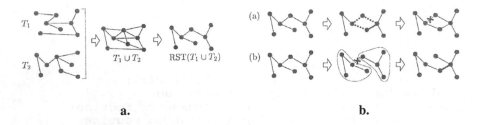

a.   b.

Fig. 2. 2.a. Recombination-crossover of spanning trees (a random spanning-tree algorithm is applied to the union of the parental edge sets) - 2.b. Mutation is implemented either by including a new edge and removing another to avoid cycles or by removing a randomly chosen edge and reconnecting the two subgroups of nodes by a new edge.

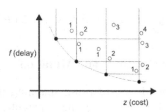

Fig. 3. Non-dominated solutions on the known Pareto front (black circles) and dominated solutions (white circles) in objective space. Each dominated solution is assigned the depicted rank.

3 Numerical Simulations

Numerical simulations are carried out for artificial data. A total of twenty access nodes each aggregating on average twenty DSLAMs is assumed. Links to the closest neighboring nodes are considered as possible edges of the optimum MST solution. Basic link capacity is 10 Gbps. The topology of the nodes is illustrated in Fig. 4. The active users per node are assumed to be 500. Depending upon the requirements set by the provider, the real number of users served by an aggregation node may be significantly higher. The traffic requirements per active user are detailed in Table 1 whereas the delay per link between nodes i and j is derived from queuing theory (see for example [17]) as

$$d_{ij} = \frac{1}{active\ users} \sum_{l=1,2} \Gamma(y_{ij}^l - u_{ij}) = \sum_{l=1,2} \frac{y_{ij}^l}{u_{ij}^l - y_{ij}^l}, \qquad (9)$$

where $u_{ij}^l - y_{ij}^l$ is the unused capacity of the link for traffic of type l (y_{ij}^l) and $\sum_{all\ l} u_{ij}^l = u_{ij}$. A generation consisting from sixty (60) individuals is considered. Evolution is carried out for sixty (60) generations. Crossover probability p_C equals 0.70 whereas mutation probability p_M equals 0.50. One of the optimum solutions on the Pareto front - for the case in which one CO located at the root of the tree is used to service all users - is depicted in Fig. 5. The percentage of the nondominated solutions (*RNDS*) in each generation before selection is presented in Fig. 6.

Table 1. Cost and traffic parameters

Traffic requirements		*Implementation costs*	
Number of active users per node	500	Basic cost per Km of link	20 K€
Traffic of highest priority per active user	20 Mbps	Cost per Km for additional cable of 10 Gbps	1 K€
Packet length for highest priority traffic	2KBytes	Cost per link termination	2 K€
Best effort traffic per active user	10 Mbps	Cost per media server-central office	$(80 + 0.01 \times$ # of active users) K€
Packet length for best effort traffic	500 Bytes		
Traffic requirements between delivery servers	$q_0^1 = 200$ Mbp		
	$q_0^2 = 200$ Mbp		

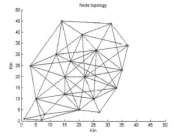

Fig. 4. Distribution of access concentration points and possible links between them (root at x_1=14 Km and x_2=45 Km)

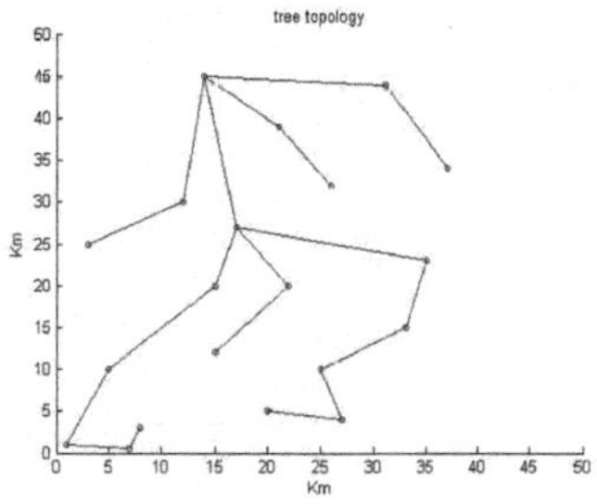

Fig. 5. Solution for one CO on Pareto front after 60 generations (27.70 msec delay per user – cost of access network 6.51 M€)

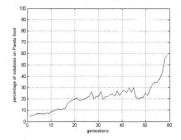

Fig. 6. Percentage of non-dominated solutions vs. generation for the population of parent and children solutions before selection (one CO at root)

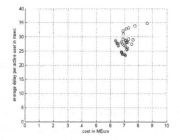

Fig. 7. Distribution of solutions after 60 generations for one CO (circles with crosses indicate solutions on Pareto front)

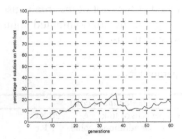
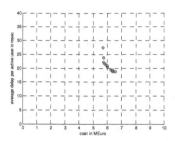

Fig. 8. Percentage of non-dominated solutions vs. generation for the population of parent and children solutions before selection (two COs)

Fig. 9. Distribution of solutions after 60 generations for two COs (circles with crosses indicate solutions on Pareto front)

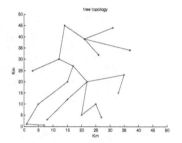
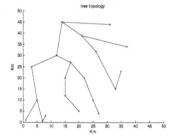

Fig. 10. Solution for two COs on Pareto front after 60 generations (2nd CO at $x_1=17$ Km and $x_2=27$ Km - 22.21 msec delay per user - cost of access network 5.74 M€)

Fig. 11. Solution for four COs on Pareto front after 50 generations (2nd CO at $x_1=17$ Km and $x_2=27$ Km, 3nd CO at $x_1=21$ Km and $x_2=39$ Km, 4nd CO at $x_1=3$ Km and $x_2=25$ Km - 16.07 msec delay per user - cost of access network 5.56 M€)

The Pareto front is moving closer to the origin of the axes for the case in which two COs are used to service all users as illustrated in Fig. 9. The delay per user (as defined in Eq. 9) as well as the implementation cost drop. The percentage of the nondominated solutions (*RNDS*) in each generation before selection is presented in Fig. 8. One of the optimum solutions on the Pareto front for the case of two COs is presented in Fig. 10. The Pareto front for the case of four COs is depicted in Fig. 13. A slight drop of the delay per user as well as of the implementation cost is observed. The percentage of the nondominated solutions (*RNDS*) in each generation for this case is illustrated in Fig. 12 whereas an optimum solution on the Pareto front is given in Fig. 11.

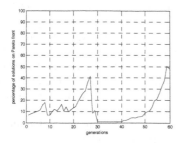

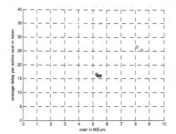

Fig. 12. Percentage of non-dominated solutions vs. generation for the population of parent and children solutions before selection (four COs)

Fig. 13. Distribution of solutions after 60 generations for four COs (circles with crosses indicate solutions on Pareto front)

4 Conclusion

In this paper we investigated the effect of the placement of COs in order to ensure optimal delivery of content related services. By employing multi-objective techniques based on evolutionary algorithms we are able to show through numerical simulations that the use of multiple CO at the access network results in cost-effective implementations and IPTV services of higher quality and enhanced end-user experience (as measured by the delay per user or -alternative- the time of buffer occupation per user for given user bandwidths). Nevertheless the total number of COs that is needed to facilitate the aforementioned advantages depends up the total number of active users and the bandwidth requirements per user. No significant improvements in implementation costs are observed for more than six COs in the examined cases.

References

1. Pioro, M., Medhi, D.: Routing, Flow and Capacity Design in Communication and Computer Networks
2. Sun, W.: QoS/Policy/Constraint Based Routing. Technical Report, Ohio State University (1999)
3. Hofmann, M., Tomsu, M. (eds.): Special Issue on Content Networking. Bell Labs Techn. J. 13(3) (2008)
4. Verhoeyen, M., Vleeschauwer, D.D., Robinson, D.: Content Storage Architectures for Boosted IPTV Service. Bell Labs Techn. J. 13(3), 29–43 (2008)
5. Krogfoss, B., Sofman, L.B., Agrawal, A.: Hierarchical Cache Optimization in IPTV Networks. In: IEEE International Symposium on Broadband Multimedia Systems and Broadcasting (BMSB 2009), Barselona, Spain, pp. 1–10 (2009)
6. Borst, S., Saniee, I., Walid, A.: Analytical Model for Provisioning of Emerging Personalized Content Distribution Services. In: Proc. of the ITC 21. LNCS. Springer, Paris (2009)
7. Sofman, L.B., Krogfoss, B., Agrawal, A.: Dimensioning of Active Broadcast Channels in Access IPTV Network. In: Optical Fiber Communication Conference (OFC), Anaheim, California (2006)

8. Deb, K.: Multi-Objective Optimization using Evolutionary Algorithms. Wiley, Chichester (2002)
9. Deb, K., Pratap, A., Agarwal, S., Meyarivan, T.: A Fast and Elitist Multiobjective Genetic Algorithm: NSGA II. IEEE Trans. on Evolutionary Computation 6(2), 181–197 (2002)
10. Zitzler, E., Laumanns, M., Thiele, L.: SPEA2: Improving the Strength Pareto Evolutionary Algorithm. In: Giannakoglou, K., Tsahalis, D., Periaux, J., Papailou, P., Fogarty, T. (eds.) Evolutionary Methods for Design, Optimization and Control with Applications to Industrial Problems, EUROGEN 2001, Athens, Greece, pp. 95–100 (2001)
11. Coello Coello, C.A., Lamont, G.B., Van Veldhuizen, D.A.: Evolutionary Algorithms for Solving Multi-Objective Problem, 2nd edn. Springer, Heidelberg (2007)
12. Lin, L., Gen, M.: An Evolutionary Algorithm for Improvement of QoS of Next Generation Network in Dynamic Environment. Artificial Neural Networks In Engineering, St. Louis, USA (2007)
13. Gen, M., Cheng, R., Lin, L.: Network Models and Optimization: Multiobjective Genetic Algorithm Approach
14. Raidl, G., Julstrom, B.: Edge Sets An Effective Evolutionary Coding of Spanning Trees. IEEE Trans. Evolutionary Computation 7(3), 225–239 (2003)
15. Lee, Y.J., Atiquzzaman, M.: Exact Algorithm for Delay-Constrained Capacitated Minimum Spanning Tree Network. IET Commun. 1(6), 1238–1247 (2007)
16. Gamvros, I., Golden, B., Raghavan, S.: The Multilevel Capacitated Minimum Spanning Tree Problem. INFORMS Journal on Computing 18(3), 348–365 (2006)
17. Zheng, Y., Akhtar, S.: Networks for computer scientist and engineers, pp. 364–372. Oxford University Press, Oxford (2000)

Application of Neural Networks to Morphological Assessment in Bovine Livestock

Horacio M. González-Velasco, Carlos J. García-Orellana,
Miguel Macías-Macías, Ramón Gallardo-Caballero,
and Antonio García-Manso

CAPI Research Group
Politechnic School, University of Extremadura
Av. de la Universidad, s/n. 10003 Cáceres - Spain
horacio@capi.unex.es

Abstract. In conservation and improvement programs of bovine livestock, an important parameter is morphological assessment, which consist of scoring an animal attending to its morphology, and is always
performed by highly-qualified staff.

We present in this paper a system designed to help in morphological
assessment, providing a score based on a lateral image of the cow. The
system consist of two main parts. First, a feature extractor stage is used
to reduce the information of the cow in the image to a set of parameters (describing the shape of the profile of the cow). For this stage, a
model of the object is constructed by means of point distribution models
(PDM), and later that model is used in the searching process within each
image, that is carried out using genetic algorithms (GAs). Second, the
parameters obtained are used in the following stage, where a multilayer
perceptron is trained in order to provide the desired assessment, using
the scores given by experts for selected cows.

The system has been tested with 124 images corresponding to 44
individuals of a special rustic breed, with very promising results, taking
into account that the information contained in only one view of the cow
is not complete.

1 Introduction

As for the control and conservation of purity in certain breeds of bovine livestock,
European legislation imposes the creation of *herd-books*, records of the information stored about existing animals of the above-mentioned race. *Morphological
assessment* is one of the parameters that are stored on those *herd-books* for each
pure-bred animal, and will be of great importance for many tasks that are done
with them. In general, the morphological assessment consist of scoring an animal considering its external morphology (hence is also known as *conformational
evaluation* or *external evaluation*) and the similarity of its characteristics to the
standard of the race. This score is usually settled between 0 and 100 points,
and is conducted by highly–qualified and experienced staff (which are known as

L. Iliadis and C. Jayne (Eds.): EANN/AIAI 2011, Part I, IFIP AICT 363, pp. 203–208, 2011.

assessors or, more generally, experts). This personnel must behave in a "neutral way" and they have to be trained in a centraliced manner in order to maintain the criteria.

There are several methods to carry out the morphological assessment, usually considering measurable traits and traits directly evaluated by visual inspection [7]. However, with rustic meat-producing breeds, normally breeded in extensive farms, morphological assessment is only based in visual inspection. This method consist of scoring ten traits, each one including several aspects of the standard of the race (see table 1). Those traits are assessed with a continuous value between 1 and 10 points, and the global score is obtained by a weighted sum of the partial scores. The weights are determined by the characteristics of the breed and the objectives to be reached with its control and selection. This is the method applied for the breed considered in this work. A similar method, but in other context, is described in [3].

Table 1. Traits to be individually assessed for the considered breed. The weights for the final sum are included.

Trait to be assessed	Weights (males)	Weights (females)
General aspect and figure	1.6	1.6
Development of the body	1.2	1.2
Head	0.5	0.5
Neck, chest, withers and back	0.5	0.4
Thorax and belly	1.0	1.0
Back and loins	1.5	1.3
Hindquarters and tail	1.2	1.3
Thighs and buttocks	1.3	1.3
Extremities	0.7	1.0
Genital organs	0.5	—
Shape and quality of the udder	—	0.5

With this method, it is worrisome the great amount of subjectivity involved in morphological assessment. This together with the need of uniformity in criteria, leads us to consider the utility of a semiautomatic system to help morphological assessment, as already discussed in [7]. In this work, as well as in the information received from the consulted experts it is suggested that the assessment could be done quite accurately using three pictures corresponding to three positions of the cow (frontal, lateral and rear), and fundamentally analyzing the profiles of the animal in those images. In this paper we present a first approach to an automatic morphological assessment system, based on images of only one of the views: the lateral position.

The proposed method has a classical structure in two stages. First, a feature extraction is performed on the image, with the aim of representing the profile of the cow with a reduced set of parameters. Later, using this parameters, a supervised neural network system is trained with samples of assessments made by the experts. This way, their knowledge about assessment can be *extracted* and their assessments can be approximately reproduced.

For the first stage we use a method based on point distribution models (PDM) [2] and genetic algorithms (GAs) [4,8], and its aim is to parameterize and extract the contours of the animals in the images. The contours are parameterized by means of PDM, and this parametrization is used, along with a potential image generated from the original colour image, to carry out an efficient search with GAs, as described in [5,6]. Later, in the second stage, we propose to use the contours extracted for a selected set of cows, and the assessments made by experts for that cows, to train a supervised neural network (a multilayer perceptron [1]). Once the neural network is trained, the complete system can provide an assessment for each image presented at its input.

In section 2 the technique used to search the contours within the images is summarized. Next, section 3 provides details about the neural network used and the training method. The results obtained by applying the whole system to a set of images can be found in section 4, whereas our conclusions and possible improvements or our work are presented in section 5.

2   First Stage: Image Analysis

The contour extraction problem can be converted into an optimization problem considering two steps: the parametrization of the shape we want to search and the definition of a cost function that quantitatively determines whether or not a contour is adjusted to the object. The general outline of the system used is shown in figure 1. As illustrated, for the contour modelling and parametrization the PDM technique [2] has been applied, which lets us restrict all the parameters and precisely define the search space. On the other hand, the objective function proposed is designed to place the contour over areas of the image where edges corresponding to the object are detected. A detailed description of this image analysis stage can be consulted in [5,6].

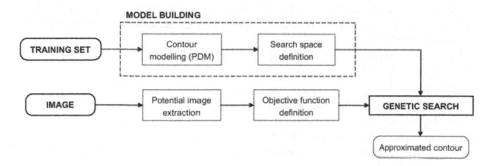

Fig. 1. General outline of the contour location system using genetic algorithms

3   Second Stage: Neural Network

Once the contour of the animal in the image has been located and parameterized, a system is needed to provide an assessment as a function of those parameters. Though our contours are characterized by 14 parameters (the transformation (s, θ, t) and 10 shape parameters b_i, see [6]), we discarded four of them (s, θ, t_x and t_y) because they provide information about the position of the animal within the image, but not about the morphology of them. Hence, we use the vector b as input for a multilayer perceptron [1], with one hidden layer, ten neurons at the input and one neuron at the output, which gives us the value for the assessment.

In order to train the network we have a database of images of cows whose morphological assessment made by experts is known. After splitting this set of data into two subsets (training and validation), the training is carried out using the backpropagation algorithm with momentum, and stops when the mean squared error (MSE) obtained over the validation set goes through a minimum. Later, we repeat this process by increasing the network size and we chose the new configuration as optimal if the MSE over the validation set is lower than the previous one.

4   Experiments and Results

We made experiments to test both stages of our system. On one hand we wanted to determine the performance of the image analysis stage. On the other hand, we intended to find out about the ability of the system to reproduce the assessments of the experts.

4.1   First Stage

We tested our method with 79 images (640x480 pixels size) from our database, to determine the performance of the system with and without fixed points and to compare results. In order to evaluate quantitatively a resulting contour, the mean distance between its points and their proper position has been proposed as a figure of merit. In our case, the distance was estimated by using only seven very significant points of the contour. Those points were precisely located for all the images in the database.

To test the performance of the method we run the GA search without fixed points and with all the possible combinations of one and two fixed points, over the 79 images. In order to define "success", we applied a hard limit of ten pixels to the distance, what we consider enough for the morphological assessment in which these contours are to be used. As a result we obtained that without fixed points the rate of success was 61.3 %, but with two fixed points, in the best of the cases (fixing significant points corresponding to the limbs) the rate of success reached 95.7 %. However, there was also another case where, fixing 2 points, we obtained only a 58 % of successes. These results indicate that the help of fixed points is very important for the system, but also that the points to be fixed must be well-selected by the operator.

4.2   Second Stage: Assessment

In order to test de morphological assessment system, and considering that we do not have a great amount of data, we have followed a *leave-one-out* strategy. For each of the 118 images (for which we had the contour extracted) we randomly divided the remaining 117 into two subsets: training and validation. Using this subsets, networks were trained with a number of neurons in the hidden layer between 5 and 40, and we selected the one offering the best results. Finally, the contour from the original image was introduced to the network in order to be assessed, and the result was compared with the assessment provided by the expert, to generate the absolute error.

Table 2. Mean and standard deviation of the absolute value of the error, for the global score and for the individual aspects

Trait	Description	Mean abs. error	σ
	Global score	5.662	4.048
1	General aspect and figure	0.666	0.469
2	Development of the body	0.619	0.484
3	Head	0.768	0.536
4	Neck, chest, withers and back	0.832	0.493
5	Thorax and belly	0.835	0.530
6	Back and loins	0.717	0.528
7	Hindquarters and tail	0.881	0.745
8	Thighs and buttocks	0.809	0.659
9	Extremities	0.671	0.635
10	Shape and quality of the udder	1.235	0.846

This process has been carried out both with the global score and with the individual scores for each of the aspects. In table 2, the mean and the standard deviation of the absolute value of the error are presented, both for the global score and for the individual aspects. As we can see, we obtain a mean error of 5.662 points in the global score with a relatively high sigma, indicating that there is high variability in the errors of the assessments. We think that the causes for these errors are, mainly, two. First, we have included the limbs in the contours, but the position of the limbs can change significantly from one image to another of the same (or different) animal, causing a great difference between the shape parameters of the contours. Also, though many of the traits to be evaluated can be observed in the image of the lateral position, there are others that can not. The clearest example is the trait 10 (shape and quality of the udder), which obtains the highest error, because the udder is not visible in the contour that we have defined.

Anyway, the results can be considered as quite good and promising, because with a partial input information, we obtain a very low error in many cases.

5   Conclusions and Future Research

In this paper, we have presented a system designed to provide a morphological assessment of a cow based on a lateral image of the animal. The system consist in two parts: one dedicated to the analysis of the image and the extraction of the profile of the animal, and the other designed to provide a score, given the parameterized contour. As we have shown, the first part performs very well with a little human intervention (fixing points), reaching a 95 % of successes. The second stage, based on a neural network, has also given very promising results, taking into account that not all the information required for the morphological assessment can be observed in one view of the animal.

In order to improve the method, two lines are being considered at this moment. First, we are considering to include the contours of the rear and frontal views of the cows as inputs to the neural network, complementing the information contained in the lateral view. Also, we intend to eliminate from the profiles all the parts that are affected by a change in the pose of the animal (for instance, the limbs in the lateral position).

Acknowledgements. This work has been supported in part by the *Junta de Extremadura* through projects PDT09A045, PDT09A036 and GRU10018.

References

1. Bishop, C.M., Hinton, G.: Neural Networks for Pattern Recognition. Clarendon Press, Oxford (1995)
2. Cootes, T.F., Taylor, C.J., Cooper, D.H., Graham, J.: Active shape models – their training and application. Comp. Vision and Image Understanding 61(1), 38–59 (1995)
3. Edmonson, A.J., Lean, I.J., Weaver, L.D., Farver, T., Webster, G.: A body condition scoring chart for holstein dairy cows. Journal of Dairy Science 72(1), 68–78 (1989)
4. Goldberg, D.E.: Genetic algorithms in search, optimization and machine learning. Addison-Wesley, Reading (1989)
5. González, H.M., García, C.J., Macías, M., Gallardo, R., Acevedo, M.I.: Application of repeated GA to deformable template matching in cattle images. In: Perales, F.J., Draper, B.A. (eds.) AMDO 2004. LNCS, vol. 3179, pp. 134–145. Springer, Heidelberg (2004)
6. González, H.M., García, C.J., Macías, M., Gallardo, R., Álvarez, F.J.: A method for interactive shape detection in cattle images using genetic algoriths. In: Kropatsch, W.G., Kampel, M., Hanbury, A. (eds.) CAIP 2007. LNCS, vol. 4673, pp. 694–701. Springer, Heidelberg (2007)
7. Goyache, F., Del Coz, J.J., Quevedo, J.R., López, S., et al.: Using artificial intelligence to design and implement a morphological assessment system in beef cattle. Animal Science 73, 49–60 (2001)
8. Haupt, R.L., Haupt, S.E.: Practical Genetic Algorithms 2e. John Wiley, Chichester (2004)

Object Segmentation Using Multiple Neural Networks for Commercial Offers Visual Search

I. Gallo, A. Nodari, and M. Vanetti

University of Insubria, Dipartimento di Informatica e Comunicazione
via Mazzini 5, 21100 Varese, Italy
{ignazio.gallo,angelo.nodari,marco.vanetti}@uninsubria.it

Abstract. We describe a web application that takes advantage of new computer vision techniques to allow the user to make searches based on visual similarity of color and texture related to the object of interest. We use a supervised neural network strategy to segment different classes of objects. A strength of this solution is the high speed in generalization of the trained neural networks, in order to obtain an object segmentation in real time. Information about the segmented object, such as color and texture, are extracted and indexed as text descriptions. Our case study is the online commercial offers domain where each offer is composed by text and images. Many successful experiments were done on real datasets in the fashion field.

Keywords: visual object segmentation, visual search, multiple neural networks.

1 Introduction

In e-commerce applications, information relating to a product are found in the textual description but in many cases it is often difficult to express in words what you want to buy, then it is much easier to choose an object watching the images associated to each commercial offer. In [1,2] many different region-based and semantic CBIR systems, that allow search with sample images, are mentioned. However, a typical search on an e-commerce site should not start with a query based on a sample image, so it is necessary to provide the user with new navigation tools, such as multi-dimensional navigation. Our method extends the common CBIR tecniques using an object class image segmentation strategy in order to combine multi-dimensional navigation and navigation by examples. Object class image segmentation aims to assign predefined class labels to every pixel in an image and therefore is a crucial step in order to find the Object of Interest (OI) in the image and then its basic features required for multidimensional navigation, like color and texture.

Recently, some applications are emerging, specialized in visual search technologies that lets people hunt online for bargains using pictures of clothing, handbags, shoes or other items they might desire. For example Google's acquisition of Like.com, was seen by some as a competitive response to Bing, the

L. Iliadis and C. Jayne (Eds.): EANN/AIAI 2011, Part I, IFIP AICT 363, pp. 209–218, 2011.

Microsoft search engine touted as a "decision engine" for shoppers. These applications are built on sophisticated machine learning and visual recognition technology and for business reasons all the details of their implementations are not revealed, so it is very difficult to make a comparison. As a demonstration of this, in [3] Skopal analyzed all the systems listed at Wikipedia[1], and declares that in many cases information about the technology used in these engines is not available.

In this work we propose a visual search web application, that takes advantage of new computer vision techniques and is deployed in a commercial version named Drezzy[2]. Figure 1 reports a screenshot of the web interface.

Fig. 1. A screenshot of the application made using the method proposed in this article. On the left column an example of color entities identified by the use of the proposed approach. The images shown on the right are the search result obtained by selecting "red" as color and "sweater" as product.

2   The Proposed Application

The basic idea of our application is the segmentation of OI in images associated with commercial offers, using a new technique based on a set of neural networks (see section 2.1). From each segmented object we can extract several information and in this paper we analyze color and texture (see sections 2.2 and 2.3). These visual information is then transformed into a linguistic description. The main advantage of this representation is the possibility in the direct use of indexing and retrieval tools for text mining. Moreover other visual information can be extracted, such as the shape of the object or its subparts.

For the color and texture extraction we used a Machine Learning method, in particular a Support Vector Machine (SVM) with Radial Basis Function (RBF) kernel, as it provides state of the art for many classification problems [4].

---

[1] Wikipedia: List of CBIR engines [Online; accessed 2-April-2011].
[2] www.drezzy.com

2.1 Object Segmentation

In this section we present the object segmentation model used in this application. The model, called Multi-Networks for Object Detection (MNOD), has already presented [5] as a tool for objects detection and is here adapted to the more complex objects segmentation problem. We chose to use a model based on supervised neural networks because neural models have a high generalization ability and good robustness, in this way the same type of performances are always guaranteed varying the classes of objects to be segmented.

The MNOD model consists of a tree of neural networks, where each network uses a sliding window of size W_S to read the features extracted from the input image. Each MNOD node $C_{I_S, W_S}^n (F_1, \ldots, F_m)$ extracts an input pattern for the neural network by concatenating the contents of the sliding window, placed over each resize input image $(F_1, \ldots, F_m)$, according to a second parameter I_S. A real example of configuration created for our application is shown in Figure 6, while in [5] you can find many details on the segmentation process that we have here omitted for lack of space. A node produces in output a soft classification map (segmentation map) where the pixels containing higher values identify the objects of interest. Only the root node of a configuration is interpreted as the segmentation map for a given object class, using a threshold in order to obtain a binary map. In the present work, the structure of a single node consists in a feed-forward Multi-Layer Perceptron (MLP), trained using the Rprop (Resilient Backpropagation) learning algorithm proposed by Riedmiller and Braun [6].

The particular aspect of this model lies in the connection between nodes, which in practice means that the output of a node becomes the input of a parent node. This means that some features of $(F_1, \ldots, F_m)$ could be the output of child nodes. Regarding the tree structure, links between nodes at different levels serves only to indicate which nodes make use of the output of a particular node.

The features set, such as information on edges, color, etc., can be directly extracted from the input images. In this work we used the normalized red ($RN_s = R/(R + G + B)$), green ($GN_s = G/(R + G + B)$) and blue ($BN_s = B/(R + G + B)$), and the Brightness (Br_s) as color features. Information about edges were extracted using a 1-D vertical (EV_s) and horizontal (EH_s) derivative filter (using the mask $[-1, 0, 1]$) and a simplified version of the *Histogram of Oriented Gradient* (HOG) [7] feature descriptors, here Oriented Gradient ($OG_{b,s}$). We first compute the gradient values and then, instead of creating the cell histograms as in [7], we create b input maps dividing the gradient orientations in b intervals. The s parameter, used in all the features, represents the scale at which the input image is resampled, before the feature computation. Figure 2 shows an example of all the features used in this work. Figure 6 shows a real configuration with 4 levels, the figure also shows the segmentation map of the OI identified.

The search space for an optimal configuration of the MNOD is very large because we have to choose the depth of tree, the number of nodes for each level, the best parameters and the features most suitable for each node. To restrict the search space, and make the configuration process much faster, we fix the depth to

Original	Br	BN	GN	RN	$OG_{3,1}$	$OG_{3,1}$	$OG_{3,1}$	EH_1	EV_1

Fig. 2. An example of features extracted for MNOD. The input image is showed on the left. In our experiments, each node can be configured with a subset of this features.

four because we have noticed experimentally that adding more than four layers, the accuracy improves very slightly. In addition, we fix the number of nodes to 4 in the first level and 3 in the two intermediate levels. We have also observed experimentally that using small values of W_S and large I_S values for all the nodes in a layer, alternated by large W_S and small I_S in the subsequent layer, results in a better segmentation accuracy. For this reason, we configure each segmentation model by choosing the parameters for each level between the following subsets $I_S = \{50, 90\}, \{10, 30\}, \{40, 70\}, \{30, 70\}$ and $W_S = \{1, 3\}, \{7, 9\}, \{1, 3\}, \{3, 5\}$, where the first subsets of parameters on the left are for the first level and the last on the right for the output level. To speed up the configuration process we used only nodes pre-configured with the following subsets of features: $C_{I_S,W_S}^n(OG_{b,s})$ choosing $b \in \{3, 5\}$ and $s \in \{1, 0.5, 0.25\}$, or $C_{I_S,W_S}^n(EV_s, EH_s)$ choosing $s \in \{1, 0.5, 0.25\}$, or $C_{I_S,W_S}^n(OG_{b,s}, RN_s, GN_s, BN_s)$ choosing $b \in \{3, 5\}$ and $s \in \{1, 0.25\}$, or $C_{I_S,W_S}^n(OG_{b,s}, Br_s)$ choosing $b \in \{3, 5\}$ and $s \in \{1, 0.5, 0.25\}$.

2.2 Object Colors

Our method, to extract the representative colors from the images, is based on a previous work [8] in which we explained an efficient and innovative approach to represent the information about colors using a textual representation. We have selected 27 representative colors based on the natural language color descriptors derived from the ISCC/NBS system as proposed by the Inter-Society Council[3]. The set of selected colors has been created in order to obtain a significative discretization of the entire RGB color space in this application domain. This set of colors is used to extract the principal colors and their quantity in the image considering all the pixels that belong to the OI identified by the segmentation mask.

The first step consist in an image quantization, associating every RGB pixel of the OI with one of the 27 principal colors. In such a way the result is an histogram of representative colors. As shown in the Figure 3 most of the pixels belonging to the OI are assigned to the color "light gray".

The second step consists in the transformation of the principal colors, taken from the previous step, in a textual description suitable for an efficient indexing. In order to keep the information on the amount of color extracted each color name is repeated in according to its occurrence in the image in such way it is possibile to use, in retrieval, the term frequency as a measurement of color

---

[3] http://www.iscc.org/

Image	Mask	Color Histogram

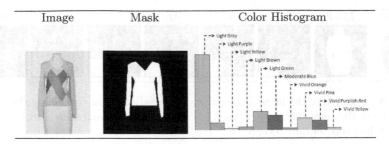

Fig. 3. An example of color extracted from an offer's image in according to the set of pixel belonging to the OI showed in the mask image. The histogram represents the amount of colors contained in the OI. For each histogram's bin the textual descriptor of the representative colors is displayed.

quantity. One of the major problems encountered in color extraction from images arises from the metric adopted to evaluate the distances between colors. The Euclidean distance on the RGB space, or one of its linear transformations, is inadequate to represent the human visual similarity, so we have adopted an approach based on a similarity metric estimated on human visual perception. We have collected a set of 2500 user judgements, every of them represents an association between the RGB space and one of the 27 principal colors selected. Using the collected data, we have trained an SVM which takes in input an RGB value and has in output one of the 27 principal colors. In this way a prediction of the trained SVM corresponds in a quantization of the RGB space in the subset of colors previous explained.

2.3   Object Textures

The texture extraction task is designed as a classification problem. Dealing with a massive amounts of offers, a key requirement of the system is the extraction speed for visual features. The texture classes with wich we deal present strongly spatial oriented patterns, this is why an extremely simple texture descriptor, based on convolution filters, is powerful enough to separate the problem classes.

Processing the original image with a convolution filters bank (see Figure 4), we obtain the maps $M_1, M_2, M_3, M_4, M_5, M_6$ from which the final features are extracted as follows: $f_k^{max} = \sum_{p \in I} \max(0, M_k(p))/|I|$,

$f_k^{min} = \sum_{p \in I} \min(0, M_k(p))/|I|$, with $k \in \{1, 2, 3, 4, 5\}$ and

$f_6 = \sum_{p \in I} \max(0, M_1(p), M_2(p), M_3(p), M_4(p))/|I|$, where I represents the set of points contained in the OI segmentation mask.

The first four maps are obtained using standard edge detection filters (convolution kernels are shown in Figure 4), M_5 is obtained using a custom convolution kernel and M_6 is computed by taking the maximum punctual value from the first 4 maps.

The feature set is small (a total of 11 features), but in our domain contains important visual information able to discriminate the chosen texture classes. An

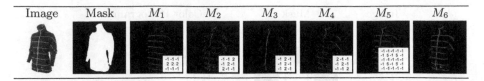

Fig. 4. An example of the input image, the segmentation mask containing the OI and the results of the convolution filters used to extract the texture features, together with corresponding convolution kernels

SVM classifier was trained using the *color-texture* dataset and using a 5-fold auto-configuration strategy to tuning the SVM parameters.

The result of the texture extraction process is a linguistic label that corresponds to the class predicted by the classifier. The label thus obtained will be inserted into the indexing engine.

3   Experiments

The application we propose has been evaluated on different datasets in order to isolate and measure the performance of the three main phases. In a first experiment (see section 3.2) we evaluated the neural segmentation algorithm that underlies the other two following steps. In particular in the section 3.3 we evaluate the automatic extraction of color and in section 3.4 we evaluate the automatic extraction of the main textures. A detailed comparison with other similar segmentation methods available in literature, was done in [5]. The two phases that follow the objects segmentation have been evaluated independently, extracting the information of color and texture only from the pixels belonging to the OI. That means in practice to involve a mask that identifies the object, created by hand for each image in the dataset.

All the tests reported in the following sections were performed using a single thread C# code, on an Intel®Core™2 Duo processor T8100 @2.10Ghz.

3.1   Datasets

Analyzing the literature we realized that there are no image datasets available to evaluate an application that deals with objects segmentation in the fashion field. For this reason we create seven datasets of images, each of which contains images of one of the following categories: *Underwear, Lingerie, Menswear, Womenswear, Tie, Shoe* and *Hat*. Each dataset contains about 200 images, divided into train and test subsets. Figure 7 contains some representative examples of each dataset.

To evaluate the performances in color and texture retrieval we have built the *color-texture* dataset containing nine classes of texture with a wide range of colors, typical in the domain of women's clothing. The texture classes represent the typical decorations found on tissues, in particular we chose horizontal lines (*horiz*), *leopard*, polka dots (*polka*), *rhombus*, *squares*, vertical lines (*vertic*),

horiz	leopard	other	polka	rhombus	color	squares	vertic	zebra

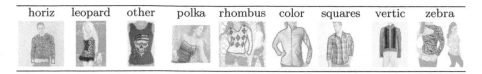

Fig. 5. Image examples taken from the *color-texture* dataset. The OI class was segmented by hand

zebra as texture classes. The solid color (*color*) and *"other"* classes were also been included to represent, respectively, tissues with homogeneous color and with decorative patterns that do not fall into the 7 textures listed above. The images in these datasets were also manually labeled associating at each image the most representative colors. In Figure 5 we show some sample images highlighting the manually segmented OI.

All the images in the datasets used in this work, were taken from the Drezzy application and are available for research purposes[4].

3.2 Object Segmentation

In this experiment we evaluated the performance of our segmentation algorithm by applying it to the seven datasets presented in Section 3.1. In order to evaluate segmentation methods we adopted the VOC2010 [9] perclass measure.

For each of the seven classes we trained an MNOD model using the configuration process described in Section 2.1. An example of MNOD configured for the dataset "Menswear" is shown in Figure 6, which also shows the maps produced by each node for a given input image, and parameters and features with which each node has been configured. Finally, we applied the trained models to the images of each test set and the results are shown in Table 1.

Table 1. Training and test results for all datasets used. Each class of objects was assessed individually by measuring the object (Obj) and background (Bg) accuracy, using the VOC2010 [9] evaluation metric.

Dataset	Obj Train -	Bg Train -	Obj Test -	Bg Test
Underwear	73%	91%	68%	88%
Lingerie	67%	91%	64%	91%
Menswear	79%	83%	73%	79%
Womenswear	64%	85%	57%	83%
Tie	84%	96%	75%	93%
Shoe	81%	94%	69%	87%
Hat	78%	91%	76%	88%

---

[4] http://www.dicom.uninsubria.it/arteLab/dataset.html

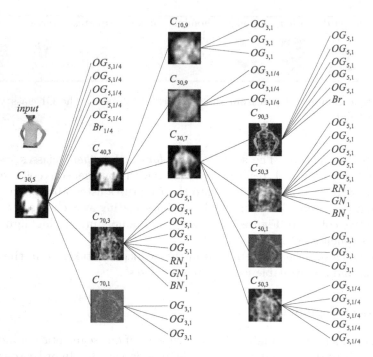

Fig. 6. MNOD configuration used for the dataset "Menswear". The maps produced by each node $C^n_{I_S, W_S}(F_1, \ldots, F_m)$ and the features used in input, all related to the same test image, are showed.

We have obtained high quality segmentation results using the trained MNOD model proposed and in Figure 7 we have included some examples for each image data set. The use of these segmentations facilitates the extraction of visual features such as color, texture, shape, etc.. These results lead to significant advantages in terms of quality of the extracted features, which are related only to the OI and are not influenced by the background. The configuration with the set of constraints established is nearly automatic, and then requires little time. Moreover, numerical results shown in Table 1 show that our algorithm can always be reliable regardless the class of objects on which you choose to work.

The computational complexity of the segmentation algorithm was computed on the seven data sets we used in our experiments. The average time to process a never seen image is $1196ms$. If an image has already been processed it is possible to cache parts of the processed information and give an answer in an average time of $1ms$.

3.3   Object Color

In order to evaluate the quality of the colors extracted by our system, we use the *color-texture* dataset. We use a metric for the evaluation of the extracted colors which takes into account the amount of color in relation to the quantity of color

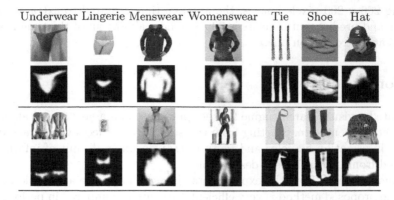

| Underwear | Lingerie | Menswear | Womenswear | Tie | Shoe | Hat |

Fig. 7. In each column two examples of input images and segmented objects, belonging to the datasets used in this work. All the images belong to the validation set.

labeled, as explained in [10]. Since the computational time of the algorithm depends on the size of the image, we have investigated the way to reduce it, resizing the images. We have thus reached a tradeoff between speed and quality of results by resizing the images to 50×50 pixels. The average time required to extract principal colors is $37ms$, obtaining the following performance: Precision: 55%, Recall: 65%, Overall Accuracy: 61%.

3.4   Object Texture

Table 2 shows the confusion matrix obtained evaluating the texture classification method, which can be summarized in an overall accuracy of 75.8% and a K coefficient of 0.73, resulting in a substantial agreement between the truth data and the classifier predictions [11]. Experiments show that the chosen features have a good discrimination power on the used texture classes.

Table 2. Confusion matrix for the texture classification problem

	horiz	leopard	other	polka	rhombus	color	squares	vertic	zebra	PA
horiz	19	0	0	0	0	0	0	0	2	91%
leopard	0	14	4	4	0	0	1	0	1	58%
other	0	2	13	7	2	0	4	0	2	43%
polka	0	0	0	10	0	0	0	0	0	100%
rhombus	0	0	1	1	13	0	0	0	2	77%
color	4	0	2	0	0	37	1	0	0	84%
squares	0	0	0	0	0	0	14	0	0	100%
vertic	0	0	2	0	0	3	0	22	0	82%
zebra	2	0	2	1	0	0	0	0	15	75%
UA	76%	88%	54%	44%	87%	93%	70%	100%	68%	

Using 200×200 pixels images, the average time required to extract texture features and predict texture class is $73ms$, where almost all of the time is spent in the feature extraction phase.

4   Conclusions

We created a visual search engine for shoppers based on a new neural algorithm for object segmentation. Starting from the segmented objects we extracted and indexed information on color and texture, transforming all unit of information extracted from images in text descriptions.

As demonstrated from the experimental phase and by the application developed, the proposed method is very efficient and can be compared in performance to a text indexing engine.

In future works we want experiment with the extraction and indexing of new visual information from images and improve the performance of the segmentation algorithm in order to obtain more accurate details for the segmented objects.

References

1. Wang, J.Z., Li, J., Wiederhold, G.: Simplicity: Semantics-sensitive integrated matching for picture libraries. IEEE Trans. Pattern Anal. Mach. Intell. 23, 947–963 (2001)
2. Liu, Y., Zhang, D., Lu, G., Ma, W.Y.: A survey of content-based image retrieval with high-level semantics. Pattern Recognition 40, 262–282 (2007)
3. Skopal, T.: Where are you heading, metric access methods?: a provocative survey. In: Proc. of SISAP 2010, pp. 13–21. ACM, New York (2010)
4. Cortes, C., Vapnik, V.: Support vector networks. Machine Learning 20, 273–297 (1995)
5. Gallo, I., Nodari, A.: Learning object detection using multiple neural netwoks. In: VISAP 2011. INSTICC Press (2011)
6. Riedmiller, M., Braun, H.: A direct adaptive method for faster backpropagation learning: The rprop algorithm. In: IEEE Conf. on Neural Networks, pp. 586–591 (1993)
7. Dalal, N., Triggs, B.: Histograms of oriented gradients for human detection. In: Proc. CVPR, pp. 886–893 (2005)
8. Nodari, A., Gallo, I., Cavallaro, A.: Real time color image indexing using a textual approach. Submitted to ICIP 2011 (2011)
9. Everingham, M., Van Gool, L., et al.: The pascal visual object classes (voc) challenge. International Journal of Computer Vision 88, 303–338 (2010)
10. Pedoia, V., Colli, V., et al.: fMRI analysis software tools: an evaluation framework. In: SPIE Medical Imaging 2011 (2011)
11. Landis, J.R., Koch, G.G.: The measurement of observer agreement for categorical data. Biometrics 33, 159–174 (1977)

Method for Training a Spiking Neuron to Associate Input-Output Spike Trains

Ammar Mohemmed[1], Stefan Schliebs[1], Satoshi Matsuda[1,2],
and Nikola Kasabov[1]

[1] Knowledge Engineering Discovery Research Institute,
350 Queen Street, Auckland 1010, New Zealand
http://www.kedri.info
[2] Department of Mathematical Information Engineering,
Nihon University, Japan
{amohemme,sschlieb,nkasabov}@aut.ac.nz, matsuda.satoshi@nihon-u.ac.jp

Abstract. We propose a novel supervised learning rule allowing the training of a precise input-output behavior to a spiking neuron. A single neuron can be trained to associate (map) different output spike trains to different multiple input spike trains. Spike trains are transformed into continuous functions through appropriate kernels and then Delta rule is applied. The main advantage of the method is its algorithmic simplicity promoting its straightforward application to building spiking neural networks (SNN) for engineering problems. We experimentally demonstrate on a synthetic benchmark problem the suitability of the method for spatio-temporal classification. The obtained results show promising efficiency and precision of the proposed method.

Keywords: Spiking Neural Networks, Supervised Learning, Spatio-temporal patterns.

1 Introduction

The desire to better understand the remarkable information processing capabilities of the mammalian brain has recently led to the development of more complex and biologically plausible connectionist models, namely spiking neural networks (SNN). See *e.g.* [5] for a comprehensive text on the material. These models use trains of spikes as internal information representation rather than continuous-value variables. Many studies investigate how to use SNN for practical applications, some of them demonstrating very promising results in solving complex real world problems. However, due to the increased complexity of SNN compared to traditional artificial neural networks, the training of these networks in a supervised fashion has proved to be difficult. See [8] for a review on supervised learning methods for SNN.

Only few algorithms have been proposed that are able to impose a precise input-output mapping of spike trains to a SNN. One of the first supervised learning methods for SNN is SpikeProb [3]. It is a gradient descent approach

L. Iliadis and C. Jayne (Eds.): EANN/AIAI 2011, Part I, IFIP AICT 363, pp. 219–228, 2011.

that adjusts the synaptic weights in order to emit a single spike at specified time. The timing of the output spike encodes a specific information, *e.g.* the class label of the presented input sample. Using SpikeProp, the SNN can not be trained to emit a desired train of spikes that has more than one spike.

An interesting learning rule for spatio-temporal pattern recognition has been suggested in [7]. The so-called Tempotron enables a neuron to learn whether to fire or not to fire in response to a specific input stimulus. Consequently, the method allows the processing of binary classification problems. However, the neuron is not intended to learn a precise target output spike train, but instead whether to spike or not to spike in response to an input stimulus.

A Hebbian based supervised learning algorithm called Remote Supervised Method (ReSuMe) was proposed in [11] and further studied in [12,13]. ReSuMe, similar to spike time dependent plasticity (STDP) [1,2], is based on a learning window concept. Using a teaching signal specific desired output is imposed to the output neuron. With this method, a neuron is able to produce a spike train precisely matching a desired spike train.

Recently, a method called Chronotron was proposed in [4]. It is based on minimizing the error between the desired spike pattern and the actual one. The error is measured using the Victor-Purpura spike distance metric [15]. This metric produces discontinuities in the error landscape that must be overcome through approximation. E-Learning is compared with ReSuMe on some temporal classification tasks and its better performance in terms of the number of spike patterns that can be classified is shown.

In this study, we propose a new learning rule allowing a neuron to learn efficiently associations of input-output spike trains. Although being principally simpler[1] compared to the methods mentioned above, we demonstrate its efficiency on a synthetic benchmark problem. The method is based on an extended Widrow-Hoff or Delta rule. In order to define a suitable error metric between desired and actual output spike trains, we convolve each spike sequence with a kernel function. Minimizing the error allows the efficient training of an output neuron to respond to specific input spikes with a desired target spike train.

We first present the new learning method. In the experiment section, we demonstrate the method using arbitrary input-output spike sequences for training an output neuron. Furthermore, we apply the learning method on a synthetic spatio-temporal classification problem and discuss the results.

2   Learning Method

In this section, we describe the neural and synaptic model used in this study, followed by a detailed description of the proposed learning algorithm.

2.1   Neural and Synaptic Model

The Leaky Integrate-and-Fire (LIF) neuron is arguably the best known model for simulating spiking networks. It is based on the idea of an electrical circuit

---

[1] For example the method does not require the definition of learning windows.

containing a capacitor with capacitance C and a resistor with a resistance R, where both C and R are assumed to be constant. The dynamics of a neuron i are then described by the following differential equation:

$$\tau_m \frac{du_i}{dt} = -u_i(t) + R\, I_i^{\text{syn}}(t) \tag{1}$$

The constant $\tau_m = RC$ is called the membrane time constant of the neuron. Whenever the membrane potential u_i crosses a threshold ϑ from below, the neuron fires a spike and its potential is reset to a reset potential u_r. Following [5], we define

$$t_i^{(f)} : u_i(t^{(f)}) = \vartheta, f \in \{0, \dots, n-1\} \tag{2}$$

as the firing times of neuron i where n is the number of spikes emitted by neuron i. It is noteworthy that the shape of the spike itself is not explicitly described in the traditional LIF model. Only the firing times are considered to be relevant.

The synaptic current I_i^{syn} of neuron i is modeled using an α-kernel:

$$I_i^{\text{syn}}(t) = \sum_j w_{ij} \sum_f \alpha(t - t_j^{(f)}) \tag{3}$$

where $w_{ij} \in \mathbb{R}$ is the synaptic weight describing the strength of the connection between neuron i and its pre-synaptic neuron j. The α-kernel itself is defined as

$$\alpha(t) = e\, \tau_s^{-1}\, t\, e^{-t/\tau_s} \Theta(t) \tag{4}$$

where $\Theta(t)$ refers to the Heaviside function and parameter τ_s is the synaptic time constant. We describe the parametrization of the model equations in the experiments section of this paper.

2.2 Learning

Similar to other supervised training algorithms, the synaptic weights of the network are adjusted iteratively in order to impose a desired input/output mapping to the SNN. We start with the common Widrow-Hoff rule for modifying the weight of a synapse i:

$$\Delta w_i^{\text{WH}} = \lambda x_i\, (y_d - y_{\text{out}}) \tag{5}$$

where $\lambda \in \mathbb{R}$ is a real-valued positive learning rate, x_i is the input transferred through synapse i, and y_d and y_{out} refer to the desired and the actual neural output, respectively. This rule was introduced for traditional neural networks with linear neurons. For these models, the input and output corresponds to real-valued vectors.

In SNN however, trains of spikes are passed between neurons and we have to define how to implement Equation 5 for this form of information exchange. In order to define the distance between spike trains, we introduce here an extended Delta rule. We transform each spike sequence into a continuous function using a kernel function. This is similar to the binless distance metric used to compare spike trains [14]. In this study, we use an α-kernel, however many other kernels appear suitable in this context. The convolved input x_i is defined as

$$x_i(t) = \sum_f \alpha(t - t_i^{(f)}) \tag{6}$$

where $\alpha(t)$ refers to the α-function defined in Equation 4. Representing spikes as a continuous function allows us to define the difference between spike sequences as the difference between their representing functions. Similar to the neural input, we define the desired and actual outputs of a neuron:

$$y_d(t) = \sum_f \alpha(t - t_d^{(f)}) \tag{7}$$

$$y_{\text{out}}(t) = \sum_f \alpha(t - t_{\text{out}}^{(f)}) \tag{8}$$

As a consequence of the spike representation defined above, Δw_i^{WH} itself is a function over time. By integrating Δw_i^{WH} we obtain a scalar Δw_i that is used to update the weight of synapse i:

$$\Delta w_i = \lambda \int x_i(t) \, (y_d(t) - y_{\text{out}}(t)) \, dt \tag{9}$$

Weights are updated in an iterative process. In each iteration (or epoch), all training samples are presented sequentially to the system. For each sample the Δw_i are computed and accumulated. After the presentation of all samples, the weights are updated to $w_i(e + 1) = w_i(e) + \Delta w_i$, where e is the current epoch of the learning process.

We note that the algorithm is capable of training the weights of a single neural layer only. Related methods such as ReSuMe [11] and the Chronotron [4] exhibit similar restrictions. Therefore, a combination with the well-known Liquid State Machine (LSM) approach [9] was suggested in these studies. By transforming the input into a higher-dimensional space, the output of the LSM can potentially be mapped to any desired spike train.

Figure 1 illustrates the functioning of the learning method. An output neuron is connected to three input neurons through three excitatory synapses with randomly initialized weights. For the sake of simplicity, each input sequence consists of a single spike only. However, the learning method can also deal with more than one spike per input neuron. The inputs $t_i^{(f)}$ are visualized in Figure 1A. In this example, we intend to train the output neuron to emit a single spike at a pre-defined time $t_d^{(0)}$.

Assume that, as shown in Figure 1B, the presented stimulus causes the excitation of the output neuron resulting in the generation of two output spikes at times $t_{\text{out}}^{(0)}$ and $t_{\text{out}}^{(1)}$, respectively, neither of them equals the desired spike time $t_d^{(0)}$. The evolution of the membrane potential $u(t)$ measured in the output

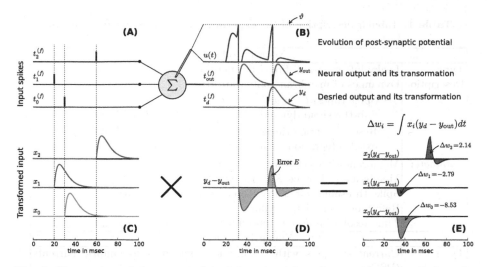

Fig. 1. Illustration of the proposed training algorithm. See text for a detailed explanation of the figure.

neuron is shown in middle top diagram of the figure above the actual and the desired spike trains, *cf.* Figure 1B.

The lower part in the figure (Figure 1C,D,E) depicts a graphical illustration of Equation 9. Using Equations 6 and 7, the input, actual and desired spikes trains are convolved with the α-kernel (Figure 1B and C). We define the area under the curve of the difference $y_d(t) - y_{\text{out}}(t)$ as an error between actual and desired output:

$$E = \int |y_d(t) - y_{\text{out}}(t)| \ dt \qquad (10)$$

Although this error is not used in the computation of the weight updates Δw_i, this metric is an informative measure of the achieved training status of the output neuron. Figure 1E shows the weight updates Δw_i. We especially note the large decrease of weight w_0. The spike train $t_0^{(0)}$ of the first input neuron causes an undesired spike at $t_{\text{out}}^{(0)}$ and lowering the corresponding synaptic efficacy potentially suppresses this behavior. On the other hand, the synaptic weight w_2 is increased promoting the triggering of spike $t_{\text{out}}^{(1)}$ at an earlier time.

We note that, unlike related methods such as ReSuMe [11], the defined learning rule does not employ any learning windows making the method easy to comprehend and to implement.

3   Experimental Results

Two experiments are conducted to demonstrate the functioning and the efficiency of the proposed learning algorithm. The first experiment intends to

Table 1. Tabular description of the experimental setup as suggested in [10]

Neural Model	
Type	Leaky integrate-and-fire (LIF) neuron

Description	Dynamics of membrane potential $u(t)$:
	  – Spike times: $t^{(f)} : u(t^{(f)}) = \vartheta$
	  – Sub-threshold dynamics: $\tau_m \frac{du}{dt} = -u(t) + R\, I^{\text{syn}}(t)$
	  – Reset & refractoriness: $u(t) = u_r \forall f : t \in (t^{(f)}, t^{(f)} + \tau_{\text{ref}})$
	  – exact integration with temporal resolution dt

Parameters	Membrane time constant $\tau_m = 10$ms Membrane resistance $R = 333.33$MΩ Spike threshold $\vartheta = 20$mV, reset potential $u_r = 0$mV Refractory period $\tau_{\text{ref}} = 3$ms Time resolution $dt = 0.1$ms, simulation time $T = 200$ms
Synaptic Model	
Type	Current synapses with α−function shaped post-synaptic currents (PSCs)
Description	Synaptic input current $I^{\text{syn}}(t) = \sum w \sum_f \alpha(t - t^{(f)})$ $\alpha(t) = \begin{cases} e\, \tau_s^{-1}\, t\, e^{-t/\tau_s}, & \text{if } t > 0 \\ 0, & \text{otherwise} \end{cases}$
Parameters	Synaptic weight $w \in \mathbb{R}$, uniformly randomly initialized in $[0, 25]$ Synaptic time constant $\tau_s = 5$ms
Input Model	
Type	Random input
Details	Population of 200 input neurons each firing a single spike at a randomly chosen time in the period $(0, T)$

demonstrate the concept of the proposed learning algorithm, while the second experiment implements the more practical scenario of a spatio-temporal pattern classification problem.

We follow the initiative recently proposed in [10] for promoting reproducible descriptions of neural network models and experiments. The initiative suggests the use of specifically formatted tables explaining neural and synaptic models along with their parametrization, *cf.* Table 1. For both experiments, we use 200 input neurons that stimulate the synapses of a single output neuron, *cf.* Figure 2. The spike trains for each input neuron are sampled from a uniform random distribution in the interval $[0, 200]$ms. For the sake of simplicity of this demonstration, we allow only a single spike for each input neuron (multiple spikes in a spike train are processed in the same way). A similar experimental setup was used in [4]. The single output neuron is fully connected to all 200 input neurons with randomly initialized connection weights. All of our experiments employ the SNN simulator NEST [6].

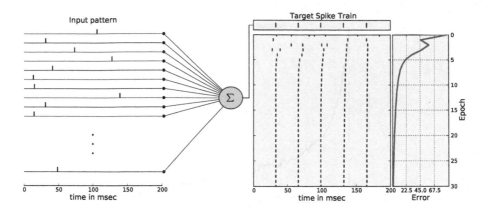

Fig. 2. A single output neuron is trained to respond with a temporally precise output spike train to a specific spatio-temporal input. The organization of the figure is inspired by [4].

3.1 Demonstration of the Learning Rule

The purpose of the first experiment is to demonstrate the concept of the proposed learning method. The task is to learn a mapping from a random input spike pattern to specific target output spike train. This target consists of five spikes occurring at the times $t_d^{(0)} = 33$, $t_d^{(1)} = 66$, $t_d^{(2)} = 99$, $t_d^{(3)} = 132$ and $t_d^{(4)} = 165$ms. Initially, the synaptic weights are randomly generated uniformly in the range $(0, 25\text{pA})$. In 100 epochs, we apply the new learning rule to allow the output neuron to adjust its connection weights in order to produce the desired output spike train. The experiment is repeated for 100 runs each of them initialized with different random weights in order to guarantee statistical significance.

In Figure 2, the experimental setup of a typical run is illustrated. The left side of the diagram shows the network architecture as defined in the experimental setup above. The right side shows the desired target spike train (top) along with the produced spike trains by the output neuron over a number of learning epochs (bottom). We note that the output spike trains in early epochs are very different from the desired target spike sequence. In later epochs the output spike converges towards the desired sequence. Consequently, the error as defined in Equation 10 decreases in succeeding epochs (right part of Figure 2). We note that the neuron is able to reproduce the desired spike output pattern very precisely in less than 30 learning epochs.

Figure 3 shows the evolution of the average error over the performed 100 runs. We note the logarithmic scale of the y-axis and the exponential decrease of the error. The slope of the curve suggests further improvement of the error, if the neuron was trained longer than the 100 performed learning epochs.

From this simple experiment, we conclude that the proposed learning method is indeed able to train a input-output behavior to a spiking neuron.

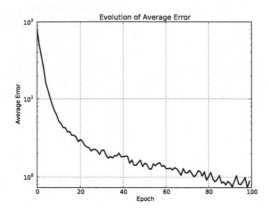

Fig. 3. Evolution of average error obtained in 100 independent runs

3.2   Classification of Spatio-temporal Data

The second experiment is a spatio-temporal classification task. The objective is
to learn to classify five classes of input spike patterns. The pattern for each class
is given as a random input spike pattern that was created in a similar fashion
as for the first experiment. Fifteen copies for each of the five pattern are then
generated by perturbing each pattern using a Gaussian jitter with a standard
deviation of 3ms resulting in a total of $15 \times 5 = 75$ samples in the training
data set. Additionally, we create $25 \times 5 = 125$ testing samples using the same
procedure. The output neuron is then trained to emit a single spike at a specific
time for each class. Only the training set is used during training, while the
testing set is used to determine the generalization ability of the trained neuron.
The spike time of the output neuron encodes the class label of the presented
input pattern. The neuron is trained to spike at the time instances 33, 66, 99,
132, and 165ms respectively, each spike time corresponding to one of the five
class labels. We allow 200 epochs for the learning method and we repeat the
experiment in 30 independent runs. For each run we chose a different set of
random initial weights.

Figure 4a shows the evolution of the average error for each of the five classes.
In the first few epochs, the value of the error oscillates and then starts to stabilize
and decrease slowly. The learning error decreases for some classes faster than for
others, *e.g.* class 3. We also note that the class reporting the highest error is
class 1. This behavior is expected and confirms a quite similar finding in [4]. In
order to classify samples of class 1 correctly, the output neuron has to emit a
very early spike at $t \approx 33$ms. Consequently, the neuron needs to be stimulated
by input spikes occurring at times before $t = 33$ms. However, due to the random
generation of the input data, only few input spikes occur before $t = 33$ms.
Most input spikes arrive after that time at the output neuron and therefore do
not contribute to the correct classification of class 1 samples. The relationship

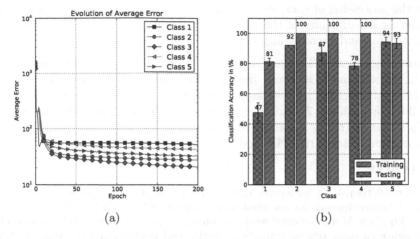

(a)   (b)

Fig. 4. Evolution of the average errors obtained in 30 independent trails for each class of the training samples (**a**). The average accuracies obtained in the training and testing phase (**b**).

between the accuracy and the output spike time was also noted in [4]. Future studies will further investigate this interesting observation.

In order to report the classification accuracy of the trained neuron, we define a simple error metric. We consider a pattern as correctly classified, if the neuron fires a single spike within $[t_d^{(f)} - 3, t_d^{(f)} + 3]$ms of the desired spike time $t_d^{(f)}$. Any other output is considered as incorrect. It is noteworthy to mention that using this definition, an untrained neuron is very likely to produce incorrect outputs resulting in accuracies close to zero. Figure 4b shows the average classification error for each class in the training and testing phase. As mentioned above, for testing, the 125 unseen patterns of the test set are used. The neuron is able to learn to classify the 75 training patterns with an average accuracy of 94.8% across all classes. Once more, we note the comparatively poor classification performance of samples belonging to the first class. For the test patterns, the neuron is able to achieve average accuracy of 79.6% across all classes which demonstrates a satisfying generalization ability.

4   Conclusion

In this paper, we have proposed a novel learning algorithm that allows the training of a precise input-output behavior to a SNN. Besides the benefits of an efficient supervised training method for a spiking neuron, we see the main advantage of the proposed approach in its algorithmic simplicity promoting its straightforward application to engineering problems. As a proof of concept, we have demonstrated the suitability of the method for classification problems on a small synthetic data set. Although the method can only train a single layer of the

SNN, it was argued that in combination with the LSM approach [9], the method allows the processing of complex non-linearly separable classification problems. Considering the difficulty of the spike-based classification task, the results are both satisfying and encouraging.

Acknowledgements. The work on this paper has been supported by the Knowledge Engineering and Discovery Research Institute (KEDRI, www.kedri.info). One of the authors, NK, has been supported by a Marie Curie International Incoming Fellowship with the 7th European Framework Programme under the project 'EvoSpike', hosted by the Neuromorphic Cognitive Systems Group of the Institute for Neuroinformatics of the ETH and the University of Zurich.

References

1. Bell, C.C., Han, V.Z., Sugawara, Y., Grant, K.: Synaptic plasticity in a cerebellum-like structure depends on temporal order. Nature 387, 278–281 (1997)
2. Bi, G.q., Poo, M.m.: Synaptic modifications in cultured hippocampal neurons: Dependence on spike timing, synaptic strength, and postsynaptic cell type. J. Neurosci. 18(24), 10464–10472 (1998)
3. Bohte, S.M., Kok, J.N., Poutré, J.A.L.: SpikeProp: backpropagation for networks of spiking neurons. In: ESANN, pp. 419–424 (2000)
4. Florian, R.V.: The chronotron: a neuron that learns to fire temporally-precise spike patterns (November 2010),
   http://precedings.nature.com/documents/5190/version/1
5. Gerstner, W., Kistler, W.M.: Spiking Neuron Models: Single Neurons, Populations, Plasticity. Cambridge University Press, Cambridge (2002)
6. Gewaltig, M.O., Diesmann, M.: Nest (neural simulation tool). Scholarpedia 2(4), 1430 (2007)
7. Gutig, R., Sompolinsky, H.: The tempotron: a neuron that learns spike timing-based decisions. Nat. Neurosci. 9(3), 420–428 (2006)
8. Kasiński, A.J., Ponulak, F.: Comparison of supervised learning methods for spike time coding in spiking neural networks. Int. J.of Applied Mathematics and Computer Science 16, 101–113 (2006)
9. Maass, W., Natschläger, T., Markram, H.: Real-time computing without stable states: A new framework for neural computation based on perturbations. Neural Computation 14(11), 2531–2560 (2002)
10. Nordlie, E., Gewaltig, M.O., Plesser, H.E.: Towards reproducible descriptions of neuronal network models. PLoS Comput. Biol. 5(8), e1000456 (2009)
11. Ponulak, F.: ReSuMe – new supervised learning method for spiking neural networks. Tech. rep., Institute of Control and Information Engineering, Poznań University of Technology, Poznań, Poland (2005)
12. Ponulak, F.: Analysis of the resume learning process for spiking neural networks. Applied Mathematics and Computer Science 18(2), 117–127 (2008)
13. Ponulak, F., Kasiński, A.: Supervised learning in spiking neural networks with ReSuMe: sequence learning, classification, and spike shifting. Neural Computation 22(2), 467–510 (2010), PMID: 19842989
14. van Rossum, M.C.: A novel spike distance. Neural Computation 13(4), 751–763 (2001)
15. Victor, J.D., Purpura, K.P.: Metric-space analysis of spike trains: theory, algorithms and application. Network: Computation in Neural Systems 8(2), 127–164 (1997)

Two Different Approaches of Feature Extraction for Classifying the EEG Signals

Pari Jahankhani[1], Juan A. Lara[2], Aurora Pérez[2], and Juan P. Valente[2]

[1] University of East London, School of Computing, Information Technology and Electronic,
London E16 2RD, United Kingdom
pari@uel.ac.uk
[2] Technical University of Madrid, School of Computer Science,
Campus de Montegancedo, 28660, Boadilla del Monte, Madrid, Spain
j.lara.torralbo@upm.es, {aurora,jpvalente}@fi.upm.es

Abstract. The electroencephalograph (EEG) signal is one of the most widely used signals in the biomedicine field due to its rich information about human tasks. This research study describes a new approach based on i) build reference models from a set of time series, based on the analysis of the events that they contain, is suitable for domains where the relevant information is concentrated in specific regions of the time series, known as events. In order to deal with events, each event is characterized by a set of attributes. ii) Discrete wavelet transform to the EEG data in order to extract temporal information in the form of changes in the frequency domain over time- that is they are able to extract non-stationary signals embedded in the noisy background of the human brain.

The performance of the model was evaluated in terms of training performance and classification accuracies and the results confirmed that the proposed scheme has potential in classifying the EEG signals.

Keywords: Wavelet, Feature extraction, EEG, Classifying.

1 Introduction

The electroencephalograph (EEG) signal is one of the most widely signal used in the biomedicine field due to its rich information about human tasks.. In practical applications of pattern recognition, there are often diverse features extracted from raw data which needs recognising. Time series modelling has many applications like, for example, feature identification across a group of time series, or model comparison measuring the likeness among groups of time series, or the evolution of one and the same group over time. In actual fact, in many domains, like medicine, the mere observation of the model by the expert can turn out to be very useful in the decision-making process.

The relation of EEG signals to the human movements and behaviour has been extensively studied in past decades [1].

A key data mining problem is the construction of feature models from set of time series.

L. Iliadis and C. Jayne (Eds.): EANN/AIAI 2011, Part I, IFIP AICT 363, pp. 229–239, 2011.
© IFIP International Federation for Information Processing 2011

In the field of time series data mining, there are well-established methods for comparing two time series, finding subsequence that are repeated several times throughout the same time series and techniques that try to determine whether a time series contains a particular sequence. Also there are techniques that try to generate a representative reference model from a set of time series [2], [3], [4], [5].

A powerful method was proposed in the late 1980s to perform time-scale analysis of signals: the wavelet transforms (WT). This method provides a unified framework for different techniques that have been developed for various applications.

Nevertheless, in many cases only particular regions of the series contain relevant knowledge and the data mining techniques should focus on these regions (known as events) [6]. This applies to domains like seismography, the stock market or medicine. In seismography, for example, the only moments of interest are when the time series indicates an earthquake, volcanic activity leading up to the quake, or replications. The lengthy periods between these events provide hardly any information. Figure 1 shows an example of an EEG time series, highlighting an event corresponding to the electrical activity generated by the nervous system in response to a stimulus.

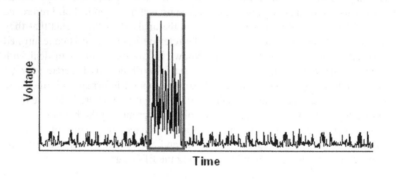

Fig. 1. Example of an EEG time series

Detecting patterns in EEG produced from the normal mental states has some problems, due to the fact that EEG signals which are recorded by surface electrodes can contain noise as a result of electrical interference and movement of the electrodes on the scalp or EEG can be corrupted by eye blinks and other muscular activity that produce signals of greater magnitude than produced by cortical activity.

In this work, two different methods are applied for feature extraction and classification.

1) Build reference models from a set of time series, based on the analysis of the events that they contain, is suitable for domains where the relevant information is concentrated in specific regions of the time series, known as events. The method enables to define regions of interest according to the knowledge extracted from the domain experts, which is a plus compared with other methods addressing the time series as a whole without taking into account that certain regions can be irrelevant in the domain in question.

2) Discrete Wavelet Transform (DWT) has been applied for the time–frequency analysis of EEG signals and an Adaptive Fuzzy Inference Neural Network System (AFINN) [7], [8], [9] scheme for the classification using wavelet coefficients.

2 Method 1: Feature Extraction of Events

Electroencephalographic devices generate time series that record scalp electrical activity (voltage) generated by brain structures. EEG signals contain a series of waves characterised by their frequency and amplitude. In EEG time series it is possible to find certain types of special waves that are characteristic of some neurological pathologies, like epilepsy. Those waves are known as paroxysmal abnormalities and can be considered as events.

During this research we have taken into account three kinds of events:

- Spike Wave: It is a wave whose amplitude is relatively higher than the rest of waves in the signal. It has a period of between 20 and 70 millisecond.
- Sharp Wave: It is a wave whose amplitude is relatively higher than the rest of waves in the signal. It has a period of between 70 and 200 millisecond. Figure 2 shows an example of a sharp wave event.
- Spicule: It is a sharp wave with an abrupt change of polarity.

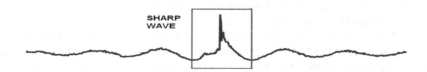

Fig. 2. Sharp wave event

The features characterising these events are as follows:

- Duration of the wave.
- Amplitude of the wave.

To identify the EEG events and determine their features, the proposed method calculates the point where the polarity of the signal changes as shown in figure 3. The method identifies points where there is a local maximum or minimum whose distance to the polarity change value is higher than a certain threshold (∂). That distance is the amplitude of the event. The duration of the wave is then calculated by analysing the two intersections between the time series and the polarity change value line. Depending on the duration, the event is classified as a spike or a sharp wave, according to the experts' criteria. Finally, those sharp waves that have an abrupt change of polarity are classified as spicules.

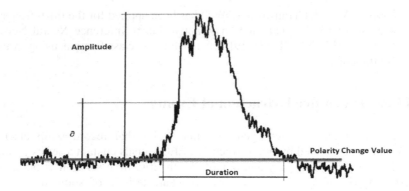

Fig. 3. Event taken from an EEG time series

2.1 Model Generation Method

The model generation method presented here is suited for domains where important information is only confined to certain regions while the remaining of the time series hardly provides any information.

In order to deal with events, each event is characterized by a set of attributes.

The model generation method receives a set of time series $S = \{S_1, S_2, ..., S_n\}$, each containing a particular number of events, and generates a reference model M that represents this set of time series. The model M is built on the basis of the most characteristic events. The most characteristic events of S are those events that appear in the highest number of timer series of S.

To find out whether a particular event in a time series S_i also appears in another time series S_j ($j \neq i$), the event has to be characterized with an attribute vector and compared with the other events of the other series. To speed up this process, all the events present in the time series are clustered, so similar events belong to the same cluster. On the one hand, the clustering process is useful to know the different groups of events. On the other hand, it facilitates the extraction of the most characteristic events. Once we have a set of clusters, the objective is to find those clusters containing events that appear in the highest number of time series, that is, characteristic events. Having located those groups with similar events, an exhaustive cluster analysis is run in order to extract the event representative of each of these groups. This will be described later (steps 5 to 9 of the algorithm). These extracted representative events are the characteristic events of S and will be part of the final model.

Let $S = \{S_1, S_2, ..., S_n\}$ be a set of n time series and m the typical number of events that appear in the time series of S. The algorithm for generating a reference model M representing the set S is as detailed below (with the purpose of making the algorithm more legible key decisions are justified at the end of the algorithm):

1. **Initialize the model**
    $M = \emptyset$.
2. **Identify events**
    Extract all the events E_v from the series of S and use an attribute vector to characterize each event. This vector covers what the expert considers to be the key

features for each type of domain event. This step is domain dependent, as the event characterization will depend on the time series type. To extract the events, the time series is examined in search of regions that meet the conditions identifying each event type defined according to the knowledge extracted from the expert.

3. Determine the typical number of events m

m is the typical number of events in each time series of S. At the end of the algorithm it will be discussed how to determine this value.

4. Cluster events

Cluster all the events extracted in step 2. Bottom-up hierarchical clustering techniques have been used. Taking into account that the proposal described here should be a general-purpose method and there is no a priori information for specifying the optimum number of clusters in each domain, bottom-up hierarchical clustering is a good option, as it is not necessary to specify the number of clusters k beforehand. We have used Hierarchical Clustering

Repeat steps 5 to 9 m times

5. Get the most significant cluster C_k

Determine which cluster C_k of all the clusters output in step 4 is the most significant. Cluster significance is measured using Equation (1).

$$ SIGNF(C_k) = \frac{\#TS(C_k)}{n} \tag{1} $$

That is, cluster significance is given by the number of time series that have events in that cluster over the total number of time series n. Events that have already been examined (step 8 and 9) are not taken into account to calculate the numerator.

6. Extract the event E_c that best represents the cluster

Extract the event that is most representative of the cluster C_k, that is, the event E_c that minimizes the distance to the other events in the cluster. Let S_j be the time series in which the event E_c was found.

7. Add the event E_c to the model

$M = M \cup E_c$.

8. Mark event E_c as examined

9. Mark the most similar events to E_c as examined

From the cluster C_k obtain, for each time series $S_i \neq S_j$, the event E_p from S_i that is the most similar to the representative event (E_c) output in step 6. Each E_p will be represented in the model by the event E_c and therefore these E_p events will also be discarded in order not to be considered in later iterations.

10. Return *M* as a model of the set *S*

The most significant clusters, that is, those clusters that contain events present in the highest number of time series were analysed to output the events that are part of the model. To do this, the process of identifying the most significant cluster is repeated *m* times, outputting a representative and marking as examined both this representative and similar events in each time series. With regard to the algorithm, note that:

a) The identification of events is domain dependent because the criteria to define events in each domain are required. The rest of the algorithm is domain independent and it can be applied to any domain without any change. Figure 4 shows the overall structure of the proposed method that receives a set of time series *S* and generates a model *M* that represents it.

b) After the representative event of the most significant cluster has been output, it should not be taken into account again for the next iteration, and it is marked as an already examined event.

c) A cluster may contain not just one but several events from each time series. For this reason, even if a cluster is selected as the most significant, the cluster in question is not omitted in later iterations. The events already processed are marked as examined and will not be taken into account in future iterations.

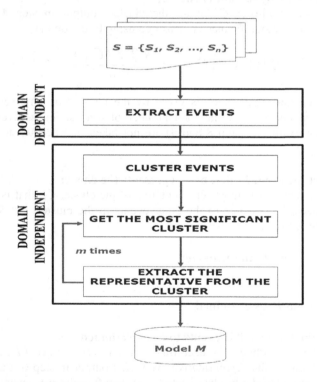

Fig. 4. Overall structure of the proposed method

Another important issue is the number of events making up the model. In this case, we have chosen the mode (*m*) of the number of events of the time series of *S*. This decision is based on the fact that if the original time series have a typical number of events *m*, it makes sense for the model that represents them to have the same number of events *m*. The typical number of events in the time series of *S* may not be unimodally distributed. This could happen especially if there are not many time series in the set *S*. For non-unimodal distributions, we have opted to take the integer value closest to the mean of the number of events.

A last point to be considered is the distance between events that has been used in the algorithm for clustering, representative event selection and discarding similar events. The *city block* distance is used. Given two vectors, the city block distance calculates the sum of the absolute value of the difference of each of the coordinates of the above vectors:

$$d(x, y) = \sum_{i=1}^{p} |x_i - y_i| \tag{2}$$

In Equation (2), *x* and *y* are the vectors (that is, the event descriptors) for comparison and *p* is the number of coordinates (dimension). Other distance measures have been studied, but the city block distance was finally chosen. The main reason for this choice is that the clustering algorithm uses the mean distance per attribute as the threshold for determining whether or not two elements are similar enough to belong to the same cluster. This mean distance per attribute is obtained simply by dividing the total city block distance *d(x,y)* by the number of attributes *p*. The use of the city block distance then saves time as it obviates additional transformations that would make the clustering process more complex to develop and more computationally intensive.

Figure 5 shows an example of the application of the proposed method to a set $S = \{S_1, S_2, S_3, S_4\}$ of 4 time series (*n*=4). In this case, S_1 contains 2 events (E_{11} and E_{12}), S_2 contains 2 events (E_{21} and E_{22}), S_3 contains 3 events (E_{31}, E_{32} and E_{33}) and finally S_4 contains 2 events (E_{41} and E_{42}). Therefore, the typical number of events is 2 (*m*=2). Once the events are extracted, they are clustered into three different clusters (C_1, C_2 and C_3). Then, the most significant cluster is obtained. To do that, it is necessary to calculate the significance of each cluster according to Equation (EQ). In this case, cluster C_1 have events present in 3 out of the 4 time series, cluster C_2 have events that appear in 1 out of the 4 time series and cluster C_3 have events present in 4 out of the 4 time series of *S*. Then, the significance of C_1 is $SIGNF(C_1) = \frac{3}{4} = 0.75$, the significance of C_2 is $SIGNF(C_2) = \frac{1}{4} = 0.25$ and the significance of C_3 is $SIGNF(C_3) = \frac{4}{4} = 1$.

Therefore, the most significant cluster is C_3. In the next step, the event E_{12} is extracted as the representative event of the cluster C_3 because E_{12} is the event in C_3 that minimizes the distance to the other events in that cluster. Thus, the event E_{12} is a characteristic event of *S* and will be part of the final model *M*. This process has to be repeated twice (because *m*=2) to build the final model that consists of the events E_{12} and E_{32}.

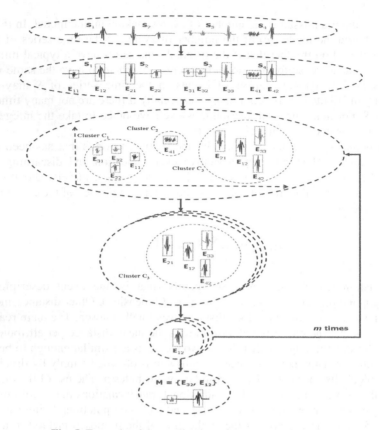

Fig. 5. Example of the application of the proposed method

3   Method 2: Feature Extraction Using Wavelet Transform

The extracted wavelet coefficients provide a compact representation that shows the energy distribution of the EEG signal in time and frequency.

In order to reduce the dimensionality of the extracted feature vectors, statistics over the set of wavelet coefficients were used. The following statistical features were used to represent the time-frequency distribution of the EEG signals:

1. Maximum of the wavelet coefficients in each sub-band
2. Minimum of the wavelet coefficients in each sub-band.
3. Mean of the wavelet coefficients in each sub-band.
4. Standard deviation of the wavelet coefficients in each sub-band.

Extracted features for the EEG recorded class A and E shown in table 1. For each of these sub-bands, we extracted four measures of dispersion, yielding a total of 20 attributes for sample window.

The complete data set consists of two sets denoted by A and E each containing 100 signal-channel EEG segments. The training and test sets of the AFINN classifier were formed by 3200 vectors (1600 vectors from each class). The extracted wavelet coefficients provided a compact representation that shows the energy distribution of the EEG signal in time and frequency. For each of wavelet sub-bands, we have extracted four measures of dispersion, yielding a total of 20 attributes per sample window. Those extracted features for two recorded classes A and E are shown in Table 1.

Table 1. The extracted features of two windows from A & E classes

Data	Extracted Feature	Sub-band D1	Sub-band D2	Sub-band D3	Sub-band D4	Approximation
Set A	Max	28.1094	101.757	131.0846	124.377	114.138
	Min	-28.4010	-60.813	-149.072	-158.797	-109.521
	Mean	-0.0022	0.0058	-0.0035	0.0388	3.7950
	Std. Dev.	5.1818	13.6442	23.3685	24.7933	35.1465
Set E	Max	123.3921	278.924	429.6621	375.0564	582.3167
	Min	-90.7055	-23851	-417.120	-468.064	-361.2154
	Mean	0.0131	-0.0281	-0.0359	-0.0071	-5.5526
	Std. Dev.	11.8488	35.9941	73.7659	78.1432	180.4493

4 Evaluation/Conclusion

A system implementing the described method has been developed. The system has been evaluated by running a battery of experiments using a 10-fold cross validation approach. These experiments were done on time series generated by electroencephalographic devices.

During this research, we have used publicly available datasets described in [10]. The complete data set consists of five sets (denoted *A-E*) each containing 100 single-channel (100 electrodes) EEG recordings of 5 separate patient classes. For this study, we focused on sets labelled *A* (healthy patients) and *E* (epileptic seizure session recordings).

The ultimate aim of the evaluation is to measure how good the model generation method is. For the evaluation of the proposed method, two models were created for each class ($M_{healthy}$ and $M_{epileptic}$).

The first model ($M_{healthy}$) was created from a training set composed of 90 of the 100 healthy patients (set *A*). The other 10 patients constituted the test set. The second model ($M_{epileptic}$) was generated from a training set composed of 90 of the 100 epileptic patients (set *E*). The other 10 patients were used as test set. The patients in the test set were chosen at random.

Once the models have been created, they have been evaluated by checking whether the $M_{healthy}$ model properly represents the group of healthy patients and whether the $M_{epileptic}$ model is representative of the group of epileptic patients. To do that, we have classified the 20 individuals in the test group according to their similarity to the two created models (that similarity was determined using the time series comparison method proposed in [11]). This process was repeated ten times changing the training set and the test set.

The training data set was used to train the AFINN model for classification of the two classes of EEG signals. The proposed system was trained and tested with the extracted features using discrete wavelet transform of the EEG signals. The simulation results reveal a perfect performance compared to a classic MLP neural network.

The results of the proposed classifier, using 2 different training sets are shown in Table 2.

Table 2. Comparison of the three methods

Class	Reference Model	AFINN	MLP
A	92%	98.12%	94.98%
E	96%	97.96%	95.86%

References

1. Zoubir, M., Bosshssh, B.: Seizure detection of newborn EEG using a model approach. IEEE Transactions on Biomedical Engineering 45, 673–685 (1998)
2. Chan, P.K., Mahoney, M.V.: Modeling multiple time series for anomaly detection. In: ICDM 2005: Proceedings of the Fifth IEEE International Conference on Data Mining, pp. 90–97. IEEE Computer Society, Washington, DC, USA (2005)
3. Caraça-Valente, J.P., López-Chavarrías, I.: Discovering similar patterns in time series. In: KDD 2000: Proceedings of the Sixth ACM SIGKDD International Conference on Knowledge Discovery and Data Mining, pp. 497–505. ACM, New York (2000)
4. Chen, Z., Yang, B.r., Zhou, F.g., Li, L.n., Zhao, Y.f.: A new model for multiple time series based on data mining. In: International Symposium on Knowledge Acquisition and Modeling, pp. 39–43 (2008)
5. Papadimitriou, S., Sun, J., Faloutsos, C.: Streaming pattern discovery in multiple time-series. In: VLDB 2005: Proceedings of the 31st International Conference on Very Large Data Bases, pp. 697–708. VLDB Endowment (2005)
6. Povinelli, R.J.: Using genetic algorithms to find temporal patterns indicative of time series events. In: GECCO 2000 Workshop: Data Mining with Evolutionary Algorithms, pp. 80–84 (2000)
7. Andrzejak, R.G., Lehnertz, K., Mormann, F., Rieke, C., David, P., Elger, C.E.: Indications of nonlinear deterministic and finitedimensional structures in time series of brain electrical activity: dependence on recording region and brain state. Physical Review. E, Statistical, Nonlinear, and Soft Matter Physics 64 (December 2001)
8. Jahankhani, P., Revett, K., Kodogiannis, V.: Classification Using Adaptive Fuzzy Inference Neural Network. In: Proceedings of the Twelfth IASTED International Conference Artificial Intelligence and Soft Computing (ASC 2008), Palma de Mallorca, Spain (September 1-3, 2008) ISBN 978-0-88986-756-7

9. Jahankhani, P., Revett, K., Kodogiannis, V.: Data Mining an EEG Dataset With an Emphasis on Dimensionality Reduction. In: IEEE Symposium on Computational Intelligence and Data Mining (CIDM) (April 1-5, 2007)
10. Jahankhani, P., Revett, K., Kodogiannis, V.: EEG Signal ClassificationUsing Wavelet Feature Extraction and Neural Networks. In: IEEE John Vincent Atanasoff 2006 International Symposium on Modern Computing, Sofia, Bulgaria, October 3-6, pp. 120–125 (2006)
11. Lara, J.A., Moreno, G., Perez, A., Valente, J.P., López-Illescas, A.: Comparing posturographic time series through events detection. In: 21st IEEE International Symposium on Computer-Based Medical Systems, CBMS 2008, pp. 293–295 (June 2008)

An Ensemble Based Approach for Feature Selection

Behrouz Minaei-Bidgoli, Maryam Asadi, and Hamid Parvin

School of Computer Engineering, Iran University of Science and Technology (IUST),
Tehran, Iran
{b_minaei,parvin,asadi}@iust.ac.ir

Abstract. This paper proposes an ensemble based approach for feature selection. We aim at overcoming the problem of parameter sensitivity of feature selection approaches. To do this we employ ensemble method. We get the results per different possible threshold values automatically in our algorithm. For each threshold value, we get a subset of features. We give a score to each feature in these subsets. Finally by use of ensemble method, we select the features which have the highest scores. This method is not a parameter sensitive one, and also it has been shown that using the method based on the fuzzy entropy results in more reliable selected features than the previous methods'. Empirical results show that although the efficacy of the method is not considerably decreased in most of cases, the method becomes free from setting of any parameter.

Keywords: Feature Selection, Ensemble Methods, Fuzzy Entropy.

1 Introduction

We have to use features of a dataset to classify data points in pattern recognition and data mining. Some datasets have a large number of features. Processing these datasets is not possible or is very difficult. To solve this problem, the dimensionalities of these datasets should be reduced. To do this, some of the redundant or irrelevant features should be eliminated. By eliminating the redundant and irrelevant features, the classification performance over them will be improved. Three different approaches are available for feature selection mechanism [1]. The first ones are embedded approaches. In these algorithms, feature selection is done as a part of the data algorithm. The second ones are filter approaches. These algorithm selected features before the data mining algorithm is run. The last ones are wrapper approaches. In these algorithms the target data mining algorithm is used to get the best subset of features.

A lot of methods for feature subset selection have been presented, such as similarity measures [2], gainentropies [3], the relevance of features [4], the overall feature evaluation index (OFEI) [5], the feature quality index (FQI) [5], the mutual information-based feature selector (MIFS) [6], classifiability measures [7], neuro-fuzzy approaches [8, 9], fuzzy entropy measures[10], etc.

In this paper we try to improve Shie-and-Chen's method. We try to solve the drawback of parameter sensitivity. To do this we use ensemble method. We get the results for different threshold values. For each threshold values, we get a subset of

L. Iliadis and C. Jayne (Eds.): EANN/AIAI 2011, Part I, IFIP AICT 363, pp. 240–246, 2011.

features. We give a score to each feature in these subsets. Finally by use of ensemble concept, we select the features which have the highest scores. This method is not a parameter sensitive one, and also it has been shown that using the method based on the fuzzy entropy results in more reliable selected features than the previous methods'.

2 Proposed Algorithm

Shie-and-Chen's Algorithm which is presented in [10] is parameter sensitive. So if these parameters change, the result of algorithm can be changed significantly. When these parameters are given by the user, the quality of algorithm results will be even weaker. Because user selects the parameters randomly and experimentally, so it is possible that they are not proper values for an exemplary dataset. So the result of algorithm is not trustable. Also the proper values are not available for some datasets which are not used in this algorithm. So to find the best result we need to test the algorithm for a lot of possible threshold values. Then we must select the threshold values which cause the best results. To solve this problem we use ensemble method.

We do not select threshold values experimentally in our algorithm. Our algorithm test different possible values for thresholds and then by doing some steps, it selects the subset of features. This algorithm has 5 steps. We employ Shie-and-Chen's method by a little change in our algorithm. The result of their algorithm is a subset of features. But we get a sequence of features instead of a subset. Actually the order of feature appearance is important in our algorithm. First step runs Shie-and-Chen's method for each pair of (T_r , T_c). The result of algorithm at this step is a table of feature sequences which are selected for each pair of threshold values. For example the result of our algorithm for Iris is shown in Table 1. We obtained this result for 5 different values for T_c and T_r. Each element in this table is a feature sequence selected by the algorithm of Fig. 1 with a different pair of threshold values.

For $T_r = base\_t_r$: step_t_r :1
      For $T_c = base\_t_c$: step_t_c :1
           AllFSeq(T_r, T_c) = Shie-and-Chen's algorithm(T_r, T_c);

Fig. 1. Pseudo code of the first step of algorithm

It has two loops. One of them slides over T_r and the other one slides over T_c. Two parameters *base_t_r* and *base_t_c* are the minimum values used for T_r and T_c respectively. Two parameters *step_t_r* and *step_t_c* determine the distance between two consecutive threshold values of parameters T_r and T_c respectively. *FSeq* is a two dimensional matrix whose elements are features sequences obtained by the algorithm of Fig. 2 with each possible tested pair of threshold values. As it is inferred from Table 1, at the first and the last rows of each column we have some similar results for some threshold values. There is a similar discussion about the first and the last columns of each row. The results of algorithm for the first and the last columns of each row and the first and the last rows of each column are not trustable to reach some proper threshold values. Since these results have strongly negative effect on the final evaluation, at the second step we have to remove these repetitions. This step has two parts. The first part removes the repetitions of columns and the second part removes the repetitions of rows. First part keeps only the results at the beginning and ending of each column to reach a dissimilar result at the beginning and ending of each column. And the second part keeps only the results at the beginning and ending of a row to reach a dissimilar result at the beginning or ending of each row. In other words, we use only one of the same results at the beginning and ending parts of each row and each column in final evaluation. The following pseudo code is the first part of second step of the algorithm.

```
New_AllFSeq = AllFSeq
For   T_r = base_t_r: step_t_r :1
      q = base_ t_c
      While (true)
                q = q + step_ t_c
                if        is_same ( AllFSeq ( T_r , base_t_c ) , AllFSeq ( T_r, q ))
                          New_AllFseq ( Tr , q ) = EmptySeq
             else
                      break
      q = last_ t_c
      While (true)
                q = q - step_ t_c;
                if        is_same ( AllFSeq ( T_r , last_t_c ) , AllFSeq ( T_r, q ))
                          New_AllFseq ( T_r , q ) = EmptySeq
             else
                      break
```

Fig. 2. Pseudo code of the first part of the second step of the algorithm

Table 1. Feature subsets selected for some pairs of threshold values over Iris dataset

Tc, Tr	0.01	0.21	0.41	0.61	0.81
0.01	4, 3	3, 4	3, 4	3, 4	3, 4
0.21	4, 3	4, 3	3, 4	3, 4	3, 4
0.41	3, 4	4, 3	3, 4	3, 4	3, 4
0.61	4, 1	4, 2	3, 1	3, 1	3, 1
0.81	3, 1	4, 3, 1	3, 4	3, 4	3, 4

Equation 1 is a function that checks the similarity of its inputs. It has two input parameters which can be two sequences of features. If they are similar, the output will be 1 and if they are not similar the output is 0.

$$is\_same \ (a,b) = \begin{cases} 1, & if \ x = y \\ 0, & otherwise \end{cases} \qquad 1$$

It checks the similarity between the first sequence of a column and the consecutive sequences of that column. By reaching the first dissimilar sequence at the beginning or ending of a column, this part of algorithm is done for each column. Output for Iris example of doing the first part of the second step of the algorithm is available in Table 2 by horizontal shading (+ sings). The second part of the second step of the algorithm is like Fig. 2. It is like the first part of the second step. It checks the similarity between the first sequence of a row and the other sequences in that column. By reaching the first dissimilar sequence at the beginning or ending of a row, this part of algorithm is done for each row. Result of doing the second part of the second step of the algorithm over the Iris dataset which is obtained from the first step is shown in Table 2 by vertical shading (* sings).

Table 2. Delete repetitions in columns of Table 1 then delete repetitions in rows of Table 1

Tc, Tr	0.01	0.21	0.41	0.61	0.81
0.01	4, 3	*	*	*	3, 4
0.21	+	+*	+*	+*	+
0.41	3, 4	4, 3	+*	+*	+
0.61	4, 1	4, 2	*	*	3, 1
0.81	3, 1	4, 3, 1	*	*	3, 4

Third step uses majority voting to reach the best subset of features. We have to give a score to each feature. There is a subset of selected features for each pair of T_r and T_c. We change this subset to a sequence of features by their ranks of appearing at the first step. In other words each feature that appears sooner has more effect on output, so it is given a higher score. Then we sum all given scores to features for each pair of threshold values. We define the score of each feature as equation 2.

After obtaining Table 2 for each dataset, we give a score to each of its features according to equation 2. In the equation 2, we give the higher weight to the first feature which appears sooner, and we give the lower weight to the last feature which appears at the end of the sequence. For example if there are 10 features, the weight of the first feature is considered 10, and the weight of the last feature is considered 1.

$$Score = \sum_{T_r} \sum_{T_c} \sum_{i=1}^{MaxSF} isequal(\ AllFSeq\ (T_r, T_c)(i), f) * (\ |AllFSeq| - i + 1) \quad 2$$

where MaxSF is obtained by equation 3.

$$MaxSF = max_{T_r, T_c, i}(|AllFSeq\ (T_r, T_c)(i)|) \qquad 3$$

Finally we sum all the weighted scores obtained by the algorithm for different pairs of threshold values. For example, in the Iris example the *MaxFS* is 3. In the example we get these results: Score (3) = 21, Score (4) = 21, Score (1) = 7 and Score (2) = 2.

Then we sort all features by their scores. After that we select the features with maximum scores. We select the same number of features as the Shie-and-Chen's method. In Iris example the subset of {3, 4} features is selected as final selected subset, because these features have the highest scores, and Shie-and-Chen's method selected two features for this example.

Table 3. Comparison between feature subsets selected by our and Shie-and-Chen's methods

Data sets	Feature subsets selected by two methods	
	Shie-and-Chen's method	Our method
Iris	{4,3}	{4,3}
Breast cancer data set	{6, 2, 1, 8, 5, 3}	{6, 2, 3, 1, 9, 5}
Pima	{2, 6, 8, 7}	{2, 4, 6, 3}
MPG data set	{4, 6, 3}	{2, 4, 1}
Cleve data set	{13, 3, 12, 11, 1, 10, 2, 5, 6}	{13, 1, 12, 3, 9}
Crx data set	{9}	{9}
Monk-1 data set	{5, 1, 2}	{5, 1, 2}
Monk-2 data set	{5}	{5}
Monk-3 data set	{5, 2, 4}	{2,5,1}

3 Experimental Results

We have implemented our feature selection algorithm in Matlab. We use Weka software to evaluate the mapped datasets into the selected features obtained by our feature selection algorithms. We compare the feature subsets selected by our method with those selected by Shie-and-Chen's method in Table 3 for all of datasets which are used to compare in [10]. Also Table 4 shows that the obtained accuracies of different classifiers on the selected features obtained by proposed method are better than the obtained accuracies of the same classifiers on the selected features obtained by Shie-and-Chen's algorithms the most datasets.

Table 4. Comparing classification accuracy rates of our and Shie-and-Chen's methods

Data sets	Classifiers	Average classification accuracy rates of different methods	
		Our method	Shie-and-Chen's method
Pima diabetes data set	LMT	76.30 ±4.84%	77.22 ± 4.52%
	Naive Bayes	76.30 ±4.84%	77.47 ± 4.93%
	SMO	75.65 ±5.61%	77.08 ± 5.06%
	C4.5	94.62 ±2.12%	74.88 ± 5.89%
Cleve data set	LMT	82.42 ± 5.34%	82.87 ± 6.23%
	Naive Bayes	80.41 ± 3.95%	84.48 ± 3.93%
	SMO	80.00 ± 5.99%	83.51 ± 6.09%
	C4.5	76.90 ± 8.40%	76.90 ± 8.40%
Correlated data set	LMT	100.00 ± 0.00%	100.00 ± 0.00%
	Naive Bayes	86.03 ± 3.75%	86.03 ± 3.75%
	SMO	89.87 ± 6.88%	89.87 ± 6.88%
	C4.5	94.62 ± 4.54%	94.62 ± 4.54%
M of N-3-7-10 data set	LMT	100.00 ± 0.00%	100.00 ± 0.00%
	Naive Bayes	89.33 ± 1.56%	89.33 ± 1.56%
	SMO	100.00 ± 0.00%	100.00 ± 0.00%
	C4.5	100.00 ± 0.00%	100.00 ± 0.00%

Table 4. (*Continued*)

	LMT	86.53 ±3.87%	85.22 ± 4.04%
Crx data set	Naive Bayes	86.53 ±3.87%	85.51 ± 4.25%
	SMO	86.53 ±3.87%	85.80 ± 3.71%
	C4.5	85.36 ± 4.12%	85.51 ± 4.25%
	LMT	100 ± 0.00%	100.00 ± 0.00%
Monk-1 data set	Naive Bayes	72.22 ± 6.33%	74.97 ± 1.95%
	SMO	72.22 ± 6.33%	75.02 ± 5.66%
	C4.5	100.00 ± 0.00%	100.00 ± 0.00%
	LMT	67.14 ± 0.61%	67.36 ± 1.17%
Monk-2 data set	Naive Bayes	67.14 ± 0.61%	67.14 ± 0.61%
	SMO	67.14 ± 0.61%	67.14 ± 0.61%
	C4.5	67.14± 0.61 %	67.14 ± 0.61%
	LMT	97.22 ± 0.47%	99.77 ± 0.10%
Monk-3 data set	Naive Bayes	97.21 ± 2.71%	97.21 ± 2.71%
	SMO	97.22 ± 0.47%	100.00 ± 0.00%
	C4.5	100.00 ± 0.00%	100.00 ± 0.00%

4 Conclusion

This paper improves one of the existing feature selection algorithms, Shie-and-Chen's method. This feature selection algorithm uses fuzzy entropy concept. The problem of Shie-and-Chen's method is that it is a parameter sensitive algorithm. User should select threshold values in that algorithm experimentally. The result of algorithm for some threshold values is very weak and it is not trustable. To solve this problem we use ensemble method. Our paper runs Shie-and-Chen's algorithm for different values as thresholds and then gives a weight to each selected features according its rank. Finally by using one of the ensemble methods, majority voting, it selects the best features which have the highest scores. So this algorithm does not need any input parameter. Also the obtained accuracies of different classifiers on the selected features obtained by proposed method are better that the obtained accuracies of the same classifiers on the selected features obtained by Shie-and-Chen's algorithms.

References

1. Tan, P.N., Steinbach, M., Kumar, V.: Introduction to Data Mining, 1st edn. Addison-Wesley Longman Publishing Co. Inc., Amsterdam (2005)
2. Tsang, E.C.C., Yeung, D.S., Wang, X.Z.: OFFSS: optimal fuzzyvalued feature subset selection. IEEE Trans. Fuzzy Syst 11(2), 202–213 (2003)
3. Caruana, R., Freitag, D.: Greedy attribute selection. In: Proceedings of International Conference on Machine Learning, New Brunswick, NJ, pp. 28–33 (1994)
4. Baim, P.W.: A method for attribute selection in inductive learning systems. IEEE Trans. Pattern Anal. Mach. Intell. 10(6), 888–896 (1988)
5. De, R.K., Basak, J., Pal, S.K.: Neuro-fuzzy feature evaluation with theoretical analysis. Neural Netw. 12(10), 1429–1455 (1999)
6. Battiti, R.: Using mutual information for selecting features in supervised neural net learning. IEEE Trans. Neural Net. 5(4), 537–550 (1994)

7. Dong, M., Kothari, R.: Feature subset selection using a new definition of classi-fiability. Pattern Recognit. Lett. 24(9), 1215–1225 (2003)
8. De, R.K., Pal, N.R., Pal, S.K.: Feature analysis: neural network and fuzzy set theoretic approaches. Pattern Recognit. 30(10), 1579–1590 (1997)
9. Platt, J.C.: Using analytic QP and sparseness to speed training of support vector machines. In: Proceedings of the Thirteenth Annual Conference on Neural Information Processing Systems, Denver, CO, pp. 557–563 (1999)
10. Shie, J.D., Chen, S.M.: Feature subset selection based on fuzzy entropy measures for handling classification problems. Springer Science+Business Media (2007)

A New Feature Extraction Method Based on Clustering for Face Recognition

Sabra El Ferchichi[1], Salah Zidi[2], Kaouther Laabidi[1],
Moufida Ksouri[1], and Salah Maouche[2]

[1] LACS, ENIT, BP 37, le Belvédère 1002 Tunis, Tunisia
[2] LAGIS, USTL, Villeneuve d'Ascq, 59650 Lille, France
{sabra.elferchichi,kaouther.laabidi,moufida.ksouri}@enit.rnu.tn,
{salah.zidi,salah.maouche}@univ-lille1.fr

Abstract. When solving a pattern classification problem, it is common to apply a feature extraction method as a pre-processing step, not only to reduce the computation complexity but also to obtain better classification performance by reducing the amount of irrelevant and redundant information in the data. In this study, we investigate a novel schema for linear feature extraction in classification problems. The method we have proposed is based on clustering technique to realize feature extraction. It focuses in identifying and transforming redundant information in the data. A new similarity measure-based trend analysis is devised to identify those features. The simulation results on face recognition show that the proposed method gives better or competitive results when compared to conventional unsupervised methods like PCA and ICA.

Keywords: Feature extraction, dimensionality reduction, similarity measure, clustering, face recognition.

1 Introduction

The recent development in information technology has induced a rapid accumulation of high dimensional data such as face images and gene expression microarrays. Typically, in many pattern recognition problems, the huge number of features that represent data makes discrimination between patterns much harder and less accurate [1]. Thus, feature extraction is an important preprocessing step to machine learning and data mining. It has been effective in reducing dimensionality and increasing learning accuracy [2]. It tries to re-describe data in a lower dimensional feature space with respect to its underlying structure and generalization capabilities [2]. Abundant techniques for feature extraction problem were developed in the literature [3-8]. Principal Component Analysis (PCA) [3-5], remains the standard approach for feature extraction. It performs a linear transformation, derived from the eigenvectors corresponding to the largest eigenvalues of the covariance matrix. PCA implicitly assume that pattern elements are random variables with Gaussian distribution. Thus, in the case of non-Gaussian distribution, largest variances would not correspond to PCA basis vectors [4]. Independent Component Analysis (ICA) [5] has been proposed to minimize both second-order and higher-order

L. Iliadis and C. Jayne (Eds.): EANN/AIAI 2011, Part I, IFIP AICT 363, pp. 247–253, 2011.

dependencies in the input data and attempts to find the basis along which the projected data are statistically independent. Unlike unsupervised method like PCA and ICA, Linear Discriminant Analysis (LDA) method [7-8], exploit label classes to make feature extraction [7]. It extracts features that minimize the within-class scatter matrix and maximize the between-class scatter matrix.

In this work, our interest is to perform a feature extraction procedure without assuming any form of knowledge, neither about data distribution nor about its class distribution, unlike already discussed methods. Actually, in high dimensional data, many features have the same tendencies along the data set: they describe the same variations of monotonicity (increasing or decreasing). Thus we can consider that these features give very similar information for the learning process. Such features are then considered redundant and useless information. Once groups of similar features have been settled, feature extraction can be realized through a linear transformation of each group of similar features. Hence, a clustering technique based on a new measure of similarity between features was used to identify and gather similar features. A linear transformation is finally made on each identified groups of original features to obtain a set of new features. Performance of our method is assessed through face recognition problem. The rest of the paper is organized as follows: in section 2, we devise the new similarity measure based trend analysis to evaluate similarity between features and we detail the proposed Feature Extraction Method based Clustering (FEMC). In section 3, experiments are carried out on face recognition problem through Yale and ORL data sets. We compare FEMC with conventional unsupervised and supervised feature extractor such as PCA, ICA and LDA. Finally in section 4, a brief conclusion is drawn with some future work.

2 Clustering Based Feature Extraction Algorithm

Actually, redundant information is an intrinsic characteristic of high dimensional data which complicate learning task and degrade classifier performance. For this reason, eliminating redundant features is one clue to reduce the dimension without loss of some important information. One existing solution is to use a filter method to select relevant features. Although redundant information is not relevant for discrimination task but it has implicit interaction with the rest of features. Eliminating them from feature space may lead to eliminate some predictive information of the inherent structure of data and thereby don't lead necessarily to a more accurate classifier. FECM seeks to transform redundant features such that the amount of predictive information lost, is minimized. Intuitively, redundancy in a dataset can be expressed by similar features in term of behavior along the data set. They describe very similar or mostly the same variations of monotonicity along the data set. Thereby we consider that they incorporate the same discriminating information. Our method seeks to identify this form of redundancy and incorporate it by a linear transformation into the new set of features. We based our method on clustering technique using a new similarity measure to identify linear or complex relations that would exist between features. Once groups of similar features are formed, a linear transformation is realized to extract a new set of features. Actually, there exists another work that exploit clustering algorithm as a feature extraction technique to find new features [9]. It focuses on the prediction of HIV protease resistance to drugs. K-means based a biological similarity function was used. However, it can be used only for a specific purpose and can't be extended to other classification problems, unlike the general concept developed in this work.

2.1 Formulation

Merely, the aim of feature extraction is finding a transform T such that $y_i = T(x_i); 1 \leq i \leq L$. Where, $x_1, x_2, ...x_L \in \mathbb{R}^D$ is the D-dimensional data set and $y_i \in \mathbb{R}^{d \ll D}$ is the transformed sample composed of d new features $v_1, v_2, ...v_d \in \mathbb{R}^L$ where $d \ll D$. Each feature vector v_i is constituted by the different values corresponding to each instance or sample $x_{1 \leq j \leq L}$. FECM uses clustering process to partition the feature space into $d \ll D$ clusters. Actually, clustering is supposed to discover inherent structure of data [1], [8]. Its goal isn't to find the best partition of a given samples but to approximate the true partition of the underlying space. Each obtained cluster C_k is composed of n_k similar features according to the new similarity measure defined in the next section. It is represented each by its centroid g_k, obtained by applying the transform f defined by:

$$g_k = f(S_k) = \frac{1}{n_k} \sum_{s=1}^{n_k} v_s$$

(1)

Where, S_k is the set of n_k feature vectors $v_{s \in S_k}$ belonging to the cluster C_k. The obtained set of centroids $\{g_k\}_{1 \leq k \leq M}$ is then considered as the set of the d new features.

2.2 Similarity Measure

Distance or similarity relationships between pairs of patterns are the most important information for clustering process to approximate true partition in a dataset. FECM focuses on defining a similarity measure that characterizes similarity in the behavior of each features pair. We propose to analyze their tendencies through studying their variations of monotonicity along the data set rather than difference between their real values. Thus, conventional distance like Euclidean distance used normally in clustering algorithm is not suitable for our objective. Using Euclidean distance may lead to erroneous results since it computes the mean of difference between each value of two vectors without use of tendency information about them. In fact, two features may have the same mean (or closer means) but they differ completely in their trend. Actually, a trend is a semi-quantitative information, describing the evolution of the qualitative state of a variable, in a time interval, using a set of symbols such as {Increasing, Decreasing, Steady}[10]. To determine the trend of a feature vector in each point, we compute firstly, the corresponding first order derivative of a feature vector v at each sample x : $\dfrac{dv(i)}{dx} = \dfrac{v_i - v_{i-1}}{x_i - x_{i-1}}$. Then, we determine the sign of the derivative in each point by:

$$
if \begin{cases} \dfrac{dv}{dx} \prec 0 \\[2mm] \dfrac{dv}{dx} \succ 0 \\[2mm] \dfrac{dv}{dx} = 0 \end{cases} then \quad \alpha = \mathrm{sgn}\left(\dfrac{dv}{dx}\right) = \begin{cases} -1 \ (decrease) \\ 1 \ (increase) \\ 0 \ (steady) \end{cases} \tag{2}
$$

A feature vector $v \in \mathbb{R}^L$ is then being represented as an L-dimensional vector composed of L variables $\alpha \in \{1, -1, 0\}$. Distance function devised to compare two feature vectors relies on verifying difference in the sign of tendency between two feature vectors. It is the squared sum of the absolute difference between occurrences of a specified value of α for two given feature vectors. It was inspired from the Value Difference Metric (VDM) [11]. Thus, the location of a feature vector within the feature space is not defined directly by the values of its components, but by the conditional distributions of the extracted trend in each component. Hence, this makes the proposed metric independent from the order of data and has a generalization capability. It is given by the following expression:

$$
d\left(v_i, v_j\right) = \sqrt{\delta_1\left(v_i, v_j\right) + \delta_{-1}\left(v_i, v_j\right) + \delta_0\left(v_i, v_j\right)}
$$
$$
\delta_\alpha\left(v_i, v_j\right) = \left| p\left(v_i / \alpha\right) - p\left(v_j / \alpha\right) \right| \tag{3}
$$
$$
p\left(v_i / \alpha\right) = \frac{\text{Occurrence of } \alpha \text{ in } v_i}{L}
$$

$p\left(v_i / \alpha\right)$ is determined by counting haw many times the value α occurs in the feature vector v_i for the learning data set. In fact, in this work we have computed the occurrence of the pair of variables $(\alpha, \beta) \in \{10, 11, 1-1, -10, -11, -1-1, 00, 01, 0-1\}$ in each vector v_i instead of computing only the probability of the single variable $\alpha \in \{1, -1, 0\}$. A similarity matrix M between all features vectors is then generated such that $M\left(i, j\right) = d\left(v_i, v_j\right); \ i, j = 1...n$.

2.3 Feature Extraction Schema

Feature extraction process is given by the pseudocode below. The similarity matrix M is computed based on the metric defined previously by (3). Then a clustering strategy based on C-means clustering, is performed. Clusters are initialized randomly. Then they are sequentially enlarged by selecting the ε first ranked features in the similarity matrix M : set of the most similar features to the corresponding centroid g_j.

Hence, this process allows an overlap between clusters. To remedy to this, we perform an intersection between each pair of the obtained clusters to determine common features and decide at which cluster they finally belong. Each common feature is then assigned to the closest cluster according to the Euclidean distance

$$\forall v_i \in \{C_{k1} \cap C_{k2}\}, \quad v_i \in C_h = \arg\min \left\| g_{j \in \{k1,k2\}} - v_i \right\|^2 \tag{4}$$

Where h is the either the index k_1 or k_2. Clusters centers are then re-computed using the current cluster memberships and the process is stopped when all d clusters are constructed.

```
{Input: Raw Data}
{Output: New features= cluster 'centers}

    Compute matrix of distance  M(i,j)=d(v_i,v_j); i,j=1..n

Clustering

    {d=Ndivε: number of clusters

    ε : number of preselected features

    C: initial number of features

    Idx: index of initial centroid

    While C > 1

        ClusterC_k = select the  ε  first features from M

        C= C- ε

    End

    Intersection between d final clusters

    Update clusters centers}
```

3 Experimental Results

Face recognition is a technically difficult task due to the varying conditions in the data capturing process like variations in pose, orientation, expressions and illumination conditions. We assess the feasibility and performance of our proposed method of feature extraction on the face recognition task using the Yale and ORL datasets, presented in the Table 1. Each image from was down-sampled into a manageable size for computational efficiency. The classification performances of FECM were compared with those of PCA, ICA and LDA. A leave-one-out schema was used to obtain the performances and K-Nearest Neighbor classifier (KNN), known for its standard performance, was used as classifier system for both datasets.

Table 1. Data sets information

Data sets	No. of features	No. of instances	No. of classes
Yale data set	783	165	15
ORL data set	952	400	40

Table 2. Classification accuracy on Yale Dataset

Methods	Error rate %	Number of features
KNN	21.82	783
PCA	24.85	30
ICA	23.03	30
LDA	8.48	14
FEMC	21.00	14

Performances of FECM for ORL dataset are detailed in the Table 3. Because there must be at least 40 PCs to get 39 features, the first 40 PCs are retained as input for LDA and ICA. Note that the number of extracted features by LDA is 39 because there are 40 classes. Our approach is close to PCA and ICA in terms of classification accuracy with smaller number of features which is 23, but LDA stay having the best accuracy classification as in Yale dataset due to its supervised nature.

Table 3. Classification accuracy on AT&T Dataset

Methods	Error rate %	Number of features
KNN	3.00	952
PCA	4.00	40
ICA	4.25	40
LDA	2.00	39
FEMC	5.00	23

4 Conclusion

This paper deals with the important problem of extracting discriminant features for pattern classification. Feature extraction techniques often trust in some interestingness criterion to search for a lower dimensional representation. However, because the true structure of the data is unknown, it is inherently ambiguous what constitutes a good low dimensional representation. This makes it difficult to define a proper interestingness criterion. In this work, we propose a new feature extraction approach based on feature clustering. The main motivation behind it was to identify redundancy in feature space and reduce its effect without losing some important information for classification task. Similar feature are recognized through analyzing their monotonicity along the data set and a new similarity measure is then devised. The proposed approach applies clustering technique into feature space to determine its underlying groups of features. Each obtained cluster is represented by one feature, computed as the mean of all features grouped in the cluster. The main difficult in the proposed method is its dependence on the partition resulting from the clustering process. In validation strategy, clustering algorithm analyses only training set, which changes every time, so clustering rules changes every time. That can produce some instability in the results of the method. Hence, further work to verify robustness of the method towards noise in data has to be engaged.

For the face recognition task, our approach produces a lower number of features than PCA and ICA, and achieves better or competitive classification accuracy. Unlike LDA, we didn't make use of class information in our procedure. It would be interesting to introduce this specific information in our procedure to approach semi supervised learning task.

References

1. Fern, X.Z., Brodley, E.C.: Cluster Ensembles for High Dimensional Clustering: an empirical study. Technical report CS06-30-02 (2004)
2. Torkkola, K.: Feature Extraction by Non-parametric Mutual Information Maximization. Journal of Machine Learning Research 3, 1415–1438 (2003)
3. Saul, L.K., Weinberger, K.Q., Sha, F., Ham, J., Lee, D.D.: Spectral Methods for Dimensionality Reduction. In: Chapelle, O., Schoelkopf, B., Zien, A. (eds.) Semi Supervised Learning. MIT Press, Cambridge (2006)
4. Delac, K., Grgic, M., Grgic, S.: Independent Comparative Study of PCA, ICA and LDA on FERET data set. Int. J. Imaging Syst. Technol. 15, 252–260 (2006)
5. Kwak, N.: Feature Extraction for Classification Problems and its Application to Face Recognition. Journal of Pattern Recognition 41, 1701–1717 (2008)
6. Wang, J., Lin, Y., Yang, W., Yang, J.: Kernel Maximum Scatter Difference based Feature Extraction and its application to Face Recognition. Pattern Recognition Letters 29, 1832–1835 (2008)
7. Xiang, C., Huang, D.: Feature Extraction using Recursive Cluster-based Linear Discriminant with Application to Face Recognition. IEEE Transcations on Image Processing 15, 3824–3832 (2006)
8. Von Luxburg, U., Budeck, S., Jegelka, S., Kaufmann, M.: Consistent Minimization of Clustering Objective Functions. In: Neural Information Processing Systems, NIPS (2007)
9. Bonet, I., Saeys, Y., Ábalo, R.G., García, M.M., Sanchez, R., Van de Peer, Y.: Feature Extraction Using Clustering of Protein. In: Martínez-Trinidad, J.F., Carrasco Ochoa, J.A., Kittler, J. (eds.) CIARP 2006. LNCS, vol. 4225, pp. 614–623. Springer, Heidelberg (2006)
10. Charbonnier, S., Gentil, S.: A trend-based Alarm System to Improve Patient Monitoring in Intensive Care Units. Control Engineering Practice 15, 1039–1050 (2007)
11. Payne, R.T., Edwards, P.: Implicit Feature Selection with the Value Difference Metric. In: The 13th European Conference on Artificial Intelligence, pp. 450–454 (1998)

A Recurrent Neural Network Approach for Predicting Glucose Concentration in Type-1 Diabetic Patients

Fayrouz Allam[1], Zaki Nossair[2], Hesham Gomma[2], Ibrahim Ibrahim[2],
and Mona Abdelsalam[3]

[1] Tabbin Institute for Metallurgical Studies, Helwan, Egypt
[2] Faculty of Engineering, Helwan Univ., Egypt
[3] Faculty of Medicine, Ain Shams Univ., Egypt

Abstract. Estimation of future glucose concentration is important for diabetes management. To develop a model predictive control (MPC) system that measures the glucose concentration and automatically inject the amount of insulin needed to keep the glucose level within its normal range, the accuracy of the predicted glucose level and the longer prediction time are major factors affecting the performance of the control system. The predicted glucose values can be used for early hypoglycemic/hyperglycemic alarms for adjustment of insulin injections or insulin infusion rates of manual or automated pumps. Recent developments in continuous glucose monitoring (CGM) devices open new opportunities for glycemia management of diabetic patients. In this article a new technique, which uses a recurrent neural network (RNN) and data obtained from CGM device, is proposed to predict the future values of the glucose concentration for prediction horizons (PH) of 15, 30, 45, 60 minutes. The results of the proposed technique is evaluated and compared relative to that obtained from a feed forward neural network prediction model (NNM). Our results indicate that, the RNN is better in prediction than the NNM for the relatively long prediction horizons.

Keywords: glucose concentration prediction, type-1 diabetes, neural networks.

1 Introduction

The current trend in research is to automatically monitor the blood glucose level and inject the insulin needed to regulate the patient glucose level. Continuous glucose sensors can be coupled with continuous insulin infusion pumps to create a closed-loop artificial pancreas. The model which is used in MPC is required to accurately predict the glucose level for long prediction horizons to compensate for the delay between the CGM readings and the blood glucose values. Since glucose-insulin interaction is a nonlinear, therefore, modeling using neural network as a nonlinear system will give better results [1]. However, if the model is required to predict more than one time step ahead, recurrent neural networks should be used. Neural network techniques have been used in the past for predicting glucose levels using CGM readings as input and also within glucose control systems [2]. Oruklu et al., [3] proposed the development of the empirical models that use frequently sampled glucose data. They used

L. Iliadis and C. Jayne (Eds.): EANN/AIAI 2011, Part I, IFIP AICT 363, pp. 254–259, 2011.
© IFIP International Federation for Information Processing 2011

autoregressive moving average (ARMA) to predict the future glucose concentration. Their model is based on the virtual subject's glucose concentration obtained from Hovorka model, and they simulate the CGM data by adding Gaussian noise to the synthetic data. The PH of their model is 30 minutes (6 steps) ahead prediction. Zainuddin et al. [4] developed four different feed forward wavelet neural networks for four intervals: morning, afternoon, evening and night, in order to predict the blood glucose at the end of each interval. The patients need to fill in information about time of glucose measurements, blood glucose values, insulin doses, food, exercises and stress. Perez et al., [1] present a NNM which can predict future glucose concentration from previous 5 glucose CGM samples and the current time stamp, while the output is the glucose concentration at the chosen PH. Three different PHs are used: 15, 30, and 45 min. Their model suffers from time delay between the original and predicted glucose concentration. Gani et al., [5] developed a glucose prediction autoregressive (AR) model of order 30 to make short term, 30-minutes ahead prediction time, without time lag. Pappada et al., [6] used a dataset of different patients obtained by CGM to construct a neural network using NeuroSolutions® software to predict glucose concentration while time varying predictive window from 50-180 minutes is used. In this paper, we present a new prediction algorithm based on a RNN. It is a fully automated prediction system which doesn't need any data to be entered from patients such as in [4]; therefore our proposed prediction algorithm is more convenient to be used during sleeping hours.

2 Subjects and Dataset

The evaluation of the proposed algorithm is performed using glucose measurements from 9 type-1 diabetic patients, the average duration of glucose measurements for each patient is 2 days, 288 samples for each day. The glucose measurements for the 9 patients were obtained using Gaurdian® Real Time CGM system (Medtronic-Minimed) which provides a glucose reading every 5 minutes. Our data set consists of 4916 samples. This data is divided into two different subsets, one subset is for training and the second is for testing and validating the model. The data was smoothed using low pass filter of order 11 before using it in training and testing the neural networks. The use of smoothed version of the CGM data reduces the time lag between the predicted glucose and measured glucose values [5].

3 The Proposed Algorithm

Our proposed prediction algorithm uses CGM readings only, it is like a nonlinear AR model. Both inputs and delayed feed backed outputs are glucose concentration values. Fig. 1 shows the architecture of the RNN predictor. The input u_i is the glucose reading of sample i (current glucose value), and the output y_i is the predicted glucose reading at time i+PH. The input u_i is entered to a tapped delay line (TDL) element to hold the previous glucose readings, $u_{i-1},...,u_{i-N}$, where N is the number of inputs. The initial outputs from this TDL are u_1 to u_N [means the glucose readings G_1, G_2, G_3, G_4,...,G_N]. The network has also feedback input which is the output y_i that enters to another TDL to hold $y_{i-1},...,y_{i-M}$, where M is the PH divided by 5 minutes sampling period. The initial outputs from this (TDL) are y_1 to y_M [means glucose readings $G_{N+1},...,G_{N+M}$]. The input u_i is updated at each new sample time by the glucose reading from the CGM sensor, this means that the prediction is based on the most recent N readings of the glucose concentration. For example, if the PH is 25 minutes, and the input is u_6 [i.e. G_6], then the predicted glucose will be y_6 which is an estimate for G_{11}. The available initial offline inputs are the first 10 samples of glucose, the first 5 samples are applied directly to the inputs and the samples from G_6 to G_{10} are applied one after the other, therefore the predicted output will be G_{11} to G_{15}, which means 5 step ahead prediction, (each step represents 5 minutes), therefore it performs 25 minutes prediction.

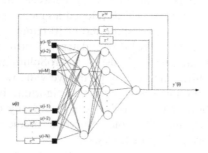

Fig. 1. The architecture of the RNN which is used in the prediction algorithm

3.1 Evaluation Metrics

The performance of the proposed prediction algorithm is evaluated using several metrics: root mean squared error (RMSE) in mmol/L, FIT, and normalized prediction error (NPE). These metrics have the following expressions.

$$RMSE = \sqrt{\frac{\sum_{i=1}^{N}(G_i - \hat{G}_i)^2}{N}} \tag{1}$$

$$FIT = (1 - \frac{\left\|G_i - \hat{G}_i\right\|}{\left\|G_i - \bar{G}\right\|}) \times 100 \tag{2}$$

$$NPE = \sqrt{\frac{\sum_{i=1}^{N}(G_i - \hat{G}_i)^2}{\sum_{i=1}^{N}G_i^2}} \tag{3}$$

Where G_i is the glucose reading of sample i, N is the total number of samples, $\hat{G}_i$ is the estimated glucose value of sample i, $\bar{G}$ is the mean of all glucose readings. In addition to the above three metrics, the Clarke error grid approach (Clarke's EGA) [7] was also used to assess the performance of the prediction algorithm with a clinically acceptable metric.

3.2 Experiments and Results

Many network architectures for the RNN are tested to optimize the predicted output. Two hidden layers and 20 neurons in the first hidden layer were found to give the best results. The prediction performance of the network is evaluated (by calculating FIT) for various numbers of inputs, when the number of inputs is changed; the network architecture that optimizes the predicted output is changed, as shown in table 1. Table 2 shows the evaluation measures calculated for several PH values when using 20-13-1 architecture which gives the best predicted output (from table 1). Table 3 shows the error matrix of EGA which contains the percentage of predicted samples that are located in each zone for different PHs.

Table 1. FIT values when using various number of inputs and PH=40 min. for different network architectures

No. of inputs	Network Architecture	FIT (%)
30	20-7-1	72.16
30	20-8-1	65.18
30	20-10-1	74.5
40	20-10-1	76.72
40	20-13-1	77.21
40	18-13-1	68.24
50	18-13-1	71.5
50	20-13-1	76.15

Table 2. Values of RMSE, FIT and NPE when using 40 inputs and (20-13-1) for different PHs

PH	FIT (%)	RMSE (mmol/L)	NPE (%)
15	95.33	0.14	1.7
30	85.83	0.42	5.27
45	72.3	0.84	10.28
60	56.61	1.32	16.2

4 Performance Comparisons

The RNN gives more accurate predicted output than the NNM because the relationship between glucose concentration and time is highly dynamic. Many NNM architectures are tested to choose the ones that give the best predicted output, the best architectures were 15-10-1, 15-13-1, 16-13-1, 20-13-1 for PH of 15, 30, 45 and 60 minutes respectively. Fig. 2 shows the difference in prediction accuracy between the NNM and the RNN for various PHs. Table 3 shows Clarke's EGA to clinically evaluate the predicted output from the NNM and RNN.

Table 3 shows that, for PHs less than 60 minutes, all the predicted values are located in clinically accepted zones A and B for RNN. At PH of 45 minutes, 2.7% of predicted outputs from the NNM lay in zone D. At PH of 60 minutes, there are 1.95% for RNN and 5.98% for NNM of predicted samples located in zone D, which can lead to incorrect treatments and detections. Table 4 shows the RMSE for results that are obtained from the RNN and the SVR model used in [8].

Table 3. The Clarke's EGA for Feed Forward Network's Output at Different PHs

PH	A		B		C		D		E	
	NNM	RNN	NNM	RNN	NNM	RNN	NNM	RNN	NNM	RNN
15	100	100	0	0	0	0	0	0	0	0
30	98.5	98.6	1.47	1.3	0	0	0	0	0	0
45	86.7	91.5	10.5	8.4	0	0	2.7	0	0	0
60	42.09	78.7	50.42	19.3	0	0	5.98	1.95	1.49	0

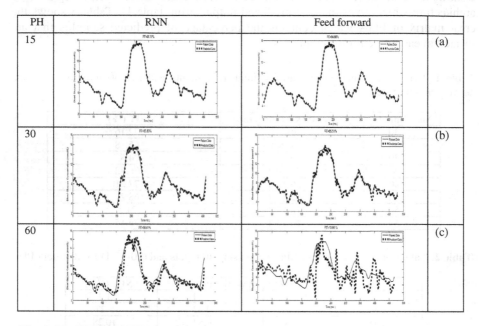

Fig. 2. The RNN and NNM prediction results for PH of (a) 15 min., (b) 30 min.,(c) 60 min.

Table 4. RMSE values for RNN prediction model and SVR based prediction model

Prediction model	15 min.	30 min.	60 min.
RNN model	0.14	0.55	1.32
SVR model	0.52	0.89	1.37

5 Discussion

From all of the previous results it can be seen that, at PH= 30 min., there is no time delay in the predicted output from both the RNN and NNM. At PH=45 min., there is a wider oscillation in the predicted profile of the NNM's output. These oscillations result in a large model prediction error. The NNM failed to predict the output for PH=60 min. For short prediction horizons our proposed RNN algorithm is comparable with others that use recurrent networks such as [9] in which they used 6 RNNs to implement the Hovorka diabetic patient physiological model. Our model used real readings of glucose obtained using CGM, and trained one RNN to predict future values of glucose. This difference makes our model more simple and based on real data instead of synthetic data. The model of Huang et al. [9] gives FIT=80.9% for PH=30 min., which is less than our result for the same PH. Our results for long PH are still incomparable with that of other algorithms that are trying to predict for longer PHs such as in [9] which predicts 2 and 4 hours.

6 Conclusion

Training the RNN using data obtained from a CGM device, which continuously reads the glucose during the full day for different patients, gives our model some generality. The RNN needs some fine tuning when it is used with a specific patient. This is one of the differences between our model and some others such as [5]. Our RNN can accurately predict the glucose values for PH=30 minutes without time delay. At PH=45 minutes the RNN can predict with very little time delay and with acceptable accuracy. But its accuracy is deteriorated for 60 minutes prediction. It is better to use the RNN than the NNM in prediction especially at longer PH, where the accuracy of the NNM is highly deteriorated. Clarke's EGA indicated that the performance of the proposed RNN prediction model is also significant from a clinical point of view. We conclude that, the RNN prediction algorithm succeeds to predict the future glucose values from CGM systems. It can be used for online glucose prediction in model prediction control systems.

References

1. Pérez-Gandía, C., Facchinetti, A., Sparacino, G., Cobelli, C., Gómez, E.J., Rigla, M., de Leiva, A., Hernando, M.E.: Artificial Neural Network Algorithm for Online Glucose Prediction from Continuous Glucose Monitoring. Diabetes Technology & Therapeutics 12, 81–88 (2010)
2. Mougiakakou, S.G., Nikita, K.S.: A neural network approach for insulin regime and dose adjustment in type 1 diabetes. Diabetes Technol. Ther. 2, 381–389 (2000)
3. Oruklu, M.E., Cinar, A., Quinn, L., Smith, D.: Adaptive control strategy for regulation of blood glucose levels in patients with type 1 diabetes. Journal of Process Control 19, 1333–1346 (2009)
4. Zainuddin, Z., Pauline, O., Ardil, C.: A Neural Network Approach in Predicting the Blood Glucose Level for Diabetic Patients. International Journal of Information and Mathematical Sciences 5(1), 72–79 (2009)
5. Gani, A., Gribok, A.V., Lu, Y., Ward, W.K., Vigersky, R.A., Reifman, J.: Universal Glucose Models for Predicting Subcutaneous Glucose Concentration in Humans. IEEE Transactions on Information Technology in Biomedicine 14, 157–165 (2010)
6. Pappada, S.M., Brent, B.S., Cameron, D., Rosman, P.M.: Development of a Neural Network for Prediction of Glucose Concentration in Type 1 Diabetes Patients. Journal of Diabetes Science and Technology 2, 792–801 (2008)
7. Clarke, W.L.: The original Clarke error grid analysis (EGA). Diabetes a Technol. Ther. 7, 776–779 (2005)
8. Georga, E., Protopappas, V.C., Fotiadis, D.I.: Predictive Modeling of Glucose Metabolism using Free-living Data of Type 1 Diabetic Patients. In: Annual International Conference of the IEEE, pp. 589–592. Engineering in Medicine and Biology Society (EMBC) (2010)
9. Huang, H.P., Liu, S.W., Chien, I.L., Lin, C.H.: A Dynamic Model with Structured Recurrent Neural Network to Predict Glucose-Insulin Regulation of Type 1 Diabetes Mellitus. In: Proceedings of the 9th International Symposium on Dynamics and Control of Process Systems (DYCOPS 2010), Belgium, pp. 228–233 (2010)

Segmentation of Breast Ultrasound Images Using Neural Networks

Ahmed A. Othman and Hamid R. Tizhoosh

Department of Systems Design Engineering, University of Waterloo, Ontario, Canada
{a4abdelr,tizhoosh}@uwaterloo.ca

Abstract. Medical image segmentation is considered a very important task for diagnostic and treatment-planning purposes. Accurate segmentation of medical images helps clinicians to clarify the type of the disease and facilitates the process of efficient treatment. In this paper, we propose two different approaches to segment breast ultrasound images using neural networks. In the first approach, we use scale invariant feature transform (SIFT) to calculate a set of descriptors for a set of points inside the image. These descriptors are used to train a supervised neural network. In the second approach, we use SIFT to detect a set of key points inside the image. Texture features are then extracted from a region around each point to train the network. This process is repeated multiple times to verify the generalization ability of the network. The average segmentation accuracy is calculated by comparing every segmented image with corresponding gold standard images marked by an expert.

1 Introduction

Most of the image thresholding methods deal with different images in a static way without paying any attention to the different properties of different images. These methods could generate good results for some images. A method of dynamic nature (with learning ability) that deals with the image based on its features is still needed. The features of the image can guide the process of calculating accurate thresholds for a given class of images sharing some common characteristics.

In this paper, we propose two different approaches to threshold medical images using neural network trained using a set of features extracted from the image. In the first approach, we use SIFT descriptors generated from a set of key points. These points seem to be the most descriptive points of the image and are used to train a supervised neural network that could be used to threshold new images. In the second approach, we use SIFT to detect a set of key points within the image. A rectangle around each point is generated and used to extract a set of second order texture features. These features are used to train a supervised neural network that could be used to threshold new images.

This paper is organized as: In sections 2 and 3 a brief survey of image thresholding and neural networks is provided. In section 4, the SIFT technique is explained. In section 5, the level set segmentation technique is reviewed since we

L. Iliadis and C. Jayne (Eds.): EANN/AIAI 2011, Part I, IFIP AICT 363, pp. 260–269, 2011.

use it for comparison purposes. In section 6, the proposed techniques are introduced and discussed. In section 7, medical images are used to test the proposed techniques. In section 8, the paper is summarized.

2   Image Thresholding

Thresholding in image segmentation is the most simplest and effective method to separate objects from the background based on image gray level. Thresholding is still used in many applications because of its simplicity and speed. Sezgin et al. [1] provide a survey of the most popular thresholding methods. They categorize thresholding methods based on the information used to six classes: histogram shape-based methods, clustering-based methods, entropy-based methods, object attribute-based methods, the spatial methods and local methods. The Otsu method is considered one of the most popular thresholding techniques. This method divides the image histogram into two classes foreground and background using a threshold that minimizes the variance between these two classes [2]. Bazi et al. [3] use the expectation-maximization algorithm to find the optimal global threshold of the image based on the estimation of the statistical parameters of object and background classes that follow generalized Gaussian distribution. Kamal et al. [4] use a genetic algorithm to generate a threshold from the histogram that has been compressed using wavelet transform. Nakib et al. [5] use the digital fractional differentiation of the image histogram to calculate the threshold of the image. Nakib et al. [6] find the optimal thresholds of the within-class criterion, the entropy and the overall probability of error criterion by using multi-objective optimization approach.

Most of the thresholding techniques depend mainly on the histogram of the image. The shape of the histogram is not the same for all images and most of the methods that depend on the histogram work well when the histogram is bi- or multi-modal. If there is a histogram with not-clear modes, then it will be difficult to detect accurate thresholds as all of these methods are static method, namely without ant ability to adjust to the features of the image. There is a need for a thresholding method that can dynamically adapt to different images. In our method we calculate the threshold of the image based on its feature.

3   Neural Network Segmentation

Because of the large number of different neural architectures used for image segmentation, it is difficult to provide an in-depth review of all proposed schemes. Hence, we will summarize only those works that may be related to our approach. Neural networks have been used in medical image analysis in different ways. Unsupervised clustering neural networks were used to segment CT and MRI brain slices [7]. A three dimensional architecture of contextual constraint-based Hopfield network [8] was used to segment medical images. An incremental neural network [9] for the segmentation of tissues in ultrasound images by using discrete Fourier transform and discrete cosine transform as a feature vectors. A survey of the image segmentation by relaxation using constraint satisfaction neural network is provided in [10]. Texture features are used with some neural networks to segment different medical images [11]. The features are extracted from a rectangle around the region of interest. The problem with this method is that prior information about the region of interest is required, otherwise manual user interaction is needed.

In our approach, the process is automated as the rectangle around the region of interest that will be used for extracting features is created by the algorithm. Our solution is a simple and efficient neural approach since fast and trainable threshold selection is still necessary for many practical applications.

4   Scale Invariant Feature Transform (SIFT)

SIFT is an approach developed by Lowe [12] as a method for object recognition. It depends on detecting a set of key points of an object and calculating a set of descriptors (features) for these points. These features, invariant to image scale and rotation, can be used to recognize one object from among different objects. The process of detecting key points and calculating descriptors consist of four stages:

Scale-space extrema detection: In this stage the points of interest (key points) are detected. First, Gaussian filters at different scales are generated and then convolved with the image at every scale. The difference of the Gaussian-blurred image are taken and the candidate key points are assigned as maxima/minima of the difference of Gaussians (DoG) $D(x, y, \sigma)$ at multiple scales. To make the scale space of an image, the convolution of a Gaussian, $G(x, y, \sigma)$, with an input image, $I(x, y)$ is taken and defined as a function, $L(x, y, \sigma)$, where

$$L(x, y, \sigma) = G(x, y, \sigma) * I(x, y), \tag{1}$$

and, (DoG) is given by:

$$D(x, y, \sigma) = (G(x, y, k\sigma) - G(x, y, \sigma)) * I(x, y). \tag{2}$$

The maxima/minima of the difference of Gaussians (DoG) are calculated by comparing each point with its eight neighbours in the current image and nine neighbours in the scale above and below. The point selected to be key point if it is larger than all of these neighbours or smaller than all of them.

Key point localization: For each candidate point, a measure of stability is calculated to discard points with low contrast or poor location along the edges.

Orientation assignment: local image gradient directions are used to assign one or more orientations to each key point location, to make sure that the candidate points are invariant to orientation.

Key point descriptor: after selecting the candidate points, the local image gradients are measured in the region around each key point. Orientation histograms are created from 4×4 pixel neighbourhoods with 8 bins each, and the magnitude and orientation values of samples in a 16×16 region around the key points are calculated. Where there are $4 \times 4 = 16$ histograms each with 8 bins, the feature vector of each key point has 128 elements.

SIFT has been used in many different applications such as object recognition, image stretching, 3D modelling, gesture recognition, video tracking, match moving, face authentication [13] and to present a self-calibration strategy to estimate intrinsic and extrinsic camera parameters [14]. Many attempts have been made to improve SIFT. Lindeberg [15] proposes a systematic methodology for dealing with the problem of how to select appropriate local scales for further analysis. Tang et al. [16] propose a modification to SIFT algorithm to produce better invariant feature points for image matching under noise. Lopez et al. [17] present a new feature matching algorithm that integrates SIFT local descriptors in the Iterative Closest Point (ICP) scheme to find the appropriate match between repetitive patterns that appear in man-made scenes.

We use SIFT in two different ways. First, we use the SIFT descriptors to train the neural network. Second, we use SIFT to locate the key points inside the image that seems to be the most descriptive points. A set of texture features is extracted from a rectangle around each point.

5   Level Set Segmentation (LS)

The level set method is a tool for modelling time-varying objects as it uses numerical techniques for tracking shape changes. The level set method uses a fixed Cartesian grid to perform numerical computations to follow shapes that change topology involving curves and surfaces without parameterizing these objects [19].

In traditional level set methods [18] a common numerical scheme is used to initialize the function ϕ as a signed distance function before the evolution to overcome the problems of sharp and/or flat shape generated during the curve evolution. This scheme periodically reshapes (or "re-initializes") the function ϕ to be a signed distance function during the evolution. Therefore, the re-initialization process is crucial and cannot be avoided in traditional level set methods [19].

As an attempt to solve the problem of re-initialization, Li et al. [20] suggest to make the level set function close to a signed distance by using internal and external energy terms. Yan et al. [21] used the object's boundary to detect the precise location of the target object and the region information to prevent the boundary leakage problem. Level set methods have been used to segment breast ultrasound images [22] by developing an energy function that employed the differences between the actual and estimated probability densities of the intensities in different regions. The initial contour and the number of iterations need to be assigned for every image which is a time-consuming task.

We used level sets for comparative studies in this paper. We have to initialize the first point that the shape uses to start to evolve. The number of iterations needs to be assigned for every image to generate perfect results which is computationally expensive.

6 Proposed Approaches

Generally, the proposed idea uses the image characteristics to train a neural network to segment images directly by assigning a threshold $T \in \{0, 1, \ldots, 255\}$. The network is trained with a set of features extracted from training images along with their best-possible threshold as a target of the network. We propose two different approaches to train the neural network. In the first approach, we use the SIFT descriptors calculated for the SIFT key points either for the whole image or within a rectangle around the region of interest (ROI). In the second approach, we use the SIFT method to detect a set of key points within the images either for the whole image or within a rectangle around the ROI. Texture features are extracted from a rectangle around each point.

6.1 Detection Algorithm

All images are processed by a detection algorithm which finds the position of the first seed point (x_s, y_s) inside the ROI. This point is calculated by tracing an $n \times n$ mask (e.g. 10×10) over the image to calculate the sum and the standard deviation of intensities inside every mask, as well as the correlation between the mask and its neighbour. Based on empirical knowledge about the test images, the ROI is rather hypoechoic (low gray-level intensities) and generally exhibits low standard deviations (many cysts and tumours in ultrasound scans of breast are usually hypo- or anechoic). The mask that has minimum sum and minimum standard deviation is considered the mask contains the seed point. The correlation coefficients between the mask and its preceding mask are used to select the mask containing the seed point if the minimum sum and minimum standard deviation are in two different masks. Hence, for every $n \times n$ part of the image the minimum sum, standard deviation and correlation are considered to mark the position of a seed point (x_s, y_s) inside the ROI. This point is used as a center for a rectangle around it.

Generating Rectangle Around ROI. The algorithm proceeds by constructing a rectangle around the point (x_s, y_s) as the center of the rectangle. The algorithm starts by finding a region around (x_s, y_s) as a window and enlarges it in small step. This process stops when the standard deviation of one region becomes greater than or less than the standard deviation of the previous region by a certain limit (e.g. 3%) and the last window is considered the rectangle region R around the ROI. These images are stored to be used for extracting feature in the training and testing phases of the proposed methods that use rectangle around the ROI. In most images, the detection algorithm detects a correct point inside the ROI. For some images, it failed to detect a correct point but we nonetheless proceeded with the rectangle generated by the algorithm to verify the overall performance.

6.2 SIFT Descriptors Neural Network (DNN)

Feature Extraction. The DNN technique uses the features generated by SIFT for training. The process of extracting features is performed using two different approaches: 1) Extracting features from the whole image (DNN$_I$). The images I is processed by SIFT to return n points and $128 \times n$ feature matrix, 2) Extracting features from a rectangle around the ROI (DNN$_R$). R is provided to the SIFT which then returns n points and a $128 \times n$ feature matrix for R.

6.3 SIFT Texture Neural Network (TNN)

Feature Extraction. In this approach we extract a set of texture features from a set of key points n assigned by SIFT method either from the whole (TNN$_I$) image or from a rectangle around the ROI (TNN$_R$). A 40×40 rectangle is generated around each point and features are calculated from the gray level co-occurrence matrix (GLCM) in the directions 0, 45, 90, and 135 degrees of this rectangle. We use a set of texture features: 1) Contrast: a measure of the intensity difference between a pixel and its neighbours, 2) Correlation: a measure of how correlated a pixel is to its neighbours over the whole image, 3) Energy: the sum of squared elements in the GLCM, 4) Homogeneity: a value that measures the closeness of the distribution of elements in the GLCM to the GLCM diagonal.

We have 4 features in four direction $4 \times 4 = 16$, for $n = 20$, the feature matrix is of size 16×20 where each column represents the features for a point. We use *Matlab* functions *"graycomatrix"* to create the co-occurrence matrix and *"graycoprops"* to calculate the features from the GLCM.

6.4 Training the Neural Network

For the two approaches, a feed-forward backpropagation network was used to learn the set of training images. The network consists of one input layer corresponding to the size of the feature matrix, one hidden layer with 60 nodes and the output layer with one output (=the estimated threshold).

For every training set, five different images are used to train the network. The best-possible thresholds for these five images are assigned as the target of the network. The network is trained using Matlab function *"trainscg"* with desired error set to $\epsilon = 10^{-7}$ to be achieved within a maximum of $N_E = 10^5$ epochs.

6.5 Testing the Neural Network

For DNN and TNN methods, we make two different tests for every new image I. For every approach DNN$_I$, DNN$_R$, TNN$_I$, TNN$_R$, the global threshold of every image is the average of the thresholds assigned by the network to every point generated for this image by SIFT. The extracted features form every point are the inputs for the neural network which assigns a suitable threshold to each point. Let N_1, N_2, N_3 and N_4 are the points generated by SIFT for DNN$_I$, DNN$_R$, TNN$_I$, TNN$_R$, respectively. The global threshold for every image is calculated as follows:

$T^* = \frac{1}{|N_j|} \sum_{i=1}^{|N_j|} T_i$ where $j = 1, 2, 3, 4$.

7   Experiments and Results

In this section, a set of 20 breast ultrasound images are employed to train and test the proposed techniques. These 20 images are quite difficult to segment as their maximum achievable segmentation accuracy is 84% (maximum achievable accuracy via pure thresholding if thresholds are optimal). For every approach, DNN and TNN, five of the images are used as a training set and the remaining 15 images are used for testing. This process is repeated 4 times to generate different training sets and investigate the generalization ability of the network. For every training set the process repeated six times and the average of the

Table 1. The first training set: The Jaccard Index J, Dice value D and their standard deviations σ_J, σ_D, the 95%-confidence interval CI of J and of D

Metrics	LS		Train	TNN_I	TNN_R	DNN_I	DNN_R
	Train	Test					
D	72	79	90	84	84	87	89
σ_D	± 19	± 18	±5	±15	±15	±11	±7
CI_D	46-96	68-89	84-97	76-93	75-92	80-94	85-93
J	59	69	82	75	74	78	80
σ_J	± 25	± 22	± 9	± 18	± 19	± 15	± 10
CI_J	28-91	56-81	72-94	65-86	64-85	69-87	74-86

Table 2. The second training set: The Jaccard Index J, Dice value D and their standard deviations σ_J, σ_D, the 95%-confidence interval CI of J and of D

Metrics	LS		Train	TNN_I	TNN_R	DNN_I	DNN_R
	Train	Test					
D	75	77	90	79	87	87	88
σ_D	± 19	± 18	± 6	± 22	± 13	± 13	± 9
CI_D	50-97	68-89	82-98	66-91	79-94	79-94	82-94
J	63	67	82	69	78	78	79
σ_J	± 23	± 22	± 10	± 25	± 17	± 16	± 13
CI_J	33-92	54-80	69-95	55-83	68-88	68-87	71-87

Table 3. The third training set: The Jaccard Index J, Dice value D and their standard deviations σ_J, σ_D, the 95%-confidence interval CI of J and of D

Metrics	LS		Train	TNN_I	TNN_R	DNN_I	DNN_R
	Train	Test					
D	76	78	90	84	86	89	89
σ_D	± 25	± 16	± 7	± 12	± 11	± 6	±6
CI_D	44-100	68-87	80-99	78-91	79-93	85-93	85-93
J	66	66	82	74	76	80	81
σ_J	± 30	± 20	±12	± 16	± 15	± 10	± 10
CI_J	28-97	55-78	67-97	66-84	67-85	74-86	74-87

Table 4. The fourth training set: The Jaccard Index J, Dice value D and their standard deviations σ_J, σ_D, the 95%-confidence interval CI of J and of D

Metrics	LS Train	Train Test	TNN$_I$	TNN$_R$	DNN$_I$	DNN$_R$
D	69	80	92	78	86	87	88
σ_D	± 23	± 16	±3	±20	± 13	± 11	± 8
CI_D	40-97	70-90	87-97	67-90	78-93	81-94	84-93
J	57	69	84	68	77	79	80
σ_J	± 27	± 20	± 6	± 23	± 17	± 14	± 12
CI_J	22-92	58-81	76-93	55-82	68-87	71-88	73-86

Table 5. Summary of the results for the accuracy J and its 95%-confidence interval

Method	1st set J	CI	2nd set J	CI	3rd Set J	CI	4th Set J	CI
LS	69%	56% -81%	67%	55% -80%	66%	55% -78%	69%	58% -81%
TNN$_I$	75%	65% -86%	69%	55% -83%	74%	66% -84%	68%	55% -82%
TNN$_R$	74%	64%-85%	78%	68%-88%	76%	67%-85%	77%	68%-87%
DNN$_I$	78%	69%-87%	78%	68%-87%	80%	74%-86%	79%	71%-88%
DNN$_R$	80%	74%-86%	79%	71%-87%	81%	74%-87%	80%	73%-86%

results was taken. For LS, the process repeated six times as well with number of iterations = 100, 200 and 300 with different sizes of initial contour and the average of the results was taken. For LS method, the algorithm is applied on the 20 images but we divide them into trained images (images that have been used to train the network) and tested images (images used for testing the proposed system) for a better comparison. All results are calculated and recorded in the Tables 1, 2, 3 and 4. The purpose of this experiment is to compare the results from the proposed techniques DNN$_I$, DNN$_R$, TNN$_I$, TNN$_R$ with the results by LS via accuracy calculation using the gold standard images. The following accuracy measures have been employed to verify the performance of the techniques under investigation (A is the binary segmented image and B is the gold standard image): 1) The Dice coefficient D of two binary images A and B: $D(A, B) = \frac{2*|A \cap B|}{|A|+|B|}$, 2) The standard deviation σ_D of the Dice coefficient, 3) The 95% confidence interval (CI) of D, 4) The average of segmentation accuracy J is calculated using the area overlap (also called Jaccard Index): $J(A, B) = \frac{|A \cap B|}{|A \cup B|}$, 5) The standard deviation σ of the average of accuracy, and 6) The 95% confidence interval (CI) of J.

It is obvious from tables 1, 2,3 and 4 that the proposed algorithms, DNN$_I$, DNN$_R$, TNN$_I$ and TNN$_R$ perform more accurately compared to LS method. Generally, it is apparent from the tables that the proposed algorithms have the highest accuracies compared with the LS algorithm for all training sets. The proposed approaches have the highest average segmentation accuracy and the lowest standard deviation for all cases. Table 5 shows a summary of the results of the four training sets with focusing on the average of segmentation accuracy J and the 95% confidence interval CI. It can be seen that the proposed approach has the highest average segmentation accuracy and the shortest confidence intervals as well, which means that the proposed approach can provide more accurate and more consistent results. For example, in the third training set, the average accuracy of the proposed system raised from 66% (LS) to 74% (TNN_I), 76% (TNN_R), 80% (DNN_I) and 81% (DNN_R). Moreover, the confidence interval is pushed higher from 55%–78% (LS) to 66%–84%(TNN_I), 67%–85% (TNN_R), 74%–86% (DNN_I)and 74%–87% (DNN_R).

8   Conclusions

Thresholding could be an efficient technique for image segmentation because of its simplicity and fastness. However, most thresholding techniques treat all images with the same static nature regardless of the properties of the image. These methods may generate good results for some images but they are not a universal solution. Intelligent segmentation by training a neural network to generate the threshold for the images based on their features seems to be a more flexible solution. In this paper, we used a neural network to segment images based on their characteristics. The network was trained using a set of features extracted from the image in different ways. The SIFT method was used to detect key points and provide descriptors. These approaches seems to be simple, efficient and accurate for designing dynamic segmentation techniques for a difficult real-world problem such as breast ultrasound imaging.

References

1. Sezgin, M., Sankur, B.: Survey over image thresholding techniques and quantitative performance evaluation. Electronic Imaging 13, 146–165 (2004)
2. Otsu, N.: A threshold selection method from gray-level histograms. Automatica 11, 285–296 (1975)
3. Bazi, Y., Bruzzone, L., Melgani, F.: Image thresholding based on the EM algorithm and the generalized Gaussian distribution. Pattern Recognition 40, 619–634 (2007)
4. Hammouche, K., Diaf, M., Siarry, P.: A multilevel automatic thresholding method based on a genetic algorithm for a fast image segmentation. Computer Vision and Image Understanding 109, 163–175 (2008)
5. Nakib, A., Oulhadj, H., Siarry, P.: Fractional differentiation and non-Pareto multiobjective optimization for image thresholding. Engineering Applications of Artificial Intelligence 22, 236–249 (2009)
6. Nakib, A., Oulhadj, H., Siarry, P.: Image histogram thresholding based on multiobjective optimization. Signal Processing 87, 2516–2534 (2007)
7. Ahmed, M.N., Farag, A.A.: Two-stage neural network for volume segmentation of medical images. Pattern Recognition Letters 18, 1143–1151 (1997)
8. Chang, C.Y., Chung, P.C.: Medical image segmentation using a contextualconstraint- based Hopfield neural cube. Image and Vision Computing 19, 669–678 (2001)

9. Kurnaz, M.N., Dokur, Z., Ölmez, T.: An incremental neural network for tissue segmentation in ultrasound images. Computer Methods and Programs in Biomedicine 85, 187–195 (2007)
10. Kurugollu, F., Sankur, B., Harmanci, A.: Image segmentation by relaxation using constraint satisfaction neural network. Image & Vision Comp. 20, 483–497 (2002)
11. Sharma, N., Ray, A.K., Sharma, S., Shukla, K.K., Pradhan, S., Aggarwal, L.M.: Segmentation and classification of medical images using texture-primitive features: Application of BAM-type artificial neural network. Medical physics/Association of Medical Physicists of India 33, 119 (2008)
12. Lowe, D.G.: Object recognition from local scale-invariant features. In: IEEE International Conference on Computer Vision, vol. 2, pp. 1150–1157 (1999)
13. Bicego, M., Lagorio, A., Grosso, E., Tistarelli, M.: On the use of SIFT features for face authentication. In: Computer Vision and Pattern Recognition Workshops, p. 35 (2006)
14. Yun, J.H., Park, R.H.: Self-calibration with two views using the scale-invariant feature transform. Advances in Visual Computing, 589–598 (2006)
15. Lindeberg, T.: Feature Detection with Automatic Scale Selection. Computer Vision 30, 79–116 (1998)
16. Tang, C.Y., Wu, Y.L., Hor, M.K., Wang, W.H.: Modified SIFT descriptor for image matching under interference. In: ICMLC, vol. 6, pp. 3294–3300 (2008)
17. Lemuz-López, R., Arias-Estrada, M.: Iterative closest SIFT formulation for robust feature matching. Advances in Visual Computing, 502–513 (2006)
18. Caselles, V., Kimmel, R., Sapiro, G.: Geodesic active contours. IJCV 22, 61–79 (1997)
19. Osher, S., Sethian, J.A.: Fronts propagating with curvature dependent speed: Algorithms based on Hamilton-Jacobi formulations. Computational Physics 79, 12–49 (1998)
20. Li, C., Xu, C., Gui, C., Fox, M.D.: Level Set Evolution Without Re-initialization: A New Variational Formulation. In: Computer Vision and Pattern Recognition (2005)
21. Zhang, Y., Matuszewski, B.J., Shark, L.K., Moore, C.J.: Medical image segmentation using new hybrid level-set method. In: Medivis 2008, pp. 71–76 (2008)
22. Liu, B., Cheng, H.D., Huang, J., Tian, J., Tang, X., Liu, J.: Probability density difference-based active contour for ultrasound image segmentation. Pattern Recognition 43, 2028–2042 (2010)

Knowledge Discovery and Risk Prediction for Chronic Diseases: An Integrated Approach

Anju Verma[1], Maurizio Fiasché[1,2], Maria Cuzzola[1], Francesco C. Morabito[2], and Giuseppe Irrera[1]

[1] CTMO - Transplant Regional Center of Stem Cells and Cellular Therapy, "A. Neri", Hospital "Morelli" of Reggio Calabria, Italy
[2] DIMET, University "Mediterranea" of Reggio Calabria, Italy
maurizio.fiasche@unirc.it

Abstract. A novel ontology based type 2 diabetes risk analysis system framework is described, which allows the creation of global knowledge representation (ontology) and personalized modeling for a decision support system. A computerized model focusing on organizing knowledge related to three chronic diseases and genes has been developed in an ontological representation that is able to identify interrelationships for the ontology-based personalized risk evaluation for chronic diseases. The personalized modeling is a process of model creation for a single person, based on their personal data and the information available in the ontology. A transductive neuro-fuzzy inference system with weighted data normalization is used to evaluate personalized risk for chronic disease. This approach aims to provide support for further discovery through the integration of the ontological representation to build an expert system in order to pinpoint genes of interest and relevant diet components.

Keywords: Knowledge discovery, knowledge representation, chronic disease ontology, personalized risk evaluation system.

1 Introduction

Populations are aging and the prevalence of chronic diseases which persists for many years is increasing. The chronic diseases such as cardiovascular disease, type 2 diabetes and obesity have high global prevalence, have multifactorial etiology. These diseases are mainly caused by interactions of a number of common factors including genes, nutrition and life-style. For ontology based personalized risk evaluation for type 2 diabetes, a Protégé-based ontology has been developed for entering data for type 2 diabetes and linking and building relationships among concepts. The ontological representation provides the framework into which information on individual patients for disease symptoms, gene maps, diet and life history details can be inputted, and risks, profiles, and recommendations derived.

A personalized risk evaluation system has been used for building the personalized modeling. Global models capture trends in data that are valid for the whole problem space, and local models capture local patterns which are valid for clusters of data. Both models contain useful information and knowledge. Local models are also

L. Iliadis and C. Jayne (Eds.): EANN/AIAI 2011, Part I, IFIP AICT 363, pp. 270–279, 2011.
© IFIP International Federation for Information Processing 2011

adaptive to new data as new clusters and new functions that capture patterns of data in these clusters. A local model can be incrementally created. Usually, both global and local modeling approaches assume a fixed set of variables and if new variables, along with new data, are introduced with time, the models are very difficult to modify in order to accommodate these new variables. However new variables can be accommodated in only personalized models, as they are created "on the fly" provided that there is relevant data for them [1]. The personalized risk evaluation using ontological based data is the main approach of the paper.

2 Chronic Disease Ontology

Ontology is a systematic account of being or existence. Ontology in terms of bioinformatics can be interpreted as the representation of the existing domain of the knowledge of life. Ontology is used to reason and make inferences about the objects within the domain [2]. Ontology is concerned with making information and knowledge explicit; it includes descriptions of concepts and their relationships. Ontology describes a hierarchical structure of concepts and the relationships built in order to extract new knowledge.

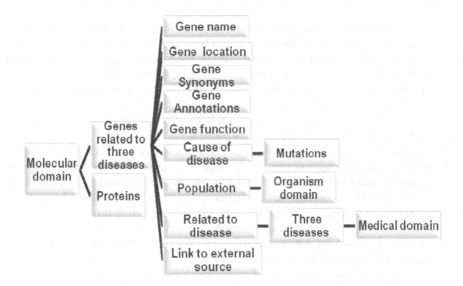

Fig. 1. General structure of molecular domain in the chronic disease ontology

Ontology is generally written as a set of definitions of the formal vocabulary of objects and relationships in the given domain. It supports the sharing and reuse of formally represented knowledge among systems [3, 4]. As a database technology, ontologies are commonly coded as triple stores (subject, relationship, object), where a network of objects is formed by relationship linkages, as a way of storing semantic information [5, 6].A standardized ontology framework makes data easily available for advanced methods of analysis, including artificial intelligence algorithms, that can tackle the multitude of large and complex datasets by clustering, classification, and rule inference for biomedical and bioinformatics applications. The main advantages of building ontology are to extract and collect knowledge; share knowledge; manage terminology; store, retrieve and analyze; find relationships between the concepts; discover new knowledge and reuse knowledge for decision support system.

Chronic disease ontology consists of five major domains namely; organism domain, molecular domain, medical domain, nutritional domain and a biomedical informatics map domain. These domains or classifications contain further subclasses and instances. Each subclass has a set of slots which provide information about each instance and have relationships among other slots, instances and concepts. Each gene instance has different information associated with the gene and also has relationships with other domains (Figure1). The chronic disease ontology can be updated manually and regularly with new knowledge and information providing a framework to keep an individual's specific information (medical, genetic, clinical and nutritional), to discover new knowledge and to adapt as required for personalized risk prediction and advice.

3 Type 2 Diabetes Personalized Risk Evaluation System

Type 2 diabetes mellitus is one of the most common chronic "lifestyle" diseases with a high prevalence throughout the world [7]. There are two main types of diabetes mellitus; type-1 and type-2. Type 2 diabetes is the most common type of diabetes and globally about 90% of all cases of diabetes are type 2 diabetes [8]. There have been several models, namely, 'The global diabetes model' [9, 10], 'The diabetes risk score' [11], the 'Archimedes diabetes model' [12, 13], the Diabetes risk score in Oman [14], the 'Genetic Risk Score' [15]. All these models predict risk of future complications associated with type 2 diabetes in people with already diagnosed type 2 diabetes.

The global diabetes model (GDM) is a continuous, stochastic micro simulation (individual by individual approach) model of type 2 diabetes. The GDM is a computer program and predicts longevity, quality of life, medical events and expenditures for groups and individuals with type 2 diabetes. The GDM calculates rates and probabilities of the medical events in diabetic individuals [9, 10]. It has been reported that from the existing methods for predicting risk of type 2 diabetes, The Archimedes Model predicts the risk with better sensitivity and specificity than other models [16]. Recently, the 'Genetic Risk Score' has been developed which uses multiple genetic as well as conventional risk factors [15]. Because these methods calculate risk of type 2 diabetes globally and they are not the same as the proposed methodology in this thesis, which involves calculations of personalized risk. The aim of the current research is to create a personalized model for predicting risk of type 2 diabetes. Genetic variables have been used along with clinical variables to create a personalized model to predict risk of type 2 diabetes. The next section of this paper describes the methods used for creating a diabetes risk model using genetic markers along with clinical variables.

3.1 Step 1: Selection of Features for Building the Personalized Risk Evaluation System for Type-2 Diabetes

The first step to build the model was feature selection which has been done by using different methods including signal to noise ratio and t-test. This analysis was done using NeuCom and Siftware. NeuCom is a computer environment based on connectionist (Neuro-computing) modules. NeuCom is self-programmable, learning and reasoning tool. NeuCom environment can be used for data analysis, modeling and knowledge discovery. Siftware is an environment for analysis, modeling and profiling of gene expression data. NeuCom and Siftware have been developed at Knowledge Engineering and Discovery Research Institute (KEDRI, http://www.kedri.info).

Results achieved from signal to noise ratio are exactly similar to student's t-test. According to signal to noise ratio and t-test for the combined male and female subjects, genes ANGPTL3, ANGPT4, TNF, FLT1, MMP2 and CHGA are ranked highest. Interestingly, gene CHGA has not been ranked at same high position for male and female subjects separately. The first six genes of highest importance for male and female subjects were selected for further analysis and to build personalized sex-specific risk prediction model. As genes are ranked differently as per signal to noise ratio for male and female subjects, different genes have been selected for personalized modeling for male and female subjects. Different methods were then used for type 2 diabetes risk prediction methods such as multiple linear regression using NeuCom (global, inductive method), WWKNN and TWNFI (personalized methods) [17].

3.2 Step2: Building Personalized Risk Evaluation Model

As every person has a different genetic admixture, therefore personalized prediction and treatment is required for each person. In personalized modeling, a model is created for a single point (subject record) of the problem space only using transductive reasoning. A personalized model is created "on the fly" for every new input vector and this individual model is based on the closest data samples to the new samples taken from a data set. The K-nearest neighbors (K-NN) method is one example of the personalized modeling technique. In the K-NN method, for every new sample, the nearest K samples are derived from a data set using a distance measure, usually Euclidean distance, and a voting scheme is applied to define the class label for the new sample [18, 19]. In the K-NN method, the output value y for a new vector x is calculated as the average of the output values of the k nearest samples from the data set D. In the weighted K-NN method (WKNN), the output y is calculated based not only on the output values (e.g. class label) y of the K, NN samples, but also on a weight w , that depends on the distance of them to x . In Weighted-weighted K nearest neighbor algorithm for transductive reasoning (WWKNN) the distance between a new input vector and the neighboring ones is weighted, and also variables are ranked according to their importance in the neighborhood area.

Transductive neuro-fuzzy inference system with weighted data normalization (TWNFI) is an improved, advanced and more complex transductive and dynamic neural-fuzzy inference system with local generalization, in which, either the Zadeh-Mamdani type fuzzy inference engine [20,21] or the Takagi-Sugeno fuzzy inference engine [22] can be used. The local generalization means that in a sub-space (local area) of the whole problem space, a model is created and this model performs generalization in this area.

Table 1. Examples of TWNFI personalized models for two different male subjects; high risk and low risk; with weight of variables and genes with global weights representing importance of the variables

Input Variables	Subject 1 (High risk male) Weights of input variables	Subject 2 (Low risk male) Weights of input variables	Global weights/ importance (male)
Age (years)	0.7729	0.9625	0.8393
Haemoglobin (g/L)	0.8521	0.7847	0.8429
Fasting blood glucose (mmol/L)	0.7507	0.9352	0.8769
Cholesterol (mmol/L)	0.7478	0.752	0.8104
Triglycerides (mmol/L)	0.6961	0.7413	0.8327
ANGPTL3	0.7617	0.9269	0.9254
FGF1	0.7295	0.641	0.8228
FLT1	0.651	0.7059	0.8096
MMP2	0.6797	0.8802	0.9009
TNF	1	0.8495	0.8699
ANGPT4	0.6705	1	0.904
Actual output			
Predicted output with Multiple linear regression	0.7963	0.1378	
Predicted output with WWKNN	1.127	0	
Predicted output with TWNFI	1.002	0	

In the TWNFI model, Gaussian fuzzy membership functions are used in each fuzzy rule for both antecedent and consequent parts. In TWNFI data is first normalized and then it looks for nearest samples. TWNFI performs a better local generalization over new data as it develops an individual model for each data vector that takes into account the new input vector location in the space. Table 1 shows results from example of personalized model built for two male subjects. Subject 1 belongs to class 1(with type 2 diabetes) and subject 2 belongs to class0 (without type 2 diabetes). It was found that highest accuracy was achieved with the TWNFI method. TWNFI not only gives highest accuracy, also gives weights of variables as per their importance for risk of disease.

For each subject in present example, separate weight of each variable has been presented and compared with global weights of variables for male subjects. It is very interesting that male subject 1 and 2 both have higher values of fasting blood glucose, cholesterol and triglycerides, the genes were more important factors to predict the risk of type 2 diabetes for male subject 2. By comparing weights for each variable of each subject, it was found that for male subject 1, gene TNF was found to be the most important gene associated with type 2 diabetes while for male subject 2, ANGPT4 gene has been weighted the highest, while for all the male subjects the ANGPTL3 gene has been found most important factor for type 2 diabetes. TWNFI along with high accuracy and importance of variables also provides set of rules based on the clusters formed based on nearest neighbors. Each rule contains a lot of information for each variable. Rules or profiles for male subjects were generated on the basis of nearest samples.

4   Integration Framework for Chronic Disease Ontology and Personalized Modeling

This section explains the framework for integrating the chronic disease ontology and a personalized risk evaluation system. The challenge is to create computational platforms that dynamically integrate the ontology and a set of efficient machine learning methods, including new methods for personalized modeling that would manifest better accuracy at a personal level and facilitate new discoveries in the field of bioinformatics. The chronic disease ontology that was described in section 2 will be used to integrate personalized modeling and ontology. The current chronic disease ontology contains most of genes which are common for three chronic interrelated diseases (cardiovascular disease, type-2 diabetes and obesity).

Data for personalized modeling was collected during a Government Research Program with the title: "Biologia e Impiego dei Progenitori Endoteliali nell' Arteriopatia Obliterante Periferica" sponsored from Italian Ministry of the Health. The collected dataset which was used for predicting risk of type 2 diabetes included clinical and genetic variables and it was found that for male and female subjects different combinations of genes are more predictive of type 2 diabetes. So these genes were updated in the chronic disease ontology and the missing genes and information related to these genes was also added in to the chronic disease ontology. Similarly, any other information derived from personalized model can be added to the chronic disease ontology and the new relationships and discoveries within the chronic disease ontology can be used to improve personalized risk evaluation system (Figure2).

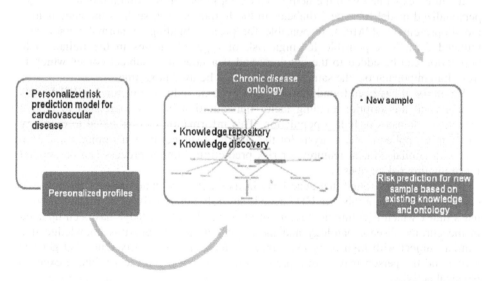

Fig. 2. Example of framework for use of knowledge from the chronic disease ontology (CDO) to personalized model

The framework uses the chronic disease ontology based data and knowledge embedded in the ontology. It also allows the adaptation of new knowledge by entering the results of the machine learning system to ontology. The main modules (Figure 3) are: an ontology module, a machine learning module (TWNFI) and an interface to import and export knowledge from and to ontology. The ontology and machine learning module evolve through continuous learning from new data. Results from the machine learning procedures can be entered back into the ontology thus enriching its knowledge base and facilitating new discoveries. Integration of the chronic disease ontology and personalized model can be done for diabetes.

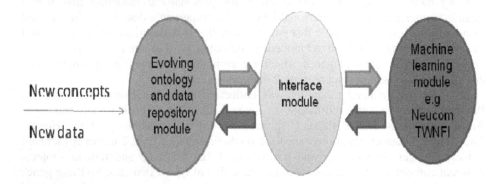

Fig. 3. The ontology-based personalized decision support (OBPDS) framework consisting of three interconnected parts: (1) An ontology/database module; (2) Interface module; (3) A machine learning module

It can be explained with the help of an example as the information obtained from personalized model for type 2 diabetes in the Italian dataset, such as the gene matrix metalloproteinase (MMP2), responsible for protein binding in normal person and mutated form is responsible for high risk of type 2 diabetes in the Italian male population can be added to the ontology and if a new male subject comes which is from Italian population, the same information can be used next time.

Similarly, it has been found that the gene hypoxia inducible factor 1 (HIF1A) acts as a normal transcription binding factor but mutation in gene is related to type 2 diabetes in females in Italian population. This information can be added to ontology and can be applied to the analysis for the next new subject from a similar population and with similar clinical features for risk prediction. Similar process can be applied for predicting risk of obesity.

Recently, it was found that gene FTO in its inactivated state protects from risk of obesity [23]. Polymorphism in FTO gene is strongly and positively correlated to body mass index which is common measure of obesity. This knowledge has been updated in the chronic disease ontology and the system is able to use this knowledge if a similar subject with high body mass index comes, it can identify that FTO gene is active and the person may have a predisposition to obesity if dietary intake exceeds physical activity.

5 Conclusions and Future Plans

It has been found that the male subjects have high values of cholesterol and triglycerides and are more prone to type 2 diabetes; For male and female subjects different combinations of genes have association with type 2 diabetes; for male subjects, genes ANGPTL3, MMP2, ANGPT4, TNF, FGF1 and FLT1 appear to be the most important genes associated with risk of type 2 diabetes; for female subjects, genes ANGPTL3, ANGPTL4. HIF1A, TNSF15, FLT1 and TNF appear to be the most important factors for determining risk of type 2 diabetes [24].

The explained framework for the integration of the ontology and the personalized modeling techniques illustrates the integration of personalized method and ontology database for better recommendations and advice and explains how existing knowledge and new knowledge can be used together for better life style, risk evaluation and recommendations[25,26]. As, Diabetes has global prevalence and none of the methods so far published have combined clinical and genetic variables together. The section 3 we have described how a model can be built using clinical and genetic variables. For personalized modeling, different methods such as WWKNN and TWNFI were used and compared [27, 28, 29, 30]. It has been found that TWNFI gives highest accuracy along with importance of each gene and variable by optimizing each variable and weight which can be used for better prediction and recommendations.

Our future plan is to extend the personalized risk evaluation system explained in this paper with more genes and more set of clinical and general variables. Still a better prediction system can be developed, if nutritional information and other environmental variables are known (e.g. exposure to sun for vitamin D) along with clinical and genetic variables are available.

We also plan to extend the chronic disease ontology with the new knowledge and information in terms of; New data, genes and also in terms of medical information such as anatomical and physiological information about the organs involved in the type 2 diabetes. The chronic disease ontology is evolving and vast project and can be carried out for years. The only limitation of evolving the chronic disease ontology is that the new information has to be added manually, at present there is no such tool which can automatically update the existing information without duplicating or removing the existing knowledge in ontology.

Acknowledgments. This study has been supported by Foundation of Research and Technology by TIF scholarship through an affiliate of Pacific Channel Limited and Knowledge Engineering and Discovery Research Institute, AUT. Many Thanks to Prof. Nik Kasabov for his support.

References

1. Kasabov, N.: Global, local and personalized modeling and profile discovery in Bioinformatics: An integrated approach. Pattern Recognition Letters 28(6), 673–685 (2007)

2. Gruber, T.R.: A translation approach to portable ontologies. Knowledge Acquisition 5, 199–220 (1993)
3. Fensel, D.: Ontologies: A Silver Bullet for Knowledge Management and Electronic Commerce, 2nd edn. Springer, Heidelberg (2004)
4. Chandrasekaran, B., Josephson, J.R., Benjamins, V.R.: What are ontologies, and why do we need them? Intelligent Systems and Their Applications 14, 20–26 (1999)
5. Owens, A.: Semantic Storage: Overview and Assessment. Technical Report IRP Report 2005, Electronics and Computer Science, U of Southampton (2005)
6. Berners-Lee, T., Hendler, J., Lassila, O.: The Semantic Web. Scientific American (May 17, 2001)
7. The FIELD Study Investigators. The need for a large-scale trial of fibrate therapy in diabetes: the rationale and design of the Fenofibrate Intervention and Event Lowering in Diabetes (FIELD) study. ISRCTN64783481. Cardiovascular Diabetology 3, 9 pages (2004)
8. New Zealand Guidelines Group. Management of diabetes. New Zealand Guidelines Group, Wellington (2003(a),
   http://www.nzgg.org.nz/guidelines/dsp_guideline_popup.cfm?guidelineID=36
9. Brown, J.B., Palmer, A.J., et al.: The Mt. Hood challenge: cross-testing two diabetes simulation models. Diabetes Research and Clinical Practice 50(3), S57–S64 (2000a)
10. Brown, J.B., Russell, A., et al.: The global diabetes model: user friendly version 3.0. Diabetes Research and Clinical Practice 50(3), S15–S46 (2000b)
11. Lindstrom, J., Tuomilehto, J.: The diabetes risk score. A practical tool to predict type-2 diabetes risk. Diabetes Care 26(3), 725–731 (2003)
12. Eddy, D.M., Schlessinger, L.: Archimedes. A trial-validated model of diabetes. Diabetes Care 26(11), 3093–3101 (2003a)
13. Eddy, D.M., Schlessinger, L.: Validation of the Archimedes diabetes model. Diabetes Care 26(11), 3102–3110 (2003b)
14. Al-Lawati, J.A., Tuomilehto, J.: Diabetes risk score in Oman: A tool to identify prevalent type-2 diabetes among Arabs of the Middle East. Diabetes Research and Clinical Practice 77, 438–444 (2007)
15. Cornelis, M., Qi, L., et al.: Joint effects of common genetic variants on the risk of type-2 diabetes in U. S. men and women of European ancestry. Annals of Internal Medicine 150, 541–550 (2009)
16. Stern, M., Williams, K., et al.: Validation of prediction of diabetes by the Archimedes Model and comparison with other predictiong models. Diabetes Care 31(8), 1670–1671 (2008)
17. Song, Q., Kasabov, N.: TWNFI - a transductive neuro-fuzzy inference system with weighted data normalization for personalized modeling. Neural Networks 19(10), 1591–1596 (2006)
18. Vapnik, V.N.: Statistical Learning Theory. Wiley Inter-Science, Chichester (1998)
19. Mitchell, M.T., Keller, R., et al.: Explanation-based generalization: A unified view. Machine Learning 1(1), 47–80 (1997)
20. Zadeh, L.A.: Fuzzy sets. Information and Control 8, 338–353 (1965)
21. Zadeh, L.A.: Fuzzy logic. IEEE Computer 21, 83–93 (1988)
22. Takagi, T., Sugeno, M.: Fuzzy identification of systems and its applications to modeling and control. IEEE Transactions on Systems, Man, and Cybernetics 15, 116–132 (1985)
23. Fischer, J., Koch, L., et al.: Inactivation of the Fto gene protects from obesity. Nature 458, 894–899 (2009)

24. Verma, A.: An Integrated Approach for Ontology Based Personalized Modeling: Chronic Disease Ontology, Risk Evaluation and Knowledge Discovery. LAP LAMBERT Academic Publishing (2010)
25. Kasabov, N., Song, Q., Benuskova, L., Gottgtroy, P., Jain, V., Verma, A., Havukkala, I., Rush, E., Pears, R., Tjahjana, A., Hu, Y., MacDonel, S.: Integrating Local and Personalised Modelling with Global Ontology Knowledge Bases for Biomedical and Bioinformatics Decision Support. In: Smolin, et al. (eds.) Computational Intelligence in Bioinformatics, ch. 4, Springer, Heidelberg (2008)
26. Kasabov, N., Hu, Y.: Integrated optimisation method for personalised modelling and case study applications. Int. Journal of Functional Informatics and Personalised Medicine 3(3), 236–256 (2010)
27. Fiasché, M., Verma, A., Cuzzola, M., Iacopino, P., Kasabov, N., Morabito, F.C.: Discovering Diagnostic Gene Targets and Early Diagnosis of Acute GVHD Using Methods of Computational Intelligence over Gene Expression Data. In: Alippi, C., Polycarpou, M., Panayiotou, C., Ellinas, G. (eds.) ICANN 2009, Part II. LNCS, vol. 5769, pp. 10–19. Springer, Heidelberg (2009) ISBN/ISSN: 978-3-642-04276-8
28. Fiasché, M., Cuzzola, M., Fedele, R., Iacopino, P., Morabito, F.C.: Machine Learning and Personalized Modeling Based Gene Selection for Acute GvHD Gene Expression Data Analysis. In: Diamantaras, K., Duch, W., Iliadis, L.S. (eds.) ICANN 2010, Part I. LNCS, vol. 6352, pp. 217–223. Springer, Heidelberg (2010)
29. Fiasché, M., Cuzzola, M., Irrera, G., Iacopino, P., Morabito, F.C.: Advances in Medical Decision Support Systems for Diagnosis of Acute Graft-versus-Host Disease: Molecular and Computational Intelligence Joint Approaches. Frontiers in Biology, doi: 10.1007/s11515-011-1124-8
30. Fiasché, M., Cuzzola, M., Iacopino, P., Kasabov, N., Morabito, F.C.: Personalized Modeling based Gene Selection for acute GvHD Gene Expression Data Analysis: a Computational Framework Proposed. Australian Journal of Intelligent Information Processing Systems 12(4) (2010); Machine Learning Applications (Part II)

Permutation Entropy for Discriminating 'Conscious' and 'Unconscious' State in General Anesthesia

Nicoletta Nicolaou[1,2], Saverios Houris[3],
Pandelitsa Alexandrou[3], and Julius Georgiou[2]

[1] KIOS Research Centre and Holistic Electronics Research Lab
[2] Department of Electrical and Computer Engineering, University of Cyprus,
Kallipoleos 75, 1678 Nicosia, Cyprus
[3] Nicosia General Hospital, Old Nicosia-Limassol Road, Nicosia, Cyprus
nicoletta.n@ucy.ac.cy

Abstract. Brain-Computer Interfaces (BCIs) are devices offering alternative means of communication when conventional means are permanently, or non-permanently, impaired. The latter is commonly induced in general anesthesia and is necessary for the conduction of the surgery. However, in some cases it is possible that the patient regains consciousness during surgery, but cannot directly communicate this to the anesthetist due to the induced muscle paralysis. Therefore, a BCI-based device that monitors the spontaneous brain activity and alerts the anesthetist is an essential addition to routine surgery. In this paper the use of Permutation Entropy (PE) as a feature for 'conscious' and 'unconscious' brain state classification for a BCI-based anesthesia monitor is investigated. PE is a linear complexity measure that tracks changes in spontaneous brain activity resulting from the administration of anesthetic agents. The overall classification performance for 10 subjects, as assessed with a linear Support Vector Machine, exceeds 95%, indicating that PE is an appropriate feature for such a monitoring device.

Keywords: Permutation Entropy, anesthesia monitor, electroencephalogram, Support Vector Machine, Brain-Computer Interface.

1 Introduction

Brain-Computer Interfaces (BCIs) are devices aimed primarily at providing an alternative means of communication through establishing a 'direct connection' between the brain and a device; in this way the conventional means of communication (through peripheral nerves and muscles) are bypassed [1]. Traditionally, in a BCI system the user consciously performs various mental tasks, voluntary modulation of brain activity or spontaneous event-related activity in order to issue different commands to control a device [2]. A BCI system can be useful not only when permanent loss of communication occurs, but also when non-permanent loss of communication occurs over a period of time. The latter is routinely performed, for example, as part of general anesthesia (GA) during surgery. This is achieved through the co-administration of neuromuscular blocking agents, together with the anesthetic agents,

L. Iliadis and C. Jayne (Eds.): EANN/AIAI 2011, Part I, IFIP AICT 363, pp. 280–288, 2011.

in order to achieve patient immobility necessary for the conduction of the surgery [3]. Under normal circumstances this drug-induced immobility is desired since the patient is under anesthesia. However, in rare cases it is possible that the patient regains consciousness during surgery unbeknown to the anesthetist; this could be a direct result of a number of factors, such as insufficient amount of administered anesthetic, and equipment failure [4]. In such cases the induced immobility leaves the patient with no means of communicating this to the anesthetist. Awareness during surgery is a highly traumatic experience with long-term psychological consequences; therefore, quick detection and subsequent intervention is important. A BCI device that monitors the general state of hypnosis of the patient can provide the means of communication necessary to alert the anesthetist. The operation of such a BCI device is based on monitoring the spontaneous brain activity as obtained from an electroencephalogram (EEG), which exhibits different characteristics under consciousness, and lack of it. By monitoring the changes in the observed characteristics of the patient's spontaneous brain activity the device is, thus, able to issue an alert when a 'conscious' state is detected. In this way, the patient can still communicate (involuntarily) to the anesthetist that he/she is conscious, despite his/her inability to do so using conventional means of communication.

Currently, commercially available EEG-based monitors are being introduced for routine patient monitoring during surgery. Two of the most commonly used devices are the BIS monitor (Aspect Medical Systems, Natick, MA) [5], and the Datex-Ohmeda S/5^{TM} Entropy Module (originally by Datex-Ohmeda Division, Instrumentation Corp., Helsinki; now with GE Healthcare) [6]. These devices usually operate by converting some combination of various EEG characteristics into a single number from 0-100 representing the level of hypnosis (100 - 'fully awake', 0 - 'isoelectricity'). At the simplest level these monitors use the loss of high frequencies and shift to low frequencies observed during anesthesia as a measure of anesthetic drug action. However, the precise algorithms utilized by some monitors are proprietary and their specifics are not known. For example, the BIS monitor integrates several disparate descriptors of the EEG, developed from a large volume of clinical data, into a single variable that correlates with behavioral assessments of sedation and hypnosis. In addition, they suffer from reliability issues, such as the inability to differentiate between an anesthetized patient or a patient who is simply asleep [7-9], unresponsiveness to specific anesthetic agents [10, 11], and being affected by the administration of other agents, such as neuromuscular blockers [12].

In addition to commercially available monitors, a number of other methods have also been utilized in order to characterize the anesthetic-induced changes observed in the EEG. The main observations concern the changes in the frequency content of the EEG after administration of anesthetic agents, thus various traditional frequency-based methods are used (see [13] for a review), as well as higher order spectral analysis [14, 15]. Other methods include various entropy-based measures [16-18] and complexity-based measures [19, 20]. Administration of anesthetic agents has also been found to affect various characteristics of auditory event-related potential activity, such as latency and amplitude [21, 22]. All these methods identify that the EEG during anesthesia becomes a more predictable signal with larger amplitude and lower frequency content. Despite the use of various measures to characterize anesthetic-induced EEG changes, only a few of them have been validated in terms of their feasibility in the discrimination between 'conscious' and 'unconscious' states, as viewed from the perspective of a pattern recognition problem.

In this paper we utilize a Support Vector Machine (SVM) to classify EEG segments into one of the two states 'Conscious' and 'Unconscious' using Permutation Entropy (PE) as a feature obtained from the EEG of 10 patients undergoing general anesthesia surgery. PE is a complexity measure based on mapping a time series on a symbolic sequence to describe the relationships between present and past samples [23]. Its previous application on EEG data obtained from anesthesia has shown that PE tracks the level of hypnosis, as its values decrease with an increasing level of hypnosis [24, 25]. The simplicity and fast speed of estimation constitute PE a good candidate for real-time and online applications. Therefore, such a feature could potentially be utilized in an anesthesia-monitoring BCI device.

2 Methods

2.1 Dataset

The data used in this study were collected from 10 male patients undergoing general and urological surgery at Nicosia General Hospital, Cyprus. The 24-channel configuration of the TruScan32 (Deymed Diagnostic) was used with sampling rate at 256Hz, and electrodes placed at positions Fp1, Fp2, F7, F3, Fz, F4, F8, T3, C3, Cz, C4, T4, T5, P3, Pz, P4, T6, O1 and O2, according to the International 10/20 system, with an FCz reference. No filtering was performed during or after data collection. Data recording usually commenced while patients were still awake prior to administration of the anesthetic agents (anesthetic induction - AI), continued throughout the entire surgery, and until patients regained consciousness (ROC) after the surgery. The point at which the patients stopped responding verbally to commands by the anesthetist occurred less than a minute after administration of the anesthetic bolus, depending on patient characteristics. ROC was defined as the point at which the patient started responding to verbal commands or tactile stimuli by the anesthetist. GA was induced by the on duty anesthetist using the regular procedures of the hospital. Standard patient monitoring was used and all patients were preoxygenated via a face mask prior to anesthesia induction with a Diprivan bolus (propofol 1%, 10 mg/ml, induction dose 2-4 mg/kg depending on patient characteristics). During induction some patients also received boluses of neuromuscular blocking agents (cisatracurium, rocuronium, or atracurium) and analgesic drugs. Maintenance of GA was achieved with an intravenous administration of propofol at concentrations ranging between 20-50 ml/h (200-500 mg/h) depending on patient characteristics and surgery requirements. In most patients remifentanil hydrochloride (Ultiva®; 2 mg, dissolved in 40ml) was also administered intravenously throughout surgery at a rate ranging between 2-15 ml/h (0.1-0.75 mg/h).

2.2 Permutation Entropy

PE is a linear complexity measure for time series [23]. The relationship between present values and a fixed number of equidistant values at a given past time is captured through a symbolic mapping of the continuous time series. This mapping is achieved by splitting the time series into segments containing m samples (where m is called the embedding dimension), and which overlap by $(m-1)$ samples. The distance between each sample is defined by a time-lag, τ. Thus, each segment is defined as:

$$X(t) = [x(t), x(t+\tau), ..., x(t+m\tau)] . \tag{1}$$

For a given embedding dimension there will be $m!$ possible permutations (motifs). If each permutation is considered as a symbol, the embedded time vectors $X(t)$ can be represented by a symbol sequence, j, each having probability distribution p_j. Thus, based on the Shannon entropy definition the normalized PE, H_p, of a given time series, $x(t)$, is defined as:

$$H_p(m) = -\frac{1}{\ln(m!)} \sum_{j=1}^{J} p_j \ln(p_j) . \tag{2}$$

where J is the distinct number of symbols for a given embedding dimension $(J \leq m!)$. The factor $\dfrac{1}{\ln(m!)}$ is a normalization factor such that $0 \leq H_p / \ln(m!) \leq 1$.

PE measures the departure of a time series from a complete random one: the smaller the value of the PE, the more regular the time series. The upper bound, $H_p = \ln(m!)$, is attained when all of the possible $m!$ permutations appear in the time series with the same probability, something which is more likely to be observed when the EEG signal is dominated by high frequencies. This implies that H_p increases with the irregulatiry of the time series. At slower frequencies the permutations corresponding to peaks and troughs are observed less frequently, i.e. the EEG is more regular, hence the permutations appear with different probabilities, which decreases the PE of the signal. With regards to the embedding dimension, m, if this is too large then it becomes difficult to detect changes in the time series. However, if this is too small, then there are very few distinct states (symbols) and the scheme will not work. For EEG signals values of $m = 3,...,7$ have been recommended [23]. For the time lag, it is adequate to use a value of $\tau = 1$ to extract most of the information in the EEG [24, 25], hence this value is commonly chosen for EEG analysis.

2.3 Support Vector Machines

SVMs belong to the family of kernel-based classifiers [26]. The main idea behind SVMs is to use kernel functions to perform operations in the "data" space, corresponding to an implicit mapping of the data in a higher dimensional "feature" space where a hyperplane (decision boundary) that can separate the classes can be found. The simplest case is a linear SVM trained to classify linearly separable data. The constructed constraints define two parallel hyperplanes whose distance from the estimated decision boundary is maximal. The points lying on the two hyperplanes are called the support vectors. Estimating the decision boundary subject to the set of given constraints is a constrained optimization problem that can be solved in the Lagrange optimization framework.

2.4 Data Analysis

The main function of an anesthesia monitor is to alert the anesthetist when a subject becomes aware during surgery. Therefore, the minimal requirement is the ability to distinguish between the two states 'Conscious' and 'Unconscious' (class 'A' and 'B' respectively). To assess this, the following was performed:

(1) Segments of a few minutes duration corresponding to the two classes were extracted from the continuous EEG recordings at AI and ROC based on markers in the EEG record of each patient indicating AI and ROC. Data from 10 subjects were available for analysis (S1-S10).
(2) The average activity over the left frontal (LF: electrodes Fp1, F7, F3, T3, C3), right frontal (RF: Fp2, F8, F4, C4, T4), left posterior (LP: T5, P3, O1), right posterior (RP: T6, P4, O2), and midline (Z: Fz, Cz, Pz) brain areas was estimated. Visual inspection of the acquired data identified electrodes with bad quality signals from bad contact or no contact; these electrodes were subsequently excluded from estimation of the average activity. For subject S4, all electrodes in the right posterior area were excluded from the analysis due to bad electrode contact. Since no artifact removal was performed this averaging removed some of the effects of artifacts.
(3) PE ($m = 3$, $\tau = 1$) was estimated over 2-second non-overlapping windows of the EEG segments from each of the five brain areas. Non-overlapping windows were used such that, at each 2-s segment, the current value of PE was estimated from new data and was not based on previous data – this is an important consideration for future online application of the method. Feature vectors consisted of the following 5-dimensional values:

$$X_C^i = \left[H_{p(LF)}^i(m) \quad H_{p(RF)}^i(m) \quad H_{p(LP)}^i(m) \quad H_{p(RP)}^i(m) \quad H_{p(Z)}^i(m) \right] . \quad (3)$$

where $C \in \{A, B\}$ corresponds to one of the two classes, and $i = 1,...N_C$ denotes the ith 2-s segment from all the available segments of each class (N_C). Since no pre-processing or artifact removal was performed, the estimated PE values were smoothed (moving average filter, $n = 10$ samples).

(4) Performance was evaluated for each subject separately over B=50 bootstrap repetitions. In each repetition, 70% of the available data for a subject was used for training, while the remaining 30% was used for testing. Classification was performed using a linear SVM. Performance was assessed as the sensitivity (4), specificity (5) and average accuracy (6):

$$Sensitivity = SE = \frac{TN}{TN_n} . \quad (4)$$

$$Specificity = SP = \frac{TP}{TP_n} \cdot \qquad (5)$$

$$Accuracy = AC = \frac{1}{2}\left(\frac{1}{B}\sum_{b=1}^{B} SE_b + \frac{1}{B}\sum_{b=1}^{B} SP_b \right). \qquad (6)$$

where TP (TN) is the number of true positives (negatives), and TN_p (TN_n) is the total number of positive (negative) examples respectively. In the following investigations, examples of class 'A' (conscious) were considered as positive, while class 'B' (unconscious) as negative.

3 Results

Induction of anesthesia causes a decrease in the estimated PE values, with return to baseline values when consciousness is recovered at the end of anesthesia. This can be seen in the grand average PE obtained over all subjects over the five pre-defined brain areas (figure 1; the right posterior area was unavailable for subject S4, hence S4 was excluded from the grand average PE estimation). This decrease in the PE is a direct result of the fact that during anesthesia the fast brain rhythms are substituted by slower brain rhythms; hence, the PE tracks this shift from faster to slower frequencies. In addition, the EEG segments representing ROC are extracted after the intravenous administration of propofol is switched off. As the blood-level concentration of anesthetic agent decreases the PE shows a more gradual return to baseline level (figure 1, thin line), compared to the PE at AI (figure 1, thick line) where a bolus of anesthetic agent is administered. It can also be seen that it is possible to separate the two classes using a linear decision boundary; hence, a linear SVM is utilized here.

Table 1 shows the single-subject and subject-average sensitivity (SE), specificity (SP) and classification accuracy (AC). Overall, SE, SP and AC greater than 0.93 (93%) are obtained. The decreased performance for subject S4 could be a result of the fact that only 4 brain areas were available for analysis, resulting in 4-dimensional PE features. Data from segments extracted at the beginning and end of surgery were classified separately. A patient awaking from surgery does not regain full alertness until sometime afterwards; this time frame is very much dependent on the rate at which each person is able to metabolize the administered drugs. Therefore, the awareness state of a patient at ROC is much more similar to the awareness state the patient will be in if awareness is experienced during surgery.

Ideally, a BCI for alerting the anesthetist in case of impending awareness should display 100% SE and SP; ideal SE means that all events of awareness are captured, an alarm is raised and appropriate action is taken, while ideal SP implies that the monitor reflects the lack of consciousness at an appropriate level of anesthesia. However, it is very difficult to have an ideal monitor and in the majority of cases a compromise between SE and SP must be made. In case of low SE, false alarms would indicate that the patient is awake, prompting the anesthetist to take action with potential disastrous consequences. In case of low SP, the alarm would not be raised in cases of awareness, no action would be taken and the patient would continue being in a conscious state, with dramatic consequences. It can be seen that in the case of an anesthesia monitor, both SE and SP are equally as important and no sacrifice of one should be made for the other. Using PE as a feature, even though SE and SP are not ideal, both are at a similarly high level. Thus, neither is sacrificed for the other.

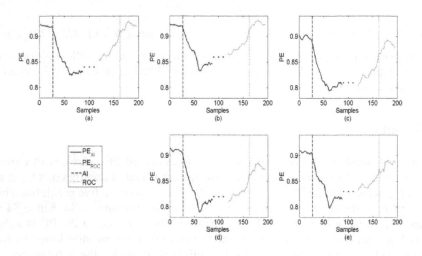

Fig. 1. Average Permutation Entropy over all patients for (a) left frontal, (b) right frontal, (c) left posterior, (d) right posterior, and (e) midline brain areas. Thick line: PE at induction (AI); thin line: PE at recovery of consciousness (ROC). Vertical lines denote the induction and recovery of consciousness (dashed and dotted lines respectively). X-axis in arbitrary samples.

Table 1. Single-subject and average sensitivity (SE), specificity (SP) and classification accuracy (AC) with 5-dimensional PE features estimated over 5 brain areas. Classification performed with linear SVM.

Subject	AI			ROC		
	SP	SE	AC	SP	SE	AC
S1	1.00	0.99	0.995	1.00	0.97	0.985
S2	1.00	0.95	0.975	1.00	0.97	0.985
S3	1.00	0.94	0.970	1.00	0.75	0.875
S4	1.00	0.90	0.950	0.73	0.84	0.785
S5	1.00	0.95	0.975	1.00	0.94	0.970
S6	1.00	1.00	1.000	1.00	0.98	0.990
S7	1.00	0.90	0.950	1.00	0.98	0.990
S8	0.99	0.96	0.975	1.00	1.00	1.000
S9	1.00	0.93	0.965	1.00	0.96	0.980
S10	1.00	0.92	0.960	0.99	0.93	0.960
TOTAL	**1.00**	**0.95**	**0.975**	**0.97**	**0.93**	**0.950**

5 Conclusion

We propose the use of Permutation Entropy as a feature in a BCI-based medical device that monitors the patients' state of hypnosis during surgery under general anesthesia in order to alert the anesthetist in cases when the patient regains awareness, but cannot voluntarily communicate this to the anesthetist. The high performance obtained encourages further investigations of PE-based classification of 'conscious' and 'unconscious' state. However, one must also bear in mind that other physiological processes, such as sleep, exhibit patterns of decreasing PE [27]. Thus, it is necessary to study both processes simultaneously in order to establish existing differences. Nonetheless, a depth of anesthesia monitor based on PE is still more advantageous than existing monitors.

Acknowledgments. The authors would like to thank the anonymous volunteers and the hospital staff who participated in this study. This work falls under the Cyprus Research Promotion Foundation's Framework for Research, Technological Development and Innovation (DESMI 2008), co-funded by the Republic of Cyprus and the European Regional Development Fund (Grant number: DIDAK-TOR/DISEK/0308/20).

References

1. Wolpaw, J.R., Birbaumer, N., Heetderks, W.J., McFarland, D.J., Peckham, P.H., Schalk, G., Donchin, E., Quatrano, L.A., Robinson, C.J., Vaughan, T.M.: Brain-computer interface technology: a review of the first international meeting. IEEE T. Rehabil. Eng. 8, 164–173 (2000)
2. Birbaumer, N.: Brain-Computer Interface research: coming of age. Clin. Neurophysiol. 117, 479–483 (2006)
3. Hammeroff, S.R.: The entwined mysteries of anaesthesia and consciousness. Anesthesiology 105, 400–412 (2006)
4. Myles, P.S., Symons, J.A., Leslie, K.: Anaesthetists' attitudes towards awareness and depth-of-anaesthesia monitoring. Anaesthesia 58, 11–16 (2003)
5. Sigl, J.C., Chamoun, N.G.: An introduction to bispectral analysis of the electroencephalogram. J. Clin. Monit. Comput. 10, 392–404 (1994)
6. Viertiö-Oja, H., Maja, V., Särkelä, M., Talja, P., Tenkanen, N., Tolvanen-Laakso, H., Paloheimo, M., Vakkuri, A., Yli-Hankala, A., Meriläinen, P.: Description of the Entropy Algorithm as applied in the Datex-Ohmeda S/5 Entropy Module. Acta Anaesth. Scand. 48, 154–161 (2004)
7. Russell, I.F.: The Narcotrend "depth of anaesthesia" monitor cannot reliably detect consciousness during general anaesthesia: an investigation using the isolated forearm technique. Brit. J. Anaesth. 96, 346–352 (2006)
8. Sleigh, J.W., Andrzejowski, J., Steyn-Ross, A., Steyn-Ross, M.: The Bispectral Index: a measure of depth of sleep? Anesth. Analg. 88, 659–661 (1999)
9. Tung, A., Lynch, P., Roizen, M.F.: Use of the BIS monitor to detect onset of naturally occurring sleep. J. Clin. Monitor. Comp. 17, 37–42 (2002)

10. Barr, G., Jakobsson, J.G., Owall, A., Anderson, R.E.: Nitrous oxide does not alter bispectral index: study with nitrous oxide as sole agent and as an adjunct to i.v. anaesthesia. Brit. J. Anaesth. 82, 827–830 (1999)
11. Hudetz, A.G.: Are we unconscious during general anesthesia? Int. Anesthesiol. Clin. 46, 25–42 (2008)
12. Liu, N., Chazot, T., Huybrechts, I., Law-Koune, J.-D., Barvais, L., Fischler, M.: The influence of a muscle relaxant bolus on bispectral and Datex-Ohmeda entropy values during propofol-remifentanil induced loss of consciousness. Anesth. Analg. 101, 1713–1718 (2005)
13. Rampil, I.J.: A primer for EEG signal processing in anesthesia. Anesthesiology 89, 980–1002 (1998)
14. Jeleazcov, C., Fechner, J., Schwilden, H.: Electroencephalogram monitoring during anesthesia with propofol and alfentanil: the impact of second order spectral analysis. Anesth. Analg. 100, 1365–1369 (2005)
15. Mi, W.D., Sakai, T., Singh, H., Kudo, T., Kudo, M., Matsuki, A.: Hypnotic endpoints vs. the bispectral index, 95% spectral frequency and median frequency during propofol infusion with or without fentanyl. Eur. J. Anaesth. 16, 47–52 (1999)
16. Li, X., Li, D., Liang, Z., Voss, L.J., Sleigh, J.W.: Analysis of anesthesia with Hilbert-Huang spectral entropy. Clin. Neurophysiol. 119, 2465–2475 (2008)
17. Anderson, R.E., Jakobsson, J.G.: Entropy of EEG during anaesthetic induction: a comparative study with propofol or nitrous oxide as sole agent. Brit. J. Anaesth. 92, 167–170 (2004)
18. Noh, G.-J., Kim, K.-M., Jeong, Y.-B., Jeong, S.-W., Yoon, H.-S., Jeong, S.-M., Kang, S.-M., Linares, O., Kern, S.E.: Electroencephalographic Approximate Entropy changes in healthy volunteers during remifentanil infusion. Anesthesiology 104, 921–932 (2006)
19. Zhang, X.-S., Roy, R.J., Jensen, E.W.: EEG complexity as a measure of depth of anesthesia for patients. IEEE T. Bio.-Med. Eng. 48, 1424–1433 (2001)
20. Ferenets, R., Lipping, T., Anier, A., Jäntti, V., Melto, S., Hovilehto, S.: Comparison of entropy and complexity measures for the assessment of depth of sedation. IEEE T. Bio.-Med. Eng. 53, 1067–1077 (2006)
21. van Hooff, J.C., de Beer, N.A.M., Brunia, C.H.M., Cluitmans, P.J.M., Korsten, H.H.M.: Event-related potential measures of information processing during general anesthesia. Electroen. Clin. Neuro. 103, 268–281 (1997)
22. Thornton, C., Sharpe, R.M.: Evoked responses in anaesthesia. Brit. J. Anaesth. 81, 771–781 (1998)
23. Bandt, C., Pompe, B.: Permutation Entropy: a natural complexity measure for time series. Phys. Rev. Lett. 88, 174102 (2002)
24. Bruzzo, A.A., Gesierich, B., Santi, M., Tassinari, C.A., Birbaumer, N., Rubboli, G.: Permutation Entropy to detect vigilance changes and preictal states from scalp EEG in epileptic patients. A preliminary study. Neurol. Sci. 29, 3–9 (2008)
25. Olofsen, E., Sleigh, J.W., Dahan, A.: Permutation entropy of the electroencephalogram: a measure of anaesthetic drug effect. Brit. J. Anaesth. 101, 810–821 (2008)
26. Burges, C.J.C.: A tutorial on Support Vector Machines for Pattern Recognition. In: Fayyad, U. (ed.) Data Mining and Knowledge Discovery, pp. 121–167. Kluwer Academic Publishers, Boston (1998)
27. Nicolaou, N., Georgiou, J.: The use of Permutation Entropy to characterize sleep electroencephalograms. Clin. EEG Neurosci. 42, 24–28 (2011)

Determining Soil – Water Content by Data Driven Modeling When Relatively Small Data Sets Are Available

Milan Cisty

Slovak University of Technology Bratislava, Faculty of Civil Engineering, Radlinskeho 11,
Bratislava 813 68, Slovak Republic
Milan.Cisty@stuba.sk

Abstract. A key physical property used in the description of a soil-water regime is a soil water retention curve, which shows the relationship between the water content and the water potential of the soil. Pedotransfer functions are based on the supposed dependence of the soil water content on the available soil characteristics. In this paper, artificial neural networks (ANNs) and support vector machines (SVMs) were used to estimate a drying branch of a water retention curve. The performance of the models are evaluated and compared in case study for the Zahorska Lowland in the Slovak Republic. The results obtained show that in this study the ANN model performs somewhat better and is easier to handle in determining pedotransfer functions than the SVM models.

Keywords: soil water regime, pedotransfer function, neural networks, support vector machines, harmony search.

1 Introduction

Modeling water content and transport in soil has become an important tool in simulating agricultural productivity as well as in solving various hydrological tasks. For instance, optimum irrigation management requires a systematic estimation of the soil-water status to determine both the appropriate amounts and timing of irrigation. That is why soil characteristics appear as a important input in the numerical simulation of a soil-water regime. A relatively large number of works have appeared which were devoted to determining the water retention curve which is needed for this purpose from more easily available soil properties such as particle size distribution, dry bulk density, organic C content, etc., e.g. [1], [2], [4], etc. Pedotransfer functions (PTF) have become the term for such relationships between soil hydraulic parameters and the more easily measurable properties usually available from a soil survey [1]. Consequently, the method for the quantification of these relationships uses various types of regression analyses. The aim of this paper is a comparison of three regression models for determining pedotransfer functions.

Besides the standard regression methods, artificial neural networks (ANNs) have become the tool of choice in developing PTFs, e.g., [1], [5], [7], [10], etc.). Authors of above works confirm that they received better results from ANN-based pedotransfer functions than from standard linear regression-based PTFs.

L. Iliadis and C. Jayne (Eds.): EANN/AIAI 2011, Part I, IFIP AICT 363, pp. 289–295, 2011.

Artificial neural networks include the ability to learn and generalize from examples with the aim of providing meaningful solutions to the problems to be solved. This process is called "training". When the training of an ANN is accomplished with a set of input and output data, the aim is to adjust the parameters of the ANN and make the ANN also provide corresponding outputs for other sets of input data (for which the outputs are not known).

Also second data driven method was used in this study- support vector machines (SVMs), which were developed by Vapnik [12] and are gaining in popularity due to their attractive features and promising empirical performance. The formulation embodies the structural risk minimization principle in addition to the traditional empirical risk minimization principle employed by conventional neural networks. It is this difference which gives SVMs a greater ability to generalize, which is the goal of statistical learning.

The objective of this work is to compare abovementioned methods while developing PTFs for the Zahorska Lowland in Slovakia, which was selected as a representative region for the investigation (e.g., while solving the regression task of determining the water retention curve from easily available soil properties).

In the following part of the paper ("Methodology") the three methods used in this study – ANN, SVM and multiple linear regression are briefly explained. Then the data acquisition and preparation is presented. In the "Results" part, the settings of the experimental computations are described in detail, and the "Conclusions" of the paper evaluates these experiments on the basis of the statistical indicators.

2 Methodology

The first approach for modeling the PTFs used in this paper is the application of *artificial neural networks* (ANNs). This approach has been described e.g. in [4] or [7]. Briefly summarized, a neural network consists of input, hidden and output layers, which contains processing elements. The number of processing elements in the input layer and output layer correspond to the number of input (e.g., the soil's bulk density, the soil's particle size data, etc.) and output variables of the model. So-called "learning" involves adjustment of the synaptic connections that exist between the neurons or weights in hidden layer, which are used for the transformation of the inputs to the outputs. A type of ANN known as a multi-layer perceptron (MLP), which uses a back-propagation training algorithm, was used for generating the PTFs in this study. The training process was performed by back propagation training algorithm of an MLP. The basic information about the application of an ANN to regression problems is available in the literature and is well known, so we will not provide a more detailed explanation here.

A second approach called *support vector machines* (SVM) for estimating the pedotransfer functions used in this study is explained hereinafter, with brief explanations of its principles. A more detailed description of the methodology can also be found in available sources, e.g., in [9].

The architecture of a SVM is similar to that of an ANN, but the training algorithm is significantly different. The basic idea is to project the input data by means of kernel functions into a higher dimensional space called the *feature space*, where a linear regression can be performed for an originally nonlinear problem, the results of which are then mapped back to the original input-output space. The linear regression is maintained by quadratic programming, which ensures a global optimum and an optimal generalization. The important idea is to fully ignore small errors (by introducing the "tube" variable ε, which defines what the "small" error is) to make the regression sparse, that is, dependent on a smaller number of inputs (called the support vectors), which makes the methodology much more computationally treatable. The uniqueness of solution produced by SVMs is often emphasized, but the actual truth is that this solution is only unique for a given set of performance parameters, which should be chosen and process of selection of them will be described later.

Objective function of mentioned linear regression in feature space SVM simultaneously minimizes both the empirical risk and the model's complexity; the tradeoff between these two goals is controlled by parameter C. An important characteristic of SVMs as a consequence of this form of objective function is that a better ability to generalize could be expected (by choosing appropriate parameter C), compared, e.g., with ANNs, because unnecessarily complex models usually suffer from over fitting.

The radial basis function was chosen on a trial and error basis as the kernel function for this work. This function has the following form:

$$K(x_i, x_j) = \exp(-\gamma \| x_i - x_j \|^2), \quad \gamma > 0 . \tag{1}$$

The parameter γ of this kernel function, the tube size ε for the ε-insensitive loss function, and parameter C should be found, which the basic task is when SVMs are applied to particular task. The *harmony search methodology (HS)* was used for this purpose instead of the usual trial-and-error principle. A harmony search is a metaheuristic search algorithm introduced by Geem [3] and is inspired by the improvisational process of musicians. In an HS algorithm, each musician corresponds to one decision variable. A musical instrument's pitch range corresponds to a decision variable's value range; the musical harmony at a certain time corresponds to a solution vector at certain iteration; and the audience's aesthetics corresponds to an objective function. Just as a musical harmony is improved time after time, a solution vector is improved iteration by iteration by the application of the improvisation's operators (the random selection of a tone, a musician's memory considerations or a pitch adjustment).

As a criterion for selecting the appropriate combinations of the parameters, the correlation coefficient could be used in regression task of determining PTF as the value of the objective function of the harmony search methodology.

3   Study Area and Data Collection

The data used in this study were obtained from a previous work [8]. An area of the Zahorska Lowland in Slovakia was selected for testing the methods described. A total of 140 soil samples were taken from various localities in this area.

The soil samples were air-dried and sieved for a physical analysis. A particle size analysis was performed utilizing Cassagrande's methods. The dry bulk density, particle density, porosity and saturated hydraulic conductivity were also measured on the soil samples. The points of the drying branches of the WRCs for the pressure head values of -2.5, -56, -209, -558, -976, -3060 and -15300 cm were estimated using overpressure equipment.

A full database of the 140 samples and their properties was used for creating the input data for the modeling from which the three subsets of the data were produced: training data (88 data samples), validation data (22 data samples), testing data (30 data samples).

A practical way to find a better generalization data driven model is to set aside a small percentage of the training set and use it for the cross validation. When the error in the validation set increases, the training should be stopped. The five divisions of the data used to the training and validation data set were used.

An ensemble of data-driven modeling was used in the present work, which means a collection of a finite number of data-driven models that are trained for the same task. This is meant as a simple variant of bootstrapping (the bootstrap scheme involves generating subsets of the data on the basis of random sampling with replacements as the data are sampled). Five data-driven models are trained independently, and their predictions are combined for the sake of obtaining a better generalization (average value was taken as result). For this reason the mentioned training fraction of the data (110 samples) was divided into the training and validation data sets alternatively in five different versions.

4 Results

The first approach used in determining the water retention curves in the presented work was an application of *ensemble neural networks*. The same network architecture for every ANN in the network was determined. In this work the multilayer perceptron (MLP) with 2, 3, and 4 neurons in the hidden layer was tested; an MLP with 3 neurons in the hidden layer was finally chosen for the ensemble neural network model. A neuron with a bias and tanh activation function was used. The Levenberg-Maquardt method was used in the context of the back propagation method.

Table 1. Regression coefficients (R1-5) of five ANN ensemble models and resulted R

h_w [cm]	R1	R2	R3	R4	R5	R
-2.5	0.914	0.921	0.937	0.934	0.888	0.930
-56	0.905	0.922	0.934	0.897	0.872	0.916
-209	0.886	0.92	0.934	0.897	0.871	0.912
-558	0.883	0.927	0.943	0.879	0.877	0.912
-976	0.872	0.923	0.937	0.871	0.865	0.905
-3060	0.858	0.92	0.93	0.846	0.848	0.892
-15300	0.192	-0.270	-0.281	-14.718	54.796	0.864

The networks were trained for computing the water content at the pressure head value h_w = -2.5, -56, -209, -558, -976, -3060, -15300 cm. Then the testing dataset was computed with the ensemble ANN. The results with five regression coefficients are summarized in Table 1 also with final (average) regression coefficient R.

Given regression problem was also solved by using *ensemble* of *support vector machines*. The estimation of the steps of the SVM regression (described in the methodology part of this paper) are the following: 1) the selection of a suitable kernel and the appropriate kernel's parameter (γ in eq.1); 2) specifying the ε parameter and specifying the capacity C.

As a criterion for selecting the appropriate combinations of the parameters, the correlation coefficient for the training and cross-validation data is calculated within the objective function of the harmony search, where the correlation coefficient of the cross-validation data was weighted by the coefficient 1.2 for the sake of a better generalization.

In the training phase, SVM models for a pressure head value of h_w= -2.5, -56, -209, -558, -976, -3060, -15300 cm were created. This was repeated five times because of the five divisions of the data used to train the model on the training and validation data set. A total of 35 computations were run because there is seven variables computed. Then the testing dataset was computed five times with the models obtained, and the final result is the average of the outputs from these five models; the results are summarized with the regression coefficients in Table 2.

Table 2. Regression coefficients (R1-5) of five SVM ensemble models and resulted R

h_w [cm]	R1	R2	R3	R4	R5	R
-2.5	0.910	0.908	0.902	0.910	0.891	0.907
-56	0.865	0.859	0.863	0.848	0.852	0.861
-209	0.860	0.857	0.867	0.862	0.855	0.863
-558	0.856	0.854	0.857	0.857	0.848	0.857
-976	0.833	0.842	0.846	0.840	0.834	0.846
-3060	0.845	0.847	0.852	0.846	0.837	0.851
-15300	0.799	0.822	0.819	0.815	0.817	0.816

A multi-linear regression for assessing the PTFs was accomplished for comparison and it was used in the form:

$$\theta_{hw} = a*1^{st} \text{ cat.} + b*2^{nd} \text{ cat.} + c*3^{th} \text{ cat.} + d*4^{th} \text{ cat.} + e*\rho_d + f. \qquad (2)$$

where θ_{hw} is the water content [$cm^3.cm^{-3}$] for the particular pressure head value h_w [cm]; 1st *cat.*, 2nd *cat.*, 3th *cat.* and 4th *cat.* are the percentages of the clay (d< 0.01 mm), silt (0.01–0.05 mm) and sand (0.1–2.0 mm); ρ_d is the dry bulk density [$g.cm^{-3}$]; and a, b, c, d, e, f are the parameters determined by the regression analysis. In the case of the multi-linear regression it was not possible to use ensemble models, because in this case no iterative process is applied which involves cross validation, so all 110 training samples were used as a whole for the development of the model and 30 samples for testing.

The PTFs designed were evaluated on a testing dataset. The results of the multi-linear regression are listed in Table 3.

Table 3. Results of the multi-linear regression (coefficients of Eq. 2 and regression coeficient)

hw [cm]	a	b	c	d	e	f	R
-2.5	-0.224	-0.427	-0.2728	-0.403	-37.251	133.466	0.888
-56	-0.803	-1.157	-0.905	-1.223	-25.193	180.218	0.798
-209	-0.794	-1.163	-1.060	-1.2781	-17.761	167.584	0.819
-558	-0.531	-0.932	-0.833	-1.024	-19.859	143.738	0.856
-976	-1.7	-2.091	-1.984	-2.174	-18.405	255.177	0.685
-3060	-1.166	-1.624	-1.499	-1.655	-1.166	199.374	0.770
-15300	-2.007	-2.459	-2.288	-2.487	-14.882	275.784	0.631

As can be seen, the results from both data driven techniques are clearly better compared with the multi-linear regression and from SVM are somewhat worse compared with the ANN. From these results, it seems that ANNs are more resistant to an insufficient amount of data (which is the case in this work), because, on the other hand, better results with the application of the SVM than with the ANN for the PTF evaluation were reported in the literature [11]. It should be mentioned that the authors of mentioned paper worked with larger data sets (2134 soil samples). For this reason the authors of the present paper hypothesize that it is advisable to use combined SVM/MLP models, because of the variability of an adequate methodology, but this should be verified in future work.

5 Conclusions

The results of this paper contain a description and evaluation of the models of an ensemble of multi-layer perceptrons and an ensemble of support vector machines for the development of pedotransfer functions for the point estimation of the soil-water content for the seven pressure head values h_w from the basic soil properties (particle-size distribution, bulk density). Both ensemble data-driven models were compared to a multiple linear regression methodology.

- The accuracy of the predictions was evaluated by the correlation coefficient (R) between the measured and predicted parameter values. The R varied from 0.631 to 0.888 for the multi-linear regression, from 0.864 to 0.930 for the MLP, and from 0.816 to 0.907 for the SVM. The MLP models perform somewhat better than the SVM models. Nevertheless, the results from both data-driven models are quite close, and the results show that they provide a significantly more precise outcome than traditional multi-linear regression.
- Although SVM training is faster, the whole process of ANN training for evaluating PTFs is accomplished in less time, because of the ability of ANNs to produce more outputs in one run, which is the advantage versus SVMs.

Because other authors have reported the better regression ability of SVMs compared with ANNs [11], the authors of the present paper hypothesize that it is advisable to use combined SVM/MLP models, because of this variability in suitable methodology. This should be verified in future work. The authors of the mentioned paper worked with larger data sets (they used 2134 soil samples; 140 samples were used in our work), and the influence of the amount of data or other statistical data set properties on the choice of the methodology suitable to use should be evaluated. Also other types of data driven models should be tested, e.g., generalized regression neural network or radial basis network.

Acknowledgement. This work was supported by the Slovak Research and Development Agency under Contract No. LPP-0319-09 and APVV-0496-10 and by the Scientific Grant Agency of the Ministry of Education of the Slovak Republic and the Slovak Academy of Sciences, Grants No. 1/1044/11.

References

1. Baker, L., Ellison, D.: Optimisation of pedotransfer functions using an artificial neural network ensemble method. Geoderma 144(1-2), 212–224 (2008)
2. Bouma, J.: Using Soil Survey Data for Quantitative Land Evaluation. Adv. Soil Sci. 9, 177–213 (1989)
3. Geem, Z.W., Roper, W.E.: Various Continuous Harmony Search Algorithms for Web-Based Hydrologic Parameter Optimisation. International Journal of Mathematical Modelling and Numerical Optimisation 1, 213–226 (2010)
4. Minasny, B., McBratney, A.B.: The Neuro-M Methods for Fitting Neural Network Parametric Pedotransfer Functions. Soil Sci. Soc. Am. J. 66, 352–361 (2002)
5. Mohammadi, J.: Testing an artificial neural network for predicting soil water retention characteristics from soil physical and chemical properties. In: 17th World Congress of Soil Science, Thailand (2002)
6. Pachepsky, Y., Rawls, W.J.: Developmennt of Pedotransfer Functions in Soil Hydrology. Elsevier, Amsterdam (2004)
7. Schaap, M.G., Leij, F.J., Van Genuchten, M.T.: Neural network analysis for hierarchical prediction of soil hydraulic properties. Soil Sci. Soc. Am. J. 62, 847–855 (1998)
8. Skalova, J.: Pedotransfer Functions of the Zahorska Lowland Soils and Their Application to Soil-Water Regime Modeling. Thesis, Faculty of Civil Engineering STU Bratislava, p. 112 (2001) (in Slovak)
9. Smola, A.J., Schölkopf, B.: A Tutorial on Support Vector Regression. Statistics and Computing 14, 199–222 (2004)
10. Tamari, S., Wosten, J.H.M., Ruiz-Suarez, J.C.: Testing an Artificial Neural Network for Predicting Soil Hydraulic Conductivity. Soil Sci. Soc. Am. J. 60, 1732–1741 (1996)
11. Twarakavi, N.K.C., Simunek, J., Schaap, M.G.: Development of Pedotransfer Functions for Estimation of Soil Hydraulic Parameters Using Support Vector Machines. Soil Sci. Soc. Am. J. 73, 1443–1452 (2009)
12. Vapnik, V.: The Nature of Statistical Learning Theory. Springer, NY (1995)

A Neural Based Approach and Probability Density Approximation for Fault Detection and Isolation in Nonlinear Systems

P. Boi[*] and A. Montisci

Abstract. A locally recurrent neural network based fault detection and isolation approach is presented. A model of the system under test is created by means of a dynamic neural network. The fault detection is performed on the basis of the statistical analysis of the residual provided by the estimated density shaping of residuals in the case of nominal value of all the parameters, made of a simply neural network. The approach is illustrated by using the Rössler hyperchaotic system.

Keywords: Locally recurrent neural networks, nonlinear systems diagnosis, gradient-based training.

1 Introduction

In this paper we introduce a neural network based approach for fault detection and fault isolation of nonlinear circuits. Several methods have been proposed for fault diagnosis of analog circuits, board, and chip levels[1]-[18]

In [2] the authors propose an optimization based multifrequency test generation method for detecting parametric faults in linear analog circuits.

In [8] a decomposition approach for diagnosis and fault prediction in large analogue and switched capacitor circuits is proposed, reduced to an analysis of the corresponding nullator-norator models at a single test frequency. Algorithms for isolation of faulty nodes and subcircuits are presented. The topological conditions for diagnosing faulty nodes and elements are given, taking into account the element parameters tolerance and measurement errors.

In [10] a coefficient-based test (CBT) is introduced for detecting deviation faults in analog linear circuits. The method uses pseudo Monte-Carlo simulation to determine the transfer function coefficients for all the test points, and the circuit is declared faulty if any coefficients falls outside the fault free range.

In [5] a fault diagnosis system for analog circuit testing based on the Simulation Before Test (SBT) approach, is presented. Frequency response analysis is carried out of the circuit under test, then parameters are extracted such that they give unique values for every configuration of the circuit.

In[6] mathematical programming models are developed for the diagnosis of soft fault in analog circuit. At the same time, the tolerance question is handled, too.

The authors in [19] and [20] propose a Generalized Algorithm of Fault Tolerance (GAFT), using time, structural and information redundancy types. In [19] it is shown that

---

[*] Electrical and Electronic Eng. Dept - Univ. of Cagliari – Italy.

L. Iliadis and C. Jayne (Eds.): EANN/AIAI 2011, Part I, IFIP AICT 363, pp. 296–305, 2011.

the design of fault tolerant systems is efficient if malfunctions are tolerated at the element level. The advantage of element malfunction tolerance is proven in reliability terms. Maximum reliability of fault tolerant system is achievable with less than a duplication system and depends on malfunction/permanent fault ratio and coverage of faults. System level of fault tolerance prerogative is the reconfiguration from permanent faults.

In [20] a scheme, is proposed to implement fault tolerant system software for routers using recovery points. It is shown that GAFT is capable of detecting, identifying, localizing faults, reconfiguring the hardware to achieve a repairable state and, if necessary, reconfiguring the software as well. Separation of malfunction and permanent fault tolerance is discussed in terms of their impact on system reliability.

In [22] is presented a fault diagnosis method for analog circuits that use a neural network classifier. The authors show that preprocessing based on the kurtosis and entropy of signals simplifies the network architecture, reduces the training time, and improves the performance of the network.

In the case of diagnosis of dynamic systems, we should to use dynamic neural networks to catch the behavior of the system. In particular, the Locally Recurrent Neural Network (LRNN) have the feed-forward multi-layer architecture and their dynamic properties are obtained using feedbacks inside the neurons, so that in spite of the neural network maintains the topological structure of a Multi Layer Perceptron, it can exhibit a dynamical behavior like recursive networks. A neural network can be trained to mimic the system behavior or to predict the next sample of the input. In the present work, a LRNN predictor has been trained, validated and tested using the input learning data, related to different operating conditions, that are collected from a simulation model of Rössler's system.

After finishing the training process, the neural network is ready for on-line residual generation. The residuals are generated by comparing the system output with the output of the neural model. A fault detection can be performed if a parameter deviation in the system under test determines a change in the dynamics of the diagnostic signal that appreciably affects the residual.

The decision on the occurrence of a fault (detection) is made when the modulus of all components of the output estimation error exceeds its corresponding threshold provided by the statistical distribution of the residual estimated in the case of nominal value of all the parameters.

We assume that a fault is said to be isolable if the fault isolation system is able to reach a correct decision in finite time. Faults are isolable if they are mutually different according to a certain measure quantifying the difference in the effects that different faults have on measurable outputs and on the estimated quantities in the isolation system.

The organization of the paper is as follows. In Section II locally recurrent neural networks are introduced. In Section III, the training algorithm is presented. Section IV, the diagnostic approach is presented. In Section V, density shaping using neural networks is explained. Section VI reports the experimental results referring to the benchmark of Rössler's system. Section VII reports conclusions.

2 The Neural Model

An artificial neural network used to model the system behavior belongs to the class of so-called locally recurrent globally feed-forward networks [23]. Its structure is similar to a multi-layer perceptron where neurons are organized in layers, but dynamic properties are achieved using neurons with internal feedbacks. The block structure of the *i-th* neuron considered is presented in Fig. 1. Thus, the i-*th* neuron in the dynamic network reproduces the past signal value with two signals: the input u t and its output y_k t. The weighted sum of inputs is calculated according to the formula:

$$s_i(k) = w_i u(k),$$ (1)

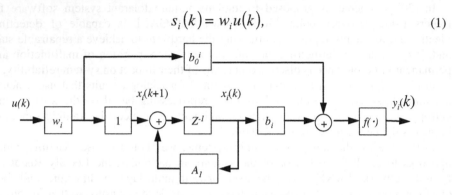

Fig. 1. i[th] locally recurrent neuron

$w_i(k) = [w_1^i, w_2^i, ..., w_n^i]$ is the input weights vector, n is the number of inputs, $u(k) = [u_1^i, u_2^i, ..., u_n^i]^T$ is the input vector (T-transposition operator). The weights w_i have the same role as the weights in the static feedforward networks. The states of the ith neuron in the network can be described by the following equation:

$$x_i(k+1) = A_i x_i(k) + W_i u(k),$$ (2)

where $x_i(k) = [x_1^i, x_2^i, ..., x_n^i]$ is the state vector. $W_i = 1 w_i$ is the weight matrix ($1 \in R^r$ and 1 is the vector of ones) and the matrix of state transition A_i has the form:

$$A_i = \begin{bmatrix} -a_1^i & -a_2^i & \cdots & -a_{r-1}^i & -a_r^i \\ 1 & 0 & \cdots & 0 & 0 \\ 0 & 1 & \cdots & 0 & 0 \\ \vdots & \vdots & \vdots & \vdots & \vdots \\ 0 & 0 & \cdots & 1 & 0 \end{bmatrix}$$ (3)

finally, the output of the neuron is described by

$$y_i(k) = f\left(b_i x_i(k) + d_i u(k), g_i\right),$$ (4)

where $f(\cdot)$ may be a linear or a non linear activation function, $d_i = b_o^i w_i$, $b_i = [b_1^i, b_2^i, ..., b_r^i]$ is the vector of feed-forward filter parameters. $g_i = [g_1^i, g_2^i]$ is the vector of the activation function parameters consisting in bias and slope of the activation function.

3 Training Algorithm

All unknown network parameters can be represented by a vector θ composed of elements A_i, W_i, b_i, d_i and g_i, where p is the number of network parameters. The main objective of training is to adjust the elements of the vector θ in such a way as to minimize some loss function

$$\theta^* = \underset{\theta \in \Theta}{arg} \, min \mathbf{J}(\theta), \tag{5}$$

where θ^* is the optimal network parameter vector Θ is the set of constraints defining the feasible values for the parameters. This network can be trained using a stochastic gradient-based algorithm [24] in the form:

$$\hat{\theta}_{k+1} = \hat{\theta}_k - lr_k \hat{g}\left(\hat{\theta}_k\right) \tag{6}$$

where $\hat{g}\left(\hat{\theta}_k\right)$ is the estimate of the gradient $\partial \mathbf{J}/\partial \hat{\theta}$ based on the measurements of $L(\cdot)$ the loss function $\mathbf{J}(\theta)$. The gradient estimate is obtained by

$$\hat{g}_{ki}(\hat{\theta}_k) = \frac{y_{1k} - y_{2k}}{2c_k \Delta_{ki}} \quad \forall i = 1,...,p \tag{7}$$

where $y_{1k} = L(\hat{\theta}_k + C_k \Delta_k) + \varepsilon_{1k}$, $y_{2k} = L(\hat{\theta}_k - C_k \Delta_k) + \varepsilon_{2k}$, ($\varepsilon_{1k}$ and ε_{2k} represent measurement noise terms), Δ_k is a p-dimensional random perturbation vector that in our work is obtained by the symmetric Bernoulli distribution ± 1. lr_k and c_k are calculated as follows: $lr_k = a/(A+k)^\alpha$, $c_k = c/k^\gamma$.

4 Diagnostic Approach

In this paper a Fault Detection approach is proposed, which can be applied to both linear and nonlinear systems. First a neural network like that in Fig. 1 is trained off-line by means of the procedure described above in order to predict one step ahead the output signal of the system. The number of hidden neurons and the number of state variables are determined by a trial and error procedure. When the trained network is used to predict the signal, unavoidably the output will exhibit a certain prediction error or residual. On the basis of a validation signal, different from the training signal, the statistic distribution of the residual is estimated both in the case of nominal value of all the parameters and when one or more of them have a value within the tolerance range. This allows us to determine a threshold for the detection of the fault.

Finally, the residual r should be used by a classifier to determine both the type and occurrence time of possible faults. To evaluate residuals and to obtain information about faults, a simple threshold can be applied. If residuals are smaller than threshold value a the tested process is considered to be healthy, otherwise it is considered faulty. The Fault isolability analysis is made by introducing a fault mismatch function between any of two types of fault. Then two faults are reciprocally isolable if the fault mismatch function exceeds its corresponding threshold.

5 Density Estimation

A random vector x of an arbitrary distribution can be transformed into a new random vector y of a different distribution maximizing the mutual information between x and y [25]. This can be achieved by maximizing the entropy of the output of the neural network that has input x and output y .

$$h(y) = -E\{\ln f_y(y)\} = -E(\ln f_x(x)) + E(\ln|\partial y / \partial x|), \qquad (8)$$

where the entropy of x, $f_x(x)$, can be neglected because it may be considered unaffected by alterations in a parameter w. Let us consider the network of Fig. 2, it has only one input x, and the activation function $f(x)$ is a sigmoidal function. The input probability density function is approximated by

$$q_x(x) = |\partial y / \partial x|, \qquad (9)$$

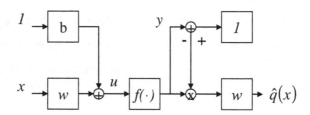

Fig. 2. Neural network model that estimates the density function

This network can be trained using the on-line version of stochastic gradient ascent rule [25] in the form:

$$\Delta v = \frac{\partial h(y)}{\partial v} = \frac{\partial}{\partial v}\left(\log\left|\frac{\partial y}{\partial x}\right|\right) = \left(\frac{\partial y}{\partial x}\right)^{-1}\frac{\partial}{\partial v}\left(\frac{\partial y}{\partial x}\right), \qquad (10)$$

where v is the generalized network parameter. The equation (10) represents a self-organizing algorithm. The equation (10) contains the anti-Hebbian term, which keeps y away from saturation at 0 and 1. The learning rule for the weight parameter w is

$$\Delta w = \frac{1}{w} + x(1 + 2y), \qquad (11)$$

similarly the rule for the bias weight parameter is

$$\Delta b = 1 - 2\mathbf{y}, \tag{12}$$

After the training, the estimated probability density function can be calculated using the scheme shown in Fig. 2. The estimation of the input probability density function takes the form:

$$\hat{q}_x(x) = |w| y(1 - y) \tag{13}$$

Then we calculate the threshold corresponding to a given significance level α.

When a fault (a deviation of the parameter) occurs in the system, a residual should deviate from the level observed to the fault-free case. The quality of the fault detection system can be evaluated using a number of performance indexes. The sensitivity of the proposed fault diagnosis system in the fault-free case is checked using the *false detection rate* $r_{fd} = n°false$ *detections/tot* $n°$ *fault signals*. This index is used to check the system in the fault-free case. Its value shows a percentage of false alarms.

The *true detection rate* is: $rsd = n°successful$ *detection/tot* $n°$ *faults*. This index is used in the case of faults and describes the efficiency of fault detection.

The *time of fault detection* t_{dt} is a period of time needed for detection of a fault measured from the instant t_0 when the threshold is exceeded the first time. A fault is considered certain when the residues of all state variables used in the diagnostic system simultaneously exceed the threshold during the period t_{dt}.

Now, Let us assume that when a fault is detected at time $t=t_d$ the fault isolation system is activated.

5.1 Fault Isolability Analysis

We introduce the fault mismatch function between the *s-th* fault and the *r-th* fault:

$$h_{jsr}(t) = e_{js}(t) - e_{jr}(t). \qquad r, s = 1...N, r \neq s \tag{14}$$

e_{js} and e_{jr} are the residuals of the *j-th* variable used in the isolation system if there are the faults s and r respectively, and N is the number of possible faults. Let us suppose that a fault s occurring at time $t=t_0$ is detected at time $t=t_d$. Then the fault s is isolable if, for each $r \in \{1,...,N\} \backslash \{s\}$, there exist some time $t_i > t_d$ and at least one variable j used in the isolation system, such that

$$|h_{jsr}(t)| > h_o \tag{15}$$

where the threshold h_0 is determined empirically, for each variable j. The sensitivity of the proposed fault isolation system is checked by calculating, for each $r \in \{1,...,N\} \backslash \{s\}$, the *true isolation rate*:

$r_{srj} = n°successful\ isolations/n°tot\ faults\ of\ type\ s$. This index is used in the case of faults and describes the efficiency of fault isolation.

6 Experiments

The Rössler's hyperchaotic system [26] has been used to validate the diagnostic approach. The difficulty to interpret the residual signal is due to the fact that the trajectory in the state space critically depends on the initial state of the system, therefore one cannot define as a reference a fault-free behavior. The equations that describe the system are:

$$\begin{cases} \dot{x}_1 = -x_2 - x_3 \\ \dot{x}_2 = x_1 + ax_2 + x_4 \\ \dot{x}_3 = x_1 x_3 + b \\ \dot{x}_4 = -cx_3 + dx_4 \end{cases} \tag{16}$$

Rössler's system has a hyperchaotic attractor when $a=0.25$, $b=3$, $c=0.5$, $d=0.05$. In order to show the suitability of the method, we tried to detect a parameter drift with respect to a point in the parameter space where the system exhibits a chaotic behavior, so that we haven't a reference behavior of the system without faults. In turn, residual evaluation is carried out by using statistical analysis discussed in Section 4. The fault diagnosis system is evaluated using several faulty conditions. An 1-5-2-1 network structure has been adopted, with 2 state variables in hidden neurons and a linear activation function. Such network is trained over 1000 samples in order to iteratively predict one step ahead three state variables (x_1, x_2, x_4) on the basis of the past samples, when all the system parameters are at their nominal value. The sum of squared errors calculated over 9000 testing samples is equal to 0.095. The reference value of the average and the variance of the residual is evaluated by performing the signal prediction being all the parameters at their nominal value but the initial state different from that one of the training signal.

Modelling results for 800 testing samples are shown in Fig. 3, where the model output is marked by the dotted line, and output of process by the solid line.

Using neural model of the process, for each system parameter, three residuals are calculated, corresponding to the prediction of three output variables. The same evaluation is performed when we decrease the parameter a of 5% and of 10% of its nominal value. The average and the variance of each residual are used as feature for the diagnosis. A greater number of experiments can aid to better describe the frontier decision for the fault detection, whereas in general further test points improve the detectability of faults. Residuals are used to train the neural network described in Section 4 to approximate the corresponding probability density function. The neural network in Fig. 2 is trained off-line for 90000 steps using an unsupervised learning (6). To perform a decision, a significance level $\alpha = 0.05$ is assumed. The test set consists of 100 signals each consisting of 1000 samples for each operating condition. In the fault-free case, the *false detection rate* r_{fd} is equal to *0.1*. In fault conditions, the results of fault detection are presented in Table 1. In each case, if the true detection rate (5) is close to 1 it means that detection of faults is performed surely. In order to perform decision about faults, and to determine detection time a time-window with the length $n = 5$ has been used. If during the following n time steps all residuals exceed the threshold then a fault is signalled. Application of time-window prevents the situation when a temporary true detection signals a fault. All faulty conditions can be classified. The results of fault detection are presented in Table 2.

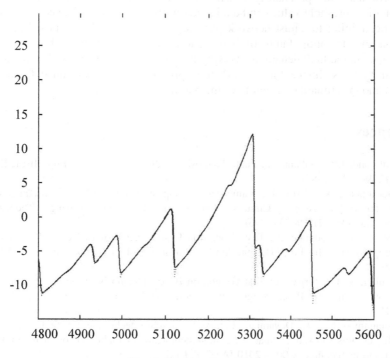

Fig. 3. Results of modelling

Table 1. Performance index for the fault conditions in to detection system when we decrease the parameter a of 5% (f1) and of 10%(f2)

	f1	f2
r_{sd}	0.7	0.78

Table 2. Performance indexes for the fault conditions in to isolation system

$r_{5\%,10\%}$	$r_{10\%,5\%}$
0.68	0.72

7 Conclusion

The purpose of this paper was to propose a model-based fault detection and fault isolation system for nonlinear circuits. The model of the system under test is realized by means of a locally recurrent neural network. The detection of faults is based on the analysis of residuals. A simple neural network trained to maximize the output entropy can approximate the probability density function of a residual and in this way a representative threshold value can be obtained with a given significance level. A self-organizing training to adjust network parameters is used. "The proposed approach, tested on the deviation faults of hyperchaotic Rossler system, exhibited a good performance in the fault detection, showing that it is suitable even for the diagnosis of nonlinear systems. In the future work the approach will be extended to the fault isolation and in estimating the entity of the parameter variation.

References

1. Bandlerand, J.W., Salama, A.: Fault diagnosis of analog circuits. In: Proc. IEEE ISCAS, pp. 1279–1325 (1985)
2. Abderrahman, A., Cerny, E., Kaminska, B.: Optimization Based Multifrequency Test Generation for Analog Circuits. Journal of Electronic Testing: Theory and Applications 9(1-2), 59–73 (1996)
3. Cherubal, S., Chatterjee, A.: Test Generation Based Diagnosis of Device Parameters for Analog Circuits. In: Proc. Design, Automation and Test in Europe Conf., pp. 596–602 (2001)
4. Cherubal, S., Chatterjee, A.: Test Generation Based Diagnosis of Device Parameters for Analog Circuits. In: Proc. Design, Automation and Test in Europe Conf., pp. 596–602 (2001)
5. Prasannamoorthy, V., Devarajan: Frequency domain technique for fault diagnosis in analog circuits-software and hardware implementation. Journal of Theoretical and Applied Information Technology 005 - 2010 JATIT & LLS
6. Zhou, L., Shi, Y., Zhao, G., Zhang, W., Tang, H., Su, L.: Soft-Fault Diagnosis of Analog Circuit with Tolerance Using Mathematical Programming. Journal of Communication and Computer 7(5) (Serial No.66) ISSN 1548-7709
7. Devarayanadurg, G., Soma, M.: Analytical Fault Modeling and Static Test Generation for Analog ICs. In: Proc. Int. Conf. on Computer-Aided Design, pp. 44–47 (November 1994)
8. Farchy, S.L., Gadzheva, E.D., Raykovska, L.H., Kouyoumdjiev, T.G.: Nullator-Norator Approach to Analogue Circuit Diagnosis Using General-Purpose Analysis Programmes. Int. Journal of Circuit Theory and Applications 23(6), 571–585 (1995)
9. Figueras, J.: Possibilities and Limitations of IDDQ Testing in Submicron CMOS. In: Proc. Innovative Systems in Silicon Conf., pp. 174–185 (October 1997)
10. Guo, Z., Savir, J.: Analog Circuit Test Using Transfer Function Coefficient Estimates. In: Proc. Int. Test Conf., pp. 1155–1163 (October 2003)
11. Halder, A., Bhattacharya, S., Chatterjee, A.: Automatic Multitone Alternate Test Generation for RF Circuits Using Behavioral Models. In: Proc. Intl. Test Conf., pp. 665–673 (November 2003)

12. Kondagunturi, R., Bradley, E., Maggard, K., Stroud, C.: Benchmark Circuits for Analog and Mixed-Signal Testing. In: Proc. 20th Int. Conf. on Microelectronics, pp. 217–220 (March 1999)
13. Panic, V., Milovanovic, D., Petkovic, P., Litovski, V.: Fault Location in Passive Analog RC Circuits by measuring Impulse Response. In: Proc. 20th Int. Conf. on Microelectronics, pp. 12–14 (September 1995)
14. Rajsuman, R.: IDDQ Testing for CMOS VLSI. Proceedings of the IEEE 88(4) (April 2000)
15. Slamani, M., Kaminska, B.: Analog Circuit Fault Diagnosis Based on Sensitivity Computation and Functional Testing. IEEE Design & Test of Computers 19(1), 30–39 (1992)
16. Frank, P.M., Köppen-Seliger, B.: New developments using AI in fault diagnosis. Artificial Intelligence 10(1), 3–14 (1997)
17. Gertler, J.: Fault detection and diagnosis in engineering systems. Marcel Dekker, New York (1998)
18. Schagaev, I.: Reliability of malfunction tolerance. In: Proc. of Int. Multiconference on Computer Science and Information Technologies, Wisla, Poland (October 2008)
19. Azam, M., Ioannides, N., Rümmeli, M.H., Schagaev, I.: System Software Support for Router Reliability. In: 30th IFAC Workshop on Real-Time Programming, and 4th International Workshop on Real-Time Software (WRTP/RTS 2009), Mragowo, Poland (October 2009)
20. Schagaev, I., Zalewski, J.: Redudancy classification for fault tolerant computer design. In: Proc. of the 2001 IEEE Systems, Man, and Cybernetics Conference, Tucson, Arizona (October 2001)
21. Yuan, L., He, Y., Huang, J., Sun, Y.: A New Neural-Network-Based Fault Diagnosis Approach for Analog Circuits by Using Kurtosis and Entropy as a Preprocessor. IEEE Transaction on Instrumentation and Measurement 59(3) (March 2010)
22. Back, A.D., Tsoi, A.C.: FIR and IIR Synapses, a New Neural Network Architecture for Time Series Modeling. Neural Computation 3, 375–385 (1991)
23. Spall, J.C.: Multivariate stochastic approximation using a simulta- neous perturbation gradient approximation. IEEE Trans. Autom. Control. 37(3), 332–341 (1992)
24. Bell, A.J., Sejnowski, T.J.: An information-maximization approach to blind separation and blind deconvolution. Neural Computation 7, 1129–1159 (1995)
25. Rössler, O.E.: An equation for hyperchaos. Physics Letters 71, 155–157 (1979)
26. Principe, J.C., Euliano, N.R., Curt Lefebvre, W.: Neural and Adaptive Systems. Wiley, Chichester (2000)
27. Bishop, C.M.: Neural Networks for Pattern Recognition. Clarendon Press, Oxford (1995)
28. Cybenko, G.: Approximation by superposition of a sigmoidal function. Mathematics of Control, Signal and Systems 2, 304 (1989)
29. The Mathworks, Neural Networks Toolbox for use with Matlab, v. 7.4.0.287, R (2007)

A Neural Network Tool for the Interpolation of foF2 Data in the Presence of Sporadic E Layer

Haris Haralambous, Antonis Ioannou, and Harris Papadopoulos

Computer Science and Engineering Department, Frederick University,
7 Y. Frederickou St., Palouriotisa, Nicosia 1036, Cyprus
{H.Haralambous,H.Papadopoulos}@frederick.ac.cy

Abstract. This paper presents the application of Neural Networks for the interpolation of (critical frequency) *foF2* data over Cyprus in the presence of sporadic E layer which is a frequent phenomenon during summer months causing inevitable gaps in the *foF2* data series. This ionospheric characteristic (*foF2*) constitutes the most important parameter in HF (High Frequency) communications since it is used to derive the optimum operating frequency in HF links and therefore interpolating missing data is very important in preserving the data series which is used in long-term prediction procedures and models.

Keywords: Ionosphere, HF communications, F2 layer critical frequency.

1 Introduction

The ionosphere is defined as a region of the earth's upper atmosphere where sufficient ionisation can exist to reflect radio waves in the frequency range 1 to 30 MHz therefore facilitating long distance HF (High Frequency) communication by skywave propagation. It ranges in height above the surface of the earth from approximately 50 km to 1000 km. The influence of this region on radio waves is accredited to the presence of free electrons.

The uppermost layer of the ionosphere is the F2 region which is the principal reflecting region for long distance HF communications [1,2,3]. The maximum frequency that can be reflected at vertical incidence by this layer is termed the F2 layer critical frequency (*foF2*) and is directly related to the maximum electron density of the layer (see figure 1). The F2 layer critical frequency is the most important parameter in HF communication links since when multiplied by a factor which is a function of the link distance, it defines the optimum usable frequency of operation. The maximum electron density of free electrons within the F2 layer and therefore *foF2* depend upon the strength of the solar ionising radiation which is a function of time of day, season, geographical location and solar activity [1,2,3]. The E-region lies below the F-region extending approximately from 90 km to 150 km (figure 1). Typically the E-region is characterised by lower electron densities than the F-region (continuous profile in figure 1). However sometimes an irregular layer of extremely high density layer called sporadic E (Es) layer appears (dashed part in the profile in figure 1) in the E-region which prevents any radio signals from reaching the F-region. Es can occur during daytime or night-time, and its characteristics vary with latitude.

L. Iliadis and C. Jayne (Eds.): EANN/AIAI 2011, Part I, IFIP AICT 363, pp. 306–314, 2011.

These regions can apparently be caused by several mechanisms, and have a wide variety of characteristics. They have been correlated in literature with solar activity, geomagnetic activity and associated with thunderstorms and meteor showers [4,5].

This paper describes the development of a neural network tool to interpolate missing *foF2* data over Cyprus. The tool development is based on 10342 hourly *foF2* measurements recorded above Cyprus from September 2008 to August 2010. The practical application of this model lies in the fact that in the presence of Es above Cyprus, due to the inability of the ionosonde to perform *foF2* measurements, this model can provide an efficient interpolation method to fill the gaps in the *foF2* data series that is used to drive long-term prediction models of *foF2*. There have not been any other efforts to apply interpolation techniques on *foF2* datasets apart from a specific dataset over UK [6]. This can be partly explained by the fact that most ionospheric stations are situated at middle latitudes where Es is not a frequent phenomenon and so data gaps may only appear because of system failure. In the case of Cyprus which is the lowest European ionospheric station in operation, the Es phenomenon is very frequent causing data gaps under normal system operation. A possible candidate for the interpolation procedure would have been the recently developed neural network approach from modelling *foF2* [7]. However the key novelty of the proposed interpolation tool is the use of TEC measurements as an additional input resulting in improved performance compared to the existing long-term (without TEC as input) model in terms of interpolation.

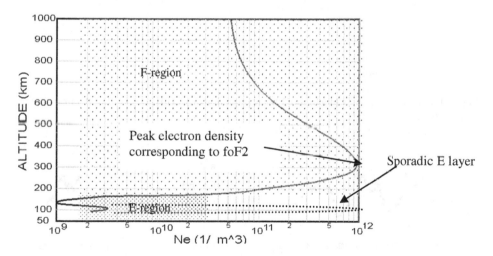

Fig. 1. Typical electron density altitude profile of the ionosphere superimposed with enhanced density in the E-region due to Es layer

2 Measurement of F2 Layer Critical Frequency and Total Electron Content

Measurements of *foF2* are conducted by ionosondes. which sweep through the HF frequency range transmitting short pulses. These pulses are reflected at various layers of the ionosphere, and their echoes are received by the receiver giving rise to a corresponding plot of reflection altitude against frequency (called an ionogram- figure 2) which is further analysed to infer the ionospheric plasma height-electron density profile (figure 1). The maximum frequency at which an echo is received is called the critical frequency of the corresponding layer. Since the F2 layer is the most highly ionised ionosperic layer its critical frequency *foF2* is the highest frequency that can be reflected by the ionosphere (figure 2b). The presence of a Es layer (figure 2a) which does not allow for ionosonde signals to reach F2 region altitudes does not allow a useful ionogram to be obtained and therefore gaps in the data series of *foF2* are formed (figure 3b). These gaps have to be interpolated in a way to preserve the inherent variability of *foF2* data. This study suggests that one way to achieve this is to incorporate Total Electron Content (TEC) measurements which is another type of ionospheric characteristic the measurement of which is not affected by Es layer. The reason is that the signals involved in the measurement of TEC are high enough (> 1 GHz) to pass through the Es layer practically unaffected as opposed to the much lower frequency of ionosonde signals (<20 MHz).

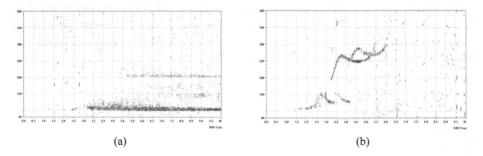

(a)   (b)

Fig. 2. Ionogram (a) with Es blocking F2 layer reflections (b) with normal F2 reflections in the absence of Es layer

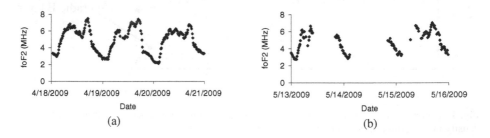

Fig. 3. Data series of foF2 (a) without gaps (b) with gaps due to ionograms with Es layer

Dual-frequency GPS data recorded by GPS (Global Positioning System) receivers enable an estimation of TEC because of the frequency dependent delay imposed on the signal due to the ionosphere [8]. By processing code and phase measurements on two frequencies in the L-band (L1=1575.42 MHz, L2=1227.60 MHz) it is possible to extract an estimate of the TEC measured in total electron content units, (1 TECU = 10^{16} el m−2). This is the total amount of electrons along a particular line of sight between the receiver and a GPS satellite in a column of 1 m^2 cross-sectional area. TEC is therefore the integral of the electron density profile (figure 1) from the E-region up to the height of the GPS satellite encompassing the electrons in the F-region as well.

The analysis used in the present work to estimate TEC from GPS transmissions was carried out by means of the procedure developed by Ciraolo [9,10]. It can be shown that the measurable GPS ionospheric delay is expressed in terms of TEC as [11]:

$$t_{ion} = \frac{40.3}{cf^2} TEC \tag{1}$$

and

$$TEC = \int_{h1}^{h2} N(h).dh \tag{2}$$

t_{ion} ... GPS ionospheric delay
c... velocity of light in free space
f... frequency of radio wave propagating through the ionosphere (GPS radio signal)
N(h) ... ionospheric electron density at the height h above the earth's surface
TEC ... total electron content along the satellite ray path.

3   Characteristics of the F2 Layer Critical Frequency and Total Electron Content

Solar activity has an impact on ionospheric dynamics which in turn influence the electron density of the ionosphere. The electron density of the F2 layer and TEC exhibit variability on daily, seasonal and long-term time scales in response to the effect of solar radiation. It is also subject to abrupt variations due to enhancements of geomagnetic activity following extreme manifestations of solar activity disturbing the ionosphere from minutes to days on a local or global scale.

The most profound solar effect on *foF2* and TEC is reflected on their daily variation as shown in figure 4. As it is clearly depicted, there is a strong dependency on local time which follows a sharp increase of *foF2* and TEC around sunrise and gradual decrease around sunset. This is attributed to the rapid increase in the production of electrons due to the photo-ionization process during the day and a more gradual decrease due to the recombination of ions and electrons during the night. The long–term effect of solar activity on both parameters follows an eleven-year cycle and is clearly shown in figure 5(a),(b) where all values of *foF2* and TEC are plotted against time as well as a modeled monthly mean sunspot number *R* which is a well established index of solar activity. We can observe a marked correlation of the mean level of both parameters and modeled sunspot number. In addition to the effects of solar activity on both parameters mentioned above we can also identify a strong effect on the diurnal variability as solar activity gradually increases through its 11-year cycle. This is demonstrated again in figure 4 where the diurnal variation of *foF2* and TEC is plotted for three different days corresponding to low, medium and high sunspot number periods. It is evident from this figure that the night to day variability is increased as sunspot number increases for both parameters.

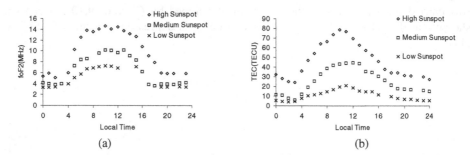

(a)   (b)

Fig. 4. Diurnal variability of (a) foF2 and (b)TEC for low, medium and high solar activity

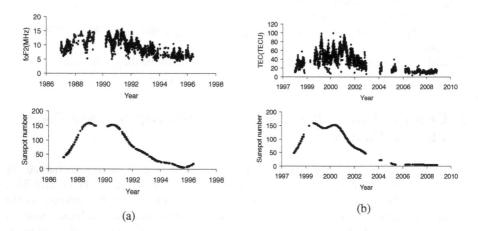

(a)   (b)

Fig. 5. Long-term variability of (a) foF2 and (b)TEC and solar activity

There is also a seasonal component in the variability of *foF2* and TEC which can be attributed to the seasonal change in extreme ultraviolet (EUV) radiation from the Sun. This can be clearly identified in figure 6 for noon values of both parameters for two different years.

From the evidence drawn from this section the incorporation of TEC as an input to the neural network interpolation tool for *foF2* data is justified based on its established correlation with TEC. However as shown in other studies this correlation varies diurnally and seasonally and also it is established that *foF2* is not linearly related to TEC [12].

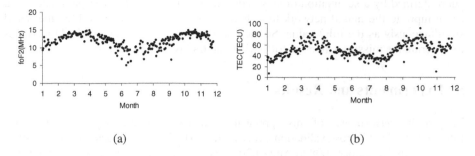

Fig. 6. Seasonal variability of (a) foF2 and (b) TEC

4 Model Parameters

The diurnal variation of *foF2* is clearly evident by observing figure 4. We therefore include hour number as an input to the model. The hour number, *hour*, is an integer in the range $0 \le hour \le 23$. In order to avoid unrealistic discontinuity at the midnight boundary, *hour* is converted into its quadrature components according to:

$$sinhour = \sin\left(2\pi \frac{hour}{24}\right) \tag{3}$$

and

$$coshour = \cos\left(2\pi \frac{hour}{24}\right) \tag{4}$$

A seasonal variation is also an underlying characteristic of *foF2* as shown in figure 6 and is described by day number *daynum* in the range $1 \le daynum \le 365$. Again to avoid unrealistic discontinuity between December 31st and January 1st *daynum* is converted into its quadrature components according to:

$$sinday = \sin\left(2\pi \frac{daynum}{365}\right) \tag{5}$$

and

$$cosday = \cos\left(2\pi \frac{daynum}{365}\right) \tag{6}$$

Long-term solar activity has a prominent effect on *foF2*. To include this effect in the model specification we need to incorporate an index, which represents a good indicator of solar activity. In ionospheric work the 12-month smoothed sunspot number is usually used, yet this has the disadvantage that the most recent value available corresponds to *foF2* measurements made six months ago. To enable *foF2* data to be modelled as soon as they are measured, and for future predictions of *foF2* to be made, the monthly mean sunspot number values were modeled using a smooth curve defined by a summation of sinusoids (figure 5). TEC is the last parameter used as an input to the neural network tool. It corresponds to the value of TEC measured simultaneously as the foF2 value. So the tool makes use of the available TEC values to generate the missing values of foF2 when the Es layer is present.

5   Experiments and Results

To test the performance of this approach in interpolating missing *foF2* values we followed a 10-fold cross-validation process; the 10342 *foF2* values (recorded above Cyprus from September 2008 to August 2010) and their corresponding inputs were split into 10 continuous parts of almost equal size and the predictions for each part were obtained by training a neural network on the other 9 parts. We chose to split the data into blocks of continuous values in order to test the performance of the approach in a worst-case scenario where the missing values cover a relatively big period of time.

The neural networks used were fully connected two-layer networks, with 6 input, 5 hidden and 1 output neuron. Both its hidden and output neurons had hyperbolic tangent sigmoid activation functions. The number of hidden neurons was determined by trial and error. The training algorithm used was the Levenberg-Marquardt backpropagation algorithm with early stopping based on a validation set created from 20% of the training examples. In an effort to avoid local minima ten neural networks were trained on each training set with different random initializations and the one that performed best on the corresponding validation set was selected for application to the test examples. The inputs and target outputs of the network were normalized setting their minimum value to -1 and their maximum value to 1. This made the impact

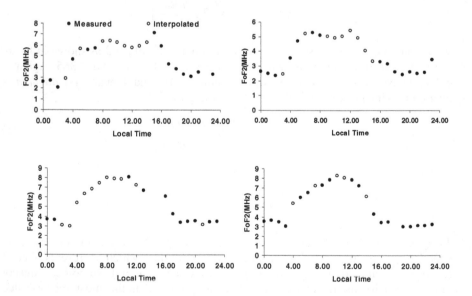

Fig. 7. Examples of measured and interpolated *foF2* values

of all inputs in the model equal and transformed the target outputs to the output range of the neural network activation functions. The results reported here were obtained by mapping the outputs of the network for the test examples back to their original scale. The whole process was implemented in Matlab with the aid of the Matlab Neural Network toolbox.

The obtained Root Mean Squared Error (RMSE) over all data was 0.508 MHz and the Mean Absolute Error (MAE) was 0.383 MHz. In order to see the improvement resulting from the inclusion of TEC in the inputs of the neural network (i.e. by using the long-term prediction approach of [7]) we performed exactly the same experiment without including TEC. In this case the resulting RMSE was 0.712 MHz and the resulting MAE was 0.545 MHz. This shows that by using TEC we achieve a much more accurate interpolation of missing foF2 values. Finally examples of the approach are demonstrated graphically in figure 7.

6 Conclusions and Future Work

In this paper we have presented the development of a neural network tool for the interpolation of missing critical frequency data of the F2 ionospheric layer (foF2) above Cyprus due to sporadic E layer conditions. The model has been developed based on a data set obtained during a period of approximately two years. The tool has produced a good interpolation capability of the gaps in the foF2 data series therefore providing a method to preserve the variability of foF2, a fact which is essential in the development of long-term time-series prediction models and procedures. The tool will be further evaluated as we collect more foF2 measurements in the next few years.

References

1. Goodman, J.: HF Communications, Science and Technology. Nostrand Reinhold, New York (1992)
2. Maslin, N.: The HF Communications, a Systems Approach, San Francisco (1987)
3. McNamara, L.F.: Grid The Ionosphere: Communications, Surveillance, and Direction Finding. Krieger Publishing Company, Malabar (1991)
4. Mathews, J.D., Sporadic, E.: current views and recent progress. Journal of Atmospheric and Solar-Terrestrial Physics 60, 413–435 (1998)
5. Whitehead, J.D.: Recent work on mid-latitude and equatorial sporadic-E. Journal of Atmospheric and Terrestrial Physics 51, 401–424 (1989)
6. Francis, N.M., Brown, A.G., Cannon, P.S., Broomhead, D.S.: Nonlinear Prediction of the Hourly foF2 Times Series in Coonjunction with the Interpolation of Missing Data Points. Phys. Chem. Earth. 25(4), 261–265 (2000)
7. Haralambous, H., Papadopoulos, H.: A Neural Network model for the critical frequency of the F2 ionospheric layer over Cyprus. In: Palmer-Brown, D., Draganova, C., Pimenidis, E., Mouratidis, H. (eds.) EANN 2009. CCIS, vol. 43, pp. 371–377. Springer, Heidelberg (2009)
8. Wild, U., Beutler, G., Gurtner, W., Rothacher, M.: Estimating the Ionosphere Using One or More Dual Frequency GPS Receivers. In: Proceedings of the Fifth International Geodetic Symposium on Satellite Positioning, Las Cruces, New Mexico, March 13-17, vol. 2, pp. 724–736 (1989)

9. Ciraolo L.: Evaluation of GPS L2-L1 biases and related daily TEC profiles. In: Proceedings of the GPS/Ionosphere Workshop, Neustrelitz, pp. 90–97 (1993)
10. Ciraolo, L.: Results and problems in GPS TEC evaluation. In: Proceedings of the Radio Communications Research Units First GPS TEC Workshop, Chilton, pp. 47–60 (2000)
11. Davis, K.: Ionospheric Radio. Peter Peregrinus Ltd., London (1990)
12. Spalla, P., Ciraolo, L.: TEC and foF2 comparison. Ann. Geofis. XXXVII (5), 929–938 (1994)

Neural Networks Approach to Optimization of Steel Alloys Composition

Petia Koprinkova-Hristova[1], Nikolay Tontchev[2], and Silviya Popova[1]

[1] Institute of System Engineering and Robotics, Bulgarian Academy of Sciences,
Acad. G. Bonchev str. bl.2, 1113 Sofia, Bulgaria
{pkoprinkova,popova}@icsr.bas.bg
[2] University of Transport, 158 Geo Milev str., bl.2, 1574 Sofia, Bulgaria
tontchev@vtu.bg

Abstract. The paper presents modeling of steels strength characteristics in dependence from their alloying components quantities using neural networks as nonlinear approximation functions. Further, for optimization purpose the neural network models are used. The gradient descent algorithm based on utility function backpropagation through the models is applied. The approach is aimed at synthesis of steel alloys compositions with improved strength characteristics by solving multi-criteria optimization task. The obtained optimal alloying compositions fall into martenzite region of steels. They will be subject of further experimental testing in order to synthesize new steels with desired characteristics.

Keywords: steel alloys, neural networks, modeling, optimization.

1 Introduction

Production of high strenght steel alloys is of big importance for the modern methalurgy. The main aim is to obtain high quality materials reducing quantitiy of used expensive compounds. Thus the production of steel alloys starts with optimization of number and content of used alloying components that improve their quality at reasonable price. Since the dependences between input and output variables in that case are strongly nonlinear, application of nonlinear modelling and optimization techniques must be applied.

The fact that neural networks are universal approximations of complex nonlinear dependences that apply "black-box" modeling approach [1, 3, 12] is well known. Therefore, they are proper candidates for modeling structure of such MIMO models. Another useful characteristic of neural networks are their training procedures that are in fact optimization algorithms aimed at minimization of error at neural network output with respect to network connection weights [12, 14]. The well-known backpropagation algorithm is procedure for propagating of derivatives of given function of network output backwards to the input [14]. Thus neural network training procedures offer a common approach to optimization tasks in process optimization and control applications [11, 14, 15].

L. Iliadis and C. Jayne (Eds.): EANN/AIAI 2011, Part I, IFIP AICT 363, pp. 315–324, 2011.

The application of intelligent modelling approaches such as neural networks is relatively new in this area but there are some examples in the literature concerning titanium alloys [9, 10] as wll as several for different steel alloys compositions and different strength characteristics accounting [2, 4, 5].

In our previous works the approach described in [14] was successfully applied to dynamic optimization [6] as well as to optimization of cultural media composition and initial conditions [7] of two kinds of biotechnological process that are other examples of highly nonlinear systems. In [8, 13] we applied that approach to optimization of steel composition having 11 alloying elements aimed at simultaneous maximization of 6 steel strength characteristics; we also showed that neural networks outperform non-linear regression models. However, it appeared that having that much input and output variables do not allow obtaining neural network model able to fit with the same accuracy all output variables and solving of six criteria optimization task showed some controversial results.

In the present paper, we continue our work with increased data set and accounting for lower number of variables. Moreover, we have created separate neural network model for each one of the considered strength characteristic. The optimization criteria were simplified and multi-criteria optimization task from [8, 13] was restricted to two simplified sub-tasks. Comparison between optimized steel compositions with respect to their mechanical characteristics was made. The obtained results will be subject of experimental proof further.

2 Experimental Data Set

Here we used data base containing 91 steel alloys with their 8 alloying elements and the corresponding strenght characterestics tested after thermal treatment of the steels: Rm – tensile strength; Re – yield strength; A – elongation; Z – reduction of area; HB – Brinell hardness. Tables 1 and 2 below summarize the minimal and maxinmal values of all considered variables.

Table 1. Alloying elements minimal and maximal values

var. name	X_1	X_2	X_3	X_4	X_5	X_6	X_7	X_8
element	C	Si	Mn	Ni	S (P)	Cr	Mo	V
min	0.120	0.100	0.300	0	0.015	0.150	0	0
max	0.520	1.400	1.750	4.220	0.035	3.250	1.500	0.150

Table 2. Steel strength characteristics minimal and maximal values

var. name	Y_1	Y_2	Y_3	Y_4	Y_5
characteristic	Rm	Re	A	Z	HB
min	500	300	7	30	179
max	1670	1375	26	55	300

For the sick of simplicity, names (X_i for alloying elements and Y_i for strength characteristics) are given to all considered variables in order to be easier to refer to them further in the text.

3 Neural Network Models of Steel Characteristics

First task of the present study was to train neural network models that approximate dependence between amounts of alloying elements in the steel for each of the five considered strength characteristics. For that purpose, the data are scaled in proper interval [0, 1]. The used neural network structure (presented on Figure 1) is multi-layered without feedback connections since the modeled dependences are static. The neurons transfer function is log sigmoid. Training procedure is resilient backpropagation. Different in number of layers and hidden neurons neural network structures were tested and the better one is chosen. Based on previous investigations [8, 13] the 8:40:1 structure was used here.

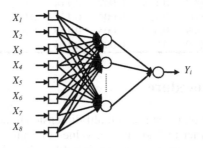

Fig. 1. Neural network models structure

We have relatively small database and we do not have guarantee that it includes all possible combinations between alloying elements. That is why for assessment of the generalization error of neural network models we apply k-fold cross-validation. In our case we split database into k=18 data subsets each containing five data samples. Next, we train 18 neural network models for each strength characteristic using all except one data subset. The left subset is further used for generalization error assessment.

The obtained training and testing mean square errors (MSE) for all five neural network models are given in Table 3 below. Since for some of the strength characteristics there were no data for all alloying element combinations (Y_4 and Y_5) smaller number of subsets was created for them (17 and 16).

For further optimization purpose, we choose to use the models with smallest testing errors as follows: models number one for Y_1 and Y_2, model number 13 for Y_3, model number 9 for Y_4, and model number 5 for Y_5.

Table 3. Training and testing errors for all NN models

No	Y_1 train MSE	Y_1 test MSE	Y_2 train MSE	Y_2 test MSE	Y_3 train MSE	Y_3 test MSE	Y_4 train MSE	Y_4 test MSE	Y_5 train MSE	Y_5 test MSE
1	0.008	0.055	0.033	0.060	0.004	0.083	0.022	0.115	0.003	0.126
2	0.007	0.445	0.015	0.224	0.006	0.143	0.007	0.200	0.006	0.197
3	0.013	0.099	0.012	0.361	0.004	0.108	0.016	0.299	0.005	0.063
4	0.013	0.064	0.010	0.112	0.009	0.079	0.012	0.137	0.006	0.099
5	0.019	0.171	0.019	0.125	0.005	0.065	0.008	0.166	0.003	0.050
6	0.010	0.170	0.015	0.217	0.006	0.088	0.009	0.115	0.005	0.135
7	0.012	0.130	0.010	0.086	0.006	0.112	0.006	0.160	0.004	0.063
8	0.012	0.104	0.017	0.083	0.005	0.162	0.005	0.382	0.004	0.075
9	0.014	0.131	0.010	0.114	0.007	0.058	0.008	0.091	0.005	0.101
10	0.010	0.087	0.012	0.222	0.007	0.135	0.025	0.213	0.005	0.085
11	0.023	0.127	0.018	0.156	0.009	0.112	0.008	0.168	0.004	0.065
12	0.013	0.136	0.006	0.085	0.010	0.067	0.013	0.157	0.006	0.140
13	0.013	0.341	0.010	0.397	0.007	0.045	0.010	0.316	0.006	0.124
14	0.009	0.195	0.010	0.159	0.006	0.108	0.019	0.289	0.005	0.089
15	0.008	0.100	0.009	0.199	0.007	0.114	0.011	0.243	0.006	0.107
16	0.010	0.080	0.008	0.124	0.004	0.157	0.009	0.123	0.004	0.118
17	0.007	0.354	0.009	0.342	0.005	0.153	0.008	0.484		
18	0.009	0.091	0.019	0.089	0.007	0.104				

4 Optimization Procedure

Since the explored input/output space is multi-dimensional and the modeling function is highly nonlinear in order to find optimal values of input variables with respect to given quality criteria that comprises output variables, there is need to explore whole region of the input space. However, because of big number of possible combinations the exhaustive search on whole variables space will take too much time. Because of this, we applied gradient optimization technique starting from several different points of input variables surface and compare the obtained results.

Figure 2 below presents the optimization procedure scheme adopted from the so-called "backpropagation of utility" method [14]. The optimization task here is defined as follows: find values of input vector X that minimize/maximize the utility function:

$$J = J(X,Y) \tag{1}$$

Here Y is vector of output variables that are related to the input once by a given function (model) F as follows:

$$Y = F(X,p) \tag{2}$$

Here, p is model parameters vector.

The optimization procedure needs calculation of utility function gradients with respect to the optimized variables as follows:

$$dX = \frac{dJ}{dX} = \frac{\partial J}{\partial X} + \frac{\partial J}{\partial Y} * \frac{\partial F}{\partial X} \tag{3}$$

In case when J does not depend explicitly on X, the first term in equation (3) is zero and thus gradient depends only on function F.

The layered neural networks structure offers a convenient way for calculating derivatives from equation (3) because the backpropagation method [12, 14] was developed initially as procedure for error derivatives calculation and their "propagation" from the output to the input of the network. From a more common point of view it is method for a given function derivative calculations with respect to variables of an ordered system of equations [14]. Hence, it could be applied to any optimization problem that can be described in appropriate way. So application of collection of neural network models trained before as model function F within optimization scheme from Figure 2 allows easy gradients calculation using backpropagation method.

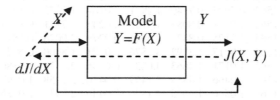

Fig. 2. Optimization procedure; dashed lines represent gradients calculation

Next, any gradient iterative optimization procedure could be applied to find optimal values of the variables X using calculated derivatives as follows:

$$X_i = X_{i-1} \pm \alpha * \Delta X_i \qquad (5)$$

Here α is parameter called learning speed and ΔX_i is step-change of X for the ith iteration calculated as follows:

$$\Delta X_i = g(dX_i) \qquad (6)$$

Here g is some function of optimized variable derivative. Usually it is proportional to the derivative dX_i but it can also depend on the old values of ΔX_i.

In present study, we used simple gradient optimization procedure with identity function for g, i.e. $\Delta X_i = dX_i$. The learning speed α is set to a relatively small value and stopping criteria is very small change of performance function gradient.

5 Optimization of Steel Compositions

Two different optimization tasks were solved here. First, one is aimed at maximization of Y_2 that is yield strength Re. The second task includes two criteria maximization: maximal yield strength and maximal ratio between Y_1 (tensile strength Rm) and Y_2. In both cases, a restriction was added to obtain low carbon steels: $X_1 \leq 0.3$. The two tasks optimization results are presented and compared in the following sections.

5.1 First Optimization Task

First, we solved one criteria optimization task:

$$J = Y_2 \rightarrow \max \tag{7}$$

We explore 15 different initial steel compositions. The obtained after optimization new 15 alloying elements "recipes" are shown in Table 4 below.

Table 4. Optimized steel compositions from the first task

No	X_1	X_2	X_3	X_4	X_5	X_6	X_7	X_8
1	0.1562	0.9180	0.4517	0.9215	0.0202	0.8730	0.2450	0.0410
2	0.1562	0.9137	0.4517	0.8663	0.0208	0.8740	0.2757	0.0423
3	0.1562	0.7997	0.7740	1.4991	0.0184	1.1572	0.1943	0.0087
4	0.1562	1.0861	0.8087	1.9735	0.0243	1.7111	0.1733	0.0087
5	0.1584	1.2125	0.8475	2.5041	0.0274	2.0026	0.1815	0.0465
6	0.1603	0.8917	1.3092	4.1876	0.0381	1.8100	0.6971	0.1025
7	0.1562	1.0171	1.4663	4.0238	0.0446	2.1378	1.0380	0.1023
8	0.1562	1.0466	1.4833	4.1469	0.0446	2.2158	1.0497	0.1146
9	0.1562	1.0566	1.4695	4.1876	0.0446	2.2936	1.0486	0.1263
10	0.1562	1.0589	1.4319	4.1876	0.0446	2.2193	0.9355	0.1440
11	0.1562	0.9196	0.4517	0.9113	0.0203	0.8721	0.2501	0.0416
12	0.1870	0.2352	0.6480	2.5490	0.0446	1.4195	0.9603	0.1583
13	0.1566	0.2352	0.7037	3.1023	0.0446	1.7221	0.9820	0.1583
14	0.2714	1.1062	1.0644	2.3624	0.0219	1.0496	0.1572	0.0087
15	0.2673	1.2441	1.1861	2.7854	0.0269	1.2693	0.2301	0.0218

Table 5. Optimized steel characteristics from the first task, optimization criteria and iterations needed

No	Y_1	$J_1=Y_2$	Y_3	Y_4	Y_5	iterations
1	1643.6	1350.4	8.5	54.7	263.8	432
2	1640.2	1349.9	8.8	54.8	260.6	445
3	1407.0	1369.5	7.8	49.5	272.6	261
4	1638.0	**1372.6**	8.1	49.8	282.7	437
5	1621.3	1359.9	9.7	54.5	290.2	530
6	1122.8	1362.1	13.7	49.9	288.2	276
7	1394.7	1360.2	16.0	42.5	282.3	378
8	1294.9	1360.7	15.0	47.2	280.8	427
9	1227.7	1360.9	14.6	51.2	279.7	362
10	1246.9	1365.3	11.9	53.1	279.8	523
11	1642.9	1350.4	8.6	54.7	263.5	442
12	662.7	1341.0	24.5	55.0	208.9	312
13	841.0	1336.3	25.0	55.0	222.5	200
14	1666.9	1370.3	11.4	51.1	281.6	160
15	1647.5	1370.9	12.2	54.1	287.4	214

The corresponding five strength characteristics of the new steel compositions and the needed number of iterations in each optimization run are presented in Table 5. The maximal value of criterion (7) was obtained in the case 4 (emphasized in bold in the table). The number of the iterations obviously depends on the starting steel composition position on the search surface; it varies between 160 and 530 iterations. In all cases, the obtained new compositions belong to the martenzite steels subset (see Figure 3 below). All the obtained new steels have relatively close values of the optimization criterion. The final decision, which composition suits better for a given purpose, should be taken considering all strength characteristics from Table 5. For some of these characteristics (e.g. 4 and 5) differences are not so big but for characteristics 1 and 3 there are significant differences observed.

5.2   Second Optimization Task

Here in addition to the first criterion (7) the second one was added as follows:

$$J_1 = Y_2, \quad J_2 = \frac{Y_1}{Y_2}$$
$$J = a_1 J_1 + a_2 J_2 \rightarrow \max, \quad a_1 = a_2 = 1$$

$$(8)$$

Table 6. Optimized steel compositions from the second task

No	X_1	X_2	X_3	X_4	X_5	X_6	X_7	X_8
1	0.1562	0.6937	0.5036	0.5673	0.0094	0.4832	0.3116	0.0301
2	0.1577	0.6915	0.5092	0.5807	0.0135	0.4832	0.2698	0.0225
3	0.1562	1.2231	0.7684	1.6164	0.0196	0.4832	0.1572	0.1255
4	0.1562	0.9408	0.7296	1.1316	0.0249	0.4832	0.1602	0.1459
5	0.1562	0.8331	1.7453	0.4564	0.0228	1.9982	0.5520	0.0632
6	0.1562	1.2004	1.7453	0.4564	0.0446	0.4832	1.4948	0.0087
7	0.1562	1.0013	1.6050	2.4654	0.0416	2.0609	1.4905	0.0570
8	0.2964	1.1273	1.4969	3.2602	0.0375	2.6033	1.2407	0.1245
9	0.2980	1.2624	1.6303	3.7373	0.0413	2.9228	1.3716	0.1427
10	0.3000	1.3968	1.7453	4.1874	0.0446	3.2287	1.4948	0.1583
11	0.1562	0.2352	0.4517	0.4569	0.0094	0.4832	0.1650	0.0093
12	0.1562	0.7446	1.4706	1.9032	0.0442	0.4832	0.9263	0.1096
13	0.1562	0.5792	1.1822	1.6692	0.0387	0.4832	1.1307	0.1441
14	0.3000	1.0140	1.1720	2.1100	0.0210	1.0760	0.2940	0.0087
15	0.2997	1.1352	1.3479	2.5514	0.0247	1.3766	0.4125	0.0246

Here we start again with the same 15 initial steel compositions. The obtained after optimization new 15 "recipes" are shown in Table 6. The corresponding to them strength characteristics iterations needed and two optimization criteria values are presented in Table 7. Again, obtained new steels are in the martenzite region on Figure 3 but there are bigger differences among them.

Because in this task we have two controversial criteria – one targeted towards increasing of yield strength and the other having Y_2 in denominator, i.e. targeted

Table 7. Optimized steel characteristics from the second task, optimization criteria and iterations needed

No	Y_1	$J_1=Y_2$	Y_3	Y_4	Y_5	$J_2=Y_1/Y_2$	iterations
1	1664.2	1233.3	7.6	52.5	261.0	1.3494	865
2	1665.5	1285.3	8.1	52.8	239.3	1.2958	157
3	1659.4	957.9	9.3	54.6	271.2	1.7323	266
4	1456.2	797.5	7.9	54.3	250.9	1.8260	605
5	499.1	300.1	11.4	40.7	185.3	1.6631	3
6	499.1	325.4	22.6	41.5	179.1	1.5338	6
7	735.5	609.3	23.3	52.5	289.3	1.2071	1353
8	1463.1	**681.1**	11.3	42.8	274.6	**2.1481**	462
9	1488.5	853.6	14.6	41.0	273.8	1.7438	839
10	1499.8	829.8	20.3	40.8	271.4	1.8074	2
11	1571.6	916.0	8.2	54.1	227.0	1.7157	289
12	1199.5	577.6	13.4	53.2	207.8	2.0767	607
13	760.0	615.1	12.2	54.7	282.1	1.2356	781
14	1635.4	**1326.0**	15.5	47.7	258.9	**1.2333**	3
15	1613.4	1308.0	15.6	53.4	267.2	1.2335	2516

towards decreasing it – the final decision about the best obtained "recipie" is not definitive. The best steel composition with respect to the first citerion is number 8 while with respect to the second – number 14 (all in bold in the table). This can explain the big variety of iterations number needed for individual optimization runs – from 3 to 2516. The variety of combinations between all stregth characteristics is also bigger making final decision more complicated too.

5.3 Results Analysis

In order to compare two optimization tasks results we present them in the form of steel types diagram accepted in metallurgy – Figure 3. It consists of Cr and Ni equivalent values calculated according to the equation on diagram axis. Here Nb denotes element niobium that is not present in our recipes, i.e. Nb=0. According to the equivalent Cr and Ni values, steels are derived in several classes shown on the diagram. The bigger is the first of the optimized characteristics – yield strength – the bigger is the steel strengh as a holle. From the other hand the ratio tensile strength/ yield strength (the second criterion) is related to local overloading steel resistance. Obtaining the good balance between these two major steel characteristics is difficult in practice. The imposed restiriction in both optimization task (low carbon concentration) was also another characteristic that guarantees obtaining of high strength steels.

From the Figure 3 we conclude that all the obtained new steel compositions belong to the targeted martenzite area. All the results from the first task are concentrated in the middle of that area while those from the second one diverge towards area borders. This result is expected having in mind controversal criteria of the second optimization task.

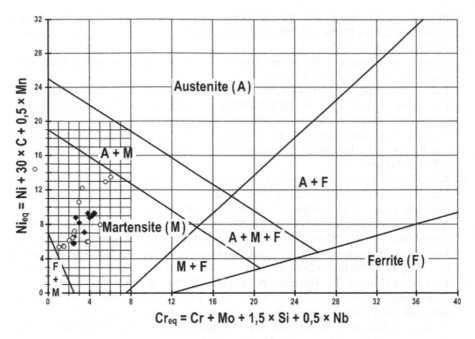

Fig. 3. Optimization results: squares represent the first optimization task solutions; circles represent the second optimization task solutions

6 Conclusions

The application of neural networks for modeling of the complex dependences of steel compositions characteristics from the relatively big number of alloying elements considered demonstrated their power as non-linear MIMO functions approximations. They allow us to carry out further optimization experiments by simulations in order to spent expensive laboratory synthesis and analysis of different steel compositions.

The results of the solved above optimization tasks are meaningful and will help further creation of high strength steel compositions for machine-building industry.

Our intensions for our future work are to include some other optimization criteria as well as to test the obtained steel "recipes" in practical experimental investigations in order to prove and refine their quality.

Acknowledgments. This work was partially supported by the Bulgarian National Science Fund under the Project No DDVU 02/11 "Characteristic modeling and composition optimization of iron-based alloys used in machine-building industry".

References

1. Ablameyko, S., Goras, L., Gori, M., Piuri, V. (eds.): Neural Networks for Instrumentation, Measurement and Related Industrial Applications. NATO Science series, vol. 185. IOS Press, Amsterdam (2003)

2. Bhattacharyya, T., Singh, B.S., Das, S., Haldar, A., Bhattacharjee, D.: Development and Characterization of C-Mn-Al-Si-Nb TRIP Aided Steel. Material Science and Engineering A 528, 2394–2400 (2011)
3. Cichoski, A., Unbehauen, R.: Neural Networks for Optimization and Signal Processing. John Wiley & Sons, New York (1993)
4. Dini, G., Najafizadeh, A., Monir-Vaghefi, S.M., Ebnonnasir, A.: Predicting of Mechanical Pproperties of Fe-Mn-(Al, Si) TRIP/TWIP Steels using Neural Network Modelling. J. Computational Materials Science 45, 959–965 (2009)
5. Esfahani, M.B., Toroghinejad, M.R., Yeganeh, A.R.K.: Modeling the Yield Strength of Hot Strip Low Carbon Steels by Artificial Neural Network. Materials and Design 30, 3653–3658 (2009)
6. Koprinkova, P., Petrova, M.: Optimal Control of Batch Biotechnological Processes using Neural Network Model. In: 9th Int. Conf. Systems for Automation of Engineering and Research, Varna, Bulgaria, September 24-26, pp. 95–99 (1995)
7. Koprinkova-Hristova, P., Angelov, M., Kostov, G., Pandzharov, P.: Neural Network Optimization of Initial Conditions of Milk Starter Culture Cultivation. Special Issue on Innovations in Intelligent Systems and Applications of the International Journal of Reasoning-based Intelligent Systems 2(3/4), 285–292 (2010)
8. Koprinkova-Hristova, P., Tontchev, N., Popova, S.: Neural Networks for Mechanical Characteristics Modeling and Compositions Optimization of Steel Alloys. In: Int. Conf. Automatic and Informatics, Sofia, Bulgaria, October 3-7, pp. I-49– I-52 (2010)
9. Malinov, S., Sha, W.: Software Products for Modeling and Simulation in Material Science. Computational Material Science 28, 179–198 (2003)
10. Malinov, S., Sha, W., McKeown, J.J.: Modelling and Correlation between Processing Parameters and Properties of Titanium Alloys using Artificial Neural Network. Computational Material Science 21, 375–394 (2001)
11. Nguyen, D.H., Widrow, B.: Neural Networks for Self-Learning Control Systems. Int. J. Control 54(6), 1439–1451 (1991)
12. Rumelhart, D.E., McClelland, J.L.: Parallel Distributed Processing, vol. 1. MIT Press, Cambridge (1986)
13. Tontchev, N., Popov, S., Koprinkova-Hristova, P., Popova, S., Lukarski, Y.: Comparative Study on Intelligent and Classical Modeling and Composition Optimization of Steel Alloys (submitted paper)
14. Werbos, P.J.: Backpropagation Through Time: What It Does and How to Do It. Proceedings of the IEEE 78(10), 1550–1560 (1990)
15. Werbos, P.J.: An Overview of Neural Networks for Control. IEEE Control Systems Mag. 11, 40–41 (1991)

Predictive Automated Negotiators Employing Risk-Seeking and Risk-Averse Strategies

Marisa Masvoula, Constantin Halatsis, and Drakoulis Martakos

Department of Informatics and Telecommunications,
National and Kapodistrian University of Athens, University Campus, Athens 15771, Greece
{marisa,halatsis,martakos}@di.uoa.gr

Abstract. Intelligent agents that seek to automate various stages of the negotiation process are often enhanced with models of computational intelligence extending the cognitive abilities of the parties they represent. This paper is focused on predictive strategies employed by automated negotiators, and particularly those based on forecasting the counterpart's responses. In this context a strategy supporting negotiations over multiple issues is presented and assessed. Various behaviors emerge with respect to negotiator's attitude towards risk, resulting to different utility gains. Forecasting is conducted with the use of Multilayer Perceptrons (MLPs) and the training set is extracted online during the negotiation session. Two cases are examined: in the first separate MLPs are used for the estimations of each negotiable attribute, whereas in the second a single MLP is used to estimate the counterpart's response. Experiments are conducted to search the architecture of the MLPs.

Keywords: forecasting opponent's offers, negotiation strategy, multilayer perceptrons for time-series forecasting, predictive negotiating agents.

1 Introduction

Negotiation is defined as an exchange mechanism between two or more parties that jointly determine outcomes of mutual interest. The field has attracted the interest of researchers from several scientific fields, providing different viewpoints and approaches [1-6]. Computer science contributes to the development of negotiation theory and examines its applied nature with the construction of negotiation tables, decision and negotiation support systems, software agents and software platforms [4]. The use of AI-based techniques to support various stages of the negotiation process has been viewed as a step towards extending the negotiator's cognitive abilities. In this paperwork focus is set on the implementation of automated agents that use predictive decision-making strategies to attain more beneficial negotiation outcomes. In this respect a negotiation strategy employed by predictive agents that engage in multi-issue negotiations is presented. Different types of behaviors with respect to the level of risk emerge, and negotiation outcomes assessed in terms of utility gain (measures of individual satisfaction) are studied. In the second section definitions and terminologies along with related work are presented, citing systems enhanced with AI-based techniques to improve the negotiation outcome. In the third section a

L. Iliadis and C. Jayne (Eds.): EANN/AIAI 2011, Part I, IFIP AICT 363, pp. 325–334, 2011.
© IFIP International Federation for Information Processing 2011

predictive decision making mechanism supporting automated negotiations over multiple issues is proposed, and in the fourth section two cases of conducting predictions with the use of neural networks are presented. Finally in the fifth section experimental results are illustrated and in the sixth section future research issues are discussed.

2 Definitions, Terminology and Related Work

In a negotiation process participants exchange offers and counter-offers in the search of an agreement. The outcome can be a compromise or a failure and satisfaction of each participant α is measured in terms of a utility function $U_\alpha(X): R^n \to [0,1]$, where X is an offer vector. The negotiable objects may consist of multiple attributes (*issues*). For each issue participants specify a range of permissible (reservation) values (a minimum and a maximum) which they are not willing to exceed. Additionally in many cases participants set a deadline indicating the maximum time they can spend in a negotiation encounter. The specific rules of communication that guide the interaction constitute the negotiation *protocol* and determine the way messages are exchanged. In this paper the negotiation protocol used to support automated negotiations is based on the one described in [7]. The decision making rules or *strategies* are used to determine, select and analyze the decision alternatives. In the simple case where negotiation is conducted between two non learning agents, alternatives are generated with the use of formal decision functions [7]. More sophisticated agents enhance their strategies with AI-based techniques and develop particular skills with the scope to maximize the incurred utility to the party they represent. In our previous work [8] a categorization of such agents is given. This research is focused on the prediction of the counterpart's future offers. Predictions can be generally grouped to single and multi lag. In cases of single–lag predictions agents estimate the very next offer of their counterpart, while in cases of multi-lag predictions they foresee future offers of their counterpart several time steps ahead. Reference [9] depicts the development of a neural network predictive model in order to facilitate "What-if" analysis and generate optimal offers in each round. A similar negotiation support tool is applied by [10] in a supplier selection auction market, where the demander benefits from the suppliers' forecasts, by selecting the most appropriate alternative in each round. In references [11],[12] an agent applies the predictive mechanism only at the pre-final step of the process, in order to increase the likelihood of achieving an agreement, and to produce an outcome of maximal utility. An older work concerning single-lag predictions in agents' strategy can be found in [13]. Trading scenarios via an internet platform are facilitated with the use of SmartAgent, enhanced with predictive decision making. The estimation of the counterparts' next move is used at each negotiation round to adjust the agents' proposal and leads to increased individual gain of the final outcome. As far as multi-lag predictions are concerned, interesting approaches can be found in [14-16], where prediction of counterpart's future offers and strategy, has been used to effectively detect and withdraw from pointless negotiations. In references [17-19] a negotiating agent enhanced with predictive ability in order to determine the sequence of optimal offers "knowing" the sequence of opponent's responses, has been implemented.

This paper is focused on single-lag predictions and builds on Oprea 's earlier work [13], extending the strategy of the predictive agents to support negotiations over multiple issues (and not just single-issued as described in Oprea). Additionally a variation of the strategic rule is provided with the scope to generate different types of behaviors with respect to the agent's attitude towards risk. In the following section the extended strategy is illustrated.

3   Extending the Strategy of Predictive Agents to Support Multi-issue (Automated) Negotiations Incorporating Different Risk Attitudes

The negotiation environment considered is tied to bilateral or one-on-one multi-issue negotiations, where all issues are bundled and discussed together (package deal). The formal model of negotiation is comprised by the set of agents A = { a, b }, a finite set of quantitative issues under negotiation I = {i_1, i_2, . . ., i_n}, the domain of reservation values D_i^a : [$\min_i^a$, $\max_i^a$] attributed by each agent α in A for each issue i in I, and the deadline T_{max}^a of each agent α. In the cases studied time variable t is discrete and expresses the interaction step (negotiation round). The possible outcomes of a negotiation can be understood in terms of utility $U^a(X_{(a \to b)}^t)$ where $X_{(a \to b)}^t$ = $\left(x_{1(a \to b)}^t, x_{2(a \to b)}^t, ..., x_{n(a \to b)}^t \right)^T$ is the negotiation offer sent from agent α to b at time t, and each x_i denotes the offered value of negotiable issue i. Utility of the offered value is computed as the weighted sum of utilities attributed to each issue, thus:

$$U^a(X_{(a \to b)}^t) = \sum_{i=1}^{n} w_i^a * U^a(x_i) \tag{1}$$

where $U^a(x_i)$: D_i^a →[0,1] is the utility function specified by agent α to evaluate the value x_i of issue i and w_i^a is a normalized weight signifying the relative importance of issue i to agent α.

Each agent α is configured with a default strategy S^a , which determines the level of concession in each round. Classification of strategic families to time dependent (TD), resource dependent (RD) and behavior dependent (BD) is used as in [7], reflecting the agent's behavior with respect to the elapsing time, resources and counterpart's responses respectively. In each time step t agent α estimates the next offer of his counterpart, $\hat{X}_{b \to a}^{t+1} = \left(\hat{x}_{1(b \to a)}^{t+1}, \hat{x}_{2(b \to a)}^{t+1}, ..., \hat{x}_{n(b \to a)}^{t+1} \right)^T$. The proposed decision rule makes use of the default strategy (S^a) of the predictive agent to generate offers until the detection of a "meeting point" (MP) with the "opponent". MP is a point which would result an established agreement if the agent was guided solely by his default strategy. When such point is detected, and according to the agent's attitude towards risk, agent risks staying in the negotiation in order to maximize the utility of the final agreement. In this respect two extreme attitudes can be generated:

risk-seeking and risk-averse. The risk-seeking agent is willing to spend all the remaining time until expiration of his deadline engaging in an adaptive behavior to turn the estimations of his counterpart's responses to profit. This risk-seeking behavior is based on the one discussed [13], and is extended to support multiple issues. More specifically:

Risk-seeking Behavior:
For each issue i
If issue value is increasing with time
$$x^t_{i(a \to b)} = \hat{x}^{t+1}_{i(b \to a)} - \varepsilon$$
Else
$$x^t_{i(a \to b)} = \hat{x}^{t+1}_{i(b \to a)} + \varepsilon$$
End For
Generate Offer $X^t_{a \to b} = \left(x^t_{1(a \to b)}, x^t_{2(a \to b)}, ..., x^t_{n(a \to b)} \right)^T$

where ε is a domain dependent parameter.

On the other hand risk-averse agents follow a more conservative behavior when they detect an MP. They do not make any further concessions and insist on sending their previous offer, waiting for the opponent to establish an agreement.

Risk-Averse Behavior:
For each issue i
$$x^t_{i(a \to b)} = x^{t-2}_{i(a \to b)}$$
End For
Generate Offer $X^t_{a \to b} = \left(x^t_{1(a \to b)}, x^t_{2(a \to b)}, ..., x^t_{n(a \to b)} \right)^T$

Fusions of the two extreme attitudes have led to the specification of risk portions (RPs) which characterize the predictive agent's behavior after the detection of MP. RP_α determines the percentage of the distance between MP and deadline T^a_{max} that agent α is willing to adopt the risk-seeking behavior. After RP_α is consumed agent adopts the risk-averse behavior. For a predictive agent who is not willing to take any risks RP_α is set to 0%, while for an agent who is willing to risk until expiration of his deadline RP_α is set to 100%. The decision making rule repeated in each step is thus formulated as follows:

If $U^a \left(\hat{X}^{t+1}_{b \to a} \right) > U^a \left(X^t_{a \to b} \right)_{default}$ *(detection of MP)*
   If **RP$_\alpha$** is not consumed
      Generate Offer adopting Risk-Seeking Behavior
   Else
      Generate Offer adopting Risk-Averse Behavior
  Else
      Generate Offer $\left(X^t_{a \to b} \right)_{default}$

Where $\left(X^{t}_{a\rightarrow b}\right)_{default}$ is the offer generated by agent α at time t based on his default strategy.

Figure 1(a) illustrates how the predictive agent with RP 100% may "tease" his opponent until an agreement is established. At the other end, Figure 1(b) illustrates a risk-averse agent with RP 0% who reaches an agreement faster than the risk-seeking agent, but incurs smaller increase in utility. Negotiation is conducted between a provider and a consumer agent, over service terms of electricity trade, characterized by four negotiable attributes (number of Kwh, Price per Kwh, Penalty terms (returns), and Duration of service provision). The latter agent uses the predictive decision rule.

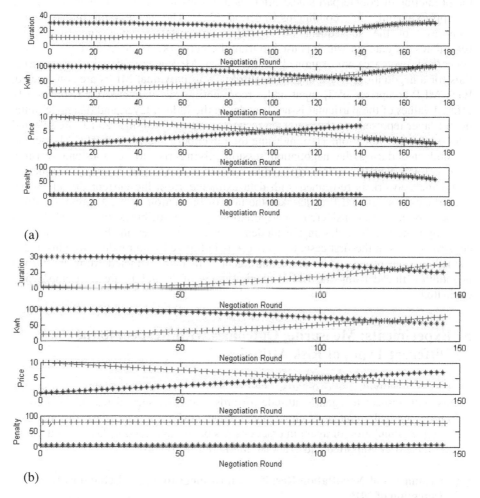

(a)

(b)

Fig. 1. (a) a risk-seeking consumer adjusts his offer with respect to the counterpart response and (b) a risk-averse consumer "freezes" his offer after MP is detected

4   Forecasting Tools Employed by Predictive Agents

Forecasting techniques employed by predictive agents are mainly summarized into statistical approaches (particularly non-linear regression), mathematical models based on differences, and neural networks. As discussed in [20], what is most appealing in neural networks is that they are data-driven, self adaptive, capable of modeling non-linear relations and do not require specific assumptions of the underlying data distributions. Current trend on providing offer forecasts lies on neural networks. In this research, a Multi-layer Perceptron (MLP) with one hidden layer using sigmoid activation functions and one output layer using linear activation functions is used for the prediction of counterpart's next offer, as it is shown that such network is capable of approximating any continuous function [21]. The negotiation thread which comprises of the subsequent offers and counteroffers of the engaged parties formulates the data set which is used to train the network. As far as design issues are concerned, two cases are examined; in the first an MLP is considered for each issue, thus for a negotiation over n negotiable attributes n individual MLPs are constructed. Each MLP comprises of J_1 input nodes representing the counterpart's J_1 previously offered values of the particular issue, J_2 nodes in the hidden layer, and one node in the output layer representing the predicted response. The values of J_1 and J_2 are selected after empirical evaluation. Training using the Levenberg and Marquardt (LM) method is conducted during the negotiation session, giving rise to session-long learning agents. Each network is initialized with random weights and in every negotiation round the network is re-trained with data extracted from the current thread. In the second case a single MLP undertakes the task of prediction. If the J_1 previous offers of the opponent are considered for negotiations over n attributes, then an MLP with $n*J_1$ input nodes, J_2 nodes in the hidden layer and n nodes in the output layer is constructed. As in the first case, the network is initialized with random weights and is trained in each round of the predicting agent with data extracted from the current negotiation thread using the LM method. Values of J_1 and J_2 are also empirically evaluated.

5   Experiments: Measuring Outcomes with Respect to the Different Types of Risk Attitudes

This section is divided in two parts. The first part is focused on assessing negotiation results with respect to agent's attitude towards risk. The second part is focused on searching optimal number of input and hidden nodes for each case discussed in section 4. A simulation of agent interactions has been developed in Java, and the Java classes have been imported and extended in Matlab (R2008a).

5.1   Evaluation of Negotiation Results with Respect to Agent Behavior after Detection of MP

The proposed strategy is tested with consumer agents with perfect predicting skills (yielding zero errors) and providers following TD strategies. The experimental workbench issues nine different scenarios with respect to deadline, and overlap of agreement zones of the two negotiators ({ $T_{max}^{Con} = T_{max}^{Pr}$, $T_{max}^{Con} < T_{max}^{Pr}$, $T_{max}^{Con} > T_{max}^{Pr}$ }

× {Φ=0, Φ=0.33, Φ=0.66}), where T_{max}^{a} ∈ [50:100:350], α={Con,Pr}, and Φ is a parameter which indicates overlap of the agreement zones [7]. In each scenario a variety of concession curves is considered in order to build the default strategies of the opposing agents. For each of the 2352 generated negotiation environments different RPs are set to predictive agent (consumer) (RP_{Con} ∈ [0:5:100]), leading to an overall of 49392 experiments. The objective is to measure the gain of consumer agent with respect to his attitude towards risk, and highlight the value of forecasting counterpart's next offer in multi-issued negotiations. Results are summarized in Figure 2 where the average gain of the agent adopting the learning strategy illustrated in section 3 is depicted with respect to Risk Portion (RP).

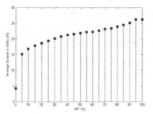

Fig. 2. (%) Average gain in Utility with respect to RP

As it is shown in Figure 2 an agent with RP 0% incurs an average increase of 2.4% in utility, while an agent with RP 100% incurs an average increase of 26.2% in utility. Figure 2 also illustrates the smooth increase of the percentage of utility gain with the increase of RP. Similar experiments are conducted for single-issued negotiations and in cases where an agreement is feasible average utility of the learning agent is increased up to 2% when RP is set to 0%, and up to 30.6% when RP is set to 100%.

5.2   Empirical Search of (Sub)Optimal Network Architectures Considering the Two Cases

Results of section 5.1 are extracted when agents with perfect predicting skills are employed. In this section, agents enhanced with neural networks are considered. More specifically the two cases discussed in section 4 are implemented and assessed. Taking the first case, the predicting agent constructs an MLP for each negotiable issue. Negotiations with RP set to 100% are conducted and the average error of the predictive mechanism is computed. In each decision making step the agent makes an estimation of the counterpart's next offer. This estimation is compared to the true offer vector of the counterpart and the absolute error is computed in terms of Euclidean distance. The subset of input features J_1 expressing the past offers of the opponent for a particular issue, as well as the number of hidden nodes are empirically searched in the space {2,3,4,5}×{2,3,4,5}. The search space comprises of 16 neural networks and is selected to be small since only a few patterns extracted from the current thread will be available for training. Preprocessing, in terms of normalization, is applied to the input data set. At the end of each negotiation, the mean of the absolute errors is computed for each network. The same procedure is also repeated in the second case, where a single neural network is used to predict the counterpart's next offer vector. For an offer which consists of n=4 attributes and for the case where the $J_1 \in \{2,3,4,5\}$ previously sent offers of the opponent are considered, the optimal number of input and hidden nodes is searched in the space $\{8,12,16,20\} \times \{2,3,4,5\}$. For each case 192 negotiation environments are generated and 16 ANNs are tested, leading to a total of 3072 experiments. The overall mean of the absolute errors is used to assess the predictive models. Results show that the neural network yielding the smallest error and smallest standard deviation comprises of 5 input and 4 hidden nodes, when an MLP is constructed separately for each issue (first case). For this ANN the average increase in utility attained by the predictive agent is 10.78%. On the other hand, in the second case where a single MLP is employed for the prediction of the counterpart's response, the smallest average error is yielded when 8 input nodes (stemming from the counterpart's 2 previous offer vectors) and 5 hidden nodes are used. This model returns an average increase in utility of 10.5%. The smallest average standard deviation is yielded when 20 input and 5 hidden nodes are used. The last ANN yields 10.34% average increase in utility. The low value of the average standard deviation signifies smoother predictive curves, as estimations do not deviate much from the mean. Table 1 summarizes the results with respect to the combination of input-hidden nodes.

Table 1. Mean errors and mean standard deviations for each combination of (input,hidden) nodes in the MLP, are illustrated for each case. Minimum values are depicted in bold style.

Input	Hidden	Mean Error				Mean Std Deviation			
		2	3	4	5	2	3	4	5
Case 1									
	2	1.62	1.36	1.6	1.81	3.49	1.67	1.97	2.07
	3	1.60	1.20	1.17	1.26	3.03	1.72	1.38	1.47
	4	1.69	1.11	1.03	1.08	3.44	1.37	1.19	1.29
	5	1.57	1.07	**0.98**	1.07	2.91	1.32	**1.16**	1.26
Case 2									
	8	1.19	0.63	0.53	**0.49**	3.63	1.38	1.03	0.97
	12	1.14	0.64	0.50	0.51	3.21	1.18	0.88	0.92
	16	1.00	0.61	0.55	0.51	2.27	1.14	0.98	0.89
	20	1.10	0.69	0.53	0.52	3.02	1.35	0.97	**0.83**

6 Conclusions and Future Research

In this paper a predictive strategy adopted by agents who engage in multi-issue negotiations is presented and assessed. Different behaviors emerge from the specifications of risk portions (RP) after the detection of a point of agreement, also termed a meeting point (MP), with the opponent. At one extreme an agent may be guided by a highly risk seeking behavior, where he risks staying in the negotiation until expiration of his deadline so as to maximize the utility of the final outcome. Maximization may be accomplished through adaptation of the predictive agent's offers based on the estimations of the counterpart's responses. At the other extreme an agent may be guided by a risk-averse behavior "freezing" his final offer and not making any further concessions. It is shown that intermediate behaviors, controlled by the RP parameter, lead to smooth increases of the average utility gain. Negotiation forecasts are undertaken by Multilayer Perceptrons (MLPs). Training data are extracted online and are composed of the previously sent offers of the opponent agent. The MLPs are retrained in each round as the data set augments with the counterpart's incoming offer. Two cases are illustrated. In the first an MLP is used to guide the prediction of each individual attribute, while in the second case a single MLP is used to estimate the vector of the counterpart's response. MLPs prove capable of capturing the negotiation dynamics if retrained in each round. However retraining is often time consuming, and time is crucial in most negotiation cases. For this reason as a future research issue we plan on focusing on the resources required, as well as on examining more flexible, evolving structures which engage in online, life-long learning, with one-pass propagation of the training patterns. These characteristics are met by Evolving Connectionist Structures (ECoS), discussed in [22].

Acknowledgment. This research was partially funded by the University of Athens Special Account of Research Grants no 10812.

References

1. Raiffa, H.: Contributions of Applied Systems Analysis to International Negotiation. In: Kremenyuk's, V.A. (ed.) International Negotiation: Analysis, Approaches, Issues, 2nd edn., pp. 5–21. Jossey-Bass, San Francisco (2002)
2. Goh, K.-Y., Teo, H.-H., Wu, H., Wei, K.-K.: Computer Supported Negotiations: An experimental study of bargaining in electronic commerce. In: Proc. of the 21st Int. Conf. on Information Systems, pp. 104–116 (2000)
3. Bichler, M., Kersten, G., Strecker, S.: Towards a Structured Design of Electronic Negotiations. Group Decision and Negotiation 12(4), 311–335 (2003)
4. Kersten, G.: E-negotiations: Towards Engineering of Technology-based Social Processes. In: Proc. of the 11th Eu. Conf. on Information Systems, ECIS 2003, Naples Italy (2003)
5. De Moor, A., Weigand, H.: Business Negotiation Support: Theory and Practice. International Negotiation 9(1), 31–57 (2004)
6. Schoop, M.: The Worlds of Negotiation. In: Proc. of the 9th Int. Working Conf. on the Language-Action Perspective on Communication Modeling, pp. 179–196 (2004)
7. Faratin, P., Sierra, C., Jennings, N.R.: Negotiation Decision Functions for Autonomous Agents. Int. Journal of Robotics and Autonomous Systems 24(3-4), 159–182 (1998)
8. Masvoula, M., Kanellis, P., Martakos, D.: A Review of Learning Methods Enhanced in Strategies of Negotiating Agents. In: Proc. of 12th ICEIS, pp. 212–219 (2010)
9. Carbonneau, R., Kersten, G.E., Vahidov, R.: Predicting opponent's moves in electronic negotiations using neural networks. Expert Systems with Applications: An International Journal 34(2), 1266–1273 (2008)

10. Lee, C.C., Ou-Yang, C.: A neural networks approach for forecasting the supplier's bid prices in supplier selection negotiation process. Expert Systems with Applications 36(2), 2961–2970 (2009)
11. Papaioannou, I.V., Roussaki, I.G., Anagnostou, M.E.: Comparing the Performance of MLP and RBF Neural Networks Employed by Negotiating Intelligent Agents. In: Proc. of the IEEE/WIC/ACM Int. Conf. on intelligent Agent Technology, pp. 602–612 (2006a)
12. Papaioannou, I.V., Roussaki, I.G., Anagnostou, M.E.: Towards Successful Automated Negotiations based on Neural Networks. In: Proc. of the 5th IEEE/ACIS Int. Conf. on Computer and Information Science, pp. 464–472 (2006b)
13. Oprea, M.: The Use of Adaptive Negotiation by a Shopping Agent in Agent-Mediated Electronic Commerce. In: Mařík, V., Müller, J.P., Pěchouček, M. (eds.) CEEMAS 2003. LNCS (LNAI), vol. 2691, pp. 594–605. Springer, Heidelberg (2003)
14. Hou, C.: Predicting Agents Tactics in Automated Negotiation. In: Proc. of the IEEE/WIC/ACM Int. Conf. on Intelligent Agent Technology, pp. 127–133 (2004)
15. Roussaki, I., Papaioannou, I., Anangostou, M.: Building Automated Negotiation Strategies Enhanced by MLP and GR Neural Networks for Opponent Agent Behaviour Prognosis. In: Sandoval, F., Prieto, A.G., Cabestany, J., Graña, M. (eds.) IWANN 2007. LNCS, vol. 4507, pp. 152–161. Springer, Heidelberg (2007)
16. Papaioannou, I., Roussaki, I., Anagnostou, M.: Detecting Unsuccessful Automated Negotiation Threads When Opponents Employ Hybrid Strategies. In: Huang, D.-S., Wunsch II, D.C., Levine, D.S., Jo, K.-H. (eds.) ICIC 2008. LNCS (LNAI), vol. 5227, pp. 27–39. Springer, Heidelberg (2008)
17. Brzostowski, J., Kowalczyk, R.: Modelling Partner's Behaviour in Agent Negotiation. In: Zhang, S., Jarvis, R.A. (eds.) AI 2005. LNCS (LNAI), vol. 3809, pp. 653–663. Springer, Heidelberg (2005)
18. Brzostowski, J., Kowalczyk, R.: Adaptive Negotiation with On-Line Prediction of Opponent Behaviour in Agent-Based Negotiations. In: Proc. of the IEEE/WIC/ACM Int. Conf. on Intelligent Agent Technology, pp. 263—269 (2006a)
19. Brzostowski, J., Kowalczyk, R.: Predicting Partner's Behaviour in Agent Negotiation. In: Proc. of the 5th Int. Joint Conf. AAMAS, pp. 355–361. ACM, New York (2006b)
20. Zhang, P.: Neural Networks in Business Forecasting. Idea Group Publishing, US (2004)
21. Hornik, K., Stinchombe, M., White, H.: Multilayer feed-forward networks are universal approximators. Neural Networks 2(5), 359–366 (1989)
22. Kasabov, N.: Evolving Connectionist Systems: The Knowledge Engineering Approach. Springer, London (2007)

Maximum Shear Modulus Prediction by Marchetti Dilatometer Test Using Neural Networks

Manuel Cruz[1,2], Jorge M. Santos[1,2], and Nuno Cruz[3,4]

[1] ISEP - Instituto Superior de Engenharia do Porto, Portugal
[2] LEMA - Laboratório de Engenharia Matemática, Porto
[3] Mota-Engil, Portugal
[4] Universidade de Aveiro, Portugal
{mbc,jms}@isep.ipp.pt, nbdfcruz@gmail.com

Abstract. The use of Neural Networks for modeling systems has been widespread, in particular within areas where the great amount of available data and the complexity of the systems keeps the problem very unfriendly to treat following traditional data analysis methodologies. In the last two decades, small strain shear modulus became one of the most important geotechnical parameters to characterize soil stiffness. Finite element analysis have shown that in-situ stiffness of soils and rocks is much higher than was previously thought, and that stress-strain behaviour of these materials is non-linear in most cases with small strain levels, especially in the ground around retaining walls, foundations and tunnels typically in the order of 10^{-2} to 10^{-4} of strain. Although the best approach seems to be based in measuring seismic wave velocities, deriving the parameter through correlations with in-situ tests is usually considered very useful for design practice. In this work, a new approach using Neural Networks is proposed for sedimentary soils and the results are discussed and compared with some of the most common available methodologies for this evaluation.

1 Introduction

Maximum shear modulus, G_0, has been increasingly introduced in stiffness evaluations for design purposes, for the last 10-15 years. At the present moment, one of the best ways for measuring it is to evaluate compression and shear wave velocities and thus obtain results supported by theoretical interpretations. The advantages of this approach are widely known, mainly because test readings are taken through intact soil in its in-situ stress and saturation levels, thus practically undisturbed, and also dynamic stiffness can be close to operational static values [1,2]. However, the use of seismic measures implies a specific test and so, many atempts have been made to correlate other in-situ test parameters, such as those obtained by Standard Penetration Test, SPT [3], Piezocone Test, CPTu [4] or Marchetti Dilatometer Test, DMT [5,6,7] with G0, using cross calibrations (e.g.,seismic or triaxial among others).

L. Iliadis and C. Jayne (Eds.): EANN/AIAI 2011, Part I, IFIP AICT 363, pp. 335–344, 2011.
© IFIP International Federation for Information Processing 2011

The DMT test is one of the most appropriated for this task (although some relations can be settled using SPT or CPTu) since it uses a measurement of a load range related with a specific displacement, which can be used to deduce highly accurate stress-strain relationship (E_D), supported by Theory of Elasticity. Moreover, the type of soil can be numerically represented by DMT Material Index, I_D, while in situ density, overconsolidation ratio (OCR) and cementation influences can be represented by lateral stress index, K_D, allowing for high quality calibration of the basic stress-strain relationship [7].

The present paper is organized as follows: In Section 2 an overview of the most important correlations used in this subject is reported, in order to get a clear view of the problem context. In Section 3 the data set is presented, as well as the methodology used for the Neural Networks application on this subject and its results and subsequent discussion. As usual, the last section will be used for conclusions and final remarks.

2 G_0 Prediction by DMT

Marchetti dilatometer test or flat dilatometer, commonly designated by DMT, has been increasingly used and it is one of the most versatile tools for soil characterization, namely loose to medium compacted granular soils and soft to medium clays, or even stiffer if a good reaction system is provided. The test was developed by Silvano Marchetti [5] and can be seen as a combination of both Piezocone and Pressuremeter tests with some details that really makes it a very interesting test available for modern geotechnical characterization [7]. The main reasons for its usefulness deriving geotechnical parameters are related to the simplicity (no need of skilled operators) and the speed of execution (testing a 10 m deep profile takes around 1 hour to complete) generating quasi-continuous data profiles of high accuracy and reproducibility.

In its essence, dilatometer is a stainless steel flat blade (14 mm thick, 95 mm wide and 220 mm length) with a flexible steel membrane (60 mm in diameter) in one of its faces. The blade is connected to a control unit on the ground surface by a pneumatic-electrical cable that goes inside the position rods, ensuring electric continuity and the transmission of the gas pressure required to expand the membrane. The gas is supplied by a connected tank/bottle and flows through the pneumatic cable to the control unit equipped with a pressure regulator, pressure gauges, an audio-visual signal and vent valves. The equipment is pushed (most preferable) or driven into the ground, by means of a CPTu rig or similar, and the expansion test is performed every 20cm. The (basic) pressures required for lift-off the diaphragm (P_0), to deflect 1.1mm the centre of the membrane (P_1) and at which the diaphragm returns to its initial position (P_2 or closing pressure) are recorded. Due to the balance of zero pressure measurement method (null method), DMT readings are highly accurate even in extremely soft soils, and at the same time the blade is robust enough to penetrate soft rock or gravel (in the latter, pressure readings are not possible), supporting safely 250kN of pushing force. The test is found especially suitable for sands, silts and clays where the grains are smaller (typically $\frac{1}{10}$ to $\frac{1}{5}$) compared to the membrane dimension [8].

Four intermediate parameters, Material Index (I_D), Dilatometer Modulus (E_D), Horizontal Stress Index (K_D) and Pore Pressure Index (U_D), are deduced from the basic pressures P_0, P_1 and P_2, having some recognizable physical meaning and some engineering usefulness [5], as it will be discussed below. The deduction of current geotechnical soil parameters is obtained from these intermediate parameters covering a wide range of possibilities. In the context of the present work only E_D, I_D and K_D have a physical meaning on the determination of G_0, so they will be succinctly described as follows [7]:

1. Material Index, I_D: Marchetti [5] defined Material Index, I_D, as the difference between P_1 and P_0 basic pressures measured normalized in terms of the effective lift-off pressure. The I_D parameter is one of the most valuable indexes deduced from DMT, due to its ability to identify soils throughout a numerical value that can be easily introduced in specific formulae for deriving geotechnical parameters. In a simple form, it could be said that I_D is a "fine-content-influence meter"[7], providing the interesting possibility of defining dominant behaviours in mixed soils, usually very difficult to interpret when only grain size is available, thus it may be associate to an index reflecting an engineering behaviour.

2. Horizontal Stress Index, K_D: The horizontal stress index [5] was defined to be comparable to the at rest earth pressure coefficient, K_0, and thus its determination is obtained by the effective lift-off pressure (P_0) normalized by the in-situ effective vertical stress. K_D is a very versatile parameter since it provides the basis to assess several soil parameters such as those related with state of stress, stress history and strength, and shows dependency on several factors namely cementation and ageing, relative density, stress cycles and natural overconsolidation resulting from superficial removal, among others. The parameter can be regarded as a K_0 amplified by penetration effects [5] and displays a typical profile very similar in shape to OCR profiles, giving useful information not only about stress history but also on the presence of cementation structures [7]. Since undrained shear strength of fine soils can be related and obtained via OCR and the relation between K_0 and angle of shearing resistance is well stated by soil mechanics theories, then the parameter is also used with success in deriving shear strength.

3. Dilatometer Modulus, E_D: Stiffness behaviour of soils is generally represented by soil moduli, and thus the base for in-situ data reduction. Theory of Elasticity is used to derive dilatometer modulus, E_D [5] , by considering that membrane expansion into the surrounding soil can be associated to the loading of a flexible circular area of an elastic half-space, and thus the outward movement of the membrane centre under a normal pressure ($P_1 - P_0$) can be calculated. In short, E_D is a parameter that includes both Young modulus (E) and Poisson's coefficient (ν) and can be expressed as follows:

$$E_D = \frac{E}{1 - \nu^2} = 34.7(P_1 - P_0) \tag{1}$$

Generally speaking, soil moduli depend on stress history, stress and strain levels drainage conditions and stress paths. The more commonly used moduli are constrained modulus (M), drained and undrained compressive Young modulus $(E_0$ and $E_u)$ and small-strain shear modulus (G_0), this latter being assumed as purely elastic and associated to dynamic low energy loading.

Maximum shear modulus, G_0, is indicated by several investigators [2,7,9] as the fundamental parameter of the ground. If properly normalized, with respect to void ratio and effective stress, could be seen as independent of the type of loading, number of loading cycles, strain rate and stress/strain history [9]. It can be accurately deduced through shear wave velocities,

$$G_0 = \rho v_s^2 \tag{2}$$

where ρ stands for density and v_s for shear wave velocity.

However, the use of a specific seismic test imply an extra cost, since it can only supply this geotechnical parameter, leaving strength and insitu state of stress information dependent on other tests. Therefore, several attempts to model the maximum shear modulus as a function of DMT intermediate parameters for sedimentary soils have been made in the last decade. Hryciw [10] proposed a methodology for all types of sedimentary soils, developed from indirect method of Hardin & Blandford [11]. Despite its theoretical base, references on this method are scarce and in general it is not applied for practical analysis due to some scatter around the determination, as illustrated by the results obtained in Portuguese normally consolidated clays [6]. The reasons for this scatter may be related to an expectable deviation of K_0 due to the important disturbance effects generated by penetration. On the other hand, this methodology ignores dilatometer modulus, E_D, commonly recognized as a highly accurate stress-strain evaluation, and also lateral stress index, K_D, and material index, I_D, which are the main reasons for the accuracy in stiffness evaluation offered by DMT tests [6]. Being so, the most common approaches [12,13,14] with reasonable results concentrated in correlating directly G_0 with E_D or M_{DMT} (constrained modulus), which have revealed linear correlations with slopes controlled by the type of soil. In 2006, Cruz [6] proposed a generalization of this approach, trying to model the ratio $R_G \equiv \frac{G_0}{E_D}$ as a function of I_D. In 2008, Marchetti [15] using the commonly accepted fact that maximum shear modulus is influenced by initial density and considering that this is well represented by K_D, studied the evolution of both R_G and G_0/M_{DMT} with K_D and found different but parallel trends as function of type of soil (that is I_D), recommending the second ratio to be used in deriving G_0 from DMT, as consequence of a lower scatter. In 2010, using the Theory of Elasticity, Cruz [7] approximate G_0 as a non-linear function of I_D, E_D and K_D, from where a promising median of relative errors close to 0.21 with a mean(std) around 0.29(0.28) were obtained. It is worth mention that comparing with the previous approach - R_G - this approximation, using the same data, lowered the mean and median of relative errors in more than 0.05 maintaining the standard deviation (Table 2).

In this work, to infer about the results quality it will be used some of the same indicators used by Hryciw, Cruz and others that are: the median, the arithmetic mean and standard deviation of the relative errors

$$\delta^i_{\widetilde{G}_0} = \frac{|\widetilde{G_0}(i) - G_0(i)|}{|G_0(i)|}; i = 1, 2, ..., N \tag{3}$$

where $\widetilde{G_0}(i)$ stands for the predicted value and $G_0(i)$ for the measured value seismic wave velocities (which is assumed to be correct). A final remark to point out that since in this work the no-intercept regression is sometimes used, the R^2 values will not be presented as they can been meaningfull in this case [16]. It is also worth to remark that in the context of DMT and from the engineering point of view, median is the parameter of choice for assessing the model quality [7] since the final value for maximum shear modulus relies on all set of results obtained in each geotechnical unit or layer.

3 Data Set, Experiments and Results

The data set used in the model is exactly the same used in the development of the non-linear G_0 approximation used by Cruz [7], resulting from 860 DMT measurements performed in Portugal by Cruz and world wide by Marchetti et al. [15] (data kindly granted by Marchetti for this purpose), which included data obtained in all kinds of sedimentary soils, namely clays, silty clays, clayey silts, silts, sandy silts, silty sands and sands. The main statistical measures of I_D, E_D, K_D and G_0 parameters are given in Table 1 as well as in Figure 1.

Several types of neural networks (NN) were used in order to improve the results obtained with traditional approaches and to achieve the best results with this kind of tool. The purpose was to find the best NN algorithm for the DMT problem. This process started by performing some experiments with traditional Multi Layer Perceptrons (MLP's) with different learning algorithms, namely Quasinewton, Conjugated Gradient and Scaled Conjugated Gradient (SCG) but, as it will be shown latter, the results were not as good as expected, and so Radial Basis Function (RBF), Bayesian and Fitting neural networks were then applied. The results obtained with this neural networks were slightly better than those with MLP's but still not significantly better. The last approach was to use

Table 1. Sample statistical measures

Values	I_D	E_D	K_D	G_0
min	0.0507	0.3644	0.9576	6.4300
max	8.8143	94.2600	20.5000	529.2000
median	0.5700	13.4450	3.5750	77.9100
mean	0.9134	18.8282	4.9161	92.5165
std	1.0739	18.8264	3.6079	69.6096

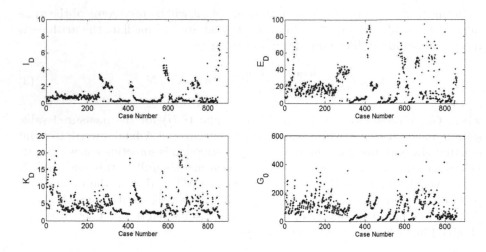

Fig. 1. Sample values for I_D, E_D, K_D and G_0

Support Vector Regression in order to improve the results with the previous NN. For all the experiments the 10 fold cross validation method with 20 repetitions was used, since this is the most common and widely accepted methodology to guarantee a good neural network generalization. For each NN a huge set of experiments was performed, varying the involved parameters such as the number of neurons in the MLP hidden layer, the number of epochs or the minimum error for stopping criteria. The results presented in Tables 3 to 7 are therefore the best ones for each regression algorithm and represents the mean of the 10×20 performed tests for each best configuration. It is important to stress the fact that, when compared to traditional approaches where all the data is used to build the model, this methodology tends to produce higher standard deviations since in each experiment only a fraction of the available data is used to evaluate the model.

As stated in Section 2, Cruz [7] was able to improve older results applying non-linear function approximation. In Table 2 the median and mean (standard deviation) of the relative errors obtained by that approaches are presented.

Table 3 shows the best results for the first performed experiments with common MLP regression using three different learning algorithms: Quasinewton,

Table 2. The results obtained with non-linear regression [7]

	Type	Median/Mean(std)
Non-Linear	$G_0 = \alpha\, E_D\, (I_D)^{\beta}$	0.28/0.34(0.29)
Regression	$G_0 = E_D + E_D\, e^{(\alpha + \beta I_D + \gamma \log(K_D))}$	0.21/0.29(0.28)

Table 3. The results (Median/Mean(std)) obtained with Multi Layer Perceptrons

	Type	Hidden neurons	$G_0 = f(I_D, E_D, K_D)$
	Quasinewton	50	0.20/0.38(0.72)
NN	Conj.Grad.	100	0.19/0.30(0.38)
	SCG	40	0.20/0.28(0.33)

Table 4. The results (Median/Mean(std)) obtained with Bayesian, RBF and Fitting neural networks

	Type	Hidden neurons	$G_0 = f(I_D, E_D, K_D)$
	MLP-Bayesian	20	0.20/0.29(0.30)
NN	RBF	200	0.20/0.31(0.39)
	Fitting	60	0.17/0.27(0.29)

Conjugated Gradient and SCG. It can be seen that there was a small improvement in the results when compared to those of Table 2 but not very significant.

The second set of experiments was performed using Bayesian, RBF's (with thin plate spline activation function) and Fitting neural networks regression, by applying several combinations for the number of iterations in RBF's or the number of inner and outer loops for the Bayesian NN's. The best obtained results with these algorithms are presented in Table 4.

These results are not significantly better than those obtained with common MLP's, with the exception of the fitting neural network that shows a significant improvement when compared with the others and also with traditional approaches.

An attempt to improve the quality of results was carried out by using Support Vector Regression (SVR). Support Vector Machines [17] are based on the statistical learning theory from Vapnik and are specially suited for classification. However, there are also algorithms based in the same approach for regression problems known as Support Vector Regression (SVR). Two different kinds of SVR algorithms: ϵ-SVR, from Vapnik [18] and ν-SVR from Schölkopf [19] were applied, which differ in the fact that ν-SVR uses an extra parameter $\nu \in (0, 1]$ to control the number of support vectors. For these experiments different values for the parameter C (cost) and for parameters ϵ and ν were used.

The best results obtained with both ϵ-SVR and ν-SVR are shown in Table 5 reveling slightly better results when compared with those obtained with the fitting neural network and better than those obtained with MLP's and the traditional regression algorithms.

In all the previous experiments it was tried to estimate G_0 as a function of I_D, E_D and K_D. Following the same strategy as Cruz [7], other experiments

Table 5. The results (Median/Mean(std)) obtained with Support Vector Regression

Type	Cost/$\epsilon(\nu)$	$G_0 = f(I_D, E_D, K_D)$
ϵ-SVR	200/0.1	0.16/0.27(0.43)
ν-SVR	200/0.8	0.16/0.27(0.41)

Table 6. The results (Median/Mean(std)) obtained with Support Vector Regression using only two input variables

Type	$G_0 = f(E_D, K_D)$	$G_0 = f(I_D, E_D)$	$G_0 = f(I_D, K_D)$
ϵ-SVR	0.19/0.32(0.46)	0.20/0.32(0.42)	0.29/0.55(0.88)
ν-SVR	0.19/0.32(0.47)	0.20/0.32(0.44)	0.30/0.55(0.96)

Table 7. The results (median/mean(std)) obtained using the subsets of the original data set and for the estimation of G_0 as a function of I_D, E_D and K_D

	Subsets	$G_0 = f(I_D, E_D, K_D)$
	$I_D < 0.6$	0.16/0.29(0.41)
ϵ-SVR	$0.6 \leq I_D < 1.8$	0.15/0.24(0.35)
	$I_D \geq 1.8$	0.15/0.39(0.57)
	$I_D < 0.6$	0.17/0.29(0.37)
ν-SVR	$0.6 \leq I_D < 1.8$	0.15/0.24(0.38)
	$I_D \geq 1.8$	0.16/0.37(0.60)

were performed which results are presented in Table 6. In these experiments G_0 was estimated only as a function of two of the three available variables. As last option E_D was used as a single input variable but the results were worst than those obtained using more input variables (due to lack of space they are not shown here). In these experiments only SVR's were used, as they presented the best results in the previous experiments.

After the last set of experiments it can be seen that the best results are still those presented in Table 5, the ones that were obtained by using the three available parameters K_D, I_D and E_D.

The final experiments were conducted splitting I_D values in coherent groups, namely those related with clay, silt and sandy soils, respectively represented by the following I_D intervals: $I_D < 0.6, 0.6 \leq I_D < 1.8$ and $I_D \geq 1.8$. This operation made a partition of the original 860 data set elements in subsets with 449, 259 and 152 elements respectively. Experiments with these data sets (subsets) were performed using only SVR algorithms since they were the ones with better results in the previous experiments. Results are presented in Table 7.

Although these final results can be pointed as very interesting, specially with
ϵ-SVR, it can not be concluded that these are better than those obtained with
the complete data set (Table 5) once there are one larger subset with a result
slightly higher and two smaller subsets with a slightly lower result (remember
I_D-values distribution in Figure 1). This indicates that the methodology can
produce interesting results in some particular cases, deserving a more detailed
study. Nevertheless from a geotechnical point of view it may be considered a
very promising result.

4   Conclusions

A new approach was applied to predict maximum shear modulus by DMT using
Neural Networks. Based on performed experiments it is possible to outline the
following considerations:

- Neural Networks improve the current state-of-the-art in terms of G_0 prediction through DMT intermediate parameters.
- The results show that, in general, NN lead us to much smaller medians,
  equivalent means and higher standard deviations in respect to relative errors,
  when compared to traditional approaches.
- Regarding the problem characteristics the SVR approach gives the best results considering the median as the main quality measure as discussed earlier.
- The Fitting NN seems to be the most robust in terms of the three quality
  control parameters used, improving the results of traditional approaches.
- The unbalanced data distribution, regarding the I_D partition, postpone a
  final conclusion about the improvement of model quality to the availability
  of a more balanced sample.

References

1. Clayton, C., Heymann, G.: Stiffness of geomaterials at very small strains.
   Géotechnique 51(3), 245–255 (2001)
2. Fahey, M.: Soil stiffness values for foundation settlement analysis. In: Proc. 2nd
   Int. Conf. on Pre-failure Deformation Characteristics of Geomaterials, vol. 2, pp.
   1325–1332. Balkema, Lisse (2001)
3. Peck, R.B., Hanson, W.E., Thornburn, T.H.: Foundation Engineering, 2nd edn.
   John Wiley & Sons, Chichester (1974)
4. Lunne, T., Robertson, P., Powell, J.: Cone penetration testing in geotechnical practice. Spon E & F N (1997)
5. Marchetti, S.: In-situ tests by flat dilatometer. Journal of the Geotechn. Engineering Division 106(GT3), 299–321 (1980)
6. Cruz, N., Devincenzi, M., Viana da Fonseca, A.: Dmt experience in iberian transported soils. In: Proc. 2nd International Flat Dilatometer Conference, pp. 198–204
   (2006)
7. Cruz, N.: Modelling geomechanics of residual soils by DMT tests. PhD thesis,
   Universidade do Porto (2010)

8. Marchetti, S.: The flat dilatometer: Design applications. In: Third Geotechnical Engineering. Conf. Cairo University (1997)
9. Mayne, P.W.: Interrelationships of dmt and cpt in soft clays. In: Proc. 2nd International Flat Dilatometer Conference, pp. 231–236 (2006)
10. Hryciw, R.D.: Small-strain-shear modulus of soil by dilatometer. Journal of Geotechnical Eng. ASCE 116(11), 1700–1716 (1990)
11. Hardin, B.O., Blandford, G.E.: Elasticity of particulate materials. J. Geot. Eng. Div 115(GT6), 788–805 (1989)
12. Jamiolkowski, B.M., Ladd, C.C., Jermaine, J.T., Lancelota, R.: New developments in field and laboratory testing of soilsladd, c.c. In: XI ISCMFE, vol. 1, pp. 57–153 (1985)
13. Sully, J.P., Campanella, R.G.: Correlation of maximum shear modulus with dmt test results in sand. In: Proc. XII ICSMFE, pp. 339–343 (1989)
14. Tanaka, H., Tanaka, M.: Characterization of sandy soils using CPT and DMT. Soils and Foundations 38(3), 55–65 (1998)
15. Marchetti, S., Monaco, P., Totani, G., Marchetti, D.: In -situ tests by seismic dilatometer (SDMT). In: Crapps, D.K. (ed.) From Research to Practice in Geotechnical Engineering, vol. 180, pp. 292–311. ASCEGeotech. Spec. Publ. (2008)
16. Huang, Y., Draper, N.R.: Transformations, regression geometry and R2. Computational Statistics & Data Analysis 42(4), 647–664 (2003)
17. Cortes, C., Vapnik, V.: Support-vector Networks. Journal of Machine Learning 20(3), 273–297 (1995)
18. Vapnik, V.: Statistical Learning Theory. Wiley, New York (1998)
19. Schölkopf, B., Smola, A., Williamson, R.C., Bartlett, P.L.: New support vector algorithms. Neural Computation 12, 1207–1245 (2000)

NNIGnets, Neural Networks Software

Tânia Fontes[1], Vânia Lopes[1], Luís M. Silva[1],
Jorge M. Santos[1,2], and Joaquim Marques de Sá[1]

[1] INEB - Instituto de Engenharia Biomédica, Campus FEUP (Faculdade de Engenharia da
Universidade do Porto), Rua Dr. Roberto Frias, s/n, 4200-065 Porto, Portugal
[2] ISEP - Instituto Superior de Engenharia do Porto
Rua Dr. António Bernardino de Almeida, 431, 4200-072 Porto, Portugal
{trfontes,vaniadlopes,lmsilva,jmfs,jmsa}@fe.up.pt

Abstract. NNIGnets is a freeware computer program which can be used for teaching, research or business applications, of Artificial Neural Networks (ANNs). This software includes presently several tools for the application and analysis of Multilayer Perceptrons (MLPs) and Radial Basis Functions (RBFs), such as stratified Cross-Validation, Learning Curves, Adjusted Rand Index, novel cost functions, and Vapnik–Chervonenkis (VC) dimension estimation, which are not usually found in other ANN software packages. NNIGnets was built following a software engineering approach which decouples operative from GUI functions, allowing an easy growth of the package. NNIGnets was tested by a variety of users, with different backgrounds and skills, who found it to be intuitive, complete and easy to use.

Keywords: artificial neural networks, software application, freeware tool.

1 Introduction

NNIGnets includes several state-of-art tools of Artificial Neural Networks (ANNs) training and analysis, namely stratified Cross-Validation [1] with train/test statistics, Learning Curves, novel cost functions such as Generalized Exponential [2], Cross Entropy [3] and Shannon Entropy of the Error [4], [5], Adjusted Rand Index [6], [7] and Vapnik–Chervonenkis (VC) dimension estimation [8], [9], among others that are not usually covered by other software implementations. NNIGnets can be used for teaching, research or, under certain conditions, business applications. Over the last five years, this software has been used as a support tool for the practical sessions of the Neural Networks Summer School yearly held at Porto (http://www.isep.ipp.pt/nn/) and was tested by many users with different backgrounds and skills, who showed great interest in the functionalities available and agreed that it was a very complete package and easy to use. In the following sections we describe NNIGnets in detail.

2 Model Description

NNIGnets is a freeware computer program developed in C# at INEB (PSI/NNIG) - *Instituto de Engenharia Biomédica* and is available for download from

L. Iliadis and C. Jayne (Eds.): EANN/AIAI 2011, Part I, IFIP AICT 363, pp. 345–350, 2011.
© IFIP International Federation for Information Processing 2011

http://paginas.fe.up.pt/~nnig. It is composed by a number of menus that allow ANN (presently only Multilayer Perceptrons (MLPs) and Radial Basis Functions (RBFs)) configuration and evaluation. The Settings menu is used to set the essential information for ANN design by specifying the training and test data, the network architecture and the learning algorithm type. On the other hand, the Results menu provides access to the design outcomes such as tables and graphs that help the user to interpret the ANN performance. Although NNIGnets presently only provides MLPs and RBFs, the software structure was designed having in view an easy insertion of other ANN types within an uniform philosophy.

2.1 ANN Inputs – Settings Menu

The Settings menu is divided into three main submenus: Data, Architecture and Learning Algorithm. These three submenus are related to each other and several definitions affect one another.

The ANN inputs are specified through an input file chosen on the Data panel. The user uploads data through a graphical user interface, by selecting a text file (.txt). Each text file line must comply with either of the following formats: tab separated columns or semi-colon separated columns (possibly with spaces in between).

After data file uploading, the graphical interface shows the respective variable names and values. Each data column (variable) can be used as one of four types:

a)   input: if the variable is to be used as input to the neural network (NN);
b)   nominal output: if the variable is to be used as target in classification mode;
c)   continuous output: if the variable is to be used as target in regression mode;
d)   Ignore: variable to be discarded from the NN design.

The Pre-processing frame holds two options that provide two different types of data pre-processing: data randomization and data standardization. For data randomization, data rows are randomly shuffled. For data standardization, three methods are provided: range scaling (1), where data is scaled to an user-specified real interval $\lfloor a, b \rfloor$; mean centering (2), where data is centered around the mean; and standardization (3), corresponding to the usual zero mean and unit variance standardization. Let x_i be the $i - $th original variable where $i = 1, ..., i_{max}$ and $\tilde{x}_i$ the standardized x_i; a and b the lower and upper interval respectively; μ the mean value of x_i; and σ the standard deviation value of x_i. Then we have:

$$\tilde{x}_i = \frac{b-a}{x_{i_{max}} - x_{i_{min}}} \left(x_i - x_{i_{min}} \right) + a \ . \tag{1}$$

$$\tilde{x}_i = x_i - \mu \ . \tag{2}$$

$$\tilde{x}_i = \frac{x_i - \mu}{\sigma} \ . \tag{3}$$

Another option available is the evaluation frame. Here the user can choose the type of performance evaluation between train/test evaluation, Cross-Validation evaluation and Learning Curves. In train/test evaluation data is divided into two subsets, train and test. The subset sizes can be specified as percentages of the whole dataset.

In Cross-Validation, the data is divided into a number of approximately equal sized subsets. The user defines the number of subsets and decides whether or not the class ratio of the data should be kept (the so-called *Stratified Cross-Validation*).

The Learning Curves allow the user to analyze ANN convergence and generalization abilities by performing multiple designs with incremental data sizes. The user defines the starting and ending sizes of the training set, the increment, the number of experiments in each subset and the format to be carried out. The format can be one of the following: i.i.d., where the instances for the test sets are randomly picked up from the data, and off-train-sets: the same process as i.i.d. but discarding instances already present in the training set.

The Architecture panel allows the specification between a MLP or a RBF network. Notice that we consider that each neuron in a given layer is connected to every neuron on the next layer and there is a weight assigned to each of these connections and a bias in each layer. The number of neurons in the input layer depends on the number of inputs chosen from the data and the number of neurons in the output layer depends on whether the user chooses classification or regression mode. In regression mode only one neuron is needed, since the network output is regarded as the expected value of the model at a given point in input space, whereas in classification mode the number of neurons depends on the number of classes: 1 output for two-class problems, c outputs for c > 2 classes problems, using 1-out-of-c coding.

For each ANN architecture, the user can choose different activation functions: Sigmoid, Hyperbolic Tangent or Linear Heaviside for MLPs and Gaussian or Multiquadric for RBFs. By default, the initial weights of the MLP architecture are set to zero, but the user can specify their initial values in two ways: by initializing the weights randomly within a specify range, or by specifying values using a text file. In latter the file must follow the format specified for input data. For RBFs the weights of neurons in the hidden layer are set according to x and y centroid coordinates. In both ANN architectures the user can change the network properties by inserting and removing layers or neurons and by changing the layer's activation function (i.e. setting weights). There is also an option for viewing the connections of a specific neuron. To ease the visualization, neurons are identified using a color scale: black for bias, red for input neurons, and blue for the remaining neurons.

The selection of the learning algorithm is available on the Learning Algorithm window. For MLP networks, either the Batch Back-Propagation or the Sequential Back-Propagation algorithm can be chosen, while for RBF networks a hybrid learning algorithm is available.

Unlike other ANN programs where only the Mean Squared Error (MSE) cost function is provided (4), NNIGnets avails (presently) three further possibilities: Exponential (Exp) cost function [2] (5), Cross-Entropy (CE) cost function [3] (6) and Shannon Entropy of the Error (HS) cost function [4], [5], (7), which have the following definition for two-class problems:

$$E_{MSE} = \sum_{i=0}^{n}(t_i - y_i)^2 \, , \tag{4}$$

$$E_{Exp} = \exp\left(\frac{\sum_{i=0}^{n}(t_i - y_i)^2}{k}\right) * k \, , \tag{5}$$

$$E_{CE} = -\sum_{i=0}^{n} t_i \ln y_i + (1 - t_i) \ln(1 - y_i) , \qquad (6)$$

$$E_{HS} = -\frac{1}{n}\sum_{i=0}^{n} \log \hat{f}(t_i - y_i) , \qquad (7)$$

where n is the number of patterns, t_i and y_i are the target and network output (respectively) values for pattern i, $k \neq 0$ is the Exponential cost function parameter and $\hat{f}(x)$ is an estimate of the error density obtained with the Parzen window method.

For MLP algorithms the following parameters can be adjusted: the learning rate which can be adaptive [10] or specified, the momentum, the number of epochs in one run and the minimum squared error. The hybrid learning algorithms only uses the number of weights which depends on the number of neurons on the hidden layer.

2.2 ANN Outputs – Results Menu

The Results menu has several submenus: the Classification Matrix, the Error Graph, the Error Surface and the Decision Border.

The Classification Matrix menu provides the classification error matrices resulting from the train/test learning process. The classification results can be adjusted to several types of priors: equal priors, with an equal weighting factor for every class, structured priors, with weights proportional to the set class sizes, and specified priors with weights specified by the user. The output varies according to the evaluation type selected in the Data panel: train classification matrix, whenever the user chooses 100% of the available data for the training set; train and test classification matrices, Cross-Validation, or the Learning Curves. NNIGNets software provides an estimate for the classification error rate (Error mean). Several performance indicators for two-class problems are also included (Sensitivity and Specificity, Balanced Error Rate and Adjusted Rand Index [6], [7]). Let c be the number of classes, j the class index, m_j the number of misclassified cases in class j, n_j the number of cases in class j and p_j the prior of class j; let fp be the number of false positives, fn the number of false negatives, tp the number of true positives and tn the number of true negatives. Then we have:

$$\text{Error Mean} = \sum_{j=0}^{c} \frac{m_j}{n_j} p_j . \qquad (8)$$

$$\text{Sensitivity} = \frac{tp}{tp + fn} . \qquad (9)$$

$$\text{Specificity} = \frac{tn}{tn + fp} . \qquad (10)$$

$$\text{Balanced Error Rate (BER)} = \frac{\frac{fp}{tn+fp} + \frac{fn}{tp+fn}}{2} . \qquad (11)$$

$$\text{Adjusted Rand Index} = \frac{\binom{n}{2}(tp+tn) - [(tp+fn)(tp+fp) + (fp+tn)(fn+tn)]}{\binom{n}{2}^2 - [(tp+fn)(tp+fp) + (fp+tn)(fn+tn)]} . \qquad (12)$$

The outputs resulting from the training process are shown on the Output panel, and include the ANN output, the target value, the deviation value and the class confidence value (H). The misclassified instances are represented in dark grey. On the options frame the user can choose which output layer will be displayed. For two-class problems the target value can be either in [0, 1] or [-1, 1] depending on the activation function chosen. For multi-class problems the targets are coded in a 1-out-of-c (where c is the number of classes) mode. The class confidence value H, as a function of each pattern is given by [11]:

$$H = -\sum_{\Omega} P(\omega_i|x)\ln(\omega_i|x),$$
(13)

where:

$P(\omega_1|x) = y_i(x), P(\omega_0|x) = 1 - y_i(x)$, for two-class problems;

$P(\omega_i|x) = \frac{y_i(x)}{\sum_{\Omega} y_i(x)}$, for multi-class problems.

For classification problems, the confidence level CC is given by:

$$CC = \begin{cases} \ln(c) - H, & \text{if well classified} \\ -\ln(c) - H, & \text{otherwise} \end{cases},$$
(14)

where c is the number of classes.

This Output panel also shows the Class Confidence Mean (Mean H) which is the average value for all cases, such that $-\ln(c) \le H \le \ln(c)$.

The Error Graph panel is one of the most useful tools available in this software. This panel is composed by a graph that shows the evolution of the mean classification error for the select cost function along the train/test epochs and helps the user to identify the minimum number of epochs for a specified ANN configuration.

If Cross-Validation method is selected, this graph also shows the MSE standard deviation for train and test over the number of epochs. Right clicking on the graph, a pop-ups menu provides several options such as saving the graph as an image on a pre-specified location, or showing x and y coordinates (visualization mode) when the user moves the mouse over the graph line.

From the Results menu the user can also choose to display the Decision Border and the Error Surface. The first is a two dimensional representation of the ANN behavior for a given range of values for two variables/characteristics specified by the user. Patterns are represented in different colors depending on the class and the border curve, which divides the classes, is represented in black. The user can set the grid resolution, the dots size and can also choose to display a grid with class labels. The Error Surface is a three dimensional plot of the ANN cost function for any pair of weights. Each ANN output can be regarded as a function of n input variables, which form a response surface on an n+1-dimensional space.

Another aspect that is not usual to find in other similar software is the estimation of the VC-dimension, which is part of the VC-theory [8]. VC-dimension assesses the model complexity and the generalization ability of a learning machine. Phatak demonstrates the inter-relationships between generalization and the VC-dimension of feed-forward ANNs [12] and a practical setup to estimate the VC-dimension of a binary classifier is proposed by Vapnik et al. [8]. NNIGnets uses the optimized design proposed by Shao and Li [9] to obtain a more accurate estimate of the VC-dimension.

The user selects the option VC-dimension from the Actions menu, which is only available for two class datasets, since the empirical process proposed in [9] is defined only for binary classifiers. On the VC Dimension window two inputs are defined: the number of experiments to be performed and the initial guess of the VC-dimension (h), which is a non negative number.

NNIGnets also includes a help tool that explains the software usage, describing each menu option, as well as the meaning of the fields on each panel.

3   Conclusions

The NNIGnets software has been used as a teaching tool for the practical sessions of the last editions of the Neural Networks Summer School, held in Oporto. The School involved over thirty participants of diverse backgrounds and practical interests from several countries. NNIGnets raised great interest among the participants who found it very intuitive, pleasant and easy to use, even for an inexperienced user. Since it offers a large set of options, including new functionalities that are not usually found in other similar software, and participants agreed it to be very complete and appealing.

New tools and ANN types are planned to be included in NNIGnets in the near future.

References

1. Hastie, T., Tibshirani, R., Friedman, J.: The Element of Statistical Learning: Data Mining, Inference, and Prediction, 2nd edn. Springer, Heidelberg (2009)
2. Silva, L., Marques de Sá, J., Alexandre, L.A.: Data Classification with Multilayer Perceptrons using a Generalized Error Function. Neural Networks 21(9), 1302–1310 (2008)
3. Bishop, C.M.: Neural Networks for Pattern Recognition. Oxford University Press, Oxford (1995)
4. Silva, L., Marques de Sá, J., Alexandre, L.A.: The MEE Principle in Data Classification: A Perceptron-Based Analysis. Neural Computation 22, 2698–2728 (2010)
5. Silva, L.: Neural Networks with Error-Density Risk Functionals for Data Classification. PhD thesis, University of Porto (2008)
6. Hubert, L., Arabie, P.: Comparing Partions. J. of Classification 2, 193–218 (1985)
7. Santos, J.M., Ramos, S.: Using a Clustering Similarity Measure for Feature Selection in High Dimensional Data Sets. In: Innovation and Sustainable Development in Agriculture and Food 2010, vol. 1, pp. 900–905. IEEE Computer Society Press, Montpellier (2010)
8. Vapnik, V., Levin, E., Le, Y.C.: Measuring the VC-Dimension of a Learning Machine. Neural Computation 6(5), 851–876 (1994)
9. Shao, X., Li, W.: Measuring the VC-Dimension using optimized experimental design. Neural Computation 12, 1969–1986 (2000)
10. Santos, J.M.: Data classification with neural networks and entropic criteria. PhD thesis, University of Porto (2007)
11. Wan, E.A.: Neural Network Classification: A Bayesian Interpretation. IEEE Tr NN (1990)
12. Phatak, D.: Relationship between fault tolerance, generalization and the Vapnik-Chervonenkis (VC) dimension of feed-forward ANNs. In: Proceedings of the International Joint Conference on Neural Networks (IJCNN) (1999)

Key Learnings from Twenty Years of Neural Network Applications in the Chemical Industry

Aaron J. Owens

DuPont Company, Engineering Research and Technology,
POB 80356, Wilmington, DE, 19880-0356, U.S.A.
aaron.j.owens@usa.dupont.com

Abstract. This talk summarizes several points that have been learned about applying Artificial Neural Networks in the chemical industry. Artificial Neural Networks are one of the major tools of *Empirical Process Modeling*, but not the only one. To properly assess the appropriate model complexity, combine information about both the *Training* and the *Test* data sets. A neural network, or any other empirical model, is better at making predictions than the comparison between modeled and observed data shows. Finally, it is important to exploit synergies with other disciplines and practitioners to stimulate the use of Neural Networks in industry.

Keywords: Artificial Neural Networks, Neural Network Applications, Stopping Criteria, Empirical Model Validity.

1 Introduction

DuPont has had a long history of supporting neural network applications in the chemical industry. Initial efforts were aimed at commercial applications in digital image processing during the 1980s. In 1990, the Neural Network Resource Center was established to catalyze the use of artificial neural network models, particularly the Back Propagation Network [1], [2], internally throughout the Company. The author has personally been involved in this these efforts ever since, except for a brief, misguided detour into management. This talk summarizes some of the "key learnings" about neural network applications resulting from those efforts.

2 Neural Networks as an Empirical Process Modeling Tool

Empirical Process Modeling is data driven, rather than emphasizing fundamental equations. It can be described colloquially as *Modeling a Spreadsheet*. The spreadsheet metaphor has been useful in helping our internal practitioners to decide what type of model to use. The *Process* being modeled can be of any kind: chemical, physical, biological, business, financial, marketing, etc. DuPont is a large, international Science company. Our *Empirical Process Modeling* efforts have spanned many products, functions, and regions.

L. Iliadis and C. Jayne (Eds.): EANN/AIAI 2011, Part I, IFIP AICT 363, pp. 351–360, 2011.
© IFIP International Federation for Information Processing 2011

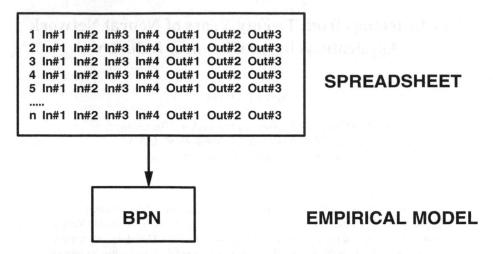

1	In#1	In#2	In#3	In#4	Out#1	Out#2	Out#3
2	In#1	In#2	In#3	In#4	Out#1	Out#2	Out#3
3	In#1	In#2	In#3	In#4	Out#1	Out#2	Out#3
4	In#1	In#2	In#3	In#4	Out#1	Out#2	Out#3
5	In#1	In#2	In#3	In#4	Out#1	Out#2	Out#3

Fig. 1. The Spreadsheet Metaphor. In *Empirical Modeling,* data are arranged into a Spreadsheet with real-valued *Inputs* and *Outputs* from the process being modeled.

DuPont's proprietary neural network software, called the *Neural WebKit*, uses a simple spreadsheet-based data format. Each *Exemplar* or case appears on a row. It consists of the following columns: a unique integer *Exemplar Number* followed by the numerical values of all of the process *Inputs X* and then of all the process *Outputs Y*. See Figure 1.

The empirical modeling tool, here illustrated by the Back Propagation Network (BPN), is applied to the data set to obtain the parameters for an Empirical Model. The goal of Empirical Modeling is to maximize accuracy of the prediction of the Ys from the Xs.

The software requires that the data set be pre-processed so that there are no missing entries and that all variables are real-valued. Categorical variables need to be unary encoded, with the Machines A, B, or C coded as the three variables [1 0 0], [0 1 0] and [0 0 1].

The appropriate modeling technique to use in building the empirical model is determined by the *shape* of the spreadsheet, as illustrated in Figure 2, along with the data's *Signal to Noise* ratio. For *Short and Fat* spreadsheets, there are fewer (often many fewer) exemplars than variables, so a sub-linear method is necessary. To identify the model coefficients, the number of model parameters needs to be less than the number of observations. Even simple *Multiple Linear Regression* (MLR) cannot be used for these cases.

For *Short and Fat* spreadsheets, the recommended *Chemometric* technique is *Partial Least Squares (PLS)* [3]. Classical statistical techniques (like MLR and polynomial regression) deal with cases in which the spreadsheet matrix is close to *Square*. In fact, classical statistical *Design of Experiments* (DOE) minimizes the number of experiments so that it is just a few more than the number of parameters to be estimated, so the spreadsheet is nearly *Square*.

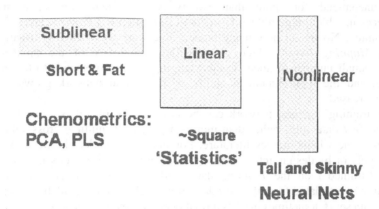

Fig. 2. What *shape* is your spreadsheet? *Chemometrics* techniques like *Partial Least Squares* [PLS] are best suited to *Short and Fat* matrices. Classical statistical techniques are appropriate with *Square* matrices. Neural network can be applied to *Tall and Skinny* matrices. For low *Signal to Noise* data sets, more *Exemplars* are required to accurately determine model parameters.

Neural networks are more appropriate only in the relatively data-rich case of a *Tall and Skinny* data matrix. Then there are enough observations to allow the system to identify a model with more coefficients than *Inputs* [4], [5].

There are a couple of *caveats* with respect to selecting the appropriate model. First, while a matrix may appear *Tall and Skinny*, if the underlying process has a small *Signal to Noise* ratio (i.e., it is dominated by noise), then more -- perhaps many more -- observations are required to accurately identify the model parameters. So it may be appropriate to use PLS for a *Tall and Skinny* matrix with low *Signal to Noise*. Second, both PLS and neural networks can successfully model linear systems. So in *Empirical Modeling* the classical statistical tools are actually seldom needed, as long as the objective of the model is accurate *Prediction*. While PLS and neural networks have tools to assess variable importance, only classical statistical techniques allow you -- for example -- to point to a specific coefficient as the cross term between variables x(3) and x(4), as well as give its statistical uncertainty.

Most of the time needed to prepare an Empirical Process Model comes from collecting and checking the data. Once the data are in a *Spreadsheet*, the time to do an analysis is usually trivial, especially with PLS. So it is recommended to *always* run a PLS analysis before proceeding to use a neural network on the same data set. Note that you can transform a single hidden layer Back Propagation Network to the PLS structure simply by eliminating the squashing functions. In addition, commercial PLS software has good graphical tools for interpreting the models with multiple-input, multiple-output mappings.

3   Use Both Training and Test Data to Find Model Complexity

More than 90% of the neural network applications at DuPont have used the Back Propagation Network with a single hidden layer [6]. That methodology has remained basically unchanged for more than twenty years. There are some special circumstances in which more hidden layers are used, often a *Bottleneck* layer [7], but they are limited. No matter how many hidden layers are used, there is usually one called the *Mapping Layer*, which controls the complexity of the input-output mapping. A small number of nodes in the Mapping layer corresponds to low model complexity, and the representational ability of the neural network grows as that number is increased.

Because training a neural network can be time-consuming, it is usual to use a single *Train/Test* data split, rather than more sophisticated multiple cross-validation methods from the Chemometrics literature. For neural networks, the data are split, either randomly or by design, into a Training data set and a Test data set. Models are developed ('trained') on the *Training* data, and their expected performance for generalization is estimated from the *Test* data. If enough data are available, a separate Validation data set is sometimes used as a final check on the accuracy of the system.

3.1 Three Train/Test Methods: Scattergun, Train and Grow, and Early Stopping

There are at least three competing methods for developing neural network models of the appropriate complexity. In the *Scattergun* method, neural networks with 1 through M hidden nodes in the *Mapping* layer are randomly initialized. They are all trained to completion, and the choice is the one with the minimum *Test* error. Because it uses multiple random initializations, this method is not robust.

A method with wide application in DuPont is *Train and Grow* [6]. Start with one node in the Mapping Layer, and train the model on the Training data to completion. Note the performance on the Test data. Grow the trained network by adding a second mapping node, with small random values for the new connection weights, and then train it. Continue training and growing until the Test error increases with increasing nodes. This method gives a more robust and reproducible Train/Test path, because the models usually stay in the same basin of attraction in weight space.

Early Stopping is a viable alternative to *Train and Grow*, particularly if modeling similar systems has given you a reasonable starting point. In this method, a single, large number of mapping units is selected, more than are actually needed. The weights are randomly initialized and then training begins. Rather than training to completion, the Root Mean Square (RMS) Errors of the *Train* and *Test* data sets are monitored as a function of the number of training iterations. Select the *Number of Training Iterations* giving the minimum *RMS Test* error as the appropriate model complexity [8].

Note that with Early Stopping, training is stopped before the weights reach their final optimum values. This method runs much more quickly than Train and Grow, since only one model is developed. But *Early Stopping* is more sensitive to initial conditions, particularly for multiple-hidden-layer models.

For all of these methods, the important piece of information is the minimum RMS *Test* error, since that should predict performance on new data. As a final step, it is always recommended to re-train the model using *All* of the data and stopping when the appropriate *RMS Test* error limit is reached.

Historically at DuPont, the *Shotgun* method was first tried but quickly abandoned as too unreliable. *Train and Grow* continues to be used for most applications with a single hidden layer [6]. For multiple-hidden-layer *Bottleneck Neural Networks, Early Stopping* has been adopted for decreased training time [8].

3.2 A Complexity Criterion Using Both Train and Test Errors

To select the best model, the neural network community has heavily weighted one criterion – minimum *RMS Test* error – but ignored some additional relevant information. A good model would be one that has a clear minimum in the *RMS Test* error but *also* has *Train* and *Test* errors similar to each other. In other words, we should also consider the *RMS Training* error in selecting the appropriate model complexity. If it is significantly less than (or greater than) the *RMS Test* error at its minimum (as a function of *Number of Hidden Units* for *Train and Grow* or *Number of Iterations* for *Early Stopping*), that indicates a modeling failure. The *Train* and *Test* data sets are, for some reason, not compatible.

We propose a new metric that takes into account both *RMS Train* and *Test* errors. It optimizes *both* the *Test* error and the difference between *Train* and *Test*. An equation that accomplished this is to minimize

$$\alpha*(\text{RMS Test error}) + (1-\alpha)*|\text{RMS Train error} - \text{RMS Test Error}| . \tag{1}$$

If $\alpha = 1$, only the RMS Test error matters (as has been conventional). If $\alpha = 0$, the criterion assures that the *RMS Train* and *Test* errors are the same. After looking at dozens of cases, we propose $\alpha = 0.5$ as a good compromise. That is a 50/50 combination of the two parts of Equation (1).

The process is to enter the RMS Train and RMS Test errors, along with the corresponding *Number of Hidden Units* or *Iteration Number*, into a spreadsheet. The spreadsheet locates the minimum of the function of Equation (1) and records the appropriate *Model Complexity* at that point.

See the example in Figure 3 below. The appropriate model complexity (*Number of Iterations*) is selected by minimizing the RMS *Test* error (plus symbols) and the absolute difference between RMS *Train* error (filled circles) and RMS *Test* error. A table with the plotted values, for this hypothetical example, appears on the right, where *Train* and *Test* refer to scaled RMS errors and *Crit.* is the new criterion of Equation (1) with $\alpha = 0.5$. The solid curve shows this new criterion.

The usual procedure, considering only the minimum RMS Test error, gives an optimum at Iteration 10 (underlined), where the Train and Test errors are 0.0071 and 0.0264, respectively (differing by a factor of 3.7!). The New Criterion selects 8 Iterations (bold and underlined), where the train and Test errors are 0.0139 and 0.0285 (a smaller factor of 2.1).

Adopting this *New Criterion* should give a more balanced selection of the appropriate model complexity. Incidentally, it works well for PLS models too, where the *Train* and *Test* errors are replaced by *Calibration* and *Cross-Validation* errors, and the complexity parameter is the *Number of Latent Variables* selected.

An important final step is to re-train the neural network model using *All* of the data (*Training + Test* data sets), stopping at the appropriate *Model Complexity*: the selected optimum *Number of Hidden Units* for *Train and Grow* or the *Number of Iterations* for *Early Stopping*.

4 An Empirical Model Is Better Than the Data Show

The discussion in this section may be well known to statisticians, but many people in the neural network and chemometrics communities may not be aware of it. Quite simply, any empirical model fit by least squares has its model coefficients and hence its prediction accuracy improved with additional data from the same process. However, by looking at model predictions compared with just the (noisy) data from that process itself, you cannot prove this.

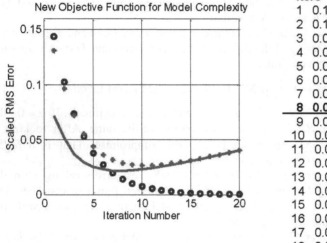

Iters	Train	Test	Crit.
1	0.1433	0.1310	0.0717
2	0.1027	0.0964	0.0513
3	0.0736	0.0722	0.0368
4	0.0527	0.0554	0.0291
5	0.0378	0.0440	0.0251
6	0.0271	0.0364	0.0228
7	0.0194	0.0315	0.0218
8	**0.0139**	**0.0285**	**0.0216**
9	0.0100	0.0270	0.0220
10	0.0071	0.0264	0.0229
11	0.0051	0.0266	0.0240
12	0.0037	0.0273	0.0255
13	0.0026	0.0284	0.0270
14	0.0019	0.0297	0.0288
15	0.0013	0.0312	0.0305
16	0.0010	0.0329	0.0324
17	0.0007	0.0346	0.0343
18	0.0005	0.0364	0.0362
19	0.0004	0.0383	0.0381
20	0.0003	0.0402	0.0401

Fig. 3. New Objective Function for Selecting Model Complexity

Suppose that there is a Process with multivariate Inputs X and Outputs Y. There will also be noise (ε) in the process. A model for this kind of process is

$$Y_k = f(X_k) + \varepsilon_k . \tag{2}$$

Here the subscript k refers to the kth *Exemplar*.

The function $f(X_k)$ is the *True Relationship* between X and Y, but each observation or *Exemplar* has an associated noise (ε). As is customary, the random errors ε for the exemplars are assumed to be *Independent and Identically Distributed* (IID), sampled from a *Normal* distribution with mean 0 and standard deviation σ.

In a neural network, the True Relationship is approximated by a neural network model $f^{NN}(X)$ with many parameters. After the training of neural network to get the optimum values of the model parameters, we assume that the neural network model approximates the truth, or:

$$f^{NN}(X) \sim f(X) . \tag{3}$$

Note that even if Equation (3) represents full equality, when we use $f^{NN}(X)$ to estimate the (noisy) observed value of Y, we see from Equation (2) that the difference between predicted and observed is equal to the noise (with standard deviation σ). While the model can get very accurate, as more and more data points are added, when we compare it with the noisy real data we still get a *Root Mean Square* error of σ.

4.1 Simple Linear Example: Numerical Simulations

The effect can be illustrated with a very simple example, with univariate x and y related by a linear relationship. If Equation (3) is applicable (i.e., the neural network, when trained, approaches the true X-Y noise-free relationship), the same kind of results would be obtained with a Neural Network model rather than this linear model. The linear results are easier to explain.

Equation (2) with this underlying model becomes:

$$y_k = c^* x_k + \varepsilon_k . \tag{4}$$

Equation (4) is used to generate the *Observed* data. For specificity, take $c = 6$ and $\sigma = 1$.

Numerical simulations were performed using a simple Matlab script. Each of N *Exemplars* has x values between uniformly sampled between 0 and 1, then added random noise with $\sigma = 1$ to get *Observed y* values from Equation (4).

To simulate the model-building phase, a simple linear regression model (Equation 5) was fitted to the N data pairs (x,y).

$$y = a^* x . \tag{5}$$

The slope a and the RMS error between the *Observed* and *Predicted* values of y were recorded for each realization. Calculations were made with the number of observations N = [10 30 100 300 1000 3000 10000]. The simulation was repeated with each value of N for a total of 1000 iterations and averaged over all 1000 of them to reduce sampling noise.

See the results in Figure 4. The RMS error between the model and the (noisy) Observed data is shown with the symbol 'x'. The RMS error between model and the underlying True (noise-free) data is shown with the symbol 'o'. The RMS error between the true slope ($c = 6$) and the model-estimated slope (a) is shown with the symbol '*'. The line is drawn to guide the eye; its equation is 1/sqrt (N), where N is the Number of Samples.

Note that the RMS error between *Predicted* and *Observed* y is close to $\sigma = 1$, as discussed above. (It is labeled 'Observed' in the figure.) Increasing N does not change this estimate, which is roughly constant with N. With added data, the RMS error of the model prediction compared with the (noisy) *Observed* data does not decrease.

Next consider the value of the modeled slope, a. It is close to the true value of c = 6 for N = 10, but it gets increasingly closer, with error varying as 1/sqrt (N), as N is increased. While standard statistical packages would estimate the error limits on the slope, there is no direct way in most PLS or neural network calculations to extract that information. The modeler may not realize that the model is getting more accurate with additional data, especially if RMS error of model predictions versus the observed noisy data is the only evaluation factor.

Finally, since this is a *Simulation*, one can 'play God' and look at how the model predicted the *underlying actual relationship*, y = 6*x, ignoring the noise in Equation (4). The points labeled 'True' in Figure 4 shows that the model prediction accuracy, compared with the underlying noise-free generating model, does in fact get better as 1/sort(N). In this simulation, the RMS prediction error from the noisy observed data remains close to $\sigma = 1$, while the model's prediction of the true underlying relationship has an RMS error of about 0.01 with 10,000 samples.

So the empirical model predictions actually are much more accurate than a comparison between the predicted and observed data show. The law of large numbers applies here, so the model prediction error of Neural Networks and PLS models really does decrease as 1/sqrt(N), as in standard statistical model estimation.

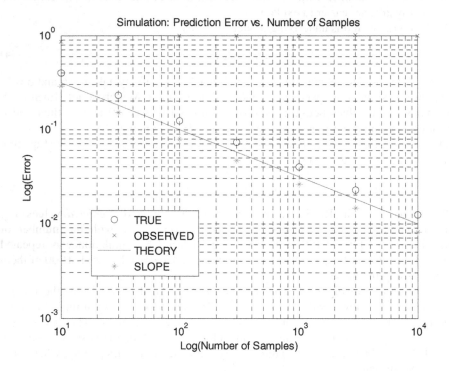

Fig. 4. Summary of Numerical Simulations of Model Accuracy, on a Log-Log Plot

5 Synergies to Increase the Use of Neural Networks in Industry

As discussed in Section 2 above, the experience at DuPont has shown Neural Networks are best used as an Empirical Process Modeling tool, in conjunction with traditional statistical analysis and methods from Chemometrics. In light of this, the

Neural Network practitioner in industry (as well as in research) should not be isolated from their colleagues who are applied statisticians and chemometricians.

Whatever success achieved in introducing Neural Networks at DuPont [9] was catalyzed by neural net modelers interacting with these other groups. As early as 1990, when few statisticians would deign to consider Neural Networks, a close working relationship was established with the Applied Statistics group. Industrial statisticians are very appropriate Neural Network practitioners, because of their understanding of nonlinear function fitting and their appreciation for the effects of uncertainty. The neural network and statistics groups had cross-training sessions about Neural Networks, Exploratory Data Analysis, and Design of Experiments. The internally developed Neural Network software was enhanced by adding Analysis of Variance tables, incorporating Degrees of Freedom thinking into the r^2 calculations, and surface and contour plots of results. Our group presented one of the first papers on Neural Networks (for process modeling and control) at an American Statistical Association in 1992 [10]. Two statisticians reported on different kinds of cross-validation for Neural Networks at the same conference the following year [11].

About the same time, Mike Piovoso introduced us to chemometrics and began our interactions with the process control community. We learned how to interpret the Hidden Layer outputs using Principal Component Analysis and recognized the similarity between the structure of a Back Propagation Network (with one hidden layer) and Partial Least Squares (PLS). Effectively, PLS is a BPN *without the squashing function*. PLS software packages showed us the utility of the Modeled versus Observed plot (Goodness of Fit), and the graphical presentation in PLS's Variable Importance Plot guided our Sensitivity Analysis plot. Interactions with process control engineers prompted the early adoption of Neural Networks as *Virtual Sensors* for model-based control [12]. Neural Networks were subsequently integrated by the major process control vendors into their software.

More importantly than just improving our Neural Network methodology, the contacts with the statisticians and process control engineers gave a wide variety of novel and important applications.

6 Summary

The primary "value add" of Neural Networks is that they are extremely good at extracting complex, nonlinear interactions between process input and outputs, particularly when there are enough observations to fit a model with high signal to noise. There are many and varied applications for that kind of tool in industry [13], [14], [15], [16].

Acknowledgments. DuPont colleagues who have contributed significantly to our neural network technology and applications include Tom Lynch, Alicia Walsh, Dewey Donovan, John van Stekelenborg, Vivek Bhide, and Tony Liu. Supporters in the businesses include Dave Alman, Allan Rodrigues, Mahnaz Mohammadi, Tariq Andrea, John Kinney, Arun Aneja, and John Locke. I learned about Chemometrics from Mike Piovoso, Barry Wise (Eigenvector), and John MacGregor (Prosensus).

References

1. Rumelhart, D.E., Hinton, G.E., Williams, R.J.: Learning Internal Representations by Error Propagation. In: Rumelhart, McClelland (eds.) Parallel Distributed Processing. Foundations, vol. 1, pp. 318–335. MIT Press, Cambridge (1986)
2. Hertz, J., Krough, A., Palmer, R.G.: Introduction to the Theory of Neural Computation. Addison-Wesley, New York (1991)
3. Software User Guide, PLS Toolbox for Matlab: Eigenvector Research, Inc., Wenatchee, Washington (2011), http://wiki.eigenvector.com
4. Ljung, L., Sjoberg, J.: A System Identification Perspective on Neural Nets. In: Kung, et al. (eds.) Neural Networks for Signal Processing II, pp. 423–435. IEEE, Piscataway (1992)
5. Bishop, C.M.: Neural Networks for Pattern Recognition. Clarendon Press, Oxford (1995)
6. Piovoso, M.J., Owens, A.J.: Sensor Data Analysis Using Artificial Neural Networks. In: Arkun, Ray (eds.) Chemical Process Control CPC IV, pp. 101–118. AIChE, New York (1991)
7. Owens, A.J.: Using Fundamental Knowledge to Guide Empirical Model Structure. In: International Conference on Engineering Applications of Neural Networks (EANN 2001), Cagliari (2001)
8. Owens, A.J.: Neural Network Based Product Formulation Models: Early Stopping Saves Training Time. In: International Conference on Engineering Applications of Neural Networks (EANN 2007), Stockholm (2007)
9. Owens, A.J.: Neural Network Based Empirical Modeling in the Chemical Industry. In: International Conference on Engineering Applications of Neural Networks (EANN 1998), Gibraltar (1998)
10. Owens, A.J.: Artificial Neural Networks for Process Modeling and Control. In: Proceedings of the Annual Joint Statistical Meetings of the American Statistical Association, Boston (1992)
11. Bhide, V., Banerjee, A.: Bootstrap Estimates in Neural Network Models. In: Proceedings of the Annual Joint Statistical Meetings of the American Statistical Association, San Francisco (1993)
12. Schnelle Jr., P.D., Fletcher, J.A.: Using Neural Network Based Process Modeling in Process Control. In: Proceedings of the I.S.A./90 International Conference and Exhibition (1990)
13. Hu, Y.H., Hwang, J.-N. (eds.): Handbook of Neural Network Signal Processing. CRC Press, Boca Raton (2001)
14. Badiru, A.B., Cheung, J.Y.: Fuzzy Engineering Expert Systems with Neural Network Applications. Wiley-Interscience, New York (2002)
15. MacKay, D.J.C.: Information Theory, Inference and Learning Algorithms. Cambridge University Press, Cambridge (2003)
16. Suzuki, K. (ed.): Artificial Neural Networks - Methodological Advances and Biomedical Applications. InTech, Rijeka (2011)

Incremental – Adaptive – Knowledge Based – Learning for Informative Rules Extraction in Classification Analysis of aGvHD

Maurizio Fiasché[1,2], Anju Verma[2], Maria Cuzzola[2], Francesco C. Morabito[1], and Giuseppe Irrera[2]

[1] DIMET, University "Mediterranea" of Reggio Calabria, Italy
[2] Transplant Regional Center of Stem Cells and Cellular Therapy, "A. Neri", Reggio Calabria, Italy
maurizio.fiasche@unirc.it

Abstract. Acute graft-versus-host disease (aGvHD) is a serious systemic complication of allogeneic hematopoietic stem cell transplantation (HSCT) that occurs when alloreactive donor-derived T cells recognize host-recipient antigens as foreign. The early events leading to GvHD seem to occur very soon, presumably within hours from the graft infusion. Therefore, when the first signs of aGvHD clinically manifest, the disease has been ongoing for several days at the cellular level, and the inflammatory cytokine cascade is fully activated. So, it comes as no surprise that to identify biomarker signatures for approaching this very complex task is a critical issue. In the past, we have already approached it through joint molecular and computational analyses of gene expression data proposing a computational framework for this disease. Notwithstanding this, there aren't in literature quantitative measurements able to identify patterns or rules from these biomarkers or from aGvHD data, thus this is the first work about the issue. In this paper first we have applied different feature selection techniques, combined with different classifiers to detect the aGvHD at onset of clinical signs, then we have focused on the aGvHD scenario and in the knowledge discovery issue of the classification techniques used in the computational framework.

Keywords: EFuNN, gene selection, GvHD, machine learning, wrapper.

1 Introduction

Recently, there have been major advances in our knowledge of basic immunology. In parallel, although much of information has been obtained from preclinical models and far less from correlations with clinical observations or treatment, our awareness of the complexity of the pathophysiology of aGvHD is significantly increased [1].

At the same time, the interplay with bioinformatics, defined as the branch of information sciences for the analysis, modelling, simulation and knowledge discovery of biological phenomena, such as genetic processes, has stimulated synergistic research in many cross-disciplinary areas.

L. Iliadis and C. Jayne (Eds.): EANN/AIAI 2011, Part I, IFIP AICT 363, pp. 361–371, 2011.

Identifying a compact set of informative genes from microarray data (gene expression data) is critical in the construction of an efficient clinical decision support system. The potential applications of microarray technology are numerous and include identifying markers for classification, diagnosis, disease outcome prediction, target identification and therapeutic responsiveness [2]. Microarray analysis might help to identify unique markers (e.g. a set of gene) of clinical importance. Diagnosis and prediction of a biological state/disease is likely to be more accurate by identifying clusters of gene expression profiles (GEPs) performed by macroarray analysis. Based on a genetic profile, it is possible to set a diagnostic test, so a sample can be taken from a patient, the data related to the sample processed, and a profile related to the sample obtained [2]. This profile can be matched against existing gene profiles and based on similarity, it can be confirmed with a certain probability the presence or the risk for a disease. We apply this approach here to detect acute graft-versus-host disease (aGvHD) in allogeneic hematopoietic stem cell transplantation (HSCT), a curative therapy for several malignant and non malignant disorders. Acute GvHD remains the major complication and the principal cause of mortality and morbidity following HSCT [3]. At present, the diagnosis of aGvHD is merely based on clinical criteria and may be confirmed by biopsy of one of the 3 target organs (skin, gastrointestinal tract, or liver) [4]. There is no definitive diagnostic blood test for aGvHD. We have already published a review paper about classification and predictive strategies for validating a novel and not invasive method to confirm the diagnosis of aGvHD in HSCT patients at onset of clinical symptoms [1]. In previous works we have employed global and local models [9][18] and obtained good results using personalized modelling for selecting genes and other important informative biomarkers from clinical, biological and genetic data collected [1][5]. In this paper we want to focus onto another aspect of aGvHD scenario analysis not still approached from anyone. Here we want to extract knowledge and rules from modelling of this disease, so we approached this issue with an incremental adaptive modelling with preliminaries but significant results.

The organization of the rest of this paper is as follows: section 2 explains the data analyzed; two feature selection techniques are applied in pre-processing step in section 3; section 4 describes results obtained with our incremental- adaptive-knowledge based- learning method; section 5 discusses the results of the diagnostic method and section 6 gives conclusions inferred with possible future applications.

2 Experimental Data

The goal of this study is to design a model to select a compact set of genes that can profile the pattern of objective microarray data.

For this purpose fifty-nine HSCT patients were enrolled in our study between March 2006 and July 2008 in Transplants Regional Center of Stem Cells and Cellular Therapy "A. Neri" Reggio Calabria, Italy, during a Governative Research Program of minister of the Health with the title: *"Project of Integrated Program: Allogeneic Hemopoietic Stem Cells Transplantation in Malignant Hemopathy and Solid Neoplasia Therapy - Predictive and prognostic value for graft vs. host disease of chimerism and gene expression"*. Because experimental design plays a crucial role in a successful biomarker search, the first step in our design was to choose the most informative specimens and achieve adequate matching between positive cases aGvHD (YES) and negative controls aGvHD (NO) to avoid bias. This goal is best achieved through a database containing high-quality samples linked to quality controlled clinical information. Patients with clinical signs of aGvHD (YES) were selected, and in more than 95% of them aGvHD was confirmed by biopsy including those with grade I. We used 25 samples from aGvHD (YES) patients that were taken at the time of diagnosis and we selected 60 samples from patients that didn't experienced aGvHD (NO). All together YES/NO patient groups comprised a validation set. Total RNA was extracted from whole peripheral blood samples using a RNA easy Mini Kit (Qiagen) according to the manufacturer's instructions. Reverse transcription of the purified RNA was performed using Superscript III Reverse Transcriptase (Invitrogen). A multigene expression assay to test occurrence of aGvHD were carried out with TaqMan® Low Density Array Fluidic (LDA-macroarray card) based on Applied Biosystems 7900HT comparative dd CT method, according to manufacturer's instructions. Expression of each gene was measured in triplicate and then normalized to the reference gene 18S mRNA, who was included in macroarray card. About the project of macroarray card, we selected 47 candidate genes from the published literature, genomic databases, pathway analysis. The 47 candidate genes were involved in immune network and inflammation pathogenesis.

3   Gene Selection Methods

The advent of microarray technology emphasized the problem to identify which genes are most important for diagnosing different diseases (e.g. cancer diagnosis) and prognosis task. Feature selection is the process of choosing the most appropriate features (variables) when creating a computational model [2][6]. Generally, most developed gene selection methods can be categorized into two groups: filter and wrapper methods. In this paper we consider two general approaches to feature subset selection, more specifically, wrapper and filter approaches, for gene selection.

Wrappers and filters differ in the way the feature subsets are evaluated. Filter approaches remove irrelevant features according to general characteristics of the data, measuring the intrinsic characteristic of genes. Wrapper approaches, by contrast, apply machine learning algorithms to feature subsets and use cross-validation to evaluate the score of feature subsets. In theory, wrappers should provide more accurate classification results than filters [6][7]. Wrappers use classifiers to estimate the usefulness of feature subsets.

The use of "tailor-made" feature subsets should provide better classification accuracy for the corresponding classifiers, since the features are selected according to their contribution to the classification accuracy of the classifiers. The disadvantage of the wrapper approach is its computational requirement when combined with sophisticated algorithms such as support vector machines.

As a filter approach, CFS was proposed by Hall [8][9]. The rationale behind this algorithm is "a good feature subset is one that contains features highly correlated with the class, yet uncorrelated with each other." It has been shown by Hall[8] and by some of the authors that CFS gave comparable results to the wrapper and executes many times faster [10]. It will be shown later in this paper that combining CFS with a suitable classifier, provides a good classification accuracy for diagnosis of aGvHD.

3.1 Gene Selection: CFS

Feature Selection is a technique used in machine learning of selecting a subset of relevant features to build robust learning models. The assumption here is that not all genes measured by a macroarray method are related to aGvHD classification. Some genes are irrelevant and some are redundant from the machine learning point of view [2], [11]. It is well-known that the inclusion of irrelevant and redundant information may harm performance of some machine learning algorithms. Feature subset selection can be seen as a search through the space of feature subsets. CFS evaluates a subset of features by considering the individual detector ability of each feature along with the degree of redundancy between them.

$$CFSs = \frac{k\bar{r}_{cf}}{\sqrt{k + k(k-1)\bar{r}_{ff}}}$$

(1)

Where:

- CFS_S is the score of a feature subset S containing k features,
- $\bar{r}_{cf}$ is the average feature to class correlation ($f \in S$),
- $\bar{r}_{ff}$ is the average feature to feature correlation.

The distinction between normal filter algorithms and CFS is that while normal filters provide scores for each feature independently, CFS presents a heuristic "merit" of a feature subset and reports the best subset it finds. To select the genes with CFS, we have:

a) Choose a search algorithm;
b) Perform the search, keeping track of the best subset encountered according to CFS_S,
c) Output the best subset encountered.

The search algorithm we used was the best-first with forward selection, which starts with the empty set of genes. The search for the best subset is based on the training data only. Once the best subset has been determined, and a classifier has been built from the training data (reduced to the best features found), the performance of that classifier is evaluated on the test data. The 13 genes selected by CFS are reported in Table 1. A leave-one-out cross validation procedure was performed to investigate the robustness of the feature selection procedures. In 29 runs, the subset of 13 genes was selected 28 times (96%) by CFS. Now it is possible to use a classifier to estimate the usefulness of feature subsets, and to extract rules describing knowledge about pattern disease.

3.2 Gene Selection: Wrapper Methods

While CFS assigns a score to subset of features, Wrapper approaches take biases of machine learning algorithms into account when selecting features. The wrapper method applies a machine learning algorithm for a feature subset selection and uses cross-validation to compute a score for them.   In general, filters are much faster than wrappers. However, as far as the final classification accuracy is concerned, *wrappers* normally provide better results. The general argument is that the classifier that will be built from the feature subset should provide a better estimate of accuracy than other methods. The main disadvantage of *wrapper* approaches is that during the feature selection process, the classifier must be repeatedly called to evaluate a subset.

To select the genes using a wrapper method, we have to:

(a)   Choose a machine learning algorithm to evaluate the score of a feature subset.
(b)   Choose a search algorithm.
(c)   Perform the search, keeping track of the best subset encountered.
(d)   Output the best subset encountered.

As a machine learning algorithm, here we used three classifier techniques: simple Bayesian classifier naïve Bayes, a SVM, and an Evolving Fuzzy Neural Network (EFUNN) as knowledge discovery connectionist approach [2]. The naïve Bayes classifier assumes that features are independent given the class. Its performance on data sets with redundant features can be improved by removing such features. A forward search strategy is normally used with naïve Bayes as it should immediately detect dependencies when harmful redundant features are added. SVMs use a kernel function to implicitly map data to a high dimensional space. Then, they construct the maximum margin hyperplane by solving an optimization problem on the training data. Sequential minimal optimization (SMO) [10] is used in this paper to train a SVM with a Linear Kernel after several test emplyed. SVMs have been shown to work well for high dimensional microarray data sets [11]. However, due to the high computational cost it is not very practical to use the wrapper method to select genes for SVMs. Also here the search algorithm was the best-first with forward selection, starting with the empty set of genes. We report here the accuracy of classifiers built from the best feature subset found during the search. The search for the best subset is based on the training data only. Once the best subset has been determined, and a classifier has been built from the training data (reduced to the best features found), the performance of that classifier is evaluated on the test data. The 5 Genes selected using the wrapper method are shown in table 1. Most of the genes selected are also similar to those of the 13 genes selected using the CFS method and the only two genes that are different are actually correlated to other genes from the set of 13 genes. A leave-one-out cross validation procedure was performed to investigate the robustness of the method over the training set: in 29 runs, the subset of 7 genes was selected 26 times (90%) by the naïve Bayes wrapper and the group of 5 genes, 29 times (100%) by the SMO. Section 5 has shown the performance of this technique estimated on the testing data.

4   Connectionist Model Proposed for Knowledge Discovery Using the Selected Gene Diagnostic Markers

EFuNNs are learning models that can learn in an incrementally adaptive mode any dataset, regardless of the problem (function approximation, time-series prediction, classification, etc.) in a supervised, unsupervised, or hybrid learning mode, subject to appropriate parameter values selected and a certain minimum number of examples presented. Some well-established Neural Networks (NNs) and Artificial Intelligence (AI) techniques have difficulties when applied to incrementally adaptive, knowledge-based learning, for example catastrophic forgetting [12], local minima problem, difficulties to extract rules [2][13], are typical problems in multilayer perceptrons (MLP) and in backpropagation learning algorithm, not being able to adapt to new data without retraining on old ones, and too long training when applied to large datasets. The radial basis function RBF neural networks require clustering to be performed first and then the backpropagation algorithm applied. They are not efficient for incrementally adaptive learning unless they are significantly modified. Many neurofuzzy systems, such as ANFIS [14], FuNN [15], and neofuzzy neuron [16] cannot update the learned rules through continuous training on additional data without suffering catastrophic forgetting. Several analysis and experiments [2] shows that the EFuNN evolving procedure leads to a similar local incrementally adaptive error of other techniques e.g. Resource Allocation Network (RAN) and its modifications, but EFuNNs allow for rules to be extracted and inserted at any time of the operation of the system thus providing knowledge about the problem and reflecting changes in its dynamics. In this respect the EFuNN is a flexible, incrementally adaptive, knowledge engineering model. One of the advantages of EFuNN is that rule nodes in EFuNN represent dynamic fuzzy-2 clusters. Despite the advantages of EFuNN, there are some difficulties when using them, the major is that there are several parameters that need to be optimised in an incrementally adaptive way. Such parameters are: error threshold Err; number, shape, and type of the membership functions; type of learning; aggregation threshold and number of iterations before aggregation, etc. A possible way for solving this problem is a genetic algorithm (GA) use, better a cGA more faster [17]. In the next future an interesting issue could be a study about performance of optimization approach for solving this and other disvantages.

5 Results

The dataset described in section 2 that consists of two classes, GvHD(Yes) and GvHD(No) (that is ~GvHD(Yes)) and a compact input space, has been used, the expression values of 47 genes has been obtained with the applied biosystem (see section 2). The whole dataset has been divided into training and testing dataset for validation of a classifier system. These two sets came from different patients in different period. A suitable subset of samples for biological peculiarities has been chosen as training data set. The training data set had 29 patient samples (13 aGvHD(Yes) and 16 aGvHD(No)). The test data set consisted of 30 patient samples (13 aGvHD(Yes) and 17 aGvHD(No)). The test set shows a higher heterogeneity with regard to tissue and age of patients making any classification more difficult.

The task is: (1) to find a set of genes distinguishing Yes and Not; (2) to construct a classifier based on these data; and (3) to find a gene profile for each classes. After having applied points 1 and 2 from the methodology above, different subset of genes has been selected. Several EFuNNs are evolved through the N-cross-validation technique (leave one-out method) on the 59 data samples (EFuNN parameters as well as are given in Table 2). In the case of data being made available continuously over time and fast adaptation on the new data needed to improve the model performance, online modelling techniques would be more appropriate, so that any new labelled data will be added to the EFuNN and the EFuNN will be used to predict the class of any new unlabelled data. This is an aim for future developments.

Different EFuNN were evolved with the use of different sets of genes as input variables. The question of which is the optimum number of genes for a particular task is a difficult one to answer. Table 3 shows an example of the extracted rules after all samples, each of them having only 13 genes filtered by CFS, are learned by the EFuNN. The rules are 'local' and each of them has the meaning of the dominant rule in a particular subcluster of each class from the input space. Each rule covers a cluster of samples that belong to a certain class. These samples are similar to a degree that is defined as the radius of the receptive field of the rule node representing the cluster. For example, Rule 1 from Table 3 shows that 7 samples of class 1 (GvHD YES) are similar in terms of having genes g1, g2 and g9 overexpressed, and at the same time genes g6 and g7 are underexpressed. One class may be represented by several rules, profiles, each of them covering a subgroup of similar samples. This can lead to a new investigation on why the subgroups are formed and why they have different profiles (rules), even being part of the same class (in this case for the four grading of aGvHD). The extracted rules for each class comprise a profile of this class, our next issue will be visualize this pattern in a significant way.

6 Biomedical Conclusions and Future Work

We examined the immune transcripts to study the applicability of gene expression profiling (macroarray) as a single assay in early diagnosis of aGvHD. Our interest was to select fewer number of molecular biomarkers from an initial gene panel and exploiting this to develop a fast, easy and non-invasive diagnostic test [1][5] [18], being able to extract rules and knowledge for modelling the disease. The proposed method provides a good overall accuracy to confirm aGvHD development in HSCT setting. From a biological point of view, the results are reliable. Others have reasoned that Th2 cell therapy could rapidly ameliorate severe aGvHD via IL-4 and IL-10 mediated mechanisms [19][20]. It is noteworthy that in our study a set of genes, indicated by computational analysis, included same mediators of Th2 response such as IL10, and signal transducer and activator of transcription 6, interleukin-4 induced (STAT6). All these were strongly down-regulated in aGvHD (YES) setting, suggesting absence of control mediated by Th2 cells. Therefore, we highlight the fact that defective expression of ICOS impaired the immune protective effectors during clinical aGvHD. This evidence is supported by a previous report about ICOS as regulatory molecule for T cell responses during aGvHD. It has been showed that ICOS signal inhibits aGvHD development mediated by CD8 positive effector cells in HSCT [20]. According to previous reports, mediators of apoptosis cells and dendritic cell activators were involved. In our study increased expression levels of CXCL10 and CCL7 were identify as informative biomarker of alloreactive disease. Altogether our results strongly outlined the importance and utility of non-invasive tool for aGvHD diagnosis based on GEP. We believe that to achieve an advantage from GEP performance, it is very important to know: a) the transcript levels of immune effector cells in early time post-engraftment in order to better understand polarization of Th2 cells; b) the CD8 positive cell action. As a clinical trial, tissue biopsies were performed to confirm the above diagnostic results. In conclusion, our models may prevent the need for an invasive procedure as already discussed in [1][5][9] and it is possible to extract knowledge and rules after features selection task with wrappers and filters combined with a suitable classifier. This study demonstrated, for the first time, that the proposed incremental- adaptive- knowledge based learning procedure used for integrating the framework tool for diagnosis of aGvHD [1][5][18] confirms a satisfactory 97% accuracy over independent test data set of HSCT population and return rules for individuating gene profiles for this complex disease. We plan to extend the system as a personalized model [18][21] including all clinical and genetic variables, testing with new data samples this method and for a larger group of patients to capture their peculiarity. Moreover a visualization technique for distinguishing different profiles needed and at last novel classifiers can be explored. The authors are engaged in this direction.

Table 1. The 13 genes selected from CFS with their names and meaning, the 7 genes selected through the wrapper- naïve Bayes method are marked with °, the 5 genes selected with SVM are marked with*

Gene Name	Official full name	Immune function
BCL2A1	BCL2-related protein A1	Anti- and pro-apoptotic regulator.
CASP1°*	Caspase 1, apoptosis-related cysteine peptidase	Central role in the execution-phase of cell apoptosis.
CCL7	chemokine (C-C motif) ligand 7	Substrate of matrix metalloproteinase 2
CD83	CD83 molecule	Dendritic cells regulation.
CXCL10°	chemokine (C-X-C motif) ligand 10	Pleiotropic effects, including stimulation of monocytes, natural killer and T-cell migration, and modulation of adhesion molecule expression.
EGR2°	Early growth response 2	transcription factor with three tandem C2H2-type zinc fingers.
FAS	TNF receptor superfamily, member 6)	Central role in the physiological regulation of programmed cell death.
ICOS°*	Inducible T-cell co-stimulator	Plays an important role in cell-cell signaling, immune responses, and regulation of cell proliferation.
IL4	Interleukin 4	Immune regulation.
IL10°*	Interleukin 10	Immune regulation.
SELP	selectin P	Correlation with endothelial cells.
SLPI°	Stomatin (EPB72)-like 1	Elemental activities such as catalysis.
STAT6	transducer and activator of transcription 6, interleukin-4 induced	Regulation of IL4- mediated biological responses.
Foxp-3 *	forkhead box P3	Regulatory T cells play important roles in the maintenance control of transplantation tolerance.
CD52 °*	CD52 antigen	B-cell activation.

Table 2. (a)EFuNN-1: Experimental results of wrapper with EFuNN as classifier and EFuNN-2: Experimental results of a CFS with EFuNN classifier. The parameter values and error results of N-cross-validation (leave-one-out method) EFuNN models for dataset described in section 2.(b)Experimental results of a CFS with EFuNN classifier and a wrapper method combined with SVM. The starting set has been divided in training set and test set, a leave one-out cross-validation has been calculated for the two subsets.

(a)

Model	Errthr	Rmax	Rule Nodes	Classification Accuracy – Training data	Classification Accuracy – Test data
EFuNN-1	0.9	0.4	6.3	97.4	97.0
EFuNN-2	0.9	0.5	4.0	95.0	97.2

(b)

Method	Training set	Test set
CFS-EFuNN	28(29)	29(30)
Wrapper-SVM	29(29)	29(30)
Wrapper-NaiveB.	26(29)	29(30)
Wrapper- EFuNN	28(29)	29(30)

Table 3. 7 samples of class 1 (GvHD YES) are similar in terms of having genes g1, g2 and g9 overexpressed, and at the same time genes g6 and g7 are underexpressed

Rule 1:
if [g1] is (1 0.8) & [g2] is (1 0.96) & [g6] is (2 0.7) & [g7] is (2 0.9) & [g9] is (1 0.89) receptive field = 0.1 (radius of cluster), then class 1, accomodated training samples = 7/30
Rule 4:
[g3] is (2 0.87) & [g5] is (1 0.83) & [g6] is (2 0.8) & [g7] is (1 0.9) & [g9] is (1 0.78) & [g11] is (2 0.95) receptive field = 0.102 (radius of cluster), then class 2, accomodated training samples = 9/30

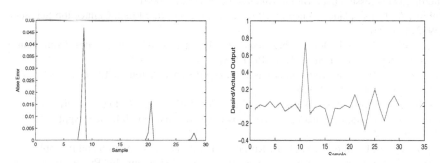

Fig. 1. Absolute error and desidere output plots for aGvHD data after filtering dataset with CFS. EFuNN-1 has been applied for obtaining these results.

Acknowledgments. This study has been supported by Italian Minister of the Health and from Calabria Region. Many thanks to doctors and biologist of CTMO and to Prof. Nik Kasabov for their support during this project.

References

1. Fiasché, M., Cuzzola, M., Irrera, G., Iacopino, P., Morabito, F.C.: Advances in Medical Decision Support Systems for Acute Graft-versus-Host Disease: Molecular and Computational Intelligence Joint Approaches. In: Frontiers in Biology. Higher Education Press and Springer -Verlag GmbH, doi:10.1007/s11515-011-1124-8
2. Kasabov, N.: Evolving Connectionist Systems: The Knowledge Engineering Approach, 2nd edn. Springer, London (2007)
3. Weisdorf, D.: Graft vs. Host disease: pathology, prophylaxis and therapy: GvHD overview. Best Pr. & Res. Cl. Haematology 21(2), 99–100 (2008)
4. Ferrara, J.L.: Advances in the clinical management of GvHD. Best Pr. & Res. Cl. Haematology 21(4), 677–682 (2008)
5. Fiasché, M., Cuzzola, M., Iacopino, P., Kasabov, N., Morabito, F.C.: Personalized Modeling based Gene Selection for acute GvHD Gene Expression Data Analysis: a Computational Framework Proposed. Australian Journal of Intelligent Information Processing Systems 12(4) (2010), Machine Learning Applications (Part II)
6. Langley, P.: Selection of relevant features in machine learning. In: Proceedings of AAAI Fall Symposium on Relevance, pp. 140–144 (1994)
7. Guyon, I., Elisseeff, A.: An introduction to variable and feature selection. The Journal of Machine Learning Research 3, 1157–1182 (2003)
8. Hall, M.A.: Correlation-based feature selection for machine learning. Ph.D. Thesis. Department of Computer Science, University of Waikato, New Zealand
9. Fiasché, M., Verma, A., Cuzzola, M., Iacopino, P., Kasabov, N., Morabito, F.C.: Discovering Diagnostic Gene Targets for Early Diagnosis of Acute GvHD Using Methods of Computational Intelligence on Gene Expression Data. Journal of Artificial Intelligence and Soft Computing Research 1(1), 81–89 (2011)
10. Platt, J.: Fast training of support vector machines using sequential minimal optimization. In: Advances in Kernel Methods–Support Vector Learning. MIT Press, Cambridge (1998)
11. Furey, T.S., Cristianini, N., Duffy, N., Bednarski, D.W., Schummer, M., Haussler, D.: Support vector machine classification and validation of cancer tissue samples using microarray expression data. Bioinformatics 16, 906–914 (2000)
12. Robins, A.: Consolidation in neural networks and the sleeping brain. Connection Sci. 8(2), 259–275 (1996)
13. Duch, W., Adamczak, R., Grabczewski, K.: Extraction of logical rules from neural networks. Neural Proc. Lett. 7, 211–219 (1998)
14. Jang, R.: ANFIS: Adaptive network based fuzzy inference system. IEEE Trans. Syst. Man Cybern. 23(3), 665–685 (1993)
15. Kasabov, N., Kim, J.S., Watts, M., Gray, A.: FuNN/2 - A fuzzy neural network architecture for adaptive learning and knowledge acquisition. Inf. Sci. Appl. 101(3-4), 155–175 (1997)
16. Yamakawa, T., Uchino, E., Miki, T., Kusanagi, H.: A neo fuzzy neuron and its application to system identification and prediction of the system behaviour. In: Proceedings of the Second International Conference on Fuzzy Logic & Neural Networks, Iizuka, Japan, pp. 477–483 (1992)
17. Harik, G.R., Lobo, F.G., Goldberg, D.E.: The compact genetic algorithm. IEEE Trans. Evolutionary Computation 3(4), 287–297 (1999)

18. Fiasché, M., Cuzzola, M., Fedele, R., Iacopino, P., Morabito, F.C.: Machine Learning and Personalized Modeling based Gene Selection for acute GvHD Gene Expression Data Analysis. In: Diamantaras, K., Duch, W., Iliadis, L.S. (eds.) ICANN 2010, Part I. LNCS, vol. 6352, pp. 217–223. Springer, Heidelberg (2010)
19. Foley Jason, J.E., Mariotti, J., Ryan, K., Eckhaus, M., Fowler, D.H.: The cell therapy of established acute graft-versus-host disease requires IL-4 and IL-10 and is abrogated by IL-2 or host-type antigen-presenting cells. Biology of Blood and Marrow Transplantation 14, 959–972 (2008)
20. Paczesny, S., Hanauer, D., Sun, Y., Reddy, P.: New perspectives on the biology of acute GvHD. Bone Marrow Transplantation, 45-1–45-11 (2010)
21. Kasabov, N.: Global, local and personalised modelling and profile discovery in Bioinformatics: An integrated approach. Pattern Recognition Letters 28(6), 673–685 (2007)

An Intelligent Approach to Detect Probe Request Attacks in IEEE 802.11 Networks

Deepthi N. Ratnayake[1], Hassan B. Kazemian[1], Syed A. Yusuf[1],
and Azween B. Abdullah[1,2]

[1] Faculty of Computing, London Metropolitan University,
166-220 Holloway Road, London N7 8DB London N7 8DB
{d.ratnayake,h.kazemian,s.yusuf}@londonmet.ac.uk
[2] Universiti Teknologi PETRONAS, Bandar Seri Iskandar, 31750 Tronoh, Perak, Malaysia
azweenabdullah@petronas.com.my

Abstract. In Wireless Local Area Networks (WLAN), beacon, probe request and response messages are unprotected, so the information is visible to sniffers. Probe requests can be sent by anyone with a legitimate Media Access Control (MAC) address, as association to the network is not required at this stage. Legitimate MAC addresses can be easily spoofed to bypass Access Point (AP) access lists. Attackers take advantage of these vulnerabilities and send a flood of probe request frames which can lead to a Denial-of-Service (DoS) to legitimate stations. This paper discusses an intelligent approach to recognise probe request attacks in WLANs. The research investigates and analyses WLAN traffic captured on a home wireless network, and uses supervised feedforward neural network with 4 input neurons, 2 hidden layers and an output neuron to determine the results. The computer simulation results demonstrate that this approach improves detection of MAC spoofing and probe request attacks considerably.

Keywords: IEEE 802.11, DoS Attacks, Probe Request Flooding Attacks, Wireless. Supervised Feedforward Neural Network.

1 Introduction

The wireless technology today comes in several forms and in a multitude of solutions to provide availability and security. However, many risks remain unmanaged [1]. IEEE 802.11 is a set of standards specified by Institute of Electrical and Electronic Engineers (IEEE) for WLAN computer communication. IEEE 802.11 was first created in 1997 and improved over the years. IEEE 802.11w-2009 is currently the most powerful security standard available for WLAN users [2,3]. The MAC layer of the 802.11 protocol is based on the exchange of request/response messages i.e. each request message sent by a station (STA) must be responded with a response message sent by the AP. Probe Request Flood (PRF) attacks are designed to take advantage of this request and respond design flaw [4]. Flooding attacks cause serious performance degradation or prevent legitimate users from accessing network resources such as the bandwidth, access points, gateways, servers and target user systems. This vulnerability is increased

L. Iliadis and C. Jayne (Eds.): EANN/AIAI 2011, Part I, IFIP AICT 363, pp. 372–381, 2011.

due to the unprotected beacon or probe request and probe response frames which can be read by anyone to learn about the network.

We learned that before an attack, the attacker actively or passively monitors the network to learn vital network information. MAC address spoofing is the next step. Therefore, we recognised that any Wireless Intrusion Detection System (WIDS) should address these initial stages of an attack before moving on to more advance steps. After analysing the previous research work and the progress of IEEE 802.11 sub committees, it is understood that there is a gap of knowledge to develop a realistic WIDS that could detect MAC spoofing and probe request attacks on IEEE 802.11 networks. This research analyses real-time traffic captured on a wireless home network. This research works with real WLAN traffic as opposed to data from a sample database or synthetic traffic generated by a test bed used in many studies. Our work aims to detect an attack during an early stage of the communication. During our initial experiments, we observed that WLAN traffic pattern is usually unpredictable and also depends on the usage, operating system and applications of the user. Further, the monitoring STA can miss many frames due to its traffic load, or receive them out of order due to packet delay, packet jitter and lost packet or prioritisation services of network traffic such as Quality of Service (QoS)[5]. These inherent complexities and unpredictable nature of data made this research a good candidate for Artificial Neural Networks (ANN). Additionally, WLAN traffic and parallel processing nature of ANNs cause a considerable amount of overhead on the monitoring STA and therefore, can affect the performance of the monitoring STA. This research analyses only 4 parameters to detect an attack. This considerably reduces the overhead of the monitoring machine whilst producing the results expected.

The rest of the paper is organized as follows. Section 2 discusses the related work. Section 3 discusses the IEEE 802.11 security policy agreement and the basic concepts behind probe request attacks. Section 4 explains the philosophy behind our research. Section 5 presents WLAN environment of the experiment and computer simulation prototype and Section 6 discusses simulation results.

2 Related Work

Intrusion detection is to identify an unauthorised user trying to gain access, or has already gained access or compromised the computer network [6]. Many researchers have worked in this area looking for possible solutions. For example, [7] presents a detailed review of most popular non-intelligent methods of detecting and preventing DoS attacks in MAC layer and [8] evaluates some commonly used non-cryptographic methods of MAC spoof detection in WLANs. They identify use of cryptography, sequence number analysis, Time Difference Of Arrivals (TDOA), decreasing re-try limits, and Network Interface Card (NIC) profiling: Signal Strength Indicator (SSI) and Radio Frequency (RF) finger printing for detecting and preventing PRF attacks. Cryptography may be the most reliable solution. But, it is expensive, may require a protocol repair and can easily be a DoS target itself. [9] proposes security improvement in management frames by a shared key. However, this solution requires a change in the wireless card. A hardware upgrade is an unrealistic solution considering the number of wireless cards that will have to change.

Detection of spoofed frames plays a major role in detection of other attacks including probe request attacks. [10] introduces an algorithm to detect MAC spoofing based on sequence number gaps by leveraging the structure and behaviour of the sequence number field. [11] introduces time difference between consecutive frames and a sliding window of received signal strengths for spoof detection. [12] utilise a combination of window of sequence numbers and traffic inter-arrival statistics (FRR - Forge Resistance Relationship Method) to detect spoofing and anomalous traffic in wireless networks. [1] argue that these solutions work only when both the attacker and victim are transmitting and, also may be difficult to differentiate an attacker from a victim, when the victim is offline. They improved [12] solution by utilising transmission rate and by sending a probe request after every 9th frame. However, this solution generates an additional overhead on the network. [13] proposes detecting identity-based attacks in wireless networks using only signal prints. However, this solution is ineffective when there is a single AP serving all STAs. Further, RSSI measurements by itself may not distinguish a genuine STA from an adversary if they are too close to each other [7]. Above discussed non-intelligent WIDS methods use statistical, rule based, expert knowledge or pattern recognition approaches on known vulnerabilities or attack signatures and therefore consumes time, lacks flexibility to adaptation to environmental changes, and eventually becomes out-dated.

[14] presents a comparative analysis of IDS approaches. ANN is currently the most established approach for IDS considering the unpredictable behaviour of WLAN networks and attacks. Most intelligent IDSs for TCP/IP networks use Self Organizing Maps, Artificial Immune systems, Fuzzy Logic and Neural models, Adaptive Neural-Fuzzy Inference Systems and hybrid models. [15] introduces a prototype of a stand-alone WID and response system based on NetStumbler attacks. This solution detects attacks only by calculating probe requests per second. It also responds to the attacker with a DoS attack in return, which can lead to attacking a own user. [16] presents a corporative detection architecture based on intelligent agents with power of auto-learning, incorporating NN and Fuzzy logics. This large and complex system was never implemented according to our knowledge. [17] also propose a distributed and collaborative architecture using IDS agents but falls short of an implementation. [18] presents a multi-agent architecture using fuzzy decision support system which performs anomaly detection for ad-hoc and infra-structure networks. This solution does real time monitoring, but the solution is based only on sequence number anomalies. [19] discusses a range of research architectures and open source and commercially available WIDSs. They propose a comparatively complex architecture for WIDS using ANNs based on real time data and tests virtual carrier sense, association flood, and de-authentication attacks. The solution focuses on the behaviour of the complete network, which can be challenging in a real network which has larger number of users.

The research observed that many of these solutions are designed based on non-real data sets and/or also identifies intrusive behaviours based on the exploration of known vulnerabilities [20,21,22]. Further, it is observed that some of these solutions are extremely complex and are simulated and tested without considering the practical implementation and computing power they may require. Therefore, these solutions are limited for academic research world as implementing is too complex or expensive.

3 WLAN Security and Probe Request Attacks

Fig. 1 shows the security policy agreement phase of IEEE 2007. A STA seeking to connect to a WLAN has a choice of passive scan or active scan. In passive scan, STA listens to successive channels, waiting to hear a beacon frame from an AP, while in an active scan, the STA broadcasts a probe request message on every channel its physical layer supports, until the STA finds an AP. These frames are unprotected and information passed between the frames can be read using freely available software like Wireshark [23,24,25].

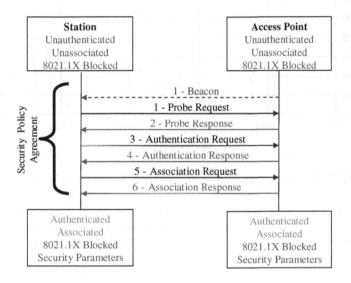

Fig. 1. Security policy agreement phase of IEEE 2007 [24]

APs keep a list of legitimate MAC addresses that can access its services to prevent unauthorised access. However, MAC addresses can easily be spoofed using ifconfig, macchanger (Linux) or using SMAC2 (Windows) to pretend it is a legitimate STA. Association to a network is not required to probe and receive a response. Hence, an adversary only requires a legitimate MAC address to send Probe Requests. Usually, probing is the initial phase of any other attack in computer networks [19].

4 The Philosophy

[24] defines three frame types namely Management, Control and Data. The management frames establish and maintain communications. The control frames help in the delivery of data. The data frames encapsulate the Open System Interconnection (OSI) network layer packets. Each frame consists of a MAC header, frame body and a Frame Check Sequence (FCS). MAC header comprises of frame control, duration, address, sequence control information, and for QoS data frames, QoS control

information. Frame body contains information specific to the frame type and subtype. FCS contains an IEEE 32-bit Cyclic Redundancy Check (CRC).

The below is a simple analysis of data captured during an attack on a test-bed.

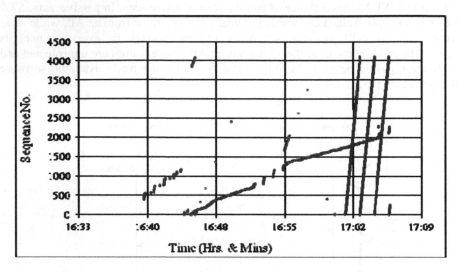

Fig. 2. Analysis of sequence numbers generated by a single MAC address

Sequence number of the MAC frame is a 12-bit counter that starts from 0 when a NIC starts or resets, and wraps on 4095 at the overflow. Theoretically, a NIC can generate only one set of sequence numbers at a time [24]. However, Fig. 2 shows

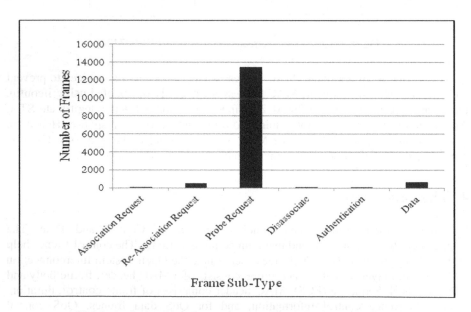

Fig. 3. Analysis of frame types generated by a single MAC address

several parallel sequence number patterns generated from the same MAC address. The straight sharp lines (starting at 17.01) were formed due to a high frequency of sequence numbers generated during a spoofed attack whilst other fluctuating and scattered lines are from the genuine user (16.39- 17.08). These parallel sequence number patterns may have generated due to QoS or packet delays [5].

Frame sub-type of the MAC frame identifies the type of the data frame [24]. Fig. 3 illustrates a high occurrence of probe request frames which complements the attack identified by the sequence number analysis in Fig. 2. Spoofed attacker cannot associate with the network without knowing the network key. Hence, other frame-sub-types have a lower frequency.

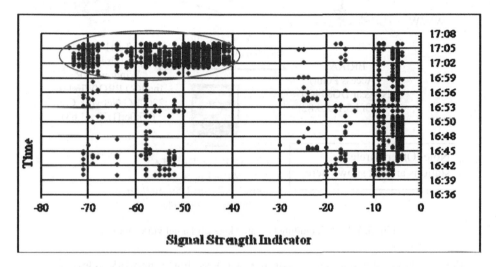

Fig. 4. Analysis of SSIs of frames received from a single MAC address

SSI of a frame captured by Wireshark provides an indication of received transmission power of a NIC, which also gives an indication of the location [8]. Therefore, SSI patterns are useful in detecting spoofed attacks. In Fig. 4, from 16.36-17.00, shows the SSI pattern generated by the genuine user. Unusual SSI patterns were generated during the spoofed attack (from 17.01 to 17.08).

The delta time value of a Wireshark captured frame indicates the time since the previous packet was captured. This is also useful in detecting attacks, as it gives an indication of the server response time, network round-trip time, and other delays.

Analysing frames of a WLAN test bed manually or statistically and detecting probing attacks are possible due to its controlled nature. However, a WIDS should be able to capture and analyse frames, and detect attacks automatically in a live environment that is unpredictable by nature. Therefore, after considering different models and their possible realistic and efficient application on detection of probe request attacks, the research utilised a supervised feed-forward NN architecture with 4 input neurons, 2 hidden layers with 20 sigmoid hidden neurons and an output layer with one linear output neuron which classify genuine frames from rogue frames.

5   WLAN Environment and Computer Simulation Prototype

This research designed to capture delta time value, sequence number, received signal strength and frame sub-type of the packets transmitted between an AP, users, and attackers of a wireless home network with 8 user stations.

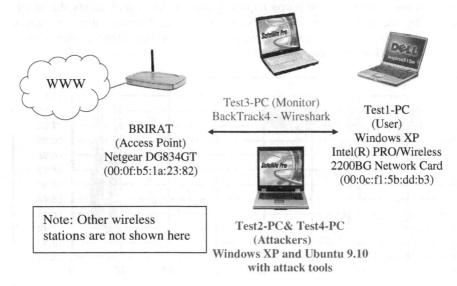

Test3-PC (Monitor)
BackTrack4 - Wireshark

Test1-PC
(User)
Windows XP
Intel(R) PRO/Wireless
2200BG Network Card
(00:0c:f1:5b:dd:b3)

WWW

BRIRAT
(Access Point)
Netgear DG834GT
(00:0f:b5:1a:23:82)

Note: Other wireless
stations are not shown here

Test2-PC& Test4-PC
(Attackers)
Windows XP and Ubuntu 9.10
with attack tools

Fig. 5. WLAN including two attackers and a network monitor

Fig. 5 shows the components of the wireless home network relevant to the research. Wireshark network monitoring software was used for data capturing. Ifconfig and SMAC2 were used to change the MAC address of the attackers Test2-PC and Test4-PC. Test3-PC was kept on promiscuous mode. Monitoring was restricted to IEEE 802.11 WLAN channel number 11 - 2462 MHz due to heavy frame loss experienced when capturing on all channels. Therefore, monitoring statistics of the entire bandwidth for STA's behaviour on the entire bandwidth is unavailable.

Data capturing was performed for 75 minutes. User Test1-PC accessed internet to browse information, download software, watch a live TV channel, listen to a live radio channel and check/send emails. Attacker Test2-PC with its spoofed MAC address sent a flood of probe request frames to the AP. Both user and attacker performed start-up and shut down procedures, network scans, a network connect and disconnect procedures, and a NIC repair. The captured data set consisted of 190K frames. Frames generated from MAC address 00:0c:f1:5b: dd:b3 were filtered using to prepare a training sample and labelled manually as rouge or genuine.

The prototype to detect probe request attacks using neural networks is designed and trained using MATLAB. The training sample consisted of approximately 175K frames that were generated from MAC address 00:0c:f1:5b:dd:b3. This was filtered to obtain delta time, sequence number, SSI and frame sub- type of each frame and fed into 4 input neurons. This sample was randomly divided and 70% of the data was used to train the network. 15% each was used for validation and testing respectively.

The network is trained using Levenberg-Marquardt back propagation algorithm. The mean squared errors of training, validation and testing were 3.86409e-3, 3.75033e-3 and 3.67129e-3 respectively. Training, validating and testing were converged outstandingly resulting overall regression value 0.98043.

6 Simulation Results and Discussion

The trained NN was tested using pre-defined scenarios (Table 1). The results were generated based on 1000 frame samples. Target output of a user's frame considered as 1 (genuine), whilst a frame from an attacker considered as 0 (not-genuine).

Table 1. Summary of tests conducted

Capture Code	Test Scenario	Detection Rate (genuine/rouge)	False +ve rate	False -ve rate
Cap21	Unseen data set from user	96%	n/a	4%
Cap29	Unseen data set from user far away from AP	98%	n/a	2%
Cap24	Unseen data set from attacker using NetStumbler	99%	1%	n/a
Cap25	Unseen data set with attacker closer to user	75%	25%	n/a
Cap26	Unseen data set with attacker far away from user	100%	0%	n/a
Cap27	Unseen data set with new attacker (attacker 2) using NetStumbler	99%	1%	n/a
Cap28	Unseen data set with 2 attackers using NetStumbler	100%	0%	n/a
Cap30	Unseen data set with an attacker using a Linux network scanning tool	89%	11%	n/a

The results in Table 1 shows that the trained NN is capable of detecting known attacks 99%-100% (Cap24-28) and unknown attacks 89% (Cap30).The NN is also tested against the mobility effect of an attacker and a user. The user's mobility within the signal range does not affect the detection rate. However, when the attacker was at the same location as the user, the detection rate dropped to 75%. The detection rate of genuine frames of a user is about 98-100%. The detection rate drops when a genuine user scans a network excessively which generates unusually a large number of probe requests. This can occur due to an ill-configured WLAN card, a weak signal strength or user deliberately scanning the network which may require network administrator's attention. However, the issue can be solved within the system by setting a threshold value of warnings to be tolerated per second to suit to specific users or network.

The research considered choosing only few variables to develop a WIDS considering the large data volume and computation power required for real-world implementation. Sequence number and frame sub-type of a MAC frame and signal attributes SSI and delta time values are the 4 independent variables that were carefully chosen by the research based on the following situations; Manipulation of these variables is nearly impossible. Some argue that attackers use sequence number synchronising software to generate sequence number patterns to match with the user STA. However, the precision and effectiveness of this technique is doubtful as they cannot predict the behaviour of the user STA, whether the STA is starting or resetting its NIC card or transmitting data or idling. Some argue that SSI can be manipulated by attackers controlling the NIC signal strength, moving close to the user STA or signal strength can simply fluctuate due to environmental factors. This is also more of a theoretical issue than a practical one as the attacker cannot perform all these activities in a WLAN without exposing itself. Some argue that excessive probe request frames can be generated by an ill-configured STA or a genuine user repeatedly attempting to log-in to the AP. In this instance, network administrator can correct if there are any problems with a genuine STA or the user. This solution also works when the genuine user is offline. Finally, each of the individual variables has the potential of indicating the possibility of a spoofed STA and a probe request attack. However, it is expected to be supported by other 3 variables if there is an uncertainty.

7 Conclusion

This research has been carried out to identify an external attacker by analysing the traffic generated from a user MAC address in a single frequency band of a Wireless Local Area Network. A supervised feed-forward neural network with four distinct inputs, delta-time, sequence number, signal strength and frame sub-type is applied to identify and differentiate a genuine frame from a rogue frame. The experimental results show that the use of neural network can detect probe request attacks to a very high precision. This solution also allows WLAN users to be mobilised freely within the signal area. Further research will be conducted to enhance this experiment by monitoring the entire bandwidth, using coordinated multiple monitoring stations.

References

1. Goel, S., Kumar, S.: An Improved Method of Detecting Spoofed Attack in Wireless LAN. In: 1st International NETCOM, pp. 104–108 (2009)
2. Sood, K., Eszenyi, M.: Discover how using the IEEE standards approach plugs vulnerabilities and thwarts attacks (2008), http://software.intel.com/en-us/articles/secure-management-of-ieee-80211-wireless-lans/
3. IEEE: IEEE Std 802.11w, pp. C1-91 (2009)
4. Bernaschi, N., Ferreri, M., Valcamonici, L.: Access points vulnerabilities to DoS attacks in 802.11 networks. Wireless Networks 14(2), 159–169 (2008)
5. Rumín, A.C., Guy, C.: VoIP over WLAN 802.11b simulations for infrastructure and ad-hoc networks. In: Proceedings LCS 2006, pp. 61–64 (2006)
6. Karygiannis, T., Owens, L.: Wireless network security, 802.11, bluetooth and handheld devices: recommendations of the national institute of standards and technology, NIST Special Publication 800-48 (2002), http://www.itsec.gov.cn/webportal/download/74.pdf
7. Bicakci, K., Tavli, B.: Denial-of-Service attacks and countermeasures in IEEE 802.11 wireless networks. Computer Standards and Interfaces 31(5), 931–941 (2009)

8. Bansal, R., Tiwari, S., Bansal, D.: Non-cryptographic methods of MAC spoof detection in wireless LAN. In: IEEE ICON 2008, pp. 1–6 (2008)
9. Malekzadeh, M., Ghani, A.A.A., Desa, J., Subramaniam, S.: Security improvement for management frames in IEEE 802.11 wireless networks. IJCSNS 7(6) (2007)
10. Guo, F., Chiueh, T.: Sequence Number-Based MAC Address Spoof Detection. In: Valdes, A., Zamboni, D. (eds.) RAID 2005. LNCS, vol. 3858, pp. 309–329. Springer, Heidelberg (2006)
11. Madory, D.: New Methods of Spoof Detection in 802.11b Wireless Networking (2006), http://www.ists.dartmouth.edu/library/195.pdf
12. Li, Q., Trappe, W.: Detecting Spoofing and Anomalous Traffic in Wireless Networks via Forge-Resistant Relationships. IEEE Transactions on Information Forensics and Security 2(4), 793–808 (2007)
13. Faria, D.B., Cheriton, D.R.: Detecting identity-based attacks in wireless networks using signal prints. In: Proceedings of the 5th ACM Workshop on Wireless Security (2006)
14. Ahmad, I., Abdullah, A.B., Alghamdi, A.S.: Comparative Analysis of Intrusion Detection Approaches. In: UKSim, pp. 586–591 (2010)
15. Lim, Y.-X., Yer, T.S., Levine, J., Owen, H.L.: Wireless intrusion detection and response. In: IEEE SIA Workshop, Man and Cybernetics Society, pp. 68–75 (2003)
16. Pleskonjic, D.: Wireless Intrusion Detection Systems (WIDS). In: 19th Annual Computer Security Applications Conference (2003)
17. Yang, H., Xie, L., Sun, J.: Intrusion detection solution to WLANs. In: Proceedings of the IEEE 6th Circuits and Systems Symposium on Emerging Technologies: Frontiers of Mobile and Wireless Communication, vol. 2, pp. 553–556 (2004)
18. Dasgupta, D., Gomez, J., Gonzalez, F., Kaniganti, M., Yallapu, K., Yarramsetti, R.: MMDS: Multilevel Monitoring and Detection System. In: Proceedings of the 15 the Annual Computer Security Incident Handling Conference, Ottawa, Canada, pp. 22–27 (2003)
19. Ataide, R.L.D.R., Abdelouahab, Z.: An Architecture for Wireless Intrusion Detection Systems Using Artificial Neural Networks. In: Novel Algorithms and Techniques in Telecommunications and Networking, pp. 355–360. Springer, Netherlands (2010)
20. Chavan, S., Shah, K., Dave, N., Mukherjee, S., Abraham, A., Sanyal, S.: Adaptive neuro-fuzzy intrusion detection systems. In: Proceedings of ITCC, vol. 1, pp. 70–74 (2004)
21. Toosi, A.N., Kahani, M.: A Neuro-Fuzzy Classifier for Intrusion Detection Systems, CSICC (2006), http://profdoc.um.ac.ir/articles/a/15.pdf
22. Ahmad, I., Abdullah, A.B., Alghamdi, A.S.: Application of artificial neural network in detection of DOS attacks. In: Proceedings of the 2nd International Conference on SIN (2009)
23. He, C., Mitchell, J.C.: Security analysis and improvements for IEEE 802.11i. In: Proc. of the 12th Annual Network and Distributed System Security Symp., pp. 90–110 (2005)
24. IEEE: IEEE Std 802.11-2007, pp. C1-1184 (2007)
25. Ahmad, I., Abdullah, A.B., Alghamdi, A.S.: Application of artificial neural network in detection of probing attacks. In: IEEE Symp. on ISIEA, vol. 2, pp. 557–562 (2009)

An Intelligent Keyboard Framework for Improving Disabled People Computer Accessibility

Karim Ouazzane, Jun Li, and Hassan B. Kazemian

T10-03, Tower Building, London Metropolitan University,
166-220 Holloway Road, London, UK N7 8DB
{k.ouazzane,jul029,h.kazemian}@londonmet.ac.uk

Abstract. Computer text entry may be full of noises – for example, computer keyboard users inevitably make typing mistakes and their typing stream implies all users' self rectification actions. These may produce a great negative influence on the accessibility and usability of applications. This research develops an original Intelligent Keyboard hybrid framework, which can be used to analyze users' typing stream, and accordingly correct typing mistakes and predict users typing intention. An extendable Focused Time-Delay Neural Network (FTDNN) n-gram prediction algorithm is developed to learn from the users' typing history and produce text entry prediction and correction based on historical typing data. The results show that FTDNN is an efficient tool to model typing stream. Also, the computer simulation results demonstrate that the proposed framework performs better than using the conventional keyboard.

Keywords: Focused Time-Delay Neural Network, Intelligent Keyboard Hybrid Framework.

1 Introduction

It is inevitable that users will make typing mistakes, which is particularly the case for disabled users. These are different kinds of mistakes such as spelling errors and adjacent key press errors etc. [1] [2]. A series of research based on words vocabulary which apply both, neural network and language modeling have been carried out; Bengio and Ducharme [3] suggested a model using neural network probabilistic language modeling to learn distributed representation for words that allow each training sentence to inform the model about exponential number of semantically neighboring sentences. Schwenk and Gauvain [4] addressed a related problem further by carrying out probability estimation in a continuous space and enabling a smooth interpolation of the probabilities. However, due to the curse of dimensionality in the discrete space representation, they still have to narrow the vocabulary by using a shortlist which damages the prediction accuracy and fail to learn a long-span language model with n >> 3 gram. An alternative way is to install filters which modify the control signals generated by the device. Such filters can have a significant effect on the speed and accuracy with which a device can be used. Attempts have also been made by IBM to devise intelligent mechanisms that could adjust the settings of the

L. Iliadis and C. Jayne (Eds.): EANN/AIAI 2011, Part I, IFIP AICT 363, pp. 382–391, 2011.

keyboard accessibility features by detecting the usage problems as introduced in Trewin and Pain [5].

Dasher [6] is an information-efficient text-entry interface, driven by natural continuous pointing gestures [7]. It is based on language model prediction, through which the space of interface is determined to each piece of text. It is useful to the users who operate a computer onehanded, by joystick, touch screen, trackball or mouse, which might be an inspiration for QWERTY keyboard [8] tools development. Although the Dasher project is a good step forward, it still has some limitations. For example, Dyslexia can cause significant problems in remembering even short sequences of numbers in the correct order. Those types of disability frequently cause typing mistakes, which haven't been well solved. ProtoType [9] is a piece of software used to type text into other programs such as a word processor based o lists of words, which includes word prediction, spelling correction and word banks. ProtoType is designed to improve spelling for people with dyslexia or spelling difficulties, but it is dysfunctional to correct the keystrokes mistakes made by most motor disabled people. Research works have been carried out to address this problem, these include Metaphone [10] and n-grams [11], each of them may have its unique features, but they all have limitations.

Intelligent models such as neural network models have been implemented in various directions, however, they are hardly seen to apply to noisy text entry processing such as user typing stream. Moreover, although efforts have been made in multiple directions such as language modeling, natural language processing and user interface design, those technologies, if used alone, will fail to meet the user's particular needs which have been presented above. It is also worth arguing that combination of models such as Jianhua & Graeme word prediction model [12] emphasizes excessively on providing a global method, and lack 'user-oriented' feature. Furthermore current models are short of self-adaptive ability (i.e. learning ability), and fail to fully recognize the right patterns from user's distinct performance.

Ouazzane et al. [1] presented a hybrid framework based on machine learning model to offer an efficient solution for people having difficulties using QWERTY keyboard; it integrates neural network, language model and natural language processing technologies, to provide users with two fundamental functions, namely, word prediction and typing correction. Also, Li et al. [13] combined distinct word correction algorithms, using neural network approach, to produce an optimal prediction. It was demonstrated that neural network, as a learning means, can provide an optimum solution through combining distinct algorithms in order to achieve a high ranking performance. Hence, the main purpose of this research is to develop an Intelligent Keyboard hybrid novel framework which is based on the combination of multiple technologies (i.e. neural network and language modeling) and therefore to put all merits of those distinct solutions. It is desirable to develop a solution that is evolutionary and adjustable, which can learn from users' past mistakes and then to predict and/or correct these mistakes. In order to achieve the text correction and prediction, in this investigation a Focused Time-Delay Neural Network (FTDNN) [14] is chosen, which can represent the unclear and complex relationship between current typed sequence and its precedent one. In this paper, the Intelligent Keyboard hybrid system's case study is developed and the conclusion of the work alongside future recommendations is provided at the end.

2 Intelligent Keyboard Hybrid Framework

As to cognitive tasks it is shown that rather than seek solutions based on the symbolic Artificial Intelligence, a more potentially useful approach is to build a structured connectionist model or a hybrid system. Then it is able to combine more functions for some specific purposes, which includes four fundamental elements, namely, Environment Analysis, Learning Elements, Knowledge Base and Performance element [15]. All of these units could be divided into more subdivisions to form a highly efficient hybrid system. Therefore, an Intelligent Keyboard (IK) hybrid system which combines neural network, statistics and natural language model together, is designed and intends to provide users with fundamental functions such as typing prediction and correction. User's typing data stream can be checked, rectified, and predicted in sequence by going through each unit following user's typing process. Through this way, the typing stream's noises are filtered significantly and the language interaction between a user and a computer becomes smoother. Multiple units and a database separated by a long-term memory and a short-term memory have been presented according to the technologies. The architecture is shown in Figure 1, which includes four processing units: Text prediction, Inference, Natural Language Processing and Error correction units; and two additional modules: User interface module and Noise process module to enable the interaction of the user with the outside environment (i.e., computer keyboard).

The two additional modules function as data pre-processing, post-processing and interaction interface. They correspond to machine learning model's Environment Element and part of Performance Element respectively. The Knowledge Base element is represented by Long-term Memory and Short-term Memory. The rules inferred from Inference Engine and some other facts such as user profile and frequently used texts, are saved in the Long-term Memory. Other facts such as recently used new words are stored in the Short-term Memory which will be transferred to the long-term memory if a certain threshold is reached. The framework is invoked by user's key strokes. As much of data stream typing could be un-preprocessed, incomplete and noisy, for example, a long key press generates more than one Window's message, the data stream needs to undergo Noises Processing module first. Through this module the input vectors are further exploited, which would include the key-up signals, key-down signals, the time difference between two consecutive strokes and so on. The definition of noises can be given according to the user profile. Subsequently, a representation vector which includes time stamp and Virtual Key Code (VKC) [16] message is chosen to be sent to the processing units, namely, Text Prediction unit and Error Correction unit. Both units process the vectors based on the association rules, dictionaries and some other facts retrieved from the memory.

Text prediction unit is composed of different algorithms developed based on different scientific methods such as statistics and phonemics while Error Correction unit is designed based on users' performance. Firstly, a spell checker function is used to detect if a mistake had occurred. In the case of no mistakes being traced, the unit processing is stopped and the result is passed on to Inference Engine. Otherwise, the function such as motor checker, to process motor disability errors, would be evoked if spell checker fails to present a result. These two units (i.e. Text Prediction unit and Error Correction unit) can process data stream simultaneously. The typing mistakes which are still under doubt are further checked by Natural Language Processing unit to check syntax and semantics' errors. Finally, the results are refurbished and shown to the user by User Interface unit.

The results (e.g. a list of words) generated from Text Prediction unit and Error Correction unit, which are usually more than one, are presented to Inference Engine unit. The Inference Engine unit ranks the results based on their probabilities to generate a word-list or directly presents a highest ranking presentation to the user. The user's feedback such as selections and correction actions is recorded by the inference algorithms (here is a neural network algorithm), and transferred to rules or rewards to be stored into the memory.

Shown as in Figure 1, an input of a sentence is a process passing through different structure status from letter, word to sentence, during which distinct units are evoked up according to the structure status' changes.

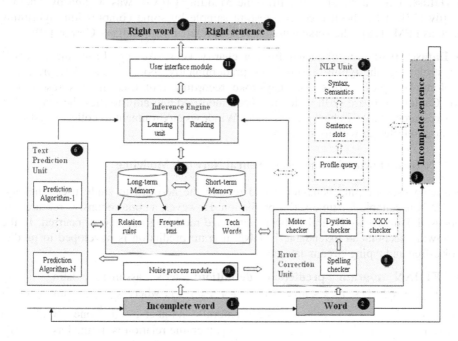

Fig. 1. The Architecture of Intelligent Keyboard; blue boxes and their connections represent the system's input and output process. The processing units from left to right, which has been marked as light yellow (or light grey in the case of black/white printing), are named as Text prediction unit (No. 6), Inference engine unit (No. 7), Error correction unit (No. 8), and Natural Language Processing (NLP) unit (No. 9). Data storage (No. 12) is divided into short-term memory and long-term memory, where the temporary and permanent information are stored. There are two additional modules: Noise process module (No. 10) and User interface module (No. 11), which are responsible for the interaction with the outer environment such as keyboard.

3   Intelligent Keyboard Framework Demonstration Using N-Gram Focused Time-Delay Neural Network Modeling

3.1   Modeling Data Sets

As illustrated above, IK framework provides two fundamental functions namely, prediction and correction. Typing stream prediction and correction can be achieved based on historical data by using neural networks through designing two models; or can be developed using a single neural network architecture if the correction can be considered as one specific case of prediction – the model produces the right symbol based on the inaccurate historical data. At this point a model based on Focused Time-Delay neural network modeling associated with different datasets is designed and implemented in the following sections. The used datasets are shown below;

♦ **Dataset one:** a novel – 'Far from the Madding Crowd' was written by Thomas Hardy [17]. It has been used as a testing sample by some compression algorithms such as PPM* [18]. The version used here is extracted from Calgary Corpus [19].

♦ **Dataset two:** it is extracted from a charity keystroke log. From the reflected keystroke log, the typing mistakes are predominantly about adjacent key press and prolong key press errors. The keystroke recording tool used in this research is KeyCapture software [20], which has been modified and adjusted for the purpose of this research. It runs in background under Windows environment to collect keystrokes without interfering with user's work.

3.2   N-Gram Focused Time-Delay Neural Network Modeling

Studying user's typing behavior would require the network to study user's history. FTDNN is suitable for time-series prediction. However, a comprehensive research on Focused Time-Delay Neural Network language modeling has never occurred. In the following sections an extendable FTDNN n-gram prediction is developed to predict noise-free and typing stream datasets.

♦ **FTDNN n-gram prediction definition:** let's assume existing string $S = \{s_1.s_i.s_j.s_k.s_m \mid i \leq j \leq k \leq m\}$ and $(j-i) = n, (k-j) = l$, where s_i, s_j, s_k, s_m are symbols and i, j, k, l, m, n are natural numbers, if one builds a relation $R_n = \{x, y \mid x = (s_i...s_j)_n \rightarrow y = (s_{j+1} -> s_k)_l\}$, then the relation is defined as n-gram's l – prediction; if one considers the special case $l = 1$, then the relation is called n-gram's one-prediction, or n-gram prediction for short. For example, given string $S=$ {*student*}, some 2-gram prediction cases are,

$$\begin{array}{ccc} \text{'st'} & \rightarrow & \text{'u'} \\ \text{'tu'} & \rightarrow & \text{'d' ...} \end{array}$$

♦ **Symbol-distribution definition:** Given a certain ranking level m and a symbol set $A = \{a,...,z, space\}$, one defines the n-gram Symbol-Distribution in ranking level m as $D_n^m = \{x, y \mid x_i -> y_i\}$, where $x_i \in$ symbol set A, and y_i is the level m Hitting Rate corresponding to each symbol.

Due to the system environment's limitations in this research, rather than adopting the whole dataset, a chunk of data ranging from zero to 100k is selected from the dataset one. The dataset is subsequently divided into training, validation and testing data. A symbol set with twenty-seven elements, A = {a...z, space}, is applied to simplify the dataset. The processing logic is shown as follows,

> *for each symbol* $S_i \in$ *context C, where* $C = \{s_1...s_n\}$
>
> *if* '*a*' $< S_i <$ '*z*' *then* write unary code to file
>
> *else if* '*A*' $< S_i <$ '*Z*' *then* convert to $\{a,...,z\}$ and write unary code to file
>
> *else* convert to blank and write unary code to file
> *end for*

```
%a b c d e f g h i j k l m n o p q r s t u v w x y z "
0 0 0 0 0 0 0 0 0 0 0 0 0 0 0 0 0 0 0 1 0 0 0 0 0 0 0          %'t'
0 0 0 0 0 0 0 1 0 0 0 0 0 0 0 0 0 0 0 0 0 0 0 0 0 0 0          %'h'
0 0 0 0 1 0 0 0 0 0 0 0 0 0 0 0 0 0 0 0 0 0 0 0 0 0 0          %'e'
```

First, all of the capital alphabets are converted to their corresponding lower case. The other symbols which do not belong to symbol set A are converted to space. Then each symbol is converted to a twenty seven length unary code. As shown in the example above, the word 'the' is successfully converted.

For this n-gram prediction, a three layer FTDNN network with 27 input neurons, 27 output neurons, extendible numbers of hidden layer neurons and extendible numbers of time delays is designed. Both input and output are encoded in unary code. A post processing function which ranks the twenty-seven output in a descending order has been used to produce the unary code results: the maximum value is converted into one and the rest of the values are converted into zeros.

3.3   Simulation with Plain Text Data Using Dataset One

In order to weight the computer simulation results, two concepts are introduced here, namely, Hitting Rate and First Three (FT) Hitting Rate. If given a testing metrics P, a target metrics T and a testing result metrics R with their numbers of lines and columns equal and expressed as n, m respectively, then the Hitting Rate is $HR = \{hr_i \mid hr_i = zeros(T - R_i)/n, i \in m\}$, where R_i is a vector of the ith Rank Conversion Value of R, and $zeros()$ is the function to compute the numbers of zero vectors included in the metrics. For instance, the second Hitting Rate is the second best option for the symbol prediction in all output neurons of FTDNN, while the third Hitting Rate is the third best option etc. Obviously the sum of all Hitting Rates is $HR = \sum_{i=1}^{k} HR_i = 100\%$.

During the FTDNN model training and testing using the dataset one, the numbers of grams – [1, 2, 3, 5, 7, 9, 11, 13] which are represented by time delays, and the numbers of hidden neurons – [1, 2, 3, 5, 7, 9, 15, 25, 50, 100] are cross-designed and implemented. Thereinto, as the gram reaches 11 and the number of hidden neurons reaches 100, or as the gram reaches 13 and the number of hidden neurons reaches 15 or onwards, the memory of current system is beyond its limit. Therefore, the computer simulation results are abandoned from G-11 & H-100 onwards.

In order to demonstrate the effect of different grams on the hitting rate, a type of plots is produced based on the same computer simulation results, as shown in Figure 2. It has [*1, 2, 3, 5, 7, 9, 11*] grams associated with various number of hidden neurons. It is evident that *2, 3 & 5*-gram give the best three First Hitting Rates while *1, 2 & 3*-gram give the best three FT Hitting Rates (Note: in a small margin *2*-gram gives the best FT hitting rates and *3*-gram gives the best First hitting rate).

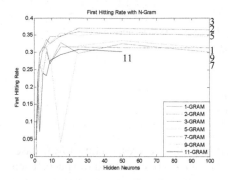 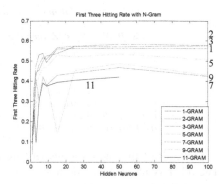

Fig. 2. N-gram First and First Three Hitting Rate curves; both have [1, 2, 3, 5, 7, 9, 11] grams associated with various number of hidden neurons

From both plots of Figure 2, the lower grams (*1, 2 & 3*) show a better convergence toward the maximum Hitting Rate (i.e. FT HR is around *56%*, First HR is around *33%*). Both figures illustrate that smaller Hitting Rates occur from *4*-gram onward. This proves that the more historical dataset input the more learning neural network space is needed, and the more training is needed toward convergence. Under the current training sample the results suggest that there is a best gram with certain number of hidden units to suit the prediction best. Beyond a critical point of prediction rate, further increase of gram or hidden unit doesn't help to achieve a better performance. Figure 2 also shows that the number of neurons in hidden layer affects the model's learning ability and Hitting Rate. For example, the number of neurons in hidden layer should not be too small to a structured symbol set {*a, ... , z, space*} distribution; otherwise, it would be difficult for neural network to reach a good hitting rate. The *11*-gram testing stops at fifty neurons; a *27-100-27* three layer FTDNN model has failed to complete the training process under the current system environment.

3.4 N-Gram Prediction with Typing Data Using Dataset Two

As analyzed, the designed *n*-gram FTDNN models have shown that it can be applied to data prediction with a high capability. Here a user's typing data stream (i.e. dataset two) is used to further test the model. The users typing history is analyzed by the model to predict user's next typing intention. As the typing data stream is a typical noisy dataset which includes user's typing mistakes as well as self correction strokes such as symbols 'backspace' and 'delete', the model will not only learn the habits of user using language but also learn the self-correction actions which occurs in typing stream. For example, a self-correction action from a wrong typing word '*desj*' to the right word '*desk*' can be broken down in a typing data stream as,

$$d => e => s => j => backspace => k \dots$$

This is a typical adjacent-key-press error usually made by some people with motor disability or Parkinson disease. Through training, the FTDNN model is able to learn 2-gram prediction rules between the predecessor and successor, for instance,

$$d \rightarrow e$$
$$e \rightarrow s$$

From the typing stream shown above, the model learns not only the existing noises such as 's' → 'j', but also the correction actions such as 'j' → 'backspace'. In practice, users just continue their typing without stop in spite of the mistakes, while the model should be able to correct the mistakes automatically or specify recommendations later on.

The collected data stream in dataset two is expressed in Virtual Key Codes [16]. In this research only editing virtual keys are adopted, other keys such as arrows are discarded. Then, the size of symbol set originally used by the model is extended into fifty three individual symbols, which apart from alphabet it also includes some other symbols such as,

VK_BACK	=>	*BACKSPACE key*
VK_RETURN	=>	*ENTER key*
VK_SHIFT	=>	*SHIFT key*
VK_DELETE	=>	*DEL key*

Based on the original design of FTDNN model, an extension to fifty-three units both at the input and output layer has been made. The dataset two has recorded both the key press 'down' status and 'up' status. Considering some disabled people specific typing behavior such as prolonged key press which would generate more 'down' keys corresponding to one 'up' keys, the keystrokes with 'down' status are selected by the pre-processing function for neural network training and testing. A comparison among the gram set [1, 3, 5, 7, 9] based on various numbers of hidden neurons - [3, 5, 7, 9, 15, 25, 50, 100] is shown in Figure 3. The first plot demonstrates a comparison of several grams' First Hitting Rates with an increase of hidden neurons. The second plot is a comparison of FT Hitting Rate between different grams.

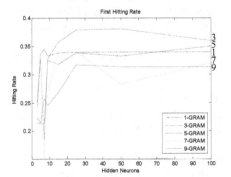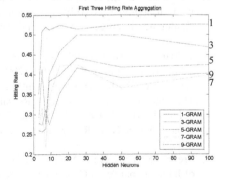

Fig. 3. [1, 3, 5, 7, 9] gram typing stream Hitting Rates; the first plot demonstrates a comparison of several grams' First Hitting Rates with an increase of hidden neurons. The second plot is a comparison of FT Hitting Rate between different grams.

Figure 3 shows that *1*-gram produces the maximum FT Hitting Rate of *53%* whereas *3*-gram with fifty hidden neurons produces the maximum First Hitting Rate of *38.1%*. Similar results have been obtained using dataset one; the lower grams (*1, 2 & 3*-gram) show a better solution using FTDNN model prediction under current circumstances. Both datasets demonstrate a highly accurate prediction rate (FT Hitting Rate, approximately *50%*) with FTDNN model.

4   Conclusion

This research work brings forth an original concept, Intelligent Keyboard hybrid framework for noisy language processing. It is developed as a hybrid solution based on FTDNN and n-gram technologies. Plain text dataset and user typing stream are tested in sequence based on extendable input and hidden neurons. Considering the user's typing history, a *38%* First Hitting Rate and a *53%* First Three Hitting Rate are obtained. The size of a training dataset, the occurrence of each symbol in a training dataset and the relationships among symbols of a training dataset all play an important role in the determination of a neural network language modeling prediction accuracy. The results further demonstrate that *1, 2 & 3*-gram generate better outcomes than other grams.

For future work, a distributed representation method to preprocess the typing symbols, where each symbol is represented by several features such as key distance, time stamp and symbols can be applied to the FTDNN models. In such a case, the prediction will not be solely based on the symbols themselves but also on related n-gram features.

Acknowledgments. The research is funded by Disability Essex [21] and Technology Strategy Board [22]. Thanks to Pete Collings for helpful advice and discussions.

References

1. Ouazzane, K., Li, J., Brouwer, M.: A hybrid framework towards the solution for people with disability effectively using computer keyboard. In: Proceedings of International Conference Intelligent Systems and Agents, Amsterdam, The Netherlands, pp. 209–212 (2008)
2. Trewin, S.: An invisible keyguard: Proceedings of ACM SIGACCESS ASSETS, Edinburgh, Scotland, pp. 143–149 (2002)
3. Bengio, Y., Ducharme, R., Vincent, P., Janvi, C.: A neural probabilistic language model. The Journal of Machine Learning Research 3, 1137–1155 (2003)
4. Schwenk, H., Gauvain, J.: Connectionist Language Modeling for Large Vocabulary Continuous Speech Recognition. In: Proceedings of ICASSP, Orlando, pp. 765–768 (2002)
5. Trewin, S., Pain, H.: A Model of Keyboard Configuration Requirements. In: Proceedings of International ACM Conference on Assistive Technologies, pp. 173–181 (1998)
6. The Dasher Project, Inference Group of Cambridge (November 14, 2007), http://www.inference.phy.cam.ac.uk/dasher/ (accessed March 03, 2008)

7. Ward, J., Blackwell, A., et al.: Dasher - a Data Entry Interface Using Continuous Gestures and Language Model, http://www.inference.phy.cam.ac.uk/djw30/papers/uist2000.html (accessed March 03, 2008)
8. QWERTY (November 13, 2009), http://en.wikipedia.org/wiki/QWERTY (accessed November 13, 2009)
9. Prototype, n.d., http://www.sensorysoftware.com/prototype.html (accessed March 03, 2008)
10. Metaphone, Wikipedia (October 18, 2008), http://en.wikipedia.org/wiki/Metaphone (accessed January 23, 2009)
11. N-gram, Wikipedia (November 26, 2008), http://en.wikipedia.org/wiki/N-gram (accessed January 23, 2009)
12. Li, J., Hirst, H.: Semantic Knowledge in Word Completion. In: Proceedings of the 7th International ACM SIGACCESS Conference on Computers and Accessibility, pp. 121–128 (2005)
13. Li, J., Ouazzane, K., Jing, Y., Kazemian, H., Boyd, R.: Evolutionary ranking on multiple word correction algorithms using neural network approach. In: Palmer-Brown, D., Draganova, C., Pimenidis, E., Mouratidis, H. (eds.) EANN 2009. Communications in Computer and Information Science, vol. 43, pp. 409–418. Springer, Heidelberg (2009)
14. Focused Time-Delay Neural Network (newfftd), The MathWorks, http://www.mathworks.com/access/helpdesk/help/toolbox/nnet/dynamic3.html (accessed January 23, 2009)
15. Haykin, S.: Neural Networks – A comprehensive Foundation, 2nd edn. Tom Robbins (1999)
16. Virtual key codes, http://api.farmanager.com/en/winapi/virtualkeycodes.html (accessed February 05, 2009)
17. Hardy, T.: Wikipedia (January 21, 2009), http://en.wikipedia.org/wiki/ (accessed January 22, 2009)
18. Cleary, J., Teahan, W.J., et al.: Unbounded length contexts for PPM. IEEE Computer Society Press, Los Alamitos (1995)
19. Bloom, C.: PPMZ–High Compression Markov Predictive Coder, http://www.cbloom.com/src/ppmz.html, ftp://ftp.cpsc.ucalgary.ca/pub/projects/text.compression.corpus/text.compression.corpus.tar.Z (accessed January 18, 2009)
20. Soukoreff, W., MacKenzie, S.: n.d. KeyCapture, http://dynamicnetservices.com/~will/academic/textinput/keycapture/ (accessed January 18, 2009)
21. Disability Essex, http://www.disabilityessex.org (accessed January 18, 2009)
22. Knowledge Transfer Partnership, http://www.ktponline.org.uk/ (accessed January 18, 2009)

Finding 3g Mobile Network Cells with Similar Radio Interface Quality Problems

Pekka Kumpulainen[1], Mika Särkioja[2], Mikko Kylväjä[3], and Kimmo Hätönen[4]

[1] Tampere University of Technology, Department of Automation Science and Engineering,
Korkeakoulunkatu 3, 33720 Tampere, Finland
[2] Nokia Siemens Networks, BSO OSS Radio Network Optimizer, Espoo, Finland
[3] Aditro Software, Espoo, Finland
[4] Nokia Siemens Networks, CTO Research, Espoo, Finland
pekka.kumpulainen@tut.fi,
{mika.1.sarkioja,kimmo.hatonen}@nsn.com,
mikko.kylvaja@aditro.com

Abstract. A mobile network provides a continuous stream of data describing the performance of its cells. Most of the data describes cells with acceptable performance. Detecting and analysing mobile network cells with quality problems from the data stream is a tedious and continuous problem for network operators. Anomaly detection can be used to identify cells, whose performance deviates from the average and which are potentially having some sub-optimal configuration or are in some error condition. In this paper we provide two methods to detect such anomalously behaving cells. The first method estimates the distance from a cell to an optimal state and the second one is based on detecting the support of the data distribution using One-Class Support Vector Machine (OC-SVM). We use the methods to analyse a data sample from a live 3G network and compare the analysis results. We also show how clustering of found anomalies can be used to find similarly behaving cells that can benefit from the same corrective measures.

Keywords: Mobile network monitoring, radio interface quality, problem detection, OC-SVM.

1 Introduction

Monitoring the mobile network is a crucial task for operators to maintain the service quality level and keep their subscribers satisfied. Efficient monitoring is needed to reduce the waste of network resources and to solve network performance related problems in a short time. The network produces massive amounts of data and a lot of experts' time is required for analysis. The majority of the available data are irrelevant in supporting troubleshooting and solving a particular network problem. Relevant observations need to be identified from the mass and presented for an expert. Therefore efficient tools are required to assist in the management of the network.

In 3G networks cells in the same layer are sharing the same frequency and air interface bandwidth is utilized more efficiently than in GSM networks. Therefore in

L. Iliadis and C. Jayne (Eds.): EANN/AIAI 2011, Part I, IFIP AICT 363, pp. 392–401, 2011.

3G networks interference control is more important. 3G networks are designed to support a range of different services that have different behaviour and problems. [7]

The purpose of performance monitoring is to reveal problems in network elements, which have similar symptoms and therefore are more likely to require the same corrective actions. Analysis results produced by automated algorithms are independent of human operator's domain knowledge and experience. Therefore identification of problems can be automated and results obtained with greater average speed and accuracy. This helps in reducing the analysis time and implementing automated corrective actions.

In this paper we propose a methodology for detecting the most severe problems in the network and categorizing them into user friendly form that enable rapid and efficient actions in the network performance management. We compare two methods for detecting the problems. The first one is based on distances from ideal state of the network. It has been used in monitoring the radio interface quality measurements of GSM network [11]. This is enabled by the scaling method we use, which transforms the primarily unsupervised anomaly detection problem into a special case of semi supervised task [10, 11]. The second method we use is based on detecting the support of the distribution of the data using One-Class Support Vector Machine (OC-SVM) [14]. Finally, we cluster the detected anomalies into groups that present possible performance problems in the network.

First, in the following section, we introduce some measurements that are used for monitoring in daily routines. Next, we present a scaling procedure that utilizes the knowledge of the experts of the network operator. In section 4 we introduce two methods to detect possible problems in the network. We give examples of the behaviour of both methods using two quality variables for 2-dimensional visualization. We compare the results that these methods produce for quality variables of 3G network.

Finally, in Section 5, we cluster the detected problems to reveal problem groups and present descriptions given by network experts. Concluding remarks are given in the last section.

2   Radio Interface Performance Data

A huge amount of various events in the 3G network are counted and summed along time into counters. Although the counters contain all the information available about the network, it is too scattered to be of practical use. Therefore the counters are aggregated into Key Performance Indicators (KPI). They depict more understandable higher level information such as ratios of dropped calls or successful data connections. Each KPI is calculated from several counters using formulas, some of which are confidential.

In this study we use a limited set of radio network performance KPIs. We focus in clustering of call setup problems using the following KPI's:

- *Dropped call rate* (DCR) measures the proportion of initiated calls that are terminated abnormally.
- *HSDPA Setup Success Rate* indicates the proportion of successful HSDPA connection attempts. HSDPA is an enhancement for 3G network that enables fast mobile internet in downlink direction.

- *HSUPA Setup Success Rate* indicates the proportion of successful HSUPA connection attempts. HSUPA is similar to HSDPA, but in uplink direction.
- *R99 Setup Success Rate* measures the packet data connection attempt success ratio defined in basic 3G standard. HSUPA and HSDPA are newer technologies than R99 and they provide more radio interface capacity and throughput.
- *Voice call setup success rate* measures the ratio of successful voice call establishments.

We use a data set that is collected from a real functioning 3G network The KPIs are cell specific daily averages. The data consists of 123 cells from a period of 135 days. Due to missing values, the number of observations of individual cells varies from 120 to 135.

3 Scaling

Scaling the variables is an essential preprocessing procedure in practically all data mining tasks. Proper scaling is especially important in clustering as Gnanadesikan et al. [5], who refer to scaling as one method of weighting the variables, have pointed out: *When done efficiently, weighting and selection can dramatically facilitate cluster recovery. When not, unfortunately, even obvious cluster structure can be easily missed.*

We use a piecewise linear scaling procedure that utilizes the knowledge of the network experts [11]. The variables are scaled to interval [0, 1] so that 0 equals the worst and 1 equals the best possible performance as depicted in Fig. 1.

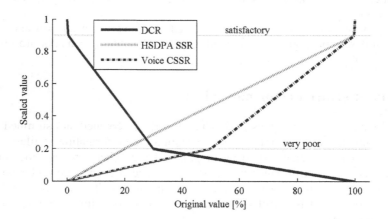

Fig. 1. Piecewise linear scaling of three radio performance KPIs

A network management expert defines two corner points that correspond to very poor and satisfactory performance levels of each KPI. These corner points are scaled to appropriate values, 0.2 and 0.9 for example and the rest of the values are linearly interpolated. Scaling equalizes the importance of the variables in distance measures. This scaling method unifies the interpretation of the variables in the scaled space; the ideal performance will be 1 for all KPIs and the worst possible 0. Each value in the scaled space indicates the same level of performance for all KPIs.

4   Problem Detection

Mobile networks, as well as other industrial processes are controlled and mostly function in acceptable states of operation. Therefore the majority of the recorded performance data represent normal, acceptable behaviour. Possible problems show up as anomalous deviations from normal and anomaly detection methods can be used to reveal the problems.

We propose two methods for detecting problems in the performance of 3G mobile network. The first one is a simple distance based method that has been found working well in GSM network monitoring [10, 11]. The second one is based on OC-SVM which is an efficient tool for identifying the support of multivariate distributions [14].

4.1   Distance Based Detection

The scaling method maps the best performance values of all variables to 1. This converts the anomaly detection into a special semi supervised case. The ideal state is now known to consist of all ones. Thus, the distance from ideal can be used as a measure of total performance, larger distances representing more severe problems [10, 11]. Scaling each variable according to the severity of their performance level equalizes their effect in the distance calculation. An example of the distance based (DB) detection of two performance KPIs is presented in Fig. 2.

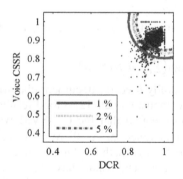

Fig. 2. Equal distance from ideal. 0.5%, 1% and 2% thresholds.

Equal Euclidean distance from ideal forms a circular area around the ideal. The threshold for detection can be set to a specific required distance or it can be identified from the data. This example displays percentage thresholds of the data.

4.2   One-Class Support Vector Machine

Support Vector Machine (SVM) is a classifier that uses hypothesis space of linear functions in a high-dimensional kernel-induced feature space [3]. The basic SVM classifies a training vector x_i of l observations into two classes, defined by a class variable $y_i \in \{-1, 1\}$. Extensions, such as "one-against-one" have been developed for multiclass classification [8, 9].

One-class SVM (OC-SVM) was proposed by Schölkopf et al. for estimating the support of a high-dimensional distribution [14]. The strategy is to separate the data from the origin with maximum margin in the feature space induced by the kernel. Parameter $v \in (0, 1]$ controls the fraction of the observations that are allowed to be classified to the class of the origin. Those observations, lying outside the support of the distribution are considered as anomalies. A variety of nonlinear estimators in input space is achieved by using different kernel functions.

The maximum margin classifier to separate the data set from the origin is achieved by solving the following quadratic program:

$$\min_{\mathbf{w}, \xi, \rho} \quad \frac{1}{2}\mathbf{w}^T\mathbf{w} - \rho + \frac{1}{vl}\Sigma_{i=1}^l \xi_i$$
$$subject\ to \quad \mathbf{w}^T\phi(\boldsymbol{x}_i) \geq \rho - \xi_i, \quad (1)$$
$$\xi_i \geq 0, i = 1, \ldots, l.$$

In this study we use a software package LIBSVM [1]. Its implementation of OC-SVM solves a scaled version of the dual form of (1):

$$\min_{\alpha} \quad \frac{1}{2}\alpha^T\mathbf{Q}\alpha,$$
$$subject\ to \quad 0 \leq \alpha_i \leq 1, i = 1, \ldots, l, \quad (2)$$
$$\mathbf{e}^T\alpha = vl, \mathbf{y}^T\alpha = 0.$$

where $\mathbf{Q}$ is a positive semidefinite matrix $\mathbf{Q}_{ij} \equiv y_i y_j K(\mathbf{x}_i, \mathbf{x}_j)$ and the kernel $K(\mathbf{x}_i, \mathbf{x}_j) \equiv \phi(\mathbf{x}_i)^T\phi(\mathbf{x}_j)$. The kernel function can be selected freely. One commonly used and versatile [6] kernel is the Radial Basis Function (RBF) kernel: $K(\mathbf{x}_i, \mathbf{x}_j) = \exp(-\gamma\|\mathbf{x}_i - \mathbf{x}_j\|^2)$, $\gamma > 0$.

The decision function classifies the outliers to class -1 and the bulk of the data to class +1 by:

$$sgn\left(\Sigma_{i=1}^l \alpha_i K(\boldsymbol{x}_i, \boldsymbol{x})\right). \quad (3)$$

OC-SVM has been successfully used for document classification [12] and novelty detection for multi-channel combustion data [2]. Good results were achieved in both cases. However, both papers reported that the OC-SVM was very sensitive to the parameter γ of the RBF kernel function. As there is no classification information available, it is not possible to use methods based on error rates, such as cross validation, for parameter selection. The results have to be verified by the end users, application experts, and the parameters selected according to their subjective judgement. It should be noted that OC-SVM is not the only method that faces this challenge but it is reality with all unsupervised methods.

Fig. 3 presents anomaly thresholds detected from the same two KPIs as in earlier, now by OC-SVM with RBF kernel. In OC-SVM the ideal state (all 1) has no special meaning. In order to prevent the ideal cases from appearing as anomalies, the "definitely good enough" data points, within distance 0.1 from the ideal, have been removed. The parameter v in (2) is adjusted so that the fraction of detected anomalies is 5% of the whole data set. When applied to these two KPIs from a 3G network the OC-SVM is not very sensitive to the kernel function parameter. Only minor changes are visible in Fig. 3 where two extreme values for the γ of the RBF kernel are used.

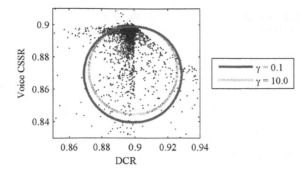

Fig. 3. Example of OC-SVM thresholds

4.3 Results of Problem Detection

We applied both methods, DB and OC-SVM to a data set consisting of the 5 KPIs described in section 2. We set the threshold in the DB method to find the worst 5% of the data set, 816 observations. We applied OC-SVM to a subset of the data, where the data within 0.1 distance from **1** were removed as in the previous example. We used RBF kernel in OC-SVM with 5 values of γ and v was 0.2061 which corresponds to 5% of the whole data set.

The number of detected anomalies for different γ varies between 831 and 832. There are 766 observations detected with all the γ values. Thus, for these date the OC-SVM does not seem to be too sensitive to the kernel function. However, only about half of the detected anomalies were common to those detected by the DB method. The numbers common observations are presented in Table 1.

Table 1. Number of common observations, detected by both methods

Kernel parameter	$\gamma = 0.1$	$\gamma = 0.5$	$\gamma = 1$	$\gamma = 5$	$\gamma = 10$
Common with DB	412	415	419	442	463

The detected anomalies present potential problems in the network. The characteristics of the common and divergent observations are discussed in the following section where the problems are described by network experts.

5 Problem Categorization for Quality Monitoring

The end users of the monitoring applications appreciate simple but informative presentations of the results. Clustering is an effective way to summarize the information [4]. We use agglomerative hierarchical clustering with Ward linkage [15]. Hierarchical clustering requires the interpoint distances between the observations and therefore it is not suitable for large data sets. However, we are clustering a relatively small number of detected anomalies. One advantage is that the

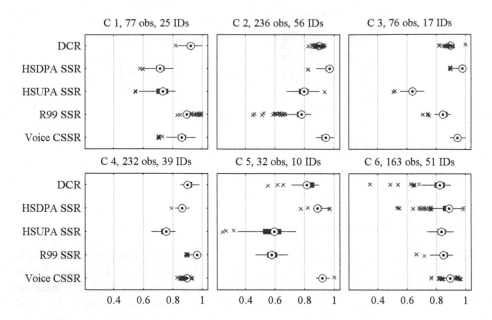

Fig. 4. Distance based problem clusters

clustering is deterministic; there are no random elements as in the initialization of another popular clustering, k-.means [4].

We use box plots [13] of the problem clusters produced to depict the characteristics of the clusters. The clustered anomalies detected by DB method are presented in Fig. 4 and those detected by OC-SVM in Fig. 5. Interpretation of the problem clusters is presented in Table 2.

The identified clusters are mapped into known network problems based on symptoms. In general, DCR correlates with bad radio conditions, and in (Cluster 5/5) there are both setup and DCR problems. This is an indication of bad radio conditions. On the other hand, BTS unit capacity is one typical problem, as the system has limitations in handling a large number of connections simultaneously. In (Cluster 6/2) this can take place depending on the amount of traffic and capacity available. Independent of the physical hardware capacity there can be licensed capacity limitations; in (Cluster 3/6) this takes place in one direction, generating HSUPA connection setup problems. HSDPA does not benefit from soft handover like other channels and is more sensitive to channel conditions because of cell overlap, in (Cluster 1/4). R99 data traffic is used when a user requests small data packets or cannot have a HSPA connection, in case of Cluster (2/-) repeated R99 setup problems due to user location or system reservation failures. The voice connections share the same resource pool as HSUPA connections, but with higher priority. In normal conditions voice setup performance should be better than HSUPA. This indicates specific voice service problem in (Cluster -/1).

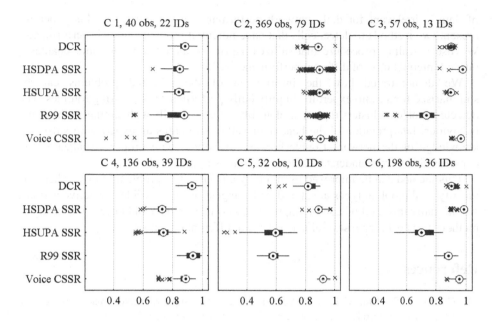

Fig. 5. OC-SVM problem clusters

Table 2. Descriptions of the problem clusters

Problem	Distance based	OC-SVM
HSDPA channel conditions (bad quality because of cell overlap or no good dominant server)	Cluster 1 (77)	Cluster 4 (136)
Limited HSUPA license capacity, or limited channel elements available for HSUPA	Cluster 3 (76)	Cluster 6 (196)
Limited uplink coverage (probably because of indoor users.) Users make call attempts in bad radio conditions.	Cluster 5 (32)	Cluster 5 (32)
Radio access setup failures for R99 packet data connections, UL interference, configuration error or equipment failure.	Cluster 2 (236)	-
Channel element capacity limitation – Omniproblem. Probably heavy resource utilization	Cluster 6 (163)	Cluster 2 (369)
"Check HSUPA licenses and coverage map"	Cluster 4 (232)	-
"Analyze more detailed setup failure reason codes for Voice". Behavior similar to Cluster 2		Cluster 1 (40)
Unexpected behavior, can be caused by particular mobile terminals or smart phones		Cluster 3 (57)

6 Conclusion

Monitoring the mobile network is a crucial task for operators in order to maintain the service quality level and keep their subscribers satisfied. Majority of the vast amounts of data is irrelevant for daily network performance management. In this paper we present two methods to detect cells that have potential problems in their performance. We use a scaling procedure that utilizes a priori expert knowledge and enables a unified interpretation of different performance KPIs.

We demonstrated how the information of the potential problems can be summarised for a radio expert to simplify daily performance monitoring routines. The detected problem clusters represent plausible groups of cells with similar problematic behaviour. Interpretation of the behaviour patterns requires an expert with sufficient knowledge of the network troubleshooting. However, with proper visualization an expert is able to give understandable explanations to the problems.

This method can be improved in future by introducing a problem library, where the most typical problem types are stored with suggestions of possible corrective actions. Additionally this method can be improved by collecting data and developing analysis method using data from several networks and different operators.

References

1. Chang, C-C., Lin, C-J.: LIBSVM: a library for support vector machines (2001), http://www.csie.ntu.edu.tw/~cjlin/papers/libsvm.pdf
2. Clifton, L., Yin, H., Zhang, Y.: Support Vector Machine in Novelty Detection for Multi-channel Combustion Data. In: Wang, J., Yi, Z., Zurada, J., Lu, B.-L., Yin, H. (eds.) ISNN 2006. LNCS, vol. 3973, pp. 836–843. Springer, Heidelberg (2006)
3. Cristianini, N., Shawe-Taylor, J.: An Introduction to Support Vector Machines and Other Kernel-based Learning Methods. Cambridge University Press, Cambridge (2000)
4. Everitt, B., Landau, S., Leese, M.: Cluster analysis. Arnold, London (2001)
5. Gnanadesikan, R., Kettenring, J.R., Tsao, S.L.: Weighting and selection of variables for cluster analysis. Journal of Classification 12(1), 113–136 (1995)
6. Hsu, C-W., Chang, C-C., Lin, C-J.: A Practical Guide to Support Vector Classification, http://www.csie.ntu.edu.tw/~cjlin/papers/guide/guide.pdf
7. Kaaranen, H., Ahtiainen, A., Laitinen, L., Naghian, S., Niemi, V.: UMTS Networks. John Wiley & Sons, Chichester (2009)
8. Knerr, S., Personnaz, L., Dreyfus, G.: Single-layer learning revisited: a stepwise procedure for building and training a neural network. In: Fogelman, J. (ed.) Neurocomputing: Algorithms, Architectures and Applications. Springer, Heidelberg (1990)
9. Kreßel, U.: Pairwise classification and support vector machines. In: Schölkopf, B., Burges, C.J.C., Smola, A.J. (eds.) Advances in Kernel Methods – Support Vector Learning, pp. 255–268. MIT Press, Cambridge (1999)
10. Kumpulainen, P., Kylväjä, M., Hätönen, K.: Importance of Scaling in Unsupervised Distance-Based Anomaly Detection. In: Proceedings of IMEKO XIX World Congress. Fundamental and Applied Metrology, Lisbon, Portugal, September 6-11, pp. 2411–2416 (2009)
11. Kylväjä, M., Kumpulainen, P., Hätönen, K.: Information Summarization for Network Performance Management. In: Laszlo, M., Zsolt, J.V. (eds.) Proceedings of the 10th IMEKO TC10 International Conference on Technical Diagnostics, Budapest, Hungary, pp. 167–172 (2005)

12. Manevitz, L., Yousef, M.: One-class svms for document classification. The Journal of Machine Learning Research 2, 139–154 (2002); Special issue on kernel methods
13. McGill, R., Tukey, J.W., Larsen, W.A.: Variations of Boxplots. The American Statistician 32, 12–16 (1978)
14. Schölkopf, B., Platt, J., Shawe-Taylor, J., Smola, A.J., Williamson, R.: Estimating the support of a high-dimensional distribution. Neural Computation 13(7), 1443–1472 (2001)
15. Ward Jr., J.H.: Hierarchical grouping to optimize an objective function. Journal of the American Statistical Association 58(301), 236–244 (1963)

Analyzing 3G Quality Distribution Data with Fuzzy Rules and Fuzzy Clustering

Pekka Kumpulainen[1], Mika Särkioja[2], Mikko Kylväjä[3], and Kimmo Hätönen[4]

[1] Tampere University of Technology, Department of Automation Science and Engineering,
Korkeakoulunkatu 3, 33720 Tampere, Finland
[2] Nokia Siemens Networks, BSO OSS Radio Network Optimizer, Espoo, Finland
[3] Aditro Software, Espoo, Finland
[4] Nokia Siemens Networks, CTO Research, Espoo, Finland
pekka.kumpulainen@tut.fi,
{mika.1.sarkioja,kimmo.hatonen}@nsn.com,
mikko.kylvaja@aditro.com

Abstract. The amount of data collected from telecommunications networks has increased significantly during the last decade. In comparison to the earlier networks, present-day 3G networks are able to provide more complex and detailed data, such as distributions of quality indicators. However, the operators lack proper tools to efficiently utilize these data in monitoring and analyzing the networks. Classification of the network elements (cells) into groups of similar behavior provides valuable information for a radio expert, who is responsible of hundreds or thousands of elements.

In this paper we propose fuzzy methods applied to 3G network channel quality distributions for analyzing the network performance. We introduce a traditional fuzzy inference system based on features extracted from the distributional data. We provide interpretation of the resulting classes to demonstrate their usability on network monitoring. Constructing and maintaining fuzzy rule sets are laborious tasks, therefore there is a demand for data driven methods that can provide similar information to the experts. We apply fuzzy C-means clustering to create performance classes. Finally, we introduce further analysis on how the performance of individual network elements varies between the classes in the course of time.

Keywords: 3G mobile network, quality variable distribution, channel quality, fuzzy clustering, fuzzy rules, unsupervised classification.

1 Introduction

The amount of data collected from telecommunications networks has increased during last decade significantly [6]. The data available today is richer in detail and complexity, which creates more requirements also for automated data analysis tools [2, 10]. In this research we propose unsupervised classification methods for analyzing the quality of cells. A cell is a geographical area that one sector of a base station covers. For classification we use daily performance metric data from 3G network [4]. The channel quality distributions describe the quality of radio conditions of HSPA channel in 3G network cells. The target is to provide methods that can support radio experts in monitoring the network and to detecting problematic behavior.

L. Iliadis and C. Jayne (Eds.): EANN/AIAI 2011, Part I, IFIP AICT 363, pp. 402–411, 2011.
© IFIP International Federation for Information Processing 2011

In the following section we first introduce the data with examples of their characteristics. Next, we introduce a fuzzy rule bases system for classification. In section 4 we present fuzzy clustering and interpretation of the clusters as quality classes. In section 5 we propose methods to monitor the variation of the behavior of individual cells. We summarize the results in the last section.

2   Quality Variable Distributions

The data used in this study are 3G network channel quality indicator (CQI) measurements [3]. The data consist of distributions from high speed packet access (HSPA) connections in 3G network. The collected channel quality measurement samples are grouped into 31 classes, each of which represents a different quality category. These reported measurement samples are collected from every HSPA connection when mobile terminal sends channel quality report indicators, that takes place constantly during the active connection. Class 1 contains the samples that have the worst radio channel quality, providing the worst radio interface throughput for mobile. Class 31 contains samples that have the best radio quality. The measurements are used during high speed packet call for deciding the optimal packet size and modulation coding scheme. Naturally, more samples in higher quality range in the CQI statistics of a 3G cell implies higher throughput for users of the cell. Throughput is one of the most significant contributors to user experience in packet data transfer.

Counting the samples in each quality class during one day constitutes a quality histogram. Dividing the counts by the total number of samples results in proportions of the samples in each quality class; producing a daily quality distribution.

The data set consists of daily CQI measurement distributions of 771 3G cells over a time period of 15 days. Most of the cells (747) have complete data for all days. The rest have smaller subset of CQI distribution profiles available. However, all cells are included in the analysis. The total amount of daily distributions is 11441.

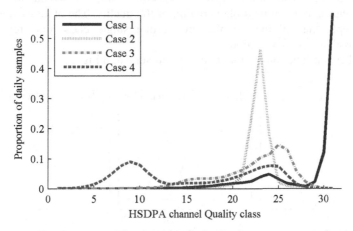

Fig. 1. Example distributions

The original data consists of absolute amount of reported measurement samples in each CQI bin. The data is scaled so that sum of samples for a cell CQI distribution profile is one. To illustrate the differences in CQI distribution profiles, some handpicked examples of distributions are shown in Fig1.

Case 1 is an example of a cell, which has very good radio channel conditions. Case 2 is a cell that provides satisfactory radio conditions. CQI distribution profile of case 3 is distributed to wide quality range, which most probably means that the cell is providing service for users in different channel conditions. In case 4 the users are probably located in two different locations, one of which provides good channel conditions and the other one much worse. These examples present extreme behavior and especially cases 1 and 4 are very rare in practice.

3 Quality Classification with Fuzzy Rules

Fuzzy sets were first introduced by Zadeh in 1965 [9]. Fuzzy logic has been successfully used in a wide variety of application areas ever since.

We implement a Mamdani type fuzzy interference system [6] to classify the cells according to their CQI distributions. Using the full 31 dimensional distributions as inputs would end up in very high numbers of membership functions and fuzzy rules. Therefore we extract 3 features from the distributions to present the most interesting aspects of the distributions: the average (or most common) quality and the variation of the quality during the day. The features are named: *MaxPosition*, *MaxValue* and *NLowValues*.

MaxPosition is the number of the quality class that contains maximum number of samples, thus representing the average quality of the day. *MaxValue* is the maximum value of the distribution, the proportion of all samples in the most common quality class. It represents the width of the peak in the distribution and can be thought as a confidence weight of the average quality. It is also related to the variation of the quality. *NLowValues* describes the variation of quality. It is the number of values below 1/31 in the distribution. Lowest possible value, 0 would mean equal distribution, thus maximum possible variation of the quality. The other extreme value 30 would imply that all the samples are in one single class, thus representing minimum possible quality variation.

The membership functions of the inputs are presented in Fig. 2.

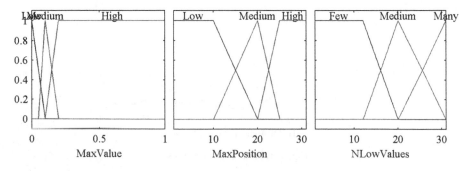

Fig. 2. Membership functions of the inputs

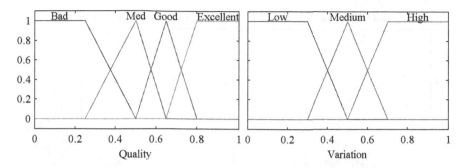

Fig. 3. Membership functions of the outputs

We have two outputs: Quality and Variation. Quality describes the average quality of the distribution and Variation represents the stability of the quality. The Quality has four fuzzy values: Bad, Medium, Good and Excellent. The variation has outputs: Low, Medium and High. An ideally performing cell would have excellent Quality and low Variation. The membership functions of the outputs are presented in Fig. 3.

We formed a total of 15 rules to map the inputs to appropriate fuzzy outputs. Some of the rules are given below as examples.

```
1. If (MaxValue is High) and (MaxPosition is High) then
(Quality is Excellent) (1)

2. If (MaxValue is High) and (MaxPosition is Low) then
(Quality is bad) (1)

5. If (MaxValue is Low) or (NLowValues is Few) then
(Variation is High) (1)

7. If (MaxValue is High) or (NLowValues is Many) then
(Variation is Low) (1)

15. If (MaxValue is Medium) and (MaxPosition is Low)
then (Quality is bad) (1)
```

The resulting classes of the outputs of the 11441 daily distributions are collected in Table 1.:

Table 1. Number of cells in the fuzzy performance classes

Quality \ Variation	Low	Medium	High
Bad	77 (0.7%)	268 (2.3%)	300 (2.6%)
Medium	981 (8.6%)	2312 (20.2%)	956 (8.4%)
Good	2923 (25.5%)	1516 (13.3%)	169 (1.5%)
Excellent	1870 (16.3%)	69 (0.6%)	0 (0%)

Most of the data have either good or excellent quality. 12.5% of the daily distributions have high variation. 0.7% have bad quality and low variation which means constant poor quality.

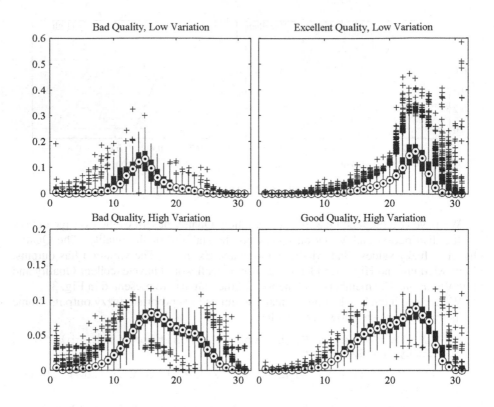

Fig. 4. Boxplots of the data in 4 classes

We present examples of the behavior in four classes in Fig 4. The selected classes are Bad and Excellent Quality with Low Variation as well as Bad and Good Quality with High Variation. All the distributions in these classes are shown as boxplots [5].

These examples of four CQI cluster classes describe cluster channel quality behavior and expected end user throughput: In [Bad Quality, Low Variation] – cluster large numbers of bad samples represent low channel quality. When a cell is in this cluster end users are not able to get a high throughput. In contrary [Excellent Quality, Low Variation] - cluster channel conditions are constantly excellent. If a cell is in this class the users are likely to experience good throughput. In [Bad Quality, Low Variation] –cluster users are experiencing both bad and good channel conditions. This means that radio conditions in cells in this class extend over several quality classes. This is likely to take place. In [Good Quality, High Variation] most users are experiencing good channel conditions. Behavior is similar to previous example, but most users are having good channel conditions.

4 Quality Classification with Fuzzy Clustering

Clustering is a term for unsupervised methods that discover groups of similar observations in multivariate data [1]. Each observation is assigned into one of the discovered groups. Thus, clustering is unsupervised classification, where the classes are not known beforehand, but identified from the data. Instead of a strict assignment into one group only, fuzzy clustering allows each observation to be a member of all clusters with varying degree of membership [7]. Fuzzy C-means (FCM) clustering identifies a predefined number, C, of cluster centers so that the fuzzified sum of Euclidean distances from observations is minimized [8]. FCM produces the centers of fuzzy clusters and for each observation the degree of membership in the C clusters. In case the observations need to be assigned to one cluster, the ones where the observations have the highest degree of membership are selected. On the other hand, if the maximum degree of membership is low and does not differ significantly from the others, it is a sign that the observation does not belong well to any of the clusters and is most likely an unusual case or an outlier.

In this study we apply FCM to the 31-dimensional data of CQI distributions. After testing several values of C, the number of clusters, we decided to use 8 clusters. That is still a reasonable number of classes for the radio expert to interpret and assign labels to. Yet, that is sufficient to cover the most of the variations in the behavior. Centers of the 8 clusters are presented in Fig. 5. The legend also shows the number of daily distributions that have the maximum membership in each cluster. The data are relatively evenly distributed across the clusters.

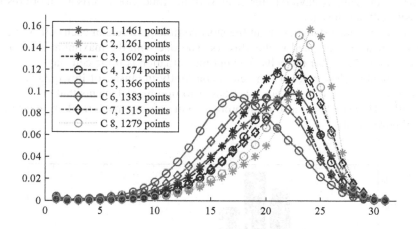

Fig. 5. Centers of 8 fuzzy clusters

It is easy to see from the centers that the main differences between the clusters are the position of the peak value, which is the most common quality class, and the width, which describes the variation of the quality in the cluster. These two features of CQI distribution are the most relevant factors for radio expert to define the behavior of the cells in the cluster.

Clusters 1 and 4 have peak values close to each other. However, cluster 4 represents better behavior, since the variation of the quality (width of the distribution) is smaller. Cluster 1 has more samples in the range that represents poor quality classes.

Clusters 1, 5 and 6 (solid red lines) have similar shape of distribution, representing similar level of variation of the quality. However, as the location of the peak differs, they represent cells that have different quality conditions. A radio expert can tell that at least most of the variation is caused by mobiles that are located in wide range of distances around the cell.

Clusters 3, 4 and 7 (dashed blue lines) provide better channel quality for users. In other words, most probably the customers are often close to the cell.

Clusters 2 and 8 (dotted green lines) represent very well behaving cells. In these clusters it is typical to have the quality distribution biased to high quality range. Also the variation is low. This behavior is common in indoor cells. They do not experience much interference outside and users are mostly located nearby.

Altogether, it is possible for radio experts to introduce descriptions to the clusters that are similar to those generated by the fuzzy rules.

5 Tracking the Changes in Quality Behavior

Tracking how the cells change clusters in the course of time provides valuable information for analyzing their behavior. Here we assign each distribution to the cluster of the maximum membership. Some cells behave constantly, and are a member of the same behavioral cluster most of the time. Some cells are more restless and visit multiple clusters.

First we introduce statistics about the most common clusters of each cell. We count the assignments of each cell in the clusters. The one with the maximum count is the most common cluster for the cells. The optimal situation is if the cell stays constantly in a high quality cluster. Even if a cell is constantly in cluster of low quality, that is reasonably good situation, because it is easier to optimize elements that are behaving constantly. These cells are also most probably not causing much random interference to neighboring cells.

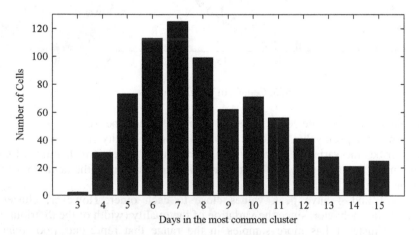

Fig. 6. Histogram of days the cells spend in their most common cluster

Histogram of the maximum counts is presented in Fig. 6. As the monitoring period in these data is 15 days, the maximum value of 15 means that the cell has stayed in the same cluster for the whole period. That is the case for 25 cells as depicted in Fig. 7. There are 21 cells that have the maximum value 14, thus they stay in the same cluster except for one day.

Table 2 shows which clusters are the most common ones. Column 1 displays the maximum count, the days spent in the most common cluster. The rest of the columns present the number of cells that have the corresponding cluster as the most common one.

Table 2. Deviation of the cells in the fuzzy clusters.

Max value	C 1	C 2	C 3	C 4	C 5	C 6	C 7	C 8
15	1	5	1	0	13	0	3	2
14	4	7	3	2	10	7	6	3
13	4	6	9	6	15	14	7	6
12	12	19	15	15	10	14	15	16
6 - 10	287	144	260	285	143	245	249	201
3 – 5	91	50	84	88	44	75	75	64

The first row contains the cells that spend all 15 days in one cluster. Most of them (13) stay in cluster 5, which presents the poorest quality. Also most of the cells that spend 13 or 14 days in one cluster, stay in cluster 5. This is an indication that those cells have mostly poor performance and they should be checked for possible improvements.

On the other hand, the cells that have a lot of variation in their behavior, (two bottom rows) visit cluster 5 less often than other clusters. Majority of the cells, 495 never visit cluster 5.

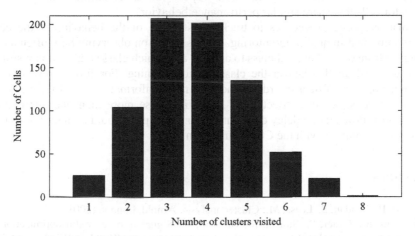

Fig. 7. Histogram of the clusters covered by cells

Clusters 2 and 8 are the ones that have the best quality. There are 64 cells that stay in either of those clusters at least 12 days out of the 15. All these are performing well and require no further attention.

Further statistics on the variation among the clusters is presented in Fig. 7. It shows a histogram of how many clusters the cells visited during monitoring period.

The same 25 cells that stay all the days in one cluster are the ones that cove only one cluster. 104 cells split between two clusters. 21 of them are divided to 14 days in one cluster and one day in another cluster, as seen in Table 2. The rest have more even distribution across the two clusters. Only one cell spreads its behavior in all 8 clusters and 21 cells in 7 clusters.

6 Conclusion

CQI distribution measures channel conditions that change according to traffic volume and user positions. Radio experts are working with thousands of elements, where channel conditions change rapidly and traffic patterns change. Identifying behavioral patterns of cell radio interface can involve a very large number of quality samples. Data abstraction and summarization are powerful ways of supporting the expert's decision making.

Fuzzy rules and fuzzy clustering can be used to create behavioral classes. Labels of these classes can be assigned to the network elements. Fuzzy rules were used to classify the distribution data based on the quality and the daily variation of the quality. Weakness of rule based analysis is that the rules need to be designed and maintaining the rule base and membership functions is laborious thus raising a demand for automated data driven methods. We used fuzzy C-means to create similar behavioral classes by clustering the distributional data. Now, the radio experts have only a handful of clusters to interpret and associate with an appropriate label. We believe that if radio experts can identify the typical behavior of a cell, it helps them to optimize or configure the cell. The radio expert can apply similar improvements methods for cells that share similar performance behavior.

We also proposed procedures to track the stability of the behavior of the cells which is important in quality monitoring. This is based on observing how often a cell is changing from one behavioral class to another and which classes the cell is visiting.

Now we used all the data in the classification training. For further research we need longer periods of data in order to acquire more information about the behavior variations of cells. Another direction in future is to use more than one distribution type indicator. Propagation delay distribution, for example, should contain interesting information to combine with the CQI distribution.

References

1. Everitt, B., Landau, S., Leese, M.: Cluster analysis. Arnold, London (2001)
2. Guerzoni, R., Zanier, P., Suman, R., DiSarno, F.: Signaling-based radio optimization in WCDMA networks. In: IEEE International Symposium on a World of Wireless, Mobile and Multimedia Networks, pp. 1–6. IEEE, Los Alamitos (2007)

3. Johnson, C.: Radio Access Networks for UMTS: Principles and Practice. John Wiley & Sons, Chichester (2008)
4. Kaaranen, H., Ahtiainen, A., Laitinen, L., Naghian, S., Niemi, V.: UMTS Networks. John Wiley & Sons, Chichester (2009)
5. McGill, R., Tukey, J.W., Larsen, W.A.: Variations of Boxplots. The American Statistician 32, 12–16 (1978)
6. Mishra, A.R.: Advanced Cellular Network Planning and Optimisation: 2G/2.5G/3G...Evolution to 4G. John Wiley & Sons, Chichester (2006)
7. Ross, T.J.: Fuzzy Logic With Engineering Applications. McGraw-Hill, New York (1995)
8. Xu, R., Wunsch II, D.C.: Clustering. John Wiley & Sons, New Jersey (2009)
9. Zadeh, L.A.: Fuzzy sets. Information and Control, 338–353 (1965)
10. Zanier, P., Guerzoni, R., Soldani, D.: Detection of Interference, Dominance and Coverage Problems in WCDMA Networks. In: IEEE 17th International Symposium on Personal, Indoor and Mobile Radio Communications, pp. 1–5. IEEE, Los Alamitos (2006)

Adaptive Service Composition
for Meta-searching in a Mobile Environment

Ronnie Cheung and Hassan B. Kazemian

London Metropolitan University,
United Kingdom
ccheung@acm.org, h.kazemian@londonmet.ac.uk

Abstract. The underlying technologies driving the World Wide Web are largely based on the assumption of wired communications and powerful desktop hardware. This is not true when a user is accessing the Web pages and documents using a PDA and moving from wireless network in a mall to a neighboring office environment. Taking into consideration on the information needs of the user, we have developed a meta-search application that can be executed on mobile devices with limited hardware capabilities. By running in the auto-configuration mode, the system detects the dynamic contextual information, and presents the results of meta-searching in a suitable format to cope with the limitations of the mobile stations. This is achieved by an adaptive service composition that is defined according to the adaptation model defined in a system configuration file.

Keywords: meta-searching, adaptive service composition, mobile computing.

1 Introduction

With the rapid development of the World Wide Web, many search engines are developed to facilitate information retrieval and filtering [1]. A meta-search engine is a kind of search engine that do not maintain its own databases, but search those of other engines [12]. Metacrawler, for instance, searches the databases of: Lycos, WebCrawler, Excite, Altavista, and Yahoo. It queries the other search engines, organizes the results in a uniform format, ranks them by relevance, and returns them to the user. In this paper, we describe the development of a meta-search engine that provides flexible and adaptive Web meta-searching service in a mobile environment. Compare with the fixed and wired network, the wireless mobile environment has smaller bandwidth, higher latency and higher error rates. A meta-search engine for mobile devices facilitates efficient web access by consolidating the search results from different search engines, and formats the results according to the requirements of mobile devices. A major issue is that many of the mobile devices have limited capabilities. For example, the size of screen, available memory and the depth of color are usually deficient. Conventional meta-search engines return the search results by using a single presentation format. In order to reduce the cost and increase the efficiency, and to provide a desirable Web meta-searching experience for the mobile

L. Iliadis and C. Jayne (Eds.): EANN/AIAI 2011, Part I, IFIP AICT 363, pp. 412–421, 2011.
© IFIP International Federation for Information Processing 2011

users, a Web meta-searching system for adaptive mobile environment is developed in this project.

The WebPADS system is employed as the underlying Web proxy framework to facilitate the adaptation requirements. Unlike other agent-based Web proxy systems, the WebPADS system offers a more flexible and adaptive platform for developing the meta-searching services. The details of the WebPADS platform are described in Section 2 of this paper. In the system, the client station acquires the contextual information by a service program running in the mobile node. The embedded service program then sends the updated information to the server periodically. Based on the dynamic contextual information of the mobile clients, the meta-search proxy server composes the service chains according to the dynamic requirements for adaptive service composition for meta-searching in a mobile environment. The client application is a user-friendly graphical user interface that is developed by Java technology. Users can interact with the system by submitting their specific requirements with a few steps. Most of the complicated tasks are processed in the proxy server. In the auto configuration mode, the users are only required to submit the keyword for the queries. The system can improve the efficiency and readability of the meta-searching, and the cost of meta-searching in mobile devices are decreased by minimizing the amount of data to be downloaded.

The major contribution of this paper is the abstraction of the dynamic service composition process using the WebPADS architecture. The integration of service composition is demonstrated using a meta-search engine application as an example. The proposed framework supports a self-organizing approach that allows a user to specify the desired adaptation and quality-of-service (QoS) requirements through adaptation rules. These QoS characteristics are broken down into requirements for individual services in the rule base using a novel approach for active service composition [9].

2   The WebPADS Platform

To provide and facilitate an effective Web meta-searching experience for mobile environments, the WebPADS system (**Web P**roxy for **A**ctively **D**eployable **S**ervice) has been employed as the underlying Web proxy framework for development. WebPADS is a object-oriented system based on the active service deployment architecture, dynamic service composition framework. Active service deployment and dynamic reconfiguration of mobile computing services accomplish the robust and efficient adaptation to mobile environment. To regulate the service configuration policies, WebPADS maintains a configuration description file within both of client and server sides. The configuration description files are in XML [3, 10] format and its acts as a declarative guide for dynamic service composition to adapt the vigorous changes of wireless environments. The condition of environment is reported by the client program and stored in an XML file in server side and its corresponding chain of service actions are defined in the configuration file.

We have previously described the WebPADS platform – a Web Proxy for Active **D**eployable **S**ervice [7, 8]. The WebPADS platform is an object-oriented system that is based on active service deployment architecture, comprising components of dynamic service objects called *mobilets*, which executes under the WebPADS execution environment. Among the system's components, the event register allows objects to locate and register for event sources. When an event occurs, the objects that have registered for that event source are notified. Event sources include various changes in the status of a network, machine resources and connectivity. Furthermore, the composition of the services of the WebPADS server can be dynamically reconfigured to adapt to the vigorous changes in the characteristics of a wireless environment.

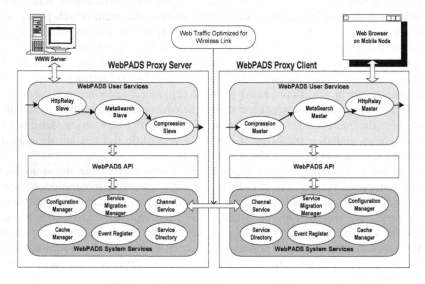

Fig. 1. The WebPADS system architecture

The unit of service is implemented as a mobilet that provides value-added services to a wireless environment. The system's components also provide generic facilities that serve the mobilets, which in turn provide services that enhance a user's Web-browsing experience. A series of mobilets can be linked together to form a processing-service composition, allowing WebPADS to benefit from the aggregated functionality of a group of services (as shown in figure 1). Services provided by the WebPADS system can be migrated from one WebPADS server to another to track the mobility of a mobile node and serve the mobile node continuously. Services can also be added, removed and updated dynamically without interrupting the service provision to other mobile nodes. Furthermore, the composition of the services of the WebPADS server can be dynamically reconfigured to adapt to the vigorous changes in the characteristics of a wireless environment.

3   Systems Architecture

With the advent of mobile computing, it is common for users to access the Web through various mobile devices such as mobile phones, hand-held PCs and PDAs etc.

Each mobile device has different characteristics. For example, a user using a personal digital assistant may have less than 480 x 640 resolution and Web access through the mobile device is normally performed through a few proxy servers, either through a home wireless network or a wireless gateway installed in a mobile user's office. To provide adaptation to suit the requirements of mobile users, we have employed the WebPADS client-proxy mobile architecture to improve web searching experience. Figure 2 shows the system's architecture of the mobile meta-searching engine. Users can interact with the system using the client application in the mobile node. The Environment Monitor on the WebPADS client reports the contextual information of the mobile node, and the dynamic information of the mobile environment is updated to the server at regular intervals. The idea is to implement the WebPADS services both in the mobile node and in the server, where all HTTP requests or responses are intercepted, transformed and optimized for transformation over a wireless network. When a meta-search query is sent to the proxy server, a chain of service is created according to the dynamic configuration of the mobile clients, to facilitate mea-searching in a mobile environment.

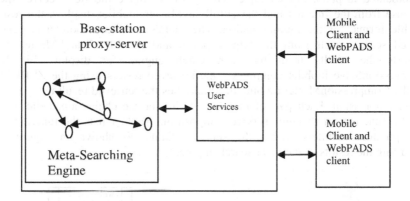

Fig. 2. System Architecture

4   Active Service Composition

Based on the user requirements of the dynamic mobile environment, the WebPADS system introduces an active service model that extends the client-proxy model to support active service composition. In this active service model, the proxy is composed of a service object called mobilets. This model offers flexibility because the chain of mobilets can be dynamically reconfigured to adapt to the vigorous changes in the characteristics of a wireless environment, without interrupting the service provision for other mobile nodes. Figure 3 shows the chain of mobilet services for providing adaptive meta-search services and Figure 4 shows the services for formatting search results.

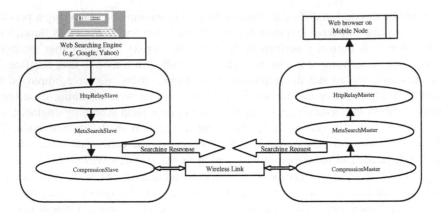

Fig. 3. The Service Chain for Meta-search

As shown in figure 3, for each service, the corresponding mobilets are implemented in pairs. For example: The HttpRelaySlave mobilet receives the http response from the Internet and the HttpRelayMaster mobilet displays the results in suitable format for the mobile station. The MetaSearchSlave mobilet searches the desired search result from the http response and the MetaSearchMaster mobilet converts the results from the meta-search engine for display. Finally the CompressionSlave mobilet compresses the retrieved results using the ZLIB library, and the CompressionMaster mobilet decompresses the retrieved result using the ZLIB for decompression. Each pair of mobilets in the service chains are dedicated for a specific function for dynamic service composition. Table 1 lists the functions of the corresponding mobilets within the service chains (as shown in Figure 4) for formatting the results of the meta-search engine.

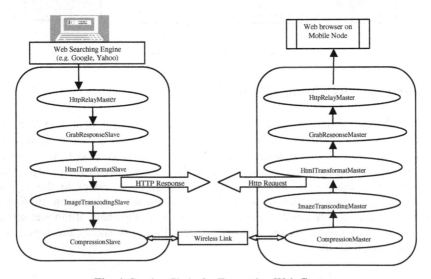

Fig. 4. Service Chain for Formatting Web Content

Table 1. Details of the services in the service chain for formatting the meta-search results

HttpRelaySlave	Receives the http response from the internet.
GrabResponseSlave	Retrieves all available image links from the html document, reformats the links with the domain and arrange the html and image link objects.
HTMLTransformatSlave	Reformats the html documents so that useless contents are removed. E.g. reformat the link of CSS, remove the javascript, applet and comments.
ImageTranscodingSlave	According to the conditions specified in the system configuration file, ImageTranscoding Slave can be used to transcode the image into a suitable format for the mobile client.
CompressionSlave	Compresses the retrieved result using the popular ZLIB compression library.
CompressionMaster	Decompress the retrieved result using the popular ZLIB compression library.
ImageTranscodingMaster	Stores the retrieved image in the client machine.
HTMLTransformatMaster	Stores the retrieved html documents in the client machine.
GrabResponseMaster	Commits the result storage and backup the old versions of the search result (if the same page is requested more than once).
HttpRelayMaster	Displays the results in a suitable format.

5 Adaptation Rules

The WebPADS platform has been used to implement mobile applications to provide efficient Web browsing experience for mobile users [4, 5, 6]. Table 2 lists the contextual information that is identified for the mobile devices. The information collected is used to configure the service provision dynamically to meet the processing and presentation requirements of the mobile clients. To regulate the dynamic service composition policies, the WebPADS system maintains a configuration description file utilizing XML. To dynamically adapt to the changes in the environment, WebPADS employs the environment monitor and event system to monitor and communicate the changes. An environment element consists of one or more conditions, where each condition specifies an event and a relational value that will fulfill that condition.

When a WebPADS client starts, a default service composition is created that is based on the description of the XML configuration file. At the same time, a number of alternative reconfiguration service chain maps are also created. Each map is attached to an environment monitor, which regulates the time and conditions for the service reconfiguration to take place. When all the conditions monitored by a specific environment monitor are fulfilled, the current service composition will be reconfigured to the service chain map attached to that environment monitor.

Table 2. Contextual information reported by the WebPADS client

Unit Type	Contextual Information
System	CPU type, clock rate, utilization, OS name, version
Storage	RAM size, free space, Secondary Storage size, free space
Network	Network type, capacity, data rate, delay, error rate
Power	Battery maximum lifetime, remaining lifetime
Display	Color type, depth, Screen resolution
Audio	Type of sound supported
Browser	Browser name, version

```xml
<RECONFIGURATION>
    ...
    <ENVIRONMENT config_option="COMPRESSION">
        <CONDITION_ATTRIBUTE value="CPU_USAGE">
            <CONDITION>
                <RELATION operator="LESS_THAN">50</RELATION>
                <CONFIG_VALUE>BEST_COMPRESSION</CONFIG_VALUE>
            </CONDITION>
            <CONDITION>
                <RELATION operator="MORE_OR_EQUAL">50</RELATION>
                <RELATION operator="LESS_THAN">65</RELATION>
                <CONFIG_VALUE>DEFAULT_COMPRESSION</CONFIG_VALUE>
            </CONDITION>
            <CONDITION>
                <RELATION operator="MORE_OR_EQUAL">65</RELATION>
                <RELATION operator="LESS_THAN">75</RELATION>
                <CONFIG_VALUE>LOW_COMPRESSION</CONFIG_VALUE>
            </CONDITION>
            <CONDITION>
                <RELATION operator="MORE_OR_EQUAL">75</RELATION>
                <CONFIG_VALUE>NO_COMPRESSION</CONFIG_VALUE>
            </CONDITION>
        </CONDITION_ATTRIBUTE>
    </ENVIRONMENT>
    ...
    <ENVIRONMENT config_option="IMAGE_SIZE">
        <CONDITION_ATTRIBUTE value="WIDTH_PIXELS">
            <CONDITION>
                <RELATION operator="LESS_OR_EQUAL">320</RELATION>
                <CONFIG_VALUE>1/2</CONFIG_VALUE>
            </CONDITION>
            <CONDITION>
                <RELATION operator="LESS_OR_EQUAL">480</RELATION>
                <RELATION operator="MORE_THAN">320</RELATION>
                <CONFIG_VALUE>2/3</CONFIG_VALUE>
            </CONDITION>
            <CONDITION>
                <RELATION operator="LESS_OR_EQUAL">640</RELATION>
                <RELATION operator="MORE_THAN">480</RELATION>
                <CONFIG_VALUE>3/4</CONFIG_VALUE>
            </CONDITION>
            <CONDITION>
                <RELATION operator="MORE_THAN">640</RELATION>
                <CONFIG_VALUE>1</CONFIG_VALUE>
            </CONDITION>
        </CONDITION_ATTRIBUTE>
    </ENVIRONMENT>
    ...
</RECONFIGURATION>
```

Fig. 5. The XML Configuration File

The configuration file is used for constructing the user adaptation model. Figure 5 shows examples of adaptations rules that are used to compose the services for meta-search dynamically. It is implemented in an XML format file. For example, the rule segments corresponding to the adaptation rules for CPU usage can be interpreted as follows: If cpu_usage < 50 then perform Best_Compression; If cpu_usage > = 50 and cpu_usage < 65 then perform Default_Compression; If cpu_usage >=65 and cpu_usage < 75 then perform Low_Compression; If cpu_usage > = 75 then perform No_Compression.

6 Example – Dynamic Activation of Transcoding Service

The meta-searching system is implemented with a graphic user interface on the mobile client station. The current version supports meta-searching through Yahoo, Google, AltaVista and Lycos (as shown in Figure 6). Corresponding to the selected search engines and the selected configuration options (e.g. auto option for compression and image color level defined in the configuration file), the system communicates with the meta-search engine through the WebPADS server. The following example shows the results of adaptive service composition after the dynamic activation of the image transcoding service in a low bandwidth wireless network environment (as shown in figure 6 and figure 7).

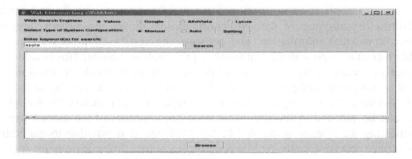

Fig. 6. The graphical user interface in the mobile station

In the meta-searching system, the size of images within the resulting pages directly affects the amount of data that is transported in the mobile environment. For example, if the bandwidth of the mobile connection is less than a threshold value (e.g. 64 K), it is desirable to transcode the graphic files (e.g. the GIF files) with a lower bit depth to reduce the image file size [2, 11]. The rules for adaptations can be configured in the configuration file in WebPADS. According to the bandwidth and contextual parameters, a scaling parameter can be defined to determine how much an image is downsampled. According to the dynamic adaptation requirements, the number of colors in a color-mapped image can be reduced (e.g. a 24-bit color image may be converted to 8-bit grayscale or even monochrome representation). Figure 7 shows the examples of the original graphic image and the retrieved image (down-sampled) after dynamic activation of the transcoding service in the system.

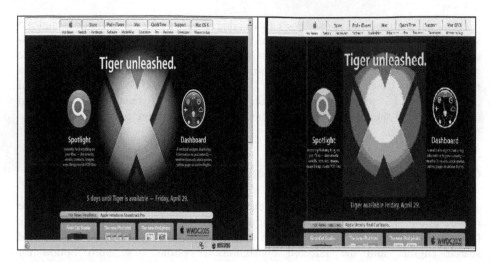

Fig. 7. The original graphic image (left) and the down-sampled image (right) in the mobile station

7 Conclusion

A meta-search application is developed for mobile devices with limited hardware capabilities. By running in the auto-configuration mode, the system detects the dynamic contextual information, and presents the results of meta-searching in a suitable format to cope with the limitations of the mobile stations. This is achieved by an adaptive service composition that is defined according to the adaptation model defined in a system configuration files. The configuration file can be stored at the mobile device and edited by the users at any time. The parameters for the adaption model can be adjusted to suit the information requirements of the mobile users. By implementing the system in the WebPADS platform, it is possible to maintain on-going service provision as the mobile node moves across different domains (e.g. from a home network to an office network in a wireless environment). A major concern about our implementation is that it is not easy to maintain the adaptation rules stored in the system confirmation file in XML format. Future directions of research include using artificial intelligence techniques to improve the flexibility in adaptation, and to provide user-friendly interfaces for the users to maintain the adaptation rules in the rule base.

References

1. Belkin, N., Croft, W.B.: Information Filtering and Information Retrieval: Two Sides of the Same Coin? Communications of the ACM 35(12), 38–39 (1992)
2. Bharadvaj, H., Joshi, A., Auephanwiriyakul, S.: An Active Transcoding Proxy to Support Mobile Web Access. In: Proceedings of the 17th IEEE Symposium on Reliable Distributed Systems, pp. 118–123 (1998)
3. Bradley, N.: The XML Companion. Addison Wesley, Reading (1998)

4. Cheung, R.: An Adaptation Control Model to Support Mobile Web Access. International Journal of Control and Automation 1(1), 9–16 (2008)
5. Cheung, R.: A Context-Aware Adaptation Model for Efficient Web Browsing on Mobile Devices. In: Kim, T.-h., Yang, L.T., Park, J.H., Chang, A.C.-C., Vasilakos, T., Yeo, S.-S. (eds.) FGCN 2008. CCIS, vol. 27, pp. 41–54. Springer, Heidelberg (2009)
6. Cheung, R.: An Adaptation Model for Accessing Document Clusters in a Mobile Environment. In: Proceedings of the 8th Asia-Pacific Conference on Computer-Human Interaction, Seoul, Korea, pp. 5–8 (2008)
7. Chuang, S.N., Chan, A.T.S., Cao, J., Cheung, R.: Dynamic Service Reconfiguration for Wireless Web Access. In: Proceedings of the Twelve International World Wide Web Conference, pp. 58–67. ACM Press, Budapest (2003)
8. Chuang, S.N., Chan, A.T.S., Cao, J., Cheung, R.: Actively Deployable Mobile Services for Adaptive Web Access. IEEE Internet Computing, 26–33 (March/April 2004)
9. Binder, W., Bonetta, D., Pautasso, C., Peternier, A., Milano, D., Schuldt, H., Stojnić, N., Faltings, B., Trummer, I.: Towards Self-Organizing Service-Oriented Architectures. In: Proceedings of the (SEASS 2011) IEEE Fifth International Workshop on Software Engineering for Adaptive Service-oriented Systems, Washington, USA (in press, 2011)
10. Extensible Markup Language (XML), http://www.w3.org/XML/
11. Han, R., Bhagwat, P., Lamaire, R., Mummert, T., Perret, V., Rubas, J.: Dynamic Adaptation in an Image Transcoding Proxy for Mobile Web Browsing. IEEE Personal Communications 5(6), 8–17 (1998)
12. Zhao, D.J., Lee, D.L., Luo, Q.: A Meta-search Method with Clustering and Term Correlation. In: Proceedings of the International Conference on Database for Advanced Applications, South Korea, pp. 543–553 (2004)

Simulation of Web Data Traffic Patterns Using Fractal Statistical Modelling

Shanyu Tang and Hassan B. Kazemian

Faculty of Computing, London Metropolitan University
166 – 220 Holloway Road, London N7 8DB, UK.
s.tang@londonmet.ac.uk

Abstract. This paper describes statistical analysis of web data traffic to identify the probability distribution best fitting the connection arrivals and to evaluate whether data traffic traces follow heavy-tail distributions – an indication of fractal behaviour, which is in contrast to conventional data traffic.

Modelling of the fractal nature of web data traffic is used to specify classes of fractal computing methods which are capable of accurately describing the burstiness behaviour of the measured data, thereby establishing web data traffic patterns.

Keywords: data traffic, patterns, fractal modelling.

1 Introduction

Data traffic is a vibrant area of queuing research. When modelling network traffic, network arrivals such as packet and connection arrivals are often modelled as Poisson processes for analytical simplicity because such processes have attractive theoretical properties [1]. However, a number of studies have shown that for both local-area [2, 3] and wide-area [4, 5] network traffic, packet interarrivals are clearly not exponentially distributed as expected from the Poisson processes. The distinctly non-Poisson nature of the arrival process has led to a substantial effort in developing statistical models of the traffic. These statistical models differ from the renewal and Markov-chain-type models that formed the basis for traditional queuing models [6], so they inspired new queuing models and solution methods.

Previous wide-area traffic studies were largely focused on FTP, TELNET, NNTP and SMTP (email) traffic [4-7], with little attention being given to web traffic [8]. The aim of this work is to tackle web traffic by providing a view of web data patterns. Since web traffic accounts for a large proportion of the traffic on the Internet, understanding the nature of web traffic is increasingly important. Like other wide-area traffic, web traffic may also have burstiness behaviour; i.e. web traffic is burst on many or all time scales. This burstiness behaviour is analogous to the self-similar or fractal-like behaviour, which exists in many natural phenomena such as Brownian motion, turbulent flow, atmospheric pressure, the distribution of stars and the activity of the stock market [9-13], which are much better characterised by fractal geometry theory than by Euclidean geometry.

L. Iliadis and C. Jayne (Eds.): EANN/AIAI 2011, Part I, IFIP AICT 363, pp. 422–432, 2011.
© IFIP International Federation for Information Processing 2011

Performance evaluation is important for assessing the effectiveness of data traffic pattern prediction, besides monitoring and verifying compliance with network performance goals [14]. Results from performance evaluation are used to identify existing problems, guide network re-optimisation, and aid in the prediction of potential future problems. Performance evaluation can be conducted in many different ways. The most notable techniques include analytical methods, simulation, and empirical methods based on measurements.

Previous research found that the light- and heavy-tailedness of web data traffic patterns. The tail weight was estimated by using the Hill method in most of the cases presented in [15, 16, 17]. The method is a statistical technique for analysing heavy-tailed phenomena. The less heavy-tailed the data traffic, the more benefit of a buffer [18]. Adding multimedia files to the set of text files led to the increase in the weight of the tail and the distribution of text files might itself be heavy-tailed [16]. For light-tailed input, the delay distribution has an exponential tail; whereas the delay distribution follows a lognormal distribution for heavy-tailed input [19]. A hypothetical example [20] of a normal probability plot for data sampled from a distribution has been illustrated from where the light-tailedness and the heavy-tailedness of the data traffic pattern can be identified by visualization.

2   Characterising Heavy-Tail Behaviour of Web Data Traffic

Several probability distributions including conventional exponential and normal distributions have been chosen to fit the web traffic traces e.g. web document size, request interval and access frequencies collected at the measurement points. Previous work [5, 6] shows that web traffic such as telnet and ftp followed heavy-tail distributions. This means that values are distributed over a very wide range and that the larger values, even if less probable, may still account for a significant portion of the traffic. Several long-tailed distributions that were chosen to fit the traces are a lognormal distribution, an extreme distribution, a log-extreme distribution, a Weibull distribution and a Pareto distribution.

Empirical distribution function (EDF) test was also used to decide whether the data (traces) were from a particular distribution and best fittings were made using the EDF statistics. Parameters (e.g. location parameter, scale parameter, shape parameter) that affect in fitting the curve are highlighted to realize their effects. The analytical expressions of some distributions are detailed in the following sections.

2.1   Log-Normal Distribution

The lognormal law or log-Gaussian frequency function is defined as

$$\frac{d\phi}{d\log x} = \frac{1}{\sqrt{2\pi}\log\sigma_g} \exp\left[\frac{(\log x - \log x_g)^2}{2\log^2\sigma_g}\right]$$

where ϕ is the general term for the frequency, x is the web file size, x_g is the geometric mean of the distribution, σ_g is the geometric standard deviation,

$\log \sigma_g = 0.5 \log\left(\dfrac{x_{84}}{x_{16}}\right)$, and $x_g = \sqrt{x_{84}x_{16}}$, where x_{16} is the size corresponding to the 16% cumulative frequency, and x_{84} is the size corresponding to the 84% cumulative frequency.

2.2 Pareto Distribution

The cumulative distribution for the Pareto (simple) random variable is obtained from

$$F(x) = P\,(X \le x) = 1 - \left(\frac{\alpha}{x}\right)^{\beta}; \quad \alpha,\beta \ge 0,\ x \ge \alpha$$

where α is the location parameter, and β is the shape parameter.

2.3 EDF Test

The EDF is a step function calculated from the sample, estimating the population distribution function. EDF statistics are measures of the discrepancy between the EDF and a given distribution function, and they are used for testing the fitting of the sample to the distribution.

Suppose a given random sample of size n is $X_1, \ldots, X_n$ and $X_{(1)} < X_{(2)} < \ldots < X_{(n)}$ be the order statistics; suppose further that the distribution of x is $F(x)$. The empirical distribution function, $F_n(x)$, is given by

$$F_n(x) = \frac{number\ of\ observations \le x}{n}; \quad -\infty < x < \infty$$

The calculation can be conducted by using the Probability Integral Transformation (PIT), $Z = F(X)$; when $F(x)$ is the true distribution of x, the new random variable Z is uniformly distributed between 0 and 1. Then Z has the distribution function $F^*(z) = z$, $0 \le z \le 1$. The following formulas can be used for calculating EDF statistics from the Z-values. The formulas involve the Z-values arranged in an ascending order, $Z_{(1)} < Z_{(2)} < \ldots < Z_{(n)}$.

$$W^2 = \sum_{i=1}^{n}\{Z_{(i)} - (2i-1)/(2n)\}^2 + 1/(12n)$$

$$U^2 = W^2 - n(\bar{z}-0.5)^2; \quad where\ \bar{z} = sample\ mean = \frac{\sum_{i=1}^{n} Z_i}{n}$$

$$A^2 = -n - \left(\frac{1}{n}\right)\sum_{i=1}^{n}(2i-1)\big[\log Z_{(i)} + \log\{1 - Z_{(n+1-i)}\}\big]$$

where $\log x$ represents $\log_e x$ (natural logarithm).

The decision can be made by comparing the calculated value with the tabulated value [3]. The hypothesis is rejected at significance level p if the calculated value is greater than the tabulated value given for level p [21].

3 Data Traffic Collection

The first step in understanding network traffic is the collection of trace data. The LBL-CONN-7 trace [22] was collected at the Lawrence Berkeley Laboratory (LBL), located in Berkeley, California, containing thirty days' worth of all wide-area TCP connections between the LBL and the rest of the world. The reduced trace was generated by TCP-reduce. TCP-reduce is a collection of Bourne shell scripts for reducing tcpdump traces to one-line summaries of each TCP connection present in the trace. The scripts are TCP-reduce, which takes a tcpdump trace file as an argument and writes a sorted summary to stdout, TCP-conn (an internal awk script that does all the work) and TCP-summary (an awk script that generates a per-protocol summary of all the TCP connections produced by TCP-reduce). The scripts were written using Bourne shell, tcpdump and the common Unix utilities sed, sort and awk. The trace was written as an ASCII file with one line per connection with the columns such as timestamp, duration, protocol, bytes sent by originator of the connection, bytes sent by responder to the connection, local host, remote host, state that the connection ended in and flags.

The trace ran from midnight, Thursday, 16 September 1993 through midnight, Friday, 15 October 1993 (times are Pacific Standard Time), capturing 606,497 wide-area connections. The tracing was performed on the Ethernet DMZ network over which flows all traffic into or out of the LBL. The raw trace was made using tcpdump on a Sun SPARC station using the BPF kernel packet filter. Fewer than 15 SYN/FIN/RST packets in a million were dropped. Timestamps had microsecond precision. The traffic was filtered to exclude connections with nearby UCB except for nntp.

A special care was taken to check the sanity of the data, as any irregularity or mistakes could set back the entire analysis for an extended period of time. The original data file was divided into smaller file and then the size (byte) of the file was arrayed into different bins for convenience of the compactness of the data file. It is very congenial to array the file size into a bin as thousands of samples can be analysed in an expected range.

4 Results and Discussion

4.1 Traffic Data in Byte Sent by Originator

Fig. 1(a) shows the web file size distribution in percentage. The highest percentage of the file size transferred is 23.4% at 500 bytes whereas the lowest is 0.30% at 23,000 bytes. The lognormal distribution does not follow the trace data satisfactorily. The t-test for one sample (web file size) in two tails distribution found to be 3.4916, which is greater than the tabulated value (Table 1), indicating that the trace data distribution may be tailed. Fig. 1(b) illustrates comparisons of the cumulative distribution between the web file data and the data generated using Pareto model. The model data somewhat fit the web data within the range 10 to 1000 byte, which is an indication of burstiness behaviour.

Table 1. T-test results for web file size data

Traffic	t (Experimental)	Degrees of freedom	t0.05 (tabulated value)
LBL-CONN-7-originator	3.4916	11	2.201
LBL-CONN-7-responder	7.3395	12	2.179

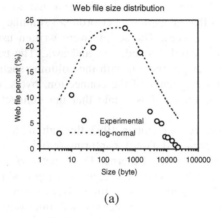
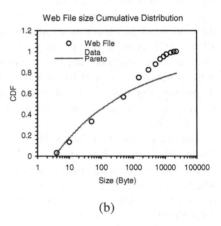

(a)   (b)

Fig. 1. Web file size distribution and Cumulative distribution of LBL_CONN_7 (byte sent by originator) data

Fig. 2 compares cumulative probability distributions of the actual trace data, the exponential, Pareto (generalized), Weibull (three parameters), logistic and extreme value distributions. The Pareto and Weibull models show the best fittings between the trace and model curves data, especially the trace data clearly follow Weibull distribution.

The experimental results show good agreements between the web data and Pareto and Weibull models, indicating that the web data distributions are heavily tailed. Such heavy-tailedness of data distributions is an indication of fractal-like burstiness behaviour of web data patterns.

The test statistics (A2, W2 and U2 tests) confirm (Table 2) that the trace data follow the normal distribution. There is contradiction between EDF test statistics and t-test as the t-test does not support the trace data for normality. The A2 test rejected the hypothesis for Weibull distribution whereas W2 and U2 tests show that the data are significant at the level $\alpha = 0.025$ which is consistent with the results shown in

Table 2. Test statistics (A2, W2 and U2) for LBL-CONN-7-originator data

Distribution	Test Statistics (TR = Test Result, α = significance level)		
	A2	W2	U2
Normal	TR = 0.6629	TR = 0.1002	TR = 0.0904
	α = 0.05	α = 0.10	α = 0.10
	Accept	Accept	Accept
Extreme value	TR = 0.5915	TR = 0.0824	TR = 0.08
	α = 0.10	α = 0.10	α = 0.10
	Accept	Accept	Accept
Weibull	TR = 2.906	TR = 0.1435	TR = 0.1218
	α = OR	α = 0.025	α = 0.025
	Reject	Accept	Accept
Exponential	TR = 0.6955	TR = 0.0807	TR = 0.0748
	α = 0.25	α = 0.25	α = 0.25
	Accept	Accept	Accept
Logistic	TR = 0.6127	TR = 0.09	TR = 0.0851
	α = 0.05	α = 0.05	α = 0.10
	Accept	Accept	Accept
Pareto	TR = 2.733	TR = 0.1427	TR=
(generalized)	α = 0.001	α = 0.025	α =
	Reject	Accept	Accept/reject

Fig. 2(c). The A2 test also rejected the hypothesis for generalized Pareto distribution where the data are significant at the level of 0.001, whereas W2 accepted the hypothesis at the level of 0.025 that makes sense with the graphical results shown in Fig. 2(b). The three test statistics show that the trace data are significant at $\alpha = 0.10$ and α=0.25 for extreme value and exponential distributions respectively, also $\alpha = 0.05$ (shown by A2 and W2 tests) and $\alpha = 0.10$ (by U2 test) for logistic distribution. The three distributions could have shown better fitness than others according to significance level. Unfortunately, poor matches were observed as shown in Figs. 2(a), (d) and (e) which is questionable. Fig. 2(f) illustrates the combination of Figs. 2(a), (b), (c), (d), and (e) from where the best fitness can be deemed by comparison.

4.2 Traffic Data in Byte Sent by Responder

Fig. 3(a) shows the web file size distribution in percentage. The highest percentage of the file size transferred is 19.48% at 150 bytes whereas the lowest is 0.12% at 600 bytes. The lognormal distribution only partly fits the web data. The t-test for one sample (web file size) in two tails distribution found to be 7.3395, which is greater than the tabulated value (Tables 1), indicating that the trace data do not follow normal distribution.

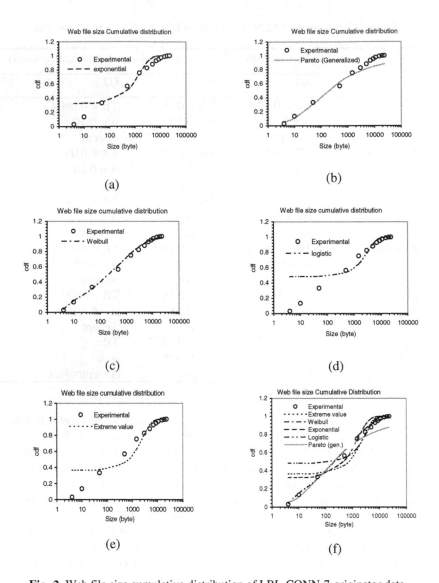

Fig. 2. Web file size cumulative distribution of LBL-CONN-7-originator data

Fig. 3(b) compares the cumulative probability distribution of the generated data points using Pareto (simple) model with the original traces. The curve does not match well with the actual data. There is consistent discrepancy between the actual distribution (web file data) and the Pareto model curve. The actual distribution seems to be light-tailed for which a good fittings can not be made as Pareto model follows heavy-tailed distribution.

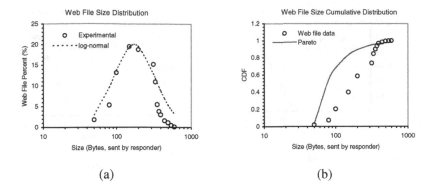

(a)   (b)

Fig. 3. Web file size distribution and Cumulative distribution of LBL_CONN_7 (byte sent by responder) data

Table 3. Test statistics (A2, W2 and U2) for LBL-CONN-7-responder data

Distribution	Test Statistics (TR = Test Result, α = significance level)		
	A2	W2	U2
Normal	TR = 0.3079	TR = 0.0474	TR = 0.0470
	α = 0.50	α = 0.50	α = 0.50
	Accept	Accept	Accept
Extreme value	TR = 0.5028	TR = 0.0894	TR = 0.0849
	α = 0.10	α = 0.10	α = 0.10
	Accept	Accept	Accept
Weibull	TR = 0.5074	TR = 0.0898	TR = 0.0836
	α = 0.15	α = 0.15	α = 0.15
	Accept	Accept	Accept
Exponential	TR = 1.1899	TR = 0.2072	TR = 0.1377
	α = 0.05	α = 0.05	α = 0.10
	Accept	Accept	Accept
Logistic	TR = 0.3321	TR = 0.0482	TR = 0.0479
	α = 0.25	α = 0.25	α = 0.25
	Accept	Accept	Accept
Pareto	TR = 1.18	TR = 0.2165	TR=
(generalized)	α = 0.05	α = 0.05	α =
	Accept	Accept	Accept/reject

Fig. 4 compares cumulative probability distributions of the actual trace data, the exponential, Pareto (generalized), Weibull (three parameters), logistic and extreme value distributions. All models show satisfactory fittings to the data points. Weibull and extreme value distributions illustrate the best fittings of curves as shown in Figs. 4(c) and (e), which is an indication of fractal-like burstiness behaviour of LBL_CONN_7 (byte sent by responder) data patterns.

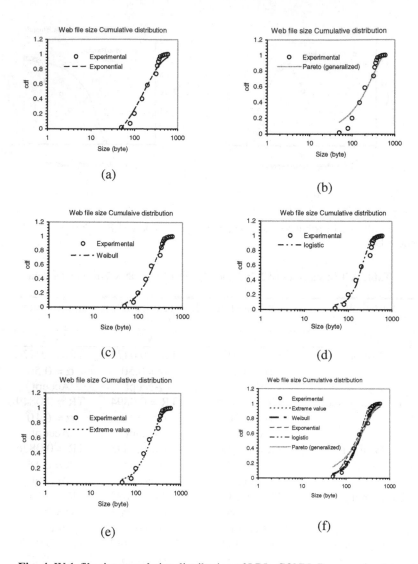

Fig. 4. Web file size cumulative distribution of LBL_CONN_7_responder data

The test statistics (A2, W2 and U2 tests) confirm (Table 3) that the trace data follow the normal distribution. The test statistics also show that the data are significant at the levels of 0.10, 0.15, 0.25, and 0.05 for extreme value, Weibull, logistic and Pareto (generalized) distributions, respectively, which is consistent with the results shown in Figs. 4(b), (c), (d), and (e). For exponential distribution, the A2 and W2 tests show the data are significant at the level $\alpha = 0.05$, and U2 shows at the level of 0.10 and the effect of these significance levels observed in Fig. 4(a) which is understandable. Likewise, there is contradiction between EDF test statistics and t-test as t-test does not support the trace data for normality.

Fig. 4(f) shows the combination of Figs 4(a), (b), (c), (d), and (e) from where comparisons of goodness-of-fit of trace data to different distributions can be made.

5 Conclusions

The T-test and EDF test statistics (A2, W2 and U2) have been used to evaluate how well a particular distribution describes the real web traffic data. The models employed in the work include lognormal, Pareto (simple), exponential, Pareto (generalized), Weibull (three parameters), logistic and extreme value distributions.

There is contradiction between EDF test statistics and t-test; the t-test results do not support the web trace data for normality, but the EDF test accepts the hypothesis that the trace data follow normal distribution. The discrepancy may be due to the different sampling methods, which has to be investigated in the future.

There are satisfactory fittings of curves observed between Weibull and the generalized Pareto model data and the real trace data, which has been confirmed by the EDF test for the two distributions. The results show that Weibull (three parameters) is the most suitable model to approximate the web traffic. In addition, the generalized Pareto model is more suitable for analysing traffic fractal-like behaviour (burstiness behaviour) than simple Pareto model.

Acknowledgements. The authors would like to thank LBL for providing the web traffic data.

References

1. Frost, V., Melamed, B.: Traffic modeling for telecommunications networks. IEEE Communication Magazine 33, 70–80 (1994)
2. Gusella, R.: A measurement study of diskless workstation traffic on an Ethernet. IEEE Trans. Commun. 38(9), 1557–1568 (1990)
3. Fowler, H.J., Leland, W.E.: Local area network traffic characteristics, with implications for broadband network congestion management. IEEE J. Select. Areas Commun. 9(7), 1139–1149 (1991)
4. Danzig, P.B., Jamin, S., Caceres, R., Mitzel, D.J., Estrin, D.: An artificial workload model of TCP/IP internetworks. J. Internetworking: Practice and Experience 3(1), 1–26 (1992)
5. Paxson, V., Floyd, S.: Wide area traffic: the failure of Poisson modeling. IEEE/ACM Trans. Networking 3, 226–244 (1995)
6. Heyamn, D.: Some issues in performance modeling of data traffic. Perform. Eval. 34, 227–247 (1998)
7. Paxson, V.: Empirically-Derived Analytic Models of Wide-Area TCP Connections. IEEE/ACM Trans. Networking 2(4), 316–336 (1994)
8. Nabe, M., Murata, M., Miyahara, H.: Analysis and modeling of world wide web traffic for capacity dimensioning of internet access lines. Performance Evaluation 34, 249–271 (1998)
9. Feder, J.: Fractals. Plenum Press, New York (1988)
10. Falconer, K.: Fractal Geometry: Mathematical Foundations and Applications, pp. 146–160. John Wiley & Sons, Chichester (1990)

11. Kaye, B.H.: A Random Walk Through Fractal Dimensions, pp. 179–188. VCH, Weinheim (1994)

12. Tang, S.: Computer simulation of fractal structure of flocs. Encyclopaedia of Surface and Colloid Science, pp. 1162–1168. Taylor & Francis, Abington (August 2006) ISBN: 978-0-8493-9615-1

13. Rezaul, K., Tang, S., Wang, T., Paksta, A.: Empirical distribution function test for World Wide Web traffic. In: Proc of International Conference on Applied Computing (IADIS), Lisbon, Portugal (March 23-26, 2004)

14. Awduche, D., Chiu, A., Elwalid, A., Widjaja, I., Xiao, X.: RFC 3272: Overview and Principles of Internet Traffic Engineering (May 2002),
    http://rfc3272.openrfc.org/

15. Judith, L.J., Wang, J.L.: From Network Management Collection to Traffic performance modelling: Challenges and lessons learned. In: CAMAD 1998 (1998)

16. Crovella, M.E., Taqqu, M.S., Bestavros, A.: Heavy-Tailed Probability Distributions in the World Wide Web, http://citeseer.ist.psu.edu/viewdoc/summary?, doi=10.1.1.29.4346

17. Bell Labs. Busier Networks create smoother traffic flow,
    http://www.informationweek.com/story/IWK20010611S0005

18. Clark, D., Lehr, W., Liu, I.: Provisioning for Bursty Internet Traffic: Implications for industry and Internet structure. MIT WISQ,
    http://www.ana.lcs.mit.edu/anaweb/PDF/ISQE_112399_web.pdf

19. Squillante, M.S., Yao, D.D., Zhang, L.: Internet Traffic: Periodicity, Tail Behaviour, and Performance Implications,
    http://www.research.ibm.com/mmaa/publication.html

20. PROPHET StatGuide. Goodness of Fit (Chi-square) Test,
    http://www.basic.nwu.edu/statguidefiles/probplots.html#Heavy-tailed%20Data

21. D'Agostino, R.B., Stephens, M.A.: Tests based on EDF statistics. In: Goodness-of-fit Techniques, ch. 4, Dekker, New York (1986)

22. Traces available in the Internet Traffic Archive,
    http://ita.ee.lbl.gov/html/traces.html

Mathematical Models of Dynamic Behavior of Individual Neural Networks of Central Nervous System

Dimitra-Despoina Pagania[1,*], Adam Adamopoulos[1,2], and Spiridon D. Likothanassis[1]

[1] Pattern Recognition Laboratory, Dept. of Computer Engineering & Informatics,
University of Patras, 26500, Patras, Greece
[2] Dept. of Medicine, Democritus University of Thrace, Alexandroupolis, Greece
{pagania,likothan}@ceid.upatras.gr, adam@med.duth.gr

Abstract. We present mathematical models that describe individual neural networks of the Central Nervous System. Three cases are examined, varying in each case the values of the refractory period and the synaptic delay of a neuron. In the case where both the refractory period and the synaptic delay are bigger than one, we split the population of neurons into sub-groups with their own distinct synaptic delay. It is shown that the proposed approach describes the neural activity of the network efficiently, especially in the case mentioned above. Various examples with different network parameters are presented to investigate the network's behavior.

Keywords: refractory period, synaptic delay, neural activity, mathematical models, asynchronous synapses.

1 Introduction

In this paper we describe and analyze mathematical models that are used for the statistical behavior of individual –without external links- neural networks of the Central Nervous System. If a neuron is activated at some point then a certain moment is necessary to pass for the neuron to be able to spike again. We consider this moment as the refractory period (r). Furthermore, we consider the moment that mediates between the spike of a neuron until the appearance of postsynaptic potential (PSP) [5] at the postsynaptic neuron being the synaptic delay (τ) [1], [2], [3]. Initially, we investigate the case where the refractory period is set to 1 (r = 1) and the synaptic delay is set to 1 too (τ = 1). The second under investigation case deals with individual neural networks with excitatory synapses where the refractory period is bigger than 1 (r > 1) while the synaptic delay is set to 1 (τ = 1) like in the first case. The third and last case studies asynchronous individual neural networks with excitatory synapses where both the refractory period and the synaptic delay are bigger than 1 (r > 1, τ > 1) [4]. Despite the fact that the last years have seen a dramatic increase of computer simulation models that were developed to investigate the issue of structure and function of the human

---

[*] Corresponding author.

L. Iliadis and C. Jayne (Eds.): EANN/AIAI 2011, Part I, IFIP AICT 363, pp. 433–442, 2011.

brain [6], [7] a few have appeared concerning neural network models with asynchronous neuron. By this term we mean the investigation of the dynamical behavior of neural network models consisting of neurons that are able to fire and cease at different time instants and not at the same time, as it is the case in neural networks consisting of synchronous neurons.

2 Individual Neural Networks with Excitatory Synapses

We study an individual neural network consisted of N neurons [4]. Each neuron has μ synapses, triggering threshold θ and refractory period r. Each synapse has synaptic weight w. All N neurons product Post Synaptic Potential (PSP) in case they are excited after τ time steps. We consider, for the moment being, that $r = 1$ and $\tau = 1$ committing that we will investigate the more general cases of $r \geq 1$ and $\tau \geq 1$ later on. If at moment n the percentage of active neurons of the network is α_n the question is to find the corresponding percentage of active neurons at the moment n+1, meaning to find the α_{n+1} versus α_n. If α_n is the percentage of active neurons at moment n, then the number of active neurons at that moment is $N \times \alpha_n$. Thus, at the moment n+1, $L = N \times \alpha_n \times \mu$ PSPs should be produced. We have to calculate the probability for a neuron to receive a total PSP that is either greater or equal to triggering threshold θ so that it is able to spike. This p_k probability is calculated by the binomial distribution

$$p_k = \binom{L}{k}(\frac{1}{N})^k (1-\frac{1}{N})^{L-k} \quad . \tag{1}$$

where L are the total PSPs produced by the active neurons and k are the ones that the neuron will receive. The neuron will be excited if $k \times w \geq \theta$ or $k \geq \theta/w$. If the synaptic weight w is set to 1, the last treaty is transformed to $k \geq \theta$. Therefore, the probability for a neuron to receive a total PSP either greater or equal to triggering threshold θ equals to the sum of p_k probabilities for $k \geq \theta$. Thus,

$$P(a_n, \theta) = \sum_{k=\theta}^{L} p_k \quad . \tag{2}$$

We must now take into consideration the refractory period r of the neurons. At the moment n, the number of active neurons is $N \times \alpha_n$. If r = 1 then at the next time step, at the moment n+1, the number of neurons that are able to spike is

$$N - N \times \alpha_n = N \times (1 - \alpha_n) \quad . \tag{3}$$

and the percentage of these neurons is

$$\alpha_{n+1} = (1 - \alpha_n) \times P(\alpha_n, \theta) \quad . \tag{4}$$

dividing by the number of neurons N the equation (3). Based on the above, we investigate the behavior of the neural network varying the following parameters: 1. Number of neurons N, 2. Number of synapses of each neuron μ, 3. Triggering threshold of each neuron θ, 4. Synaptic weight w. Specifically, we calculate the percentage of neurons that will be activated at the moment n+1, α_{n+1}, and the percentage of neurons that are active at the moment n, α_n. Also, in each case we calculate the steady states and with every change of the parameters. By steady states we mean the case where $\alpha_n = \alpha_{n+1}$.

3 Changes at the Network's Behavior

3.1 Varying the Number of Neurons N

We maintain the following values for $\mu = 70$, $\theta = 15$, $w = 0.8$. In table 1 the steady states are presented.

Table 1. Steady states for number of neurons N

Number of Neurons N	Steady States	
10	0.2000	0.4995
200	0.1700	0.5000
5000	0.1670	0.5000
10.000	0.2378	0.4997
10^{11}	0.1668	0.5000

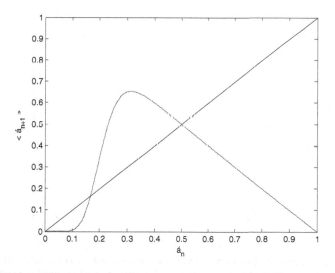

Fig. 1. We choose the number of neurons N to be 10000. While α_n increases, α_{n+1} increases too, until it reaches a percentage of the order of 0.7 where it decreases. We mention that for arbitrarily big number of neurons we choose to investigate, the behavior is still the same.

3.2 Varying the Number of Synapses μ per Neuron

We maintain the following values for $N = 10.000$, $\theta = 15$, $w = 0.8$. In table 2 the steady states are presented.

Table 2. Steady states for number of synapses μ

Number of Synapses μ Per Neuron	Steady States ss	
15	[ ]	
70	0.2376	0.4997
100	0.1493	0.5000
500	0.0227	0.5000
1000	0.0105	0.5000
7000	0.0009	0.5000

It is obvious that there are no steady states when the number of synapses per neuron is small. In this case, the neurons that could be activated at the moment n+1 do not activate at all -only a small percentage- and only when the percentage of neurons activated at the moment n is relatively big. That means that the number of synapses per neuron affects the α_{n+1} (the α_n too). As μ is increased the steady states correspond to small percentages of neurons that are activated at the moment n. That means that when each neuron is concluded with many neurons or when it has many synapses with each neuron of the network, not a big number of neurons are necessary to be activated at the moment n so that the neurons at the next time step, n+1, are activated.

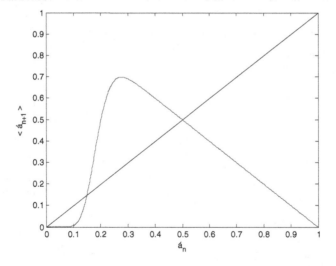

Fig. 2. When the percentage of neurons activated at the moment n overcome the 0.1 value, the percentage of neurons activated at the moment n+1 increases rapidly until it reaches a maximum limit (=~ 0.71) after which it decreases.

For a big number of synapses per neuron the behavior of the network is radically different than the case where e.g. μ = 15. The steady states are two and the first one – as already mentioned- corresponds to the activation of a small percentage of neurons.

3.3 Varying the Triggering Threshold of Neurons θ

We maintain the following values for N = 10.000, μ = 70, w = 0.8. In table 3 the steady states are presented.

Table 3. Steady states for triggering threshold of neurons

Triggering Threshold of Neurons θ	Steady States	
5	0.0468	0.5000
9	0.1186	0.5000
15	0.2376	0.4997
30	[ ]	
70	[ ]	

As the triggering threshold of neurons is increased we reach to a point where there are no steady states since the mathematical treaty k ≥ θ/w is no longer valid. The smaller the threshold θ, the faster the $α_{n+1}$ is increased versus $α_n$ and steady states exist for a rather small percentage of activated neurons.

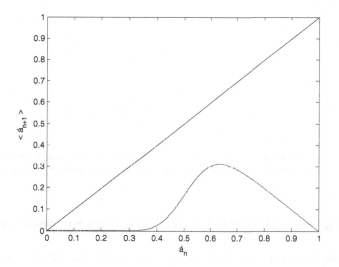

Fig. 3. For θ = 30. $α_{n+1}$ is set to 0 for a percentage of neurons equal to or bigger than 0.33. That means that neurons are not activated at all since k ≥ θ/w is no longer valid and θ is relatively big.

3.4 Varying the Synaptic Weight w

We maintain the following values for N = 10.000, μ = 70, θ = 15. In table 4 the steady states are presented.

Table 4. Steady states for synaptic weight w

Synaptic weight w	Steady States	
0.1	[ ]	
0.6	0.3668	0.4892
1.5	0.0883	0.5000

Again, since $k \geq \theta/w$ and θ is stable, as synaptic weight w is increased, the percentage of activated neurons at the moment n+1 is increased too. Contrary, for a small w, e.g. w = 0.1, α_{n+1} is set to 0 no matter how many neurons are activated at the moment n. Of course, in this case there are no steady states for the network.

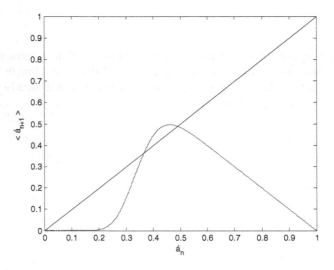

Fig. 4. For w = 0.6. By setting a bigger value to w, α_{n+1} is increased as α_n is increased. For α_n smaller than 0.19 α_{n+1} remains 0, meaning there are no neurons activated at the next time step n+1.

4   Individual Neural Networks with Excitatory Synapses and r ≥ 1

Previously, the refractory period of neurons was assumed to be equal to 1 - if of course the neuron receives $PSP \geq \theta$. In general, this restriction does not apply, therefore r should be considered bigger than 1. In equation (4) the percentage of available neurons for activation is changed, since we have to subtract the percentages of activated neurons not only at the moment n but also at the moments n - 1, n - 2, ... , n − r +1. So, the equation (4) is transformed to

$$< a_{n+1} >= (1- \sum_{i=n-r+1}^{n} a_i)*P(a_n,\theta) \qquad (7)$$

Based on the equation (7) and equation (5), it is possible to calculate the expected value α_{n+1} if the values α_n , α_{n-1} , α_{n-2} , ..., α_{n-r+1} are known [4]. The network's behavior is investigated while the refractory period r is varied and all the parameters (N, μ, θ, w) are maintained constant.

The value of the refractory period does not affect the number of neurons activated at the moment n+1 versus the number of neurons activated at the moment n since r now affects more than one time steps. For example, if r = 4, 4 previous time steps of neural activity should be taken into account. To study the affect of r > 1 on the neuron's network we investigate the evolution of the percentage of active neurons over time. We track the values for which the neural activity is identical, so we calculate the period of the repeated neural activity and the delay that the network needs to reach the periodic activity.

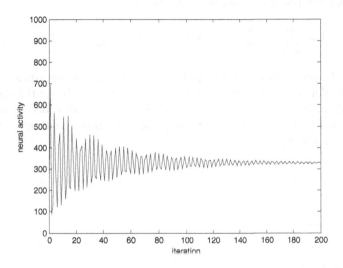

Fig. 5. For r = 2, the network reaches the periodic activity after 200 *iterations* and the period is 24. At the moment where 326 neurons *(neural activity)* are activated (of the 1000 available) the network reaches a periodic activity.

5   Asynchronous Individual Neural Networks with Excitatory Synapses and r ≥ 1, τ ≥ 1

In this case we split the total number of synapses of the network, which is equal to N × μ into sub-groups of synapses [4]. The synapses that belong to the same sub-group have the same delay τ, which means that τ time is necessary for PSP to appear in this group of synapses. Suppose that the synapses of the network are split to c sub-groups. Let f_j be the percentage of the sub-group of the synapses with synaptic delay j. Then

$$\sum_{j=1}^{c} f_j = 1 \ .$$

(8)

Due to the assumption that the synapses are asynchronous, at the moment n+1 the total PSP that is produced is a result of all the neurons that were activated at the moment n-c+1 and have synapses with synaptic delay c. If L_n, L_{n-1}, L_{n-2}, ..., L_{n-c+1} are the PSPs produced for $\tau = 1$, $\tau = 2$, etc. then:

$$L_n = a_n \times N \times \mu \times f_1$$
$$L_{n-1} = a_{n-1} \times N \times \mu \times f_2$$
$$L_{n-2} = a_{n-2} \times N \times \mu \times f_3$$

and in general :

$$L_j = a_{n-j+1} \times N \times \mu \times f_j \qquad j = 1, ..., c \ . \tag{9}$$

If L is the total PSP produced at the time n+1 then :

$$L = \sum_{j=n-c+1}^{n} L_j = \sum_{j=1}^{c} a_{n-j+1} * N * \mu * f_j = N * \mu * \sum_{j=1}^{c} a_{n-j+1} * f_j \ . \tag{10}$$

Based on the L value derived of the equation (10) we may use the equations (1), (2) and (5) to calculate the probability of neurons to be activated. Using the equation (7) the α_{n+1} is calculated for any of the r and τ values, given the networks' parameters N, μ, θ, w, r, c, and f_j, (j = 1, ..., c). Below we present the graphs concerning two cases of the network's activity.

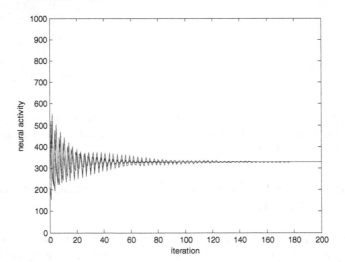

Fig. 6. For 2 sub-groups of synapses and percentage of 0.1 and 0.9 each one. The network reaches a periodic activity after 89 *iterations* while the period is 1. When 329 neurons *(neural activity)* of the 1000 available are activated, the network reaches a periodic activity.

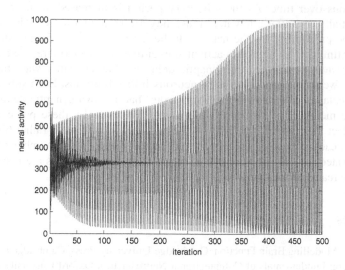

Fig. 7. For 3 subgroups of synapses. The percentage of synapses for each subgroup is 0.1, 0.2 and 0.7.

We tested the network for more sub-groups with fewer synapses per group and the result was that the bigger the number of the sub-groups, the fewer the number of the neurons are activated initially and fewer are the iterations needed for the network to reach a periodic activity. As it is shown in fig. 7, we tested the network for 500 iterations. The network reaches periodic activity after 480 iterations while the period is 3. Contrary to the case shown in fig. 6, where we had 2 sub-groups, in this case more neurons, 990, are activated (neural activity) when the network reaches a periodic activity.

6 Conclusions

By studying the aforementioned mathematical models, a few conclusions can be made: The size of the network does not affect the network's behavior, since no matter how many neurons the network is consisted of, its course remains the same. That could mean that we obtain a rather good statistical picture of the network. The number of synapses per neuron affects the network's behavior since when this number is increased, the neurons that are able to spike at the next time step are increased rapidly initially, but eventually this value decreases until it is set to zero. This phenomenon is explained by the network's training when new synapses are created. As far as the triggering threshold is concerned, when it is increased the neurons that are able to spike at the next time step are decreased to zero. For especially big triggering threshold, the neurons are never activated since the treaty $k \geq \theta/w$ (with synaptic weight stable) does not apply. By increasing the synaptic weight, the percentage of neurons that is activated at the next time step is increased rapidly while the percentage of neurons that is activated at the time n is also increased, remaining zero for a rather small α_n. For neural networks with refractory period bigger than 1, we investigate the evolution of neurons over time. As the refractory period is increased, many neurons are activated initially, but after a few iterations, they are no longer active. That is reasonable since the probability for the neurons to be active after e.g. 15 time steps is decreased over time and no neuron is activated eventually. Furthermore, the case where both the refractory period and the synaptic delay are bigger than 1 was studied. For this purpose, we split the population of neurons into sub-groups. Each sub-group has various percentages of synapses. Each sub-group had its own synaptic delay (it's the same for the members of the same sub-group). Interestingly, these percentages per subgroup affect the network's activity. If the network is split into a rather big number of subgroups each of which has a small number of synapses, the number of neurons that are activated initially is small. Also, in this case, less iterations are necessary for the system to reach periodic activity.

References

1. Amit, D.J.: Modelling Brain Function. Cambridge University Press, Cambridge (1989)
2. Trappenberg: Fundamentals of Computational Neuroscience. Oxford University Press, Oxford (2002)
3. Bear, M.F., Connors, B.W., Paradiso, M.A.: Neuroscience: Exploring the Brain, 3rd edn. Lippincott Williams & Wilkins, Baltimore (2007)
4. Adamopoulos, A.: Introduction to biological neural networks (2007)
5. Giuliodori, M.J., Zuccolilli, G.: Postsynaptic Potential Summation and Action Potential Initiation: Function Following Form. Advan. Physiol. Edu. 28, 79–80 (2004)
6. Eeckman, F.H., Bower, J.M. (eds.): Computation and Neural Systems. Kluwer Academic Publishers, Boston (1993)
7. Bower, J.M.: Modeling the nervous system. Trends Neuroscience 15, 411–412 (1992)

Towards Optimal Microarray Universal Reference Sample Designs: An *In-Silico* Optimization Approach

George Potamias[1], Sofia Kaforou[2], and Dimitris Kafetzopoulos[2]

[1] Institute of Computer Science
[2] Institute of Molecular Biology & Biotechnology,
Foundation for Research & Technology – Hellas (FORTH), N. Plastira 100,
GR - 70013 Heraklion, Crete, Greece
potamias@ics.forth.gr, kafetzo@imbb.forth.gr

Abstract. Assessment of the reliability of microarray experiments as well as their cross-laboratory/platform reproducibility rise as the major need. A critical challenge concerns the design of optimal Universal Reference RNA (URR) samples in order to maximize detectable spots in two-color/channel microarray experiments, decrease the variability of microarray data, and finally ease the comparison between heterogeneous microarray datasets. Towards this target we devised and present an *in-silico* (binary) optimization process the solutions of which present optimal URR sample designs. Setting a cut-off threshold value over which a gene is considered as detectably expressed enables the process. Experimental results are quite encouraging and the related discussion highlights the suitability and flexibility of the approach.

Keywords: Bioinformatics, microarrays, universal reference sample.

1 Introduction

Scientific experimental science is founded on the 'right' design of experiments where some common-sense principles should apply [1]. The observation is more than critical in the set-up and the complex design of microarray experiments. With more than fifteen years of research and experimentation in the field the real challenge as well as the actual tendency is moving towards the comparison of different microarray experiments originated from different platforms, from different laboratories, and from different designs. In this context, assessing the reliability of microarray experiments as well as their cross-laboratory/platform reproducibility rise as the major need.

Measuring reliable fluorescence intensities with microarrays is not a straightforward task. The basic problem rises from the variability in microarray spot geometry and the quantity of DNA deposited at each spot. So, absolute fluorescence intensity cannot be used as a reliable measure of RNA level. However, if two RNA samples are differentially labeled and co-hybridized to spots on the same microarray, the ratio of their signal intensities accurately reports the relative quantity of RNA targets in both samples – the so called, *two-color (two-channel)* hybridization set-up (2CH). Obtaining reliable and reproducible 2CH gene expression data is critically important for understanding the biological significance of perturbations made on a

L. Iliadis and C. Jayne (Eds.): EANN/AIAI 2011, Part I, IFIP AICT 363, pp. 443–452, 2011.
© IFIP International Federation for Information Processing 2011

cellular system. Moreover, and most critical, *maximizing detectable spots* on the reference image channel also decreases the variability of microarray data allowing for reliable detection of smaller differential gene expression changes. [2].

With the 2CH microarray technology there are two alternatives for the comparison between different sample conditions, C_1 vs. C_2: (i) the *'loop'* design where, direct comparisons between a series of arrays are performed with a sample of type C_1 in one channel and one of type C_2 in the other channel for all other arrays, and the comparison of samples in circular or multiple pair-wise fashion - it is a useful approach when a small number of samples is to be analyzed; and (ii) the *Universal RNA Reference* (URR) sample, C – devised by a pool of diverse (in terms of their ability to express different families of genes) cell-lines. With the URR approach a series of hybridizations are carried out with an experimental sample of type C_1 / C_2 in one channel and the URR sample in the other. Then differences in gene-expression between C_1 and C_2 are acquired by comparing the ratios C_1/C vs. C_2/C [3]. The hybridization of each (experimental) sample with a URR *mixture* serves as a common denominator between different microarray hybridizations [4]. With the employment of a reproducible URR the quantization of gene-expression levels is more reliable and offers a valuable tool for monitoring and controlling intra- and inter-experimental variation. The URR design has several practical advantages over the loop design: (i) it extends easily to other experiments if the common URR is preserved, (ii) is robust to multiple chip failures; and (iii) reduces incidence of laboratory mistakes as each (experimental) sample is handled the same way [1]. In addition, the URR design facilitates the normalization and the subsequent comparison between heterogeneous microarray data sets [5]. Typically molecular scientists and experimentalists prepare their own array-specific reference samples e.g., genomic DNA [6, 7], a mixture of clones spotted on the arrays [8], as well as complementary to every microarray spot short oligomers [9]. Many groups utilize a mixture of cell-lines for their URR (e.g., Stratagene's human URR [5]) or, clone-vectors [2]. In most of the cases the utilized URR samples are not reproducible between labs and may provide detectable signal for a low percentage of the microarray spots [10]. Subsequently, they do not provide good expression *coverage*, i.e., a high proportion of genes being adequately hybridized and expressed in order to avoid spots with zero denominators in C_1/C vs. C_2/C ratio comparisons, a fact that would force discarding those spots from the analyses [3].

It is natural to assume, and this is actual the case, that as more cell-lines are utilized to prepare the URR sample mixture then, the biggest the chance to get dilution and saturation effects. So, it is of fundamental importance to determine an *optimum number* of cell-lines so that such effects are avoided as much as possible. This is the target of the present work. In particular, our aim was to devise a general methodology that guides the determination of an optimal ("the less the better") number of cell-lines the mixture of which is capable to hybridize and express the highest possible number of array genes. The paper is organized as follows: section 2 outlines the state-of-the-art research on the field; in section 3 we introduce and formally present our optimization approach, and in section 4 we present and discuss the results of the performed experiments; finally, in section 6 we conclude and point to future research plans.

2 Background to the URR Sample Design

The MAQC (MicroArray Quality Control) project[1] systematically evaluated the reliability of microarray technology by profiling two human URR samples using different microarray and QPCR (*Quantitative PCR*) platforms [11]: Stratagene's (acquired by Agilent Technologies[2]) human Universal Reference RNA™ - derived from a mixture of cell lines [5], and Ambion's human brain URR - pooled from multiple donors and several brain regions[3].

According to Sterrenburg et al., a common reference for DNA microarrays would consist of a mix of the products being spotted on the array. Their polymerase chain reaction (PCR) reference was generated by pooling a fraction of all amplified microarray probes prior to printing. A very low number of spots could not be analyzed because reference, as opposed to target, did not give a significant signal [8]. Yang et al., suggested the use of a limited number of cell lines, each expressing a large number of diverse genes. They constructed two reference pools from those cell lines with the greatest representation of unique genes, which are also easy to grow and yield high quantities of RNA. They found that adding more cell lines to the pool would not necessarily improve the overall gene representation because some genes were diluted below the detection limit. The first reference sample exhibited similar coverage with Statagene's human URR sample (75%), and the second reference sample had coverage equal to 80%. Thus, according to Yang et al., a simple pool of RNA from diverse cell lines can provide a superior reference [10]. Human, mouse and rat reference RNA samples were considered by Novoradovskaya et al. [5] and were prepared from pools of RNA derived from individual cell lines representing different cell-lines (ten human, eleven mouse and fourteen rat). They evaluated microarray coverage based on a pre-specified threshold equal to the background intensity or twice the background intensity of each channel, using different microarray platforms. Probes with intensities above threshold were characterized as present. They reported microarray coverage greater than 80% for all arrays tested when threshold was equal to background, and greater than 60% when threshold was equal to twice the background. Consequently, they agreed with Yang et al., that pools of RNA derived from a limited but diverse set of cell lines result in an optimal reference sample.

Furthermore, in a recent study we examined whether a small number of cell-lines (in a total of 22), each of which expresses different genes, could outperform more complex reference mixtures [12]. Following different techniques (exhaustive combination of cell-lines, heuristic search and stochastic simulated annealing) we achieved an optimal cell-line mixture of 11 cell-lines with theoretical gene coverage of 57.84%. The mixture was tested with a wet-lab experiment (i.e., it was hybridized with the mixture of all 22 cell-lines), and showed coverage of 57.12% - quite near to the theoretical one. Testing (with a similar experimental set-up) the standard Stratagene URR mixture an inferior coverage of 54.02% could be reached.

The relatively low gene coverage (around 57%) but also, the need to offer a more natural, universal and robust design approach forced us to consider a straightforward

---

[1] http://www.fda.gov/ScienceResearch/BioinformaticsTools/MicroarrayQualityControlProject/default.htm

[2] http://www.genomics.agilent.com/

[3] http://www.ambion.com/catalog/CatNum.php?6050

optimization approach. In particular, we utilized the mathematical programming framework and devised a *linear/binary programming* optimization methodology. Our methodology is flexible enough and could be easily tuned to fit the specifics of different microarray platforms and heterogeneous experimental settings.

3   Towards Optimal Reference Sample Designs

Assume a set of genes, G, and a set of cell-lines, C. In addition, we assume that the URR sample is to be devised using equal shares of fixed quantity from each cell-line. A series of C two-channel microarray experiments are performed, each time hybridizing an individual cell-line with the reference-mix. After standard, cross-experiment normalization of the acquired intensities, we get the gene-expression profile for each cell-line, and the respective gene-expression matrix is formed - a matrix with G rows and C columns. Our fundamental concern is twofold: which genes are expressed over all cell-lines (i.e., across rows), and which genes are expressed by each cell-line (i.e., across columns). We address the problem by setting a *cut-off* value, with gene-expression values greater than the cut-off to be considered as detectably expressed (with the remaining considered as not detectable). In most microarray experiments expression cut-off values could be acquired either during the microarray image analysis phase where, the (manual) inspection of the underlying background intensities guides to the determination of a specific cut-off value in order to consider the gene signal as detectable or, by the inspection of the normalized gene-expression matrix and the calculation of different cut-off values for different fold-change gene expression rates. As the determination of the cut-off value is beyond the scope of the current work, we assume an absolute cut-off based on the *median* over all gene-expression values.

We consider a gene as *detectably expressed* if an *adequate number of selected cell-lines express it*, i.e., the corresponding gene's expression values for these cell-lines are over the cut-off. In the present paper we report results with two different cut-off values: one that equals the median, and one being set to the 70% of the median of all gene-expression values. Elaborating on the previous discussion, we post two *criteria* in order to consider the number of cell-lines (to be utilized in the URR) as optimal:

(i) each array gene should exhibit an *adequate* number of its corresponding expression-values over the cut-off threshold - in this case we consider the gene as expressed, and

(ii) the number of expressed genes is over a (user-defined) pre-specified percentage of all array genes. All genes considered as expressed by (i) are considered as covered, and their percentage over all the array genes presents the coverage figure of the final URR mixture.

3.1   The Optimization Methodology

In order to meet and fulfill the aforementioned criteria we devised an optimization process enabled by a linear/binary programming problem formulation.

Notation. Cell-line: given a set of m cell-lines, assume, C_j, a set of *binary* variables, $C_j \in \{0,1\}$, $0 \le j \le m$ to denote the *presence* ($C_j = 1$) or, *absence* ($C_j = 0$) status of a cell-line. We do not cope with the case of multiple (i.e., integer or, real) values for C_j. This is a more difficult problem that calls for a more elaborate and complex modeling. In such a case we need more microarray experiments in order to assess exact dilution and saturation effects when the cell-lines are taking part in a reference-mix in non-equal shares; *Gene-Expression value*: given a set of n genes, G_i, $0 \le i \le n$, we denote with G_{ij} the expression value of gene i for cell-line j; *Cut-Off*: the pre-specified cut-off threshold is denoted with T. Based on this notation we form the following Binary Programming Optimization Problem (BPOP):

minimize OF: $$\sum_{j=1}^{m} C_j \qquad\qquad (1)$$

subject to: $$\sum_{j=1}^{m} C_j \cdot G_{ij} \ge kT \qquad\qquad (2)$$

$$i, 1 \le i \le n$$

$$C \in \{0,1\}, G_{ij} \in \mathrm{R}$$

$$0 \le k \le m$$

Solutions to the BPOP problem will assign values to the binary variables C_j. If $C_j=1$ then, the respective cell-line is to be utilized in the URR sample, otherwise it will not. The objective function (1) seeks for the minimum number of cell-lines to be utilized. Each constraint in (2) states the following requirement: the weighted sum of gene-expression values (over all present cell-lines) should be greater or equal to kT, i.e., k times the cut-off value T. In other words, we try minimize the number of cell-lines, and at the same time to keep the gene-expression values over k times the (pre-specified) cut-off threshold. In this way, the constraints guide the minimization process to select those cell-lines for which at least one or more of its gene-expression values is over the cut-off. In the ideal, the corresponding gene-expression values will be greater than the cut-off in all present cell-lines – of course this may happen if all genes exhibit at least one of their expression values (across all present cell-lines) over the cut-off. What we really seek is an adequate number of cell-lines for which each gene exhibits an expression value over the cut-off. Tolerating (by varying the k control number) the required number of cell-lines covering a gene the BPOP process results into different solutions. For example, we may consider a gene as expressed if *at-least-one* of its expression values is over the cut-off, i.e., at-least-one cell-line covers it. This requirement is guaranteed by the formulation of BPOP - the constraints presented by (2) guides the optimization process to select those cell-lines for which, not only just one value is over the cut-off but also all other values are high enough in order to pass the kT threshold. So, for different and increasing values of k the actual BPOP solutions meet the aforementioned criteria for the design of an optimal reference sample.

4 Experiments

A set of 22 tissue-specific cell-lines were targeted as candidates for the design of the optimal URR (their code, name and tissue-origin are shown in Table 1). With these cell-lines a set of 22 microarray experiments were conducted on a custom-made microarray platform comprising 34771 gene transcripts (for details of cell-line hybridizations, acquisition of signal-intensities and normalization across experiments the reader may refer to [12]). As a number of missing gene-expression values were present, and in order to avoid as much as possible noise effects, we conducted a data cleaning procedure: (a) genes having more than half, across all cell-lines, missing values were eliminated, and (b) for the remaining genes we replaced missing values with the average of the respective gene's expression values. The data cleaning process concluded into a final set of 34673 genes.

Table 1. The target cell-lines

	Cell line	Tissue origin
1.	HL60	Bone marrow
2.	Hs578T	Mammary Gland
3.	McF7	Mammary Gland
4.	OVCAR3	Ovary
5.	Panc1	Pancreas
6.	SKMEL3	Skin
7.	SKMM2	Bone Marrow
8.	T47D	Mammary Gland
9.	TERA1	Testis
10.	U87MG	Brain
11.	Raji	B-lymphoblasts
12.	JAR	Genital
13.	Saos2	Bone
14.	SW872	Liposarcoma
15.	THP1	Peripheral Blood
16.	HCT116	Colon
17.	HUVEC	Umbelical Vein
18.	HepG2	Liver
19.	HeLa	Cervix
20.	LNCap	Prostate
21.	Molt4	T-lymphoblasts
22.	WERI1	Retina

We set the cut-off threshold to be equal to the median (T=368.64) of all gene-expression values, and to a proportion of 70% of the median (T = 258.05). Because of space limitations we do not report the full spectrum of results but just some observations should be reported: (a) a percentage of 28.1% and 5.0% of genes are not covered by any cell-line, (b) the percentage of genes being covered by just-one ($k=1$) time the respective cut-off threshold is 7.4% and 4.5%, respectively – in this case the respective genes are considered as *tissue-specific*, and are not taking part in the optimization process, and (c) the percentage of genes being covered by all, ($k=22$) times the respective cut-off threshold is 31.5% and 46.7%, respectively - these genes are considered as *tissue-independent,* and again are not taking part in the optimization process (whatever cell-line is to be included in the final URR, these genes will always exhibit gene-expression levels over the respective cut-off threshold; and (iv) the percentage of genes being covered by at-least-one ($k\geq1$) times the respective cut-off threshold is 71.9% and 95.0%, respectively - this observation validates the determination of the median as a rational cut-off value.

4.1 Results and Discussion

We run the BPOP process for each of the specified cut-off thresholds using the MOSEK optimization suite [4]. MOSEK optimization software solves large-scale mathematical optimization problems, and provides specialized solvers for linear/binary programming and mixed integer programming problems. In the sequel we present and discuss on the respective results.

$T = 368.64$ cut-off. Varying the k control number from 2 to 21 (times the cut-off threshold value - recall that genes with just one, $k=1$, and all, $k=22$ of their expression values over the cut-off are discarded), we came up with the results presented in Table 2. The 'k' row refers to the number of times the sum over all weighted gene-expression values exceeds the cut-off – it controls the lower limit for the formed BPOP constraints. Note that for $k>13$ no solutions could be found, i.e., there are no genes covered by more than 13 cell-lines.

Table 2. Gene coverage results of the BPOP process for cut-off $T=368.64$

at-least	one				two				three					three
k	1	2	3	4	5	6	7	8	9	10	11	12	13	
C_j=1	2	4	6	7	9	10	12	13	15	16	18	19	21	22
0	45.4%	40.4%	38.1%	36.7%	34.7%	33.9%	33.0%	32.3%	30.9%	30.1%	29.4%	29.2%	28.3%	28.1%
1	54.6%	59.6%	61.9%	63.3%	65.3%	66.1%	67.0%	67.7%	69.1%	69.9%	70.6%	70.8%	71.7%	71.9%
2	45.9%	51.9%	55.0%	56.2%	58.1%	58.1%	59.7%	60.5%	61.7%	62.2%	63.1%	63.4%	64.2%	64.5%
3		47.1%	51.3%	52.4%	54.5%	54.5%	56.1%	57.0%	58.0%	58.5%	59.4%	59.7%	60.4%	60.7%
4		40.4%	48.0%	49.6%	51.9%	51.9%	53.7%	54.7%	55.7%	56.2%	57.0%	57.3%	58.1%	58.3%
5			44.4%	46.7%	49.6%	49.6%	51.7%	52.9%	53.9%	54.5%	55.3%	55.6%	56.3%	56.5%
6			38.7%	43.2%	47.4%	47.4%	49.9%	51.3%	52.5%	53.0%	53.8%	54.1%	54.9%	55.2%
7				37.7%	44.8%	44.8%	48.1%	49.8%	51.2%	51.8%	52.6%	53.0%	53.8%	54.1%
8					41.7%	41.7%	46.2%	48.3%	49.9%	50.5%	51.5%	51.9%	52.7%	53.0%
9					36.2%	36.2%	43.8%	46.6%	48.5%	49.2%	50.4%	50.9%	51.7%	52.1%
10							40.6%	44.8%	47.2%	48.0%	49.3%	49.8%	50.8%	51.2%
11							35.2%	42.6%	45.7%	46.7%	48.2%	48.8%	49.8%	50.3%
12							24.7%	39.8%	44.0%	45.2%	46.9%	47.6%	48.8%	49.4%
13								31.6%	41.8%	43.5%	45.7%	46.4%	47.8%	48.4%
14									38.9%	41.1%	44.4%	45.2%	46.7%	47.5%
15									33.8%	38.1%	42.7%	43.9%	45.7%	46.4%
16										33.1%	40.4%	42.2%	44.5%	45.4%
17											37.6%	39.9%	43.2%	44.3%
18											32.6%	37.1%	41.3%	42.9%
19												32.2%	39.2%	41.2%
20													36.4%	39.0%
21													31.6%	36.3%
22														31.5%

(COVER indicated along the left vertical axis for rows 0–22)

The respective non-zero binary variables in each solution are shown in row '$C_j=1$', for example, when $k=4$ the solution includes 7 non-zero, i.e., the sum of genes' expression values is greater or equal to four times the cut-off is satisfied. In other words, all constraints are satisfied at an optimal selection of seven cell-lines. Setting a lower (user specified) coverage limit of 60%, and in the case that all 22 cell-lines are to be included in the final URR mixture, all genes should exhibit gene-expression levels over the cut-off in <u>at-least-three</u> cell-lines. For $k=3$ the corresponding adequate number of cell-lines is equal to <u>at-least-one</u>. On this level of adequacy, i.e., when we

---

[4] http://www.mosek.com

want the genes to exhibit in at-least-one cell-line an expression value over the cut-off, we achieve coverage of 61.9% with the inclusion of just 6 cell-lines. For $k=4$ the corresponding adequate number of cell-lines is still to at-least-one. On this level of adequacy we achieve coverage of 63.3% with the inclusion of just 7 cell-lines. For $k=8$ the corresponding adequate number of cell-lines is equal to at-least-two. On this level of adequacy, i.e., when we want the genes to exhibit in at-least-two cell-lines expression values over the cut-off, we achieve coverage of 60.5% in the presence of 13 cell-lines. When the corresponding adequate number of cell-lines is equal to at-least-three, we may achieve a coverage of 60.4% but with a costly reference sample design of 21 cell-lines being present ($k=13$). With a careful inspection of the results we devised a map of the cell-lines being present in the aforementioned solutions (Table 3).

Table 3. Present cell-lines (marked) in the solutions for the design of an optimal reference sample for cut-off $T=368.64$

k	3	4	7	8	12	13
# CELL-LINES	6	7	12	13	19	21
COVERAGE	61.9%	63.3%	59.7%	60.5%	59.7%	60.4%
CELL-LINE	PRESENCE					
HL60	✓	✓	✓	✓	✓	✓
Hs578T			✓	✓	✓	✓
McF7					✓	✓
OVCAR3					✓	✓
Panc1	✓	✓	✓	✓	✓	✓
SKMEL3			✓	✓		
SKMM2				✓	✓	✓
T47D				✓	✓	✓
TERA1		✓	✓	✓	✓	✓
U87MG			✓	✓	✓	✓
Raji						✓
JAR	✓	✓	✓	✓	✓	✓
Saos2				✓	✓	✓
SW872			✓	✓	✓	✓
THP1				✓	✓	✓
HCT116	✓	✓	✓		✓	✓
HUVEC						✓
HepG2	✓	✓	✓	✓	✓	✓
HeLa	✓	✓	✓	✓	✓	✓
LNCap					✓	✓
Molt4					✓	✓
WERI1			✓		✓	✓

From table 3 we may observe that there are exactly four cell-lines, HL60, Panc1, JAR and HepG2, being present in all solutions. So, it is natural to consider them as the most promising and the only components of the optimal URR sample mixture. With just these cell-lines in the final URR reference mixture we were able to achieve coverage of 60%. Note, that two of these cell-lines (Panc1, HepG2) are also included in the experimentally tested URR mixture that achieves coverage of 57.12% (refer to [12]).

$T=258.05$ *cut-off.* The BPOP process was also applied on the same data with a lower cut-off threshold T = 258.05 (70% of the median) but with a higher coverage limit of 75%. Because of space limitations we do not report results analogue to Tables 2 and 3. With a careful inspection of the results we again came up with a map of the cell-lines being present in the solutions that meet the aforementioned criteria. There are thirteen of them with just six cell-lines, HL60, Hs578T, Raji, HepG2, LNCap, and WERI1 being present in at least eleven of the thirteen solutions. So (as in the case of the 368.64 threshold) it is natural to consider them as the most promising and the only components of the optimal URR sample mixture. With just these six cell-lines we were able to achieve a coverage of 87.8%. Again, five (Hs578T, Raji, HepG2, LNCap, and WERI1) of the six cell-lines are included in the experimentally tested URR mixture (refer to [12]). So, and provided that with the presence of less cell-lines saturation and dilution effects are avoided as much as possible, we may hypothesize that the presented optimization approach greatly improves previous URR sample designs.

5 Concluding Remarks

We have presented an *in-silico* methodology for the design of optimal URR samples suited for 2CH microarray experiments. The biological problem to overcome relates to the avoidance (as much as possible) of dilution and saturation effects taking place when a big number of cell-lines are present. In the final URR mixture sample. We approached the problem with the careful formation of a binary programming optimization methodology (BPOP). In particular, we tried to minimize a set of binary variables that represent the inclusion or not of a cell-line in the final URR mixture, and maximize the overall expression of genes. Setting different cut-off values, to determine if a gene is detectably expressed or not, we achieved high enough gene coverage percentages. In particular, setting the cut-off to the 70% the median of gene expression values, we were able to achieve a quite high coverage of 87.8% with the presence of just six cell-lines. A figure that outperforms current state-of-the-art URR sample designs.

Our future R&D plans include: (a) testing and assessment of the introduced optimization methodology on other cell-line configurations, and especially on integrated microarray data from different platforms and studies, and (b) elaboration of more advanced optimization techniques, e.g., integer and/or real programming optimization in order to extend our approach to varying cell-line shares in the final URR mixture.

References

1. Design of Microarray Experiments. Genomics & Bioinformatics Group, Laboratory of Molecular Pharmacology, Center for Cancer Research, NCI, NIH, DHHS, http://discover.nci.nih.gov/microarrayAnalysis/Experimental.Design.jsp
2. Khan, R.L., Gonye, E.E., Gao, S., Schwaber, J.S.: A universal reference sample derived from clone vector for improved detection of differential gene expression. BMC Genomics 7, 109 (2006), doi:10.1186/1471-2164-7-109
3. Manduchi, E., White, P.: Issues Related to Experimental Design and Normalization. WhitePaper-20040629, Report, Computational Biology and Informatics Laboratory, University of Pennsylvania, http://www.cbil.upenn.edu/downloads/EPConDB/download/Protocols/WhitePaper-20040629.doc
4. Eisen, M.B., Brown, P.O.: DNA arrays for analysis of gene expression. Methods Enzymol. 303, 179–205 (1999)

5. Novoradovskaya, N., Whitfield, M.L., et al.: Universal Reference RNA as a standard for microarray experiments. BMC Genomics 5, 20 (2004), doi:10.1186/1471-2164-5-20
6. Williams, B.A., Gwirtz, R.M., Wold, B.J.: Genomic DNA as a cohybridization standard for mammalian microarray measurements. Nucleic Acids Res. 32(10), e81 (2004)
7. Gadgil, M., Lian, W., Gadgil, C., Kapur, V., Hu, W.S.: An analysis of the use of genomic DNA as a universal reference in two channel DNA microarrays. BMC Genomics 6, 66 (2005)
8. Sterrenburg, E., Turk, R., Boer, J.M., van Ommen, G.B., den Dunnen, J.T.: A common reference for cDNA microarray hybridizations. Nucleic Acids Res. 30(21), e116 (2002)
9. Dudley, A.M., Aach, J., Steffen, M.A., Church, G.M.: Measuring absolute expression with microarrays with a calibrated reference sample and an extended signal intensity range. Proc. Natl. Acad. Sci. 99(11), 7554–7559 (2002)
10. Yang, I.Y., Chen, E., et al.: Within the fold: assessing differential expression measures and reproducibility in microarray assays. Genome Biology 3 (2002), doi:10.1186/gb-2002-3-11-research0062
11. Shi, L., Reid, L.H., Jones, W.D., et al.: The MicroArray Quality Control (MAQC) project shows inter- and intraplatform reproducibility of gene expression measurements. Nat. Biotechnol. 24(9), 1151–1161 (2006)
12. Tsiliki, G., Kaforou, S., Kapsetaki, M., Potamias, G., Kafetzopoulos, D.A.: A computational approach to microarray universal reference sample. In: 8th IEEE International Conference on BioInformatics and BioEngineering, pp. 1–7 (2008), doi:10.1109/BIBE.2008.4696690

Information-Preserving Techniques Improve Chemosensitivity Prediction of Tumours Based on Expression Profiles

E.G. Christodoulou[1], O.D. Røe[2], A. Folarin[3], and I. Tsamardinos[1,4]

[1] Bioinformatics Laboratory, ICS-FORTH, Heraklion, Crete, Greece
[2] Dept. of Cancer Research and Molecular Med., NTNU
[3] University College London
[4] Computer Science Department, University of Crete

Abstract. Prior work has shown that the sensitivity of a tumour to a specific drug can be predicted from a molecular signature of gene expressions. This is an important finding for improving drug efficacy and personalizing drug use. In this paper, we present an analysis strategy that, compared to prior work, maintains more information and leads to improved chemosensitivity prediction. Specifically we show (a) that prediction is improved when the GI50 value of a drug is estimated by all available measurements and fitting a sigmoid curve and (b) application of regression techniques often results in more accurate models compared to classification techniques. In addition, we show that (c) modern variable selection techniques, such as MMPC result in better predictive performance than simple univariate filtering. We demonstrate the strategy on 59 tumor cell lines after treatment with 118 fully characterized drugs obtained by the National Cancer Institute (NCI 60 screening) and biologically comment on the identified molecular signatures of the best predicted drugs.

Keywords: chemosensitivity prediction, variable selection, feature selection, regression, classification.

1 Introduction

Prior work shows that the sensitivity of a tumour to a drug can be predicted better than chance based on the gene-expressions of the tumour [1], [2]. This finding paves the way to personalized therapy models. However, the machine learning and statistical analysis employed in prior work processes the data in a way that reduces the available information with potential detrimental effects both on the models' prediction performance as well as the identification of the molecular signatures [1], [2], [3].

First the estimation of the response to a drug in prior work is sub-optimal [1], [2]. The response of a tumour depends of course, on the dosage. The National Cancer Institute has treated a panel of 60 cancer cell lines with several thousands drugs and has created a dosage-response profile for each combination of

L. Iliadis and C. Jayne (Eds.): EANN/AIAI 2011, Part I, IFIP AICT 363, pp. 453–462, 2011.

drug and tumour. Often, this profile is summarized with a single value such as the $\log_{10} GI50$ where GI50 is the dosage (in μM) of the drug that reduces the natural tumour growth to 50% within 48 hours. NCI, in the majority of cases, estimates $\log_{10} GI50$ by piece-wise linear interpolation which are then employed by all prior work (e.g., [1], [4], [3]). In this paper, *we show that estimating the $\log_{10} GI50$ values by fitting a sigmoid to the dosage-response profile preserves more information about the effects of the drug that lead to statistically significantly improved predictive performance.*

Second, prior work typically quantizes the $\log_{10} GI50$ values to create classes of tumours: [1] and [2] categorize tumours as sensitive and resistant, while [3] and [4] as sensitive, intermediate, and resistant. This type of quantization allows the application of machine learning classification techniques, variable selection methods for classification tasks, and statistical hypothesis testing techniques for discrete outcomes. Our computational experiments demonstrate that maintaining the exact $\log_{10} GI50$ values and *employing regression analysis instead of classification is often preferable as it improves chemosensitivity prediction in approximately half of the cases.*

Third, prior work often employs simple methods for identifying molecular signatures such as selecting the top k genes that are mostly differentially expressed between different classes of tumours. *We show that more sophisticated methods such as the Max Min Parents and Children (MMPC) algorithm for multi-variate feature selection [5] select more predictive signatures for the same parameter k. We biologically interpret these signatures for the 5 better predicted drugs.*

2   Data and Problem Description

Data Description: Gene-expression profiles were obtained for the NCI-60 cell-line panel [6] (these actually contain expressions only for 59 of the 60 cell lines) representing nine types of cancers: 5 Breast, 6 Central Nervous System (CNS), 7 Colon, 6 Leukemia, 10 Melanoma, 8 Lung, 7 Ovarian, 2 Prostate, 7 Renal. The expressions were measured on AffymtrixU133plus2 array containing 54,675 probesets that correspond to about 47,000 transcript variants which in turn represent more than 39,500 of the best characterized human genes. We denote with X_i the vector of expressions for cell-line i, X_i^v the expression value for probeset v on cell-line i, and with $\mathcal{X} = \{X_i\}$ the matrix of expressions. The raw data have been subjected to GCRMA normalization before analysis as implemented in the BioConductor platform [7]. The drug-response data for all 59 cell-lines were obtained from the CellMiner database [8] for a panel of 118 drugs that are fully characterized. Specifically, for each combination of drug and cell-line, the data contain several pairs of $\langle d, r \rangle$, where d is the log_{10} drug dosage and r is the percentage of tissue that survived at 48 hours after treatment. We denote with $R_{i,j}$ the set of such pairs for cell-line i and drug j.

Problem Definition: The analysis task we address is to predict the response to a drug of a tissue with expression vector X. The response of cell-line i to a drug j is often characterized with a single number that we denote with $GI50_{i,j}$

and corresponds to $\log_{10} GI50$. $GI50_{i,j}$ is typically not available in the raw data, thus the value of $GI50_{i,j}$ is estimated from the data in $R_{i,j}$. Learning predictive models for $GI50_{i,j}$ given a vector X is a regression task. Additionally, we are interested in identifying minimal molecular signatures that are optimally predictive of response and that could provide insight into the molecular mechanisms of the drug.

3   Improving the Estimation of $GI50$

The $GI50_{i,j}$ values in the publicly available NCI data are usually estimated as follows : The mean response $\bar{r}(d)$ for each dosage d is calculated and a piecewise linear function is interpolated through these mean values. The estimated GI50 value is the concentration that corresponds to $r = 50\%$ on this function, denoted as $GI50_{i,j}^{PLI}$. According to the official NCI-60 site [9], this is the methodology followed for estimating the 55% of the $GI50_{i,j}$ values. The remaining 45% were either approximated (manually, we presume) or chosen to be the highest concentration tested.

We now present an estimation method that employs all available measurements in $R_{i,j}$. We assume the dosage-response curve to have a sigmoid shape where at 0 dosage (i.e., its logarithm approaches $-\infty$) there is no reduction of the tumour (r=100%) and at infinity the tumour size is reduced to zero (r=-100%).

The equation of a sigmoid that ranges asymptotically between α and $\alpha + \beta$ and crosses the mid-range at γ is

$$r = \alpha + \frac{\beta}{1 + e^{(d-\gamma)\delta}} \tag{1}$$

where δ is a parameter controlling the slope of the function, r the response and d the dosage (expressed by its logarithm). Considering that asymptotically the drug has no effect at small dosages we set $\alpha = -100\%$; equivalently, at high dosages the tumour is eradicated completely which corresponds to -100% growth, and so we set $\beta = 200$. The remaining two parameters γ and δ were estimated using least-squares numerical optimization. Specifically, we used the function *nlinfit* of Matlab with initial values $\gamma = -5$ and $\delta = 1$. This function performs a number of steps towards the steepest descend direction for the parameters γ and δ in order to converge to a good value. In the cases where the procedure would not converge with these initial values, we repeated it 100 times with different initial values for the parameters γ and δ uniformly sampled within [-15 2] (the range of all concentrations in the data). Out of these 100 repetitions the parameter pair that led to the least mean squared error (MSE) was selected. The estimated $GI50_{i,j}$ values are found by setting r=50% and solving Eq. 1. In certain cases, fitting a sigmoid leads to extreme values. In order to detect the outliers we applied the matlab function *deletoutliers*. This implements iteratively the Grubbs Test that tests one value at a time [10]. If outliers are found they are trimmed to $\pm 2 * \sigma_j$, where σ_j is the standard deviation of all currently fitted values to drug j. We denote the final estimates as $GI50_{i,j}^{Sig}$. Figure 1(a)

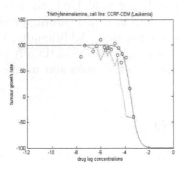 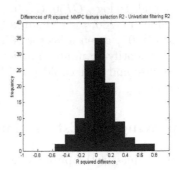

Fig. 1. (Left)The drug-response measurements for cell line CCRF-CEM (Leukemia) and Carmustine (BCNU). The $R_{i,j}$ values are shown, as well as the fitted sigmoid curve (red color) and the respective piece-wise linear interpolation segments (green color), (Right) Histogram of differences of leave-one-out cross validated R^2 when MMPC is used as the feature selection procedure minus the leave-one-out cross validated R^2 when univariate filtering is used as the feature selection procedure.

shows a graphical depiction of $R_{i,j}$ for the CCRF-CEM (Leukemia) cell-line and Carmustine (BCNU) with the fitted sigmoid superimposed. The corresponding piece-wise linear interpolation segments are also shown in the figure. We now show that this method of estimation leads to improvements in chemosensitivity prediction. The analysis includes the following steps:

Feature Selection: The most commonly applied feature (variable) selection method in the field of personalized medicine is to rank the genes according to their association with the class (equivalently the p-value) and select the top k. We call this method univariate filtering. In our work we additionally employed the Max Min Parents and Children algorithms (**MMPC**) [5] to select a minimal-size, optimally predictive set of probe-sets. MMPC is an algorithm that seeks to identify the neighbors of the variable-to-predict in the Bayesian Network capturing the data distribution by taking into account multivariate associations. It has been shown very effective in recent extensive experiments [11] against an array of state-of-the art feature selection methods. In this work, the causal explorer implementation of MMPC was used [12] with the default values for the parameters.

Regression: We employed SVM Regression to construct the predictive models [13]. In our implementation we used the Radial Basis kernel and all other parameters set to default(we have experimented with other values but they did not lead to better results).

Estimation of Performance: We used a leave-one-out cross validation protocol due to the small number of samples that we had (59). For each training set, the combination of MMPC and SVM regression produced a predictive model that was applied on the hold-out test sample.

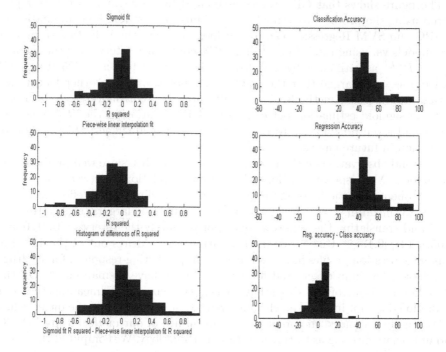

Fig. 2. (Left) Histogram R^2 for $GI50^{Sig}$ (GI50's fitted by a sigmoid), $GI50^{PLI}$ (standard estimation), and their difference, from top to bottom respectively. (Right) Histograms of cross validated classification accuracies A_j, discretized regression accuracies D_j and the $A_j - D_j$ differences, from top to bottom, respectively

Metric of performance: The metric to measure prediction performance is the leave-one-out cross-validated R^2 (coefficient of determination), which is a conservative metric [14]. Specifically, for a given drug j, let $\mu_{\backslash i}$ be the mean value of GI50 in the data excluding cell line i (training data), $\widehat{GI50}_{\backslash i}$ the predicted GI50 by the model constructed excluding cell-line i, and $GI50_i$ the GI50 as estimated by the experiments in the corresponding cell line i for drug j. We define:

$$R_j^2 \equiv 1 - \frac{\sum_i (GI50_i - \widehat{GI50}_{\backslash i})^2}{\sum_i (GI50_i - \mu_{\backslash i})^2} \qquad (2)$$

The interpretation of R^2 is that it corresponds to variance explained (uncertainty) by the models, or the reduction of variance by the use of the gene-expression models.

We have computed R_j^2 for all 118 drugs both when the GI50 values are estimated using piece-wise linear interpolation as well as when fitting a sigmoid function, as described above. We denote the corresponding values as R_j^{PLI} and R_j^{Sig}. The results are shown in Figure 2(a).

The figure shows that GI50 values estimated by the sigmoid are better predicted using the protocol described above. Thus at least for the combination of MMPC and SVM Regression $GI50^{Sig}$ values facilitate the induction of predictive models vs. using the $GI50^{PLI}$. The 95% confidence interval for the median $R_j^{Sig} - R_j^{PLI}$ as estimated by a Wilcoxon signed-rank test is $[0.025, 0.122]$. Of course, one could argue that the results may not transfer to other feature selection or regression methods. The results however, corroborate our intuition that the sigmoid estimation better preserves information in the $R_{i,j}$ measurements and given no evidence to the contrary, we would suggest this method of estimation in future analyses.

A second observation on the results is that several drugs are well predicted by the models. More specifically, for the Pearson correlation r between two quantities, Cohen gives the following interpretation guidelines: small effect size, r = 0.1 - 0.23; medium, r = 0.24 - 0.36; large, r = 0.37 or larger. Interpreting R^2 as r^2 and translating the values we get approximately the intervals $[0.01, 0.05)$, $[0.05, 0.13)$, $[0.13, 1]$. Under this interpretation for 21 drugs out of the 118, the tumour expression profiles have a large effect in predicting response; for 12 drugs they have a medium effect, and for 19 drugs they have a small effect. On the other hand, 65 out of 118 drugs have a negative size effect, meaning that our prediction does not improve much compared to the prediction by the mean value.

We finally compared the prediction performance of our models using MMPC and univariate filtering as feature selection methodology. We computed the cross-validated R^2 for both methods on all drugs using the same protocol as before. The k parameter is set to the number of genes returned by MMPC, so that both methods return the signatures of the same sizes. Figure 1(b) presents a histogram of the results. The figure shows that, on average, MMPC returns more informative signatures and thus, it should be preferred.

4   Comparison of Regression versus Classification

In all related prior work, to the best of our knowledge, classification models have been constructed for predicting GI50 values [1,3,4]. Given that the latter values are continuous, the authors have quantized them before applying any classifiers, as described in the previous sections. We now show that quantization is sometimes detrimental to performance and regression techniques have greater predictive power.

In this next set of computational experiments we pre-process the GI50 values of each drug to discretize them as described in [4]. Specifically, the class $C_{i,j}$ of a cell-line i and drug j is computed as sensitive, intermediate, or resistant if $GI50^{Sig}_{i,j}$ falls within $(-\infty, \mu_j - 0.5\sigma_j]$, $(\mu_j - 0.5\sigma_j, \mu_j + 0.5\sigma_j]$, and $[\mu_j - 0.5\sigma_j, \infty)$ respectively, where μ_j is the average GI50 value over all cell lines for drug j and σ_j the standard deviation.

To evaluate classification, we employed the same overall protocol described in Section 3 with the following modifications: we used multi-class SVM classification instead of SVM Regression [15]. SVMs have been very popular and successful classifiers, particularly in bioinformatics [16]. We used the *libsvm* implementation of SVMs with the Radial Basis kernel and all other parameters set to default. In addition, the metric of performance for classification is accuracy, i.e., the percentage of samples whose class is correctly predicted. We denote with A_j the leave-one-out cross-validated accuracy of the method on drug j.

Comparing regression vs. classification is not straightforward given that regression outputs a continuous prediction for $GI50_{i,j}^{Sig}$ while classification outputs its class. To overcome this issue we discretize the output of the regression models to the three stated classes using the same intervals as above. This allows us to compute the cross-validated accuracy of the regression for each drug j, denoted as D_j. In other words, A_j are computed by first discretizing the data, then using classification, and measuring the accuracy of the output, while D_j is computed by using regression, then discretizing the predictions, and computing accuracy.

Figure 2(b) shows the histograms of A_j, D_j, and their difference $D_j - A_j$. In some cases regression accuracy scores higher than classification accuracy and in other cases the reverse happens. For example, for drug Vincristine-sulfate (NSC:67574) regression accuracy D is 55,9322 while classification accuracy A is 18,6441. On the other hand, for drug Guanazole (NSC:1895) A is 57,6271 while D is 27,1186.

5   Biological Interpretation of the Molecular Signatures

The biological correlates of these findings are quite interesting. Below we will discuss the target systems which may connect these genes with tumour resistance and tumour response. Due to space limitation we consider only the top five drugs with the highest R^2, i.e., the drugs for which we get the larger improvement in prediction when gene expressions are employed. These drugs and their signatures are shown in Table 1.

Carmustine (BCNU) is a mustard compound and an alkylating and cross-linking agent, used in oncology since 1972, and still in use for tumours of the central nervous system, Hodgkin, non-Hodgkins disease and myelomatosis [17]. FDZ6 (Frizzled homolog 6) belongs to the family of catenin molecules and involved in various processes in developing and adult organisms, but is also implicated in carcinogenesis through the WNT/FZD signaling pathway. IKZF1

Table 1. The 5 best predicted drugs (highest R^2) along with their gene signatures

Compound	R^2	Selected Probesets and Their Gene Symbols
Carmustine (BCNU)	0.3960	1558517_s_at (not mapped), 202574_s_at (CSNK1G2), 202957_at (HCLS1), 203987_at (FZD6), 207868$_a$t (CHRNA2), 220176_at (NUBPL), 224391_s_at (SIAE), 227346_at (IKZF1), 227485_at (DDX26B)
Nitrogen mustard hydrochloride	0.3617	205739_x_at (ZNF107), 209694_at (PTS), 221679_s_at (ABHD6), 232543_x_at (ARHGAP9), 232909_s_at (BPTF), 235320_at (not mapped), 240458_at (not mapped), 242314_at (TNRC6C)
Chlorambucil	0.3564	209694_at (PTS), 225853_at (GNPNAT1), 232543_x_at (ARHGAP9), 240458_at (not mapped), 241935_at (SHROOM1), 243678_at (not mapped), 57516_at (ZNF764)
Amsacrine	0.3503	202538_s_at (CHMP2B), 203600_s_at (FAM193A), 204336_s_at (RGS19), 227539_at (not mapped), 229280_s_at (FLJ22536), 229389_at (ATG16L2) 230424_at (C5orf13), 241935_at (SHROOM1), 244551_at (not mapped)
Dichloroallyl-lawson	0.3071	200595_s_at (EIF3A), 203147_s_at (TRIM14), 208260_at (AVPR1B), 217917_s_at (DYNLRB1), 218130_at (not mapped), 222549_at (CLDN1), 223915_at (BCOR), 228124_at (ABHD12), 237726_at (not mapped), 243007_at (not mapped)

or Ikaros zinc finger 1 alteration status accurately predicts relapses [18] and a nine-gene signature including deletion of IKZF1 is predictive of chemotherapy response in pediatric acute lymphoblastic leukemia [19].

Chlorambucil and Nitrogen mustard hydrochloride compounds are derived from mustard gas and are used in chemical warfare since the first world war. They are both alkylating agents, that interfere with DNA replication and transcription of RNA, and ultimately result in the disruption of nucleic acid function. These compounds are very toxic as well as mutagenic, and thus a more tailored use by genomic signatures would be very important. The indications for Chlorambucil are chronic lymphocytic leukemia, Hodgkin's disease, and other lymphomas. Nitrogen mustard hydrochloride or chlorethamine is active on small cell, non-small cell and prostate cancer cell lines (NCI cell line database), and is indicated for the palliative treatment of Hodgkin's disease (Stages III and IV), other hematological malignancies as well as bronchogenic carcinoma. These two drugs share three genes of interest in their signatures: ARGHAP9 and zinc finger proteins (ZNF107 and ZNF764 respectively) and PTS. ARGHAP9 contains the RhoGAP domain and is a GTPase activator protein. It is responsible for the transduction of signals from plasmamembrane receptors and for the control of cell adhesion, motility and shape by actin cytoskeleton formation [20]. Zinc finger proteins are involved in DNA recognition, RNA packaging, transcriptional activation, regulation of apoptosis, protein folding and assembly, and lipid binding [21]. PTS, encoding 6-pyruvoyltetrahydropterin synthase is crucial in folate metabolism and neutransmitter synthesis [22]. This has not been associated to cancer previously.

Amsacrine is an aminoacridine derivative and a potent intercalating antineoplastic agent. It is effective in the treatment of acute leukemias and malignant lymphomas, but has poor activity in the treatment of solid tumors. It is frequently used in combination with other antineoplastic agents in chemotherapy protocols. The gene CHMP2B is involved in protein sorting and transport from the endosome to the vacuole/lysosome in eukaryotic cells. It affects the MVB sorting pathway, which plays a critical role in the decision between recycling and degradation of membrane proteins [23]. Individuals with mutations of this gene develop neurodegenerative disease, probably due to dysfunctional autophagy [24]. RGS19 belongs to the RGS (Regulator of G Protein Signalling) multi-functional, GTPase-accelerating proteins. Recently it was discovered that RGS19 overexpression can enhance cell proliferation [25]. Single nucleotide polymorphism in FLJ22536 was associated to clinically aggressive neuroblastoma, a childhood malignancy [26]. Interestingly, hypermethylation of the autophagy related gene ATG16L2 was associated with poorer prognosis in terms of molecular response to Imatinib treatment in acute lymphoblastic leukemia, which is also the target disease of amsacrine [27]. C5orf13 or P311 is involved in invasion and migration of glioblastoma cells [28].

Dichloroallyl lawson is not an anti-cancer drug yet, and is largely inactive in most cell lines screened. Interestingly, the eIF3a mRNA is found elevated in a number of cancer type and it shown that suppression of eIF3a expression can reverse the malignant phenotype and change the sensitivity of cells to cell cycle modulators [29].

In summary, four of the five signatures predict activity in drugs with a similar mechanism of action, that is DNA damage through alkylation, and mainly active in hematological diseases as lymphomas and central nervous system tumours. Something also worth noticing is that three of our top drugs are nitrogen mustards. The signatures include several genes that are not directly related to the classical DNA damage and repair systems and may infer novel associations and actions of these genes.

6 Conclusion

Predicting chemosensitivity of tumours from gene expressions is important for selecting treatment, understanding the molecular mechanisms of drug response, and selecting molecular signatures. In this paper, we show that predictive performance can be improved by employing a new method for estimating the GI50 (indication of response to drug), regression algorithms instead of classification, and state-of-the-art, multivariate feature selection. The signatures identified here have several links to cancer progression and resistance to chemotherapy, but the direct relations between the genes and the respective drugs are missing. Knowledge on these relations are still expanding and the methods used to identify those signatures may be important tool for novel biological hypotheses.

Acknowledgements. We would like to thank Matina Fragoyanni for parts of the code, Sofia Triantafyllou, Vincenzo Lagani and Angelos Armen for suggestions and feedback. Finally, we thank FORTH for funding and support of the work.

References

1. Potti, A., Dressman, H.K., Bild, A., Riedel, R.F., et al.: Genomic signatures to guide the use of chemotherapeutics (2006)
2. Augustin, C.K., Yoo, J.S., Potti, A., Yoshimoto, Y., et al.: Genomic and molecular profiling predicts response to temozolomide in melanoma. Clinical Cancer Res. 15(2) (2009)
3. Staunton, J.E., Slonim, D.K., Coller, H.A., et al.: Chemosensitivity prediction by transcriptional profiling. Proc. Natl. Acad. Sci. 98(19), 10787–10792 (2001)
4. Ma, Y., Ding, Z., Qian, Y., et al.: An integrative genomic and proteomic approach to chemosensitivity prediction. Int. J. Oncol. 34(1), 107–115 (2009)
5. Tsamardinos, I., Brown, L.E., Aliferis, C.F.: The max-min hill-climbing bayesian network structure learning algorithm. Journal of Machine Learning 65, 31–78 (2006)
6. http://dtp.nci.nih.gov/index.html
7. http://www.bioconductor.org
8. Shankavaram, U.T., Varma, S., Kane, D., et al.: Cellminer: a relational database and query tool for the nci-60 cancer cell lines. BMC Genomics 10(277) (2009)
9. http://dtp.nci.nih.gov/docs/compare/compare$_$methodology.html
10. http://www.itl.nist.gov/div898/handbook/eda/section3/eda35h.htm

11. Aliferis, C.F., Statnikov, A., Tsamardinos, I., Mani, S., Koutsoukos, X.D.: Local causal and markov blanket induction for causal discovery and feature selection for classification part i: Algorithms and empirical evaluation. Journal of Machine Learning Research, Special Topic on Causality 11, 171–234 (2010)
12. Statnikov, A., Tsamardinos, T., Brown, L.E., Aliferis, C.F.: Causal explorer: A matlab library of algorithms for causal discovery and variable selection for classification. Challenges in Causality 1 (2009)
13. Chang, C.C., Lin, C.J.: LIBSVM: a library for support vector machines (2001), software http://www.csie.ntu.edu.tw/~cjlin/libsvm
14. Steel, R.G.D., Torrie, J.H.: Principles and Procedures of Statistics. McGraw-Hill, New York (1960)
15. Boser, B., Guyon, I., Vapnik, V.: An training algorithm for optimal margin classifiers. In: Fifth Annual Workshop on Computational Learning Theory, pp. 144–152 (1992)
16. Statnikov, A., Aliferis, C.F., Tsamardinos, I., Hardin, D., Levy, S.: A comprehensive evaluation of multicategory classification methods for microarray gene expression cancer diagnosis. Bioinformatics 21(5), 631–643 (2005)
17. Egyhazi, S., Bergh, J., Hansson, J., Karran, P., Ringborg, U.: Carmustine-induced toxicity, dna crosslinking and o6-methylguanine-dna methyltransferase activity in two human lung cancer cell lines. Eur. J. Cancer. 27, 1658–1662 (1991)
18. Waanders, E., van der Velden, V.H., van der Schoot, C.E., van Leeuwen, F.N., et al.: Integrated use of minimal residual disease classification and ikzf1 alteration status accurately predicts 79% of relapses in pediatric acute lymphoblastic leukemia. Leukemia 25, 254–258 (2011)
19. Zuo, Z., Jones, D., Yao, H., et al.: A pathway-based gene signature correlates with therapeutic response in adult patients with philadelphia chromosome-positive acute lymphoblastic leukemia. Mod. Pathol. 23, 1524–1534 (2010)
20. http://pfam.sanger.ac.uk/
21. Laity, J.H., Lee, B.M., Wright, P.E.: Zinc finger proteins: new insights into structural and functional diversity. Curr. Opin. Struct. Biol 11(1), 39–46 (2001)
22. Meili, D., Kralovicova, J., Zagalak, J., Bonafe, L., et al.: Disease-causing mutations improving the branch site and polypyrimidine tract: pseudoexon activation of line-2 and antisense alu lacking the poly(t)-tail. Hum. Mutat. 30, 823–831 (2009)
23. Babst, M., Katzmann, D.J., Estepa-Sabal, E.J., Meerloo, T., Emr, S.D.: Escrt-iii: an endosome-associated heterooligomeric protein complex required for mvb sorting. Dev. Cell. 3, 271–282 (2002)
24. Rusten, T.E., Simonsen, A.: Escrt functions in autophagy and associated disease. Cell Cycle 7, 1166–1172 (2008)
25. Tso, P.H., Wang, Y., Wong, S.Y., Poon, L.S., Chan, A.S., et al.: Rgs19 enhances cell proliferation through its c-terminal pdz motif. Cell Signal 22, 1700–1707 (2010)
26. Maris, J.M., Mosse, Y.P., Bradfield, J.P., et al.: Chromosome 6p22 locus associated with clinically aggressive neuroblastoma. N. Engl. J. Med. 358 (2008)
27. Dunwell, T., Hesson, L., Rauch, T.A., Wang, L., et al.: A genome-wide screen identifies frequently methylated genes in haematological and epithelial cancers. Mol Cancer 9(44) (2010)
28. Mariani, L., McDonough, W.S., Hoelzinger, D.B., Beaudry, C., Kaczmarek, E., et al.: Identification and validation of p311 as a glioblastoma invasion gene using laser capture microdissection. Cancer Res. 61, 4190–4196 (2001)
29. Saletta, F., Rahmanto, Y.S., Richardson, D.R.: The translational regulator eif3a: the tricky eif3 subunit! Biochim Biophys Acta 1806(2), 275–286 (2010)

Optimizing Filter Processes on Protein Interaction Clustering Results Using Genetic Algorithms

Charalampos Moschopoulos[1], Grigorios Beligiannis[2],
Sophia Kossida[3], and Spiridon Likothanassis[1]

[1] Computer Engineering & Informatics,University of Patras, GR-26500 Rio, Patras, Greece
(mosxopul,likothan)@ceid.upatras.gr
[2] Department of Business Administration of Food and Agricultural Enterprises,
University of Western Greece, G. Seferi 2, GR-30100, Agrinio, Greece
gbeligia@cc.uoi.gr
[3] Bioinformatics & Medical Informatics Team,
Biomedical Research Foundation of the Academy of Athens,
Soranou Efesiou 4, GR-11527, Athens, Greece
skossida@bioacademy.gr

Abstract. In this manuscript, a Genetic Algorithm is applied on a filter in order to optimize the selection of clusters having a high probability to represent protein complexes. The filter was applied on the results (obtained by experiments made on five different yeast datasets) of three different algorithms known for their efficiency on protein complex detection through protein interaction graphs. The derived results were compared with three popular clustering algorithms, proving the efficiency of the proposed method according to metrics such as successful prediction rate and geometrical accuracy.

Keywords: protein-protein interactions, protein interaction graph, genetic algorithm, protein complexes prediction.

1 Introduction

The importance of protein interactions is given as they play important role on fundamental cell functions. They are crucial for forming structural complexes, for extra-cellular signaling, for intra-cellular signaling [1]. Recently, new high throughput experimental methods [2-5] have been developed which detect thousands protein-protein interactions (PPIs) with a single experiment. As a result, enormous datasets have been generated which could possibly describe the functional organization of the proteome. However, these data are extremely noisy [6], making it difficult for researchers to analyze them and extract valuable conclusion such as protein complex detection or characterizing the functionality of unknown proteins.

Due to the vast volume of PPI data, they are usually modeled as graphs G=(V,E) where V is the set of vertices (proteins) and E the set of adjacent edges between two nodes (protein interactions). The model of graph makes it easy for bioinformatics researchers to apply various algorithms derived from graph theory in order to perform clustering and detect protein complexes which are represented as dense subgraphs [7-9]. According to [10, 11], the most prevailed algorithms are MCL (Markov clustering) [12]

L. Iliadis and C. Jayne (Eds.): EANN/AIAI 2011, Part I, IFIP AICT 363, pp. 463–470, 2011.
© IFIP International Federation for Information Processing 2011

and RNSC (Restricted Neighbourhood Search Clustering) [13]. Besides them, spectral clustering can achieve similar results [14]. While these methods use the PPI graph structure to detect protein complexes, additional information could also be used such as gene expression data [15], functional information [16] as well as other biological information [17]. However, the use of additional information has the disadvantage that can not cover the aggregation of proteins that constitute the PPI graph.

The aforementioned algorithms assign each protein of the initial PPI graph to a cluster, constructing clusters that could hardly be characterized as dense ones. As a result, their prediction rate of protein complexes is pretty low. One way to deal with this problem is to filter the results of such an algorithm using additional information such as Gene Ontology [13]. However, the sources of the additional information usually do not cover all the recorded interactions that form the PPI graphs. Moreover, the parameters of these filters are almost always empirically defined, leading to biased solutions.

In this contribution, a filter is constructed by four methods which are based on graph properties such as density, haircut operation, best neighbor and cutting edge and it is applied on the results of MCL, RNSC and spectral algorithm. Furthermore, the parameters of the filter methods are optimized by a Genetic Algorithm (GA) which takes into account the rate of successful prediction, the absolute number of valid predicted protein complexes and the geometrical accuracy of the final clusters. Extended experiments were performed using five different PPI datasets. The derived results were compared with the recorded protein complexes of the MIPS database [18], while statistical metrics were calculated such as sensitivity (Sn), positive predictive value (PPV) and geometrical accuracy (Acc_g). To demonstrate the efficiency of the proposed filter, we compare the derived results with 3 other algorithms (SideS [8], Mcode [7], HCS [9]).

2   Our Method

We chose to perform our filtering method on the results of 3 clustering algorithms that assign each protein of the initial PPI graph to a cluster and they are considered as the best of their category: MCL, RNSC and spectral. The MCL algorithm [12] is a fast and scalable unsupervised clustering algorithm based on simulation of stochastic flow in graphs. The MCL algorithm deterministically computes the probabilities of random walks through a graph and uses two operators transforming one set of probabilities into another. It does so by using the language of stochastic matrices (also called Markov matrices) which capture the mathematical concept of random walks on a graph. The RNSC algorithm [13] performs an initial random clustering and then iteratively by moving one node from one cluster to another is trying to improve the clustering cost. In order to avoid local minima, it maintains a tabu list that prevents cycling back to a previously explored partitioning. Due to the randomness of the algorithm, different runs on the same input data produce different outputs. For the spectral clustering algorithm, we used [19] spectral graph decomposition and mapped the set of nodes of PPI graph into the k-dimensional space. Following the spectral decomposition, the EM algorithm [20] was applied to produce the final clusters.

The developed filter was based on four graph metrics that would help to detect the denser clusters out of the above algorithms results and it was first introduced in [21]. These graph metrics are:

- **Density** of a subgraph is calculated as 2|E|/|V|(|V|-1) where |E| is the number of edges and |V| the number of vertices of the subgraph.
- **Haircut operation** is a method that detects and excludes vertices with low degree of connectivity from the potential cluster that these nodes belong to.
- **Best neighbor** tends to detect and enrich the clusters with candidate vertices that the proportion of their edges adjacent to the cluster divided by the total degree of the vertex is above a threshold.
- **Cutting edge** metric is used to detect those clusters that are more isolated than the remaining of the graph by dividing the number of edges that are adjacent to two cluster vertices with the total number of edges of the cluster.

The difference of the filter presented in this manuscript with the filter presented in [21] is that its parameters are optimized by a genetic algorithm in order to achieve better quality results concerning the rate of successful prediction, the detection of more real protein complexes and the highest accuracy.

2.1 Optimizing Clustering Results Filter

Genetic Algorithms (GAs) are one of the most popular techniques to solve optimization problems with very satisfactory results [22, 23]. In this manuscript, a GA is used to optimize the fitness function containing metrics such as successful prediction, absolute number of valid protein complexes and accuracy by choosing the appropriate values for the filter parameters. In order to implement the GA, we used GALIB library [24] which is a set of C++ GA objects and well known about its computing efficiency.

The chromosome used in our case is represented as a one dimensional array, where each cell represents a filter parameter: the first parameter is used in density method, the second one in best neighbor method, the third in cutting edge method and the fourth in haircut method.

The proposed GA uses simple mutation and crossover operations while as a selection scheme we decided to use Roulette Wheel selection [25]. The mathematical representation of the evaluation function is as follows:

$$Max(10*percentage+0,05*\#valid\_clusters+5*Acc\_g)$$

where percentage is the percentage of successful predictions, #valid_clusters is the absolute number of valid clusters, Acc_g is the geometrical accuracy. Depending on how important each metric of the fitness function is, we multiplied it with a constant number. In our case, we considered as best solutions those that succeed high prediction rate without having small absolute number of valid predicted protein complexes. These values were selected after performing exhaustive experiments.

Finally, in order to retain the best chromosome in every generation, as elitism schema [25, 26] is used. The best chromosome of each generation is copied to the next generation (and not to the intermediate one, the individuals of which may crossover or mutate) assuring that it is preserved in the current population for as long as it is the best compared to all other chromosomes of the population. This choice assures that the best chromosome of each generation will be, if not better, at least equal to the best chromosome of the previous generation. Furthermore, it helps GA to converge faster to a near optimal solution.

3 Experimental Results

In order to prove the efficiency of our method, we performed experiments with 5 different yeast datasets derived by online databases (MIPS [18], DIP [27]) or individual experiments (Krogan [28], Gavin_2002 [29], Gavin_2006 [30]) and compared the results with the algorithms: SideS, HCS and Mcode. As an evaluation set, we used the recorded yeast complexes stored in MIPS database.

For all the results presented in this section the same set of GA's operators and parameters were used in order to provide a fair comparison of the algorithm's efficiency and performance. The crossover probability was equal to 0.7, while the mutation probability was equal to 0.1. The size of the population was set to 20 and the algorithm was left to run for 200 generations (the number of generations was used as termination criterion).

In Figure 1, the percentage of successful predictions is presented. As it can easily be seen, the optimized filtered algorithms achieve better percentages than those of the other algorithms in all cases. The combination of the MCL algorithm with the optimized filter gives the best results except in the case where the MIPS dataset is tested.

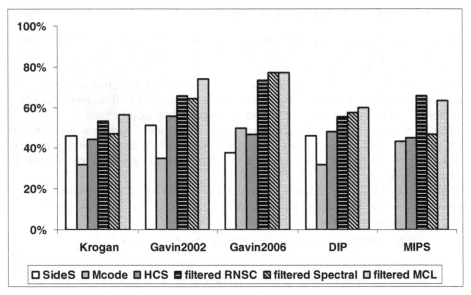

Fig. 1. Percentage of successful prediction

Concerning the geometrical accuracy metric, the results are satisfactory comparing to all other algorithms (Figure 2). In most of the cases, our methodology surpasses the other algorithms. In contrast with Figure 1, it seems that the combination of RNSC algorithm and the optimized filter is equally good with the one which uses MCL.

On the other hand, as it is shown in Figure 3, the absolute number of valid predicted clusters is lower than the other algorithms. The variables used in the fitness function of the GA caused those results. There is a trade off between the absolute number of valid predicted clusters and the other metrics used in the fitness function. We decided to give a priority to the quality of the produced solutions even if this leads to fewer final clusters.

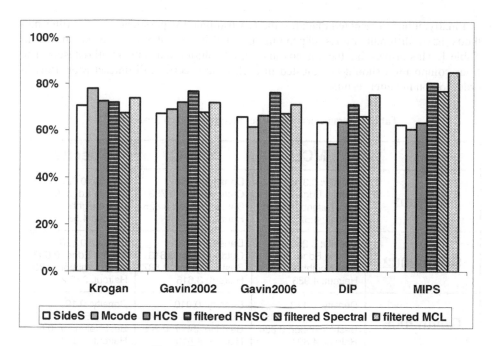

Fig. 2. Geometrical accuracy of results

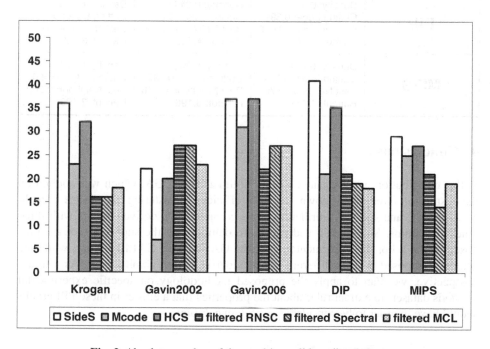

Fig. 3. Absolute number of the resulting valid predicted clusters

Finally, it has to be noted that after the GA training, the parameters of the filter methods have different values depending on the input dataset, as it is shown in Table 1. This proves that there is not an optimal solution that suits in all datasets. The filter composition should be adjusted in each time specific PPI dataset properties in order to obtain better results.

Table 1. Parameters of the filter methods in each time dataset

	MCL	**RNSC**	**Spectral**
Krogan	Density: 0.370 Cutting Edge: 0.455 Best Neighbor: 0.216 Haircut: 4.528	Density: 0.306 Cutting Edge: 0.753 Best Neighbor: 0.825 Haircut: 0.059	Density: 0.027 Cutting Edge: 0.584 Best Neighbor: 0.670 Haircut: 4.539
Gavin2002	Density: 0.250 Cutting Edge: 0.609 Best Neighbor: 0.887 Haircut: 4.983	Density: 0.342 Cutting Edge: 0.613 Best Neighbor: 0.587 Haircut: 3.615	Density: 0.123 Cutting Edge: 0.602 Best Neighbor: 0.836 Haircut: 3.672
Gavin2006	Density: 0.173 Cutting Edge: 0.685 Best Neighbor: 0.824 Haircut: 4.807	Density: 0.010 Cutting Edge: 0.674 Best Neighbor: 0.905 Haircut: 4.610	Density: 0.196 Cutting Edge: 0.647 Best Neighbor: 0.695 Haircut: 3.357
DIP	Density: 0.503 Cutting Edge: 0.399 Best Neighbor: 0.616 Haircut: 1.174	Density: 0.344 Cutting Edge: 0.398 Best Neighbor: 0.606 Haircut: 4.785	Density: 0.153 Cutting Edge: 0.398 Best Neighbor: 0.630 Haircut: 3.152
MIPS	Density: 0.711 Cutting Edge: 0.365 Best Neighbor: 0.798 Haircut: 2.729	Density: 0.700 Cutting Edge: 0.237 Best Neighbor: 0.958 Haircut: 3.196	Density: 0.437 Cutting Edge: 0.050 Best Neighbor: 0.209 Haircut: 3.196

4 Conclusions

In this contribution, we presented a filter, optimized by a GA, which was applied on the results of three well known for their efficiency clustering algorithms namely MCL, RNSC and spectral. Furthermore, we compared the derived results with three other algorithms: SideS, HCS and Mcode to demonstrate the superiority of the proposed method. For the implementation of the GA we used GALIB library, while the filter is composed by four different methods derived from graph theory. As a future prospective, we plan to apply the proposed methodology on specific experimental methods datasets to extract rules about the properties that a cluster in these PPI graphs should have in order to be considered as protein complex.

References

1. Ryan, D.P., Matthews, J.M.: Protein-protein interactions in human disease. Curr. Opin. Struct. Biol. 15(4), 441–446 (2005)
2. Ito, T., et al.: A comprehensive two-hybrid analysis to explore the yeast protein interactome. Proceedings of the National Academy of Science 98(8), 4569–4574 (2001)
3. Puig, O., et al.: The tandem affinity purification (TAP) method: a general procedure of protein complex purification. Methods 24(3), 218–229 (2001)
4. Stoll, D., et al.: Protein microarrays: applications and future challenges. Curr. Opin. Drug. Discov. Devel. 8(2), 239–252 (2005)
5. Willats, W.G.: Phage display: practicalities and prospects. Plant Mol. Biol. 50(6), 837–854 (2002)
6. Sprinzak, E., Sattath, S., Margalit, H.: How Reliable are Experimental Protein-Protein Interaction Data? Journal of Molecular Biology 327, 919–923 (2003)
7. Bader, G.D., Hogue, C.W.: An automated method for finding molecular complexes in large protein interaction networks. BMC Bioinformatics 4, 2 (2003)
8. Koyuturk, M., Szpankowski, W., Grama, A.: Assessing significance of connectivity and conservation in protein interaction networks. J. Comput. Biol. 14(6), 747–764 (2007)
9. Hartuv, E., Shamir, R.: A clustering algorithm based on graph connectivity. Information Processing Letters 76(4-6), 175–181 (2000)
10. Brohee, S., van Helden, J.: Evaluation of clustering algorithms for protein-protein interaction networks. BMC Bioinformatics 7, 488 (2006)
11. Li, X., et al.: Computational approaches for detecting protein complexes from protein interaction networks: a survey. BMC Genomics 11(suppl. 1), S3 (2009)
12. Enright, A.J., Van Dongen, S., Ouzounis, C.A.: An efficient algorithm for large-scale detection of protein families. Nucleic Acids Res. 30(7), 1575–1584 (2002)
13. King, A.D., Przulj, N., Jurisica, I.: Protein complex prediction via cost-based clustering. Bioinformatics 20(17), 3013–3020 (2004)
14. Kritikos, G., et al.: Spectral Clustering of Weighted Protein Interaction Networks (2010) (submitted)
15. Eisen, M.B., et al.: Cluster analysis and display of genome-wide expression patterns. Proc. Natl. Acad. Sci. USA 95(25), 14863–14868 (1998)
16. The Gene Ontology (GO) project in 2006. Nucleic Acids Res. 34(Database issue), D322–D326 (2006)
17. Huh, W.K., et al.: Global analysis of protein localization in budding yeast. Nature 425(6959), 686–691 (2003)
18. Mewes, H.W., et al.: MIPS: analysis and annotation of proteins from whole genomes in 2005. Nucleic Acids Res. 34(Database issue), D169–D172 (2006)
19. Ng, A.Y., Jordan, M.I., Weiss, Y.: On Spectral Clustering: Analysis and an algorithm. Advances in Neural Information Processing Systems 14, 849–856 (2001)
20. Bishop, C.M.: Pattern Recognition and Machine Learning (Information Science and Statistics). Springer-Verlag New York, Inc., New York (2006)
21. Moschopoulos, C.N., et al.: An enchanced Markov clustering method for detecting protein complexes. In: 8th IEEE International Conference on BioInformatics and BioEngineering (BIBE 2008), Athens (2008)
22. Goldberg, D.: Genetic Algorithms in Search, Optimization and Machine Learning. Addison-Wesley, Reading (1989)
23. Bandyopadhyay, S., Pal, S.K.: Classification and Learning Using Genetic Algorithms: Applications in Bioinformatics and Web Intelligence. Springer, Heidelberg (2007)

24. GALIB, http://lancet.mit.edu/galib-2.4/
25. Mitchell, M.: An Introduction to Genetic Algorithms. MIT Press, London (1995)
26. Michalewicz, Z.: Genetic Algorithms + Data Structures = Evolution Programs. Springer, New York (1999)
27. Xenarios, I., et al.: DIP: the database of interacting proteins. Nucleic Acids Res. 28(1), 289–291 (2000)
28. Krogan, N.J., et al.: Global landscape of protein complexes in the yeast Saccharomyces cerevisiae. Nature 440(7084), 637–643 (2006)
29. Gavin, A.C., et al.: Functional organization of the yeast proteome by systematic analysis of protein complexes. Nature 415(6868), 141–147 (2002)
30. Gavin, A.C., et al.: Proteome survey reveals modularity of the yeast cell machinery. Nature 440(7084), 631–636 (2006)

Adaptive Filtering Techniques Combined with Natural Selection-Based Heuristic Algorithms in the Prediction of Protein-Protein Interactions

Christos M. Dimitrakopoulos[1], Konstantinos A. Theofilatos[1],
Efstratios F. Georgopoulos[2], Spyridon D. Likothanassis[1],
Athanasios K. Tsakalidis[1], and Seferina P. Mavroudi[1]

[1] Department of Computer Engineering & Informatics,
University of Patras, Rio, GR-26500, Patras, Greece
{dimitrakop,theofilk,likothan,tsak,mavroudi}@ceid.upatras.gr
[2] Technological Educational Institute of Kalamata, 24100, Kalamata, Greece
sfg@teikal.gr

Abstract. The analysis of protein-protein interactions (PPIs) is crucial to the understanding of cellular organizations, processes and functions. The reliability of the current experimental approaches interaction data is prone to error. Thus, a variety of computational methods have been developed to supplement the interactions that have been detected experimentally. The present paper's main objective is to present a novel classification framework for predicting PPIs combining the advantages of two algorithmic methods' categories (heuristic methods, adaptive filtering techniques) in order to produce high performance classifiers while maintaining their interpretability. Our goal is to find a simple mathematical equation that governs the best classifier enabling the extraction of biological knowledge. State-of-the-art adaptive filtering techniques were combined with the most contemporary heuristic methods which are based in the natural selection process. To the best of our knowledge, this is the first time that the proposed classification framework is applied and analyzed extensively for the problem of predicting PPIs. The proposed methodology was tested with a commonly used data set using all possible combinations of the selected adaptive filtering and heuristic techniques and comparisons were made. The best algorithmic combinations derived from these procedures were Genetic Algorithms with Extended Kalman Filters and Particle Swarm Optimization with Extended Kalman Filters. Using these algorithmic combinations high accuracy interpretable classifiers were produced.

Keywords: Protein-Protein Interactions, Adaptive Filtering, Genetic Algorithms. Particle Swarm Optimization, Least Squares Algorithm, Recursive Least Squares, Kalman Filtering.

1 Introduction

In each living cell of the human organism, a variety of protein interactions take place. In recent years, researchers have tried to approach the problem of predicting all

L. Iliadis and C. Jayne (Eds.): EANN/AIAI 2011, Part I, IFIP AICT 363, pp. 471–480, 2011.

possible protein interactions in the human organism by implementing different computational techniques. At the beginning, most of them were based on the analysis of a sole feature, indicative of interaction between two proteins. Several examples of such features are features concerning the genomic sequence of the genes-generators of the reference proteins, features concerning the structure of the reference proteins, features concerning the sequences of the references proteins and many others [1,2]. The most recent computational approaches use various features as inputs for their classifiers in order to take advantage of all the available information [3,4].

In the present paper, we applied to the problem of PPI prediction several adaptive filtering techniques combined with the most contemporary heuristic methods which are based in the natural selection process. From this combination, a novel computational framework has been formed for the creation of a mathematical equation that gives the best classifier. We consider three classical parameter estimation algorithms (LMS, RLS and Kalman Filter) and one gain adaptation algorithm (IDBD). The gain adaptation algorithms have been shown to perform comparably to the best algorithms (Kalman and RLS), but they have a lower complexity [6].

Concerning the heuristic methods, each adaptive filtering technique was combined with a genetic algorithm and a Particle Swarm Optimization (PSO) heuristic technique. Genetic algorithms [7] and PSO [8] are the most contemporary heuristic methods and their process is based on the principle of natural selection. They are implemented in order to find the best subset of mathematical terms that constitutes the optimal mathematical model that can be used as the optimal classifier in the adaptive filtering techniques. In the RLS and LMS algorithms, the forgetting and convergence factors are been optimized respectively through the heuristic algorithms used.

In [5], genetic algorithms were firstly combined with Extended Kalman Filters for the problem of predicting PPIs. That method has been demonstrated to achieve higher classification performance than the PIPS naive Bayesian method [9] on the same dataset. In the terms of the current paper, the research has been extended by implementing different adaptive filtering techniques and heuristic algorithms in order to establish a novel classification framework. The proposed methodology was tested with a commonly used dataset and the advantages and disadvantages of each method selection are discussed. The mathematical equation that produced the best classifier in terms of classification performance and interpretability was presented and some first biological hypotheses about the classification model were derived.

2   Materials and Methods

2.1   Dataset

The dataset used in this paper was created by retrieving material from the PIPS database [9] which contains information for about 17.643.506 human protein interactions. The positive samples in the dataset were the 16536 known human protein interactions extracted from Human Protein Reference Database (HPRD) [10]. The negative dataset was built using randomly chosen protein pairs provided by the PIPS Database. A 1:1 ratio of positive and negative samples was selected in our original dataset, in order to force our classifiers to achieve higher sensitivity and discover a large number of protein-protein interactions. The dataset was split into two equal subsets, training and testing, keeping the 1:1 ratio between the positive and negative samples.

For every protein pair the following features as in [9] were used as inputs:

- Expression: Gene expression profiles from 79 physiologically normal tissues (Pearson correlation of co-expression over all conditions).
- Orthology: Interactions of homologous protein pairs from yeast, fly, worm and human. The similarity function used is the InParanoid score function [11].
- Fully Bayesian combination of the following features:
  - o Localization: Here PLST predictions are used [12].
  - o Domain co-occurrence: Chi-square score of co-occurrence of domain pairs.
  - o Post-translational modifications (PTM) co-occurrence: PTM pair enrichment score has been calculated as the probability of co-occurrence of two specific PTMs in all pairs of interacting protein pairs divided by the probability of occurrence of both of these PTMs separately.
- Transitive: This is a module that considers local topology of the underlying network predicted using combinations of above features and it works on the premise that a pair of proteins is more likely to interact if it shares interacting partners.

All feature values were normalized in a range from 0 to 1.

2.2 Adaptive Filtering Techniques

The adaptive filtering techniques used in this survey are the least mean squares (LMS) [13], the recursive least squares (RLS) [14], the Extended Kalman filtering method (EKF) [15] and the incremental delta-bar-delta algorithm (IDBD) [16].

The LMS algorithm is by far the most widely used algorithm in adaptive filtering because of its low computational complexity, proof of convergence in stationary environment and stable behavior when implemented with finite-precision arithmetic.

To guarantee the convergence of LMS it is good practice to set the learning rate in the range,

$$0 < \mu < \frac{1}{\lambda max} \tag{1}$$

where λ_{max} is the largest eigenvalue of $R = E[x(k)x^T(k)]$, where $x(k)$ is the vector of the input variables.

Least-squares algorithms aim at the minimization of the sum of the squares of the difference between the desired signal and the model filter output. When new samples of the incoming signals are received at every iteration, the solution for the least-squares problem can be computed in recursive form resulting in the recursive least-squares (RLS) algorithms.

Kalman filter is a set of mathematical equations which constitutes an efficient means to estimate the state of a process by minimizing the mean of the square error. The Extended Kalman Filter (EKF) is the nonlinear version of the Kalman Filter, and its goal is to approach the situation where the process to be estimated or the measurement relationship to the process is nonlinear. The specific equations for the time and measurement updates are divided into two groups. The time update equations and the measurement update equations.

Gain adaptation algorithms [16] implement a sort of meta-learning in that the learning rate is adapted based on the current inputs and on the trace of previous modifications [17]. The incremental delta-bar-delta (IDBD) uses a different adaptive learning rate for each input. This action can lead to the improvement of the system, when some of the inputs are irrelevant. In IDBD, each element of the $k_i(t)$ of the gain vector $k(t)$ is computed separately.

2.3 Heuristic Methods

Heuristic methods are implemented to fasten the process of finding a "good enough" solution to a problem, where the usage of an exhaustive search is impractical. Because of the large search space of our problem (2^{113} possible solutions), 2 classical heuristic methods were used, genetic algorithms and particle swarm optimization.

Genetic Algorithms (GAs) [7] are search algorithms inspired by the principle of natural selection. They are useful and efficient when the search space is big and complicated or when there is not any available mathematical analysis of the problem. A population of candidate solutions, called *chromosomes,* is optimized through a number of evolutionary cycles and genetic operations, such as *crossovers* or *mutations.*

In our approach, a simple GA was used where each chromosome comprises *term genes* that encode the best term subset and *parameter genes* that encode the best choice of parameters for each adaptive method used. The term genes are binary genes with the value of 1 indicating that this specific term should be included in the final classification model and the value of 0 indicating the opposite. The parameters which are optimized using GA are the convergence factor μ for the LMS adaptive filtering method and the forgetting factor λ for the RLS adaptive filtering method.

For the genetic algorithm used in our hybrid methodology, the one-point crossover and the mutation operators were used. Crossover and mutation probabilities for the GA where set to 0.9 and 0.01 respectively. Crossover is used in hope that new chromosomes will have good parts of old chromosomes and maybe the new chromosomes will be better. However it is good to leave some part of population survive to next generation. This is the reason a high (but not equal to one) crossover probability was used. As already mentioned, mutation is made to prevent falling GA into local extreme, but it should not occur very often, because then GA will in fact change to random search. That is the main reason why a small mutation probability was applied. Furthermore, roulette selection was used for the selection step and elitism to raise the evolutionary pressure in better solutions and to accelerate the evolution.

The size of the initial population was set to 30 chromosomes after experimentation in the training dataset. The termination criterion is the maximum number of 100 generations to be reached combined with a termination method that stops the evolution when the population is deemed as converged. The population is deemed as converged when the average fitness across the current population is less than 5% away from the best fitness of the current population. Specifically, when the average fitness across the current population is less than 5% away from the best fitness of the population, the diversity of the population is very low and evolving it for more generations is unlikely to produce different and better individuals than the existing ones or the ones already examined by the algorithm in previous generations.

The particle swarm optimization (PSO) [8] algorithm is another population based heuristic search algorithm based on the simulation of the social behavior of birds within a flock.

In our approach PSO searches the best mathematical term's subset for building the optimal classifier and the best parameters for each adaptive filtering method. Thus its particle is consisted of 113 variables indicating whether to include a term in the subset or not, plus one variable for the parameter selection of the adaptive filtering method. The values of the variables for the term selection range from 0 to 2. Values bigger than 1 indicate that this specific term should be included in the final classification model and the values less than 1 indicate the opposite.

In order to make a fair comparison with the GA search method, the initial population size of the swarm was set to 30 particles and the total number of iterations was set to 100. The termination criteria of convergence was not applied here because of the adaptive search behavior used in our PSO implementation which needs the total number of iterations to be used in order to perform in its full strength and effectiveness.

As mentioned above, the convergence factor μ for the LMS adaptive filtering method and the forgetting factor λ for the RLS adaptive filtering method are been optimized through the GA and the PSO algorithms. According to the theory, the convergence factor μ for LMS algorithm has been selected in the range $[0, 1/\lambda_{max}]$, in order to guarantee convergence of the mean square error, where λ_{max} is the largest eigenvalue of the autocorrelation matrix of the input x(k). Concerning RLS algorithm, the forgetting factor λ is chosen such that $2\mu = 1 - \lambda$, where μ is the corresponding convergence factor of the LMS algorithm. Hence, the values of the parameter λ are close to 1 and the values of the parameter μ are close to 0.

2.4 Evaluation in the Hybrid Methodology

The main idea of our proposed classification method is to use a heuristic method to find a "good enough" subset of terms in order to build the mathematical model for our predictor and then apply an adaptive filtering technique to find its optimal parameters. The search space of our problem consists of 2^{113} possible solutions and hence is extremely large. GAs and PSOs are heuristic methods that can deal with large search spaces and do not get trapped in local optimal solutions. The 113 mathematical terms that were used in our method were taken from 3 known nonlinear mathematical models, which are the Volterra Series, the exponential and the polynomial model, as described in [5].

In our approach, a simple Genetic Algorithm and PSO were used as heuristic methods. Each chromosome in these methods comprises of genes that encode the best subset of mathematical terms to be used in our classifier. Roulette selection was used for the selection step including elitism to accelerate the evolution of the population in the Genetic algorithm.

The evaluation process in both heuristic techniques is described in the following steps:

- For every individual of the population, use the Adaptive Filtering method (using the training dataset) to compute the best parameters for the subset of terms that arises from the individual's genes.
- Use the mathematical model found at the previous step to compute the fitness of the classifier in the validation set.
- For every individual compute the output of the following function:
  $F = a* G_m + b*sensitivity + c*specificity - d*terms$ (2),
  where G_m is the geometric mean of sensitivity and specificity. Hence, the proposed method tries to produce one mathematical model that optimizes the combination of sensitivity and specificity measures, sensitivity and specificity alone and simultaneously minimize the number of mathematical terms to be used in the mathematical model.
- Rank the individuals from the one having the lower fitness value to the one having the bigger fitness value. Using this ranking in the evaluation procedure, better scaled fitness scores can be achieved.
- Give as fitness value for every individual their ranking number. For example, the worst individual will take fitness equal to 1, the next fitness equal to 2 etc.

During the training we used 5-fold cross validation.

3   Experimental Results

In order to evaluate the performance of each combination of algorithms we applied it to the dataset described in Section 2.1. In order to make a fair comparison between all combinations, their classification thresholds were optimized. For all methods we experimented running them 100 times and in Table 1, the average values for each combination of algorithms are presented.

Table 1. Classification performance of all possible combinations between adaptive filtering and heuristic algorithms. Gm is the geometric mean of sensitivity and specificity.

Algorithm Combination	Gm	Sensitivity	Specificity	# of terms
Kalman with GA	0.7911	0.7540	0.8302	12.3
Kalman with PSO	0.7927	0.7568	0.8304	39.3
RLS with GA	0.7826	0.7291	0.8400	14.6
RLS with PSO	0.7797	0.7308	0.8319	26.1
LMS with GA	0.7012	0.6388	0.7698	15.6
LMS with PSO	0.6845	0.6418	0.7300	38.6
IDBD with GA	0.6704	0.4976	0.9033	26.6
IDBD with PSO	0.6694	0.5516	0.8124	37.3

As it is clear from Table 1, Kalman Filtering algorithm when combined with the PSO heuristic method achieves the highest geometric mean, which is the combination of sensitivity and specificity. Hence, we can assume that Kalman with PSO achieves the highest classification performance. However, at the same time it is observed that the optimal mathematical models generated by Kalman with GA are the simplest ones concerning complexity. Particularly, classifiers generated from Kalman with GA algorithm have an average of 12.3 mathematical terms. While IDBD and RLS succeed to achieve higher specificity than Kalman algorithm, they cannot achieve a higher overall classification performance through the geometric mean measure, because of their low sensitivity values.

In general, GAs lead to less complexity classifiers than the classifiers produced by PSO for all possible adaptive filtering algorithms. According to the classification performance, adaptive filtering techniques can be ranked from the best one to the worse as Kalman, RLS, LMS and IDBD. This fact can also be observed at figure 1, where the performance of each algorithm has been depicted based on the evaluation measure, as described in equation (2). The evaluation measure is a multi-objective measure, as it considers more than one metrics simultaneously. Kalman and RLS perform almost the same, but Kalman achieves a slightly higher accuracy. LMS algorithm is known for its computational simplicity, but RLS algorithm and Kalman filter have higher performance as they focus on the minimization of the mean square error between the desired signal and the model filter output. IDBD, which is a gain adaptation algorithm, fails to compete with the other algorithms. Maybe this happens because the learning rate of the IDBD algorithm is not optimized through the heuristic algorithms, but within the algorithm itself (meta-learning parameter). When dealing with the PPI prediction problem our first objectives are classification performance and interpretability and not computational complexity because of the off-line nature of the problem. Thus, among the local search algorithms explored in the present paper, Extended Kalman filters are the best solution.

Another observation is that the results of the adaptive filtering techniques combined with PSO have larger variance than the corresponding algorithms combined with GA. This means that PSO is more unstable than GA algorithm, and hence, GA has a smoother convergence. Moreover, we can observe that RLS, LMS and IDBD have -in general- larger variance than the Kalman algorithm which is more stable. This fact can be attributed to the parameters that RLS, LMS and IDBD try to optimize through the heuristic algorithm. As a result, they have a larger search space to explore and the complexity of the heuristic problem rises making them difficult to converge using the same iterations. In the Kalman case, both GA and PSO have low variance in the measures' results and PSO achieves to overcome the classification accuracy of the GA.

Next, we present the classifier with the higher evaluation value (equation 2), that resulted from the Kalman with GA combination. We observe that there are a lot of nonlinear mathematical terms in the model, like exponential or polynomial, revealing the complexity of the real model and indicating that this classification model cannot be derived with simple classification algorithms. The model attributes higher importance to terms including the third feature x_3, which is a combination of three distinct features. Furthermore, the third feature dominates the model, as 4 terms out of 9 consist only of the third feature.

$$out = -4.0961x_3{}^3 - 0.5481x_2x_4{}^3 - 0.4992x_4{}^4 + 1.1192x_2e^{-x_3{}^2} + 4.2501x_3e^{-x_3{}^2}$$
$$+ 0.7043x_4e^{-x_2{}^2} + 0.3599e^{-x_3{}^2} + 3.5403x_3{}^7 - 0.6968x_2{}^9$$

$$(3)$$

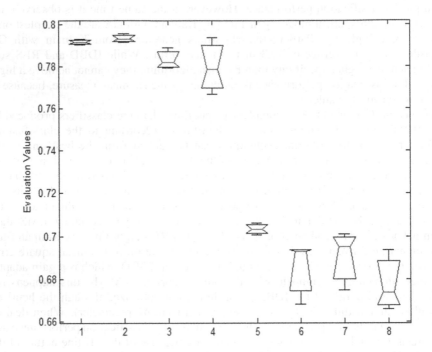

Fig. 1. Evaluation value is the average of the three main measures (geometric mean, sensitivity, specificity), for each combination of algorithms. 1: Kalman GA, 2: Kalman PSO, 3: RLS GA, 4: RLS PSO, 5: LMS GA, 6: LMS PSO, 7: IDBD GA, 8: IDBD PSO.

4   Conclusions

We have studied the influence of different combinations between adaptive filtering techniques and heuristic algorithms on PPI prediction problem in order to produce the optimal hybrid method for this problem. A search space of possible mathematical models is been searched through the heuristic algorithms (GA, PSO) and the optimal parameters for each specific model are been calculated by using an adaptive filtering technique (Kalman, RLS, LMS, IDBD). The mathematical model resulted from the above process constitutes our optimal classifier. All methods were tested in a human protein interaction dataset extracted from the PIPS database.

Our research concluded that the combination of an Extended Kalman Filter combined with PSO – as described in Section 2.3 – gives us the highest classification performance. Moreover, the Extended Kalman Filter when combined with GA produces the less complicated classifiers. In general, PSO heuristic has a larger variance than GA technique, except for the Kalman algorithm where both are stable. In the Kalman algorithm, PSO achieves to overcome the classification accuracy of GA.

In this paper, we presented a new classification framework for predicting PPIs combining heuristic algorithms with adaptive filtering techniques. According to the need of the researchers for high classification accuracy or low complex classifiers, the most convenient combination of algorithms can be used. Finally, we intent to use our method for the prediction of novel human PPIs.

Acknowledgments. This research has been co-financed by the European Union (European Social Fund - ESF) and Greek national funds through the Operational Program "Education and Lifelong Learning" of the National Strategic Reference Framework (NSRF) - Research Funding Program: Heracleitus II. Investing in knowledge society through the European Social Fund.

References

1. Bock, J.R., Gough, D.A.: Predicting protein-protein interactions from primary structure. Bioinformatics 17, 455–460 (2001)
2. Chua, H.N., Sung, W.K., Wong, L.: Exploiting indirect neighbors and topological weight to predict protein function from protein-protein interactions. Bioinformatics 22(13), 623–1630 (2006)
3. Chen, X., Liu, M.: Prediction of protein-protein interactions using random decision forest framework. Bioinformatics 21, 4394–4400 (2005)
4. Fariselli, P., Pazos, F., Valencia, A., Casadio, R.: Prediction of protein-protein interaction sites in heterocomplexes with neural networks. European Journal of Biochemistry 1 FEBS 269, 1356–1361 (2002)
5. Theofilatos, K.A., Dimitrakopoulos, C.M., Tsakalidis, A.K., Likothanassis, S.D., Papadimitriou, S.T., Mavroudi, S.P.: A new hybrid method for predicting protein interactions using Genetic Algorithms and Extended Kalman Filters. In: 10th IEEE International Conference on Information Technology and Applications in Biomedicine (ITAB 2010), November 3-5 (2010)
6. Diniz, P.S.: Adaptive Filtering: Algorithms and Practical Implementation. Springer, Heidelberg (2002)
7. Holland, J.: Adaptation in Natural and Artificial Systems: An Introductory Analysis with Applications to Biology, Control and Artificial Intelligence. MIT Press, Cambridge (1995)
8. Kennedy, J., Eberhart, R.C.: Particle Swarm Optimization. In: Proceedings of the IEEE International Joint Conference on Neural Networks, pp. 1942–1948 (1995)
9. Scott, M., Barton, G.: Probabilistic prediction and ranking of human protein-proteininteractions. BMC Bioinformatics 8, 239 (2007)
10. Mishra, G.R., Suresh, M., Kumaran, K., Kannabiran, N., Suresh, S., Bala, P., Shivakumar, K., Anuradha, N., Reddy, R., Raghavan, T.M., Menon, S., Hanumanthu, G., Gupta, M., Upendran, S., Gupta, S., Mahesh, M., Jacob, B., Mathew, P., Chatterjee, P., Arnn, K.S., Sharma, S., Chandrika, K.N., Deshpande, N., Palvankar, K., Raghavnath, R., Krishnakanth, R., Karathia, H., Rekba, B., Nayak, R., Vishnupriya, G., Kumar, H.G.M., Nagini, M., Kumar, G.S.S., Jose, R., Deepthi, P., Mohan, S.S., Gandhi, T.K.B., Harsha, H.C., Deshpande, K.S., Sarker, M., Prasad, T.S.K., Pandey, A.: Human protein reference database 2006 update. Nucleic Acids Research 34, 411–414 (2006)
11. O'Brien, K.P., Remm, M., Sonnhammer, E.L.: Inparanoid: a comprehensive database of eukaryotic orthologs. Nucleid. Acids Res. 33(Database issue), D476–D480 (2005)
12. Scott, M.S., Thomas, D.Y., Hallett, M.T.: Predicting subcellular localization via protein motif co-occurrence. Genome Research 14, 1957–1966 (2004)
13. Widrow, B., Hoff, M.E.: Adaptive switching circuits. WESCOM Conv. Rec. pt. 4, 96–140 (1960)

14. Goodwin, G.C., Payne, R.L.: Dynamic System Identification: Experiment Design and Data Analysis. Academic Press, NewYork (1977)
15. Welch, G., Bishop, G.: An Introduction to the Kalman Filter. University of North Carolina at Chapel Hill (1995)
16. Sutton, R.S.: Adapting bias by gradient descent: An incremental version of delta-bar-delta. In: Proceedings of the Tenth National Conference on Artificial Intelligence, pp. 171–176. MIT Press, Cambridge (1992)
17. Prediction Update Algorithms for XCSF: RLS, Kalman Filter, and Gain Adaptation
18. Ratnaweera, A., Halgamuge, S., Watson, H.: Particle Swarm Optimization with Self-Adaptive Acceleration Coefficients. In: Proceedings of the First International Conference on Fuzzy Systems and Knowledge Discovery, pp. 264–268 (2003)

Investigation of Medication Dosage Influences from Biological Weather

Kostas Karatzas[1], Marina Riga[1], Dimitris Voukantsis[1], and Åslög Dahl[2]

[1] ISAG – Informatics Systems and Applications Group, Department of Mechanical
Engineering, Aristotle University of Thessaloniki, 54124, Thessaloniki, Greece
kkara@eng.auth.gr, {mriga,voukas}@isag.meng.auth.gr
[2] Gothenburg Atmospheric Centre/ Aerobiology, Department of Plant and Environmental
Sciences, University of Gothenburg, SE 405 30, Gothenburg, Sweden
aslog.dahl@dpes.gu.se

Abstract. Airborne pollen has been associated with allergic symptoms in
sensitized individuals, whereas atmospheric pollution indisputably aggravates
the impact on the overall quality of life. Therefore, it is of major importance to
correlate, forecast and disseminate information concerning high concentration
levels of allergic pollen types and air pollutants to the public, in order to
safeguard the quality of life of the population. In this study, we investigate the
relationship between the Defined Daily Dose (DDD) given to patients in a
triggered allergy reaction and the different levels of air pollutants and pollen
types. By profiling specific atmospheric conditions, specialists may define the
need for medication to individuals suffering from pollen allergy, not only
according to their personal medical record but also to the existing air quality
observations. Paper results indicate some interesting interrelationships between
the use of medication and atmospheric quality conditions and shows that the
forecasting of daily medication is possible with the aid of proper algorithms.

Keywords: Allergy, Pollen, Medication Dosage Forecasting, Information Gain
Criterion, Self-Organizing Maps, Decision Trees.

1 Introduction

Allergies related to airborne pollen are very common in the general population and
also act as a factor with a considerable impact on quality of life in urban areas [1].
Atmospheric pollen counts are positively correlated with symptoms of allergic rhinitis
and/or conjunctivitis [2-3], emergency visits or hospitalization because of asthma [4-
6] and stroke [7]. In addition, even a short term exposure to allergic pollen has been
found to increase the prescribed anti-allergic medicines [8]. The dosage and duration
of medication primarily depends on interaction between an individual's immune
system and pollen allergens, but also, presumably, on environmental pressures, such
as air pollution. Air pollutants can induce respiratory inflammation and affect the
response to aeroallergens. The evidence of interaction between pollen and air
pollution in their health impact comes from many laboratory and experimental
studies, as well as from long-term epidemiological studies [9-11] (and references

L. Iliadis and C. Jayne (Eds.): EANN/AIAI 2011, Part I, IFIP AICT 363, pp. 481–490, 2011.

therein). The number of studies indicating short-term, acute effects are fewer but at least ozone and aeroallergens have been found to interact in promoting asthma [12-15], and this stands also for the combination of particulates and pollen [16-17].

2 Materials and Methods

The aim of the current paper is to study the relationship between aeroallergens, air pollution and the use of anti-allergic medication (antihistamines) to citizens, during spring and summer seasons. More specifically, we investigate the relationship between the so called Defined Daily Dose (DDD) prescribed to allergic patients and the levels of air pollutants and pollen concentrations in the atmosphere. For this reason, a dataset of corresponding observation data was provided by the Gothenburg Atmospheric Centre (GAC), from the Department of Plant and Environmental Sciences at the University of Gothenburg in Sweden.

The available dataset is a time series (corresponding to middle-spring and summer seasons) for the years 2009 and 2010, consisting of heterogeneous data (air quality concentrations, pollen counts and medication dosage). Due to the heterogeneity of the dataset and the existence of some missing values in the time series, it became evident that a robust computational methodology was required, which may tolerate missing data and can also handle parameters of varying nature. For this reason, we adopted Self-Organizing Maps (SOMs) in the first phase of our study, as an unsupervised learning approach to extract hidden patterns and produce visualizations of interrelationships between the available parameters (data set attributes). In the second phase, we utilize the Information Gain criterion and produce forecasting models based on decision trees, for the prediction of the medication levels provided to patients on aggravated air quality conditions. The evaluation of the models' performance is made through the calculation of specific statistical indexes.

2.1 Study Area

Gothenburg is the second largest city in Sweden and the fifth largest in the Nordic countries, accounting for approximately 510,000 inhabitants in a total area of 1,029km^2. It is located on the west coast in South-West Sweden, at the mouth of the river Göta Älv. The city contains an adequate rate of green space, estimated at 175m^2 per citizen, while there are several parks and nature areas that reserve space ranging from tens of meters to hundreds of hectares. The climate of Gothenburg is characterized as suboceanic, with warm summers and cool, windy winters, pointing a narrow annual temperature range. During the summer, daylight extends 17 hours, but lasts only 7 hours in late December. The quality of the atmospheric environment is generally good in the city of Gothenburg, which is not extremely polluted due to its moderate size and location near the coast. Nevertheless, the climatic conditions of the last years accumulated the air pollutants emitted at the ground level and air quality became poorer than in the past [18].

2.2 Pollen Collection and Identification and Air Quality Monitoring

For pollen monitoring, Burkard 7-day volumetric spore traps were used. The Gothenburg trap is situated approx. 30m above ground at the roof-top of the Central

Clinic at Östra sjukhuset, at the eastern border of Gothenburg and 20km from the sea (57°72'N, 12°05'E). In the microscope, pollen grains were counted along twelve latitudinal transects of the exposed tape, corresponding to an exposure to 1 cubic metre of air. The value used in the calculations is the number of pollen grains per cubic metre and 24 hours.

Gothenburg air pollution data originated from a monitoring station owned by the Environment Department of Gothenburg City, approx. 20m above ground at the roof top of the shopping centre "Femman" in the very city centre (57°42'N 11°58'E), and 8km away from the pollen trap. All pollution data used are 24-hour sums of hourly values.

2.3 Exploration of the Initial Dataset

A diverse collection of air quality, pollen and medication information was under investigation, forming a daily time series of observations from middle spring to summer season (1/4/2009 to 31/8/2009 and 1/4/2010 to 31/8/2010).

More specifically, the data used in this study consisted of daily pollen counts of 7 main pollen types (*Alnus*, *Betula*, *Corylus*, *Fagus*, *Quercus*, *Poaceae* and *Artemisia*) and 3 features concerning overall pollen related measurements (total birch related pollen, i.e. the sum of *Alnus*, *Betula*, *Corylus*, *Fagus* and *Quercus*, total allergenic pollen and total pollen counts). Daily sums of hourly concentrations of 9 air pollutants (SO_2, NO, NO_2, NO_x, CO, O_3, PM_{10}, $PM_{2.5}$ and Soot) and additional time information (year, month, day of the week and day of year) were taken into account. The DDD of medication given to allergic patients was used as a class attribute. This attribute is defined as the average "maintenance" dose per day for a drug used in adults. The available dataset was divided into 2 subsets and was investigated for the years 2009 and 2010 separately. Overall, 153 daily datasets per year were made available, each one including 24 different attributes.

2.4 Methods

The primary investigation of the relationships between air quality, pollen concentrations and medication dosage was performed using Self-Organizing Maps [19]. In addition, and in order to support patients in managing the quality of their everyday life, a number of forecasting models for the DDD was developed, by employing the well known *C4.5* Decision Tree algorithm [20]. In order to select the appropriate features from the dataset that will feed the prediction model with valuable information, the Information Gain criterion was adopted. It should be noted that Computational Intelligence methods have already been applied in the analysis of allergenic pollen types [21-22]. Moreover, a detailed analysis of interconnections between pollen and air quality data has been performed in [23], by introducing a two-step clustering process consisting of the application of SOM and K-means algorithms.

In the current study, SOM visualizations have been deployed using the function package SOM Toolbox 2.0[1] in the Matlab environment, while J48 decision trees models have been developed using the open source Data Mining tool WEKA[2].

---

[1] Available at: http://www.cis.hut.fi/projects/somtoolbox/
[2] Available at: http://www.cs.waikato.ac.nz/ml/weka/

Self-Organizing Maps (SOMs). A self-organizing map is a form of an artificial neural network that uses a competitive, unsupervised learning algorithm, in order to model high-dimensional data into low-dimensional (usually 2-dimensional) visualizations, by also preserving constant their spatial/ topological interrelationships. SOM consists of neurons, each one of which is a set of coefficients corresponding to the variables of the data set. The number of neurons and the interconnection between them is determined by the user. Results of the method are visualized by the production of Kohonen maps, with specific characteristics, meaning: data with similar "behavior" are grouped together and displayed in the same 2-D space of maps [19]. It is a robust and computationally efficient method that not only compresses the dimensions of data but also explores and extracts hidden information of them. On this basis, SOMs are capable of identifying complex, non-linear relations within data, and representing them in a convenient and understandable way. In the current study, the map grid size of the topology structure was 24x16 (parameter size: 'normal'), arranged on a hexagonal lattice in a sheet shaped map.

Information Gain Criterion. In order to obtain an optimum performance of the modeling process, several parameters need to be evaluated, concerning the information gain they give. The method adopted in the current study for feature selection is the Information Gain (IG) criterion which evaluates the worth of an attribute by measuring the information gain with respect to the predicted class variable. The method is based on the notion of entropy that, in this context, characterizes the impurity of an arbitrary set of attributes.

In the current case, the target variable is the DDD. Since the IG criterion requires for the target variable to be nominal, the numeric values of DDD per 1000 inhabitants were transformed into nominal ones, according to the classification table bellow (Table 1).

Table 1. The transformation table of defined daily dose from numeric values to nominal

DDD per 1000 inhabitants	Nominal value (class name)
<25	Class1: Very low
25-32.5	Class2: Low
32.5-40	Class3: Medium
40-47.5	Class4: High
>47.5	Class5: Very high

Continuing, by calculating IG for each variable through the WEKA software, a ranking of each parameter's impact became available, giving their relative importance in descending order (Table 2):

The IG values of the parameters within the studied data set (Table 2) suggest that certain pollen types are the least important variables in the modelling process of DDD while air quality data (and specifically concentrations of O_3, PM_{10} and NO) seem to play a significant role in medication usage.

Table 2. Classification of each considering variable, according to their information gain value estimation (descending order)

Dataset of 2009		Dataset of 2010	
1. DayOfYear	13. Soot	1. DayOfYear	13. Year
2. Month	14. NO_2	2. Month	14. Day
3. NO	15. Day	3. Artemisia	15. SO_2
4. Artemisia	16. $PM_{2.5}$	4. O_3	16. NO_2
5. TotalBirchRelated	17. O_3	5. TotalBirchRelated	17. TotalPollen
6. TotalAllergenicPollen	18. SO_2	6. NO	18. NO_x
7. PM_{10}	19. Quercus	7. Betula	19. CO
8. Betula	20. Fagus	8. Corylus	20. Fagus
9. NO_x	21. Corylus	9. Alnus	21. TotalAllergenicPollen
10. TotalPollen	22. Poaceae	10. PM_{10}	22. Quercus
11. Alnus	-	11. $PM_{2.5}$	23. Poaceae
12. Year	-	12. Soot	-

Decision Trees. Decision trees are a set of classifiers that produce a top-down structure of interconnected nodes (a tree), by selecting a root node and partitioning the data properly following *"if... else"* rules. The most significant variables (those with high information gain value) are located in the upper layers of the tree, while the least valuable are the leaf-nodes. They are considered especially attractive as classification techniques, due to their following characteristics:

- their intuitive representation allows for easy interpretation of the resulting classification model, as their structure "inherits" the basic characteristics of the knowledge domain they are mapping, and
- they are non-parametric, thus especially suited for exploring datasets where there is no prior knowledge about the probability distributions of the target class or data attributes.

In the current study, calculations were made with the J48 classifier (implementation of C4.5 algorithm in the WEKA data mining tool), which achieves fast execution times and adequate scale of large datasets. As this method requires the class attribute to be nominal, arithmetic values of DDD per 1000 inhabitants were transformed according to classification rules given in Table 1. In order to create the forecasting models, the input data were selected via a process by which certain data were excluded from the initial data set, in the frame of consequently executed data modification steps. After every step, a classification model was constructed and evaluated by using 10-fold cross validation.

The accuracy of the models was measured according to percentage (%) of correctly classified instances and Kappa-statistic. In more detail, the first measure is giving a success rate by dividing the sum of correctly predicted instances to the total number of predicted instances, but this metric is not sensitive to class distribution. On the other hand, Kappa-statistic is a more robust statistical measure that is used to calculate the agreement between predicted and observed categorizations of a dataset, while correcting for agreement that occurs by chance. It estimates the error cost of a classification model, by being a more fair measure of the overall success of the model.

3   Results and Discussion

The aforementioned methodology was applied at both datasets of the years 2009 and 2010 separately. The objective was to identify interrelationships between pollen concentrations and DDD or air quality observations and DDD, by adopting the SOM method and then constructing efficient decision trees.

3.1   SOM Analysis of the Initial Dataset

High values of DDD seem to be a multi-parametric phenomenon, i.e. influenced by various parameters. On this basis, synergies can be expected between pollen and air quality. Figure 1 represents the map resulted using SOM on the overall dataset of 2009. The most important conclusions from the analysis are listed below:

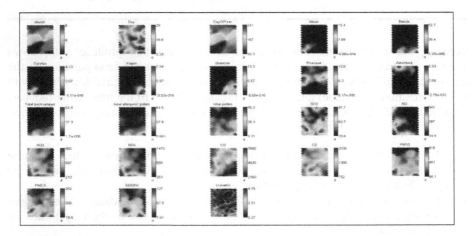

Fig. 1. Self-organizing maps of air quality, pollen and medication data for the year 2009

- The use of medication is lower when *Artemisia* is in its highest concentration levels, while *Poaceae* is correlated with medium levels of medication.
- *Alnus* and *Corylus* seem to be related with high levels of NO, NO_2 and PM_{10}, while additionally they are related with medium to high levels of medication.
- High levels of medication use is observed when air pollution is high, especially for PM and O_3 levels.
- The existence of high NO and NO_2 concentration levels is correlated to medium levels of medication.

No efficient conclusions could be derived as far as CO levels are concerned, since the corresponding levels of medication vary from low to high. Overall, it becomes evident that DDD is positively correlated with air quality and some specific pollen taxa.

By repeating the SOM analysis on the overall dataset of 2010 the following basic conclusions are derived:

- Medication usage is related to high levels of air pollution, and especially to PM_{10}, O_3 and Soot, with the latter revealing a very similar topological pattern with DDD in the derived SOM visualizations.
- NO_2 and NO_x seem to play an important role in high medication usage.
- High total pollen measurements increase medication.

3.2 Decision Trees Application

The development of models for the use of medication was performed by testing a number of scenarios concerning the types of data to be included. The results of this process in terms of model performance are described in Table 3.

Table 3. Evaluation of developed decision trees in modelling medication usage for 2009 and 2010 separately, according to two different dataset variations (case scenarios)

	Dataset 2009		Dataset 2010	
Data scenario	Correctly classified %	Kappa Statistic	Correctly classified %	Kappa Statistic
A	**56.86%** **(87/153)**	**0.3874**	54.90% (84/153)	0.3250
B	52.94% (81/153)	0.3271	**59.48%** **(91/153)**	**0.3991**

Data scenario A: Exclusion of the variables Year, Soot and *Fagus* (no measurements were available for both years).
Data scenario B: Removing all pollen data observations and total birch related variable and keeping only relative information about total allergenic pollen and total pollen counts.

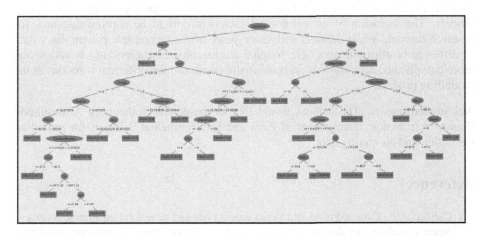

Fig. 2. J48 decision tree with the best performance (Case A) for the dataset of 2009

The accuracy of developed decision trees models, concerning the best performing scenario per year, ranges from 56% to 59%, in terms of correctly classified instances. This method outperforms a completely random approach, where the probability of correct classifications, by choosing randomly one of the five pre-defined classes as a forecasting result, equals 20%.

While interpreting the developed decision trees for best case scenarios per each year (see Figure 2 for year 2009), it is interesting to note that the day of the year seems to be the most decisive parameter in the modelling process. Other parameters of importance include PM_{10} and NO_2 (for 2009) and PM_{10} and O_3 (for 2010), followed by pollen type parameters. Overall, there is evidence that air quality parameters play an important role in modelling medication use, for the aforementioned years.

4 Conclusions

The motivation in the current study was to develop self-organizing maps that would exploit interrelationships between the use of medication and air quality conditions, concerning pollution and pollen concentrations, so as to evolve computationally effective decision trees for daily medication prediction. The preliminary analysis of the Gothenburg dataset indicates that there are some interesting relationships between the parameters under investigation. More specifically:

- Air quality seems to play a synergetic role in the use of medication, influencing the total DDD per 1000 inhabitants. Thus, an interaction between air quality levels and medication usage (i.e. symptom development) is suggested from the results of the preliminary analysis.
- The medication being used seems to be also influenced by the total allergenic pollen.
- The role of Particulate Matter seems to be away from neutral or independent, yet more research is certainly required in this subject.

Further investigation need to be done, in order to enhance the efficiency of prediction models. The inclusion of meteorological factors seems to be a promising task for research through, while datasets with more years of data, complete patient diary data or different health indicators (like hospital admissions, mortality, etc.) would reveal more complicated relationships and potentially result to more efficient solutions in the modelling process.

Acknowledgments. The authors would like to thank the Gothenburg Atmospheric Center/ Aerobiology Department of Plant and Environmental Sciences for providing the pollen and air quality data.

References

1. Cariñanos, P., Casares-Porcel, M.: Urban green zones and related pollen allergy: A review. Some guidelines for designing spaces with low allergy impact. Landscape and Urban Planning 101(3), 205–214 (2011)
2. Breton, M.C., Garneau, M., Fortier, I., Guay, F., Louis, J.: Relationship between climate, pollen concentrations of Ambrosia and medical consultations for allergic rhinitis in Montreal, 1994-2002. Science of the Total Environment 370, 39–50 (2006)
3. Takasaki, K., Enatsu, K., Kumagami, H., Takahashi, H.: Relationship between airborne pollen count and treatment outcome in Japanese cedar pollinosis patients. European Archives of Oto-Rhino-Laryngology 266, 673–676 (2009)

4. Carracedo-Martinez, E., Sanchez, C., Taracido, M., Saez, M., Jato, V., Figueiras, A.: Effect of short-term exposure to air pollution and pollen on medical emergency calls: a case-crossover study in Spain. Allergy 63, 347–353 (2008)
5. Tobias, A., Galan, I., Banegas, J.R., Aranguez, E.: Short term effects of airborne pollen concentrations on asthma epidemic. Thorax 58, 708–710 (2003)
6. Jariwala, S.P., Kurada, S., Moday, H., Thanjan, A., Bastone, L., Khananashvili, M., Fodeman, J., Hudes, G., Rosenstreich, D.: Association between tree pollen counts and asthma ED visits in a high-density urban center. Journal of Asthma 48, 442–448 (2011)
7. Low, R.B., Bielory, L., Qureshi, A.I., Dunn, V., Stuhlmiller, D.F., Dickey, D.A.: The relation of stroke admissions to recent weather, airborne allergens, air pollution, seasons, upper respiratory infections, and asthma incidence, September 11, 2001, and day of the week. Stroke 37(4), 951–957 (2006)
8. Fuhrman, C., Sarter, H., Thibaudon, M., Delmas, M.C., Zeghnoun, A., Lecadet, J., Caillaud, D.: Short-term effect of pollen exposure on antiallergic drug consumption. Annals of Allergy, Asthma and Immunology 99, 225–231 (2007)
9. D'Amato, G., Liccardi, G., D'Amato, M.: Environmental risk factors (outdoor air pollution and climatic changes) and increased trend of respiratory allergy. Journal of Investigational Allergology and Clinical Immunology 10, 123–128 (2000)
10. Lubitz, S., Schober, W., Pusch, G., Effner, R., Klopp, N., Behrendt, H., Buters, J.T.: Polycyclic aromatic hydrocarbons from diesel emissions exert proallergic effects in birch pollen allergic individuals through enhanced mediator release from basophils. Environmental Toxicology 25, 188–197 (2010)
11. Peden, D., Reed, C.E.: Environmental and occupational allergies. Journal of Allergy and Clinical Immunology 125, 150–160 (2010)
12. Dales, R.E., Cakmak, S., Judek, S., Dann, T., Coates, F., Brook, J.R., Burnett, R.T.: Influence of outdoor aeroallergens on hospitalization for asthma in Canada. Journal Allergy and Clinical Immunology 113, 303–306 (2004)
13. Higgins, B.G., Francis, H.C., Yates, C., Warburton, C.J., Fletcher, A.M., Pickering, C.A., Woodcock, A.A.: Environmental exposure to air pollution and allergens and peak flow changes. The European Respiratory Journal 16, 61–66 (2000)
14. Lierl, M.B., Hornung, R.W.: Relationship of outdoor air quality to pediatric asthma exacerbations. Annals of Allergy. Asthma and Immunology 90, 28–33 (2003)
15. Fco Brito, F., Mur Gimeno, P., Martínez, C., Tobías, A., Suárez, L., Guerra, F., Borja, J.M., Alonso, A.M.: Air pollution and seasonal asthma during the pollen season. A cohort study in Puertollano and Ciudad Real (Spain). Allergy 62, 1152–1157 (2007)
16. Renzetti, G., Silvestre, G., D'Amario, C., Bottini, E., Gloria-Bottini, F., Bottini, N., Auais, A., Perez, M.K., Piedimonte, G.: Less Air Pollution Leads to Rapid Reduction of Airway Inflammation and Improved Airway Function in Asthmatic Children. Pediatrics 123, 1051–1058 (2009)
17. Ghosh, D., Chakraborty, P., Gupta, J., Biswas, A., Gupta-Bhttacharya, S.: Asthma-related hospital admissions in an Indian megacity: role of ambient aeroallergens and inorganic pollutants. Allergy 65, 795–796 (2010)
18. Grundstrom, M., Linderholm, H.W., Klingberg, J., Pleijel, H.: Urban NO2 and NO pollution in relation to the North Atlantic Oscillation NAO. Atmospheric Environment 45, 883–888 (2011)
19. Kohonen, T.: Self-Organizing Maps (2001)
20. Salzberg, L. S.: C4.5: Programs for Machine Learning by J. Ross Quinlan. Morgan Kaufmann Publishers, Inc., San Francisco (1993); Machine Learning 16, 235–240 (1994)

21. Voukantsis, D., Niska, H., Karatzas, K., Riga, M., Damialis, A., Vokou, D.: Forecasting daily pollen concentrations using data-driven modeling methods. Atmospheric Environment 44(39), 5101–5111 (2010)
22. Mitrakis, N., Karatzas, K., Jaeger, S.: Investigating pollen data with the aid of fuzzy methods. In: Diamantaras, K., Duch, W., Iliadis, L.S. (eds.) ICANN 2010, Part III. LNCS, vol. 6354, pp. 464–470. Springer, Heidelberg (2010)
23. Voukantsis, D., Karatzas, K., Rantio-Lehtimaki, A., Sofiev, M.: Investigation of relationships and interconnections between Pollen and Air Quality data with the aid of Computational Intelligence Methods. In: 23rd Conference on Environmental Informatics and Industrial Environmental Protection: Concepts, Methods and Tools, pp. 189–198. Shaker Verlang, Aachen (2009)

Combination of Survival Analysis and Neural Networks to Relate Life Expectancy at Birth to Lifestyle, Environment, and Health Care Resources Indicators

Lazaros Iliadis and Kyriaki Kitikidou

Democritus University of Thrace,
Department of Forestry and Management of the Environment and Natural Resources,
Pandazidou 193, 68200, Orestiada, Greece
kkitikid@fmenr.duth.gr

Abstract. This paper aims to shed light on the contribution of determinants to the health status of the population and to provide evidence on whether or not these determinants are producing similar results from two different statistical methods, across OECD countries. In this study, one output – Life Expectancy (LE) at birth of the total population – and three inputs are included. The inputs represent the three main dimensions of health outcome production: health resources (measured by health spending or the number of health practitioners), socioeconomic environment (pollution, education and income) and lifestyle (tobacco, alcohol and diet). A variable expressing country specificities is also used. Two independent statistical analyses, resulted that health resources and country specific effects are more closely related to LE.

Keywords: Artificial Neural Networks, Cox regression, Health status, Survival analysis.

1 Introduction

The health status of the population has many determinants. Lifestyle factors (tobacco, alcohol and diet) have numerous health effects. Excessive alcohol consumption increases the risk for heart stroke and vascular diseases, as well as liver cirrhosis and certain cancers. Alcohol consumption has fallen in many OECD countries since the early 1980s but some countries are standing out; consumption has increased sharply in Ireland and has remained broadly stable in Nordic countries. The empirical results suggest that differences in alcohol consumption can help to explain a gap in Life Expectancy (LE) at birth of up to 1.8 years between low-consumption countries (such as Turkey) and high consumption ones (including France, Hungary and Ireland) [24]. Tobacco consumption is another important factor for health status. Influenced by public awareness campaigns, smoking prohibition in public areas and in the workplace, advertising bans and increased taxation, tobacco consumption has declined steadily in most OECD countries since the early 1980s, in particular in the United States, Canada and New Zealand where consumption has more than halved. However, disparities in tobacco consumption across countries remain large, with

L. Iliadis and C. Jayne (Eds.): EANN/AIAI 2011, Part I, IFIP AICT 363, pp. 491–498, 2011.

heavy smoking in the Czech Republic, Greece, Japan, the Netherlands and Turkey [24]. In addition to the lifestyle factors mentioned, a healthy diet is widely recognized as a major factor in the promotion and maintenance of good health. Low intake of fruits and vegetables is estimated by the World Health Organization (WHO) to be one of the main risk behaviors in developed countries. The consumption of fruits and vegetables has tended to increase over the past two decades in most OECD countries, with Japan and Switzerland being the main exceptions [24].

As regards socio-economic factors, the impact of pollution, education and income is increasingly recognized [17]. Per capita emissions of nitrogen oxide (NOx) have been widely used as a proxy for pollution. By contributing to the formation of fine particulate matter pollution, NOx emissions aggravate respiratory illness and cause premature death in the elderly and infants. They also play a major role in the formation of ground-level ozone (smog) pollution. On high ozone days, there is a marked increase in hospital admissions and visits for asthma and other respiratory illnesses. Since the early 1990s, however, NOx emissions per capita have declined in many OECD countries, partly reflecting technological improvements of combustion processes, in particular in power production and vehicle engines, and government plans aimed at reducing NOx emissions, e.g. Canada, European Union (World Health Report 2002). Although the strong relation between health and education is well established, the direction of causality is still debated and may well be both ways. Better health is associated with higher educational investment, since healthier individuals are able to devote more time and energy to learning. Because they live longer, they also have a greater incentive to learn since they have a higher return on human capital. On the other hand, education causes health if better-educated people use health care services more effectively; they tend to comply better with medical treatments, use more recent drugs and better understand discharge instructions. Education, as measured by the share of population aged 25 to 64 with an uppersecondary degree or higher, has been increasing steadily in particular in most of the countries with the lowest levels in the early 1980s (e.g. Belgium, Greece and Spain; Mexico, Portugal and Turkey being notable exceptions to this catch-up process) [17]. The level of income is even more correlated with the population health status across OECD countries than education. Higher GDP per capita affects health by facilitating access to many of the goods and services which contribute to improving health and longevity (e.g. food, housing, transportation). The relation between GDP per capita and health may also reflect working conditions – richer countries tend to have a higher share of service activities, which are considered to be less health damaging than others such as construction or industrial activities ([4]; [13]).

While recent studies invariably conclude that socio-economic and lifestyle factors are important determinants of the population health status, the contribution of health care resources has been much debated. Berger and Messer [1] as well as Or ([18];[19]) conclude that health care resources have played a positive and large role up to the early 1990s for a panel of OECD countries. Crémieux et al. [3] and Soares [22] reach similar conclusions for Canadian provinces and Brazilian municipalities, respectively. Hitiris and Posnet [8] and Nixon and Ulmann [15] both find that an increase in health expenditure per capita has an impact on health status, which is statistically significant but quite small. Likewise, Thornton [23] concludes for the United States that additional medical care utilization is relatively ineffective in lowering mortality and increasing life expectancy, and thus that health care policy which focuses primarily on the provision of medical services and ignores larger economic and social considerations may do little to benefit the nation's health. Finally, Filmer and Pritchett [5] as well as Self and Grabowski [21] find that health care resources have no significant impact on the population health status. Controversy about the link between health care resources and health status could reflect measurement problems and/or the fact that health-care resources represent too broad a concept, with some components having a more marked impact on health status than others.

The aim of this paper is to relate lifestyle factors, socioeconomic factors and health care resources to health status, using survival analysis (Cox regression) and Artificial Neural Networks (ANN). Similarity in the results from two different statistical analyses could lead us in a combination, for examining health data.

2 Materials and Methods

Regressions on a panel of 23 OECD countries over the period 1981-2003 have been used to assess the impact of health care resources on the health status of the population. This approach allows both changes over time in each country and differences across countries to be taken into account. Socio-economic and lifestyle factors affecting the population's health status, such as income and education, diet, pollution and consumption of alcohol and tobacco are examined [12].

The dependent variable is a measure of the population health status, alternatively:
LE at birth, for males and females,
LE at 65, for males and females,
Premature mortality, for males and females,
Infant mortality.
Inputs consist of:

- spending = health care resources per capita, either measured in monetary terms (total spending including long-term care at GDP PPP exchange rates and constant prices) or in hysical terms (*e.g.* health practitioners).
- tobacco = tobacco consumption in grams per capita.
- alcohol = alcohol consumption in liters per capita.
- diet = consumption of fruits and vegetables per capita in kgs.
- pollution = emissions of nitrogen oxide (NOx) per capita in kgs.
- education = share of the population (aged 25 to 64) with at least upper secondary education.
- GDP = Gross Domestic Product per capita.

Panel data regression results suggested that health care resources, lifestyle and socio-economic factors are all important determinants of the population health status. All regression coefficients for these inputs were highly statistically significant, and carried the expected sign, with health care resources measured either in physical or monetary terms. The choice of health status indicator (LE at birth, at older age, premature mortality, etc.) was not crucial to the analysis. Regression results provided estimates of the impact of the factors identified above on health status proxies, both over time and across 23 OECD countries

In addition to the level of the exogenous variables described above, countries differ according to a number of characteristics which may also affect the health status of their population. Institutional features of their health system may play an important role. Failing to account for these country specificities would lead to biased estimates of the model coefficients. The introduction of country fixed-effects allows taking into account cross-country heterogeneity not reflected in other explanatory variables [12].

The analyses applied to these data were Cox regression ([9]; [14]; [16]) and Multiple Linear Perceptron (MLP) ANN. For the performance of the analyses, the SPSS v.19 statistical package was used ([10];[11]).

The Cox Regression procedure is useful for modelling the time to a specified event, based upon the values of given covariates. The basic model offered by the Cox Regression procedure is the proportional hazards model. The proportional hazards model assumes that the time to event and the covariates are related through the following equation.

$$h_i(t) = [h_0(t)] e^{b_0 + b_1 x_{i1} + \ldots + b_p x_{ip}}$$

where

h_i(t)   is the hazard rate for the ith case at time t
h_0(t)   is the baseline hazard at time t
p is the number of covariates
b_j is the value of the jth regression coefficient
x_{ij} is the value of the ith case of the jth covariate

The hazard function is a measure of the potential for the event to occur at a particular time t, given that the event did not yet occur. Larger values of the hazard function indicate greater potential for the event to occur.

The baseline hazard function measures this potential independently of the covariates. The shape of the hazard function over time is defined by the baseline hazard, for all cases. The covariates simply help to determine the overall magnitude of the function.

The value of the hazard is equal to the product of the baseline hazard and a covariate effect. While the baseline hazard is dependent upon time, the covariate effect is the same for all time points. Thus, the ratio of the hazards for any two cases at any time period is the ratio of their covariate effects. This is the proportional hazards assumption.

$$S_i(t) = e^{-\int_0^t [h_0(t)] e^{b_0 + b_1 x_{i1} + \ldots + b_p x_{ip}}}$$

where $S_i(t)$ is the probability the ith case survives past time t.

The concept of "hazard" may not be intuitive, but it is related to the survival function. The value of the survival function is the probability that the given event has not occurred by time t. Again, the baseline hazard determines the shape of the survival function.

In our study, we putted as dependent variable the LE at birth and spending, education, tobacco, alcohol, diet, pollution, GDP and country specific effect as covariates, and we applied the forward stepwise (Wald) algorithm. The status variable identifies whether the event has occurred for a given case. If the event has not occurred, the case is said to be censored. Censored cases are not used in the computation of the regression coefficients, but are used to compute the baseline hazard. In our study, the status variable is the country specific effect (1 if the effect is positive, 0 if the effect is negative).

For the performance of the ANN analysis, an MLP network model was used, applying the Back Propagation (BP) optimization algorithm. In BP the weighted sum of inputs and bias term are passed to the activation level through the transfer function to produce the output ([2]; [6]; [7]; [20]). The automatic architecture selection was used and the hyperbolic tangent function was applied. The architecture of the developed ANN included only one hidden layer, in an effort to keep the network as simple as possible.

Xiang et al. [25] report that neural network methods do not outperform Cox regression. Both methods have advantages and disadvantages; i.e. neural networks can detect complex patterns among the inputs, but they can be overlearned. On the other hand, in Cox regression, coefficients can be interpreted as the likelihood of an outcome given some value(s) of the risk factor, while neural networks weights usually do not lend themselves to such interpretation. Perhaps a combination of the two methods could give us interesting results.

3 Results-Discussion

In Cox regression, the model-building process took place in two blocks (Table 1). The omnibus tests are measures of how well the model performs. The chi-square change from previous step is the difference between the −2 log-likelihood of the model at the previous step and the current step. If the step adds a variable, the inclusion makes sense if the significance of the change is less than 0.05. If the step removes a variable, the exclusion makes sense if the significance of the change is greater than 0.10. In the first step, Country specific effect is added to the model. In the second step, spending is added to the model.

Table 1. Omnibus Tests of Model Coefficients

		Overall (score)			Change From Previous Step			Change From Previous Block		
Step	-2 Log Likelihood	Chi-square	df	Sig.	Chi-square	df	Sig.	Chi-square	df	Sig.
1[a]	17.498	6.296	1	0.012	6.865	1	0.009	6.865	1	0.009
2[b]	6.791	8.374	2	0.015	10.707	1	0.001	17.572	2	0.000

a. Variable(s) Entered at Step Number 1: country specific effect
b. Variable(s) Entered at Step Number 2: spending

The Exp(B) in Table 2 can be interpreted as the predicted change in the hazard for a unit increase in the predictor. The value of Exp(B) for spending means that the hazard is reduced by $100\% - (100\% \times 0.00047) = 99.95\%$ for each monetary unit a country adds in health care resources. Likewise, the value of Exp(B) for Country_specific_effect is reduced by $100\% - (100\% \times 0.00458) = 99.54\%$ for each unit a country adds in its effects. Variables left out of the model have score statistics with significance values greater than 0.05.

Table 2. Variables in the Cox regression model

		B	SE	Wald	df	Sig.	Exp (B)	95,0% CI for Exp(B)	
								Lower	Upper
Step 1	Country _specific _effect	-1.077	0.485	4.932	1	0.026	0.34069	0.132	0.881
Step2	Spending	-7.645	3.880	3.883	1	0.049	0.00047	0.000	0.960
	Country _specific _effect	-5.387	2.483	4.706	1	0.030	0.00458	0.000	0.595

From the ANN analysis, 13 cases (86.7%) were assigned to the training sample, and 2 (13.3%) to the testing sample. The choice of the records was done randomly. Eight data records were excluded from the analysis because dependent variable values in the testing sample did not occur in the training sample. Nine units were chosen in the hidden layer.

Table 3 displays information about the results of training. Sum-of-squares error is displayed because the output layer has scale-dependent variables. This is the error function that the network tries to minimize during training. The relative error for each scale-dependent variable is the ratio of the sum-of-squares error for the dependent variable to the sum-of-squares error for the "null" model, in which the mean value of the dependent variable is used as the predicted value for each case.

The average overall relative errors are not constant across the training (0.025) and testing (1.173) samples. This could be due to limited data.

Table 3. ANN model summary

Training	Sum of Squares Error	0.149
	Relative Error	0.025
	Stopping Rule Used	1 consecutive step(s) with no decrease in error[a]
	Training Time	00:00:00.000
Testing	Sum of Squares Error	0.003
	Relative Error	1.173

a. Error computations are based on the testing sample.

The importance of each independent variable (Table 4) shows that the variable that affects the most LE is country specific effect, followed by spending.

Table 4. ANN independent variable importance

	Importance	Normalized Importance
Country_specific_effect	0.249	100.0%
Spending	0.167	66.9%
Pollution	0.129	51.8%
Alcohol	0.110	44.0%
Education	0.107	43.0%
Diet	0.089	35.7%
GDP	0.075	29.9%
Tobacco	0.074	29.6%

4 Conclusions

In this work, we have done an attempt to compare two completely different statistical analyses, in order to examine the similarity of the results. For this purpose, we used a health status variable as dependent (life expectancy at birth) and eight independent variables (spending, tobacco, alcohol, diet, pollution, education, GDP and country specificities), closely related to health status. Two analyses were applied: survival analysis (Cox regression) and Artificial Neural Networks (Multiple Linear Perceptron ANN). Results from both methods indicate that country specificities and health care resources (spending) are most important. Cox regression gives us a measure of hazard (health status decrease) for changes in the two independent variables, while MLP ANN classifies all independent variables, according to their importance. Combining the two methods could be useful and intriguing, for exploring and interpreting health data.

Aknowledgements. We wish to thank Mr James Kitchen, Marketing Manager of Public Affairs & Communications Directorate of OECD, who gave us online access to the OECD publications.

References

1. Berger, M., Messer, J.: Public Financing of Health Expenditure, Insurance, and Health Outcomes. Applied Economics 34(17), 2105–2113 (2002)
2. Bishop, C.: Neural Networks for Pattern Recognition, 3rd edn. Oxford University Press, Oxford (1995)
3. Crémieux, P., Ouellette, P., Pilon, C.: Health Care Spending as Determinants of Health Outcomes. Health Economics 8, 627–639 (1999)
4. Cutler, D., Deaton, A., Lleras-Muney, A.: The Determinants of Mortality (2005), http://www.princeton.edu/~rpds/downloads/cutler_deaton_llera s-muney_determinants_mortality_nberdec05.pdf
5. Filmer, D., Pritchett, L.: Child Mortality and Public Spending on Health: How Much Does Money Matter? The World Bank (1997), http://www.worldbank.org/html/dec/Publications/Workpapers/WP S1800series/wps1864/wps1864.pdf

6. Fine, T.: Feedforward Neural Network Methodology, 3rd edn. Springer, New York (1999)
7. Haykin, S.: Neural Networks: A Comprehensive Foundation, 2nd edn. Macmillan College Publishing, New York (1998)
8. Hitiris, T., Posnett, J.: The Determinants and Effects of Health Expenditure in Developed Countries. Journal of Health Economics 11, 173–181 (1992)
9. Hosmer, D., Lemeshow, S.: Applied Survival Analysis. John Wiley and Sons, New York (1999)
10. IBM SPSS Complex Samples. SPSS Inc. (2010)
11. IBM SPSS Neural Networks 19. SPSS Inc. (2010)
12. Joumard, I., André, C., Nicq, C., Olivier, C.: Health Status Determinants: Lifestyle, Environment, Health Care Resources and Efficiency. OECD Economics Department Working Papers No. 627. OECD Publishing (2008)
13. Kiuila, O., Mieszkowski, P.: The Effects of Income, Education and Age on Health. Health Economics (2007),
    http://www3.interscience.wiley.com/
    cgi-bin/fulltext/114050615/PDFSTART
14. Kleinbaum, D.: Survival Analysis: A Self-Learning Text. Springer, New York (1996)
15. Nixon, J., Ullmann, P.: The Relationship between Health Care Expenditure and Health Outcomes – Evidence and Caveats for a Causal Link. European Journal of Health Economics 7(1), 7–19 (2006)
16. Norusis, M.: SPSS 13.0 Advanced Statistical Procedures Companion. Prentice Hall, Inc., Upper Saddle-River (2004)
17. OECD. OECD Environmental Outlook to 2030, Paris (2008)
18. Or, Z.: Determinants of Health Outcomes in Industrialised Countries: A Pooled, Cross-country, Time Series Analysis. OECD Economic Studies (30), 2000/I (2000a)
19. Or, Z.: Exploring the Effects of Health Care on Mortality Across OECD Countries. OECD Labour Market and Social Policy, Occasional Paper No. 46 (2000b)
20. Ripley, B.: Pattern Recognition and Neural Networks. Cambridge University Press, Cambridge (1996)
21. Self, S., Grabowski, R.: How Effective is Public Health Expenditure in Improving Overall Health? A Cross-country Analysis. Applied Economics 35, 835–845 (2003)
22. Soares, R.: Health and the Evolution of Welfare across Brazilian Municipalities. Journal of Development Economics 84, 590–608 (2007)
23. Thornton, J.: Estimating a Health Production Function for the US: Some New Evidence. Applied Economics 34(1), 59–62 (2006)
24. World Health Report - Reducing Risks, Promoting Healthy Life. World Health Organization, France (2002)
25. Xiang, A., Lapuerta, P., Ryutov, A., Buckley, J., Stanley, S.: Comparison of the performance of neural network methods and Cox regression for censored survival data. Computational Statistics & Data Analysis 34, 243–257 (2000)

An Artificial Intelligence-Based Environment Quality Analysis System

Mihaela Oprea[1] and Lazaros Iliadis[2]

[1] University Petroleum - Gas of Ploiesti, Department of Informatics,
Bd. Bucuresti nr. 39, Ploiesti, 100680, Romania
mihaela@upg-ploiesti.ro
[2] Democritus University of Thrace, Greece
liliadis@fmenr.duth.gr

Abstract. The paper describes an environment quality analysis system based on a combination of some artificial intelligence techniques, artificial neural networks and rule-based expert systems. Two case studies of the system use are discussed: air pollution analysis and flood forecasting with their impact on the environment and on the population health. The system can be used by an environmental decision support system in order to manage various environmental critical situations (such as floods and environmental pollution), and to inform the population about the state of the environment quality.

1 Introduction

The continuous improvement of life quality is related directly, among others, to the improvement of environmental quality. This can be achieved by using adequate intelligent monitoring, analysis, forecasting, decision and control systems, based on intelligent tools and techniques. Such integrated intelligent systems are very useful decision support tools for the management of environmental critical situations (events or incidents): floods, severe air/water/soil pollution, earthquakes, tsunami, storms, land sliding, avalanches and others. Also, they can be used in everyday life in order to inform the population of a certain region: urban region (city/town), metropolitan area, or wider areas such as a whole county, continental or intercontinental areas. The complexity of such systems is high due to the interdependencies of various environment parameters. For example, the meteorological factor of precipitations has a direct impact to the evolution of the flow in a specific hydrographic basin as well as to the degree of environmental pollution (air, water or soil). If the volume of precipitation is very high it can contribute to a flood in a certain region of a river and also it can lead to soil pollution, if the water of the river has been polluted.

An environmental decision support system (DSS) capable of handling environmental crises requires an efficient forecasting and analysis approach that can guide the development of a proper strategy. The implementation of such a system can be obtained by employing artificial intelligence (AI) methods that might be combined in an optimal and hybrid manner. AI approaches that can be employed include rule-based expert systems, machine learning techniques like artificial neural networks (ANN)

L. Iliadis and C. Jayne (Eds.): EANN/AIAI 2011, Part I, IFIP AICT 363, pp. 499–508, 2011.

and inductive learning, data mining algorithms, case based reasoning and optimization methods like genetic algorithms.

As the majority of the environmental processes have a certain degree of uncertainty, and a variety of interdependencies between environmental factors and as we do not always have complete datasets (with recorded timeseries or real time accurate measurements) the environmental forecasting and analysis systems have to deal with uncertain knowledge.

A hybrid method is proposed in this paper that combines two AI techniques: a feed forward artificial neural network (doing the forecasting) and a rule-based expert system (doing the analysis). The INTELLEnvQ system (**INTELL**igent **En**vironment **Q**uality) was developed as a tool for environmental quality analysis, that provides information to environmental decision factors and to the population, about the state of the environment of a specific region in a certain period of time, with the possible consequences on human health and on the whole environment (air, soil, water, vegetation, fauna). The system provides also alert codes associated to the specific environmental event/incident.

2   Environmental Forecasting and Analysis

The quality of life is affected by various factors and critical environmental situations. It is important to have forecasting intelligent systems capable of alerting the population in order to prevent or to reduce the effects of an extreme environmental incident.

Figure 1 shows the possible effects of some environmental critical situations to other parts of the environment. For example, a severe air pollution problem would affect the soil, and the water. Also, if two problems are combined, the impact on the environment could increase significatly. For example, if there is a severe air pollution and flood in a given region, than the impact on the water and soil is greater, increasing the pollution degree.

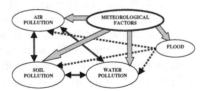

Fig. 1. Interdependencies between different environmental critical situations

Figure 2 presents an overview of the dependencies between the meteorological system and the environment (air, water, soil, vegetation, humans). The system is linked to a network of meteorological stations (MSN) which provides measurements and observations from specific locations. Also, the environment can be associated to specific networks of air, water or soil quality monitoring stations capable of providing measurements and observations of various environmental parameters (e.g. concentration of air pollutants). For example, the air stations network (ASN) can provide measurements of air pollutants in urban regions (SO_2, CO, NO_2, NH_3, O_3, PM_{10}, $PM_{2.5}$) whereas the water stations network (WSN) can measure the level of water pollution in a hydrographic basin or hydrometric station and soil stations network (SSN) can offer information on soil pollution in the agricultural (farming) regions. Also, WSN can include hydrometric stations networks which monitor and analyze various hydrologic parameters in specific hydrographic basins in order to allow management of torrential phenomena. Some events or incidents that have to be predicted and managed (through alerting systems) are also specified in Figure 2. For example, rainfalls and storms in case of the meteorological system, air pollution in case of air monitoring system, soil pollution and land sliding in case of the soil monitoring system, and flood and tsunami in case of the water monitoring system, just to name some of the most important.

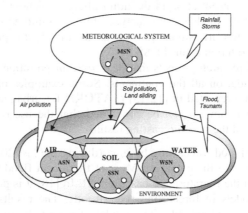

Fig. 2. Overview of the dependencies between the meteorological system and the environment (air, soil, water)

3   Artificial Intelligence and Environment Quality Analysis

3.1   Literature Review

The potential benefits of using various artificial intelligence techniques and in particular, machine learning (ML) techniques for solving different environmental problems were emphasized by various research efforts that have been reported in the literature [1-7] and by new research opportunities such as those mentioned in [8]. Several environmental problems (monitoring, analysis, diagnosis, forecasting, planning, control) can be solved efficiently by using AI techniques. In this paper we shall focus on the analysis problem of two particular cases: air pollution and flood forecasting. The solution that was adopted is the use of a rule-based system that receives the values of the forecasted parameters by an ANN.

The main AI techniques that can be applied to forecasting problems solving are ANN, fuzzy logic, case-based reasoning, Fuzzy Inference Systems (ANFIS), expert systems, adaptive neuro-fuzzy systems. Other hybrid techniques that can be used are those based on Genetic Algorithms (GA), Hidden Markov Models (HMM), Support Vector Machines (SVM).

Air Pollution Forecasting. In the last years, several AI-based forecasting systems were presented in the literature for the prediction of different air pollutants. In [9], the authors describe a novel feature scaling method, named neighbor-based feature scaling that is combined with an ANN model and an ANFIS model for the prediction of sulfur dioxide (SO_2) concentration. The performance of the proposed method was evaluated by using four statistical indicators, including the index of agreement (IA). The results were very good showing the benefits of using the proposed method for sulfure dioxide concentration forecasting in a specific region of Turkey (the Konyia province).

In [4] it is presented an overview of several soft computing approaches like ANN, SVM, fuzzy logic as a feasible solution for urban air forecasting. Another work that reported a successful use of ANN and ANFIS models for the prediction of daily carbon monoxide (CO) concentration in the atmosphere of Tehran is described in [10]. The performances of the models were analyzed by taken into account the uncertainty in forecasting (a Monte-Carlo simulation was used). In [11] it is presented knowledge modelling in an air pollution control DSS.

There are several research projects that deal with air pollution forecasting in various regions worldwide, on all the continents. Some examples of such projects and research initiatives are reported in [12-15] (SATURN for urban air monitoring), [16-17]. From this brief review, it can be concluded that the use of ANN and ANFIS models provides one of the best forecasting results.

Flood Forecasting. Flood forecasting became (during the last 20 years) an intensive research topic for most of the countries. Most of the recent flood forecasting systems that were reported in the literature are based on AI. In [18] it is presented an analysis of using ANFIS models in forecasting river floods. The results showed that such models are accurately and reliable. The models forecast the discharge at a downstream station by using the flow information at various upstream stations. The research work described in [19] focuses on three models of flood forecasting used in India, ANN, ANFIS and ANGIS (Adaptive Neuro-GA Integrated System). The conclusion of the research was that ANFIS performs better than ANN, whereas ANGIS provides maximum accuracy in predicting flood events. The ANGIS model uses GA to optimize the ANN weights. In [20] it is presented a hybrid solution, based on ANN and kernel algorithms for the water resources management in the Thasos islands. In this case, SVM were used to optimize the ANN. The most significant result of this research is that the optimal ANN was validated by using a kernel approach. In [21] it is described an expert system prototype for flood forecasting and river monitoring. The knowledge base of the system consists in expert rules that take into account the specific hydrographic basin parameters, and some meteorological factors. The system was experimented as a simulation for the Prahova hydrographic basin from Romania.

Finally, we have to mention that there are several research projects and initiatives to develop flood monitoring, forecasting and management systems ([12], [13], [16], [22]).

From the brief review presented in this section we can conclude that the most succesfully AI techniques that were used both in air pollution forecast and flood forecasting are ANN and ANFIS. In this paper we shall focus our discussion on the rule-based system considering that the ANN provides the forecasting values for the parameters that are analyzed by the rule-based system in a specific environmental event/incident scenario.

4 The INTELLEnvQ System

The architecture of the INTELLEnvQ system is presented in Figure 3. The main components of the system are a knowledge base under the form of rule base, an inference engine, both components being parts of a rule-based expert system and a forecasting module that is composed by a feed forward artificial neural network. The rules from the knowledge base provide the environmental quality analysis result by taking into account the forecasting result provided by the ANN and other factors (such as the meteorological ones) that influence the environment quality.

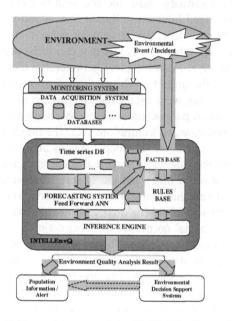

Fig. 3. The architecture of the INTELLEnvQ system

The information about a certain environmental incident is described by the facts from the facts base. The forecasting system uses the meteorological timeseries and the timeseries with the values of the parameters specific to the environmental incident (real measurements, taken from publicly available databases), and provides the values of the forecasted parameters that are taken by the facts base of the rule-based system, and that are used during the reasoning process of the environmental quality analysis. Therefore, the integration of ANN with the rule-based system is facilitated by the facts base, which apart from the current context of a certain environmental incident will contain the values of specific forecasted parameters that will fire certain rules during the reasoning process. The INTELLEnvQ system provides the environmental quality analysis results that might be announced to the population of a region affected by an environmental incident and to environmental DSS. Also, the system can be used as a daily information tool about the state of the environment (air, water, soil) and the potential effects on the population's health in regions with environmental problems, such as urban regions where air pollution can affect seriously the health of people.

The data acquisition system is included in an environmental monitoring system that records the environmental data (meteorological, air, water, soil) in databases. As most of the EU countries have implemented the air pollution monitoring system and some of them have implemented also the hydrometric stations network, we have developed the knowledge base of the INTELLEnvQ system for air quality analysis and flood forecasting. In the next section we focus on these two case studies.

The rules from the knowledge base include standard checking rules, that make comparisons with predefined limits of pollutant concentration (i.e. admissible values in a certain interval of time), dependences analysis rules, that make an extensive analysis by taking into account other parameters that can influence the analyzed environment quality parameter (e.g. meteorological parameters), alert coding rules, and impact analysis rules (e.g. the impact on the environment or on the population health). The standard checking rules were established by taking into account real measurements of the environmental parameters and the environmental quality standards with pre-defined limits of pollutants concentrations (e.g. the maximum admissible concentration in a certain period of time). The dependences analysis rules were established by taking into account the timeseries with real measurements of the environmental parameters (their evolution in time) and the experts' knowledge (about the interdependences between different environmental parameters derived from their experience) that provides some heuristic rules. The alert coding rules were established by taking into account the environmental norms in critical situations. The impact analysis rules were derived from experts' knowledge. The dependences analysis rules and the impact analysis rules depend also on the characteristics of the region for which it is made the environment quality analysis. The problem of combinatorial explosion was phased by developing decision tables in a rather heuristic manner. This minimized the number of rules to a rational extend. Some examples of rules from the knowledge base of INTELLEnvQ system are given in Figure 4 (rules for air quality analysis), and in Figure 5 (rules for flood analysis).

```
RULE 62
IF AP_PM10 = greater_increase AND AP_SO2 = greater_increase
   AND AP_NO2 = greater_increase
THEN AQ = severe_air_pollution;

RULE 102
IF AQ = possible_air_pollution THEN Alert_Code = yellow;

RULE 103
IF AQ = severe_air_pollution  THEN Alert_Code = red;

RULE 201
IF Alert_Code = yellow THEN
   Impact = possible_impact
   DISPLAY "Attention - keep monitoring and analyzing very carefully";

RULE 202
IF Alert_Code = red THEN
   Impact = real_impact
   DISPLAY "ALERT - persons with asthma and other respiratory diseases";
```

Fig. 4. Rules for air quality analysis from the knowledge base of the INTELLEnvQ system

```
RULE R22
IF Temp = high AND PrecipitationS = high
    AND Type_precip = snow   AND Season = winter
THEN Flood_Warning = Yes;

RULE R23
IF Temp = normal AND PrecipitationS = high
    AND Type_precip = rains   AND Season = summer
THEN Flood_Warning = Yes;

RULE T27
IF Flood_Warning = Yes AND Flow >= (Attention_TH)
    AND Flow < (Flood_Danger_TH)
THEN Flood_Forecast = possible_flood;

RULE T28
IF Flood_Warning = Yes AND Flow >= (Flood_Danger_TH)
    AND Flow < (Real_Flood_TH)
THEN Flood_Forecast = very_possible_flood;

RULE A1
IF Flood_Forecast = no_flood THEN   Alert_Code = green;

RULE A2
IF Flood_Forecast = possible_flood THEN   Alert_Code = yellow;

RULE A3
IF Flood_Forecast = very_possible_flood THEN Alert_Code = orange;

RULE A4
IF Flood_Forecast = severe_flood THEN   Alert_Code = red;
```

Fig. 5. Rules for flood forecasting from the knowledge base of the INTELLEnvQ system

5   Case Studies

For the first version of the INTELLEnvQ system we have used the Neural Network Toolbox from Matlab 7.7.0 (2008b) for the development of the forecasting system (i.e. the ANN), and we have implemented the rule-based expert system in VP-Expert, an expert system generator. We have tested the system on two case studies: flood forecasting and air quality analysis in urban regions from Romania. We have used the timeseries with public available data from the National Meteorology Agency (http://www.meteoromania.ro), the Romanian Statistical Institute (http://www.inss.ro), and the National Air Quality Monitoring Network (http://www.calitateaer.ro). The ANN employed in both application cases were back propagation multi layer feed forward using the Extended Delta Bar Delta algorithm and one hidden sub layer. The number of hidden layers was kept as minimum as possible in order to avoid complexity.

5.1   Flood Forecasting

The first case study is a flood forecasting problem. We have extracted the timeseries from the publicly available databases with precipitations and rivers flows data for some Romanian hydrographic basins.

Each hydrographic basin has a number of hydrometric stations that provide measurements and observations for precipitations, rivers flows and other specific parameters (e.g. the three flow thresholds: attention, danger, flood). We have run several scenarios for each hydrographic basin. Figure 6 presents a screenshot of the INTELLEnvQ system run in the case of a scenario with real flood and possible pollution of the soil, while Figure 7 shows a screenshot of a system run in the case of a scenario with a possible flood with no additional impact on the environment pollution.

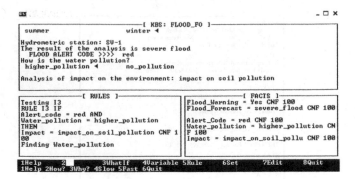

Fig. 6. Screenshot of the INTELLEnvQ system run (flood forecasting - alert code - red)

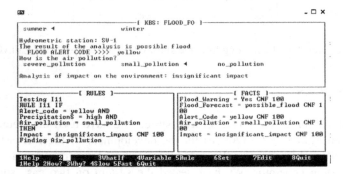

Fig. 7. Screenshot of the INTELLEnvQ system run (flood forecasting - alert code - yellow)

5.2 Air Quality Analysis

The second case study is an air quality analysis in urban regions. We have considered three air pollutants: PM10, SO_2 and NO_2. The possible impact of these pollutants to human health was also analyzed. Figure 8 presents a screenshot of the INTELLEnvQ system run in the case of a scenario with serious air pollution with great impact on the population health, while Figure 9 shows a screenshot of a system run in the case of a scenario with no air pollution and no impact on the population health.

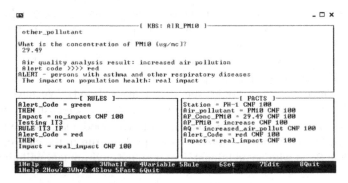

Fig. 8. Screenshot of the INTELLEnvQ system run (air pollution - alert code - red)

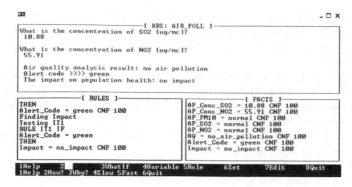

Fig. 9. Screenshot of the INTELLEnvQ system run (air pollution - alert code - green)

6   Conclusion

The paper presented an AI-based environment quality analysis system, INTEL-LEnvQ, that can be mapped to different scenarios of environmental events or incidents with the adaptation of its knowledge base accordingly, by taken into account the specific parameters and environmental context that need to be instantiated. The system uses an artificial neural network for short term forecasting and a rule-based expert system that makes the analysis or forecasting, depending on the type of environmental problem that need to be solved. The main purpose of the system is to give a quick answer to the population or to the environmental decision factors in order to reduce the impacts on the environment and on the population. In this paper we have presented two case studies of the system use: a flood forecasting problem and an air quality analysis problem. Such a system can be integrated in an environmental decision support system.

References

1. Dunea, D., Oprea, M.: Fuzzy-APA: Employing Fuzzy and Neural Networks Techniques in Data Analysis of Industrial Wastewaters Monitoring. WSEAS Transactions on Environment and Development 6(8), 581–590 (2010)
2. Fdez-Riverola, F., Corchado, J.M.: Improved CBR System for Biological Forecasting. In: Proceedings of the ECAI WS – Binding Environmental Sciences and Artificial Intelligence, Valencia (2004)
3. Karatzas, K.D.: Artificial Intelligence Applications in the Atmospheric Environment: Status and Future Trends. Environmental Engineering Management Journal 9(2), 171–180 (2010)
4. Li, M., Hassan, M.R.: Urban air pollution forecasting using artificial intelligence-based tools, ch. 9 (2009)
5. Núñez, H., Sànchez-Marrè, M., Cortés, U., Comas, J., Martinez, M., Rodríquez-Roda, I., Poch, M.: A comparative study on the use of similarity measures in case-based reasoning to improve the classsification of environmental system situations. Environmental Modelling & Software 9(9), 809–819 (2004)

6. Sànchez-Marrè, M., Gibert, K., Sevilla, B.: Evolving GESCONDA to an Intelligent Decision Support Tool. In: Proceedings of the International Congress on Environmental Modelling and Software Modelling for Environment's Sake, Fifth Biennial Meeting, Ottawa, Canada (2010)

7. Tsataltzinos, T., Iliadis, L., Spartalis, S.: An intelligent Fuzzy Inference System for Risk Estimation Using Matlab Platform: the Case of Forest Fires in Greece. In: IFIP International Federation for Information Processing. Artificial Intelligence Applications and Innovations III, vol. 296, pp. 303–310 (2009)

8. Dietterich, T.: Machine Learning in Ecosystem Informatics and Sustainability. In: Proceedings of IJCAI 2009, pp. 8–13 (2009)

9. Polat, K.: A novel data preprocessing method to estimate the air pollution (SO_2): neighbor-based feature scaling (NBFS). Neural Computing & Applications (2011)

10. Noori, R., Hoshyaripour, G., Ashrafi, K., Araabi, B.N.: Uncertainty analysis of developed ANN and ANFIS models in prediction of carbon monoxide daily concentration. Atmospheric Environment 44(4), 476–482 (2010)

11. Oprea, M.: A case study of knowledge modelling in an air pollution control decision support system. AiCommunications 18(4), 293–303 (2005)

12. Ebel, A., Davitashvili, T. (eds.): Air, Water and Soil Quality Modelling for Risk and Impact Assessment. Springer, Heidelberg (2007)

13. Kim, Y.J., Platt, U. (eds.): Advanced Environmental Monitoring. Springer, Heidelberg (2008)

14. Kolehmainen, M., Martikainen, H., Ruuskanen, J.: Neural networks and periodic components used in air quality forecasting. Atmospheric Environment 35, 815–825 (2001)

15. Moussiopoulos, N. (ed.): Air Quality in Cities. Springer, Berlin (2003)

16. Von Storch, H., Tol, R.S.J., Flöser (eds.): Environmental Crises – Science and Policy. Springer, Heidelberg (2008)

17. Xu, H., Xue, H.: Improved ANFIS to Forecast Atmospheric Pollution. Management Science and Engineering 2(2), 54–61 (2008)

18. Ullah, N., Choudhury, P.: Flood Forecasting in River System Using ANFIS. In: AIP Proceedings of the International Conference on Modeling, Optimization, and Computing, vol. 1298, pp. 694–699 (2010)

19. Mukerji, A., Chatterjee, C., Raghuwanshi, N.S.: Flood Forecasting Using ANN, Neuro-Fuzzy, and Neuro-GA Models. Journal of Hydrologic Engineering 14(6) (2009)

20. Iliadis, L.S., Spartalis, S.I., Tachos, S.: Kernel Methods and Neural Networks for Water Resources Management. Environmental Engineering Management Journal 9(2), 181–187 (2010)

21. Matei, A.: Flood forecasting and river monitoring expert system in the Prahova river basin. In: Proceedings of the IFAC Workshop on Intelligent Control Systems, vol. 8, part 1, pp. 82–86 (2010)

22. The European Flood Alert System (EFAS) EFAS-IS Portal,
http://efas-is.jrc.ec.europa.eu

Personalized Information Services for Quality of Life: The Case of Airborne Pollen Induced Symptoms

Dimitris Voukantsis[1], Kostas Karatzas[1], Siegfried Jaeger[2], and Uwe Berger[2]

[1] Informatics Systems & Applications Group, Dept. of Mechanical Engineering,
Aristotle University, P.O. Box 483, 54124, Thessaloniki, Greece
[2] Medizinische Universität Wien, Universitätsklinik für Hals-,
Nasen- und Ohrenkrankheiten, Währinger Gürtel 18-20, 1090 Wien, Austria

Abstract. Allergies due to airborne pollen affect approximately 15-20% of European citizens; therefore, the provision of health related services concerning pollen-induced symptoms can improve the overall quality of life. In this paper, we demonstrate the development of personalized quality of life services by adopting a data-driven approach. The data we use consist of allergic symptoms reported by citizens as well as detailed pollen concentrations of the most allergenic taxa. We apply computational intelligence methods in order to develop models that associate pollen concentration levels with allergic symptoms on a personal level. The results for the case of Austria, show that this approach can result to accurate and reliable models; we report a correlation coefficient up to r=0.70 (average of 102 citizens). We conclude that some of these models could serve as the basis for personalized health services.

Keywords: Allergy, Computational Intelligence, Personalized Health Services.

1 Introduction

Allergy due to airborne pollen is a reaction of the human immune system to certain allergens carried by the pollen grains. It is estimated that approximately 15-20% of the European citizens suffer from pollen-related allergies [1]; additionally, there are well-established, yet not fully understood, associations with certain respiratory diseases, e.g., asthma [2]. During the last years, there has been an increasing trend in pollen-induced allergic symptoms, while the World Allergy Organization [3], reports an increase in severity of the symptoms.

In this context, there is an emerging need for quality of life information services that could assist sensitized citizens in making decisions concerning their daily life. This issue has already been partially addressed by existing information systems that provide information of pollen concentration levels of allergenic taxa [4]. However, the severity of allergic symptoms is strongly dependent on the citizen under consideration. Therefore, a more personalized approach that addresses symptoms rather than pollen concentration levels seems more appropriate.

The design and development of personalized information services addressing citizen-specific symptoms is a challenging task due to the lack of a generic (universal)

L. Iliadis and C. Jayne (Eds.): EANN/AIAI 2011, Part I, IFIP AICT 363, pp. 509–515, 2011.
© IFIP International Federation for Information Processing 2011

mechanism responsible for the triggering of allergic symptoms. Moreover, airborne pollen concentration levels have not been regulated as in the case of chemical air pollutants [5], thus there is no regulatory or management framework, based on common limit values and threshold levels to serve as a reference for any health related decision. In order to avoid these difficulties, we adopt a data-driven modeling approach by utilizing the database of pollen-induced symptoms reported by citizens themselves through the Pollen Diary system [6]. Additionally, we use detailed pollen concentration levels, monitored in several sampling sites, for the area of interest. We demonstrate the development of such models for the case of Austria, using data collected during the year 2010. The resulting personalized models could serve as the main modeling tool of existing or future information systems, providing citizen-specific warnings concerning the occurrence and severity of airborne pollen-induced symptoms.

2   Materials and Methods

2.1   Data Presentation

The modeling approach adopted in this study has been based in two distinct databases. i) Pollen concentration data of 65 distinct taxa sampled at several monitoring sites across Austria during 2010, and ii) Pollen-induced symptoms reported by users of the Pollen Diary system. The total number of users was 716, with an average of 57 records per user. The symptoms were reported in detail (eye itching, eye watering, nose, etc.); however, in this case we have identified the "overall symptoms" as the main parameter of interest. The latter one ranges from 0 (no symptoms) up to 25 (strong symptoms in eyes, nose and lungs).

Table 1. Variables included in the preprocessed data set

Temporal Variables	Pollen Concentration	Symptoms (target)
Day of Year	Acer, Alnus, Ambrosia, Betula, Carpinus, Corylus, Cupress, Fraxinus, Juglans, Pinus, Plantago, Platanus, Poaceae, Populus, Quercus, Rumex, Salix, Sambucus, Tilia, Urtica	Overall Symptoms

The data were preprocessed excluding taxa with more than 10% missing values, resulting to a final of 20 taxa (Table 1). Furthermore, users with less than 100 records were not included in this study, resulting in a total of 102 users. The final preprocessing step was to normalize the data using variance scaling. The latter one results to variables with average value $\mu=0$ and standard deviation $\sigma=1$. Fig.1 presents the overall symptoms (average of all citizens) and average pollen concentrations (average of all taxa) as a function of time. It is evident that during spring (days 80-130) peak values of overall symptoms and pollen concentrations coincide.

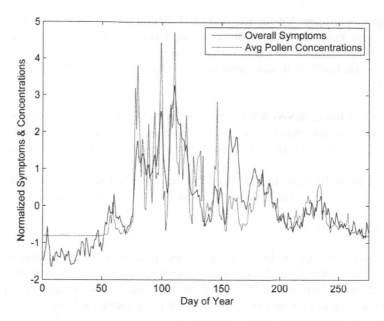

Fig. 1. Overall symptoms (average of all citizens, solid line) and pollen concentration (average of all taxa, dash-dot line). Both variables are normalized, using variance scaling ($\mu=0$, $\sigma=1$).

2.2 Computational Intelligence Methods

In order to model the inter-relations between pollen concentrations and citizen-specific symptoms, we have applied a series of Computational Intelligence (CI) methods. The task under consideration has been addressed as a regression problem (the target was the numerical value of "overall symptoms"). Therefore the proper versions of the following CI methods were considered:

Multi-Layer Perceptron (MLP). MLP [7] models are probably the most popular artificial neural network models, capable of modeling complex and highly non-linear processes. In this case, we have evaluated network architectures consisting of one hidden layer, setting the number of neurons equal to $N=(inputs+outputs)/2$ [7]. Where *inputs* is the number of input variables of the model and *outputs* the number of output variables; in this case, outputs=1. Furthermore, we have use the Levenberg-Marquardt backpropagation algorithm during the training of the models, with a maximum number of epochs at 500.

Support Vector Regression (SVR). SVR is a modification of the original algorithm introduced by Vapnik [8] capable of tackling regression problems. In this case we have chosen the SVR kernel to be the Radial Basis Function (RBF). Furthermore, we optimized the regularization parameter (C) and the ε-intensive zone of the model, as well as the γ parameter of the kernel. The SVR models have been developed using the Spider Toolbox for Matlab [9].

Least Squares Support Vector Regression (LS-SVR). LS-SVR is a modification of support vector machines [10]. In this case, we have used the RBF kernel and optimized the regularization (C) and kernel parameter (γ) using leave-one-out cross-validation. The LS-SVR models were developed using the LS-SVMlab toolbox for Matlab [11].

k-Nearest Neighbors (kNN). kNN is non-parametric CI algorithm that can be used to tackle regression problems. In this case, we have set the number of nearest neighbors to be k=5 and we applied the $1/r$ (r is the distance to the neighbor) weighting scheme.

Multiple Linear Regression (MLR). MLR is a traditional statistical method that provided the reference frame for comparison of the other CI methods.

2.3 Feature Selection

The selection of the appropriate features as input parameters of the models is an important modeling step as irrelevant or noisy features may result to poor performing models. Mutual Information (MI) as well as other information related criteria have been used in the past in order to identify relevant input variables. In this case, we have used MI following the approach presented in [12].

2.4 Training and Evaluation

Due to the limited number of available instances per citizen, the training of the models was based on the 10-fold cross validation, in order to utilize all instances. The Root Mean Square Error (RMSE), the Correlation Coefficient (r), as well as the Index of Agreement (d) have been used to validate the models. The latter index is defined by the following formula:

$$d = 1 - \frac{\sum_i \left| p_i - a_i \right|^2}{\sum_i \left(\left| p_i - \overline{a} \right| + \left| a_i - \overline{a} \right| \right)^2} \tag{1}$$

where p_i refers to predicted values and a_i to observed ones, whereas with $\overline{p}$ and $\overline{a}$ are denoted the average of the predicted and observed values, respectively. The index of agreement ranges from 0.0 (theoretical minimum) to 1.0 (perfect agreement between observed and predicted values).

3 Results and Discussion

Table 2 summarizes the performance of the resulting 102 citizen-specific models. The results are presented as averages (and standard deviations) of the statistical indices presented in section 2.4. It is clear that the performance differs significantly depending on the algorithm used to develop the model. The non-parametric kNN models as well as the LS-SVR models indicate superior performance compared to the SVR and MLP models. This may be attributed to the limited number of training examples in the data set (at least for the MLP models). Furthermore, all CI methods perform on average better than the reference (MLR) method. This indicates that CI algorithms are more suitable to model the pollen-induced symptoms.

The results presented in Table 2 indicate that modeling pollen-induced symptoms on citizen level can result to models of acceptable performance. In contrast, a global approach, i.e., using the same data and algorithms to build a model for all citizens, does not result to acceptable performances ($d<0.4$, $r<0.25$, rmse>4).

Table 2. Performance (average and standard deviation) of 102 citizen-specific models. The unit of RMSE is the number of symptoms.

Model	d	r	RMSE
MLR	0.74 ± 0.14	0.61 ± 0.20	2.26 ± 1.05
MLP	0.76 ± 0.15	0.63 ± 0.22	2.17 ± 0.93
kNN	0.80 ± 0.11	0.67 ± 0.17	2.07 ± 0.86
SVR	0.74 ± 0.14	0.64 ± 0.19	2.11 ± 0.88
LS-SVR	0.79 ± 0.14	0.70 ± 0.18	1.92 ± 0.80

The prevalence of allergic symptoms in humans is a highly complex process that dependants on several factors such as pollen concentrations, meteorological and chemical (i.e. air quality) weather conditions, citizen habits (outdoor activity, travelling, medication). Therefore, in some cases the available data cannot result to accurate models. This can be demonstrated in more detail for the case of two specific citizens (Citizens with ID number 80 and 85, hereafter denoted as Cit.#80 and Cit.#85), with similar data records and maximum overall symptoms. Table 3 presents the performance of the two citizen-specific models (Cit.#80, Cit.#85). The results show that the allergic symptoms indicated by Cit.#85 can be successfully modeled; however, this is not the case for Cit.#80. Fig.3 presents the overall symptoms for both citizens, as a function of time. It is evident that the pattern of symptoms for both citizens is different.

Table 3. Typical detailed performance (10-fold cross validation) of models for two citizens

ID	Model	MLR	MLP	kNN	SVR	LS-SVR
Cit.#80	d	0.67 ± 0.16	0.73 ± 0.16	0.74 ± 0.15	0.71 ± 0.13	0.79 ± 0.12
	r	0.54 ± 0.23	0.65 ± 0.26	0.59 ± 0.28	0.61 ± 0.19	0.68 ± 0.21
	rmse	4.51 ± 0.95	4.16 ± 1.33	4.44 ± 1.18	4.48 ± 1.08	3.83 ± 1.20
Cit.#85	d	0.92 ± 0.09	0.95 ± 0.06	0.97 ± 0.02	0.94 ± 0.02	0.95 ± 0.03
	r	0.88 ± 0.15	0.93 ± 0.06	0.94 ± 0.04	0.92 ± 0.04	0.93 ± 0.05
	rmse	2.87 ± 0.90	2.30 ± 1.02	2.08 ± 0.78	2.70 ± 0.35	2.34 ± 0.67

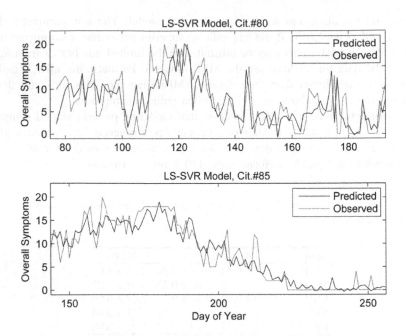

Fig. 2. Overall symptoms (solid line: predicted, dash-dot line: observed) for Cit.#80 and Cit.#85

4 Conclusions and Future Work

In this paper, we have demonstrated the use of CI methods in order to develop models capable of estimating pollen induced symptoms on a personal level. The results show that the data collected by the Pollen Dairy system can provide a solid foundation to build accurate citizen-specific models in most of the cases. The latter ones can serve as the basic modeling tool to develop personalized health services.

Future work in this field includes i) the use more databases and more advanced CI methods in order to improve the performance of the personalized models and ii) the use of the Pollen Diary database in order to categorize citizens into several sensitized groups and identify common characteristics. These goals will advance the accuracy and interpretability of the models, therefore providing a more solid background for the development of personalized health services.

Acknowledgments. The authors greatly acknowledge the contribution of all colleagues involved in the pollen concentration data collection. Manfred Bobek, Sigmar Bortenschlager, Inez Bortenschlager, Uschi Brosch, Edith Bucher, Bernard Clot, Pramod Harvey, Veronika Kofler, Andreja Kofol-Seliger, Herta Koll, Sabine Kottik, Margit Langanger, Rudolf Litschauer, Karol Micieta, Anna Paldy, Ondrej Rybnicek, Hanna Schantl, Jutta Schmidt, Roland Schmidt, Ingrid Weichenmeier, Helmut Zwander.

References

1. Huynen, M., Menne, B., Behrendt, H., Bertollini, R., Bonini, S., Brandao R., et al.: Phenology and Human Health: Allergic Disorders. Report of a WHO meeting, Rome, Italy (2003)
2. Taylor, E.P., Jacobson, W.K., House, M.J., Glovsky, M.M.: Links between Pollen, Atopy and the Asthma Epidemic. International Archives of Allergy and Immunology 144, 162–170 (2007)
3. World Allergy Organization, http://www.worldallergy.org/
4. Europe: Polleninfo.org, http://www.polleninfo.org/
5. CAFE - Derective 2008/6/EC of the European Parliament and of the Council (2008)
6. Pollen diary, https://www.pollendiary.com/Phd/
7. Haykin, S.: NeuralNetworks: A Comprehensive Foundation. Prentice Hall, Upper Saddle River (1994)
8. Vapnik, V.: The Nature of Statistical Learning Theory. Springer, New York (1995)
9. Spider Toolbox for Matlab,
   http://people.kyb.tuebingen.mpg.de/spider/index.html
10. Suykens, J.A.K., Van Gestel, T., De Brabanter, J., De Moor, B., Vandewalle, J.: Least Squares Support Vector Machines. World Scientific, Singapore (2002)
11. LS-SVMlab, http://www.esat.kuleuven.be/sista/lssvmlab/
12. Peng, H., Long, F., Ding, C.: Feature selection based on mutual information: criteria of max-dependency, max-relevance, and min-redundancy. IEEE Transactions on Pattern Analysis and Machine Intelligence 27(8), 1226–1238 (2005)

Fuzzy Modeling of the Climate Change Effect to Drought and to Wild Fires in Cyprus

Xanthos Papakonstantinou[1], Lazaros S. Iliadis[1], Elias Pimenidis[2], and Fotis Maris[1]

[1] Department of Forestry and Management of the Environment and Natural Resources,
Democritus University of Thrace, Pandazidou 193, Orestiada, PC 68200, Greece
pxanthosster@gmail.com, liliadis@fmenr.duth.gr
[2] School of Computing IT and Engineering, University of East London UK

Abstract. This is an intelligent modeling of the evolution of drought and forest fires, due to climate change in Cyprus. Original annual wild fire data records (1979-2009) and data regarding meteorological parameters were used. A flexible modeling approach was proposed towards the determination of drought risk indices in all of the country. Cyprus was divided in eight polygons corresponding to eight meteorological stations. A Fuzzy Inference Rule Based System (FIRBS) was developed to produce the drought risk indices vectors for the forest regions under study. An analysis of the spatial distribution of the heat index vectors was performed. Forest fires distribution through the island was addressed. All of the results were stored by using an ArcGIS, (version 9.3) spatial data base that enables more comprehensive presentation of the most risky areas. There is a significant increase of drought in the island and this has a serious effect in the problems of forest fires and heat indices.

Keywords: Climate Change, Fuzzy Inference System, Fuzzy Drought Indices, Heat Index, Wild Fires.

1 Introduction

According to Olej and Hardi [1-2] sustainable development is understood as the one that ensures the fulfillment of the needs of contemporary society without jeopardizing the opportunity to meet the needs of future generations and at the same time it improves the quality of life while living within the carrying capacity of supporting ecosystems. Drought is an extreme local climate phenomenon, difficult to be defined scientifically and this is one of the reasons that make its rational management more complicated [3]. Regardless the efforts for a general definition the specialists did not manage so far to agree in one that would be globally acceptable. Some of the existing descriptions for the term refer to *"Meteorological drought"*, "Agricultural drought" and "Hydrological drought" as a result of looking at the problem from different points of view. When the word *drought* is used commonly, the most often intended definition is meteorological drought. However, when the word is used by urban planners, it is more frequently in the sense of hydrological drought.

Sustainable development is and it will be one of the main objectives of the contemporary societies and thus this study concentrates not only in recording the situation in

L. Iliadis and C. Jayne (Eds.): EANN/AIAI 2011, Part I, IFIP AICT 363, pp. 516–528, 2011.
© IFIP International Federation for Information Processing 2011

terms of climate change but also in producing new Artificial Intelligence tools that can provide significant assistance towards the design of effective natural disasters management policy. The drought in the island of Cyprus is slowly but continuously getting worse during the last decades due to the fact of the climate change. The Republic of Cyprus has recognized several years ago the need for the control and management of desertification with its complicated potential consequences [4-6]. The problem is influenced by natural phenomena and also by human activities. The United Nations contract on the problem became an official law of the Cyprus Republic (Act 23 (III)/1999) and it contains a special Annex for the Mediterranean countries (Annex IV) [7]. According to this Act it is obligation of each state to design a National planning towards facing the problem.

This research effort aims first in modeling establishing and testing new flexible and efficient drought risk indices (DRI) and also in investigating the effect of climate change to a major natural disaster like forest fires. A main achievement of this effort is the design and implementation of an Intelligent Fuzzy Rule based System under the MATLAB platform where the DRI model is embedded. It is a System that performs local analysis of the drought and forest fire and estimates the degree of risk. The results are stored visually in a spatial database using ARCGIS 9.3 using actual coordinates for all of the areas.

1.1 Area of Research, Changes in the Climate Conditions

The main characteristics of the Mediterranean Cyprus climate are hot and dry summer from mid May till mid September, the rainy but soft winter which lasts from mid November till March. There are two short transition periods spring and autumn. During the 20th century the climate of Cyprus and especially the two main climate parameters namely rainfall and temperature have followed significant variations. More specifically in Cyprus during the last century the average rain height has dropped significantly whereas the average temperature has risen. The change rate of these meteorological features has been much higher in the second half of the 20th century. The warmest cases of the last 100 years have been recorded during the last 20 years [7]. The problem of desertification in Cyprus is a crucial one.

1.2 Literature Review

Previous research efforts estimate risk mainly based on specific imposed instructions and they do not consider major aspects and features related to the problem. They use crisp boundaries in order to classify areas based on their risk. This approach is quite error prone because an area for example with 10mm of rain height can be classified as "dry", whereas an area with 10.0001 mm as "not dry". More specifically the following stochastic research efforts have been proposed recently for modeling drought [8] and some research has been done in the direction of evaluating existing models [9]. Fuzzy modeling efforts have been done recently towards forest fire risk classification in Greece [10-14]. Finally a limited number of Soft Computing Approaches applied in drought modeling has been published in the literature [15].

2 Materials and Methods

2.1 Data Vectors and Data Gathering

The meteorological and cartographic data have been generously provided by the Cypriot public services. More specifically the meteorological data have been provided by the Cyprus Meteorological Service. Average monthly maximum and minimum temperatures and rainfall from eight meteorological stations located in the island for a period of thirty nine years 1979-2009 were gathered. The forest department of Cyprus provided detailed forest fire data (forest fire frequencies, cause of ignition, burned areas) and an ArcGIS shape file (.shp) with spatial and land data on the forest areas of Cyprus. Wild fire data are related to period 30th of April 1979 to the 24th of October 2009. Real coordinates of the center of each wild fire from 1994 till 2009 were gathered.

2.2 A Fuzzy Inference System for the Determination of DRI

In fuzzy algebra every piece of data belongs to a fuzzy set with a degree of membership (in the closed interval [0, 1]) that is determined by a fuzzy membership function (FMF) [16-17]. Thus each case can belong to both of *"Risky area"* and *"High Risk area"* fuzzy sets with a distinct degree of membership [17]. This research aims in proposing a reliable, flexible and rational *Drought Risk Index* (DRI). This is achieved with the use of fuzzy sets in order to determine the partial risk indices (due to each risk parameter). These partial risk indices can be unified to a unique risk index by the employment of fuzzy relations and more specifically fuzzy conjunction Norms. *Average monthly maximum temperature, average monthly minimum temperature, average monthly relative humidity, average total rainfall* were considered in this research.

2.3 Fuzzy Degree Membership Functions

Semi-Triangular and *Triangular* membership functions (functions 1 and 2 respectively) were used to determine the degree of membership (DOM) of each area under study to each corresponding fuzzy risk set ([10], [12], [16]). The choice of these functions was based on the fact that they offer only one single peak point where the DOM equals 1 and thus they distinguish the areas in a more straightforward manner.

$$\mu_s(X) = \begin{cases} 0 \text{ if } X < a \\ (X - a)/(c - a) \text{ if } X \in [a, c] \\ (b - X)/(b - c) \text{ if } X \in [c, b] \\ 0 \text{ if } X > b \end{cases} \tag{1}$$

$$\mu_s(X) = \begin{cases} 0 \text{ if } X < a \\ (X - a)/(c - a) \text{ if } X \in [a, c] \end{cases} \tag{2}$$

Unification of Partial Risk Indices. After the determination of the partial degrees of risk due to each separate feature, the final target was the unification of all indices to a unique risk index (the DRI) for each of the eight areas under evaluation. In fact the DRI would express the degree of membership of each area to the fuzzy set *"Area of* *high Drought"*. A special case of fuzzy relation namely the Minimum T-Norm was applied in order to perform the fuzzy conjunction. The following function 3 presents the *Minimum T-Norm* approach where μA(X) and μB(X) are the DOM of element X to the fuzzy sets A and B respectively ([12], [13], [17], [18]).

$$DRI= MIN(\mu_A(X), \mu_B(X)) \tag{3}$$

The fuzzy conjunction performs the fuzzy "AND" operation between two fuzzy sets. This means that the minimum T-Norm determines the DOM of an element x to the fuzzy set A AND B. After the determination of the fuzzy sets that correspond to each parameter, the next step was the design and construction of the "Linguistic" fuzzy rules to be used for the operation of the fuzzy controller. Thus a Mamdani FIS ([18-21]) was designed built and tested. The System was designed to use four risk parameters and three FMF (corresponding to "Low", "High", "Middle" linguistics) for each parameter. So according to Olej and Hajek ([1], [17]) totally $3^4 = 81$ fuzzy rules should be built, which leads to an acceptable degree of complexity.

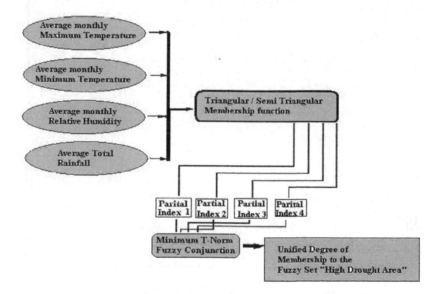

Fig. 1. Structure of the fuzzy inference system

Thus, the System was built to contain totally 81 fuzzy rules, derived from properly designed Decision Tables. It is a fact that fuzzy sets $\mu_1(y), \mu_2(y),.... \mu_{pk}(y),.... \mu_o(y)$ represent the actual assignment of linguistic variables values to set Y. Let $[x_1, x_2,...x_i,...x_m]$ be the input variables vector defined on the reference sets $X_1, X_2,....,X_i,....X_m$ and let y be an input variable defined on the reference set Y. In this case the FIS has m input variables and one output and each set X_i (i=1,2,..,m) can be divided in p_j (where $j=1,2,...,n$) fuzzy sets.

In a *Mamdani* FIS the fuzzy rules can be written as follows:

IF x_1 is A_1 and x_2 is A_2 AND …..AND x_i is A_{pj} AND…AND x_m is A_n THEN y is B
(where i=1,2,….,m j=1,2,….n) The fuzzy rules that were actually applied had the following form:

IF (H is LOW) and (N is HIGH) and (J is MIDDLE) and (C is LOW) THEN (DRI is HIGH). The developed FIS outputs a matrix that contains pure numbers in the closed interval [0, 1] that express the degree of membership of each area to the fuzzy set *"Area of high Drought"*.

Of course this can be considered as the matrix of the drought risk indices. Each single index is produced after the consideration of all involved meteorological parameters for each area of study and for a specific temporal value. Due to the fact that the obtained indices matrix has quite low values that are not easy to follow and to use, the risk indices were multiplied by 100.

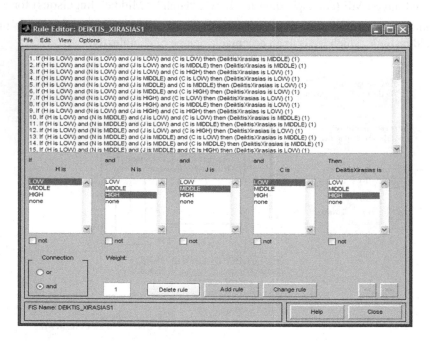

Fig. 2. Design of the fuzzy Ruleset in MATLAB

2.4   Average Monthly Maximum Heat Index

The determination of the average maximum Heat Index (HI) value for each area was done by using the respective average monthly maximum temperature and relative humidity values from all of the meteorological stations used. For this reason the temperatures were converted from Celsius °C to Fahrenheit °F. The most widely used deterministic approach was employed for the estimation of the HI, namely the methodology proposed by the Unite States meteorological service which can be seen in the following function 4 [23].

$T_{HI}= 16,923 + 1,85212*10^{-1}*T + 5,37941*RH - 1,00254*10^{-1}*T*RH + 9,41695*$
$10^{-3}*T^2 + 7,28898*10^{-3}*RH^2 + 3,45372*10^{-4}*T^2*RH - 8,14971*10^{-4}*T*RH^2 +$
$1,02102*10^{-5}*T^2*RH^2 - 3,8646*10^{-5}*T^3 + 2,91583*10^{-5}*RH^3 + 1,42721*10^{-6}*T^3*$ (4)
$RH + 1,97483*10^{-7}*T*RH^3 - 2,18429*10^{-8}*RH^2 + 8,43296*10^{-10}*T^2*RH^3 -$
$4,81975*10^{-11}*T^3*RH^3$

The obtained values were manipulated by a FIS to determine the risk due HI.

3 Using Geographic Information Systems ArcGIS

Geographic Information Systems as dynamic tools of spatial data analysis and manipulation can be combined with fuzzy systems. They can join their forces in order to reach decisions in complex non linear and non deterministic problems such as risk modeling.

3.1 Defining Zone Areas Using GIS

Using ArcGIS (version 9.3) a spatial database has been developed towards the analysis and spatial representation of the most risky areas in terms of drought and according to the estimated average heat index. Also the cases were studied based on their average burned area during the last fifteen years (1994-2009). A shape ARCGIS file (.shp) of Cyrpus was employed and the free part of Cyprus (as a polygon) was divided from the occupied one, by using the cut-polygons approach. Before this division our research team performed "*georeport*" of the scanned map. This was done because scanned maps do not contain any piece of real coordinate data. Thus in all cases a spatial report had to be performed to the raster data in order to define the application of the data to the coordinates of the map. In other words the geo-report offered real world coordinates to each part of the map. The fact that the actual coordinates of each point of each station were known enabled the division of the limits of each meteorological station. In this way several polygons were formed in the free part of the island. This task was performed by using the ArcGIS *Spatial Analyst* which is an actual Extension of the System. Spatial Analyst enables the construction, analysis and mapping of raster data and the performance of an integrated raster–vector analysis [24-25]. More specifically the *Path Distance Allocation* methodology was employed [26].

Fig. 3. Division in polygons based on the Path Distance Allocation method

This approach recognizes for each cell the zone of the source cell which may be approached with the minimum cost. More specifically, it calculates the nearest source for each cell based on the least accumulative cost over a cost surface, while accounting for surface distance and horizontal and vertical cost factors. Finally a cut of the raster files was performed (cut polygons) and the new data were stored to correspond to the new polygons-regions.

4   Results

4.1   Results Related to Drought Indices

Figure 4 shows that the area corresponding to the meteorological station of "*Athalassa*" is assigned with the highest and the most stable values of the *Average Maximum Drought Index* (AMDI) for the period 1979-2009.

For the other areas the AMDI does not have a stable rate and it has the highest peaks during the decade 1999-2009. The highest AMDI value ever, has been recorded in the "*Athalassa*" meteorological station in 2008 and it is equal to 86.62706905. It should be clarified that though the obtained AMDI indices are fuzzy numbers and thus they take values in the closed interval [0, 1] they have been multiplied by 100 in order to be more easily understood.

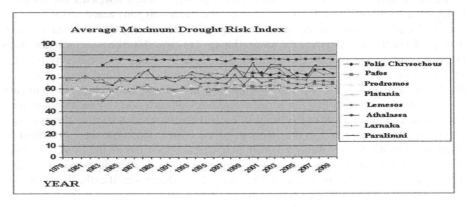

Fig. 4. Average Maximum Drought risk indices 1979-2009

The following maps (Figure 5a, 5b) are indicative graphical displays of the AMDI and of the *Average Actual Values of Drought Indices* (AAVDI) for the specific year 2006 and they confirm that the driest area is the one of "*Athalassa*".

The following graph (Figure 6), the area of "*Athalassa*" has also the highest AAVDI for the period 1979-2009. This area includes the central part of the country where the capital *Nicosia* is located and where is the residence and the working place of the majority of the population. This area has the highest CO_2 emissions by vehicles and the smallest forest cover as a percentage of its surface. However the most significant result is that the AAVDI values are constantly increasing for all of the areas under study during the last decade. Even in areas such as "*Prodromos*" and "*Platania*" with the lowest AAVDI values and with the 2/3 of the island's forested area, the problem of drought has been increasing constantly during the last decade, without any significant decrease as it used to happen during the previous two decades.

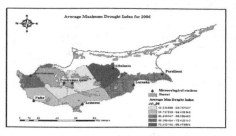

Fig. 5a. (AMDI) for 2006   **Fig. 5b.** (AAVDI) for 2006

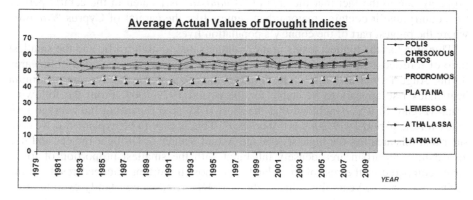

Fig. 6. AAVDI risk indices values for the period 1979-2009

From table 1 it is concluded that for the areas of *"Prodromos"* "Polis *Chrysochous"* and *"Platania"* which are located mainly in the center of the island the most risky month due to drought is July followed by August whereas for *"Larnaka"*, *"Athalassa"*, *"Pafos"*, *"Lemesos"* and *"Paralimni"* the worst month is August followed by July. The most important result is the fact that the area of *"Athalassa"* which is far from the seaside has the highest average drought risk value equal to 86.6270 during August. The areas of *"Prodromos"* "Platania" and *"Larnaka"* appear 31 times to have the highest values of the average maximum drought risk index whereas *"Paralimni"* 26 times, *"Athalassa"* and *"Pafos"* 27 *"Lemesos"* 17 and *"Polis Crysochous"* 10. This means that though the area of *"Athalassa"* has the highest average values of drought risk index, the areas of *"Prodromos"*, *"Platania"* and *"Larnaka"* have more often extreme maximum values of drought.

4.2 Results Related to the Heat Index

From the following graph (Figure 7) it is concluded that the area of *"Athalassa"* has the highest values of average maximum heat index for the period 1979-2009. This is

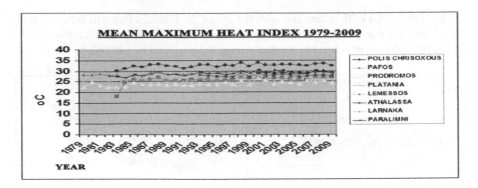

Fig. 7. Mean Maximum Heat Index 1979-2009

probably due to the fact that the area of "*Athalassa*" is located in the central part of the country and it contains major urban centers like the capital of Cyprus "*Nicosia*" where the biggest part of the country's population lives.

This area has the highest levels of air pollutants due to high traffic and the smallest ratio of forested area to the total surface. The highest value was recorded in this area during August 1998 and July 2000. In all of the other areas, the average maximum heat index risk appears to be stable for the period 1979-2009. From the following graph (Figure 8) it is concluded that the most risky area regarding the average heat index for the period 1979-2009 is "*Athalassa*". This is easy to be explained if we consider that this area has the highest Average Actual Values of Drought Indices and it is also mainly an urban area densely inhabited with the smallest proportion of forest cover compared to the rest of the island. The most important obtained result is that during the last five years the value of the AAVDI increases constantly even in areas with the smallest heat index values.

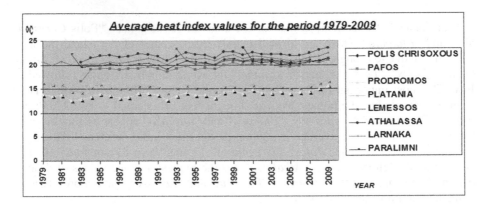

Fig. 8. Average heat index values for the period 1979-2009

It is impressive that the areas with the smallest average heat index values namely "*Prodromos*" and "*Platania*" which have a very high proportion of forest cover (they contain almost 66% of the whole forested area of Cyprus) appear to have a continuously increasing heat index values in the last five years.

From the following table 1 it can be seen that the most risky month regarding the heat index for the areas of "*Prodromos*" "*Polis Chrysochous*" and "*Platania*" is July followed by August whereas for "*Larnaka*" "*Paralimni*", "*Pafos*" and "*Lemesos*" the most risky month is August followed by July. For "Athalassa" the two months are equally risky regarding the heat index. Again the area of "Athalasa" has the highest heat index values which have been recorded in July and in August. The areas of "*Prodromos*" "*Larnaka*" and "*Platania*" have the highest average heat index risk values 31 times, "*Paralimni*" 26 times, "Athalassa" and "*Pafos*" 27, "*Lemesos*" 17 and "*Polis Chrysochous*" 10 times.

Table 1. Average Maximum Heat Index and AMDI X100

Area	Month	Frequency of inclusion in highest DRI	Maximum Average DRI	Frequency of inclusion in highest HI risk	Average Maximum HI risk
Prodromos	July	61,29%	682,651	64,52%	26,7
	August	38,71%	657,319	35,48	25,4
Platania	July	64,52%	658,913	64,52%	27,8
	August	35,48%	673,197	35,48	27,3
Larnaka	August	61,29%	789,141	64,52%	29,8
	July	38,71%	775,406	35,48	29,6
Paralimni	August	61,29%	810,530	69,23%	30,3
	July	38,71%	829,690	30,72	30,1
Athalassa	August	66,67%	866,270	48,15	34
	July	29,63%	855,613	51,85%	34
Pafos	August	77,78%	643,002	77,78%	27,1
Lemesos	August	76,47%	723,669	70,59%	29
PolisChrisochous	July	100%	770,234	100%	29

4.3 Results Related to Forest Fire Risk

A few reports are available in the literature on the forest fire problem of Cyprus [27]. The problem has not been analyzed by the use of spatial decision support systems like ARCGIS or Intelligent Systems. From Figure 9 it is concluded that the majority of forest fire incidents were recorded during the last decade whereas the year 2008 was the worse so far. It should be mentioned that year 2008 had the highest average maximum drought risk index for the period 1979-2009. Obviously these two findings are related. Totally from the 1226 forest fires of the period 1979-2009 the 804 were recorded during the last decade 1999-2009.

The area of "*Pafos*" has the least number of forest fire breakouts (only 21 cases). "*Athalassa*" appears to be significantly risky with a high number of wild fires although only a small percentage of this area is forested. This finding is very important and it shows that the urbanization and land value together with the high heat index influence the problem significantly. The influence of the human factor is obvious [28].

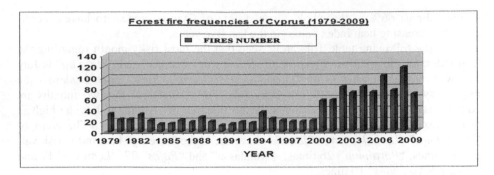

Fig. 9. Forest fire frequencies of Cyprus (1979-2009)

Totally 917 wild fires incidents appear in Figure 10, with 211 incidents in "*Platania*", 158 in "*Prodromos*" 140 in "*Polis Chrysochous*", 131 in "*Lemesos*" and 123 in "*Athalassa*". The area of "*Pafos*" has the least number of forest fire breakouts (only 21 cases). "*Athalassa*" appears to be significantly risky with a high number of wild fires although only a small percentage of this area is forested.

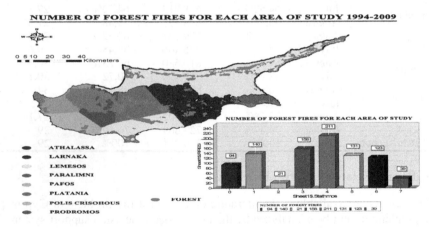

Fig. 10. Number of forest fires for each area of study

This finding is very important and it shows that the urbanization and land value together with the high heat index influence the problem significantly. The influence of the human factor is obvious [28].

5 Discussion

For the first time Cyprus was divided in eight polygons based on the *Path Distance Allocation* approach. This enabled the more comprehensive and reliable analysis of each area that demonstrated different and distinct special characteristics and properties. These areas were ranked based of the estimated DRI and on their HI values. It is worth mentioning that the DRI was estimated based on the equal contribution of several meteorological features something that offers a high degree of innovation to this effort. It is obvious that in Cyprus the climate conditions are changing to the worse especially during the last decade and this has an influence to the burning of forest ecosystems and to the obtained heat indices vectors that are continuously growing to higher maximum and average values A very interesting result of this research is related to the urban area of *"Athalassa"* where the capital Nicosia is located. Though this region has a small ratio of forest cover (forested area divided to its area) it has a very high number of wild fire incidents something that was not expected initially. This shows the influence of the drought increase and perhaps the influence of the urbanization and land value to the problem. Another crucial point is the conclusion that the DRI and the heat index are both increasing significantly during the last decade even in the areas which are located near the cost yard. This should alarm the authorities towards the design of a more effective planning. This research will continue in the future with more sophisticated Soft Computing techniques and of course with more available data.

References

1. Olej, V., Obrasalova, I., Krupka, J.: Modelling of Selected Areas of Sustainable Development by Artificial Intelligence and Soft Computing. Grada Publishing (2009)
2. Hardi, P., Barg, S.: Measuring Sustainable Development: Review of Current Practice. International Institute for Sustainable Development, Ontario, Canada (1997)
3. NAGREF: Drought A dangerous extreme climate phenomenon with special management requirements, vol. 24, pp. 10–13 (2006) (in Greek)
4. Dorflinger, G.: Assessment of Sedimentation and Erosion, Kalavasos Reservoir and Catchments, Cyprus. M.Sc. Dissertation, University of Wales, U.K (2003)
5. Kosmas, C., Kirkby, M., Geeson, N.: The Medalus project - Mediterranean desertification and land use: Manual on key indicators of desertification and mapping environmentally sensitive areas to desertification. Project ENV4 CT 95 0119, EC (1999)
6. Photiou, C.: Wastewater Treatment and Reuse-Conference on: Integrated Water Management, Policy Aspects, A.R.I. Cyprus (2003)
7. Cyprus Ministry of Agriculture, Natural Resources and Environment, National Plan for fighting the desertification, Nicosia, Cyprus (2008)
8. Ghanbarpour, M.R.: Groundwater for Sustainable Development Problems, Perspectives and Challenges. In: Bhattacharya, P. (ed.) Stochastic Modeling of Groundwater Discharge for Hydrological Drought Forecasting, ch. 14. Taylor & Francis, Abington (2008)
9. Stockwell, D.R.B.: Critique of drought models in the Australian drought exceptional circumstances report (DECR). Energy & Environment 21(5), 425–436 (2010)
10. Iliadis, L.: A decision support system unifying partial environmental risk indices by using fuzzy intersection operators: the case of forest fires. In: Proceedings of the HAICTA International Conference, Thessaloniki, pp. 7–16 (2004)
11. Iliadis, L.: A Decision Support System Applying an Integrated Fuzzy Model for Long-Term Forest fire Risk Estimation. Environmental Modeling and Software 20, 613–621 (2005)
12. Iliadis, L., Vangeloudh, M., Spartalis, S.: An intelligent system employing an enhanced fuzzy c-means clustering model: Application in the case of Forest Fires. Journal Computers and Electronics in Agriculture 70(2), 276–284 (2010)

13. Iliadis, L., Skopianos, S., Tachos, S., Spartalis, S.: A Fuzzy Inference System Using Gaussian Distribution Curves for Forest Fire Risk Estimation. In: Papadopoulos, H., Andreou, A.S., Bramer, M. (eds.) AIAI 2010. IFIP AICT, vol. 339, pp. 376–386. Springer, Heidelberg (2010)
14. Iliadis, L., Zigkrika, N.: Performing Fuzzy Multi-feature Scenarios for the Determination of Forest Fire Risk. In: Proceedings of the 3rd ITAFFE 2010 International Conf., pp. 170–177 (2010)
15. Yang, D.W., Nadarajah, S.: Drought modeling and products of random variables with exponential kernel. Journal Stochastic Environmental Research and Risk Assessment 21(2), 123–129 (2006)
16. Iliadis, L.: Intelligent Information Systems and Applications in Risk Estimation. Stamouli Publishing, Thessaloniki (2007) (in Greek)
17. Kecman, V.: Learning and Soft Computing. MIT Press, London (2001)
18. Cox, E.: Fuzzy Modeling and Genetic Algorithms for Data Mining and Exploration. Elsevier Inc., USA (2005)
19. Kuncheva, L.I.: How good are Fuzzy IF-THEN Classifiers? IEEE Transactions on Systems, Man and Cybernetics 30(4), 501–509 (2000)
20. Pedrycz, W.: Fuzzy Control and Fuzzy Systems, 2nd extended edn. John Wiley & Sons Inc., New York (1993)
21. Vascak, J., Madarasz, L.: Automatic Adaptation of Fuzzy Controllers. Acta Polytechnica Hungarica 2(2), 5–18 (2005)
22. Hajek, P., Olej, V.: Municipal Creditworthiness Modelling by means of Fuzzy Inference Systems and Neural Networks. In: Proceedings of the 4th International Conference on ISTM, TECSI-FEA Sao Paolo Brazil, pp. 586–608 (2007)
23. SCONC (State Climate Office of North Carolina) (2009), http://www.nc-climate.ncsu.edu/climate/heat_index_climatology.php
24. ArcGIS Desktop 9.3 Help 2009 Spatial Analysts (2009), http://resources.arcgis.com/content/arcgisdesktop/9.3/about
25. Hillier, A.: Working with ArcView 9.3 (2008)
26. ArcGIS Desktop 9.2 Help 2008 Path Distance Allocation, http://webhelp.esri.com/arcgiSDEsktop/9.2/index.cfm?TopicNam e=path_distance_allocation
27. IFFN Forest Fire Management in Cyprus International Forest Fire News (33), 38–43 (2005) ISSN 1029-0864
28. Cyprus Department of Forests forest fires, http://www.moa.gov.cy/forest

Author Index